THE CRUCIBLE OF RACE

The
CRUCIBLE
of
RACE

Black-White Relations in the American South
Since Emancipation

Joel Williamson

New York   Oxford
OXFORD UNIVERSITY PRESS
1984

099468

Library of Congress Cataloging in Publication Data

Williamson, Joel.
The crucible of race.

Includes index.
1. Southern States—Race relations.   2. Afro-Americans
—Southern States—History.   3. Afro-Americans—Civil
rights—Southern States.   I. Title.
E185.61.W738   1984   305.8'96073'075   83-24985
ISBN 0-19-503382-5

Printing (last digit): 9 8 7 6 5 4 3 2 1

Printed in the United States of America

For

Joelle
William
Alethea

Preface

This is a book about relations between blacks and whites in the South, but the ultimate object of the book is to promote an understanding of the nature of race relations in the whole of America today and how race relations came to be what they are. The black-white story in America began at Jamestown with the arrival of some twenty black people in 1619, within a dozen years of the first permanent white settlement in British North America, and it has continued through almost four centuries. The greater part of black-white relations that has occurred in America happened in the South because black people in the mass have lived in the South. As late as 1910 nearly 90 percent of America's blacks lived south of Mason's and Dixon's line, and only within the last two decades have less than half done so. One can hardly overemphasize the fact that black people living outside the South in large numbers is a very recent phenomenon.

There are and there have been, of course, other races in America—Indians and Orientals—so that the study of race relations is not alone the study of the interaction between blacks and whites. Yet American Indians diminished in numbers relative to the white population so drastically and were so isolated as to have only limited contact with the white population as a whole. Orientals were never mixed among Caucasians widely enough or in sufficient numbers to occasion high levels of contact.

There have been other groups separated from the British American core by culture rather than by race—the French in Louisiana, the Spanish in Florida, and Germans, Irish, Scandinavians, Slavs, Jews, and Italians elsewhere. But these too have not long persisted as significantly different from the mainstream culture, and, indeed, they accommodated rapidly and largely melted into the main current, adding to its power. Today, the Hispanic-American population is large and growing, but the tendency of Hispanic-Americans to merge into the dominant flow is also great, and it is fully possible that the third and fourth generations born in America will hardly be identifiable by sight and sound. Both as a race and as a culture, only the Afro-Americans seem to persist in large numbers over the centuries, physically proximate to other Americans, and yet significantly outside of the mainstream. Standing today at more than 22,000,000 people, they are still the great minority, the seemingly permanent minority, the perpetually important main subject in the study of race and ethnic relations in America.

During the last sixty years very able historians have poured their energies into the study of black-white relations in the pre-emancipation South, both within and outside of the framework of slavery. There exist virtually whole libraries on this subject, and any young professor of American history can name at least a dozen stars that shine brightly in that vast historiographical sky. On the other hand, the study of blacks and whites after emancipation is barely a generation old, and the printed literature springing from that movement remains relatively thin, both in narrow factual studies and in broad interpretative efforts. The single book that has attempted to cover the whole ground is the same book that opened the field, C. Vann Woodward's *The Strange Career of Jim Crow,* published in 1955. In his preface, Professor Woodward judged his work a "somewhat premature effort" and invited scholars both to investigate the subject further and to profit from the perspectives of later times. In a modest way scholars have investigated further, and the writing of the history of the Jim Crow era has now aged some thirty years. Professor Woodward also wrote in that preface that "I shall expect and hope to be corrected."[1]

This book does contain a revisionist interpretation of race relations in the South since emancipation, but the goal is not at all to revise the original thesis advanced by Woodward. The always elusive ideal is to tell the truth as exactly as possible—to be faithful to the story as it happened. There is no attempt to stand the Woodward thesis upon its head. Indeed, to succeed in that effort would be to construct a lesser thesis, to confine one's self within a circle of perspectives and categories fully appropriate only a generation ago. Also there will be no effort to measure point by point the facts and the interpretation in the original work against the facts others and I have developed over these years and the interpretation to which I have come. It will seem to the reader, perhaps, that this work ignores and by-passes the Woodward interpretation. Actually, it is more accurate to say that I simply move to one side, and begin again. I cover much the same historical ground, the same years, the same geography, the same several dozen millions of people. But necessarily, I view the subject from another perspective, one that incorporates new research and profits from the experiences of the last twenty-five years. While measurements are not taken, the scholarly reader will easily see that there are congruences between the Woodward interpretation and the one advanced here. Most especially in concentrating upon the South in the 1890s, Professor Woodward, with something akin to intuitive genius, chose the right place and the right time to catch the critical phase of race relations for twentieth-century America. However, I conclude that what happened then was essentially and vitally different from what he suggested. With all of this, I mean merely to say that this is how the pursuit of truth in history works when it works well. We do not so much build upon one another as we build alongside one another. We are stimulated to seek the golden fleece by the most worthy work of our predecessors. Professor Woodward gave us a direction and a push. It seems to have been the right direction, and the launching was effective. We can only be grateful to him, and also to the other historians who pioneered in opening the field, most especially to those earliest pioneers Vernon Lane Wharton, George Brown Tindall, Charles E. Wynes, and Richard Wade.[2]

Chapel Hill   J.W.
January 1984

Acknowledgments

During nearly twenty years of researching and writing this book, I have incurred debts that I can, indeed, only "acknowledge" and never fully repay. In research, the text and endnotes will reveal that I relied heavily upon manuscript sources, following the model established by my mentor Kenneth M. Stampp in his book *The Peculiar Institution.* The first draft of roughly a thousand pages, written in 1970–71 under a Guggenheim Fellowship, offered an array of theses built almost exclusively upon the letters, diaries, journals, and scrapbooks of contemporaries.

In the fall of 1971, I began to teach a course on race relations in the University of North Carolina in Chapel Hill. It was, essentially, the book as it then stood. It was taught each semester for a dozen years, with enrollment rising early on to about two hundred students. More recently, reflective of the general decline of interest in America in race relations, the class musters about fifty students. At Harvard, where I gave the course in the fall of 1981, the class numbered twice that many, an increase not easily explained. Over these twelve years, my many fine students hammered away, critically and uncritically, at my theses, and I have gratefully responded. In reading the book, I hope that now and again some of them will see a specific result of their scholarly valor. It was, for instance, a black student sitting near the back of a large lecture hall who raised his hand and asked the question that led me to think, over the years, more deeply and pointedly about the relation between the psychological principle of "projection" and the ritual of lynching in the South. Indeed, in the early 1970s, my best students pressed me into a continuous reassessment of the meaning of my material. The central thesis in the bundle of theses, an interplay of three "mentalities" on race, held up well, but the illustrations, the elaborations as to implications and interconnections, in short the fine tune, evolved appreciably.

In the fall of 1976, I was invited to spend the academic year 1977–78 as a Fellow in the Center for Advanced Study in the Behavioral Sciences in Stanford, California, a fellowship that was financed by the National Endowment for the Humanities. I went—ostensibly to rewrite and complete what had come to be called, with fitting humor, the "big book."

Within ten minutes of settling in my study at Stanford, which was within thirty minutes of my arrival at the Center, I began to write a book and finished it in seven months. But it wasn't the big book. Rather it was one that I had thought about generally for several years and pointedly during my slow and solitary two weeks' drive across the country. It was a book that traced out the history of mixing between black and white in America and the story of the children of that mixing—mulattoes. In the writing, physical mixing became a metaphor for cultural mixing. Black culture in America, like black people in America, are a mixture and an evolution of Africa and Europe in a new land. They are distinctly, as the short title of the book declared, a "New People," and, as the book argues, best understood as such. They are unique, valuable, and evolving to become increasingly powerful among the peoples of the world.

Writing *New People* forced me to rethink closely yet again the whole history of black-white relations in America. What emerged from that process was a mutation in my conception of the big book. The primary thesis involving the three mentalities still remained intact, but it came to be re-set in a framework that was global and reached back a thousand years. Race relations in the South are, of course, world history, but more immediately race relations in twentieth-century America took their basic form from a change that occurred during the lives of the three generations of Southerners, black and white, who matured between about 1850 and 1915. At the end of that period, race relations crystallized into the system with which we still live, not only in the South, but in the nation at large. That transition was tied inextricably to the industrial revolution, to the "explosion" of Europe and the United States into the rest of the world, and to the phenomenon labeled "modernization." In the book, I call this fundamental shift in race relations and white culture in the South "The Great Changeover."

I mailed off *New People* one day, and I began to rewrite the big book the next, recasting the whole in the model of The Great Changeover. I had been easy with not writing the book for several years before; now I was ready, willing, and eager. In three months at the Center in 1978, I rewrote the first three chapters and by the time I finished I knew that in the end this book would be published. During each of the next three years, I returned to the Center as a Summer Fellow and, in 1981, completed rewriting the text.

If I have done anything worthwhile as a scholar during the last seven years, most of the credit belongs to my association with the Center for Advanced Study: to the truly marvelous staff, to the generations of fine progressive scholars I have known there, and to the spirit of inquiry into the affairs of humanity that flourishes on that usually sunny acre. Specifically, I would like to thank Director Gardner Lindzey, who appreciates academic freedom and battles for it; strong, gentle Preston S. Cutler, the founding Associate Director of the Center; and Katherine Jenks, who manages a vast support system with obvious grace and apparent ease. At the Center, I bow specially to Librarian Margaret Amara, Receptionist Kat Kohlsaat, and Secretaries Gen Carter and Agnes Page whose generosity to me seems endless.

During the academic year 1981–82 and the ensuing summer, I was a Fellow in the Charles Warren Center at Harvard, a visiting professor in the Department of History, and a resident associate in Lowell House. During this year, I completed the manuscript and committed it to Oxford University Press for publication. In this last stage, I was generously aided by my colleagues in the Center, in the Department, and especially by my friends and fellow students in Lowell House and in Harvard-Radcliffe College. I came to value them most highly, both for their talents and for their responsible use of those gifts. I owe particular thanks to Stephan Thernstrom, the Director of the Center, and Wallace McCaffrey, Chairman of the Department, for arranging my visit, and to Patricia Denault, Administrative Assistant for the Center, and Diane Draine of the staff for full support given with unflagging good cheer.

Having written a "big book," the next task was to cut it down to a publishable size. Stephanie Golden, Leona Capeless, and Sheldon Meyer, truly a prince among publishers, did hard labor in that stony field. Most of all they have been perfectly faithful to the book and steadily supportive of the author, for which I am lastingly grateful.

Because of limitations of space, many fine scholars who have worked in the history of race relations in the South will not find themselves cited here. However, if they read the text, they will see by particular word choice or syntax that I have woven my understanding of their work into the story and thus make respectful if silent salute. Similarly, there is no bibliography because even a bare listing of every study relevant to this broad subject would fill half again as many pages as we have used, and a "select" bibliography would be distortive.

Essentially, this book is built from manuscript sources, and I happily acknowledge a great debt to the manuscript archivists who made this possible. In researching this subject, I lived with them in close intimacy for over a decade, and I feel that I know them well. I see in that calling a dedication to service that is nearly Franciscan—in every sense of the vow of that saintly person. In expressing my appreciation, I am led to appropriate and reword the lines from Omar Khayyam:

> I wonder often what the archivists buy
> One half so precious as the stuff they absolutely give away.

Most of the archives I used are cited in the endnotes. Among the archivists who helped me, I owe special thanks to the late James W. Patton, long-time Director of the Southern Historical Collection in Chapel Hill and a close friend; to his successors as Director, Isaac Copeland and Caroline Wallace; and to their cordial and highly efficient staff. I spent literally years in the collection in the 1960s; and I also spent whole months with Mattie Russell and her staff in the manuscript collection at Duke University nearby. Together, these two collections remain the lodestone for research in Southern History, but beyond these the South is rich and getting richer in manuscript archives and archivists. In every state there are a dozen or more of the former and, lamentably, all too few of the latter. I wish I could say thank you personally to each of the several hundred fine archivists who have helped me.

The University of North Carolina has proved ever-ready to facilitate my work by giving me free time, a galaxy of stimulating collegues, and the help of a highly congenial staff. Much of that happy ambience in which I move in Chapel Hill springs from the adept management of Jane Lindley, the many-talented Administrative Assistant for the Department of History. My chairpersons, Carl Pegg, James L. Godfrey, George V. Taylor, Donald R. Higginbotham, and Gillian T. Cell have been good friends personally and totally supportive professionally. Other than the author, no one has invested so much time and energy in this book as has my secretary Rosalie I. Radcliffe. She typed the whole thing once and many parts of it more than once. Her patience, intelligence, and heartening cheerfulness have been a large factor in bringing this long and sometimes tedious work to an end.

Among my academic colleagues, I owe very special gratitude to three people. I was careful to show the full manuscript to C. Vann Woodward before all others. I did so, first, as a symbol of my great regard for his scholarship and deep humanity, and, secondly, in deference to the fact that he set me upon this sea by his own early work. I am in his debt once more for a close reading and characteristically cogent comments. Shortly afterward, Daniel Aaron read the same draft and offered encouragement and ideas from a perspective in American Studies, a field in which he pioneered and one that I find increasingly valuable. Finally, my colleague Nell Painter has been steadily supportive, exhibiting yet again her salient capacities for high intelligence and selfless friendship. For all of my caring colleagues, I feel deeply thankful.

J.W.

Contents

PART TWO

THE RAGE OF RADICALISM, 1889–1915

THE CRUCIBLE OF RACE

Introduction

The essence of what happened in the South in race relations after emancipation can be largely explained by a description of the evolution and interplay of three Southern white "mentalities." These mentalities could be aptly labeled "Liberal," "Conservative," and "Radical."

1

It would be much more convenient if we could use a single mentality, a model "mind of the South," to explicate the history of race relations—as writers in the past have often done. But the concept that Wilbur J. Cash, born in the year 1900, used in 1941 in his book of that name has meaning limited for the most part to the time and place in which he conceived it. The plight of all thinkers, writers, and artists is, of course, to be the captive of his or her age. Yet, Cash and his book constitute a case specially exaggerated. This is a special case, first, because his work builds out from the black presence to interpret the whole of Southern society, next because he took his understanding of what had been the nature of the black presence from the Southern white world in which he came to maturity, and, finally, because that society was uniquely out of touch with the realities of black history in America and with the history of race relations. It fixed upon the conviction that Negroes were by nature substantially inferior to white people, that such had always been true and always would be true, and that Negro history and the history of race relations in America—in so far as there was a Negro history and a history of race relations that deserved any attention at all—amounted simply to the story of what happened to or about Negroes rather than what Negroes had done. These histories were most remarkable in instances in which the inferior nature of the

1

Negro had not been recognized, usually by Yankees, and bad things had happened, such as the Civil War and Reconstruction. Blacks had been slaves, and then they were free . . . that was black history. All whites had always been steadily together against all alien colors from antiquity . . . that was the history of race relations. Race was at the core of Southern culture, they declared, and the essential nature of the Negro and the thinking of whites about Negroes were unitary and fixed.

Cash appropriated the concept of white supremacy whole-bodied from his society and called it the "Proto-Dorian" bond.[1] However, both Cash and his society argued that in the South the harshness of that color exclusiveness had come to be meliorated by a pervasive ethos of paternalism among the white elite. Southern racism, then, was kindlier than racism elsewhere. Such was the way things were, and such they had always been, monolithic and essentially unchanging. Like every thoughtful person in his time, Cash knew that somehow the Negro was the root cause of it all. What he did not know, nor rightly guess, was in what way the black presence had functioned to shape the particular white world that existed around him. Cash could only grope searchingly, dragging a rigid white supremacy awkwardly up through time, bumping and jerking it across the hard places of history like some stiff mannequin, toward historical realities his society had chosen to forget, and, moreover, worked diligently to prevent his recalling. He was closed out from a workable understanding from the very beginning because he could never actually understand that there was no such thing as Negro, that there were only Negroes, and black culture was always changing. He matured in a white world in which blacks had become, to use Ralph Ellison's perfect phrase, "Invisible Man," and he probably never really knew any of them, and neither did the great mass of his contemporaries.[2]

The mind of the South that Cash depicted was the mind of himself as tutored, essentially, by that post-1915 Southern world in which he came to maturity. Admitting all of Cash's considerable virtues and talents, admitting even that he was brilliantly right in many parts of his book, he was after all relatively untraveled, white belt, piedmontese, small town, Baptist college, and small factory New South in his origins, environs, and experience. While there are no footnotes in his book, the materials from which it is drawn are clearly derivative rather than original. The sources do not include the manuscript letters and diaries of his subjects, nor even the easily accessible newspapers, journals, and official documents. It is derived from his own memory, from tales told to him by others, and from a somewhat chance choice of historical authorities. Interpretatively his work labors under a heavy burden of Turnerian frontier history, textile economics and New South paternalism as supplied by Broadus Mitchell, Odumian regional sociology, and Menckenesque "Dutch uncle" social criticism. All of this was fused and rendered in print by a vastly patient and peculiar literary process that might be called "Knopfian extrusion" in honor of the publishing genius who drew the book from the author in more than a decade of careful ministration.[3]

The most useful thing about *The Mind of the South* is that it is, in itself, an artifact. It is a book that captures its own time superbly even as it sought to capture times past. Like a monument over a grave, it speaks more accurately of the living than of the dead. Cash's book could have been written only by a totally native Southerner who came of age in the 1920s and ripened in the 1930s. Certainly never since and probably never before, with the possible exception of the months surrounding the beginning of the Civil War, had the South come so close to generating what was, in truth, a single mind. More or less age in the author would have spoiled the document because he would have had evidence that there had been or were later other minds. Even a brief sojourn in a contemporary culture that was biracial, such as those in Brazil, Trinidad or Jamaica, would have suggested to Cash that things were even then not everywhere the same, and that there were, indeed, alternatives in race relations. In reality, of course, there had been many Souths, but in that certain place and in that particular time, it was uniquely possible for an intelligent and highly perceptive Southerner to conceive of the mind of the South as singular and to bring it forth with a lusty cry of "Eureka."

The Cashian view of the cultural history of the South gained high credibility, in part, because there was no one to challenge it. Any white Southerner who vibrated sympathetically to that world might have written essentially the same book that Cash wrote. It was a time and place in which virtually everyone who was anyone did vibrate sympathetically. No Southern writer just then was prepared to see an alternative history of Southern culture and print it, and no one outside the South seemed much to care. Indeed, among American intellectuals at large, Cash's "mind of the South" was a cultural indulgence for the South, a promotion and levitation for the region above anything that had gone before. Northern intellectuals had long preached that there was in fact no mind of the South and never had been. Only slavery and ignorance had thrived below Mason's and Dixon's line before the war, and emancipation had left only half of that. Cash, at least, gave the South a mind, even if it was a minimally single one. His interpretation, seemingly licensed and let loose upon the world by the South itself, immediately gained the high currency that it has long enjoyed. After 1941 if one needed to say something, almost anything, about the Southern ethos, one simply cited Cash and moved confidently and comfortably on.

Actually, sectional pride need not have relied upon Cash to prove that the South did indeed have a life of the mind and that Southern culture had at least some value. Exactly the same unitary world that matured Wilbur Cash and *The Mind of the South* gave rise to a whole wave of impressive artists and works. Cash's era was the same that produced Margaret Mitchell and *Gone with the Wind;* U. B. Phillips, the explication of plantation culture, and a grand plan of Southern history that featured the "central theme" of race control; the Nashville agrarians; and a literary rebellion that gave birth to a wellspring of creativity that yet runs full. Most signally, perhaps, it produced William Faulkner, *The Sound and the Fury* (1929), *Light in August* (1932), *Absalom, Absalom!* (1937), the saga of the Snopes family, and a body of work that won for its author international acclaim and, in 1950, a Nobel prize for literature.

It will be one of the theses of this book that this flowering of the Old South in the New—including Wilbur Cash, William Faulkner, *et al.*—was the direct result of the black presence, that it was in fact the tangible fruit of a tri-generational and complex interplay of black and white reaching a new plateau in the decades after World War I and deployed upon new ground. Ironically, each of these thinking Southerners knew as did Cash that somehow the Negro was at the center of things. They all worried about the edges of the problem, but none was able to transcend his times, drive to the core, and perceive that racial thinking in the minds of white Southerners had been vari-parted and evolutionary, and that they themselves had been shaped by coming of age at a peculiar juncture in the culture resulting from that process. The next generation, ideationally if not by raw date of birth, the generation of, for instance, C. Vann Woodward, would attack the problem with greater focus, with an awareness more cosmopolitan, and with greater insight. They would harry it with great energy and would come to see important patterns of diversity and change, to see, in short, that things had not always been the same.

2

In dealing with Southern white thinking on race, I will define and use a special term: "mentality." By mentality I mean to suggest something less perfectly formed than a philosophy. Like a philosophy, a mentality will have certain discrete ideas, but those ideas are not tightly knit into a smoothly finished and comprehensive web such as might be the case, for instance, with "Platonic" philosophy or "Christian" philosophy. On the other side, I use mentality to indicate something that includes but is more than "notions," "opinions," and "attitudes," all of which suggest vagueness, impermanence, individual thought rather than social thought, and thinking that does not compel action and is very often at variance with behavior. By mentality I want to suggest an intellectual atmosphere of a distinctive, clearly identifiable quality. It is derived from the broad society, touches a large number of individual minds, and flows and changes over time, influencing behavior and being influenced by behavior, and by the physical world. It is in part emotional, and it does compel action. Like a prevailing wind, it does not prevail perfectly in all times and places, but in the wide sweep of human history and total flow is virtually uniform and prevalent.

In this study I use mentality much as Marvin Meyers used the term "persuasion" to describe the thinking of the Jacksonians in his book *The Jacksonian Persuasion* (1957). The Jacksonians were united by a persuasion, he asserted, consisting of "a matched set of attitudes, beliefs, projected actions: a half formulated moral perspective involving emotional commitment."[4] However, I use mentality to suggest intellectual systems somewhat better integrated, more consciously and closely thought out, and more steadily and positively purposeful than were those of the early Democracy. My use of mentality is nearer to the adaptation of Meyers's concept of persuasion made by Arthur F. Wright in 1960 in his book *The Confucian Persuasion*. Wright used the term to describe "the mix of mind and matter" that shaped and directed Confucian leadership in China over the ages. The men who have led China, Professor Wright asserted, "are not systematic thinkers, but men of thought and action. Each, in his way is selecting and adapting inherited ideas to the peculiar complexities of his time and milieu."[5] Precisely the same could be said of the leaders in each of the racial mentalities in the South, and of their followers as well. They were thoughtful people, but they were not philosophers. They were men and women who fused thought and action.

I can identify in the mind of the white South during the last century and a half three rather clear and distinct "matched sets" of thought about Negroes as Americans. All three mentalities made a judgment, among many other judgments, as to the future of Negroes in America. In this relation, the three can be easily ranged on a scale running from optimistic to pessimistic. As a way of beginning to understand the nature of each mentality and how it interacted with the others, it is useful to lay out the spectrum here.

At the top of the array was a mentality that I will style as "Liberal." Liberalism said, in brief, that it did not yet know the potential of the Negro. Racial Liberalism was strongest in the 1880s, and it was deeply impressed with the progress that black people had made under Northern leadership during Reconstruction, progress that antebellum whites would have declared impossible. Liberals rued the desertion of Negroes by Northern tutors after Reconstruction and the subsequent failure of Southern whites to pick up again the cross of missionary labor to blacks that they had, in their own eyes, carried before the war. In the 1880s Liberalism felt that the capacity of Negroes to absorb white culture in America had not yet been fairly tested, and it refused to close them out brusquely and across the board somewhere far below the white man. It was relatively open-ended in its view of the future of the Negro in the nation; and, most essentially, it possessed a sanguine faith, an optimistic adventurousness, a willingness to experiment in a search for progress that other mentalities lacked. Liberals were very few, but those few were articulate, highly energetic, and conspicuous.

Second, there was a "Conservative" mentality on race. Conservatism always began, proceeded, and ended upon the assumption of Negro inferiority. The Negro problem for Conservatives was simply a matter of defining the nature and the degree of Negro inferiority and of accommodating society thereto. It looked quite literally to the conservation of the Negro. It sought to save him by defining and fixing his place in American society. *Place* was the vital word in the vocabulary of Conservatism, and it applied to whites as well as to blacks. Conservatism probably had its effective beginning in the 1830s. It is the long-running and mass mode of thought on race in the white South, and, stubborn at its core and subtly pliant on its surface, it persists strong and essentially unchanged even today. Indeed, the other two mentalities, the Liberal and the Radical, are only the legitimate children of Conservatism. In the fashion of Professor Wright's Confucian leaders who evoked the past to meet the present, each in novel circumstances ran elements of orthodox Conservative thought out to extremes, each acted aggressively upon its new racial lights, and each eventually lost its patricidal struggle.

At the bottom of the scale, most significant for race relations in the twentieth-century South, and most pessimistic, was "Radicalism." The Radical mentality emerged vigorously about 1889 and ran until 1915. Between 1897 and 1907 it possessed terrific power. Radicalism envisioned a "new" Negro, freed from the necessarily very tight bonds of slavery and retrogressing rapidly toward his natural state of savagery and bestiality. Liberalism may have been, in essence, merely an improved version of Conservatism, but Radicalism differed sharply from Conservatism in that it anticipated the ultimate demise of the Negro in America. Radicals insisted that there was *no place* for the Negro in the future American society, and, moreover, that his disappearance was imminent.

Racial Radicalism was indeed radical, and the term is fitting. The seeds of Radicalism were old, as old as the first meetings between blacks and whites, but until the 1890s they had not taken root in America for long enough nor among a sufficient number of whites to have great effect. During the generation after 1889 the seeds took life, the plants flourished, and they covered the racial earth in the black belts of the South, almost to the exclusion of other growths. For a time the Radical persuasion profoundly altered public and private institutions to effect real reductions in the quality of life for black people. It also caused white people to reorder the white world in response to their changing perceptions of the nature of black people. Then, it dissolved. The transition is very intricate and complex in detail and in process, but it constituted a coherent pattern of evolution that eventuated in the particular Southern world of the 1920s and 1930s in which blacks as people were lost and Conservatism again reigned supreme. This was the world of Wilbur Cash in which both Liberalism and Radicalism had died as thought-sets, and each carefully buried in an unmarked grave somewhere behind conscious memory. But Radicalism, by far the more powerful of the two, had left a real legacy in the Negro much reduced. A part of that legacy was that black people lost visibility in white eyes unless they behaved in some acceptable Sambo-like manner. In the popular mind of the white South in the decades after World War I, there was no race problem, no black history, and no history of race relations if the Yankees and Communists, Catholics and Jews, outsiders and aliens would simply leave black people alone.

3

In the chapters that follow I will trace out this story. The primary burden of the first two chapters is to describe the black background, to essay an interpretation of what black people in the South were actually doing in the years up through the turn of the century. Interwoven into that tale is a description of the beginnings of the Conservative mentality among whites in the South in the late 1830s and its history up to the Civil War. Chapter III deals with the Conservative resurgence at the end of Reconstruction and afterward, with the Liberal revolt of the 1880s, and with the defeat of Liberalism. Chapters IV and V trace out the intellectual origins of Radicalism and seek to personalize that story through close studies of three important Radical leaders: Benjamin Ryan Tillman, a politician; Rebecca Latimer Felton, a leader in the movement for women's rights; and Thomas Dixon, Jr., a minister, writer, and social activist. These are people of "thought and action," the Confucian-like leaders of the Radical persuasion. Chapter VI seeks to identify the effects of Radicalism at the popular level by an examination of interracial violence. Chapter VII looks at Radicalism working in disfranchisement and segregation, and the Conservative response thereto. Chapter VIII describes the Conservative reaction to Radical violence and the retreat of Conservatism into certain areas of education, medicine, religion, and elsewhere. Chapter IX is an interpretation of how the three mentalities interplayed to educe, after about 1915, a new orthodoxy in race relations. Again, this was the world in which Cash and others of his generation matured. Chapters X and XI shift northward to examine, first, the white North looking at the South after Reconstruction, and then specifically at Northern politics working in the South in that era. Chapter XII follows Radicalism and Conservatism as both came eagerly to Washington with Woodrow Wilson in 1913 to play out in faithful echo the struggle in which they had engaged in the South over the preceding generation. Chapter XIII picks up black history again with "The Souls of Black Folk" and argues that the DuBoisian system was heavily influenced by Hegelian thought. Chapter XIV, "White Soul," builds upon the same philosophical foundation and traces out the impact of nineteenth-century idealism, and particularly Hegelianism, upon a rapidly changing South during the turn of the century years. Finally, Chapter XV begins with the end of Radicalism as a thought system about 1915 and sweeps through to the present, suggesting in its title "Legacy" that the story of race relations in the twentieth century is largely the *denouement,* the unwinding in the modern world of what had gone before. The Conclusion offers an overall interpretation of the evolution of Southern culture from the last generation of slavery to the present, a grand changeover in which the ruling elite shifted the basis of its power from a reliance upon the black mass through slavery to one that allied the white elite to the white mass through a broad array of essentially new institutions.

PART ONE

Slavery and After, to 1889

CHAPTER I

The Genesis of the Organic Society

BETWEEN TWO WORLDS

It is possible to construct an interpretation of the experience of the African in British America and subsequently the United States upon the assumption that black life has oscillated between two extremes of perfect separation and perfect integration. At one extreme, blacks might have found themselves practically outside of personal contact with white Americans—for instance, detached and settled upon a reserve that included South Carolina, Georgia, Alabama, and Mississippi. At the other extreme, they might have found themselves in a world in which no cultural distinction was attached to skin color, and they were melting physically and mentally into the white world. However, the nature of the society in which blacks have found themselves in America has prevented them from achieving the relative stability promised by either extreme. Rather has it cast them into a perpetual motion, moving first toward the one and then toward the other. Like some giant pendulum, the weight of black existence swings with a rush through a center line between separation and integration, but even as it moves beyond, the forces pulling it back increase with geometric rapidity.

The fluctuation between a perfect integration and a perfect separation began in the middle of the sixteenth century when white men from an aggressively expanding England came by sea to meet blacks south of the Sahara. Through enslavement, through the crossing of the Atlantic in the infamous "middle passage," and in the careful system of acculturation called "seasoning" in which the African was married to the plantation system and learned to survive in the New World, the process of depriving black people of their natal culture and of force-drafting them into European, English, and English-American culture proceeded very far, even in the first generation of those

11

taken. But when the very first black child was conceived, and born, and bred in America, a cultural mutation occurred. That child, and the brothers and sisters who came after, were lost to Africa far more than were their parents. No child can know precisely what its parents knew, and the life experience, the consciousness of a black born a slave in America was vastly different from that of an African born free. Each succeeding generation in America, by its very birth, moved a quick half-step farther away from the primal culture of Africa.

From the beginning, simple economics made it necessary that whites educate blacks into plantation living and, in some minimal degree, into life in the British-American world. But after about 1750, when the first great waves of African migrations had passed, there was no broadly concerted and highly effective attempt by the owners or the authorities to acculturate the African. Rather did the African in America seem to experience a kind of cultural neglect born of white indifference. Even so, as the generations passed, black Americans probably drifted rather vaguely toward whiteness.

Among white people, the Revolutionary generation was the first to pause and squarely face the broad issue of what was to be the future of black people in America. Generally speaking, they decided with relative ease that they were against slavery. But they evinced a profound and persistent ambivalence about black people, the great majority of whom were slaves. One could end slavery by legislative fiat, but blackness was another and much less tractable problem. What did the blackness of these people signify in cultural terms? Could black people once freed join the cultural communion of whiteness? And what did their blackness mean for the future of the new nation? In the North, emancipation was made easier by the relatively low proportion of Negroes in the total population. The same fact made freed blacks less threatening. In the South, large numbers of Negroes made both slavery and blackness very difficult problems. In the upper South, meaning North Carolina and points west and north to Mason's and Dixon's line (the southern border of Pennsylvania), the Revolutionary generation of Jefferson, Madison, and Monroe responded to the problem with a focus that their ancestors had lacked. They did so, in part, because theirs was the first generation in that part of America who knew what it was to be born white in small seas of black humanity. In the lower South, where the black population often outnumbered the white, the Revolutionary generation hardly recognized any problem with slavery. For them, slavery itself was the solution to the problem of blackness.

Black people had come to the South early, in 1619, close upon the heels of the English who settled at Jamestown in 1607. Slavery, too, came early and was fairly well defined in practice, concept, and law within fifty years of the arrival of the first blacks. But in this formative period, British America remained vastly white, even in the South. In 1648 in Virginia, for instance, only 300 blacks lived among 15,000 English. As late as 1681, blacks comprised only some 4 percent of the total population in this first settled British North American colony. The great majority of "bound" labor in the seventeenth century consisted not of black slaves, but of white people held to work for a fixed term of several years under the system of "indentured servitude," essentially a device for exchanging work for passage across the Atlantic to the New World. It was only in the early eighteenth century, about 1715, that Africans existed in such massive numbers as to stir the imagination, and the anxieties, of the already solidly entrenched whites. When blacks did come in great numbers in and after the 1690s, they came, of course, to the South, into Maryland and Virginia and the eastern portions of the Carolinas and Georgia. In Maryland and Virginia the black population rose to roughly 30 and 40 percent of the total by the middle of the eighteenth century. In South Carolina blacks outnumbered whites as early as 1708.[1]

Much of the leadership of Revolutionary Virginia was born amid waves of black migration and to parents wealthy in slaves. Thomas Jefferson's first remembrance was of being carried on a pillow held by a slave mounted on horseback from Albemarle, in western Virginia, to the plantation Tuckahoe, near Richmond. His father had undertaken the management of Tuckahoe for one of the Randolphs, his landed and slave-rich kinsman by marriage. There young Thomas grew up white and favored among a black slave population so numerous as to require seven overseers. Thomas Jefferson shared a color-conscious youth with many of the leaders of the Revolution in the South. He and they grew to manhood with a perspective on blackness that their parents born to whiter worlds could not have known.[2]

Nation-building compelled leaders in the Revolutionary generation to study slavery and black people with unprecedented intensity. The Founding Fathers were forced to think deeply and deliberately, as people not often do, about the far future of a whole people that was yet to be. Slavery emerged as a difficulty susceptible to solution. Both economics and Revolutionary ideology militated against it. In the upper South by the 1750s labor-intensive tobacco culture was rapidly losing ground to the cultivation of cereals, and the demand for slave labor was declining. At the same time, the idea of the natural rights of man was gaining currency, and that principle did not explicitly except black people from its rule. Jefferson himself, in 1776, drew the approval of his colleagues in the Continental Congress by beginning the Declaration of Independence with the ringing assertion that "all men are created equal, that they are endowed by the Creator with certain unalienable Rights, that among these are Life, Liberty and the pursuit of Happiness." Furthermore, in first drafting that document, he had indicted King George III for disallowing colonial laws attempting to halt the further importation of slaves, an item that was later deleted.[3] In 1784 Jefferson proposed, in an ordinance for the governance of western territories ceded to the national government by the states, that slavery be prohibited after the year 1800 west of the Appalachian Mountains. That proposal was defeated in the Confederation Congress by a vote of seven states to six.[4] However, in 1787 the Northwest Ordinance did pass. It prohibited the further introduction of slavery north and west of the Ohio River, and thus the whole of that vast territory from Indiana to Wisconsin was set in the direction of freedom at home and, when the struggle came, antislavery in the nation.[5]

Revolutionary society as a whole reflected Jefferson's antislavery inclinations. In 1776 slavery existed in each of the thirteen colonies. However, the "First Emancipation" began in New England with the beginning of the Revolution and proceeded southward over the next generation as state after state down through New Jersey and Pennsylvania either abolished slavery immediately or implemented some plan of gradual emancipation.[6] Antislavery sentiment by no means stopped at Mason's and Dixon's line. Indeed, there were more antislavery societies in the South in the 1820s than there were in the North, even though there seems to have been no organized antislavery movements in South Carolina and Georgia. Where slavery was not abolished, the various states, at least for economic if not for ideological reasons, acted independently to prohibit the importation of slaves from abroad. In 1794 no state licensed such additions to its black population. South Carolina and Georgia soon reversed themselves, but in 1808 Congress exercised the option offered by the Constitution and outlawed the further importation of slaves from abroad. Thus the total effect of the Revolutionary generation's actions on slavery was to press the institution southward below Mason's and Dixon's line and to push it into an isolation that led finally to extinction.

In the sense that slavery was ultimately eradicated by Americans themselves, it became a manageable problem. Blackness, on the other hand, proved to be perpetually unmanageable. Thought in the Revolutionary era tended against slavery, but it decided practically nothing about the meaning of blackness.[7] The perplexity of the Founding Fathers is fully understandable. To that generation and for at least a century afterward, culture was tied directly to color and blood. Inevitably they saw in the physical mixing of white and black a dilution of superior European culture. Shortly many of them thought that they saw precisely that phenomenon occurring in Latin America. To them the vital question of race relations was what color the complexion of the future American would be, and it was a question that gave them serious pause. Would future Americans be purely white by dint of excluding blacks from their society? Or would they be a mixture of white and black, a mongrel breed in a mongrel nation? What followed by way of answer were a few fretful starts, a rising hesitancy, ambivalence, indecision, and then drift. For a time after 1817, with the foundation and support of the American Colonization Society by such eminents as John Jay, Thomas Jefferson, and James Monroe, the resettlement of blacks abroad, particularly Africa, seemed a possible solution. The idea of inducing masses of people voluntarily to export themselves across the seas seemed not unrealistic to a white population that had so recently shipped itself to America by the tens of thousands. Liberia, a child state created by America in Africa in the 1820s, began to be peopled by Americanized blacks. Liberia survived and grew, but only slowly, and it did not flourish, primarily because the great majority of American blacks simply refused to go.[8] America, to them, was home.

In the long, hot summer of 1831 the drifting suddenly ceased. In August in southside Virginia, Nat Turner led a band of rebel slaves to slaughter, in the most horrible way with knives, axes, and crude guns, some fifty-seven whites and to be slaughtered themselves. The whites thus killed were nonslaveholders as well as slaveholders, kind slaveholders as well as unkind, women and children was well as men. The single clear condition that held all the massacred together was that they were white—a fact not lost upon contemporaries of the same color.[9] The message of the Turner insurrection was that when blacks rebelled, all whites died. There had been large-scale insurrections and insurrectionary plots in the United States and abroad before, and whites were never totally free of the fear. But for nearly a century any real plots in the South had been nipped in the bud. Before the advent of Nat Turner reasonable people could believe that it could not happen here, that the American South was different, and that fears of servile insurrection were for the faint-hearted who overreacted to plots and rumors of plots. Turner's rebellion had one transcendent result: massive slave rebellion in the South was lifted from the realm of possibility and conjecture and placed with terrific bluntness in the realm not only of the possible, but of the probable. With that great traumatic convulsion, the broad current of race relations in the South was wrenched up and out of its former channel. Like a great river disrupted by some giant earthquake, it poured out over the land in a rushing search for a new bottom, a new place to flow smoothly in the natural order of things.

THE HARD-SOFT PERIOD OF SLAVERY

The signal response of the white South to Nat Turner's insurrection came in the meeting of the Virginia legislature in the winter of 1831–32. Virtually the whole of that session was devoted to a great debate on slavery. Antislavery Virginians insisted upon facing the issue of what the state should do about that institution. While no vote was taken upon the precise question of whether to end slavery or not, a vote was taken on a motion that is often considered to have been an effective test of the question. If that assumption is warranted, emancipation in Virginia was defeated by a very narrow margin of 65 to 58.[10]

It would appear, then, that at times before Nat Turner there was a fair chance that Virginia would go the way of New England and the Middle States and become a free state. Had it done so, it is very possible that the Civil War would not have occurred, and the Southern nation that existed from 1861 to 1865 would never have come to be. In 1830 nearly a quarter of the 2,000,000 slaves in America lived in Virginia.[11] Without slavery in Virginia there would have been far fewer slaves to supply the slave frontier to the southwest, to help make cotton a self-crowned king to defy the world. Without slavery the state's political weight would have been thrown into the balance with the free states in the face of threats of secession and civil war from the lower South. Without Virginia, Robert E. Lee, a host of able generals and other officers, and more than 200,000 soldiers would have been denied to any future Southern Confederacy and their numbers added to those against the rebels. Without it, the war would have been fought, if there had been a war at all, in South Carolina and south and west of that testy state, and it would have been a very abortive affair. One can, of course, exaggerate the importance of Nat Turner's insurrection, the Virginia debates, and of Virginia itself at this juncture. There was rebelliousness among the slaves before 1831 and a response among whites. There was always dissent against slavery among whites in the South. Always some people opposed the evil, and some of these spoke out against it. Nevertheless, the Turner insurrection and its sequel marked the last time that slavery was seriously challenged in Dixie by both blacks and a powerful combination of Southern whites. Thereafter, there would be no more slave rebellions in the South approaching such magnitude, and organized antislavery action would become an exclusively Northern phenomenon.

The debates in the Virginia legislature and their result were a signal, an indicator of how the upper South in the post-Revolutionary generation was going to respond to slavery. In 1834 Tennessee and in 1835 North Carolina held constitutional conventions in which they followed Virginia's lead. In the end, the upper South decided that it could not dismount from the tiger of slavery. It must, therefore, take the animal by the ears and ride. That decision was one of the critical turning points in the creation of a distinctive Southern people and in the genesis of a racial universe within which we in America still struggle today.

After the Virginia debates and during the last generation of slavery, a paradox occurred in race relations in the South. Even as white society came to impose a more rigid police control over black people, it also moved across the race line to touch blacks with unprecedented intimacy. This era may well be called the "hard-soft" period of slavery. On the one hand, white society elaborated and tightened the laws dealing with blacks, both slave and free, and revamped the police system for enforcing those laws. On the other side, white people went among black people in a new style. Whites strove hard to make a place for black people in the white-dominated world, to integrate them, as it were, into a harmonious order—almost to make them white. Ultimately what had begun as an effort to change blacks ended in the reconstitution of white society itself. Out of the labor of race control was born an altered Southern character. That character and the culture that supported it grew in the face of a North that at first saw and repudiated William Lloyd Garrison and a passion for immediate emancipation but finally came, by 1861, with its 22,000,000 people, to deny slavery and the Southern order the right to expand beyond the limits then imposed upon them.

After Turner's insurrection and the decision that they must ride the tiger, Southern states generally enacted more stringent laws for the control of black people, both slave and free. For example, black people were not allowed to assemble together in any considerable numbers, even to worship, without a white person present. It became universally illegal in the South to teach slaves to read or write for fear that they would use those skills to foment insurrection. Slaves were not, of course, allowed to have weapons; but they were also not to have drums or trumpets that might be used to pass signals, nor to work in pharmacies where they might have access to poisons. The curtailing of the rights of free Negroes was also striking. In North Carolina after 1835 free Negroes were not allowed to vote. In South Carolina restrictions upon their worship were so tight that the African Methodist Church felt constrained to close its doors and withdraw from the state.[12] Finally, new laws regulated more closely the behavior of white people in relation to blacks. For instance, a Richmond ordinance of 1859 imposed a fine of up to twenty dollars upon any white person who beat a slave unlawfully, and inflicted lashes or a fine upon any free person of color who did so.[13]

In addition to special slave laws, brought together from time to time in the so-called slave codes, blacks were regulated by the master's rules on the plantation itself. Those rules, built around a desire to utilize the labor of the slave to the maximum, closely fixed such details as hours of work and rest, feeding, and care of tools and clothing. The law of the plantation left few hands idle for the devil's use. Above the slave codes were provisions in the general laws of the states that paid special attention to blacks. For instance, criminal codes often prescribed lashes for blacks and fines for white people, and the crimes for which a black person might be punished by death far outnumbered those for which a white person might suffer the same fate. There were also national laws that impinged especially upon black people. The federal government itself guaranteed the rendition of fugitive slaves and, in its commitment to suppress "domestic insurrection," was bound to put down slave revolts. In the revamping of the fugitive slave law in 1850 to facilitate the return of runaway slaves and in the ready repression of John Brown's rebellion in 1859, the federal government showed itself not remiss in honoring these commitments.

Effective police control of Southern blacks was a function of both white numbers and white alertness. In the black belts of the South where slaves were heavily concentrated and in a majority, vigilance was the crucial element. Antebellum Southern whites knew well enough that eternal vigilance was the price of slavery as well as freedom—and the price, too, of the security of their own lives and property. The local police, the state militia, and, ultimately, the armed forces of the United States stood ready to control the slaves. But the immediate instrument by which white society as a whole consciously and officially kept black people in check was the "patrol." The patrol was the front line of defense in what was, in essence, an undeclared war between the races.

The patrol began as early as the seventeenth century, and it varied in constitution and function from state to state and from time to time. In the colonial period it was usually made up of masters and overseers, people with a direct stake in slavery who banded together with full legal authority to enforce the laws of slavery. In the nineteenth century the constitution of the patrol shifted; its essential feature in this new phase was that, typically, every white male of military age and capacity—not only masters and overseers—was required to serve, sometimes without pay. Increasingly the patrol assumed the aspect of a *posse comitatus* enlisted by the state in an emergency. It savored of the power of the government to command the services of its citizens in cases of fire, flood, or foreign invasion. The patrol had authority not only over slaves, but over free blacks as well, and over any white person who might be suspected of conspiring with blacks in illegal activities. It was, in short, a system in which virtually all white men came together to enforce the racial establishment. In the patrol every white man was a policeman in the face of every black person. In the institution of the patrol in the years before the Civil War, one can see the racial system meshing smoothly into the slave system. Slavery was no longer simply a matter of economics, nor of masters controlling slaves in a somewhat separated segment of society. It had become a matter of all whites controlling all blacks ... a matter of race.

Particularly, it was the duty of the patrol to ride the highways and byways at night while the masters slept. In effect, patrols were courts on horseback. They arrested blacks away from their plantations without passes, searched their persons and cabins for arms and stolen goods, and broke up meetings. Patrols were often made up of three, six, nine, or a dozen men; they were juries or fractions of juries with the power to try, judge, sentence, and punish offenders on the spot. These were summary courts over which masters had little immediate control. Most especially the patrol enforced the laws regulating blacks, but the design of those laws and the raison d'être of the patrol were very clearly to stop insurrections before they began. So central to the concerns of white people in the black-belt states was the problem of racial control that the very term applied to the area for which a patrol was responsible, the "beat," came to be applied to the smallest area of civil administration. What was a "township" in New England and the Northwest and a "community" or a "parish" in other areas, in the deep South was a "beat." In South Carolina the term "beat" was replaced by "township" only in 1868 after the carpetbaggers assumed control, and in Alabama and Mississippi to this day "beat" remains the designation for the smallest governmental and political subdivision in rural areas. The persistence of the term in these three states is but indicative of the lastingly high ratios of blacks to whites, the danger to which white lives and limbs were subjected, and the intensity of racial feelings there.[14]

The militant South, the military South prone to shoot first and answer questions later, did and still does exist. It sprang from the necessity of controlling a potentially explosive black population. In the nineteenth-century South the key to control lay in possessing all the guns and the mobility that horses afforded. Given blacks armed only with knives, axes, and hoes, it was very possible that a single white man could match twenty slaves. On the other side, Negroes were well aware of the facts of life, and of death, and of the odds against them in an insurrection. It is possible that every major insurrectionary plot from the Stono affair in South Carolina in 1739 to John Brown's raid in Virginia in 1859 included some plan for seizing an arsenal, and it is certain that whites saw that red thread woven into every scheme for slave rebellion. The fact that John Brown struck at the federal arsenal at Harper's Ferry was an awfully accurate testimony to Southerners of the deadly seriousness of the threat he represented.

White Southerners were alert to rebelliousness among their slaves, and they by no means relaxed between open outbreaks. They were fearful of the insidious attacks of arsonists and poisoners; and they took anything less harmless than a childlike face and manner among blacks as an open threat to peace and good order. In one sense they were too fearful, but in another they could hardly be fearful enough. Masters and mistresses were terribly vulnerable, in themselves and vastly more so through their loved ones. They could not long forget the tortuously precarious way of their lives. After 1830, as Southerners saw themselves threatened by the North from the outside, their fears of the enemy within increased. They took small comfort in John Brown's defeat by United States Marines under Colonel Robert E. Lee when every night might hide the infiltration of dozens of other John Browns into the South. Secession offered some protection, but even secession itself was accompanied by a great well-poisoning scare that swept eastward from Texas through the lower South in 1860 and 1861. Indeed, there seemed to be no safe place, and armed surveillance the best and only refuge.

The military personality that we call Spartan arose in an ancient society where a master class confronted a slave population some twenty times its size. The South was not another Sparta, but it was Spartan-like, and from a comparable necessity. The message of the South to its young men in the last decades of slavery was to be, perhaps, more Spartan than the Spartans. If people are told early and late, and often and long, that they are the very sons of Mars, if their rewards and pleasures—night and day, before whites and blacks, men and women, fathers and mothers, powerful and powerless—tend to come from striking the military pose, then they will strike it. And if they play the martial role long enough, intensively enough, and without relief, then they tend to become precisely what they play.

The martial spirit in the South was further advanced by the fact that the militia in the various states was inextricably bound up with the patrol system. Every state supported a militia in which every white male of military capacity was enrolled. Typically the militia was organized by counties, each county supplying one or more regiments. The county was subdivided into districts that supplied the men for a company. These were usually townships, parishes, communities, or "beats." Whatever the civil designation, the beat of the patrol, the area of its responsibility, was exactly the same one that supported the militia company. Usually the county sheriff or the county court was responsible for organizing the patrol. Immediate supervision most often was assigned to the company officers of the militia. The militia captain was also the captain of the patrol, and the same men served in both organizations under the same officers. Consequently, the South was a social order in which every able-bodied white man was a trooper in the service of the racial state. The antebellum South was military-minded, and it was full to overflowing with military titles, not only with colonels but with a plethora of majors and captains as well. Those titles sprang from a central and vital function—race control. They were not ludicrous, or empty, or even merely honorific. When one Southerner addressed another as "Cap'n," it did mean something.

It was no accident that the Southern landscape was dotted with preparatory schools run rigidly along the military model and that the various states established military academies in the style of West Point. In 1859 when Louisiana recruited William Tecumseh Sherman to open its State Seminary and Military Academy, Braxton Bragg, a fellow West Pointer who had become a successful Louisiana planter, advised him that "every plantation is a small military establishment—or it ought to be." It was not slaves as soldiers that he had in mind, but rather management. "Give us well-disciplined masters, managers, and assistants," he urged the commandant, "and we shall never hear of slave insurrections."[15] Louisiana was late in starting, but the Virginia Military Institute (1839) and South Carolina's academy, The Citadel (1842) in Charleston, had for nearly a generation produced officers who did not need to blush deeply in the presence of graduates of the United States Military Academy.

Black-belt white Southerners of military age were conditioned to leap into the saddle at the mere suspicion of a black revolt, and, apparently, after Nat Turner they had an abundance of exercise in that drill. Young Southerners understood that a large part of their mission was to avoid large and disastrous outbreaks by suppressing small ones quickly and with exhibitory ruthlessness. "Overkill" was a way of interracial life in the South. An insurrection, a threat of insurrection, or a presumption of insurrectionary intent was a mandate to chase, seize, search, lash, and to scar psychologically as much as physically, to squelch the rise this time and to deter its happening again. White men also understood that divisiveness among whites in the face of the enemy had to be minimized, and that they ought to be as ruthless against deviation among whites as among blacks. It was literally a living fact in the world of the antebellum South that every white man, ideally, had to be more than a man to face the rising enemies both within and outside the walls of the peculiar institution. It is probably true that most Southerners conditioned to martial postures by the travail of slavery and by a generation of militancy really believed, in 1861, that one of them could lick ten Yankees.

Even as they were moving to enforce a more stringent slavery upon blacks, Southern whites were also moving to reach across the race line to contact black people in a softer style. Most clear in this regard were the activities of the churches, and especially those of the evangelical sects. In South Carolina in 1858, for example, Baptists counted 22,000 blacks among their formally enrolled members. In addition they probably ministered separately to several times that number without having enlisted them in the white-dominated congregations. In 1860 Methodists in the Palmetto State carried 42,000 Negroes on their rolls, and the Presbyterians counted 5,000 blacks in a membership that totaled only 13,000. Interestingly the Presbyterians in South Carolina offered both some of the most ardent and effective proslavery protagonists, such as James Henley Thornwell, sometime president of the South Carolina College, and some of the most conscientious laborers among black people, such as Dr. J. L. Girardeau. In 1850 Girardeau organized Zion Church in Charleston with special provision for a Negro membership that grew to several hundred. The church building itself, designed to seat 2,000, became the frequent meeting place of the liberated Negro community after the occupation of the city by the Union Army early in 1865. The Episcopalians were also influential in reaching across the race line into the Negro world. On the eve of the Civil War they claimed some 3,000 Negro members. Given the facts the churches regularly touched more people than they took in as members and that the entire black population in South Carolina numbered about 400,000 including children, a formal enrollment of some 72,000 was indeed impressively large.[16]

The indications are that South Carolina was not unique, that in and after the 1830s all over the South the movement of white churchmen into black worlds proceeded with purposeful vigor.[17] In fact, in the last generation of slavery many eminent churchmen earned their fame as missionaries to the slaves. It was, for a time, the frontier of Southern religion, and ambitious young clerics went there to seek their fortunes.

In the last three decades before the Civil War, Southern churchmen were also in the vanguard of those who constructed what came to be called the proslavery argument. In its beginning, this was a defense of slavery that drew upon every aspect of thought and art from theology to science to literature. The argument was based, ultimately, upon race. The truth was, it asserted, that black people were creatures inferior to white people. God had made black people precisely to be slaves, and it was the genius of white Southerners to recognize that fact. Thus, racism was finally turned fully to the service of slavery. It was, in effect, married to slavery, and as the marriage matured race became the junior partner in the union. At its crest, the proslavery argument was so vital, so dynamic that it reached out to anticipate, for its own peculiar purposes, evolutionary science and sociology. It was fantastically imaginative, informed by masses of research, and profoundly and intricately worked out. On the eve of conflict it was a weirdly beautiful flower, the black orchid of antebellum Southern intellectual culture.[18]

Elaborate as it was, the proslavery argument was only a small part of a larger effort involving a tremendous outpouring of energy. Whites worked diligently, desperately, and, given their particular lights, one must say brilliantly to build a place for black people in their economy, their religion, politics, philosophy, literature, and even in their families. They were amazingly successful in this vast endeavor, and their success was still growing when the war came.

Out of the mix of mind and matter involved in the evolution of Southern culture, whites in the last decades of slavery began to build a stereotypical image of the black person as simple, docile, and manageable. They labored hard to see all blacks as, essentially, perpetual children. In time, that image of the Negro came to be labeled "Sambo." Sambo, the name given to the second son in some African cultures, was one of the several most popular among male slaves in the South. In colonial times there had been no single ruling image of black people in the white mind. Indeed, slave traders and buyers had closely marked the differences between Africans because the traits, real or imagined, of various peoples were directly related to their prices as slaves. It was only in the last generation of slavery that all blacks came to look alike in the eyes of Southern whites, and the person they chose to see was Sambo. The Sambo of imagination was a child adopted into the white family, an adult black body with a white child's mind and heart, simultaneously appealing and appalling, naturally affectionate and unwittingly cruel, a social asset and a liability. Sambo had within him, then, two terrific and opposite capacities. Improperly cared for, he became bestial, an animal in human form and all the more dangerous because of his human capabilities. Properly managed, on the other hand, he was like a white child—and dear.

Seen from the black side, playing Sambo was simply a way to survive. When local whites panicked into color-coded hysteria (which they did recurrently), Sambo was a mask behind which black people might survive the holocaust. Downcast eyes, shuffling feet, soft uncertain words, and a totally pliant manner were white-invented signals to be used by a black person to say that this individual was no threat. The role sometimes saved blacks. Indirectly, it also sometimes saved whites themselves from the wild and murderous behavior that did damage to their flattering image of themselves as protecting parents to these childlike people.

The Sambo role also worked toward building up a social structure designed to afford stability and security to all. In the role, black people were called upon to perform like white people, but to stop short of being totally white. In the role, black people were here to stay, perpetually, as slaves. No longer did Southerners talk of recolonizing all American blacks in Africa, the Caribbean islands, or out West among the displaced Indians. The positive inducements offered to black people to become like whites were great. To be Christian, to labor well and faithfully in their place within the slave system, to be family people, in brief to be "civilized," was to gain a certain measure of respect and security from the whites that slaves might value. At the living level, survival for slaves depended upon their seeming to be white-like, as well as upon their not being too white to threaten the whites. It seems that many things conspired in those last three decades of slavery to cause black people to learn the ways of the white world and to practice them, even as they evolved a consciousness of the great chasm that separated them from a happy entry into that world.

In reality, of course, Sambo was a creature purely of the white mind, a device by which white slaveholders day by day masked a terror that might otherwise have driven them over the edge of sanity. In time, however, the Sambo role functioned to build white egos. The role was, after all, beautifully fitted to flatter the white man's image of himself. He was the superior, the Spartan warrior and the winner. The Negro was the subordinate. The white man was the Christian, civilized gentleman carrying the message to the heretofore heathen and savage black. He was doing God's work in the Southern world, and it was a labor that would earn him grace in the hereafter. The slaveholder's women were worthy and willing helpmates in that effort. If Sambo came to have a role with certain moves to make on the Southern stage and certain lines to speak, so too did his masters.

Black people probably did not much internalize the Sambo role because it was ultimately unflattering.[19] It seems clear enough that they had the strength to resist that role, to wear it as a mask when necessary and to set it aside at will. Tight as it was, the slave system was simply not tight enough to force blacks to become the Sambos they played. Negroes were not always under the eyes of the whites. There were some blacks who were not slaves, and even the slaves could build other roles for themselves in the woods and swamps, in the cabins at night, and even in the fields by day. Moreover, in song, dance, religion and folk tales they lived through metaphor beyond the ken of whites.[20]

THE ORGANIC SOCIETY

White people could not prescribe and enforce a precise role upon black people without prescribing and enforcing a precise role upon themselves. If blacks were to be held in place, white people would have to assume a place to keep them there. In brief, if there were to be Sambos, there would have to be Sambos' keepers, and the keeper role, being superior, had to be even more firmly fixed than the role of the kept. In practice, of course, there would have to be a broad range of Sambos (male and female, house servants, artisans, drivers, field hands, adults and children) and a broad range of keepers (masters, mistresses, overseers, nonslaveholders, physicians, merchants, and ministers). But the varieties, obviously, were not nearly so important as the species.

The movement to reform the late Old South into an ideal, unitary order of masters and slaves, whites and blacks, was a drive to achieve what might be called an "organic" society. In that order there would be various parts in the social body, and every part would have its place and function. In that society everyone would have a role to play. To use the image that prevailed in late-medieval Western civilization, the head would not want to be the heart, and the hand would not pine to be the head. Rather each would function contentedly in its place according to its nature. In the organic society, people would know their own places and functions and those of others around them. They would govern themselves in those places with keen awareness of the approval of others within their circle. As a personality, the individual would be "other directed" rather than "inner directed."[21] His or her values would be relative and fluid in response to society rather than fixed and absolute. Diversity would be the complement of unity; conscious individuality and power within the accepted circle of society would be its strength. This ideal world would need many different parts, each with distinct functions, but each would mesh smoothly with the others into one harmonious whole. When things had found their places, real dissent from within was inconceivable, and criticism from without would become inconsequential.

In the organic society idealized by the Old South the key people were the men and women of the white elite. They were, one might say, the head and the heart of society. Their roles were rather precisely prescribed. The white elite was dominated by the large slaveholders. In 1860 there were some 10,000 individuals who possessed fifty or more slaves whom they worked on tobacco, rice, sugar, and cotton plantations from Maryland down to Florida and across into Texas and Arkansas.[22] Since the average family in that period contained about five people, this meant that some 50,000 men, women, and children belonged to the planter elite. Some lesser planters belonged to the elite because of birth, education, or manner. Planters themselves often served as leading ministers, lawyers, merchants, politicians, professors, and physicians; at other times these special functions were performed by their faithful allies. In the organic society, Southern men of the higher order were supposed to play a paternalistic role. They were to behave as fathers not only to blacks, but also to white women and children of their own sort and to the lower orders of whites of both sexes.

The roles of upper-class men and women in the Old South were generally reinforced and given specific form by Victorian concepts of the family. Essentially the Victorian family was the early-nineteenth-century creature of the industrial revolution and a Romantic reaction against the extreme rationalism of the Enlightenment. The Victorian family cast men as the physical protectors of society, and women as its moral conservators. It was specially the function of each man to protect physically and provide materially for his wife and children. It was he who was to venture forth into the harsh world to succeed and "bring home the bacon." It was the function of the wife to be submissive to her husband and to make the home morally strong and physically comfortable. At home every evening the husband would find physical ease and, most important, moral sustenance after a hazardous day in a world of open competition. Most of all, women were to be the conservators of piety. Pious and pure, domestic and submissive, they were the veritable angels of the earth, God's agents in human form. As such, it was the wife and mother who was most responsible for the spiritual education of the children.[23] The Victorian world thoroughly loved the idea that "the hand that rocks the cradle rules the world." Thus the chain of command, the flow of moral energy so to speak, ran from God to mother, to boys and girls, to men, and through men out into the world and back home again to women for spiritual regeneration every evening, weekend, and holiday. The family, the hearthstone, the heavenly sanctioned and harmonious union between husband and wife, was the very center of earthly good.

Victorian ideas were imported into the North just as they were into the South. The difference was that in the South the roles were intensified to an extraordinary degree because all roles among Southern whites had to be deeply internalized and earnestly played in order to keep Sambo in his place. White women and white men in the South became something that their contemporaries in the North did not. Southern men had to be gentlemen, or aspire to be, and all women were ladies. In the South in and after the 1830s Victorian prescriptions of role were woven firmly into fabrics of male and female identity already reshaping themselves to meet the black threat.

Threads of high feudalism were also woven into the culture of the late Old South. The relishing, for instance, of the idea of men as chivalrous knights and women as castellated ladies was not merely coincidental, nor was it frivolous. On the contrary it was immanent and deadly serious. The concept of the organic society is, of course, ancient, but its modern phase is late medieval in origin. It sprang from the centuries around 1200 when a rather desperate Western society, having barely survived invasions by the barbarians, then the Moslems, and at last the Vikings, drew itself together into rather rigid orders of churchmen, royalty, nobles, serfs, and, finally, townspeople. Everyone recognized by the society was fixed in place and function. The purpose of such fixedness was no less than the survival of Western civilization against external threat and internal dissolution.

Before the nineteenth century, the late medieval period was also the last great age of idealism, revolving, of course, around Christian idealism. During the Renaissance the philosophical center began to shift toward realism, a process that continued with the scientific revolution and led to the Age of the Enlightenment in which rationalism and realism were virtually enshrined. In the minds of many people in the West, the bloody chaos of the French Revolution and the subsequent rampage of the beast Napoleon became associated with an excess of realism. In a sense, when Napoleon went down at Waterloo, so too did the philosophy of the Enlightenment. After 1815 the center of thinking shifted again, this time back in the direction of idealism. By the 1830s, when Victorianism came to America, the reaction was in full swing, and America imported along with Victorianism a heavy cargo of idealism. Idealism saw truth in the idea of the thing rather than in the thing itself. Ideas of the monarchy, of the church, and of man and woman were the realities. Truth was approximated best not by natural laws, but by such ideas as love, duty, and honor, piety, purity, and motherhood. Idealism, like Victorianism, flooded the North as well as the South. In the North it helped give rise to Emerson, Thoreau, and the Transcendentalists. In the South it rendered legitimate the abstraction of ideas of slavery, gentility, and paternalism. Again there was no difference between the idealism that came into the North and that which came into the South. What differed was the use each made of it. In the South it was turned to the support of slavery, and it was woven into the cultural fabric being created out of old threads and new. The new threads were the roles of black and white, the Victorian roles of men and women, and of knights and ladies with their retainers.

Thus a process of change that had begun with a readjustment to the presence of menacing blacks and resulted first in the creation of a Sambo role for blacks and a paternalistic role for whites, now added roles drawn from the Victorian order, roles that were reinforced by overtones that smacked of the high feudal ages—all overlaid by a template of idealism in the form of its post-Napoleonic Western revival. There remained to be infused into the reconstructed Southern order one more vital element, that of Romanticism.

Romanticism went with idealism and Victorianism, like, one might say, a soft hand in a velvet glove. The Romantics sought truth through feelings rather than reason. They raised emotions, intuition, faith, and sentiment from the level of the despicable to the divine. Romanticism was primarily a mood, verbalized most succinctly in the words from Keats's "Ode on a Grecian Urn":

> "Beauty is truth, truth Beauty."—that is all
> Ye know on earth, and all ye need to know.

—probably the most quoted lines in the nineteenth-century South. When the South adopted Romanticism, it had abandoned Thomas Jefferson and the Age of Reason. In time the North would move through Romanticism and into other things, but in the South Romanticism and its allies would persist long after the cause of its being there had died.

At the height of the Romantic era in the mid-nineteenth century, Western civilization looked admiringly back to that seemingly static and secure age of high feudalism as some beau ideal. It appropriated for itself the chivalric image in which the best men were knights who donned their armor and went out to fight for noble, and indeed holy, causes. It also absorbed the courtly manners ascribed to that era. Gentlemen respected ladies of proper birth, and relations between gentlemen and ladies were governed by precise and well-understood rules. The United States at large shared in the Romantic revival of the chivalric ideal. The South, however, not only accepted the basic formula, it elaborated upon and practiced it to an extraordinary degree. Elite Southerners knew about Richard the Lion-Hearted, they knew about Eleanor of Aquitaine, and they emulated what they understood to be their styles. *Ivanhoe* (1820), one of Sir Walter Scott's knightly stories, was the most popular novel in the South before the Civil War. Southerners actually engaged in tournaments in which men on horseback "jousted" with relatively harmless lances and played other knightly games. The victor won the right to name the "Queen," often styled the "Queen of Love and Beauty," who "reigned" with her ladies-in-waiting at the evening ball that followed the tournament. The winner's prowess was thus dedicated to her honor. During the "combat" he carried her handkerchief hidden in his clothes at his bosom, and that was his real reward—to battle for her. Publicly, his victory was gladly surrendered to her triumph. It was all very Romantic, very idealistic, and very Victorian, even as it seemed very medieval. Knightly combat between gentlemen often enough passed beyond social games into games that were deadly serious. In the South the code *duello* persisted as a way of life among gentlemen unmatched in intensity elsewhere in America.

Placeness was the key word in the organic society, and thus in the social order of the Old South. Inevitably placeness included hierarchy. Some parts of the body are more vital than others. A hand is expendable, a head is not. Andrew Jackson's revolution notwithstanding, the elite in the Old South on the eve of the Civil War was not democratic in its attitudes. It believed in an aristocracy of talent and that talented people should rise. But it did not believe that all men were equal or ought to be treated equally. Some people were better than others, it declared, and a proper society, a proper ordering of persons, would recognize that fact. Southern law itself was not blind to color, frankly unequal, and seemed not vastly disturbed by the split-level justice it meted out. Black people, slave and free, got lashes and white people got fines. And above and beyond the written law was the "code," the private law by which gentlemen organized relations among themselves and with others. A gentleman owed it to his honor to respect himself and to respect others in their proper places. If anyone got out of place and offended, a gentleman had clearly prescribed methods for rectifying the situation and "satisfying" his honor.

In private law, as in public law, different punishments were meted out to different sorts. The last resort in a difference with another gentleman was the duel, which constituted a penultimate recognition of equality between gentlemen. Disagreements with men of the lesser sort were to be settled by means less honorable to the offender, by horsewhipping, beating with a stick, or even by having someone else administer the punishment in behalf of the gentleman offended. The perfect illustration of the latter is the famous Sumner-Brooks affair. When Massachusetts Senator Charles Sumner made a speech on the floor of the Congress in 1856 in which he alluded to the fact that South Carolina Senator Andrew Butler expectorated when he talked, which that elderly gentleman did, he forfeited any claim to gentility by referring to an unfortunate, unavoidable personal infirmity. By the code, the task of exacting justice from Sumner fell to Butler's proximate kinsman, the very physical Congressman Preston Brooks. After due deliberation and in a seemingly calm mood, Brooks selected a walking cane of proper heft. He walked onto the Senate floor where Sumner sat at his desk writing. Brooks called Sumner's name. When Sumner turned to face him, Brooks struck him over the head. When Sumner tried to stand, Brooks struck him again and continued to strike him until the cane shattered and Sumner fell to the floor bleeding profusely. It was two years before Sumner returned to the Senate chamber, and all over the

South gentlemen made up purses to buy Brooks new canes, usually with highly complimentary inscriptions. These men understood precisely what Brooks had done. He had punished a man of the lower orders for an offense against the honor of an aged kinsman who was physically too infirm to exact justice for himself. He did not give Sumner a gentleman's chance to defend himself, and he did not simply shoot him. He chastised Sumner, ignominiously, calmly, without putting his hand upon him, almost as he would whip a rebellious dog.[24]

By their acts Southerners of the upper orders frankly repudiated any Jeffersonian inclination to treat all men equally. They went rather with John C. Calhoun, who exalted the inequality of men, and they sought to organize society hierarchically to accommodate their various capacities. It was precisely fitting that the Confederacy should elect Jefferson Davis as its president. The essential facts of his life are nearly perfectly symbolic of the evolution of Southern culture. Davis was born of farmer stock in Kentucky in 1808, ironically not a hundred miles from the place where Abraham Lincoln was born a year later. Both were born in modest material circumstances, but each was vastly rich in talent. By 1861 Davis was wealthy in Mississippi land and slaves, but, more important to the South, he was a paragon of the gentlemanly ideal, the living representative of the potential high elegance of Southern culture. Jefferson Davis was named for Thomas Jefferson, but his very life had marked the travels of the South away from Jeffersonian ideals.[25] By the time of the Civil War the elite in the South saw itself as aristocratic, and they saw Northern leadership as plebeian. Abe Lincoln as the "common man" in the White House might have had great appeal in the North and West, but in the South he was an anathema. His election struck incisively at one great difference between Northern and Southern culture. The ruling elite in the South was bending strongly in the direction of a hierarchic social universe, while the North was tending democratic.

The idealized organic society of the Old South featured placeness in time as well as function. In that increasingly structured society, there was a time for every event and a procedure for carrying it through. Courtship, marriage, birth, death, and social relations of all kinds had their forms, as they do in all societies. But in the South, the forms were more important, and they were very closely prescribed. Behavior after marriage, for example, was specified in detail, especially for women. The demeanor of ladies, the behavior of gentlemen, the lower orders of whites, and blacks all came to be increasingly ritualized. Forms of address denoted station. Hats on heads or off and yielding walkways established order in personal encounters all the way up and down the social pyramid. As young people grew up in this system, they behaved almost as if they had been drilled in a military fashion in the rituals of human interaction. Behavior came to be delivered as promised in the contract implied by accepting membership in the social order, namely, by being born there.

"The principals are to be respectful in meeting and neither by look or expression irritate each other," South Carolinian John Lide Wilson instructed the would-be duelists who read his 1838 booket on the etiquette of maintaining one's honor. "They are to be wholly passive . . . ," he continued, moving beyond a prescription for behavior to one for mood. The pistol, he directed, is to be handed to the duelist in a certain way, and the duelist grasps it "midway the barrell," As in a play, even the words of the participants are prescribed. When the first pair of shots has been fired, the second of the challenged party approaches the second of the challenger and says: "Our friends have exchanged shots, are you satisfied, or is there any cause why the combat should be continued?" One could hardly imagine more precise instructions and a stricter ritual.[26]

Duels were tied to honor, and honor very often involved women; James Marion Sims, a pioneer gynecologist, declared that he was "educated to believe that duels inspired the proprieties of society and protected the honor of women."[27] It was then, perhaps, no accident that Wilson also edited the Southern edition of the beautifully romantic tale of Cupid and Psyche, and that he also authored the manuals for sword and artillery drills for the South Carolina militia. Psyche might well have been the genteel Southern lady. Psyche was mortal, but fairer than Venus. Though cursed by the jealous goddess and afflicted with the frailties of humankind, Psyche strove and, with the help of the gods (particularly Jupiter), triumphed.[28] *Psyche,* the Greek word for "butterfly," was also the word for "soul." The butterfly represents a height in beauty achieved out of the lowly and earthly caterpillar, a loveliness that has a brilliant moment in the sun and dies. Soul is the essential reality, the ultimate truth of God as given to man. Sweet ephemeral beauty and lasting truth was the Southern woman. All else were but aspiring shadows, and all found life through her. Put on a pedestal, enshrined like a holy object, woman was to be approached only through a set ritual. Cupid is a handsome young god, the son of Venus and Jupiter, and Psyche's lover. Ironically, he brings love with an instrument of death. He smites the intended through the heart with an arrow. Love begins with a wound, open and bleeding.

"Upon the word swords being given," John Lide Wilson instructs the South Carolina militia soldier in one of his manuals, "direct the eyes to the sword hilt, bringing the right hand with a brisk action across the body and seize the hilt, at the same time seize the scabbard with the left hand; draw the sword about four inches, and wait in that position for the next word of command."[29] Swords and pistols, love, sex, and violence, women, blood, and death, were all becoming inextricably mixed in that Southern world before the Civil War. It was a world in flux and under pressure, and rituals gave the planter elite a feeling of order, a sense that certain acts, certain words, and even certain emotions ought to and did follow one another with predictable, reassuring regularity.

Southerners had cast off from the ideals of the Revolutionary generation, and they were moving into a separate culture that was both like and increasingly unlike that of other Americans. It was as if they took the common qualities of Western civilization, the qualities that all Americans shared, and exaggerated them terrifically. Occasionally the exaggeration approached the point of caricature, constructs that might seem humorous were they not so dangerous. If upper-class women in Western civilization generally were being pedestalized, in the South the pedestal was higher and rising. If private violence was legitimate in America, it was more legitimate in the South. If American men had individual honor, Southerners saw themselves as having more of it. It was a strung-out, tension-laden society where vast energies were spent simply holding one's self together. The tension was there because the blacks were there. In a real way, the Southern white was the person black people made simply by being in the South in such numbers and in such manner as they were. That manner was recurrently rebellious—in the fields, in the kitchens, and in the cabins—and it made of Sambo's keepers a peculiar people.

The drive for a harmonious, unitary culture produced an outpouring of intellectual energy in the Old South that is no less than astounding. The proslavery argument—horrible in its purpose of enforcing perpetual bondage upon a whole race of people—was yet an impressive example of how gymnastic, how muscular, how imaginative and driven the human mind can be under pressure. Nourished in the rich soil of economic prosperity, warmed by the sun of social necessity, the black flowers of the proslavery argument thrived marvelously in the Old South. As there had been an earlier flowering of genius in New England, now there was a flowering in the South. But there the flowers turned their faces heliotropically toward slavery, and they drew life from that false, that brilliant and bogus sun.

Although it could be said that this drive began negatively for the purpose of keeping black people under control by a total and perfectly rationalized slavery, by the late 1850s Southern thought and culture were beginning to transcend that narrow goal by assuming that it was already nearing accomplishment. What had begun as a movement to keep the Negro down ended by raising the white man and Southern culture up. Slavery was the "mudsill" upon which a societal superstructure marvelous for the time was to be constructed. Slavery was not the end of Southern society, it was rather the beginning. On the very eve of conflict, Southern culture—as seen by itself—was attaining flight speed and about to soar. Southerners were fully aware of the necessity of slavery and generally convinced of its beauty. But it was not slavery itself that exhilarated them. It was the sense of moving up and out in a limitless ascent where none had been before. Southern culture was risingly self-confident and aggressive. Southerners felt that they knew who they were, and they had images of what they were becoming. They were expansive—in the West, in Latin America, and in the Caribbean—because they thought they had found a new and better order for humanity and felt that that order should spread.[30]

Practically speaking, to realize the unitary society the planter elite had to move into place three great classes of people, each more or less dissident: Negroes, nonslaveholding whites, and women—among the last, particularly plantation women.

Of these, the problem of Negroes, free as well as slave, was most critical. A more stringent system of control and a Sambo image worked for the slaves, but the quarter-million free Negroes scattered across the South posed a more delicate problem. Free Negroes were a contradiction in an organic world in which whites were free and Negroes were slaves. In the last generation of slavery, the controlling whites exerted tremendous social pressure, largely successfully, either to drive free Negroes out of the South or else reduce them practically to slavery and thereby de facto integration into the organic society.[31]

Mulattoes also constituted a threat to the organic society. In the lower South, three-quarters of the free Negroes were mulattoes, and their claims to whiteness were often deeply disturbing to the social order. On the other side, the number of slaves who were seen as mulattoes increased tremendously in the years from 1850 to 1860. While the number of blacks in slavery rose in that decade only 20 percent, the number of mulattoes in slavery rose an astounding 67 percent. Slavery was undoubtedly getting lighter—indeed, some slaves were indistinguishable from whites—and yet , as South Carolina judge William Harper indicated in 1835, "a slave cannot be a white man." Slavery and whiteness were incompatible. Whites could drive free mulattoes out of the South and devalue those who remained, but it soon became clear that they could not halt the alarming proliferation of mulattoes among slaves. In the end, they did in their imagination what they could not do in reality. In the last years of slavery, the white South generated a great mythology about people of mixed blood. One concept in the myth, an idea that took firm root and flourished in the twentieth century, was that one drop of black blood made a person all black. Thus, a slave could seem to be as white as snow and yet be essentially black. Another idea, one that faded and died early in the twentieth century, was that such hybrids could not last. Like that other ubiquitous Southern creature, the mule, mulattoes could not bear children or would do so only poorly. Mulattoes were weak, effete, delicate, and failing things who would soon wither away and die. Although clearly visible to the eye, in the mind of the South mulattoes were already seen as dead, and, hence, unthreatening.[32]

There were no Nat Turners in the 1850s, but there were other disturbing indications that elements in the institution of slavery needed correction. For instance, slaves in the cities and slaves who hired out their own time were tending to break down the system.[33] In 1859 Edward A. Pollard, a young Virginian who had just returned from travels in which he actively supported a briefly successful attempt by Southerners to gain control of Nicaragua and who was later to win eminence by explaining the Civil War as essentially a constitutional debate, most famously in a book entitled *The Lost Cause* (1866), was outraged by the sleek, well-fed, well-dressed "slave gentry" in the cities and on the large plantations who condescended to notice and make slurs about the untutored whites of the lower orders. He ardently sought the reduction of all blacks to "the uniform level of the slave." On the other side, seemingly few things afforded Pollard and other Southerners more pleasure than the image of the black man playing the Sambo role. Returning home to Virginia from wanderings that took him to the California gold fields and the Orient, Pollard grew ecstatic over the first venerable black uncle that he saw. "I love the simple and unadulterated slave," he rhapsodized, "with his geniality, his mirth, his swagger, and his nonsense...."[34]

Similarly, the organic society of the Old South concerned itself with finding a place for the great mass of nonslaveholding whites. It was, perhaps, least effective in that area. When the war came, Southern leadership was groping simultaneously toward two solutions. Either nonslaveholding whites would be instituted as a squirearchy in support of the aristocratic knighthood of the South, or they would be dissolved by a universal elevation of all whites into the upper class through slaveholding. In pursuit of the latter end, some Southerners pressed for the reopening of the international slave trade so that every white family might partake of the liberating and elevating effects of the peculiar institution. As Pollard indicated, the purchase of a slave for $150 would allow a poor man to "at once step up to a respectable station in the social system of the South."[35] The alternative was to fix the white mass as a dependent and loyal class. The role finally handed to nonslaveholding whites was that of willing and permanent squires to the knightly order. Plain folk but genteel, they were to accept the values of the upper class and emulate the manners of the aristocracy in so far as their means allowed. In the organic society, nonslaveholders were to have an honorable place somewhere between the earth of Sambo and the sky of aristocracy, but certainly closer to the former.

Although the Southern elite was less than totally effective in its drive to integrate the lower orders of whites, it had already developed a capacity for defusing potential rebelliousness by preempting leadership talent as it emerged in the lower orders. In South Carolina, for instance, rather clearly there was a multi-layered "aristocracy" consisting of successive appropriations of new leadership. It began when the royal governors allied themselves with those who gained affluence in the rice-indigo culture, and later added those who rose through the cultivation of long-staple cotton in the Sea Islands, and finally the barons of the short-staple fleece. In the South at large on the eve of the Civil War, ruling elite whites were properly anxious about their capacity to control the lower order. There were men in the South like Andrew Johnson, the Tennessee senator, and Albert Gallatin Brown, the governor of Mississippi, who preached democracy and behaved rather mulishly in what was supposed to be a stable of exclusively fine horses. Still the people at the top managed well enough and, on the whole, successfully. For every Andy Johnson there were dozens of Jefferson Davises who rose into the elite from somewhere and accepted its values, and the leadership did manage to carry a constituency of about seven million nonslaveholding whites into the Confederacy and to put well over a million of those into butternut gray.

Southern women, and especially some of those plantation women who lived with their families closest to large numbers of slaves, were also restless under the rising regime of the slave-based society. The wives and mothers of slaveholders had probably long been anxious about their men in the midst of a village of subordinate if not submissive dark women. However much they might relish and want to believe in a world in which superbly loyal Negro women existed only to nourish fondly their own white children, the fact was that numbers of mulatto children were constantly appearing. Particularly during late slavery, apparently whole plantation communities fell into a morass of interracial sexuality as men of the master class spawned one child after another with their female slaves, usually mulattoes and usually maids in the manor house. Perhaps pedestalizing the white mistress of the plantation was an attempt to salve the wound that had been done, and was being daily done deeper, to the Southern lady by husbands, sons, and fathers in liaisons with slave women.

Probably in no other area was the drive for a unitary society so effective as it was in wooing white women of the elite group into the system. Blacks might well have been reluctant to see themselves as Sambos, and nonslaveholding white men might have still somehow resented the imperious airs of the gentry; but it is perfectly understandable that people who were constantly told, night and day, day in and day out, that they were the most beautiful, the purest, the most divine thing ever wrought in human clay might have been tempted to believe it. The Southern woman did sometimes internalize the image of the plantation lady, and sometimes grew blind to the fact that the darkling boys and girls with whom her children played were their own brothers and sisters and a living insult to her integrity.

The Romanticism of the late Old South might have been formed, in part, by the retreat of the female gentry from painful reality. They were being hard pressed to accept a system inimical to their most vital interests; and if they did retreat into make-believe worlds, it is understandable. It is probably no accident that students of literature have come to characterize the decade when a rash of romance broke out in Southern writing as "the feminine fifties." It was a literature by women, about women, and for women's peace of mind.

The attempt to press women into the mold was aggressive. Historian Dorothy Ann Gay, after extensive research in the diaries and letters of Southern women between 1830 and 1861, concluded that they were, indeed, a threat to the continuation of slavery, especially in their reaction against the sexual abuse of black women by white masters. The frequency with which white mobs in the South attacked, beat, and demeaned white men suspected of antislavery sentiments was a warning, she argued, to white women to stay in their place and support the peculiar institution. In addition, "Southerners always stressed the physical threat black revolt posed for white women." Either the women must support the system of slavery or find themselves ravished and their children slaughtered.[36] In the 1830s Professor Thomas R. Dew of the College of William and Mary urged women to keep their place in the home. Two decades later the Carolina fire-eater William Porcher Miles wanted them to participate more fully in the life of society. But what he wanted out of that increased association was a more perfect complement to maleness in the Victorian model. By their beauty, by their queenly grace and purity, they would elevate the society of men. That women should come out in the world seemed to be his message, but in doing so they should clearly keep their place.

BLACK CULTURE

The result of the push-pull tension operating in Southern society was to suspend Negroes between two worlds.[37] Of necessity, black people generated a culture that was certainly neither purely African in America nor simply a reflection of whiteness. For convenience of description, it is useful to divide black life in the Old South into four parts.

First, a large part of black culture in the antebellum South was slave culture, and much of that was defined by what it meant to be a slave—either by conformity to the system or rebellion against it. The slave system, for instance, might forcefully promote habits of hard work, sobriety, and temperate language because the master class insisted upon this sort of behavior and had the power to enforce it. At the same time, the slave system produced other indirect cultural effects among black people. Unlike the great majority of white people, slaves in the mass simply did not have clocks or watches, or even calendars. Their sense of time must have differed from that of the whites. They lived by the sun and by the season. The South was vastly rural and agrarian, but Negroes as a people lived closer to the soil than anyone in America save, perhaps, the Indians. As a people they worked harder than white people, and they had different attitudes about their work. Slavery produced effects that white people did not want. There was always an undercurrent of rebellion among slaves, whether it took the form of a sullen manner, running away, dropping a rock among the fine teeth of the cotton gin, or outright and murderous rebellion. As slaves, black people generated attitudes about property that varied from those of whites. Northerners who came South to teach the freedmen during and after the Civil War were delighted at the temperate nature of their black protégés, but they were astounded and dismayed by their tendency to take things of small value found lying about. One Northerner might have had her curiosity satisfied by being told the old joke that from the slave's point of view no breach of morality was involved when he simply "put massa's chicken into massa's nigger." These whites had never been property themselves, of course, and the logic of property as seen by slaves and freedmen largely escaped them. Further, slaves might answer the demands of slavery but still, internally and beyond the eye of the master, evolve a life-style quite independent of it. Their religion, their entertainment, their diet, and their sense of family, justice, and self might all have dimensions well beyond the slave system as conceived by the white mind.

Second, black culture included free blacks as well as slave blacks, On the eve of the Civil War there were about half a million free blacks in America, half of whom lived in the South. As with slaves, most but not all of their culture was circumscribed by the world the whites made. To some extent, black culture resulted from black people's perception and imitation of the white way. Another part of it was made up of resentment and rebellion against the white world—much of this because white people would not accept the full humanity of black people in their world. Thus, for instance, in the years around 1800 the Negro Methodists in Philadelphia, Baltimore, and New York withdrew from white-dominated churches to establish their own institutions, the African Methodist Episcopal Church and the African Methodist Episopal Church Zion. In the first third of the century, these churches gradually spread into the free Negro communities in the South, in the second third they were largely forced out, and again in the last third of the century they returned to become, along with the Baptists, the largest Negro denominations in America. These churches were undeniably Methodist, but they were also undeniably black and different by dint of their blackness.

It has been profitable to think of white culture in America as evolving in terms of a "frontier thesis," that is, as European culture altered by the physical and social environment of a new land. It is also useful to think of black culture in America as evolving, in part, in the same vein. Imagine, for example, that some pre-Columbian African adventurers had built a raft, some "kon tiki," and drifted with the currents across the Atlantic into the American South and established a colony there. That culture soon would not be African simply because the geography, the climate, the flora and fauna of the South were not African. In reality each locale in the South—the sea islands, the river basins, the swamps—had its own natural logic, and the Africans in America, no less than the English people in America, came to terms with a new physical universe. A third part of black culture came out of those physical conditions and did not depend upon slavery or blackness or even whiteness for its existence. On the large plantations and in the black belts where blacks were numerous and white people least often seen, black people met the land and created lifestyles that had least to do with color of skin. Over the years the love of the land, the fondness for the place of their birth and breeding, marked American Negroes as it does all peoples. It was they who delved in that earth, and planted and reaped its harvests. It was they who trod its paths by day and by night. With their hands and feet they minutely mapped its topography and with their bodies measured its heat and cold. White Southerners, so specially possessive of the land themselves and so idolatrous of the legalities of ownership, could hardly contemplate, much less understand, and still less sympathize with, the feelings of Negroes about their mutually natal soil. Some whites later assumed that the hatred of slavery among blacks, which did exist, extended to the place of slavery. Quite the contrary was true. Blacks, like whites, tended to love the land upon which they were born and spent their lives.

A fourth part of black culture in the American South was African in its origins. The question here is not whether the African legacy has survived into modern times. Certainly it has, and not merely in the form of physical characteristics. Nor even is it a matter of how much of the legacy has survived. The real historical problem is how the African heritage was transmuted in the American circumstance: how it was changed by slavery, by the African's blackness in a white world, and by the novel physical setting. That problem is, at least, every bit as difficult as defining European survivals in white culture. And it is probably more difficult because the black experience was refracted through slavery and through a moral code reigning in the white world in which black quite literally often meant "bad" and therefore was to be suppressed. There is a peculiar and distressing insensitivity in the persisting argument that blacks have to "make it" in America just as the Irish, the Italians, and other more recent immigrant groups have done. Would that it were so simple. To dismiss the distinctive black experience in this facile way, one has to ignore a history profoundly shaped by white Americans' special perception of blackness in humans and their reaction to that perception. If in fact blacks have sometimes rotted at the doorstep, it is not because they take a perverse pleasure in giving their lives to offend white nostrils.

The problem of identifying African survivals is raised still one more level in difficulty by the truth that as whites invaded black life with a new intensity in the middle of the nineteenth century, they not only changed blacks; they were changed by blacks. Then and later whites would have been vastly resentful at the suggestion that blacks had educated them, so proudfully intent were they on unilaterally educating blacks. But without attempting to catalogue the entire range, it seems fairly clear that whites learned much from blacks in language, literature, and religion, in music and manners, and in cuisine and conjuring. It is probably not too much to say that a significant amount of the African heritage that survived in the slave South survived outside the black world in the white. Southern whites would have passed beyond resentment and into outrage at the idea of themselves being Africanized, but the idea is not without an element of reality.

A FUSION OF CULTURES AND COLORS

White people not only adopted and adapted African survivals from Negroes, they also drew more broadly from the well of post-African black culture to fill their own lives. For instance, Southern white religion owed something to black religion. Southern whites did attend the sermons of black ministers, and sometimes they did so eagerly. "There was a Negro meeting down at church and we hurried dinner to go," Ella Thomas, the young wife of a Georgia planter, wrote in her diary in 1855. At church she found a large crowd, overflowing the building and seated on benches outside. "I procured a seat in church and heard an exhortation from the Baptist minister Peter Johnson," she wrote. "A very fine looking mulatto man, dressed very nice, with a gold watch and fob chain." Afterward Thomas was led to make a generalization about black ministers. "In their exhortations they very often do much good," she concluded. "They appeal to the heart more than the understanding." Johnson was impressive, but Thomas thought him "not so polished nor by no means so talented" as another black minister, Sam Drayton. In the following month, she and several white friends went to hear Drayton. "I find it very delightful to do down and hear Sam Drayton preach to the servants," she asserted after that event. "He is a negro of extraordinary talent and cultivation and well repays one for listening to his sermon." Drayton earned her admiration, so too did his wife. Thomas judged Mrs. Drayton to be "one of the most ladylike persons I have ever seen."[38]

In magic, as in religion, whites were also indebted to blacks. Black "conjurers" were often sought out by whites for their services. A native of Knott's Island, in the northeastern tip of North Carolina, remembered having seen cartloads of whites going to the settlement of a conjuring black family headed by Clarenda Cartwright in the Moyock Backwoods near the Dismal Swamp, "and the loads were from Virginia," he said, "the land of the 'F.F.V.'" Once, while working with a surveying party there, he saw a Negro man coming with a "woman in tow, a white woman at that." The surveyor was told "that she was a subject whom this negro had brought to have a 'spell' taken off by Clarenda." Later, he reported, "I saw the patient seated on a stock or log, and in front of her was Clarenda with a circle drawn on the ground in her front, blowing her incantations. She would turn her face north, east, south, west, cut all manner of figures with her body, arms and hands, her eyes following her extended fingers, and all the while making mumbling that I could not understand."[39]

No one has yet described in detail the manner in which Southern white children in the slave period were reared, or the effects the process might have had upon the adult. But we do know that upon the large plantations typically the older slave women oversaw the young slave children and that often white children shared some of the life of black children until puberty, when a more careful separation began. Many whites later claimed a close childhood association with some adult who was a slave. Usually they claimed a "mammy," but now and again a white son of the master class found his mentor in a sable hero, some black and accomplished Nimrod who tutored the boy in riding, hunting, and woods lore. Possibly, the planter class learned its famous manners from its close association with blacks and especially, perhaps, with black mammies. Blacks, being subject to sudden, violent, and often arbitrary punishments from whites, developed a super-sensitivity to the thoughts and moods of others, an interest and a capacity that they conveyed to the white children in their charge.

Ultimately, the process was probably much more intricate than one race simply teaching the other. What we have in the South are two cultures in symbiosis, each constantly taking from the other, but each filtering what it takes and absorbing it relative to its special perspectives. White culture feeds off of black and grows and changes, and black culture feeds from white and grows and changes. Finally, it is possible to speak of two cultures, one white and the other black, but it is also proper to speak of a fusion of cultures. This fusion, which occurred in the last three decades of slavery, forms the substratum that joins black and white today—it is the substantial beginning of the oneness of modern Southern life. It is why black people and white people in similar situations perform very much alike. It is why they share many of the same values. It is why they can, if need be, sometimes relate to one another with great intensity and understanding.

A fusion of colors in the South paralleled the fusion of cultures. Many contemporaries thought that the number of people of mixed blood was rapidly growing. Quantitatively, most of the mixing of black and white in the last generation of slavery probably resulted from what social scientists later called "internal miscegenation," that is, the marriage of Negroes of purely African ancestry to Negroes whose ancestry was partially European. The marriage of blacks to mulattoes was most pronounced on the frontiers of the cotton kingdom of the lower South where slaves of lighter color were being imported in unusually large numbers from the upper South.[40] Qualitatively, the most important mixing was by the planter elite itself. It seems that in almost every community in the slave South there existed at least one slave woman whose distinctly lighter-colored children testified to a falling from racial grace by one or more white men. Typically, the woman worked as a domestic in the house of a planter and was herself very light in color. Now and again, it appears that whole plantations were lost in the social void of interracial sex and a mixed progeny. The signs were that all too often for the integrity of an idealized Southern society, whole settlements were losing the color line in a welter of browns, yellows, and reds. In the last years of slavery, thoughtful whites in the South and in the nation came to fix upon race mixing as a clear and present problem. In 1850 the United States Census, for the first time, counted people in whom mixed ancestry was visible and labeled them "mulatto." By the end of the Civil War whites had invented the term "miscegenation" to cover the whole phenomenon of mixing black and white, and it was a term that carried dire implications.[41]

Like the geological fault line that exposes the layers underlying the earth's crust, the disparity between what mulattoes actually were and what whites insisted that they were revealed much about the composition of the racial world of the South. The public myth was that the mulatto population grew out of the midnight marauding of lower-class white males. The fathers of mulattoes were said to be poor whites, itinerant Irish laborers, and Yankee overseers who simply seized upon occasional targets of sexual opportunity and passed on. Doubtless some mulattoes did come from such casual connections. But significantly often these children were the sons and daughters of relatively well-to-do slave owners. However lightly or brutally the liaison might have begun, it sometimes ended with white fathers taking care about the upbringing, education, and economic security of their darker offspring. Related to the myth that socially sanitized the conception of the mulatto population was a publicly professed ignorance of the fatherhood of specific mulatto children. Yet, in every community it seems that whites privately knew well enough who fathered each light child.

Mary Boykin Chesnut, a highly observant and superbly intelligent plantation woman, recalled the "magnate who runs a hideous black harem with its consequences under the same roof with his lovely white wife, and his beautiful and accomplished daughters. . . ." One of her friends marked another awful example. "He was high and mighty," the friend averred, "but the kindest creature to his slaves—and the unfortunate results of his bad ways were not sold, had not to jump over ice blocks. They were kept in full view, and were provided for, handsomely, in his will." In the situation, the women in his family perfected their membership in the cult of true womanhood. "His wife and daughters, in their purity and innocence, are supposed never to dream of what is as plain before their eyes as the sunlight, and they play their parts of unsuspecting angels to the letter. They prefer to adore their father as the model of all earthly goodness."[42]

The increasing mulatto population was a profound indictment of the biracial Southern system. In the South's ideal world, all slaves were black and all blacks were slaves. Further, the black as slave was locked into place as the perfect complement to the white as free. A rising rage for identity among whites left increasingly little room for a blurring of the color line, and a civilization on the make took great pains to blind itself to the whiteness of its mulatto children. The white world tried to ignore mulattoes, but mulattoes repaid that attempted neglect with an intense scutiny of the white world and, generally, with that best form of flattery—imitation. Mulattoes usually knew who were their white fathers and mothers, and they were led by their society often to value their lighter color and to relish the culture that it represented.

On the eve of the Civil War, the problem of the mulatto in Southern society took on a new and, had it continued, an unbearable strain. Some eminent white men were having not only one child by a Negro woman but several children. Further and worse, far from having the decency to apologize for their transgressions and to go and sin no more, they compounded racial outrage with social confusion. Rather than casting aside this strange fruit of the Southern racial tree, they tended to acknowledge the relationship and to honor it by bequests of property. Tensions were rising—tensions between masters and slaves, between plain folk and patricians, between free Negroes and whites, and between slaveholders and their wives, daughters, and mothers. But probably nowhere was the social order more visibly fractured and loyalty to the system more severely taxed than by the presence of increasing numbers of mulattoes in the homes of leading Southerners. It raised doubts as to the moral capacities of the men of the planter elite themselves.

By way of illustration, witness the experience of one deep South plantation family. In 1856 Samuel Townsend of Madison County, Alabama, died, freeing by his will some forty of his slaves and leaving to them an estate valued at over $200,000, including other slaves. Shortly before, another man in the family, perhaps his father, had died leaving a will in which he bequeathed an estate worth some $500,000 to his two mulatto children. The earlier will was successfully contested by white heirs, but Samuel Townsend's testament was honored and executed with great fidelity by his friend and neighbor, S. D. Cabaniss. Cabaniss sent agents north and west to search out homes and possible schools for the Townsend people. Shortly he had resettled some of the Townsends in Leavenworth, Kansas, and others in Xenia, Ohio. Over the next twenty years, in war and in peace, in slavery and in freedom, Cabaniss continued to manage the estate. He sent some of the children to Wilberforce University, a vigorously antislavery black school in Ohio. Indeed, on the eve of the war, the estate owed the university the considerable amount of $593.08 for the education of these children.[43]

It is almost certain that this peculiar Alabama story occurred because the master family, perhaps for two generations or more, became inextricably mixed with several of its own slave families. These were set aside and freed. Their separateness and freedom were underscored by the facts that other slaves labored for their prosperity and that the very capable administrator of the estate actually bought and sold other blacks for their benefit. Because they were men of large affairs and because they took care to state their intentions in wills, the Townsends left a clear trace of their mulatto progeny. More and more, available evidence suggests that the Townsends were hardly unique. Rather was it that in almost every community there were mulattoes of recognized and respectable white parentage. In certain communities, perhaps, white society was losing the landmarks afforded by a distinctly biracial human geography. If white was right, was half-white half-right? On dark seas and in high hot winds some men—and women too—were running wild, dashing their culture to pieces upon the rocks of miscegenation. When the culture crumbled and sank in 1865, it left a flotsam and jetsam of human fragments adrift upon the social sea, united only retrospectively in the great ship of slavery that had gone down.

Thus, in 1861, at one level white life was driving hard toward realizing an idealized, unitary, organic society in which there was a place for everything and everything was being put in its place. At another level, the South as such an entity could not last because things were not staying in their places. Not only was the master class, seemingly, too often losing control of itself emotionally and sexually, but Sambos, women, and even the lower orders of whites were all beginning to stir and dissent.[44] Inevitably the system, as a system, would have collapsed before it reached maturity. It fell, however, before its own weaknesses became manifest. Perhaps unfortunately for the future tranquility of the South and the nation, it fell not because it was a society based upon unreal assumptions about the basic natures of blacks and whites, men and women, and not because it was a society committed to a hierarchical ordering of people, a concomitant inequality in the administration of justice, and a crudely color-coded split-level view of humanity. It fell, finally, by the raw physical power of a North that flatly would not tolerate first disunion and then slavery. The great moral defection of the North, the great sin of the

North against the South, was to destroy slavery and yet not destroy the culture that slavery had generated. The result was to doom a whole people to the fate of the Flying Dutchman, to abandon them to pursue a culture whose primal base, whose very reason for existence, had been forever lost, to ride a social ship that could never find haven or harbor.

CHAPTER II

Black Life in the South,
1865–1915

In the hard-soft life of the last days of slavery, then, black people identified with white ideals as they never had before. Slavery and other devices of race control not only provided the white community with instruments to promote that education, they also gave them the means to dam up black behavior and to prevent blacks from living the very life they were taught to idealize. Emancipation and the disordered times that followed broke that barrier, and black behavior tended to flow quickly, easily, and smoothly into channels already pre-set in black minds. It should occasion no surprise that while white politicians in Washington were still trying to decide what black people ought to be, black people in the South were already becoming what they would be. Further, it should occasion no embarrassment that they aspired to be what generations of example and one generation of intensive indoctrination had taught them that everyone—white and black—ought to be. In the first flush of freedom, black people in the South wanted families; they wanted farms; they wanted schools; and they wanted full citizenship and a recognition of their equal humanity, not only in their governments, but in their churches and in their society.[1]

BLACK RECONSTRUCTION

Black people were in motion all over the South during the summer and fall of 1865. White observers looked at the seething mass of black atoms and interpreted the movement as a simple minded, child-like jubilee. Blacks were indeed jubilant at the end of slavery, but their motion was highly purposeful and calculated to give very solid substance to their freedom. Usually black travelers were simply going home, having fled during the war when Union armies drew near or having been taken away by their masters to prevent flight. Frequently, they moved to rejoin families broken by slavery. Much of this movement was only local as a husband or a wife used freeedom to join his or her mate on a neighboring plantation, or a son or a daughter who had been hired out as a slave came home as a free person. Now and again, a freedman who had been sold away to the southwest in the flush times of the 1830s crossed half a continent and half a lifetime to come again to the people and the land that had given him birth. Increasingly, the evidence seems to indicate that, once together again, fathers and mothers; aunts, uncles, and cousins; brothers, sisters, and children, all slipped familiarly and comfortably into roles already well defined in their minds. Those roles would prove to be deeply and persistently Victorian.

The typically quiet and certain way of family re-making, often in spite of the wishes of either their late owners, or of the occupation officials who urged blacks to stay where they were until the harvest was completed, was caught by R. B. Anderson on his father's plantation in piedmont North Carolina. Anderson was a a Princeton graduate and a Presbyterian minister. He had married the daughter of James H. Thornwell, recently the president of South Carolina College and one of the foremost of the proslavery protagonists. "A few changes have taken place, since you left, amongst the negroes," Anderson wrote to his wife in September 1865. "Carolina & Sally with their families moved the next morning after my return. C. was greatly distressed & couldn't help weeping aloud. Father gave her a cow to begin housekeeping with. A few days before I got back Henry left; & Franky had gone to live with her husband. This morning a boy nearly grown—Strephon—whom father hired to a man in the neighborhood [at the] beginning of this year, came home & wanted to work: he is in the field. Ellen's daddy went after her & first thing father knew she was here on the place. He gave out nothing but a quart of meal for her & told Minerva that she, that is E., must leave; but I believe she is lurking about still."[2]

Black men in agriculture, like white men in agriculture, visualized an ideal in which each man worked his own farm. The ideal had been given substance in the nation at large in the various land laws before the war. During the war, the concept was further promoted by the Homestead Act that allowed heads of families to claim 160 acres of public lands essentially by using them. The same spirit showed itself briefly during the war in sporadic attempts to divide up the plantations of the conquered South into forty-acre plots for the settlement of the freedmen. Ultimately, the sanctity of private property—even the property of rebels—overruled such a division of the land.

However, even as Congress and the national executive faltered and failed in programs of land redistribution, individual blacks in the South were acquiring farms for themselves precisely as the white ideal had long and rather ostentatiously espoused as a proper American goal. Further, they were doing it without violating current concepts of the rights of property. In some cases they bought land with savings put together during the war, but in the mass they did it by renting farms for a share of the anticipated crop. Sometimes the farms were carved out of the very plantations upon which they had labored as slaves, almost always out of plantations within a few miles of the home place. In securing farms, either by purchase or by renting as tenants, blacks moved against the explicit desires of white landowners. Whites wanted neither to sell their lands nor even to break them up into individual farms for renting. The plantation system had not arrived at its relatively high state of efficiency by accident, and planters were not eager to sacrifice that efficiency by dividing their land into so many small parcels and, in a large measure, losing control over its management. The great majority of planters would have much preferred to keep their estates intact, to work the available labor day by day as they saw fit, and thus to maintain the closest control. But the freedmen themselves simply would not have it that way. They much preferred to rent their forty acres for a share of the crop, to borrow—as it were—their mules, and to live upon their own small farms, tenanted if necessary rather than owned, and to do so even if it was less economic than the plantation system. The Negroes were, as one planter phrased it, "rent crazy."

Thus, the breakup of the plantation system in the South was caused in a major way, not by whites, but by black people refusing to work in gangs under white supervision as they had in slavery. Shortly the slave quarters were well nigh deserted as ex-slave families moved onto the lands they either bought or rented. Sometimes new tenants agreed to build a cabin on their plot of ground in lieu of the first year's rent. Occasionally the cabins of recent slaves were hitched to teams of animals and pulled away from the plantation village to the new farm. One could hardly imagine a more graphic declaration of independence by the freedman than his literally dragging his home away from the home of the late master.

Quite clearly, the freedman wanted to work his own farm under his own supervision, and he also wanted his family on that farm. Once made, the division of the plantation into family farms tended to perpetuate itself. The family needed a farm; and, hardly less, the farm needed a family—not a man alone, nor a woman with children, but a family in which each played his role. The black family patterned itself on the Victorian model. The father ruled in worldly matters, the mother in things spiritual. Fathers were the breadwinners, mothers were the conservators of morality. Men generally went into the broad world, women stayed home. Negro men ran the farm. They did the heavy, muscular labor, and they removed their women from the fields whenever they could. Ideally, women did the housekeeping, the cooking, washing, and sewing, and very often they managed a garden for vegetables and flowers.

As with the whites, it was the women, primarily, who reared the chilren. Much of the decline in agricultural productivity that came to the South immediately after emancipation resulted, first, because, black people simply refused to work in the fields as they had in slavery and, secondly, because the men strove to keep their women at home with the children and out of the fields. Much of the return to productivity had to do with the lavish use of commercial fertilizers beginning in the late 1860s.

The family on the farm was the massively usual pattern of black life in postwar America, a pattern that lasted well into the twentieth century. Until World War I, when the need for labor brought a flood of blacks into the North and West, roughly 90 percent of the black population lived in the South, and the vast majority of those lived in rural settings as did a large proportion of those who lived in the North and West. The evolution of the black yeomanry was not, then, simply a process in which whites in freedom developed a mastery of the land and credit as tools of social control to replace a mastery of people exercised in slavery. Black people themselves created the black yeomanry. Outside of racial considerations, there was nothing at all revolutionary in the in the move. The family farm was, after all, the realization of an ideal that was as respectable as Thomas Jefferson and greatly valued, at least rhetorically, by this nation of farmers, North and South, black and white.

Blacks also used their freedom to refine their Christianity. In none of the white churches were they accepted as fully equal members, and from each the withdrawal began with emancipation and proceeded rapidly. Most freedmen went into denominations that were totally black. Still the black church strived to be what the white church ought, ideally, to have been. In structural terms, the congruity was high. Just as there had been white churches named Trinity and St. Mark's, Mt. Zion, and St. John's, so too would black churches have the same names, and in them congregations ostensibly would practice the same ritual and profess the same theology. Precisely as there were bishops, presiding elders, ministers, and probationers in the white church, so too would there be blacks with the same titles in its sable sister. And yet the black church was not white . . . nor was its God. The division between the white church and the black, between white Christianity and black, that existed in slavery persisted in freedom. Impressionistic accounts then and later asserted that the black church was more spiritual and less formal, more emotional and spontaneous and less philosophical and structured than its white counterpart.

In three vital areas of their lives, then—in their families, on the farms, and in their churches—blacks were moving physically away from whites. Ironically, even as they moved away in the physical sense, they gained the freedom they needed to be more like whites. These things they did almost coincidentally with freedom, beginning even in the war years when their freedom was uncertain. In a large measure, this exodus to whiteness was a playing out of an impetus that had been pressed upon them in the last years of slavery. The freedman was the black man that the slave South wittingly and unwittingly had made, and in freedom he seemed to be getting whiter every year. But even as blacks were first moving to realize this special vision of the promise of American life as taught by Southerners, a relief team of Northern teachers was moving southward to expand black expectations and to elaborate details in a multitude of ways.

Black Southerners did not wait for the arrival of Northern teachers to commence their efforts in education and politics, but those teachers obviously added important new dimensions to black efforts in these and other areas. Through the army of occupation which penetrated every community in the South, through the Freedmen's Bureau which was nearly as pervasive, and through the host of educational, religious, and political missionaries who flooded in after the war, the instruction of black people went on. It was an instruction marked by high intensity and sharp focus. Northern white ministers preached to Southern Negro ministers and congregations. Northern educators taught Negro teachers and students, and they taught behavior and values as well as academics from the homely homilies of Guffey's readers, Webster's *Blueback Speller,* and Morse's *Geography.* Carpetbaggers instructed Negro politicians and voters; Northern lawyers indirectly taught Negro lawyers, jurymen, and witnesses. Northern businessmen sometimes established connections with Negro merchants. And the great mass of blacks, being farmers of one sort or another, immediately entered the same hard school of colonial economics in which their white neighbors were already establishing records for perfect attendance and poor grades. Thus the Northern message of whiteness was carried to the Southern Negro in massive, pointed, "professional," person-to-person encounters that rivaled in intensity the black-white bonds of late slavery and has not yet been matched—even in the Second Reconstruction. Finally, there were in the new wave of tutors a highly significant few who taught that Negroes were, after all, only white men with black skins. These whites held up a very special mirror in which the Negro might see himself, a revolutionary mirror that tended to filter out black as a meaningful part of his self-image.

If Negroes in the South during Reconstruction were not in fact white people with black skins, the thrust of the times—at least briefly and upon many levels—was to make them so. This is not to say that Northern whites were not conscious of the darkness of Negroes. Only a few of the missionaries were nearly aracial in their thought and behavior. Most Northerners were, in fact, racists who equated dark skin with inferior capacity. But the racism of Northerners in the South during Reconstruction usually wore the benevolent clothes of paternalism. It was seldom spoken and almost never—if we can exclude the soldiery of the occupation forces—violent. They dwelt upon, and they were obsessed with the current lacks of the Negro. Indeed, that was at the heart and soul of their profession. But they seldom ventured to predict any natural limits to his elevation. In the cultural sense, for black people Northern Reconstruction in the South was an invitation to whiteness—even though Northerners seldom forgot the color of the freedman's skin.

In Reconstruction, Negroes, too, were sensitive to their blackness. There was a positive pride in blackness, a pride that sprang in part from having survived great tribulations together. Further, there was a distinct and impressive racial solidarity. At the very least, black people were joined together in their opposition to white prejudice and the unwillingness of whites to afford them full citizenship. A black legislator in Reconstruction South Carolina, chided by a white member about black members all voting together on issues, answered that blacks voted together because whites voted together to deny them full citizenship. He predicted that when blacks were treated as citizens equally with whites, they would divide their votes as did whites. Often it seemed that the force of the bond between blacks was equal and opposite to the force that oppressed them and excluded them from the culture espoused by whites. Indeed, in the Reconstruction South there was very little that could be called Black Nationalism, if one means to suggest by that term an exclusive black culture, fully self-conscious, and determined to carve for itself a permanent and separate place in the cultural federation in America. On the contrary, black leaders in the South saw themselves as pioneers in a progressive age in which color in people would rapidly lose significance. Further, there was very little concern among Southern blacks to recover their African heritage. Such interest as existed was designed, it seems, not to separate themselves from their white neighbors. Rather was it directed toward building an admirable trans-Atlantic past, a laudable antiquity much as white Americans claimed.

It is not too much to say that blacks in the South during Reconstruction were becoming the most American of Americans. In those areas, like South Carolina, where Negroes were in the majority and the promise of true democracy did hold up a reasonable prospect of effective black power, that power was turned—not to black exclusiveness or the cultivation of a black mystique—but toward pressing the whole society up to its own best ideals. Black power worked for public education for all children, full civic equality for all peoples, and the humane treatment of the insane, the sick, and the criminal. The system of public schools in existence in South Carolina today, for example, was begun by a predominantly black legislature. Before the war, public school systems were nearly universal north of slavery. In the South, only North Carolina had made real progress on that front. After the war, black legislators in every state participated in making the American ideal of public education a reality. So, too, of American ideals in almost every area of life. It is a true, and intriguing, and a revealing paradox that if every Southern white person had deserted the South after the war, if the whites had left the task of rebuilding on that land entirely and exclusively to Negroes, that a perfectly Black Reconstruction would have been, in cultural terms, very white.

DISENGAGEMENT AND ALIENATION

In Reconstruction black people came to be relatively deeply engaged in the mainstream of American culture. That engagement, in itself, lent a structure to black life that was marked initially by very great disparities. Some blacks, for instance, had just been freed from the darkest and most brutal slavery on the southwestern frontier. Others had been slaveholders and planters them-selves, often possessed of large estates. In New Orleans and Charleston and in parts of Louisiana the mulatto elite approached the white elite in culture and wealth. When emancipation came, however, the mulatto elite joined mission-aries from the North—white, mulatto, and black—in moving into the hinter-land to raise up the freedman in the scale of Western civilization as they under-stood it. Close engagement in the economy as free individuals, in national patterns of education, family, and society, and in politics and civic affairs— along with a lingering engagement in white Christianity and with white denominational orders—plugged black people into a ready-made cultural sys-tem and gave them a valuable degree of unity. Pre-schooled even in slavery, black people were prepared to flow with striking rapidity into the molds ready-made by the white world. Emancipation broke the dam, Northern tutors replaced Southern, and a gold team trotted onto the field to work in tandem, push-pull, with the blue. It was during Reconstruction, this complex time of national transition, that modern black America had its signal beginning. For a time the prefabricated structure of white culture afforded black people a framework within which they might shape their lives in a meaningful and satisfying way. The end of Reconstruction, however, brought a rising disen-gagement and alienation of black people from the white world, and with that phenomenon a loosening of the threads in the fabric of black life. When the weave was made tight again, the cloth would be unique, and the uniqueness would be distinctly black. But that end, the crystallization of modern black culture in America, was not achieved without much searching and a great struggle.

The disengagement of black people from the white way began, paradoxi-cally, even during Reconstruction when black life was rushing into the white mainstream with unprecedented mass and strength. The very separation of the races in the physical sense, for example on the land and in the churches, reduced interracial contacts and inevitably made it impossible for blacks to maintain a high level of awareness of the ever-changing white world. More-over, while black people were moving more deeply into the white world in some areas such as politics and family and civil life, they were moving out in others such as religion.

Even Northern educational efforts, which did so much of the labor in hold-ing up white models for emulation by blacks, did not follow the smoothly progressive path that a reading of the general record would imply. In 1868 the Freedmen's Bureau had hardly completed the organization of a widespread and increasingly effective system of schools in the population centers of the South when it began drastically to curtail its efforts in that area. Officials explained their withdrawal on the grounds that state governments, installed in nearly all the South in that year by Congressional action, were traditionally and constitutionally responsible for public education. Also, Northern benev-olent associations, anticipating the resumption of educational activities by the reconstructed state governments, having sent hundreds of Yankee teachers into the South during and immediately after the war, began to redeploy their forces by withdrawing from elementary education and moving into trade and normal schools, and into secondary and college level education. Lamentably, both the federal government and the associations acted prematurely. It was two years and more before the Reconstruction state governments got their educational programs under way, and even then those programs were modest enough in the face of the gigantic task to be done. Taken all together, the beginning of public education by the Bureau and the benevolent associations, the stopping after 1868, and the beginning again by the Reconstruction state governments was a crippling blow to the quick integration of blacks into the main current of American life through education.

If a firm plan for educational reconstruction had been implemented at the war's end (including, for example, integrated public schools), a great deal of suffering might have been prevented. Given even that failure, if the recon-structed state governments had continued in power for a generation, previous interruptions might have been rendered insignificant. But with Redemption, as conservative native whites termed their return to dominance in 1877, came not only another stoppage of the scholastic heart, but the beginning of an erosion. It was not so much an absolute decline as it was a relative one. Gen-erally speaking, the statistics of enrollment, attendance, length of school year, and adult literacy recovered and progressed nicely. This in spite of the fact that after Redemption the per capita amount spent on black school children declined steadily compared with that spent on white children. Rather was it most essentially an erosion of vision, a loss of clarity among young black peo-ple in perceiving the goals of white American life and how those goals were to be achieved. Indicative of the broad trend was the fact that white teachers were disappearing from Negro schools. The visible example of whiteness was evaporating, as well as the substance of what they taught. Increasingly, Negro students were taught by Negro teachers, and later by Negro teachers who had been taught by Negro teachers. The number of Northern whites working closely and helpfully with blacks dropped drastically with the end of Reconstruction. Further, by the turn of the century, Southern whites who had sometimes taken jobs teaching in black schools in the hard times of Reconstruction had almost disappeared. Individual white models became less visible as Negro schools became thoroughly black, a consummation not much resisted by black teachers and administrators. With all of this came a rising loss of capacity among black people to perceive clearly the white ideals and an evaporation at the mass level of the resources necessary to pursue those ideals.

What began as day by day disengagement ended as lasting alienation. As the black world moved away from the white world and solidified, disengagement became institutionalized. Schools and churches, for instance, became all black as black people filled the places that had once been filled by whites. The growing alienation of the black world from the white that was evident in education proceeded also at various rates and in various forms in religion, civic affairs, and politics, on the farms, in commerce, industry, the professions, transportation, libraries, music, drama, the opera, the arts, restaurants, bars, ice cream parlors, and even in the rites of death. It seems that even the language of the whites was increasingly foreign to blacks as they lost access to white culture.

THE FEUDALIZATION OF BLACK LIFE

It is indeed an irony that focus upon the white world of Reconstruction and early post-Reconstruction times gave the black experience a basic centrality. The pursuit of white cultural forms gave black life what some social scientists call "integrity." A society with total integrity has fully developed economic, political, religious, familial, and other systems, all rationally inter-related and supportive of individual personalities. In Reconstruction and for some years afterward, a firm focus upon white ideals lent integration, in this sense, to black life. It might well be that whiteness afforded a highly convenient point of communion among black people during this critical time of transition. Perhaps a rather clear focus on white values and the use of white language provided the necessary bridges upon which blacks of very disparate backgrounds might quickly cross to relate to each other, to establish, for instance, the meaning of blackness itself, to articulate goals, and to define programs of action. However, with black people increasingly separated both physically and mentally from whites, the aims and energies of the Negro community lost a measure of integration, lost clarity, and became diffused.

Possibly, in this time of rising frustration and disorientation, individual Negroes sought islands of certainty in local and highly tangible institutions such as churches, schools, and businesses. It may be that even as the total picture disintegrated, parts of the picture gained autonomous definition and strength, and that these, to some extent, commanded attention and obscured the widening loss of unity in the total round of black life. For the great mass of black people, probably the local church—the Mount Zions, the Bethels, and Ebenezers—began to support a life that included satisfying styles of politics, social structure, and entertainment as well as religion. Black educational institutions may have performed the same functions for the more fortunate and ambitious. Atlanta, Fisk, and Straight Universities, Hampton and Tuskegee Institutes, Penn School, and Mt. Holly perhaps became not only the source of employment and education for administrators, faculty, students, and alumni, but also a satisfying source of politics, religion, economics, social structure, and entertainment as well. It could be that as the messages of denial from the whites continued to crash in upon the black world, loyalties and energies that had once reached up toward nation and state were pulled down to local, more palpable and responsive institutions. It seems that many black people of talent increasingly found their lives rather completely absorbed—not with national or state politics and not with large and national concerns, but rather with local activities, as they became leading ministers, educators, or businessmen. Conversely, those who continued to concern themselves with national matters in the mid-nineteenth-century style, as did Frederick Douglass, lost relevance, audience, and influence.

In sum, energies that were encountering rejection in the broad white world were now being vested in local and very tangible enclaves. The turndown was less than obvious. In fact, it was masked by some signal successes by individuals and by an "up from slavery" rhetoric that insisted to the world that Negroes were getting better and better every day in every way. It was true that Negro churches increased in numbers, church property rose in value, and the roll of members swelled during these decades, while black education at it best was indeed impressively progressive. But it was also a fact that as the 1890s gave way to the twentieth century, the quality of life for blacks who were not privileged to be members of these enclaves degenerated to its modern low. There were great numbers of black people who fell away from farms and families and who by-passed entirely the churches and academic institutions to live on the nether side of life, usually in the cities and towns of the South.

It is not too much to say that a species of feudalization occurred in black life in these turn-of-the-century decades. The centrifugal forces in black life were losing power as the minds and motives of black people tended to fall away from the single center that a common focus upon the white ideals had previously afforded and to transfer their loyalties to more proximate and palpable institutions. The faithful pursuit of abstract ideas of democracy, freedom, and equality had proved less than fully rewarding. Tuskegee Institute, Mount Bethel AME Church, Atlanta University, and North Carolina Mutual Insurance Company, or other such concrete and serviceable institutions offered much more satisfying engagements. These enclaves became the storehouses in which black people deposited their loyalty. They drew out, in return, some measure of security and satisfaction in a life that was hazardous at best.

Out of this fragmentation, this feudalization of black life emerged what amounted to a new black "nobility." The new noble was, perhaps, a minister or a bishop, the principal of a school, the president of an insurance company, or a political boss. Like the feudal lord, he offered his followers protection and maintenance, and he demanded loyalty and labor in return. He was invariably the self-conscious strong man who brooked no opposition within his domain. He was capable of using his people and his institution as a warrior would his sword to cope with an extravagantly hostile environment. A part of his method was to impose what might seem to whites to be a harsh and arbitrary discipline upon his followers, not entirely for the inflation of his own ego as some might judge, but for the salvation of the group. He was a leader like Toussaint L'Ouverture who, in the black revolution in Santo Domingo about 1800, was alleged to have marched some of his men over a cliff to their death as an exhibit to the French general Le Clerc of the determination of the rebels to fight to the bitter end. The black feudatory in the South was hardly less determined, and he was willing to sacrifice some to save the remainder. Ralph Ellison caught the awful side of that reality perfectly in his novel, *Invisible Man*. In that story he depicted a tyrannical college president, Bledsoe, who expelled the student who became Invisible Man for a careless mistake involving a white benefactor. The expulsion consigned Invisible Man to the living death of attempting to survive alone in the white-dominated world outside the enclave, a world that seemed unable to recognize his essential humanity and was bent on his destruction.[3]

Whether avowed or not, the black feudatory was steadily at war with everyone outside the enclave. There were powerful whites sitting on his borders, often quiescent but always potentially hateful and terrifically destructive. And there were always the other black barons all around eager to grab a larger share of the limited resources available for survival. Vitually never did the black baron openly defy the local whites, but there were ways to carry on the combat covertly. In dealing with the outside world, he exhibited a Machiavellian flexibility. In so desperate a struggle, strong enemies were to be appeased and weak ones brought to their knees or destroyed. Shrewd and often secret diplomacy would be linked with the select and sometimes brutal use of power. The black feudatory might use local whites against local blacks he considered inimical to the welfare of his people. He might try to turn the local whites most favorable to blacks against those whites least favorable; and he might, while avowing all love and obedience to the Southern white neighbor, secretly and diligently woo some super-powerful Northern white force to crush him. Whites were often appeased by the syrupy accommodationism of the black feudatory, but they were appalled by what they thought was their almost mystical power over their vassals. They soon concluded that a deeply personal, almost a slavish vassalage to a black tyrant—such as Booker T. Washington, Marcus Garvey, Daddy Grace, or Father Divine—was a natural and unfortunate portion of the life of the average Negro. In some degree white perceptions of the case were true; and in a large measure they were true because a relentless hostility on the part of whites to black equality made them so.

Black life was feudalized and, inevitably, there was constant warfare between the feudatories. Independent and all-black African Methodists warred against the independent and all-black Zion Methodists. Both coldly scorned the Colored Methodists as the fawning constituency of the child church organized by the white Southern Methodists. Blacks who remained in the white-controlled Episcopal Church often assumed un-Christian airs of superiority and were repaid with disdain. "Among the people of my race, we who belong to The Church [the Episcopal Church] are regarded almost heretics and have to suffer something of a spiritual isolation at times," complained a black who had been born into the church as a slave.[4] William H. Councill in his state school at Normal struggled against Washington at Tuskegee for educational leadership in Alabama, and Washington and Tuskegee Institute, themselves, steadily resisted the ever-threatening encroachment of the denominational imperialists, such as those, for instance, who sortied out from that Congregational fortress, Atlanta University.

It may be that such rivalries were only the common lot in American life. After all, whites often opted to tie their lives closely to a profession or to a single institution, and bitter rivalries were not unknown in the white world. Even so, there seemed to be a quality of ferocity and quiet desperation among black warriors that was not usual among their white contemporaries. It was as if life were a card game in which the white man could make error after error and yet play again. But a black man who overplayed his hand lost his life at the table, instantly, violently, with table upturning, cards and chips scattering, and a body crashing to the floor. Thus black leaders were compelled to watch the game too closely, study their cards too carefully, and spend tremendous energies calculating minor and sometimes imaginary chances. A trivial error in play might become a devastating blow to a black leader. Booker T. Washington was probably the ultimate master in this intense, back-to-the-wall, super-cautious style of play. It was fully appropriate that his people should call him the "Wizard of Tuskegee." He rarely lost a hand, seeming almost to put mathematical odds in suspension, and he often finessed hands that he should by great odds have lost.

Illustrative of the desperate nature of this game was the trauma that overcame William H. Councill, the president of Alabama's State Normal School for Negroes at Huntsville, on one occasion when he thought that the carelessness of one of his students had lost him both the hand and the game. Councill was Booker T. Washington's prime antagonist for black educational hegemony in Alabama. During Reconstruction he had played Radical Republican politics to create the school. After Redemption, he had steadily developed the institution by cooperating with the all-powerful Democrats. He became, in fact, the black protégé of Alabama's most dashing Confederate general, "Fighting Joe" Wheeler. In 1887, however, the previous great harmony was broken when a party of his students took a train from Huntsville to Decatur to challenge the debating team of another school. A breach in racial etiquette occurred when some of the male students in the group attempted to seat some of the young women in the first class, or "ladies" car. They were refused, boarded the second-class car without further protest, and proceeded to Decatur. C. H. Hopkins, a leader in the group, later recalled: "I don't think one of us had thought about the matter at all. I know I had not." Meanwhile, Councill had heard of the incident and sent word for Hopkins to come to his office immediately upon his return. When Hopkins entered Councill's chambers, he found the president with "his face buried in his hands and crying as if his very heart would break. . . . He raised his head from his hands, and said to me in agony, 'Well, you all have ruined me.'" So convinced was Councill that the rage of the whites would follow that he hastened to volunteer his resignation in an attempt to save the school. The all-white board of trustees, previously unaware of the incident and aroused initially only by Councill's reaction, did grow angry and quickly accepted his resignation. Within a year, however, his long history of accommodation to whites and service to blacks redeemed him, and he was restored to office.[5] When black leaders saw themselves living in such a frightening world, it is fully understandable that they might, indeed, become dictators and tyrants, seeking to control every thought and every act of their followers. It seems almost as if they would make of them, if only they could, but physical extensions of their own minds and bodies.

In this view of black leadership at the turn of the century, Booker T. Washington becomes the most effective feudal lord of them all. Because he managed his own domain so superbly, he came in time to possess an hegemony over those who were less effective. Eventually, he evolved into a sort of overlord, a feudal monarch. Like the Capetians in tenth-century France, he began with a self-supporting, superbly administered, and totally disciplined home base. Washington's Paris was Tuskegee. This tight bastion gave him the resources and the strength to expand his influence, to prepare elaborate outworks, to undermine the power of his immediate enemies, to win allies abroad, and to wait and choose his time. Also, like the Capetians, Washington wisely settled for a manageable kingdom rather than spending himself futilely in search of an improbable empire. He pulled back from the more ambitious and exposed frontiers of earlier efforts. He retreated from an overt and exciting claim to perfect equality, and, whatever his goals were in his own mind, he seemed to white people to settle for substantially less. Thus leadership in the white world, North and South, felt safe with Washington, and they applauded the expansion and consolidation of his power in the black world. Even so, the sage of Tuskegee shrewdly pressed for possession of a realizable and very defensible territory. He claimed for his people the family farm and areas of skilled labor. His "divine right" to rule came through his discovery of the almost providentially available "Tuskegee idea," the idea that black people by "industrial education" would achieve both productivity and moral character in learning to work with their hands and their heads on the farms and in the trades. He espoused for Negroes the great virtues—simplicity, practicality, patience, and industry. Tuskegee Institute was the model for the plan, and by 1915, when he died, the South was full of Tuskegees, each run by a carefully selected Tuskegee disciple who spread the gospel with the same jealous thoroughness exemplified by his master. If the black South in the early twentieth century was a late medieval France, Booker T. Washington was its king.

NOBODY'S NEGRO

Separation and alienation from the white world loosened the threads of black life for a generation or more. For each individual black person, taken all together and totaled up, there was a measure of disorientation, an anarchy, a chaos and loneliness compared both with what their white contemporaries then knew and with what black individuals had known before and would know subsequently. The poor and the young, as usual, suffered the most.

As the black community lost integration with the white world, individual blacks tended to fall away, not only from the sun-center afforded by white ideals, but from all centers. Some black individuals seem to have shot like meteors through the gravitational fields of the lesser satellites of church and school and spun off into space, losing the power to relate to an accepted human universe. Their world became their person and their person became very much physical. Black men peculiarly suffered this fate. Out of place and out of law, they were sometimes lynched, they were sometimes quietly murdered, and they were sometimes slaughtered in murderous riots. More often they wore the stripes and chains of convict labor. In most Southern states convict labor was leased out to private entrepreneurs who used it hard and ate up black lives like some monstrous ogre. In Texas, for example, about one-quarter of the population of the state was black but more than half of the convicts were Negroes. In the United States, the normal annual mortality rate for prisoners was about 25 per 1000. Yet in the Lone Star State it was 49 for those who were leased out on the plantations, 54 for those in the iron works, 74 in railroad construction, and 250 for those so unfortunate as to be rented out to the isolated timber camps in the swamps of eastern Texas.[6]

Awful as were the quick deaths in lynchings, murders, and riots and the slower deaths of the convict lease system, these probably accounted for only a few of the vast number of victims. The great truth is that most blacks died by black hands. Walled away from the dominant white society, denied the order afforded by living in that relatively stable universe, and missing the protection of a black enclave, some black people were left to isolation, to self-denigration, and ultimately to self-hatred. At its worst, black life was cheapened in the estimation of blacks themselves, and too often individual Negroes destroyed one another or themselves in a churning, nearly formless black rage. Such, seemingly, is the lot of oppressed peoples everywhere, of colonialized and powerless peoples, of, as Franz Fanon has called them, "the wretched of the earth."[7]

Here and there individual Negroes fell entirely out of all society, white or black, and took to a roaming, reckless, and often enough violent existence. It was these that the whites most feared—the strange "nigra," as whites of the more fortunate class would have called him. As in the time of slavery, they might say, it was not my Negroes that I fear nearly so much as it is yours, and not yours nearly so much as nobody's. The "nigger loose"—without place, without the restraining, taming, legitimizing white-man link to the white man's world—was the worst of all social crises in Southern communities. The strange black man, the "nigger in the woods," only glimpsed and seldom totally seen, like Edgar Allan Poe's "Raven" or William Faulkner's Joe Christmas, menaced whites in awful ways that only a mind that did not know him could create. It was especially bad in the rural communities where whites were few and policemen fewer.

The black menace, the "nigger loose," was born in the country and moved to the city. The black family might well have been at home on the land, but the deepening agricultural depression of the late 1880s and on through the 1890s drove large numbers off the land. A tenant farm on moderately productive soil might have supported a black family in relative comfort when cotton was selling at twelve cents a pound; but it could not be worked at all at seven, six, and five because landlords and creditors would not invest in advances for food and supplies. The result was that less productive farmers on less productive soils were squeezed off the land.

By the Victorian model the young men would leave first, looking for work. The search might prove endless and lead them to a perpetually marginal existence, hovering on the fringes of organized life. Ultimately, they might come to New Orleans, Memphis, or Atlanta, or one of the lesser cities. Loosened males tended to congregate in the cities, and Negro families in the urban situation tended to lose the forms of family that farm life had supported. Ironically, it would be the women—rather than the men—who succeeded best in finding work in the cities—typically as domestics in the kitchens of the whites. Urban middle-class white women had to have Negro maids even as they actually needed them less and in spite of depressions. Negro men and their labor, in contrast, were tangential to and increasingly expendable in the commercial and risingly industrial society. Trapped in the city, young black men might sometimes take to a street-corner, pool-hall hustling, and petty criminal way of life. Of necessity, they generated a set of values to justify their lives, values that directly countered those of the Victorians. If the black male could find no decent job, it was because he was too smart to work. If he seemed to travel from one woman to another, sleeping in the bed of the white folks' maid, and eating the "take-homes" from the white folks' table, and if his children did not all live under the same roof, it was simply because he was too much man for one woman to handle. The street-corner, counter-value, male-worshiping society that became so very evident in black life in the nation later actually emerged in the urban South in the turn-of-the-century decades. Along with it, and complementary to it, was spawned the "black matriarchy," also later evident and usually imputed to slavery. In reality, both were new, and they were the unfortunate children of the marriage of the industrial revolution to white racism. Together they constituted a model diametrically opposed to the Victorian order.

Inevitably, social denigration at the hands of the dominant whites in the post-Reconstruction decades laid its special tax upon each black personality, including those highly placed as well as low. To some extent the black reaction to alienation was an aggressive one. The black psyche became suspicious, not only of whites, but of other blacks. Negro leaders were inordinately jealous of other leaders in the community, and too often they would, in effect, rather see a black project fail than a black man succeed. James A. Whitted, a school principal who was soon to be highly successful as president of North Carolina College, tried very hard in 1890 to get the black portion of federal land grant funds for his school in Durham. He experienced extreme difficulty organizing the local black leadership into a united front. "I am afraid that petty jealousies among our big men will cause them to fall out by the way," he confessed to a fellow principal. "Some men want to be sure that they are carrying all the honors, especially in the estimation of 'God's flaming chariots.'"[8] Below the top ranks of leadership, blacks with some degree of authority sometimes used that authority in picayune ways, attempting to grab back some of the self-esteem taken away in the broader social world. Blacks bent on getting things done often saw the elaborate routines invented and presided over by black petticrats as pure obstructionism. An agent trying to get exhibits from the Negro fair in Washington in 1886 to include in the North Carolina fair later in that year vented his irritation in a letter to a friend. "There is so much 'pomposity' [,] Sham dignity and red tape about everything done here of a business character, it is trying to the Soul of a man who means business to deal with these people."[9]

If some Negroes reacted to their alienation more or less aggressively, others responded passively. A black woman in Wilmington secured pledges of articles for exhibits at the fair, but placed small faith in the promises. "You know that we Wilmingtonians have but little, if any, energy, enthusiasm, race-pride, or any of those grand qualities which go so far toward the making of a people," she asserted.[10] Apathy at the mass level was distressingly apparent at voting time. George Washington Murray, the last black member of Congress from South Carolina, complained after the election of 1898 that, while many whites in Charleston voted for him, "many Negroes, who were qualified[,] abstained from voting."[11] Black leaders were appalled by the failure of Georgia Negroes to react against a disfranchising move there in 1899. Booker T. Washington, as usual playing the black man's hand as best he could, found the situation difficult and exasperating. "It is a question how far I can go and how far I ought to go in fighting these measures in other states when colored people themselves sit down and will do nothing to help themselves," he complained. "They will not even answer my letters." Shortly, he journeyed to Atlanta where he found the conservative Democratic organ in the state, *The Constitution,* the most effective force for the benefit of blacks. "If we do not win," he asserted, "we have certainly shown them that we were not cowards sleeping over our rights."[12]

The process of disintegration in black life was, as I have said, less than obvious. It never became total chaos, complete anarchy, or absolute disorientation. It was a relative matter, but it was nonetheless real. Also it was a process that has been awkward for historians to treat because it was a phenomenon that does not relate directly to statistics or the palpable things of this world, or even with thoughts that are coolly rational and logically explicable. Rather was it a matter of individual psychologies, of emotions and moods, of vague sentiments and feelings, that scholars in the past have usually preferred not to discuss.

The masses of black men who were thus cast out probably had little comprehension of what was happening to them; but the truly tragic people were those more thoughtful blacks who sensed the meaning and depth of their denial. If the ideals of the total culture were white and the most talented

Negroes were denied access to the ultimate satisfactions in the pursuit of those ideals, then there must have been a certain vacuity in the lives of gifted Negroes, and that emptiness must have existed in the life of the mind, the most vital and, potentially, the most satisfying portion of their being. The missing portion—the part denied—was sometimes lesser, sometimes greater. In Reconstruction it was less than it became after the turn of the century. But until the times of our own lives very few Negroes in America have had a chance to be totally whole, totally complete in the way that some few favored white people have been, and every white person has had at least an opportunity to be. Until very recently, black life in America began with a closed door.

CHARLES W. CHESNUTT

There were some very intelligent blacks in the South who lived through this time and recorded in their own lives and observations precisely this process of separation, alienation, and disintegration. Charles Waddell Chesnutt, probably the first Negro novelist to win national acclaim solely upon the excellence of his work, was one of these.

Born in 1858 of a family with deep roots in and around Fayetteville, North Carolina, Chesnutt spent his childhood in Cleveland where his parents, having fled from the closing society of the South, had come to settle. Soon after the war, Chesnutt returned to Fayetteville with his family. There he grew to young manhood, attending school, reading widely, and helping in his father's store. While still in his early teens, he served as an assistant teacher, first in Fayetteville and then in Charlotte. In 1875, at seventeen, he took his first school in a rural community near Spartanburg, in, as he expressed it, "this much abused negro rule State—South Carolina."[13] At that time, South Carolina, Louisiana, and Florida were still under Republican regimes, and South Carolina Republicans relied heavily upon the black majority in that state to hold themselves in power. After a term, Chesnutt returned to North Carolina where, by 1879, he was a professor in the State Colored Normal School in Fayetteville. In 1880, at twenty-two, he became the school's principal.[14]

Chesnutt's rapid rise in the teaching profession was a proper reflection of his brilliance. While still in his teens he knew Latin and Greek, played the organ and the piano, and, along with a whole generation of bright young Southerners of that time (including Woodrow Wilson), followed the vogue to master stenography. Still, his passion was for English and American literature, and in the study of these he excelled. Chesnutt had a tremendous capacity for self-teaching. For instance, in 1875 he had learned German well enough, primarily from books, to converse in German with an immigrant who had become sufficiently affluent to earn a place on a local school board.[15] In the

North later in life, Chesnutt read law and passed examinations for the bar, developed a large clientele for his stenographic service in the Cleveland that was spawning the Standard Oil Company, became the president of the national stenographic association, and generated a very comfortable middle-class life for his family. He wrote more or less steadily in his spare time, became a protégé of George Washington Cable, the New Orleans author, and about the turn of the century, when his family had been very solidly established, turned his energies largely into writing. It was unfortunate for Chesnutt himself—so patently a genius—that he chose to work intensively in literature in the very years when a black man's chance for literary success was rapidly evaporating. But it is fortunate for historians of race relations that Chesnutt did live and work precisely as he did because he gave us, as he early set out to do, a very human example of a hard test of talent against the color line.

As an adolescent, and to some extent throughout his life, Chesnutt was ambivalent about blackness, in himself and in others. Only one-eighth black and, by his own account, very light of skin, he was early tempted to flee from his darker self by crossing the color line and "passing" for white. "I believe I'll leave here and pass anyhow," he confided to his diary in South Carolinia in 1875, "for I am as white as any of them." At the swimming hole earlier that day, one fellow said, "'he'd be damned' if there was any nigger blood in me," and in town an older white man had called to a friend, "Look here tom, here's a black fellow as white as you air,"[16] After a month, he grew tired of his rural black neighbors. He pronounced them bigoted and superstitious, and denounced them as believing in "ghosts, luck, horseshoes, cloud signs, witches, and all other kinds of nonsense. . . ." A week later, he railed against the local blacks: "They accuse you indirectly of lying, almost of stealing, eavesdrop you, retail every word you say, Eavesdrop you when you're talking to yourself, twist up your words into all sort of ambiguous meanings, refuse to lend you their mules &c. They are the most suspicious people in the world, good-sized liars, hypocrites, inquisitive little wenches &c."[17]

Of course, much of Chesnutt's life in these years fell upon the dark side of the color line, and he found there much that was appealing as well as some that was distressing. He loved music, and he was profoundly moved by the spirituals he heard and sang in the black church. Journeying to Washington in 1879, he made a special effort to visit the chambers of the Senate to see Blanche K. Bruce, the Negro senator from Mississippi still filling out the term he had begun during Reconstruction.[18] En route to Washington, riding the second-class car to Norfolk, Virginia, Chesnutt participated in a vignette that revealed neatly the deep ambivalence of his own racial feelings. He had been enjoying, as he later recalled in his journal, a conversation with a "gentleman" from Weldon, apparently white. "It was pleasant enough till we took on about fifty darkies who were going to Norfolk to work on a truck farm," he wrote.

"They filled the seats and standing room, and sat in each others' laps for want of seats. As the day was warm and the people rather dirty, the odor may be better imagined than described. Although it was nothing to me, I could sympathize with my fellow traveller, who stuck his head out of the window, and swore he would never be caught in such a scrape again." Chesnutt did not explain why the odor was "nothing" to him and overpowering to his companion. But he did catch—neatly, sensitively, and sympathetically—a scene in black life that was beautiful. "It was a merry crowd however," he continued amiably, "especially one young fellow who would gravely line out a hymn and then sing it himself, with all the intonations of a camp meeting. His sister, he said, sat in his lap though the affectionate way in which he embraced her seemed, to our unsophisticated eyes, to render the relationship doubtful, at the least."[19]

As he matured, Chesnutt deliberately opted to be black, and, further, he undertook to use his abilities to assault the color line. His mission in life, he resolved, was to "test the social problem" by seeing "if it's possible for talent, wealth, genius to acquire social standing and distinction." Writing in his diary after an all night vigil that ended in the birth of his first child, a daughter, and having enjoyed a lengthy conversation with a perceptive and sympathetic white physician, Theodore D. Haigh, Chesnutt pledged himself to the cause of trying the color line. "This work I shall undertake not for myself alone," he asserted, "but for my children, for the people with whom I am connected, for humanity!" In an echo of Martin Luther, he concluded, *So will Ich strebe zu then, mitt Gottes Hilfe.*[20]

Chesnutt never lost his determination to succeed in his struggle to rise in American culture, but over the next few years awareness was pressed in upon him that such success was not to be had in Fayetteville, North Carolina. Increasingly, he encountered frustration, he felt alienated, and he began to withdraw.

In March 1880 Chesnutt recorded a conversation he had with the proprietor of the bookstore in Fayetteville, a gentleman who had, interestingly enough, allowed Chesnutt to borrow books freely when he was a youngster with a voracious appetite for reading. The same man was a brother of the sympathetic physician who had delivered his daughter. Mr. Haigh was complaining about the departure of the better class of free Negroes from the area to the North in the 1850s. That movement was, in fact, only a part of a more general exodus of free Negroes from the South. Chesnutt, who probably had in mind the flight of his own family to Cleveland in 1856, answered that living in North Carolina had become impossible. "You had taken away their suffrage," he said, referring to the disfranchisement of free blacks in 1835, "the laws were becoming more and more severe toward free colored people; and they felt that their only safety lay in emigration to a freer clime." Revealingly, he bared his sense of frustration. "As for my part, I can't see how intelligent colored people can live in the South even now. And I went on to state my reasons why;—the existing prejudice—the impossibility of a rise in the social scale, etc." Mr. Haigh replied that he "thought that these grades of society were the best preservatives of society." Chesnutt demurred and Haigh grew angry. He declared that God had made things as they were and "asserted that the condition of things would never be different, for the line must be drawn somewhere, and the best plan is to draw it where it is."[21]

A few weeks later Chesnutt encountered a more tangible and personally pointed form of white racism. He was twenty-two, a professor in a state normal school, and highly talented. He was offered the Republican nomination for the office of town commissioner and accepted it on the night it was tendered. "The next day my friends remonstrated. Mr. H. spoke of my indiscretion; and Capt. Williams, Powers, and several others contrived to put so 'many fleas in my ear' that I sent in my formal withdrawal to the Ch'rman of the committee, and backed off as gracefully as possible."[22] Chesnutt had learned that an ambitious young black man, however principled and cultured, would be wise to avoid politics in North Carolina.

Within a month, Chesnutt was complaining that after fifteen years in the South he still could not enjoy full intellectual freedom. "And my circumstances, my outward circumstances," he wrote, "are not favorable to a very high development either of mind or morals."[23] Shortly he attempted to take private lessons in German from an émigré professor named Neufeld. "He says there have been some objections made on the part of some of his patrons to his taking colored pupils. He says however, that nothing of that kind would influence him at all, as he is sufficiently independent to lose 20 scholars if necessary." Neufeld loaned him a German reader, but after Chesnutt had left, Mr. Kyles, one of Neufeld's students who happened to be present, warned him not to accept Chesnutt as a scholar. Dr. Haigh was also there and, on the contrary, urged Neufeld to take Chesnutt. Haigh later told a white friend, who repeated his words to Chesnutt, that "he could sympathize with me, for he Knew my position, and could imagine my feelings. He recognized my ability and accomplishments, and felt that my lot was a hard one, to be cut off from all intercourse with cultivated society, and from almost every source of improvement." For Chesnutt, Haigh's sympathy was "a drop of rain in the desert of discouragement by which I am surrounded. . . ."[24]

Chesnutt was persistent. Through the summer of 1880, his ultimate goal remained what it had always been—to enter the white world fully and to enjoy its fruits. He thought that the great mass of blacks would gradually but surely follow. He resolved not to allow his own vision to be "blinded by the dirt and the hazy moral and social atmosphere which surround the average negro in the south."[25] Chesnutt thought that the racist position in America "must be mined, and we will find ourselves in their midst before they think it." The Negro must quietly "prepare himself for social recognition and equality," and literature must "pen the way for him to get it—to accustom the public mind to the idea; and while amusing them to lead them imperceptibly unconsciously step by step to the desired state of feelings."[26]

Interestingly, it was the upper class in the white community that did most to alienate Chesnutt. Indeed, he had few acquaintances and no friends among lower-class whites. It was not "red-neck racism" that cut Chesnutt most deeply, but that of the most cultivated gentry of the white community. On one occasion, his sympathy for Professor Neufeld evoked a flood of sentiment. Some of the more prominent whites were "prejudiced to Neufeld because he is a foreigner and a Jew," Chesnutt wrote in his journal. "J. C. Williams, Crawford, E. F. Moore are some that he [Neufeld] mentioned. He says they are so much prejudiced that he would just like to hurt them real bad once. I wish he would. Some of these purse-proud aristocrats seem to think they own the whole world, and that other people only live because they graciously vouchsafe to permit them."[27] A trip to the North increased his resentment against his exclusion from Southern society. "I occupy here a position similar to that of Mahamets Coffin," he complained. "I am neither fish [,] flesh, nor fowl— neither 'nigger,' white, nor 'buckrah.' Too 'stuck-up' for the colored folks, and, of course, not recognized by the whites."[28]

Chesnutt's efforts to win honor across the color line did not go entirely without reward and, recurrently, he gained hope. In 1881, after he had testified eloquently for the normal school before a state senate committee in Raleigh, he was very favorably referred to on the floor of the senate and in the newspapers as a "scholar and a gentleman" and called "Prof. Chesnutt." After teachers from the white schools in Fayetteville visited his classes, Chesnutt found himself delightfully popular among the leading people there, both black and white. Further, along with many other knowledgeable blacks in the South, he thought for a time that Negro participation in the Prohibition movement, including a celebrated speech by himself at a local meeting, was bringing blacks and whites closer together. In the next year, moreover, he was enjoying Greek lessons from Mr. Hodges, a graduate of Davidson College, a fine scholar, and "a thorough Southern, but also a gentleman."[29]

Inexorably, however, the burden of race weighed down upon him. He scorned Negroes who claimed that they had white friends. "I have no white friends," he asserted disdainfully in 1882. "I could not degrade the sacred name of 'Friendship' by associating it with any man who feels himself too good to sit at table with me, or to sleep at the same hotel. To me friendship can only exist between men who have something in common, between equals in something, if not everything; and where there is respect as well as admiration."[30]

Chesnutt reacted against denial with bitterness, but he also showed the classic syndrome of withdrawal. More and more, he isolated himself in his room where, as he said, he could "enjoy the society of the greatest wits and scholars of England." Increasingly, his alienation bore down upon him. "I get more and more tired of the South," he complained in 1882. "I pine for civilization and 'equality.'" He hesitated to leave his work at the school, but, he said, he shuddered "to think of exposing my children to the social and intellectual proscription to which I have been a victim."[31] Within a year he had fled north, precisely as had his parents a generation before.[32] First he went to New York, then home again to Cleveland, where he spent the remainder of a long life.

Somewhere a black man rode in the first-class car of a train, somewhere black people sat in the back pews of a church while white people worshiped in the front pews, and now and again a very light and well-educated Negro might be served at an ice cream bar with white people. One day every other year, some black men went to the polls with white men and cast ballots for Republicans, some of whom were black. These things were important as qualities of American life. In the realm of absolutes, of ideals, there is a vast difference between one black person exercising even a minor measure of equality in the white-dominated world and no black person at all doing that thing. But in life as lived, tokens are less than vital to each separate person. The fact that somewhere, sometime black people touched the core of white American life could not have been greatly valued by a black person who had no such opportunities. Further, there was a vast throng of others who lost the dream of such possibilities.

Even for blacks who mingled with whites in these marginal ways, the effect was not always salutary. Charles Chesnutt collected all those tokens of mixing, and they seemed only to heighten his sense of alienation. Chesnutt yearned for intimate contact with minds cultivated in the Western way and many of those existed in white bodies. Most often the intellects that he admired and sought to engage belonged to people of the more affluent upper class. The color of his own skin testified to the fact that white people sometimes accepted the nearness of black bodies. Further, one strongly suspects that Chesnutt's white blood as well as his name came from the Southern slaveholding elite, from the very class with which he yearned to commune, not because of its color, of course, but because of it culture. Still, his experience witnessed that a profound and painful separation existed in the world of the mind, and that—while he might live in daily contact with white people and in himself be practically white—the most cultured and lightest mulatto would not be accepted in the world of the white South.

VARIOUSLY BLACK

Charles Chesnutt left the South, but not every thoughtful black could or would desert that native ground. Over the next several decades, those who remained exhibited a broad range of responses to the rising level of anxiety in black life. In race relations, some simply withdrew, masking their inner feelings. Others protested. Still others accommodated. Most did all three at various times and under various circumstances. Confusion in race relations was matched by confusion within the black world itself. Indeed, a mark of oppression was a confusion of personality in individual Negroes, a tendency to accrete a melange of disparate and often contradictory parts bound in a single body. Parts from the white world came sometimes to be grotesquely mixed in black persons. Holy men became unholy satyrs, philosophers were fools, and insanity was sanity.

Charles Norton Hunter was one whose life was an agony of protest and accommodation. Born a slave in 1854 near Raleigh, North Carolina, and early orphaned, he had been educated first at the hearth of his master and then in the freedmen's schools. He clerked in a freedmen's bank, taught in the public schools, and became one of the pioneers in a company that organized the annual Negro fair in the state. During the 1880s he came to be recognized as an authority on fairs within the Negro world. In 1907 he was most active in arranging the black side of the North Carolina exhibit in the Jamestown Tricentennial Exposition at Hampton Roads, Virginia. In his exhibits he always strove to illustrate the progress of the race and the validity of a black identity. "Do you ever think of the fact that we have no record?" he wrote to a school principal in 1907. "That we have no history to which we can appeal? That we are going on from day to day living, and moving, and having our being among men without making any authentic record of what we are doing or who we are? Does it not occur to you that, until we can tell who we are and what we have done we can have no standing among the other races of men?"[33]

In the 1890s Hunter settled down to become the principal of an elementary school in Raleigh, and evidently he performed excellently in that capacity. He worked hard and consistently, earning the respect and the trust of the white superintendent over him. The ordinary frustrations of his position were great, but most telling upon him were the special taxes he paid for his color. With a family of five to support, his salary as a black principal recurrently proved inadequate. His personal correspondence suggests the distressing difficulty with which he kept a charming and intelligent daughter in Hampton Institute for two years and then suddenly, tragically, lost her to some unknown disease. On one occasion the newspapers raised a furor when two of his female teachers were accused of prostitution and one of his male teachers of procuring and acting as "lookout." The specifications under the charge were patently absurd. But it was the sort of thing that many whites in the high tide of white supremacy emotionalism in North Carolina readily believed of black people. Absurd as the charge was, Hunter had strenuously to deny it. Increasingly, his notes to the superintendent grew plaintive, querulous, even paranoid. Parents of children in his school became irritated, threatened to complain to the white authorities, and did so. Hunter began to drink. In 1900 he was dismissed for drunkenness. He fled to New Jersey, leaving his wife and children. He worked first as a dishwasher. Then, ever the entrepreneur, he became an emigration agent, pulling black labor up from the South for Jersey farms and kitchens.

After his collapse and retreat to New Jersey, Hunter was a broken man. Previously, he had been relatively casual about his prewar closeness to his aristocratic masters as a slave child. In his last years, he showed himself increasingly vulnerable to flights into the protective paternalism of upper-class Southern whites. Down and out in the North, he finally appealed for aid to the rector of a local Episcopal church. He stressed his identification with the church from infancy through his master's house, and he asserted that he had been cast out by his own people for his faithfulness. But he had remained loyal, he declared, and the presumption was that the aristocracy should remain loyal to him and rescue him during this time of need.[34]

After 1902, back in North Carolina as a principal again by the protective benevolence of the white Democratic school superintendent, he assiduously cultivated his white friends. Occasionally, he lashed out at discrimination or threatened to do something Republican in politics. But, by and large, he drifted toward a shapeless, sentimental accommodationism. In an Emancipation Day address in 1910, he protested against the inferior railroad facilities set aside for Negroes traveling to and from Raleigh and the humiliation imposed upon black people by forcing them to use those facilities. Almost in the same breath, he lauded most heartily the aristocratic white families of North Carolina and sought their protection. "My brother and I were reared at the fireside of one of the grandest families of this state," he boasted to the audience. "I feel convinced that the Southern Negro has no better friend than the Southern white man who once owned him, lived in close contact with him, and whose children were raised by negroes."[35] In 1913, on the fiftieth anniversary of the Emancipation Proclamation, Hunter arranged for the Negro state fair to feature an "Old Slaves dinner." To finance the affair, Hunter solicited contributions from surviving slaveholders and their families.[36]

Late in life, Hunter began a correspondence with another disengaged black intellectual, H. A. Parris. Parris was a contemporary of Hunter who had served most of his mature life as an Episcopal priest doing missionary work among American blacks. After what appeared to be a very successful career, he retired to live in Savannah, Georgia. Like Hunter, he felt keenly his ultimate alienation from the white culture that he had striven to join. On the other side, he rued his alienation from his own people. "Do you know, I have lived a very lonely life," Parris confided. "You touched a very responsive note in my heart when you bemoaned the lack of a good and practical point of contact with the mass of people."

The alienation of the intellectual from the mass of humanity was not and is not, of course, an exclusively black phenomenon. Indeed, in varying degrees, it is the usual case. But there was an element of unreality added to the life of the black intellectual who remained in the South in the twentieth century. He suffered a special uncertainty as to where the horizons really lay and recurrently suspected that his own thinking was pointless and irrelevant. Parris caught the mood neatly in an image he often expressed to his wife. "It must be," he would say, "that I am crazy or hung in upside down." His life had been spent in the "uplift" of the Negro, and yet in that crusade he felt that he had been "a miserable failure." One of his professors at Columbia University in his student days had urged him to quit school because he was being educated away from his people, the people with whom of necessity he must spend his life. "I thought him prejudiced. . . . My brother, he was right!!!" Father Parris had found the society in which he was forced to abide "very inert, hypocritical, shamming." Secretly, he withdrew from the world even as he seemed, Franciscan-like, to go into it. "And so I have gone mostly alone," he concluded, "trying to keep step outwardly with the world as I find it; but inwardly rebellious & weary & protestant—and lonely."[37] How many black intellectuals felt precisely so in the "nadir of the Negro"?

Parris withdrew into a lonely bitterness. Hunter was aggressive and submissive. George W. Henderson, pastor of prestigious Straight University Church in New Orleans and a professor in the School of Theology, was discouraged but persistent. Ultimately, he came to recognize the necessity of defining a valid black identity. Early in 1899, in a letter to Chesnutt, he lamented the strong tendency toward divisiveness within the black community. "There is much of prejudice among colored people," he complained. For instance, "there are benevolent societies here that will not admit persons of dark complexion. And what is called *society here* is disposed to follow the same rule with a supreme disregard of character, of moral worth and native sense and ability." He captured perfectly the lack of satisfaction in even the richest of Negro life. "Our social life is somewhat chaotic from necessity," he commented sadly, "so is all our life more or less unorganized." He felt the need for points of reference that all Negroes could recognize as legitmate and thus give unity and form to their lives. Chesnutt, he thought, and Paul Lawrence Dunbar, the black poet, had a mission in that movement. "I am convinced more and more that we need a literature of our own. The current literature does not touch us in many vital points; it does not interpret our experiences, does not recognize our traditions, and has no real message for us. You and Dunbar perceive this, I think, as no one else has."

Henderson doubtless read much of his own aspiration for his people into Chesnutt's writing. He, himself, was diligently working to hold up a worthy and distinctive black experience in which his people could take pride. He had written an article on the "gallant conduct" of Negroes in the Spanish-American War and was moving to have a monument erected to honor those blacks who had fallen in the struggle. He was also publishing articles in the *African Methodist Review*. "I am trying to do in the realm of history and religion," he told Chesnutt, "what you are doing so much better in fiction—deal with the great subjects of our past and present from the Negro's standpoint."[38]

DEFINITION: WASHINGTON AND DuBOIS

By the late 1890s, black intellectuals and leaders in the South were turning their energies away from a relatively single-minded pursuit of whiteness from within their various enclaves and were falling back, in one sense or another, upon the black masses. There was always, of course, a distance between the vanguard and the rank and file, a lapse in time between the definition of a new course and its pursuit by the mass of black people. Black society moved much like some loosely organized army. Often scouts and leaders found themselves out upon new ground, in effect, without followers, alone and wasted. Some, who had previously enjoyed the followship of the masses, found themselves unaccountably deserted and irrelevant. Frederick Douglass—black abolitionist, assimilationist, and the most famous black man in America before his death in 1895—was one of the latter. With the end of Reconstruction his power steadily dwindled. With his marriage to a white woman in 1884, it practically evaporated altogether. Still others in the vanguard beat a path forward and looked back, eventually, to find—perhaps with a measure of surprise— that the masses had moved in behind them and were following. Booker T. Washington was one of these. He did not at first so much offer himself as he was chosen. His successor, W. E. B. DuBois, was at first not so much chosen as he offered himself.[39]

In the deep South blackness was most massive, chaos most frightening, and the drive for a viable structure most imperative. Out of the struggle came two grand and conflicting schemes for organizing black life in America. Booker T. Washington offered one alternative, a relatively accommodative one in which blacks would strive to be superbly white but only in areas carefully selected to appear nonaggressive to whites. Washington's appeal to both blacks and whites was almost overwhelming in the turn-of-the-century years. What he would preserve for black people were precisely those things, religion aside, they held most dear: the farm, the family, and education. What he gave up were claims to things that blacks in a large measure had already lost in fact if not in law: physical integration and full political participation. Moreover, by giving up demands for integration in public places and universal male suffrage, he seemed also to surrender any claim to the "social equality" that so thoroughly frightened whites.

Washington and his program came to stage center on the speaker's platform of the Atlanta Cotton States Exposition in 1895, the very year Frederick Douglass died. In an address given as a part of the opening ceremonies, he called upon both whites and blacks to "put down their buckets" where they were, to come to terms with one another, and to draw upon the rich resources that each afforded the other. Black people had been loyal to their masters during the war, they had labored faithfully, and they would be loyal to white employers now and work "without strikes and labour wars." The white South after emancipation had given black people "a man's chance in the commercial world." For future progress, black and white had only to band together again, to deal with one another in a spirit of trust as they had in the past. Implicit in his words was the program he had followed at Tuskegee with signal success for more than a dozen years, a program that he had evolved out of his experience at Hampton Institute. In the exchange as offered in 1895, black people would accept some things and expect others. Washington symbolized his idea with a dramatic gesture. He held up his right hand, fingers spread. "In all things that are purely social we can be as separate as the fingers," he declared. Closing his fingers into a fist, he concluded, "yet one as the hand in all things essential to mutual progress." This "Atlanta Compromise," as it came to be called, was Washington's offering to the white people as the basis for an interracial peace. The audience accepted it with thunderous applause, with, indeed, a standing ovation.[40] It was not, it must be noted, a representative audience. In fact, the stage was filled with Georgia Republicans, a Reconstruction Republican governor had introduced Washington, and a Republican federal judge followed him as speaker. Finally, the whole Exposition was gotten up by business interests as a commercial device to combat the great depression of the 1890s.

Even so, the event served to thrust the baton of black leadership into Washington's not unwilling hand. During the next several years he was, in effect, the undisputed leader of the great mass of black people in the South. Some 90 percent of the Negro population was in that region, and Washington thus became the spokesman for the great mass of black people in America. In those years, very few black leaders in the South refused to applaud Washington's stance in race relations, if not Washington himself. White leadership in the nation at large moved to take advantage of the convenience of having a single black leader, someone who could not only speak for his people, but make commitments and deliver as promised. In the fall of 1901, Theodore Roosevelt, then President by dint of the assassination of William McKinley, invited Washington to the White House to discuss political appointments in the South. Soon Washington was generally understood to be Roosevelt's principal adviser on Southern appointments. His power, even over the political affairs of Southern whites, became highly impressive. For instance, in Alabama in 1901 it was probably his endorsement that effected the appointment of a conservative white Democrat, Thomas G. Jones, to the federal bench against the wishes of the senior Alabama Senator, a Democrat.[41] Washington's power in the field of black education was even greater than in politics. Southern white leaders soon come to request Tuskegee men to manage black education in their states and communities. Finally, Northern philanthropists, eager to pour money into Southern education, called upon him to point out the deserving. Washington had no difficulty in identifying his friends.

Ironically, even as Washington's power grew, the inadequacy of his accommodationism in the face of a rapidly deteriorating state of race relations became increasingly apparent. What changed was not Washington or his racial philosophy, or even his tactics, but rather the racial posture of the white world with which he had to deal. Washington, in essence, had offered an arrangement to whites who were racially conservative, to men who thought of blacks as a people created for a subordinate and serving place in a world dominated by benevolent whites. As the years clicked over the end of the century, however, these people lost control of their communities and, in the deep South, they lost whole states to racial extremists who regarded black people as hardly more than dangerous beasts. Washington had negotiated a compromise with benevolent establishments only to find many of those establishments dissolved and replaced by ones that were positively malevolent.

The racial world changed; so also did the material one, and that change compounded racial difficulties. Washington's program was designed for the agrarian order of the nineteenth century. But even as Washington gained power, the United States and the South were moving into an industrial order that would dominate the lives of the great mass of working America in the twentieth century as agrarian orders had dominated their lives in the nineteenth century. There had been a place made for black people in the old order. In the new order, powerful elements would press for their exclusion.

The message of denial from whites was manifested in many ways—by legal segregation and disfranchisement, by a broad social proscription that went far beyond specific discriminatory laws, by an imbalance in educational resources, by a progressive squeeze upon black tenant farmers, and by a drumfire of horrendous lynchings that left the landscape dotted with hanging bodies and charred remains. Especially did it come crashing in with a wave of violence at the turn of the century. In this time of riots, beginning signally with the outburst in Wilmington, North Carolina, in 1898 and ending with a massacre in Atlanta in 1906, upper-class blacks learned that in the South there were no citadels—nor even any refuges—in which any black person could find certain security. In September 1906, at last, the black businessmen along Auburn Avenue in Atlanta, who had taken Washington's advice and put down their buckets where they were with exemplary success, found themselves pursued, beaten, and their shops demolished by white mobs. Even the black professors of the elite circle of institutions clustered around Atlanta University found that their high culture, which certainly matched that of their white neighbors, afforded them no sanctuary. Their blackness alone was license enough to line them up against walls, to menace them with guns, to search them roughly, beat them, and rob them of every vestige of dignity.

With the Atlanta riot, in particular, it became apparent to thoughtful and objective blacks that even the most yielding of postures was not working in the South. In the North where there were few blacks, and where white assimilationists were persons of unusual power, black people could assert themselves and maintain their dignity. Occasionally in the South a Negro might aspire to the special kind of manhood projected in the image of Booker T. Washington and enjoy the carefully limited respect received by that sort of personality in the white world. But by the end of 1906, it was clear enough to those who would see that in the South Washington no longer had a contract that white men in the mass were bound to respect, and black claims to parity in any sphere would be met with terrible violence. If Negroes in the South were to regain their rights and dignity, it would not be by the further pursuit of accommodation.

Awareness of the racial realities over the next several decades not only fueled anti-Washingtonian attitudes of resistance among Negroes, it also lent strength to the idea that, after all, the Negro was not a white man with a black skin, and, moreover, that he could never be free within the given organization of Southern society. If Negroes in the South were to have ideals unstunted by limitations imposed by an insistent and omnipotent white society, those ideals would have to be distinctly black and quite apart from the ideals of the white world. If Negroes in the mass were to have ideals, values, and culture, these would have to be, in some significant measure and for some time to come, separated ideals, values, and culture.

The germ of the idea that proved to be the great alternative to the Washingtonian approach appeared a scant two years after the Atlanta speech. It was offered by W. E. B. DuBois, who came to the lower South in 1897 to take a teaching post at Atlanta University. DuBois, then twenty-nine, was a brilliant young man with degrees from Fisk and Harvard. He had studied at the University of Berlin under some of the foremost German scholars in that dawning age of social science, and he was completing a study of Philadelphia Negroes when he came to Atlanta. In 1897 in two little-noticed articles he introduced the revolutionary idea that the black experience in America was not only essentially different from that of the whites, but that it was necessarily and beautifully so. In Du Bois's interpretation, every people was imbued by God at creation with a distinct genius. Throughout its life each people struggled, often in confusion and seeming contradiction with itself, to realize its special nature. Different peoples came to new and higher plateaus of self-realization at different times. Black people in America, so recently out of slavery, were a child race, only then coming to the threshold of self-understanding. There had been painful struggle, and there would be further struggle in which the true nature of black soul would become increasingly evident. But even then, he argued, even in 1897 it was clear that blacks were a specially spiritual people, living in the midst of an increasingly materialistic America. They were also an artistic people given specially to music, to colors, and language. In time, by virtue of their own striving, the genius of black people would manifest itself, and they would find themselves in close harmony with the prime being, and, presumably, through Him, with all else. Thus the path of progress, the way to harmony and a perfect assimilation lay in the pursuit of blackness not white-ness, in black people seeking communion with black people. Self-realization would not be achieved one by one, but all together or not at all. Consequently, a certain amount of black exclusiveness, a certain amount of voluntary sepa-ration from whites and confederation in all-black enclaves was essential to salvation.[42]

Du Bois's racial philosophy was fundamentally different from that of Booker Washington, but the difference was not at first apparent. Indeed, the two men could come together readily and easily upon the ground of the neces-sity of concert among black people. Washington's program featured race pride, solidarity, and self-help. Du Bois, of course, could easily endorse these. Also, Du Bois was very much in favor of the economic improvement of black people, endorsed industrial education as legitimate, and applauded the rise of black businesses able to stand upon the patronage of black people. Most of all, Washington and Du Bois agreed on the necessity of black people organizing to pursue their interests. Finally, the principal and the professor both wanted full political and civil rights for black people, though they might differ as to how to achieve those goals. For a time, Du Bois could even be contented with a degree of gradualism. During the last years of the nineteenth century, he, along with nearly every other influential black leader in the South, applauded Washington's stance and followed his lead. Washington recognized Du Bois's talents and support. On three occasions he offered the young professor appointments at Tuskegee. On each occasion Du Bois turned down the offer with reluctance.

The primary cause of the break between Washington and DuBois was the change in the interracial environment in which they labored. In effect, the white people with whom Washington had negotiated a modus vivendi in 1895 were, by 1900, rapidly losing control to people who had radically different ideas about the proper state of relations between the races. In the black belts of the South white attitudes of accommodation rapidly melted into universal rejection, and burning and bloody aggression. Whereas Conservative whites would have blacks stand in a subordinate place, Radical racists would reduce black people to supersubordination. As Radical racists gained power, they moved to effect that end. Washington, nevertheless, steadfastly maintained an overt posture of accommodation; indeed, he seemed psychologically incapable of altering that stance. Persistently he would try for the best, but he would take what he could get. Ironically even as his posture became less appropriate to the circumstances, his power to hold it and enforce it upon other blacks increased. By 1902 his command of the Southern black response to the white world was nearly complete, and even though he used that power to resist white encroachments strenuously, he did so secretly, deviously, and with only sporadic success. Under Washington and with accommodation, black resistance began from a kneeling position to face an on-rushing, powerful, and fanatical foe bent upon nothing less than rendering black people prostrate.

DuBois was the first black person to attack Washington's leadership with lasting effect. He did so initially in 1903 in his book, *The Souls of Black Folk,* the opening gun in a long and sometimes vicious battle for the leadership of black America. In 1905 Du Bois broadened the fight by organizing the so-called Niagara Falls Conference. The Conference included twenty-nine black leaders, only five of whom were from the South. Already black people in the South had been so reduced as to be practically powerless. There, overt resistance was met by galloping violence, rope and faggot, and expatriation. Any explicit contest for equality, clearly, would have to be waged, as it were, from exile. The Niagara Conference was candid in its intention to enter the fray fully erect and armed. It resolved that black people should protest vigorously against political, civil, and economic inequality. In a direct assault upon accommodationism, it denied that "the Negro-American assents to inferiority," or "is submissive under oppression and apologetic before insult." For itself, it declared that "we do not hesitate to complain and to complain loudly and insistently."[43] The Niagara Movement convened yearly thereafter. It was, indeed, very active in protest, and its impact was felt. At its peak it mustered some four hundred activists, and it sufficiently frightened Booker T. Washington that he resorted to his usual tactics of spying upon the organization, denying funds to some of its members while suborning others, and attacking the movement through the mouths of his agents. The militants responded in kind. Between 1907 and 1910 they sponsored a newspaper in the District of Columbia that attacked "King Booker" and his self-assumed absolutism, charged him with acquiescing in segregation, remaining "dumb as an oyster as to peonage," and discovering "that colored people can better afford to be lynched than the white people can afford to lynch them.[44]

In 1909 the members of the Niagara Movement began to merge with Northern white racial liberals to form a permanent organization, the National Association for the Advancement of Colored People. Washington again attempted futilely to undermine the organization. The alliance of black and white leaders proved highly effective. By 1914 the NAACP, headquartered in New York and with a permanent full-time staff, boasted 6,000 members, mostly black and Northern. However, it was very strong in Washington, D.C., and had some hard core representation in almost every large Southern city. Its journal, *Crisis* (founded in 1910 and edited by DuBois, who moved from Atlanta to New York for the purpose), had a circulation of 31,540.[45] The success of the NAACP sprang from many causes, of course, but the key factor was that it met the burning issue—it moved head-on against the unequal treatment of black people in American society. In doing so it traveled squarely in the path of the ideas of American republicanism as announced in the Declaration of Independence and the Constitution as amended. The program of the NAACP was strikingly old-line, nineteenth-century, patrician liberal. Its first president was, appropriately, Oswald Garrison Villard, the grandson of the great abolitionist William Lloyd Garrison. In 1831 Garrison had simply stood for the recognizedly American ideal that all men are and by right ought to be free. The objectives of the NAACP represented a continuation and updating precisely in that channel. It moved directly toward the immediate assimilation of black people as equal citizens in the Republic.[46] Like that early movement, it had little direct economic consciousness, and such as it had was laissez-faire and conservative. Stressing assimilation, it frowned upon black exclusivism and the drawing of race lines generally. What was radical about the NAACP was not its philosophy or even its method. It was, as with those earlier abolitionists, that it insisted upon "freedom now." That stance made it anathema to the gradualist Bookerites and compellingly attractive to W. E. B. DuBois.

Scholars have long noted that DuBois was, himself, often at bitter variance with the parent organization of his magazine. The root of that variance was philosophical and lay in the fact that DuBois was not an assimilationist in the traditional sense. The NAACP searched longingly for the key to the integration of blacks into the mainstream of American life. For it, an ideal society would be one in which color had no practical significance. DuBois, on the other hand, thought of color as the key to salvation. Far from eradicating color consciousness, he thought it essential that it be promoted, developed, and refined. In insisting that blacks were innately and perpetually different from whites, DuBois took a position that was virtually opposite from the integrative, assimilationist stance of the NAACP. Inevitably, in later times the difference would cause a breach. It came in the 1930s when Du Bois came out for black people voluntarily segregating themselves from whites in certain areas. Every other black leader, including his friends in the NAACP, vigorously opposed that program. Ultimately, Du Bois went his own way. He became a Marxist and settled himself in Africa, where he lived his last years.

Du Bois was the black radical in race relations in America; he was the revolutionary. Before his time, no broadly influential black leader, nor any white leader who was sympathetic to blacks, held that black people were God-givenly and essentially different from white people, and perpetually and beautifully so. Indeed, placed along the scale of assimilation versus nonassimilation, the NAACP and the Bookerites fell upon one side and Du Bois on the other. The NAACP was spread along the far end of the assimilation side and the Bookerites were arrayed on the same side but inward and closer to center, while Du Bois would stand close to the end on the other side. In the interest of black people winning a greater share in the good things of American life, both Washington and Du Bois would move closer to assimilation. But where Washington would aspire to achieve a perfect assimilation, Du Bois would stringently resist that end. For him, blackness was to be preserved and perfected, never totally lost. Du Boisian assimilation would be of a transcendental nature. Black people had contributed and would continue to contribute to a total American culture that was both black and white, each pursuing its own identity and thereby to know itself and to know God, and through Him to achieve harmony.

Du Bois's plan was more comprehensive, more cosmopolitan than any other. It is highly significant that he stood in sharp contrast to Washington and the NAACP in his attitude toward Africa. Before Du Bois, black American leaders as a group exhibited little interest in Africa, and most of the interest shown was in Africa as a missionary field for the spread of "American" culture, not as the homeland of soul brothers from whom one might learn as well as teach. Washington's interest in Africa was practically nil, and the NAACP did not feature an African relations department. Probably most educated blacks would have agreed with Charles Chesnutt, who confessed that he was "not greatly concerned about Africa except as an interesting foreign country."[47] But Du Bois, as early as 1899, initiated the first Pan African conference. He was ecumenical in his blackness where his cohorts were provincial or, at most, national. Washington allowed black people to join his club if they were "good" blacks and industrious. The NAACP allowed them to join their club if they were "good" Americans. Du Bois allowed them to join the club if they were, quite simply, black. Washington's tenure as the spokesman for the black mass was actually relatively brief. He enjoyed great strength from about 1895 to about 1907, and considerable strength until his death in 1915. The NAACP would have a very successful life for over half a century. Ultimately, however, it would find that it could go only so far in making white people out of black people in America. In the 1960s, DuBoisian soul would prove to be the most powerful organizing idea of all. It would pick up all black people, the lowly more easily than the high, and practically none would escape the pull of its gravity. Bookerism and the NAACP, after all, were for the qualified few, while Black Soul was for the masses . . . wherever they were.[48]

CHAPTER III

The Conservative Restoration and the Liberal Revolt

For a full generation after slavery, the dominant effort of Southern whites was to restore race relations, in so far as conditions allowed, to some semblance of what they had been—or, more accurately, what controlling whites assumed they had been— in the years before the Civil War. During Reconstruction that antebellum mode of thought (the Conservative mentality as I have called it) was embattled. In some places and during some times it seemed as if the old order would be lost beyond recall. However, Reconstruction was not deep enough, nor did it last long enough to give firm root to dissident styles. With the recapture of political control of their states by the Southern elite came a Conservative Restoration. That restoration was political and racial, but it was also broadly social. During the 1880s the Restoration regime was solidly established, and, while it was often vigorously challenged from within by native whites, it proved to have lasting strength.

WHITE RECONSTRUCTION

"Place" was the key word in the vocabulary of Conservatism, and place applied not only to blacks, but to all people and to all things. One Southern white perception of Radical Reconstruction was that it seemed to be precisely a concerted attempt to put things out of place. It was a horrendous effort, not simply to destroy the Conservative world but to make of the social order in the South a monstrosity. In the reduction of the planter elite and in the liberation of the slave and his elevation in civil life, it was as if the conquerors had lopped off a head and sewn on a foot in its place. Hearts had been removed and put where hands should be. The resulting creature was not unlike those Old World sixteenth-century depictions of New World people as misshapen

79

monsters. It is ironic and revealing of the essential disjunction between Southern white and Radical Republican perceptions of blackness that the latter frequently boasted that "the bottom rail is on top." Bottom rails have no business being on top. Some rails are better than others. In Southern minds there was an appalling imagery associated with the charge that the Radical Reconstructionists were filling the legislative halls of the South with common field "hands." Hands, simply, could not be heads. No more could heads or hearts become hands. Southern ladies and gentlemen could not become laborers and servants and remain ladies and gentlemen. From the Southern point of view, Radical Reconstruction's ultimate horror was that it mocked the Southern genius for social order by distorting it. Something of the resentment of an outraged people was shown in the seemingly endless bitterness that Southerners poured like vitriol upon the heads of Radical legislatures, even after they ceased to exist. Racially mixed Republican assemblies were called "ring-streaked and striped," like some mongrel and unlovely cat. Black legislators were described as eating "goobers" (peanuts) during sessions and making a mockery of parliamentary order by their misunderstanding of terms and procedures. The democratic faith implicit in Radical Reconstruction was almost unthinkable to Southern minds; it sat crosswise over the molds of what ought to be racially and socially. In Southern eyes, Reconstruction was, in its essence, an ordinance against nature and a denial of God.

Reconstruction was the "nadir of the Southern white" just as the turn-of-the-century years were the "nadir of the Negro." For white people, life in Reconstruction became very much a physical matter; it was a struggle for survival. The disengagement, alienation, and disintegration that marked black life after Reconstruction also marked white life during Reconstruction. The mark was especially deep in the lower South, and particularly so in those states where the proportion of blacks to whites was greatest.

In South Carolina where the ratio of blacks to whites, at 58 percent, was higher than in any other state, the contrast between the tone of white life before emancipation and after was most striking. In that state, by the early 1870s, white people were clearly suffering from a rising confusion of identity. Increasingly powerless as the war drew to a close and Reconstruction progressed, relieved of command of their collective destiny by losing their grasp upon the formal and compulsory agency of the state government, in the racial minority as they were, Carolina character began to fall away from the highly advertised, cocksure, dead-game, self-propelling personality that had reduced Fort Sumter to rubble in 1861. During Reconstruction, Carolinians saw clearly the specter of a perpetual reign of blackness and a prostrate state that would never rise in the same body again. With the dark abyss before them, white society began to disintegrate very much as black society under white domination was to do a generation later. Factionalism in white politics (nearly all

Democratic, as black politics after Reconstruction was nearly all Republican) rose and ran the gamut from stubborn reactionaries who refused to recognize an end of slavery to native white men who became black Republicans. Scalawags were, after all, often merely Uncle Toms of a different color, and Klansmen were nothing less than white militants, some of whom were willing to die with their guns in their hands, as they saw it, in the defense of their manhood, homes, and families. As white society disintegrated institutionally, so too did white values and character. Gray zone morality touched business and especially business that touched government. Probably, the first black legislator who was bribed in South Carolina took money raised for the purpose by leading and socially respectable Charleston businessmen who sought, and got, exclusive access to phosphate beds (fertilizer) owned by the state.

As Carolina whites lost their sense of self and ideals became blurred, the cement that had held their society together seemed to melt. They tended to fall away from one another, to turn their loyalties to local and sometimes isolated institutions— to the local church, the lodge, the family—and ofttimes to pull loyalties downward from ideals and institutions to individuals. It was, in brief, a sort of feudalization, a settling for less in order to have anything at all. This fragmentation in life that came to the South during Reconstruction probably had much to do with the generation of a modern Southern culture that remains distinctly different from that of the nation. It might have to do, for instance, with why the South eventually came to be characterized as the "Bible belt," possessing some extra-ordinary quality of spirituality, some richness in the goods of the next world to match its material poverty in this one. It might also have to do with why the South is a region where family identity remains remarkably strong. The clannishness as well as the Klannishness of Reconstruction ought to be understood in the context of this vast societal disintegration. It might relate, too, to the rise of a new model in Southern politics. It might be that Wade Hampton operated in the style of a latter-day liege lord for South Carolina whites during Reconstruction and Redemption very much as Booker T. Washington did for blacks a generation later. Both men seemed to function as overlords who gave lesser, more local nobles a modicum of common orientation and a formula for survival. Moreover, both men practiced the same sort of ever-ready accommodationist tactics. Each would try for the best for his people, and settle for what he could get. Each would be very patient and wait for opportunities. Finally, just as Washington's aides referred to him reverentially as the "Wizard," Hampton's lieutenants labeled him the "Chief."

In other states in the South were other Hamptons, and sooner or later they were all successful. And while there was never a single white leader to organize tightly all Southern whites as Booker T. Washington organized blacks, there was a beginning of "white soul." In the end, the essence of the old order, the sense of Southernness and whiteness as qualities uniquely valuable, was saved. An identity that had been sorely burned in the Civil War and very nearly drowned in the swirling currents of Black Reconstruction was regained, and a positive image of Southern self took root and life again. As Southerners looked back upon Reconstruction, they felt that they had been all but lost in a world that was all but lost, but then they were found. For a time they paused and contemplated the abyss that yawned at their feet, panting like victims snatched from the jaws of destruction. The term that they applied to regaining control of their states was as fully laden with meaning as the Christian view of the rebirth of the spirit. They called it "Redemption." It was indeed a secular salvation, a new infancy that began a higher and truer life. When they had caught their breath, they turned and moved on, "born-again" Southerners.

The Conservative mentality in the South was not totally unprogressive. Indeed, it seemed to possess a slow, strong, and subtle intelligence that allowed it to recognize and absorb, albeit reluctantly, new realities. Conservatism did change, and it had an uncanny ability to change just enough to survive. That carefully measured flexibility was—and is—its genius. For example, within months of Appomattox, the great mass of thoughtful Southerners accepted the death of slavery, the very foundation upon which their prewar culture had been built, and they moved out to reconstitute Southern society without the benefit of the peculiar institution.

As a part of that transition, feelings about paternalism made a most amazing travel between 1865 and the 1880s. In 1865 and 1866 many whites who had been closest to large numbers of Negroes as slaves and who previously had been most paternalistic in their expressions of sentiment about black people now evinced a bitter hatred of the freedmen. Particularly was this true among whites who had owned large numbers of slaves and who as a class had been among the most earnest in pleading paternalism as a justification of slavery before the war. It was almost as if they blamed the Negro, rather than the North or themselves, for the war that had freed him and the ruin that followed. The passage of the first Reconstruction Act in March 1867 in effect established universal male suffrage among Southern Negroes. Thereafter, some Conservatives made a brief ploy in the direction of attempting to persuade the freedmen that those who had lately been large slaveholders were their best friends, tried and true, and that blacks should vote for them rather than the new-coming Yankees and defecting scalawags who were then so sweetly wooing them. In this first blush of Radical Reconstruction in 1867 and 1868, Wade Hampton in South Carolina and others who clung to the paternal ideal indicated that they had advocated giving the ballot to educated and propertied blacks in the fall of 1865, well before there was pressure from the North for them to do so. Blacks, with a unanimity that was distressing and humiliating to their late masters, rejected such overtures. After that abortive attempt, ex-slaveholders generally turned and precipitantly fled from the concept of paternalism. As Radical Reconstruction deepened and the prospect of Redemption seemed more remote, paternalism seemed to turn to pouting and petulance. For a time, "ungrateful child" was the salient tone of white attitudes about black people.

In the 1870s paternalism was revived as a device to promote the process of Redemption. A part of the rhetoric of those campaigns asserted that aliens, foreign and domestic, had misled the Negro and brought both blacks and whites to the current sad state. Now that the Negro had learned the error of his ways, he would turn again to support his old friends, his true friends, his recent masters. In South Carolina, at least, a large part of that rhetoric was uttered in calculated bad faith. In that state, in 1876, the Redeemers copied very carefully the plan that had been used in Mississippi in 1875. A part of the Mississippi Plan was to claim during the election campaign that the vast majority of Negroes were going to vote Conservative and to insist after the election that blacks, had, indeed, cast their ballots for the Democracy. "The negro was not with us, did not vote with us, and still has an idea that he did not," a Mississippian explained to a prospective Carolina Redeemer in January 1876, "but he had no one on the spot to show him how the thing was done, but he sees that it was done, hurras for the winning side, and now, it is a hard matter to find a negro *who did not vote the people's ticket.* All that is necessary is to obtain the result, no matter how, and Mister Nigger accepts it as satisfactory, and claims that he helped to work out the problem."[1]

In South Carolina, in the campaign of 1876, the Redeemers pointedly preached the paternalistic line, organized pet clubs of Negro Deomcrats, gave them conspicuous places in parades, barbecues, and rallies, and moved the few black speakers they had from county to county to heighten the illusion of a credit-worthy black leadership within the Democratic camp. The paternalistic gambit in the Redemption campaign was made possible and highly plausible by Hampton's acting as the gubernatorial candidate and the white spokesman. There was no blot on his escutcheon either as a master of slaves or as an aristocrat among freedmen. He was the impeccable paternalist. His campaign slogan addressed to blacks was "free men, free schools and free ballots." Hampton himself was an honorable man, beyond suspicion of the deceit that his managers assiduously practiced. Even so, Hampton's paternalism was severely limited. There were no blacks on his ticket, and what he meant by free ballots was that Negroes would be free to cast their ballots for whomever among their late masters they chose. Before the election, Hampton's campaign manager Alexander C. Haskell claimed that 7,000 blacks would vote for the Democrats. After the election, he insisted that 9,000 had done so. Democrats, counting the votes to their own advantage, dared claim a total majority of only slightly over 1000. To have claimed more would have made the fraud too blatant. Nevertheless, it was a stolen election, and the rhetoric of paternalism covered the theft.[2]

Hampton, himself, meant what he said. As governor, he even made some well-advertised appointments of blacks to lowly offices. But most of the Democratic leadership regarded the rhetoric simply as a means to the all-important end of regaining power. Shortly Hampton, as Redemption leaders so often did, moved on to join the club of genteel gentlemen then sitting in the United States Senate. At home in South Carolina in the ensuing years, blacks were progressively squeezed down in their freedom—in politics, in education, in economics, and as individuals. It is probable that Hampton and many of the better sort never really recognized that fact. If less money were spent on black schools than white, it was because the educational needs of blacks were less than those of whites. If fewer blacks voted than whites, it was because fewer were qualified or really cared to do so. All of this was merely a part of solving the Negro problem. Life was getting right again in the Southern world and, if the cream was rising to the top, the baser elements were floating properly and evenly to the bottom. Men of Hampton's class steadily reiterated their paternalism, past and present, and it was a very convincing pose. In the end, probably not a few Redeemers fell victim to their own rhetoric. They really came to believe their own campaign verbiage about Negro loyalty and white noblesse oblige, in both slavery and freedom. As the actual experience of Redemption became more remote, the myth grew more comfortable. But in the decade of the 1880s, paternalism remained form without content, a sentiment without broadly effective action as black and white worlds drifted apart.

From time to time, bold realities have forced major alterations in the complexion of Conservative racial thought. The history of paternalism provides one case in point, the idea of the "black demise" provides another. If one followed out the logic of the proslavery argument, blacks in freedom would cease to exist in America. They would be as children turned together into a wilderness. The black man alone without the white man's supervision was, after all, only poorly productive. Under slavery he had been compelled to work enough to feed himself, in freedom he would starve. Improvidence would raise the incidence of disease and death among the newly freed. Furthermore, blacks were given to childish excesses, but childish natures given liberties with adult bodies could only breed destruction. Crime would rise, violence would increase, and sexual promiscuity would destroy the family. Venereal diseases would rip through the black population like wild fire and rapidly destroy the reproductive capacity of the race.

After the war, when whites saw the seemingly ceaseless motion among blacks, the apparent idleness and aimless wandering, the flocking to the cities, and the rise in violence and disease, they concluded that blacks were indeed destined to die away. When the census of 1870 failed to document the anticipated event, when instead it indicated that the Negro population had actually increased slightly over the decade, many whites insisted that the count was in error. The census throughout the South had, after all, been taken by ignorant blacks and their Radical carpetbag and scalawag masters who saw political advantage in swelling black numbers. In South Carolina, the charge actually produced a recount in several counties with the result that the initial figures were judged to be essentially correct. And yet, even today, there lingers about the census of 1870 an air of special distrust. Probably that census was not significantly less accurate in counting people than those of neighboring decades. What we have inherited in the suspicion surrounding the census of 1870 is probably a remnant of the disparity between what Southern whites assumed to be true about black people and what actually was true.

During the decade of the 1870s, various surveys made by states, including the school censuses, indicated what the federal census of 1880 (often enough taken by the Conservatives themselves) confirmed. Black numbers, far from diminishing, were undoubtedly increasing. Unfortunately, no one thought to exert himself to redeem the good name of the census of 1870 from the slander that had been fixed upon it. However, Conservative thought did react to the reality of the persisting presence of black people. The census of 1880 indicated that blacks were here to stay. Increasingly, as Conservatism faced the new realities, the "Negro problem" shifted in meaning. It was no longer a phrase that meant rebellious blacks. The Negro problem became a very mild issue, centering on the question of how far beneath white people black people were to be. The problem was very much a matter of defining and adjusting society to the limited abilities of black people. Thus, the Conservative mentality changed from an accepting, sometimes almost a gleeful (because self-vindicating) anticipation of the disappearance of blacks in the first years of freedom, to alarm and rejection during Reconstruction, and, finally, to a calm acceptance of the black presence in the future South during the decade after Reconstruction. If the attempt to put a new bottom on the boat of race relations in the South between 1865 and 1877 could be called Black Reconstruction, the same effort in the 1880s could well be called White Reconstruction.

THE LIBERAL REVOLT—PATERNALISM REVISITED

In the 1880s in the South, the Conservative mentality ruled in race relations. After the hard push for Redemption, it had, as it were, relaxed and drifted. Conservatism by its very nature tended to regard any peace as a good peace. It much preferred to let well enough alone. It was not aggressively anti-Negro, unless the Negro deserted his assigned place, and that place was always assumed to be somewhere safely below the place of white people. Conservatism was securely the mass mode of thought about race in the South in the 1880s, and it tolerated a wide range of varieties, the variety depending essentially upon various views of the innate character of Negroes. At the bottom of the scale, some Conservatives thought that the potential of black people was very poor, and they tended to regard a low level of Negro existence as his proper place, or a point on the path to finding that place. Other Conservatives were optimistic about the potential of black people for absorbing white civilization and attaining a relatively high place in the future society. Those who were most optimistic about black potentiality tended to be highly active in labor within the Negro community—in religion, in education, and much more delicately and carefully in matters economic, political, and societal.

In the early 1880s, a few thoughtful and highly perceptive Southern Conservatives became convinced that Negro life was losing sight of the ideals that whites cherished. They felt that black life, thus bereft, was in danger of disintegrating. In the crisis there was a reaction in the white community that might be called the Liberal revolt. It was a revolt against the apathy of the vast majority of whites in regard to black people, an apathy that, as Liberals saw it, sometimes bred ignorance and carelessness in interracial matters. It began as a call for a return to the paternalism of late slavery when the best masters had cared for and raised up the best blacks. But often it ended, as intensified interracial contact sometimes does, in a much less biased racial posture by some whites.

Racial Liberalism took a new view of race relations in the South by arguing that the Negro's capacity was as yet untried. It was distinguished by a faith that black people, properly nurtured, had the capacity to rise well up in the range of white culture. That nurture inevitably involved close instruction by whites and thereby a renewal of the physical propinquity between Negroes and at least some whites that had marked slavery. Indeed, the Liberal faith in Negro progress rested most heavily upon a rather roseate view of how greatly the Negro had been elevated in those last years of slavery in which whites had moved into black communities to Christianize and civilize the benighted. Liberalism was also influenced, though to a lesser degree, by an appreciation of how rapidly and how far Negroes had advanced under the aggressive tutelage of Reconstruction regimes. For instance, in 1860 Southern whites who presumed to know Negroes well were convinced that the black mind, while capable of managing simple arithmetic, would never be able to rise to the heights of abstraction necessary to master algebra, trigonometry, or calculus. Yet in Reconstruction, when the experiment was actually made on a large scale, often in schools sponsored by Northerners, that myth was dealt a crippling blow. Some blacks, obviously, were capable of taking giant steps into what had been previously regarded as an exclusive province of the white man.

Liberalism in the 1880s, then, was optimistic about the capacities of the Negro, and it called upon the best of Southern whites to pick up again the cross of labor among their darker brothers. Appropriately, Liberalism was open-ended in its view of the Negro's future place in Southern society. It could contemplate with relative equanimity, if not outright pleasure, an eventual parity of Negroes with whites in the enjoyment of many—but never all—white cultural ideals. Liberalism was also marked by adventurousness. Liberals were willing to gamble that improved circumstances and broader exposures would better the Negro, and they exhibited a disposition to be flexible and experimental in the pursuit of that end. There were limits, of course, to how liberal Southern Liberals would be. There were some Northern liberals, for instance Bishop Gilbert Haven of the Methodist Episcopal Church, who warmly espoused miscegenation as the solution to the race problem. Virtually no white Southerner expressed sympathy with that approach. The integration of black and white that Liberals envisioned was restricted very much to the mental and spiritual realm. Physical integration was licensed only to promote that end.

There was a lamentable paucity of racial Liberalism in the South even during its high time in the 1880s. But it did exist, and the current probably flowed most strongly among churchmen disturbed by what they regarded as a loss of religious values among Negro clergymen and a rise of dangerous emotionalism among the masses.

What disturbed some liberal white churchmen in the South also disturbed some thoughtful black people. It was probably very much the same phenomenon that Charles Chesnutt saw and deplored in Fayetteville, North Carolina, in 1880. He was fascinated by the unending drama in the life of a leading local minister-politician known as "Elder Davis." Looking toward the day when he would be a celebrated writer about black life, Chesnutt carefully detailed in his journal Davis's method of sermonizing. The Elder had once explained to him that he preached to three types of blacks at the same time. "The first class is educated— been to school—know what preaching is. They are in a small minority. The second class is moderately intelligent, but with very little learning. The lowest class is the ignorant, unlettered, naturally stupid ones who can't be reached by anything but excitement and extravagance." Thus, in every sermon, Elder Davis first read from a manuscript, pausing now and then to "fling in a trifle of Latin and Greek." Then he preached in colloquial style for a while, only using "a big word now and then, as a sort of puzzle you Know." Finally, "I shut up the Bible, rumple up my hair; shove up my coat sleeves . . . and fall back on my imagination! . . . I forget all about grammar, and come down to plain 'niggerisms.'" He burned them with the horrors of hell, he said, and soothed them with the joys of heaven. "About this time, the audience being worked up to the right pitch, I bring my fist down on the bible, Knock the water pitcher off the pulpit, and by a final burst of extravagance, bring down the house." Chesnutt observed the preacher in action on one occasion and verified his capacity for creating "pandemonium." Davis, he noted, seemingly with a mixture of admiration and dismay, had "animal magnetism."[3]

Chesnutt was appalled at the bold hypocrisy of Elder Davis. Within the year, he reported, with some glee, that the erring churchman was about to get his just deserts. Some of the members had pointed the accusing finger at him and a hearing was to be held at church that evening. "He has been playing fast and loose for some time," Chesnutt wrote. "His love for liquor, his abuse of the people, his conceit, arrogance, and impudence, together with his fondness for the fair sex and his lax method of conducting financial matters, have borne their legitimate fruit; and when the reaction comes, (and I think it is setting in now,) his fall will be as great as the elevation to which the people raised him when he first came here." Chesnutt seemed most eager for a public exposure of Davis's sins. Davis, he said, had "presumed too much on the ignorance of the people, and they are both beginning to find out their mistake." Later that evening, the diaryist added sadly that the flock had exonerated their shepherd. "His rheumatism accounts for his unsteady gait, his medicine for the smell of whiskey [with] which his clothes and breath are redolent, his niece must have company, and the Rosebuds must meet, so these give him frequent opportunities for enjoying the company of the fair Janes."[4]

ATTICUS GREENE HAYGOOD AND CHURCHLY LIBERALISM

Atticus Greene Haygood was one of the first and probably the greatest of the Southern churchmen to revolt against the abandonment of black Christians to what they regarded as exploitation by such men as Elder Davis. Haygood was the son of a country lawyer who had moved to Atlanta before the Civil War and had become a public spirited leader in that booming city. Reared in a devotedly Methodist family, Atticus was educated in staunchly Methodist Emory College. Resisting a strong temptation to enlist as a missionary to China, he became a minister, married into one of the leading ministerial dynasties in Southern Methodism, and very soon became the protégé of the foremost Southern Methodist bishop, George F. Pierce. During the war, he was a Confederate chaplain and did hard service among the troops in the field and in the hospitals, especially during the Atlanta campaign. After the war, Haygood rose rapidly to eminence in the church, not on the front lines of parish labor, but rather, one might say, by way of staff work at the rear. For a time, he was an editor in the Methodist publication complex in Nashville, quietly gaining recognition of his superior talents from the inmost hierarchy of the church. In the midst of the depression of the 1870s, he became the president of his alma mater, Emory College, and worked brilliantly to save the school from financial failure and dissolution. Finally, while still president of Emory, he took the editorship of *The Wesleyan Christian Advocate,* probably the most influential Methodist journal in the southeastern United States.[5]

Rather suddenly, in 1881, while he was president of Emory and editor of the *Advocate,* Haygood moved vigorously into the field of race relations when he published *Our Brother in Black.* He began that book by illustrating the childlike nature of Negro character through some two score anecdotes. Then he went on to criticize the necessity of Northern educational activity among Negroes in the South and to apologize for the lack of such activity by Southerners. The South had not produced slavery, but inherited it, he argued. Providence had not allowed abolitionism to become strong until white American civilization had reached a point where it could successfully resist amalgamation with the freedmen. Negroes were not white people, the two peoples would always remain racially separated, and white people could therefore relax in the black presence. But humanity was a single race, and whites might now safely reach down from their heights and teach Negroes to abandon their habits of thoughtlessness, drinking, fornication, and "debasement of 'worship' services." It was the duty of the white South to educate the Negro, and to include in that education a practical training that would allow him to win a stake in society and an appreciation of literacy in politics. Education, guided by whites, was the key to achieving a brotherhood of black and white. Finally, Haygood turned both to praise the Northern churches for their educational work in the South in the past and to discharge them from further responsibility.[6]

Our Brother in Black won high praise in the North. Within a year, Haygood was appointed the executive agent of the newly created Slater Fund at the insistence of ex-President Rutherford B. Hayes, one of its organizers. The Fund as dedicated largely to the industrial education of Negroes and spent some $40,000 annually in the South. As agent, Haygood decided how and by which schools the funds were to be used. The indications are that Haygood wielded this power effectively. One of the largest beneficiaries was Booker T. Washington's rapidly rising school at Tuskegee. In the early 1880s Haygood was also the moving spirit in establishing Paine College in Augusta, Georgia. Paine was begun by the Southern Methodists to train Negro teachers and ministers for the Colored Methodist Church, but it soon became a key institution of black education in that area and a symbol of Southern, as opposed to Northern, white missionary efforts among the blacks. In the early 1880s, Haygood himself became the symbol of a willingness among Southern whites to pick up again their commitments to the Negro. At a meeting in Chautauqua, New York, in 1883, he increased his popularity among racial liberals everywhere by emphasizing his conviction that all races were one in humanity.[7]

In the South, Haygood enjoyed the support of many Negro leaders and some whites. One correspondent of the *Advocate* applauded Haygood's efforts and regretted that the Methodist Church South had neglected to maintain what he called its "Protectorate" over the Colored Methodists even while it obstructed self-help or help by others.[8] Another writer excused previous Southern inaction upon the ground that Northerners had profited from slavery and hence had an obligation to return a portion of their wealth to the South in the form of missionary efforts. But, he argued, by 1882 the time had come when the South must again care for its Negroes by urging temperance upon them and by providing them with literature and church buildings.[9]

Every major Southern church shared in some degree the concern for the Negro that Haygood represented in MEC South. Each tried in some way to train a Negro ministry to work across the race line, and each attempted, at least spasmodically, to transmit the evangel directly through white ministers.

Committed as he was to Negro education and a relatively open-ended view of the potential of the Negro for elevation in the white man's civilization, Haygood's liberalism was not without limits. He was certainly not in favor of a physical merging of the races. On the contrary, he found great relief in the thought that Southern civilization had passed beyond the point where amalgamation was possible. In December 1881, speaking to a Boston audience, he noted with obvious gratitude that "very few mulattoes have been born during the last fifteen years."[10] Further, even though he himself seemed to move easily and freely among Negroes in their world, Haygood was no integrationist. He endorsed the separation of the races in the schools in the North as well as in the South, and he thought that ninety-nine out of every one hundred citizens would have agreed with him. Yet, on one occasion he endorsed integrated schools. In 1887, he protested a Georgia law passed to prevent white missionaries from sending their own children to schools, such as Atlanta University, where they themselves taught Negro students. The law prescribed the chain gang for convicted offenders, and that, of course, was an exceedingly cruel punishment and carried a high risk of death. In the previous school year, Haygood argued, there were only fourteen white children so situated, and their parents were doing the work among the blacks that Southern whites should have been doing. It was a disgraceful show of ingratitude, he thought, for Georgians to harass and punish others for doing the labor that was properly their own.[11]

Precisely why Haygood revolted against the drift of his times is not clear. There is a tradition at Emory that the revolt came quickly as a reaction to an incident in which Haygood lost his temper and upbraided his janitor, a black man. Filled with remorse at his un-Christian behavior, he rose in the night and went to the janitor's cottage to apologize. Thereafter, according to the story, he set himself in this new pattern of thought and action.[12] Haygood's intimate friend, protégé, and his own successor as the most eminent bishop in the church, Warren A. Candler (the brother of the founder of the Coca-Cola Company and Emory University's most generous benefactor), reported that there was indeed a sudden turn in Haygood's life. Troubled by the Negro problem, Candler told a friend, Haygood prayed, and he found "grace to brave the public and to publish 'Our Brother in Black,' by asking himself 'What would Christ do in my place?'" By Candler's understanding, "somewhere between midnight and morning, kneeling by his bed he put that question to himself, and answered it, he said, 'for the judgment day.'"[13]

The explanation of sudden revelation does not do justice to Haygood and to the lasting strength of that "best of Souths" that came out of the late slave period. Probably Haygood was led to take his stand by a persisting paternalism that made him not only aware of the duty of favored whites toward blacks, but of the more fortunate whites to people not so favored everywhere—to whites, browns, and yellows as well as to blacks, and of Christians to heathen peoples all over the world. Haygood as a paternalist was a perfect example of the type, and he personified clearly the bridge between the old paternalism and what was soon to became the new. His father had been one of the kindest of slaveholders, and Haygood's own youth was spent in closest intimacy with Negroes. In particular, he was for a time given over almost totally to tutelege by a male slave, a man highly knowledgeable in hunting, fishing, and woods' lore. Atticus the boy had lived a Huck Finn–Nigger Jim relationship such as Mark Twain later depicted, and it marked his life.

Within the church, Haygood's mentor was Bishop George F. Pierce, himself a representative of the paternalistic side of Southern slavery. When a Southern bishop in the antebellem Methodist church, James O. Andrew, acquired slaves through a bequest to his wife, the Northern bishops demanded that he surrender either his bondsmen or his office. Pierce vigorously supported Andrew's refusal to do either and was a leader in the secession of the Southern Methodists from the national church in 1844. Pierce soon emerged as the leading Southern bishop. But he was most widely known and admired, not for his role in creating the Methodist Episcopal Church South, but for his sermons that called upon masters to be good to their slaves.[14] Pierce was himself an excellent example of how the "travail of slavery" might produce a selfless paternalism, and Haygood was the legitimate child both of his slaveholding father and his episcopal mentor. Paternalism was his heritage, and he reclaimed that heritage in the 1880s when he picked up the cross of service beyond the color bar. By 1881, the seeming sinfulness of Negro life, the chaos, the disorder, and the wickedness of the black ministry made action imperative to one who had been born and bred to bear a sense of responsibility for his brothers in black. Haygood's work in establishing Paine College, his labor for the Slater fund, his exhortatory speaking and writing were all movements in a grand symphony of Christian endeavor in race relations, of getting back, as he saw it, to the vital relationship Southern Methodists had achieved with blacks in the last years of slavery.

Haygood's crusade had its effect upon the awareness of the Southern white community. Among the white elite, there was an odd, backhanded satisfaction with his work. Earlier Haygood had been relieved that the Northern churches had done some of the labor among blacks that the Southern churches ought to have done. Now, Southern whites seemed relieved to see that Haygood was doing the work that they themselves would not stoop to do. Further, just as there was a touch of resentment against the Northern churches precisely for performing that labor, so too was there a tinge of bitterness mixed with the respect that Southern whites accorded to Haygood. Ironically, the most effective opposition to Haygood's work came from those very persons who had been, and who remained, closest to him. Both Bishop Pierce, his mentor, and Bishop Candler, his own protégé, were not supportive of Paine College, an institution that might have efficiently and neatly executed the moral obligations of the Southern Methodists to Negroes with a minimum of physical contact. Pierce, as Haygood told Rutherford B. Hayes, thought that education prompted Negroes to claim equality and did "violence" to the "ordination of nature."[15] In 1882 Candler refused Haygood's request that he head the new college.[16] In Haygood's own Emory College in 1883 a debate was held on the question "Is Emory college sorely in favor of the education of the negro?" The negative side won a "complete victory," and one student took pains to advertise the fact, lest people get the "wrong" impression of the college.[17]

Haygood continued his labors throughout the decade of the 1880s. In 1882, he refused to accept election as a bishop of the church, probably because acceptance would have entailed, as it customarily did, removal to another diocese. Finally, in 1890, he did accept and became the Bishop of California, a post that included service as the missionary Bishop of Mexico. In 1891 he moved his family to California. Shortly thereafter, during a visitation in Mexico, an apparently already weakened Haygood contracted a fever that was to prove fatal. In 1893, when the family returned to Georgia, the fragile momentum of the revived mission to blacks that Haygood had achieved in the 1880s had been lost, and the current was running swiftly in the opposite direction.

Still, Atticus Haygood was not one to lose faith. He had never thought the race problem a simple one. Indeed, he had suggested that it might become even more complex than it was in the late nineteenth century. But he maintained a steadfast belief that, in God's good time a persistent Christian endeavor would find a way. In 1895, several months before his death, Haygood wrote his final, and perhaps his most poignant, words on the race question for *The Methodist Review,* words that were perfectly prophetic for another crusade for racial justice a century after emancipation. "One chief trouble with us in the Negro problem," he said, "as in all things, is this: we are in a great hurry about everything. But God is not in haste about anything." Time, faith, and labor, he urged, were the tools of progress, but progress would be slow. "It will be a problem not to be solved offhand, as schoolboys show off on black boards how they have learned to 'do their sums'," he warned.

Haygood felt that the Southern people were the patriotic, Christian people necessary to solve the problem. He rested his "faith in the educational missionary movement that set in before the war was over, and that moves on with increasing power for good to this day." The North and the East were hobbled. "With socialism, communism, and infidelities that curse these sections, they are not fitted to solve this Negro problem. Their best people may help the South to solve it; in Northern communities it could not be solved at all. They have far worse problems than the Negro question. . . ." He lamented the loss of hope by those who had been engaged in the education of the Southern Negro. "They expected too much, and expected it too soon. They forgot history; else idealized the Negro. Many did idealize him, and did him infinite harm at the beginning—telling him much more of his rights than his duties. Alas for them! When the actual Negro did not measure up to their romantic dreams of him—an angel in ebony—hope died within them."

"Those who are seeking the Negro's good," Haygood concluded, "deal with at least three generations—the people set free, their children, and their grandchildren. Our great-grandchildren, comparing 1865 and 1965, will rejoice, and glorify the Lord God and Father of us all. They will also help to build monuments to the heroic men and women whom their grandparents ostracised. Among and by those monuments half a dozen of our people and time will be remembered. Would God there were more!"[18]

GEORGE WASHINGTON CABLE AND SECULAR LIBERALISM

Haygood carried the banner of Liberalism into the clerical world, George Washington Cable, the writer, carried in into the secular. Cable's ancestors on his father's side had lived in Virginia for almost a century before the 1830s. Then his grandfather took his family, including Cable's father, to Pennsylvania where he emancipated his slaves and moved on to settle in Indiana. In Indiana, Cable's father met and married a woman whose family had followed the typical pattern of migration over the generations from New England to New York State and on into the Northwest Territory. Cable's father saw his financial prospects collapse in the great depression that began in 1837. Personifying the pluck and luck that was the national genius, he moved to New Orleans before the year was out and re-entered the race for prosperity. By the time of George's birth in 1844, the elder Cable had made a small fortune in various enterprises connected with steamboating.

The formative years of George's life were spent in growing luxury in a large and elegant house on Annunciation Square in one of New Orleans's best neighborhoods and in a family served, at one time, by eight slaves. However, before George was six years old, his father again failed in business. After 1850, the Cable family was never beyond the fringe of poverty. Still, far from being cast down by its varying fortunes, the Cable household was a happy and hopeful one. When Cable's father died in 1859, George, then slightly over fourteen years old, was allowed to leave school and fill a lowly place in the customshouse, the same post that his father had held. After the war broke out, Cable remained for a time in New Orleans, even after its occupation by Union forces. In fact, as a teenager, he joined the mobs that roamed the streets, defying the Union Army, and on one occasion hauled down the American flag over the United States Mint. Shortly before he was nineteen and liable to conscription by the United States Army, he slipped away into Mississippi and enlisted in the Confederate cavalry.

Cable was an excellent soldier. During the last two years of the war, he was in the saddle almost every day, ranging over northern Mississippi and Alabama and repeatedly engaging in running fights with elements of the Union Army. In February, 1864, when he charged with his unit through a detachment of Illinois infantry caught unawares marching along a country road, Cable was seriously and painfully wounded in the chest. The shot left a "bloody ragged hole," and Cable suffered from "the vile smell of that sloughing wound." After several months, he recovered sufficiently to ride again, returned to the army, and fought the war to the bitter end. But when the war was over, Cable quickly gave up the struggle. Within a month of the capitulation, he was back in New Orleans and hard at work helping to support his mother and sisters.[19]

After running through a scattering of jobs in the postwar depression in New Orleans, Cable became an accountant in one of the leading cotton trading houses in the city. It was here that a childhood interest in writing reasserted itself, and he began to contribute regularly to a leading New Orleans newspaper, the *Picayune*. Before the end of 1875, he had seven stories accepted for publication in national magazines. After that, he published no fiction for three years and turned instead to the cause of reform. By this time, he was secretary to the grand jury and had come to look closely and increasingly critically at the management of the public institutions of the city, especially the jail. By 1873 he had established a pattern he would follow all his life. Recurrently, he would interrupt his primary work to enter, usually journalistically, into the cause of social reform. Public discussion, he came to believe, was the key to human progress. As Cable himself later said, he really began to think only in the 1870s. When he did so, he began to question the justice of the social system around him. One of the things he questioned was the fairness of the Southern racial order.

Before 1871, in race, as in other things, Cable apparently reflected the thought of educated elements in his community. In 1871 as a reporter for the *Picayune* he attended a teacher's institute in the city and was shocked and offended to see that the carpetbagger Superintendent of Education had allowed black and white teachers to mix freely in the meetings. However, his sense of outrage abated shortly when he covered the annual examinations in the public high schools. New Orleans was the one city in the South where students in the public schools were, for a time, generally not separated by race. Visiting the schools, he saw Negro teachers in some of the rooms with white and black students "standing in the same classes and giving each other peaceable, friendly and effective competition." Soon, he was convinced that "the black race must share and enjoy in common with the white the whole scale of *public* rights and advantages provided under American government," and that only in this way would the race problem be solved.[20]

The really decisive turn for Cable came, however, in 1874. In December of that year a mob of white men invaded the Girls' High School in the city, thrust the teachers aside, and proceeded to expel the students visibly Negro and to conduct impromptu inquisitions on those who appeared to be white but were suspected of having Negro blood. All of this was followed by a mass demonstration in Lafayette Square to protest mixed schools. Cable published a letter in the *Picayune* in which he denounced the actions of the mob. In slavery there had been no such separating of black and white children, and Negro women had nursed white children at their breasts. Why, he asked, should there be any fear of contact with Negro students or teachers in well regulated schools now? The expense of separation would be great, and the benefits of exposing the lowest in New Orleans culture to the influence of the best would be lost. Page M. Baker, the editor of the *Picayune*, replied bitterly and rather simply to the "heretical seed" contained in Cable's letter. "The only condition under which the two races can co-exist peacefully is that in which the superior race shall control and the inferior race shall obey," he declared. Cable wrote an intemperate reply that was never printed, and for ten years thereafter, outside of his fiction, he was largely silent on matters of race.[21]

In the decade between 1875 and 1885 Cable came to full mastery in the literary profession. He published a book of short stories, *Old Creole Days* (1879), and his great novel *The Grandissimes* (1880). Both were squarely in the local color school then in vogue and were tremendously successful. After the publication of the latter, Cable was probably the most celebrated of Southern authors and approached Mark Twain in national fame during those early years of both their careers.

Soon he took to the lecture platform. Traveling from city to city, he read some of his own material, talked in Creole dialect, and sometimes sang folk-songs from the Bayou country while he played the guitar. In the winter and early spring of 1884–85, he reached the pinnacle of literary showmanship when he was chosen by Samuel Clemens, Mark Twain, to join him on the lecture circuits. Cable was the lesser attraction and, originally, his task was to "warm up" the audience by going on stage for the first fifteen minutes of the two-hour performance. But all too often, in Clemens's view, fifteen minutes stretched to nearly an hour as parts of Cable's performance were encored. In the relationship, Cable was the deep Christian, but it was Clemens who carried the cross. Sam Clemens smoked, drank, flirted, gambled, and cursed with great and satisfying roundness. Cable did none of these. He was a Presbyterian of the old school, a puritan. Writing to his friend William Dean Howells after weeks on the road, Clemens declared that Cable had shown him "how loath-some a thing the Christian religion can be made." In particular, Cable had taught him "to abhor and detest the Sabbath-day and hunt up new and trou-blesome ways to dishonor it."[22]

In the same ten-year period, Cable regularly dropped his fiction for active reform. He attacked the convict lease system in the state and the administra-tion of public institutions in New Orleans. Also he had not forgotten the mat-ter of race after the bitter-keen exchange with Page Baker over the school incident in 1875. His feelings about race had come powerfully, but not obtru-sively to the fore in the minds, words, and characters of the people with whom he populated his stories. He had revealed something of his thinking on the South and race explicitly in an 1882 commencement address at the University of Mississippi. The "melancholy mistake" of the South, he asserted, had occurred before the war when the South isolated itself intellectually from the world and sought only to defend slavery. "When the whole intellectual energy of the southern states flew to the defence of that one institution which made us the South," he said, "we broke with human progress. We broke with the world's thought. We have not entirely in all things joined hands with it again. When we have done so we shall know it by this— there will be no South. . . . Let us hasten to be no longer a unique people." Cable continued the address, indicating the perpetuation in the South of an elitist dictatorship, the idea of caste, and the survival of the semi-barbaric plantation system with Negro ten-ants instead of Negro slaves.[23] In June 1884 he was invited by the Alabama Historical Society to offer a lecture at the University of Alabama. He took that opportunity to talk pointedly about the Negro problem to a Southern audience at a time when outside pressures were minimal. Afterward, he thought he had been successful at Tuscaloosa. "I left Alabama more deeply impressed than ever before with the fact that behind all the fierce and resentful conservatism of the South there was a progressive though silent South which needed to be urged to speak and act," he later recalled. "To this end somebody must speak first, and as I was now out in the storm, and as one may say, wet to the skin, why should it not be I?"[24]

In January 1885, Cable spoke, loudly and to a national audience. His medium was an article, "The Freedman's Case in Equity," published in *The Century*, one of the leading journals of thought in the United States at that time. The freedman's case as stated by Cable in his article was a relatively simple one. The debased condition of blacks in slavery had caused the white South to exclude the freedmen from Southern and American society. Specifically, whites had concluded that the inferiority of Negroes was natural, God-ordained, and could not be removed by social action. He detailed the wrongs suffered by blacks. They had been denied participation on juries. They were the special victims of the convict lease system. They were relegated to inferior facilities on trains. He suggested that mixed schools had worked in New Orleans and would be less expensive than separated schools. He decried the "huge bugbear of Social Equality," and declared that "We may reach the moon some day, but not social equality."[25]

Why did Cable break forth in this way in 1885? He himself said that his reaction was triggered by a scene he had witnessed while traveling through Alabama by train. A well-dressed, mannerly Negro woman of light color and her daughter were forced to ride in a crowded car with nearly a score of chained convicts, while the few whites aboard rode in a nearly empty coach reserved for their color. The same woman, had she been nurse to a white child, he indicated, would have ridden in the white coach without a question being asked or an eyebrow raised.[26] It happened that the Supreme Court in 1883 had declared unconstitutional the federal Civil Rights Act of 1875 that forbade separation by race on common carriers. Thus, the Negro woman had no recourse in law. Her only resort was to plead her case in fairness, or, as lawyers would say, in equity. So, too, with every other Negro citizen in every place of public accommodation. Cable sought in his article to enter that plea, not in the courts, but before the conscience of the white South and in the view of the nation.

Of course, other whites had seen the same things that Cable saw and only a few reacted as he did. Four rather clear traits in Cable's personality go far toward explaining his special behavior. First, he was a devoutly religious man. He was a very strong, puritanical Presbyterian, experiencing a steady, intense pressure to put himself into communion with God's will. He had courage to match his beliefs, and he often took postures that were strikingly different from those of his neighbors and friends.

Secondly, Cable was a rationalist. He believed that God's will was made manifest by Him to each age. The result was that Cable was constantly sifting his impressions of the seeming world with the conviction that in the end he would find the real world—the truths of life. He thought that truth had already been made evident in three basic documents: the Bible, the Declaration of Independence, and the Constitution, including its amendments. These, he believed, squared with each other, and his logical mind was always at work to find the elements in everyday life that harmonized with them. The argument that a nation founded upon the concept of the natural rights of man could not support slavery or unequal citizenship carried irresistible weight with him. He was one of those rare Southerners before very modern times to recognize an American dilemma in its race relations. It was his great misfortune to be a realist born into the South, a land that was compulsively romantic.

Thirdly, Cable was a moralist who could not remain inactive in the face of immorality. Again and again, he left more satisfying and more promising literary or commercial pursuits to crusade—for such it was—for reform. In his reform efforts in the 1870s he had learned that a careful education of public opinion moved mountains of men. In this process, communication was all-important. Therefore, his arguments were carefully calculated not to alienate his audience and, while he was never dishonest, he did not always give first place to those considerations he considered most important. He always argued that social equality was a private matter that would settle itself, and that the South needed only to be concerned about public equality. Apparently, he never revealed his thinking on miscegenation, though he probably opposed it. His words were almost never acrimonious, or accusing, or insulting. His arguments were beautifully rational, his understanding of the errors of the ways of others sweetly reasonable, and his advice always to go and sin no more. He was not impatient, he did not expect a miracle, and he anticipated a great deal of sinning after the message and before the conversion. He thought that artificial, unsanctioned ways of life were maintained by constant reiteration of untruths. The racial shibboleths would be uttered and followed by, as he called them, "the therefores." The truth, constantly spoken in free and open discussions, would break the pattern and make possible changes in the popular mind. By 1885 he had become a master at that technique of persuasion.

Finally, the best single explanation of Cable's uniqueness was his great sensitivity. He had that rare and valuable quality of being able to put himself in other people's places, and to walk a mile—or more—in other people's shoes. That was his essential genius. As his exposures changed, as he came to know new people in different situations, he himself changed. When he saw black children abused in New Orleans in 1875, he sympathized. When, as the secretary of the grand jury three years later, he saw inmates in public institutions mistreated, he felt compassion. When he came to know one talented and warmly human actor, he abandoned a theretofore lifelong aversion to the stage. And when he came to know New England, he found a home. Cable's empathy for Creole culture sprang directly from the same source that fed his interest in black people, his capacity to feel and to know other people's lives. If Cable was critical of the more physical aspects of Creole life, it was not because he secretly lusted to lather himself in a non-puritan world in the style of some fallen angel. Rather was it that as he came to know Creoles, he came to love them. Though Cable was a puritan he was no masochist, nor even a willing martyr. But it was in his nature that as he came to know other people, he suffered for their sins. When he found a cross, he was bound to raise it up. He was a latter-day saint—and saints begin by being human. They know how to suffer greatly for the right, and they do it. Cable did not relish the abuse that fell upon his head, but he bore it, and, Christ-like, he forgave those who abused him. "I remember my favorite text," he wrote to his wife in the midst of this struggle, "and it is a great consolation: 'Woe unto you when all men speak well of you.'"[27]

Measured by that Biblical rule, in the winter of 1885 Cable was a man rarely blessed. Hardly a man spoke well of him, and many spoke ill. One man who spoke ill—very ill—was Charles Etienne Arturo Gayarré. It was he who led the first assault against Cable's racial Liberalism. Gayarré was the grandson of Etienne de Bore, a 1790's émigré from insurrection-ridden Santo Domingo who had made the technical breakthrough that established the sugar industry in Louisiana. The Gayarrés had refined their Charles fully as superbly as they had refined their sugar. He was crystal white. He was extremely well educated in schools in both France and America. Though trained as a lawyer, he never practiced. Instead, he worked at literature and, at the age of thirty, achieved a remarkable success as the author of a three-volume history of Louisiana. He was bright, a good scholar, and highly cultured. On the eve of the Civil War, he was a brilliant, if rather delicate, illustration of what a Creole gentleman ought to be. After the war, when Cable came to know him, Gayarré had lost his fortune and was living by scattered and chance employments, some of them literary. Before the end of Reconstruction, he was sufficiently desperate to take an appointment from the Radical Republicans as a minor clerk in the state judiciary. After Cable began to write about New Orleans and Creoles, contact between the two men became frequent, and, as Cable thought, friendly. However, in the 1880s it became clear that the Creole octogenarian was consumed with envy for the young *Americain* who was winning so vast an audience by writing about Creoles, an audience that Gayarré—the legitimate literary heir of the culture as well as its exemplar—had long aspired to engage.

Within a week after the appearance of "The Freedman's Case," Gayarré burst into print in the *Times-Democrat* with an article attacking its author. Cable had, Gayarré asserted, misunderstood race relations in the South and had misrepresented the Creoles in literature. Both failings, he suggested, reflected defects in the author's character. Among other things, Gayarré labeled Cable "a sentimental aspirant to notoriety" and "a self worshipping

censor of public and private morals."[28] Gayarré's attacks were widely noticed
in the South, and, before the end of the month, much encouraged, he took the
subject to the lecture platform in New Orleans.[29] Fervently, he tried to carry
the attack to a broader audience. "I wish you would have the inclosed newspaper slip reproduced in a Charlotte journal, if possible," he wrote to a friend.
"We must beat the drum. I want Georgia, South Carolina and North Carolina
to rise in arms on my behalf."[30]

Gayarré was not alone in the attack. It was as if the "Freedman's Case"
had ruptured a long festering ulcer in Cable's public image, and now the mixed
bile of literary and racial bitterness ate like acid into his reputation. The few
Southern friends who remained faithful to Cable were appalled by the prevalence and virulence of sentiment against him. Marion A. Baker, literary editor
of the *Times-Democrat* (where his brother was an editor and a constant critic
of Cable), was a lifelong friend. "The papers—one and all are peppering you
about the Century article—the T.D. heading the pack in full cry," he reported
in February. "You can form no idea of how bitter the feeling is against you,
as bitter as it used to be against Garrison and men of his way of thinking in
the antebellum times."[31] During the spring there was some abatement of the
abuse. Baker wrote that Gayarré had fallen into a squabble with someone else.
"The boys say that if you had not given him a chance to orate, at a dollar a
head, the old man would have had to go to the Almshouse before this." Still,
Baker reported, "the Southern folk, just now, are very bitter toward you."[32]

CRITIQUES OF LIBERALISM—NEW SOUTH AND OLD

A highly significant facet of the Southern response to the challenge offered by
Cable was that there were actually two responses—one from the Old South
and another from the New, and the two critiques were as much at war with
one another as they were with Cable's Liberalism. It is worth looking closely
at the nature of that conflict because it foreshadows a profound division in the
Southern sense of self, the division between the "New South" as it was called,
and the Old. The New South learned from the Civil War—as Scarlett O'Hara
would later illustrate in *Gone with the Wind*—the lesson that industry and
commerce were the keys to power, and power was what they wanted. The Old
South learned from the war the lesson—as Melanie Wilkes would later illustrate—that they had been transcendentally right in their moral order. Broadly
speaking New Southites were materialists, Old Southites were idealists. New
Southites had a rather simplex answer to the race problem. Old Southites had
a complex answer, but one that laced thoroughly into antebellum roots. In the
end, the response of the Old South would prove to have the greatest relevancy
for race relations in America.

It was probably unfortunate for the cause of meaningful debate that the editors of *Century* invited Henry W. Grady, the apostle of the New South and a commentator certain to increase the circulation of the magazine, to write the "official" reply to Cable. Like all the leading advocates of the New South, Grady was a legitimate descendant of the Old South, a graduate of both the University of Georgia and the University of Virginia. In the early 1880s he bought part interest in the Atlanta *Constitution* and became nationally famous as its editor. Before 1885, Grady had spent the last several years of his life busily—perhaps overly busily—attempting to push the Southern ship into the mainstream of American life by industrial and commercial levers. Grady's answer to Cable was neither sophisticated nor even perfectly logical. But, characteristically, it was very efficient. Grady simply declared that the kind of racial mixing that Cable envisioned would inevitably produce miscegenation and a fusion of the races. At the same time, he argued, quite inconsistently, that there was a racial instinct among both whites and blacks that would keep the two races forever apart.[33]

Cable replied in the September 1885 issue with an article entitled "The Silent South." He made a lengthy and lucid distinction between civil rights and social equality. He did not believe that there was an inherited instinct for separateness. He saw, on the contrary, a danger of amalgamation resulting from the flight of Negroes of light color into the white world to escape the oppression they suffered in the black. Rationally, it was a beautiful argument. Practically, it should have been effective, appealing to the worst fears of the whites in order to win a higher degree of fairness for blacks. Finally, Cable called upon the moral elite, the heretofore silent South, to come forward again as they had in the past and deliver to the Negro the full measure of justice to which he was entitled.[34]

Much nearer than Grady to the heart of the prewar South was Paul Hamilton Hayne, poet laureate of the Old South and still very much alive in—and detesting—the New. As early as 1883, he had recognized the menace embodied by Cable, "an effeminate little fellow," he said, who had shown himself in his Oxford, Mississippi, speech the year before to be "a mere child" as a political thinker.[35] A month before the "Freedman" article appeared, Hayne decried the New South and put Cable among its most pernicious advocates. "Have you been struck," he asked a friend, "I have, by the manner in which certain representatives of the So-called 'New South' are now in the habit of answering for their Elders? (e.g.): Mr Cable is pleased to remark in his last novel, that *everybody South* now '*execrates* the idea of Slavery.' (*or words to that effect,*); and altogether undertakes to be Spokesman, the miserable little *ci-devant* Clerk and Parvenue, a *thorough Yankee in blood,* wherever, by *accident,* he was born, for this entire section of the Country, touching past political beliefs and principles, of which he knows evidently next to nothing. (!!) Yes, and *scores* of young men are following his lead; and men also, by no means young, old Confederates, quite willing to defile the graves of their Fathers."[36]

Ironically, it was anger at Cable that first brought Hayne and Gayarré together, a meeting of the poet laureate of the Old South (East) and the palladin of the Old South (West). The two men had known each other by reputation before but had never met, even in correspondence. That they would meet in this way, over the carcass as it were of Cable and the recognized rights of black people was a sign of the times, for it did indeed signify the revival of the Old South.

From the Old South point of view, the core of Cable's crime was not simply racial and prospective. It was rather that he so willingly and crassly compromised that whole superior Southern culture—past and present as well as future—to the North, to a leveling democracy, and to Negroes. People like Gayarré and Hayne saw the struggle primarily in terms of a Southern culture abandoned for a Northern culture that had been victorious only by force of arms, not by right. "We are essentially different people," Hayne wrote to his Creole friend, "and why in the mysterious providence of God, we were allowed to be conquered by them is to me the puzzle of puzzles." His faith, he confessed, "is sometimes shaken by it. . . ."[37] The real and great harm that Cable had done was to encourage defection from the values of the Old South. He would break the molds of place. "He encourages *Renegadism* of every kind," Hayne charged, "and has evidently a large following among members of what I believe is called 'the New South'."[38] Cable would hasten a current that ran already too swiftly and too strongly. "In the 'young South,' so-called, I observe a growing tendency towards contempt for the *Past,* and a *truckling* spirit, so far as Yankee ideas, and Yankee *prejudices* are concerned. One thing is *certain,*" he declared. "If miscegenation does not occur, *amalgamation* of *North* and *South,* in blood, brain, purpose, aims, *social* affinity—*everything*— is *inevitable.*"[39] Gayarré concurred with the poet. "I fear amalgamation as much as you do," he admitted, "moral and intellectual amalgamation more than the physical, and I think that there is already too great a fusion of leveling, new fangled notions with the old *castellated* ones."[40] Southern whites who thought most profoundly about the implications of Cable's work would have agreed. It was, indeed, vastly pernicious to an aristocratic and hierarchical South.

Inextricably intertwined with the loss of the Old South was the demise of the traditionally proper relationship between ladies and gentlemen. That relationship was, of course, chivalrous. Gayarré and the Haynes themselves personified the persisting chivalric idealism of the antebellum world, and they spoke its idiom with grace and ease. When Gayarré learned that Mrs. Hayne approved of his answer to Cable, he declared that his "greatest gratification is derived from my being informed that Mrs. Hayne has condescended to favor with a smile of approbation the aged knight who has ventured to couch his lance against so youthful and vigorous an adversary as the standard bearer of Africa. I respectfully bow my thanks." Mrs. Hayne was fully equal to her complementary role as a lady fair to knights. As she read Gayarré's letter to her husband, she declared, "eh! *this* is old time courtesy which is fast departing from our So. land [.] do remember me cordially to 'the ancient knight', & tell him I hope that many years may be added to his useful, & illustrious life!" Later in the year when Mrs. Hayne had read one of Gayarré's typically romantic literary sorties entitled "Test of Love," she asserted that he was "one of the very few persons of your sex, (& mind), who comprehend *women* & comprehend *love*."[41] All of this might taste too saccharine to later generations trained up to scorn such displays. But it was superbly acceptable in the late Old South, and it was rapidly coming to be, as we shall see, warmly welcomed by certain elements in the postwar South.

Both Gayarré and Hayne realized that chivalry, and hence a proper relationship between ladies and gentlemen, depended upon a leisured upper class and that leisure demanded servants. In part the new order in both its white democratic and racial egalitarian dimensions threatened Southern ladyhood because, as Gayarré commented sadly, "it has become impossible to get any white or black son, or daughter of equality to condescend to do any menial work whatsoever. The word *servant* is offensive and has been struck out of the vocabulary of Liberty."[42] Back in Georgia, the poet laureate of the South insisted that Southern women of the elite order had been in the Civil War and Reconstruction the conservators of the ideals of the Old South. While Gayarré was indeed an "honored old Southerner, *sans peur, et sans reproche*," Hayne warmly urged that the ladies elegantly embodied the last stronghold. "Ah!" he exclaimed, "our women of the grand old Confederacy how much truer they *have been* and *are than the men*."[43] Southern ladies, then, were made the sun center of Southern culture, the bright star that kept all in place. In them, in their ladyhood, in their idealism, still burned the fire that might warm the world if only the cold and soulless minions of the New South could be frustrated.

The disjunction between the Old South and the New was more than merely generational; it was also ideological. Not only did the Old South deny Cable, it also denied young Grady. The error of the Atlanta editor in making his reply to Cable was a very special and vital one. Grady was much too ready to sell out the true South, the Old South, to the North. Hayne was disgusted to find that "he *concedes* so much to the North as this, (viz) that they were perfectly justified in abolishing Slavery, and that we ought rather to be grateful for the same." Not only did Grady make this morally damaging concession, but he also failed miserably in arguing the miscegenation point. He was "wretchedly superficial" in dismissing, in "a somewhat airy and insouciate fashion," the "dreadful problem touching the Negro." On the one side he raised the danger of racial intermixture; but on the other he stated the reverse. "He *actually* maintains that the *Negro* has no desire whatever towards social communion and *amalgamation;* that the [inferior] Race desires to keep itself apart from the white is, of course, a mere solecism!"[44] Gayarré quite agreed and commented that if the Grady article had not been perfectly "colorless" in this way, it would not have been printed in the North.[45] For Old Southerners, Grady missed the primary point that the South was fighting desperately to preserve a hard-won and precious culture, the world's one best hope for salvation, and he botched the argument for a lesser point—racial purity. To them, culture and blood were one. To debase one meant, inevitably, the debasement of the other. Racial purity was important, but the cultural purity of which it was symbolic was of transcendental importance. To say that Negroes did not really want to be white was not only unflattering to whites and flagrantly untrue; it was a misconception that was fraught with disaster for that grandest culture of them all.

Actually Hayne and Gayarré need not have concerned themselves greatly with the inadequacies of Grady's answer. Cable, simply by speaking out, was rapidly destroying his influence in the South. He was slandered in the press, and his property taxes in New Orleans suddenly increased tenfold.[46] Cable was, in fact, dead in the South, and the physical removal in the fall of 1885 of his family seat to Northampton, Massachusetts, where it remained for the rest of his life, was but a minor reflection of the alienation that the body social of the South had already imposed upon him. Southerners would not bear looking at the values to which Cable exposed them, and they resented his presumption in offering them. Well before Cable left the South, he had had his day in the court of the social South and lost it; he was beyond a fair hearing. Symptomatically, Hayne did not even bother to read "The Silent South." His wife read it and agreed with Gayarré "as to its contradictions, illogicality, hypocritical professions of devotion to the South, and general involved 'twaddle'." Hayne rendered his final verdict: "The fellow has shown his cloven *foot* so plainly that even *our own* rather *subservient* People seem disgusted with him."[47]

REFERENDUM ON RACE: THE OPEN LETTER CLUB

Cable was a solid Christian soldier who persisted in seeing in his fellow man everywhere some flicker of divinity that promised salvation. In the spring of 1887, after he had resettled his family in New England, he made a Southern tour. During that time, some of which he spent in Louisiana and in New Orleans, he met some cold and dark looks, but also some warmth and cordiality.

Out of this visit, he took renewed faith in the existence of a liberal, though silent, South. To Cable, progress was a matter of evoking that better sentiment. To that end, he launched "The Open Letter Club."

The Open Letter Club was the most aggressive—and potentially the most promising—of Cable's efforts to improve race relations in the South. In 1887 he lectured to the Monteagle Assembly, a public affairs forum held every summer in the mountains near Chattanooga and attended by local leaders from various parts of the South. His sponsor in the Assembly was William M. Baskervill, a young professor of literature at Vanderbilt University. Both men were much encouraged by the apparent benefits of free discussions among leading Southerners in meeting the region's problems. During the summer of 1888 they conceived the idea of forming a correspondence club to carry the same kind of discussions into every Southern community. Under the scheme, thinking Southerners would isolate one problem after another, collect data, argue views, and publish the results South-wide. Meanwhile, Cable had already begun to test thoughtful Southern opinion by distributing an essay "The Negro Question." From that activity, he obtained sufficient replies to collect the names of hundreds of thoughtful and judicious gentlemen in communities scattered throughout the South. Before the end of the year, the Open Letter Club was under way with Baskervill, not Cable who was much too suspect, as the apparent head. However, few people were unaware that the prime mover in the club was George Washington Cable. Soon, several hundred leaders of public thought in the South were enrolled in the organization. In October, an article by Senator J. B. Eustis of Louisiana on "Race Antagonism in the South" and an answer by Bishop Haygood entitled "Shall the Negro Be Educated or Suppressed?" formed the core of the first discussion and elicited the usual Conservative vs. Liberal debate. Cable planned others on the crop lien system, the Eight-Box Law (which practically barred Negroes from casting their votes in state-wide elections in South Carolina after 1882), and the county government system in North Carolina (which was a device to take local government out of local hands in the black counties and give it to the white controlled state government). One set of papers on the topic of education was published and another was being prepared, when a single slip by Cable opened the dike, and outraged public sentiment flooded in to drown the project.

Late in December 1889 Cable addressed the students at Fisk University in Nashville. Before he left, he wanted to meet some of the leading Negro citizens of the city. Because he knew he could not invite them to his hotel, he met them in the home of the unofficial leader of the Negro community in Nashville, John C. Napier, a wealthy lawyer and politician. After the meeting, all had left except Napier, his wife, and Cable. Cable felt their embarrassment "in a dilemma between asking a white man to sit at their board and sending him away supperless." He then announced bluntly that he had not eaten. "We broke bread together," he reported later. "Was I wrong in that? To anyone who answers yes, I can only reply, Shame on you!"[48] Cable's admonition fell upon unhearing ears. The *Nashville American,* which had praised the literary Cable as late as 1887, now concluded that the social Cable was calling for a program of equality between the races. Cable's denials that he had ever advocated the "private commingling of the two races" had no effect. His own single act at the Napiers' shouted down his words. Baskervill thought that the damage was irreparable, that Cable could not get a hearing in Nashville. Soon, he concluded that Cable's ideas would not be heard in the whole of the South, and that the Open Letter Club was doomed by its association with Cable. In the spring of 1890, he closed out the affairs of the Club and shipped its files to Cable.[49]

The hundreds of letters in the files of the Open Letter Club, preserved at Tulane University in New Orleans, indicate how hopeless was the task that Cable had set himself. They reveal that there was no such silent South as Cable had imagined. Evidently, the great truth was that the vast majority of thinking Southerners felt that the Negro was at, or very close to, his proper level in the scale of white civilization. If he were not so, a gentle evolution would soon bring him to that point. Precisely because they were so sure of the innate inferiority of the Negro and his ultimate subordination, white Southerners in the 1880s were largely inactive and not greatly concerned about race relations.

Many of Cable's correspondents asserted, in essence, that there was no race problem and refused the invitation of the Open Letter Club. An ex-Commissioner of Immigration in Louisiana judged the effort useless and felt that blacks themselves would agree. "The Negro would enjoy a mess of 'possum and taters' more than a feast of reason," he suggested, and concluded, "May the Good Lord save him from his friends!"[50] A Memphis storekeeper easily explained the silence of those who were concerned. "While the better white sentiment" opposed the oppression of the Negro, he said, "it is simply a negative opposition which, while silently existing, yet simply acquiesces in these diabolisms of active, ignorant and lawless portions of the Commonwealth."[51] The issue was, after all, not so very vital, and good men had other, more important things to do. "The trouble is that our thoughtful men are over burdened with *work* in their own lives and have no time to spare," responded the headmaster of one of the most influential private schools in North Carolina.[52] The silence of the Silent South implied, as great silences often do, that people did not want to be bothered.

Most respondents to the Open Letter Club were Conservative in their attitude, but some were beginning to think that the Negro was doomed to fall down and away from white civilization into barbarism and savagery. "Brought under the influence of the highest forms of civilization of all ages; and to a greater Extent than any people known to history, aided, encouraged and Sympathised with, they have uniformly relapsed into barbarism whenever that civ-ilized aid was withdrawn from them," declared a Tennesseean.[53] In areas where blacks were numerous and whites few, retrogression would make peaceful coexistence between the races impossible. A correspondent from Jackson, Mississippi, asked that if "it be admitted that the black increase in the extreme south faster than the white race, must it not be inferred that the blacks and whites will sooner or later come to open strife?" His solution was to strike the word "race" out of the Fifteenth Amendment and to suggest that a territory such as California or Mexico be set aside for the blacks.[54]

Historically, Cable's efforts between 1885 and 1890 have great significance. In a sense, he held a national, and especially a Southern, referendum on the race question. Had he been a lesser person, had he been less moral, sensitive, intelligent, and skillful at mass organization and education, the significance of his rejection would have been much less. But Cable was all of these, and in this half-decade, he, with the few others who joined him in making the test, offered the nation a choice in race relations. Cable's proffered alternative was a mild form of racial equality, an equality of opportunity in public places. It was not a revolutionary alternative. Yet, the great mass of thinking Southern-ers rejected Cable and Liberalism immediately. To them, public equality for the Negro was equated with social equality, and that was unthinkable. What-ever might have been their thoughts about Cable as a literary person (and they seemed recurrently willing to think well of him in that way), whenever he entered the field of race relations his artistic credentials won him no suffer-ance. The furor that had followed Cable's "Freedman's Case" article in 1885 indicated that they had already decided the question. There was, even then, no chance of a white man retaining his Southern identification while he endorsed the modest degree of racial mixing that Cable advocated.

Haygood and Cable were the two conspicuous Liberals in race in the South in these post-Reconstruction years. Haygood, who certainly had good cause to keep count, said that there were half a dozen heroes in race relations in 1895. He wished that there were more; and we could very well wish that he had named those because it is now difficult to identify even six spirits of Hay-good's caliber among his contemporaries. Ultimately, it can only be said that the Liberals were a small and embattled band, a corporal's guard thinly arrayed against a hostile frontier.

SUMMATION

Conservatism, then, was the mass mode of racial thought in the South in the generation after 1865. It prevailed among patricians and plebeians alike. Stag-gered by the blows of defeat and Reconstruction, it regained its footing in

Redemption and stood solidly through the decade of the 1880s. Liberalism, running during the 1880s, was the deviant child of Conservatism and a rebel against its parent. In the Conservative view, Liberals were Conservatives gone wild. They thought too much of the Negro's worth, and they were too willing to test that impression. Conservatives felt that they knew, rather precisely, just what was the nature of the Negro. Conservatism always began and ended with the idea that Negroes were inferior to whites in every major way. Liberals did not always make that assumption. Indeed, they flirted with the idea of equality in important categories— as in religion, in educational and economic opportunity, and civil rights.

Conservatism could remain warily aloof from and cautiously permissive of the churchly Liberalism of a Haygood. But it was shaken to its very core by the secular, organized, and pressing Liberalism of a Cable. Such racial mixing as he envisioned did in truth raise the possibility of miscegenation, just as Henry Grady said, and it also raised the much more awful threat to the traditional culture perceived by such apostles of the Old South as Gayarré and Hayne. It would be a sin and a shame, they thought, to cheat the world by allowing a dilution of that Southern culture. Caste and class together were the world's one best hope for human harmony. Conservatives might disagree as to why Cable was an enemy, but they could agree with ready ease that he was an enemy. Thus, in the late 1880s, they moved, not by any combination, nor by any great concert, but separately and spontaneously (one is tempted to say, instinctively) to snuff out that frightening spark of racial rebellion.

In the 1880s the race question in the South was not whether or not the Negro would be equal to the white in any way. It was, rather, how far beneath white people black people were to be. Reconstruction had labored hard to afford more equitable alternatives to the racial pattern that black slavery had so deeply set; but those possibilities had died with Redemption. Whatever remote promises of a more harmonious interracial world lay, germ-like, involuted in the yet-to-be history of the 1890s, no one in the 1880s assumed that any alternative style in race relations would breed equality. Quite the contrary, virtually universally white Southerners believed that the Negro was and would remain perpetually inferior to the Caucasian. Haygood and Cable had tested the question and offered an alternative that was liberally open-ended. Southerners had rejected that suggestion quickly, easily, at the threshholds of their minds. The 1890s generated other alternatives. Those alternatives included a broad range of possibilities, some that would raise the Negro slightly and others that would press him literally into extinction. None promised a reasonable parity.

PART TWO

The Rage of Radicalism, 1889–1915

It is, indeed, one of the great ironies of American history that when the nation freed the slaves, it also freed racism. After Nat Turner's insurrection, the marriage of slavery to race that had begun in America more than a century before was completed. In that union, race seemed, at first, to rise to domination. For a time, slavery was everybody's business, and race ruled slavery. By the decade of the 1850s, however, slavery clearly ruled race. White people in the South were no longer free to think what they pleased about black people. They could not, for extreme examples, think that any Negro could be totally white in the cultural sense or envision a South in which blacks did not exist. Sambo, the perpetually perfect servant to white masters, was a fair image of the black person that slavery sought and, in the white mind, found.

After the war, Southern white leaders were not eager to let Sambo go, and, with Redemption, he was regained. Racial Conservatives, ruling again in the 1880s, built their power, in part, upon the assumption that the Negro would remain in the South and that he would be willingly and harmoniously subordinate. They resisted strenuously both attempts in the 1880s to raise blacks substantially higher in the scale of white civilization and efforts in the 1890s to exclude them altogether. The basic flaw in the new structure was, of course, that Conservatives in power assumed that black people were inherently inferior to whites and naturally subordinate; they did not fear that blacks in the mass and over time would offer serious competition to whites. In a relatively open society in which black people had considerable economic, educational, and cultural opportunities, blacks would be competitive, and that assumption was disastrous to continued Conservative dominance. In the late 1880s and on through the 1890s, caught in a depression in which opportunities for everyone diminished with sickening rapidity, racial Conservatives found themselves losing power and fighting for survival. In effect, in the turn of the century years they were playing out the last losing cards in a hand dealt in the last generation of slavery. It was a hand they could not win. In the end they would concede defeat in that match, shuffle, and deal again.

CHAPTER IV

The Rise of the Radicals

In the 1880s Conservativism downed Liberalism rather quickly and with relative ease. In the generation that followed, however, it turned to face a new and much more powerful foe. The new enemy was Radical racism.

RADICAL THINKING

Radicalism appeared in strength in 1889 and spread rapidly through the South. The core of the Radical mentality was the concept that Negroes, freed from the restraining influences of slavery, were rapidly "retrogressing" toward their natural state of bestiality. Older Negroes were susceptible to fall, but, more importantly, in the mid-eighties young Negroes were coming into manhood who had been born free and had never felt the civilizing effects of slavery. By 1889 the "New Negro," as white contemporaries labeled him, might be twenty-four years old. Indeed, he *was* a new man, and his potential *was* unknown. By the end of that year, very clearly, many Southerners were concluding that the essential nature of the newly matured black was bestial, and that, unsupported by the enforced moral behavior of slavery, the New Negro was reverting to a native savagery. The reversion, they concluded, came to its most conspicuous crisis in attempts by black men to rape white women. Ultimately, Radicals believed, there would be no place for blacks in the South or in America. The end might come in a kind of race war, not always physical, that the superior whites would win, or blacks might be transported to some foreign parts, but the two races together would not last. As one Georgia woman expressed it: "Since our old-time friends, the negro, who as a slave, was trustworthy and gentle, seems to have retrograded through freedom into a dangerous beast, it is surely necessary that he be removed from among us."[1]

111

Precisely why Radicalism appeared with such dramatic suddenness in 1889 and swept so powerfully through the South in the years that followed is beyond easy explanation. Quite clearly, the seeds of Radicalism lay deep in Southern race relations. The proslavery argument itself contained the prediction that outside of slavery blacks could not exist. However, during Reconstruction that belief died away, and after Reconstruction Southerners assumed that Negroes would have a lasting presence in their midst. Further, and happily for the white South, a wave of evidence indicated that the nation at large was again surrendering black people to the control of their late masters. In 1877 President Rutherford B. Hayes withdrew the federal troops from the state capitals of the South and, after he retired as President, greatly interested himself in race relations there. As the head of the Slater Fund, in and after 1881, he labored for black education, not with the rude and heavy hand of the outsider, but sympathetically and through the instrumentality of Atticus Greene Haygood. In 1883 the United States Supreme Court struck down a large part of the Civil Rights Act of 1875 and thereby took the federal government out of the business of enforcing the integration of public accommodations. Moreover, in 1884 the nation elected a Democratic President, Grover Cleveland, marking an end to the twenty-four-year reign of Republicans. Southerners assumed that Cleveland would be especially generous to the South. Some Southern Congressmen felt so secure that they began to jest in Washington restaurants about the prospective return of slavery and loudly claimed this or that individual Negro waiter as their future property. In the early years of the 1880s, Southern whites were gladly accepting a renewed responsibility for the management of black people, and they believed that the burden would not be inordinately onerous.

There were countercurrents, however, to disturb the tranquility of Southern white minds on matters of race, and the late 1880s saw them rise menacingly to the surface. Far from proscribing the Negro further, President Cleveland in office in 1885 actually initiated the practice of appointing leading black Democrats to six certain federal offices, each of which paid a good salary and carried with it a significant measure of power and dignity. This was a step strikingly beyond those of Reconstruction, during which more than a score of blacks were elected to Congress but not a single black person was appointed to an important federal office. The Republican victory in the national elections in November 1888 jarred the South even more profoundly than Cleveland's apostasy. "The Negro question is a live one just now," wrote William Baskervill to George W. Cable from Nashville in December. "There is great uneasiness about the President elect's plans and purposes."[2] Southerners had good cause for anxiety. In the campaign, the forces of Benjamin Harrison had made a superbly well organized play for the black vote under the leadership of James S. Clarkson, co-owner with his brother of the Des Moines (Iowa) *Register*. As a teenager Clarkson had helped guide Radical abolitionist John Brown across the plains at a critical juncture in his tumultuous career, and afterward he proved himself a steady ally of the Negro. As a reward for his efforts, Harrison made Clarkson his Postmaster General in 1889, and in that capacity, Clarkson later asserted, he caused some 16,000 blacks to be appointed to federal jobs.[3] In the higher offices, Republicans could hardly do less than the Democrats had done before them, and the Harrison administration appointed six black Republicans to the places that six black Democrats had previously held. Those six offices continued to be held by Negroes until the Democrats came into power in 1913.

In the elections of 1888 the Republican party gained control of the national executive, and it also won a majority of the seats in each house of Congress. Republicans could pass any measure they could agree upon. A long-running agitation for the enactment of the so-called Blair bill providing federal aid to education, including black children as well as white, now emerged as a very real danger. The Blair bill had never come to the floor of the House, but it had passed the Senate handily in 1884, in 1886, and again in 1888. If it succeeded and black people in the South were to be educated equally with white, their capacity for challenging white supremacy would be vastly improved.[4]

The South also had good reason to fear a resumption of Reconstruction in politics. Southern elections since Redemption had been uniquely and notoriously violent and fraudulent. In December 1889 President Harrison asked Congress for an elections law. The House responded with the "Force bill," a measure introduced by Representative Henry Cabot Lodge of Massachusetts to ensure fairness in federal elections by the use of federal supervisors. Honest federal elections would have made illegal exclusion of black voters more difficult in state and local elections, especially those that occurred at the same time, and, hence, would have jeopardized an all-white Democratic supremacy at home. The Force bill actually passed the House and was halted temporarily in the Senate only by a Southern filibuster. It seemed for a time in 1889 and 1890 fully possible that both it and the Blair bill would sweep through the newly elected Republican Congress and pass on to enforcement by a fully receptive administration.[5] If these measures had passed it would have signified the beginning of another Reconstruction, and Southern white civilization would have been again sorely threatened. The danger was real, as Southern white leadership well knew, and it was present.

The South was also deeply disturbed by economic and political disintegration at home, an erosion that had profound effects in race relations. Farmers in the South in the decade of the 1880s moved from prosperity to deepening recession. As the recession deteriorated into a depression in 1892 and 1893, agricultural prices fell dramatically. Farms that had supported a family comfortably with cotton selling at twelve cents a pound became marginal at eight cents a pound, and failed totally at seven, six, and five—a point reached in 1894. The richest lands, such as those in broad river bottoms that refertilized themselves with every flood, came to be much prized because out of sheer productivity they might still show a living and even a profit at comparatively low prices. Those lands were the very lands that slavery had possessed to form the "black belts" of the South. After slavery they were most often tenanted by the freedmen and their descendants, usually, of course, as renters. In the early 1890s white farmers desperate to provide for their families resorted to violence in attempts to displace black tenants from those more desirable lands. In 1892 and 1893, for instance, in soil-rich Amite, Franklin, and Lincoln counties in southwestern Mississippi, organizations of farmers known as "Whitecaps" operated much like the Ku Klux Klan of Reconstruction years to terrorize Negroes off farms rented from landlords and country merchants. White landlords who controlled Negro labor soon took alarm, and authorities moved to squelch the terrorists. When a band of Whitecaps attacked the Lincoln County jail in the spring of 1893 in an effort to free ten of their friends who had been arrested, the governor of the state joined local officials in firmly crushing that particular movement.[6] In some areas, however, whitecapping seemed to become a habit, and even after the return of prosperity white farmers continued into the twentieth century attempts to drive blacks away so that they might themselves take up the best lands as renters.[7]

Plain white farmers probably had good reason to fear competition from black farmers. Many white landlords and merchants much preferred black tenants and creditors to white for reasons both real and imagined. Moreover, there are suggestions in agricultural statistics that black farmers, so recently out of slavery and beginning almost literally only with the clothers on their backs, farmed their lands—whether rich or poor—more intensively than their white contemporaries and that their level of indebtedness tended to be lower. In 1910, for instance, the census indicated that black farmers in the South had improved 66 percent of their land whereas white farmers had improved only 39 percent. In the North the proportions at 71 percent for blacks and 70 percent for whites were essentially equal.[8]

As the economic plight of the farmers became more extreme in the late 1880s, they began to organize themselves into the Farmers' Alliance. The repeated failure of the Democratic party to respond to their needs, capped by the nomination of conservative Grover Cleveland for the presidency, led many Southerners to join with Westerners in 1892 to form the People's, or Populist, party. The division that became official in 1892 was already profoundly present in the late 1880s. By 1889 incipient populism was visibly under way among men who still called themselves Democrats. The old order was under attack, not only economically but politically, and anxiety levels rose accordingly.

The recession of the late 1880s and the depression of the 1890s also produced profound psychological effects. Southern whites had been very much taken by sex and family roles prescribed in the Victorian era. Men saw themselves as the providers and protectors in their families. As the economic world constricted, men found themselves less and less able to provide for their women in the accustomed style, and there seemed to be no promise of an end to the decline. For those men at the lower end of the economic scale fulfillment of the provider portion of the role became nearly impossible. But even those at the top generally suffered a relative reduction in their capacity to give satisfaction in the role, and with that loss, doubtlessly, came feelings of inadequacy. It seems fully possible that the rage against the black beast rapist was a kind of psychic compensation. If white men could not provide for their women materially as they had done before, they could certainly protect them from a much more awful threat—the outrage of their purity, and hence their piety, by black men. What white men might have lost on one side in affirming their sense of self, they might more than compensate for on the other. Bread for their women was important, but it was as nothing alongside their purity. Of what earthly good was the body if the soul be lost?

The particular conjunction of sex and race that seized the South in 1889, and has not yet let go, probably had its immediate origins in Southern acceptance of the Victorian model of sex roles and familyhood by both blacks and whites in the last generation of slavery. Ironically, the same Victorianism that cut black men loose from hearth and home in the 1890s to roam the roads of the South in search of work generated in white minds a perception of them that would lead to the most awful display of interracial violence the South has yet experienced. The way in which the white South chose to react to the great depression of the 1890s is, indeed, curious. White Southerners might have responded economically with great cooperative combinations, or politically by radical new organizations. Instead they seemed to respond radically only in race, moderately in politics, and hardly at all in the sphere of direct economic action.

Whatever political, economic, and psychological realities underlay the Radical upsurge, Radicals themselves did not relate their special thinking to those causes. On the contrary, Radicals believed that their views rose solely from racial realities, easily observable. Ironically, Radicals were much like such liberals as Atticus Haygood in that they were obsessed with what they perceived to be an alarming deterioration in black life. But Radicals differed, radically, from Liberals in that they sustained no hope, ultimately, for the salvation of black people in America, and they espoused programs designed to put black people down and out rather than up.

In the Radical eye, there were many signs of black retrogression. One of the most telling was an appalling rise in Negro criminality. Whether or not

Negroes were actually becoming more criminal in their behavior we shall never know. Many whites who were most sympathetic with blacks thought so, as did indeed many well-informed blacks. Economic hard times, after all, do generate higher crime rates regardless of race. Nevertheless, Radicals could imagine no cure for the criminal propensities that they saw spreading like a plague among Negroes. In the crisis, some turned against any formal education at all for blacks. They began to argue that the New Negro was innately bad and any increase in his talents or capacities by education only heightened his potential for evil. Even the kind of industrial education that Booker T. Washington offered was dangerous. But most pernicious of all, because it held up false hopes, was the kind of liberal learning advanced by such Northern benevolent organizations as the American Missionary Association and institutionalized in such schools as Atlanta, Fisk, and Straight (now Dillard) Universities.

In the Radical mind, the single most significant and awful manifestation of black retrogression was an increasing frequency of sexual assaults on white women and girl children by black men. Above all else, it was this threat that thrust deeply into the psychic core of the South, searing the white soul, marking the character of the Southern mind radically and leaving it crippled and hobbled in matters of race long after the mark itself was lost from sight.

The assault upon idealized Southern womanhood by the "nigger beast" was the keen cutting edge of Radicalism. Let Benjamin Ryan Tillman of South Carolina catch the scene for us, as he did for his colleagues on the floor of the United States Senate in 1907. As he drew the picture, white women in the rural South were virtually besieged by Negro brutes who roamed almost without restraint, their "breasts pulsating with the desire to sate their passions upon white maidens and wives." Every Southerner returning home was fearful of finding his wife or daughter ravished. Forty to a hundred maidens, he said, were sacrificed annually to the Minotaur, and there was no Theseus in sight. Vividly, he described the victim choked or beaten by the black savage and ravaged, "her body prostituted, her purity destroyed, her chastity taken from her, and a memory branded on her brain as with a red-hot iron" for the rest of her life. Tillman described the scene that came all too easily to Southern white minds. "The young girl thus blighted and brutalized drags herself to her father and tells him what has happened. . . . Our brains reel under the staggering blow and hot blood surges to the heart. . . . We revert to the original savage." The entire countryside is aroused and exacts revenge. There was and there could be no trial because it would be a "second crucifixion" for the girl. "I have three daughters," cried Tillman, "but so help me God, I had rather find either one of them killed by a tiger or a bear and gather up her bones and bury them, conscious that she had died in the purity of her maidenhood, than to have her crawl to me and tell me the horrid story that she had been robbed of the jewel of her womanhood by a black fiend."[9]

Rapes and the lynchings that followed became the special studies of the Radicals, and provided the most vital of their statistics. It is vastly significant that the lynching of black men for the rape of white women was not the subject of intense observation and comment in the South before 1889. There had been a great fear of blacks certainly, but the older fear was that they would rise massively and kill whites, or do them bodily injury, or destroy their property—not that they would rise individually and sporadically and rape white women. In and after 1889, however, that crime and its punishment commanded a new and tremendously magnified attention.[10] Of course, lynching had long existed in the United States, and it had been common enough in the South. It derived its name, in fact, from a famous practitioner of the method upon Tories in Virginia during the American Revolution. But, generally speaking, during the 1880s lynching was a Western and all-white phenomenon, often having to do with bands of cattle rustlers. In the 1890s lynching became a special Southern occurrence in which black men were the special victims. In the decade of the 1890s, 82 percent of the nation's lynchings took place in fourteen Southern states. In the three decades from 1889 to 1918, that proportion increased to 88 percent. Beginning in the year 1889, in the South and in the nation at large, the lynching of Negroes increased markedly and within a few years reached its height. In 1892 the number peaked at 156. The sudden and dramatic rise in the lynching of black men in and after 1889 stands out like some giant volcanic eruption on the landscape of Southern race relations. There was, indeed, something new and horribly palpable on the earth. It was signalized by the mob, the rushing, swelling fury of a mass of struggling men, the bloody and mangled bodies, and the smell of burning flesh. It would be some years before anyone would earnestly contend that actually only about one-third of the lynchings were committed for the "the new crime" (the rape of white women by black men), and many more years before Southerners at large would acknowledge that lynching was itself a crime.[11]

That the number of lynchings decreased after 1892 might be attributed primarily to a rising caution among black men that led them to avoid occasions that could possibly be twisted into a semblance of rape or an attempt at rape. Almost certainly, black men came generally to avoid being alone with white women, were careful not to meet feminine eyes with a level gaze, and guarded the tone of their voices in the presence of white females. Much more were they not inviting white women to join them in adventures in interracial sex. For this and for other reasons, from decade to decade after the 1890s the number of lynchings decreased. In the nation, at large, from 1889 to 1899, on the average, one person was lynched every other day, and two out of three were black. In the first decade of the twentieth century, a person was lynched approximately every fourth day, and nine out of ten were black, a ratio of black over white that held into the 1930s. In the second decade, one person was lynched every five days, and in the third, one very nine days.[12] In the 1930s lynching declined significantly. Still, between 1889 and 1946, a year widely accepted as marking the end of the era of lynching, almost 4,000 black men, women, and children had been mobbed to their deaths.

In the 1890s, when lynching was most prevalent, no one really knew how many rapes or attempted rapes there had been, or how many lynchings, or that the whole distressing process would end this side of disaster. Furthermore, contemporaries were keenly aware that they did not know. Looking backward from the present, it seems likely that all kinds of criminal activity, including the rape of white women by black men, was on the rise in that depression-plagued decade. Whatever the realities, it is clear that contemporaries vastly exaggerated the problem. Even heads so cool and minds so fair as that of Bishop Atticus G. Haygood, in 1893 freshly home to Georgia from California, were turned and made feverish by the seeming prevalence of such outrages. Writing for a national magazine, he declared that he personally could recall but a single case of a Negro assaulting a white female before the war. That man had been burned. Now, he recognized "the unmistakable increase of this crime," and observed that "it has become so common that it no longer surprises." Haygood cited the belief of a leading Southern Methodist editor that "three hundred white women had been raped by negroes within the preceding three months," and the Bishop thought that the editor's estimate was low.[13] Black leaders too were perplexed. Some were driven to conclude that where there was so much smoke, there must be at least some fire. They gave birth to the idea that many of the rapes had actually been perpetrated by white men who disguised themselves with burnt cork to sate their sexual appetites and blame black men. In 1904, George Harvey, a leading Northern journalist, published an article on the subject in *Harper's Weekly* that by its very title, "The New Negro Crime," conceded that rape was on the rise.[14]

Radicals were generally less philosophical and less well integrated in their thinking about the race problem than were Conservatives. Also unlike Conservatives, Radicals were not given to writing out elaborate verbalizations of their ideas. They much preferred the more evanescent performance: the impromptu talk, the lecture from the platform, the speech on the stump, the newspaper interview, the editorial, and, later, the oration in the halls of Congress. It seems that each vociferous Radical soon developed a standard inventory of arguments and proofs that he ticked off eloquently and passionately, with obvious satisfaction to himself and to the decided interest of his audience. Also, Radicals did not have the relatively high degree of communication with one another that Conservatives had. The result was that virtually every Radical spokesman evinced a somewhat unique mosaic of ideas and evidences, and each offered his case with a flourish distinctly his own. It is hardly surprising then, that there were relatively few full and carefully written presentations of the Radical cause. Such offerings as the book by Charles Carroll, himself a black man, *The Negro a Beast: or In the Image of God* in which it was alleged, among other absurdities, that the tempting serpent in the Garden of Eden was actually a Negro, received little serious attention from the Radicals themselves.[15] On the other hand, Conservatives often seemed driven to pour out in ink their views on the race problem, and many of them wrote entire books on the subject.[16]

RADICAL THINKERS

Generally speaking, leaders in Radical thought could be divided into two groups. Some were primarily intellectuals who provided the ideas, the scientific and scholarly apparatus, and rationales for Radicalism. Often these people were academicians in leading universities. Others led the troops, one might say, in front-line combat.

Probably the first significant person to promote the theory of retrogression in a scientific way was Nathaniel Southgate Shaler, a professor at Harvard University, and after 1891 the Dean of the Lawrence School of Science. Shaler was a natural scientist, trained by the world famous Louis Agassiz, whose chair at Harvard he assumed upon the death of his mentor. A Kentucky gentleman and the son of slaveholders, he had graduated from Harvard in 1862. Shaler was a man of many parts. He was a Union officer of artillery during the Civil War, but near the end of Reconstruction he published a series of widely read and very unflattering articles on Radical Republican rule in the Southern states. Afterward, hardly a year's issues of any national magazine appeared without some contribution from his pen. He wrote about the earth and the universe, and about the influence of the earth upon man. He wrote fiction, history, and travelogues, and he established himself as a national adviser on higher education. He was a tremendously popular lecturer at Harvard. His general course in geology had to be moved to a large auditorium to accommodate an admiring throng of students. Shaler had a broad and already interested audience for whatever he might choose to say about the race question. And he chose, again and again, to talk about it.

As early as 1884, Professor Shaler stated the retrogression theory in an article in *The Atlantic Monthly,* one of the leading national journals. His article wove the American race problem smoothly into the new science. Nineteenth-century science had expanded the history of the earth and of man on the earth from a few thousand to several hundred thousand years. Shaler postulated that human behavior was not something that was formed within the memory of man. It had, rather, evolved over the eons. The different races, occupying different lands, had developed different traits, and those traits were deeply rooted in time. They were, in practical effect, fixed. White people were marked as great organizers and builders. Black people were imitative. The restraints of slavery had kept black people close to whites, and the imitative trait had served to make black people sufficiently white-like to survive. With the black man freed from slavery, Shaler predicted that "there will naturally be a strong tendency, for many generations to come, for them to revert to their ancestral conditions." Those conditions were, of course, savage.[17] Repeatedly, during the next two decades he sounded the same theme. In 1890 he warned whites to take care "lest the old savage weeds overcame the tender shoots of the new and unnatural culture," and he urged scholars to undertake studies of the black man in Africa in order to understand the true nature of the African when he reappeared in the freedman in America.[18]

Shaler's contributions to early Radicalism were highly significant. He gave the theory legitimacy by his position at Harvard, by his clearly superior credentials as a scientist and an intellectual, and by his perfectly paternalistic and gentlemanly attitude toward Negroes. In 1904, two years before his death, he fired his last important shot at the race problem in a widely noticed book, *The Neighbor: The Natural History of Human Contacts*. In this rather strange mixture of science and sympathy he postulated that the "currents of our fears, loves, hatred, and other streams of instinct flow in the ancient deeply carved channels which the ages of life of our pre-human ancestors have worn." Various peoples had cultivated various instincts, and those could not be immediately changed. Negroes, he repeated, possessed a "remarkable imitative faculty." In America they had used that talent so well that some whites had come to think that Negroes were, after all, simply white men with black skins. But it was becoming clear that such was not the case. "Here, as in the Old World, the Negroes have not only failed to exhibit a capacity for indigenous development, but when uplifted from without have shown an obvious tendency to fall back into their primitive estate as soon as the internal support was withdrawn." Slavery had offered such support. Personally, he had never heard of a case of rape in slavery, but he thought that the fact that "assaults of Negroes on white women in the South have increased since the emancipation appears to be clear." It was a common belief, he found, "that the Negro is sexually a very brutal creature who cannot be trusted in contact with white women."[19]

Actually, Radicalism took what it wanted of Professor Shaler's work and ignored an interesting remainder. Shaler himself was not certain that black men were specially given to the crime of rape. He was adamantly against lynching. He noted that lynch violence was peculiar to the lower South, "where the blacks are least domesticated, where they have been in the smallest measure removed from their primitive savagery." And he favored black education. Even though Negroes were severely limited (they could never comprehend higher mathematics and physical science) and without any important historical sense ("their life is immediate"), they were nevertheless possessed of rather appealing natural talents in languages, colors, and music. These capacities, Shaler believed, could add richness to American life, and they could be salvaged by the ex-slaveholders and their descendants. These elite Southerners had survived a process of natural selection in the stewardship of the Negro. They were not only specially fitted for the work, he argued, they also wanted earnestly to do it. Thus in a rather attractive extrapolation of Agassizian science, Hegelian philosophy, and Old South paternalism, Shaler managed to exalt the natural genius of both black and white Americans and meld them together to predict the synthesis of a newer, better, and higher civilization. He left a way open for the survival of blacks in America, and in this he parted company with the Radicals. Lamentably, Radicals did not seem to notice the departure.[20]

In 1884, Phillip Alexander Bruce, a young southside Virginia aristocrat, a graduate of the University of Virginia, and, later, editor of the state's most prestigious journal of history, published an article in the New York *Evening Post* in which he expressed the fear that Negroes were falling away from their prewar level of civilization. He used the term "regression" to describe the savage tendencies of blacks and called on Southern whites to labor to save the Negro and to supplant the Northerner as his tutor. In 1889, in a book entitled *The Plantation Negro as Freeman,* Bruce elaborated upon the regression theme. He found that young Negroes then coming to maturity approximated "more closely to the original African type than the character of their fathers who were once slaves." In the end, he thought, there would be no place for these two distinct peoples, and there would come "a sharp contest." The whites, of course, would win that contest. There were many evidences of black retrogression, but the most striking was the increasing frequency of crimes of impulse, especially that "most frightful crime," the rape of white women by black men. Bruce offered a detailed explanation of why black men were so driven. "There is something strangely alluring and seductive to them in the appearance of a white woman; they are aroused and stimulated by its foreignness to their experience of sexual pleasure, and it moves them to gratify their lust at any cost and in spite of every obstacle. This proneness of the negro is so well understood that the white women of every class, from the highest to the lowest are afraid to venture to any distance alone, or even to wander unprotected in the immediate vicinity of their homes; their appreciation of the danger being keen, and their apprehension of corporal injury as vivid, as if the country were in arms." When the attack occurred, whites were outraged, "and not unnaturally, for rape, indescribably beastly and loathsome always, is marked, in the instance of its perpetration by a negro, by a diabolical persistence and a malignant atrocity of detail that have no reflection in the whole extent of the natural history of the most bestial and ferocious animals. He is not content merely with the consummation of his purpose, but takes that fiendish delight in the degradation of his victim which he always shows when he can reek his vengeance upon one whom he has hitherto been compelled to fear; and, here, the white woman in his power is, for the time being, the representative of that race which has always over-awed him."[21]

Still another expert often quoted by Radicals was Frederick L. Hoffman, a statistician for the Prudential Insurance Company of America. In 1896 the superbly respectable American Economic Association published his study, *Race Traits and Tendencies of the American Negro.* Hoffman thought that the deterioration of the black race in the United States had been in process "ever since 1810, but less intense before emancipation than during the past thirty years." The census of 1890 admittedly counted more blacks than ever before, but, Hoffman contended, it also indicated a rapidly rising mortality among Negroes, especially among the young, "for the root of evil lies in the fact of an immense amount of immorality, which is a race trait, and of which scrofula, syphilis, and even consumption are the inevitable consequences."[22] Black erosion was illustrated in many areas, he declared, but a telling fact was that in 1890 there were 567 Negroes in prison for rape. Thus 47 percent of those serving prison terms for rape in this country were Negroes, whereas black men formed only about 10 percent of the total male population over the age of fifteen. In Charleston, South Carolina, in the six years 1889–94, Hoffman found that 16 of the 17 men arrested for rape were Negroes, and by his own private study of 129 lynchings attempted or accomplished, 72 involved rape and 64 of those accused were black. During slavery "the negro committed fewer crimes than the white man, and only on rare occasions was he guilty of the more atrocious crimes, such as rape and murder of white females." In the 1890s that crime was increasing at an alarming rate, he thought, and "the rate of increase in lynching may be accepted as representing fairly the increasing tendency of colored men to commit this most frightful of all crimes."[23] Hoffman concluded: "All the facts brought together in this work prove that the colored population is gradually parting with the virtues and the moderate degree of economic efficiency developed under the regime of slavery. All the facts prove that a low standard of sexual morality is the main and underlying cause of the low and anti-social condition of the race at the present time." There was no relief, he decided, either in religion, education, or economic improvement, and he predicted the "gradual extinction of the race."[24]

Interestingly, in 1881 the Prudential Insurance Company had concluded from its own experience that the mortality rate among blacks was extremely high—about 50 percent in excess of that among whites. Consequently, it began to issue policies to blacks that offered benefits one-third less than those afforded whites at the same cost. Agents using application forms, upon which the question of race had not been raised, were directed to write "on the lower margin on the back of the application the word 'white' or 'colored' as the case may be...." When the leading states in the Northeast passed laws against racial discrimination in insurance policies, the Prudential simply ceased to solicit the business of blacks. In the years from 1891 into 1898 only 2.5 percent of the policies paid off by the company in death claims were for Negroes, and by 1900 this class of business was "practically none." Other companies, however, continued "to solicit colored risks in more or less large proportions."[25] In view of the circumstance that its nationally famous statistician believed that blacks were rapidly "deteriorating" and marked for "extinction," it is small wonder that the Prudential retired from the field. In part, it was the withdrawal of the Prudential from the business of insuring black people that brought about the formation of the North Carolina Mutual Insurance Company in Durham, soon to be advertised as the "World's Largest Negro Life Insurance Company."[26] In the 1920s a black businessman thought the North Carolina Mutual was much indebted to Hoffman's "propaganda" for its origins and success. [27]

There were a number of other academic contributors to Radical theory. Walter Francis Willcox, a professor at Cornell University, Chief Statistician of the United States Census, 1899–1901, and a significant influence upon the kind of statistics gathered by the Census Bureau in and after 1900, did a special study of Negro criminality. Using the census figures of 1890, he described a massive and disastrous increase in crimes committed by blacks. He presented his conclusions, which were widely quoted, at the 1899 meeting of the American Social Science Association in Saratoga, New York. At the Montgomery Conference on Southern race problems during the next year, he went on to predict the ultimate extinction of the Negro in America. In 1902, Professor Willcox wrote a preface to a book that attempted to do precisely what Shaler had called for: to study the Negro in Africa with the idea of relating him to the African reappearing in the American Negro. This work, Willcox indicated, would help us to understand the black man in the United States, and "to realize that many faults often attributed to the debasing effects of American slavery, are faults which he shares with his African ancestors and contemporaries." The work ultimately suggested a reevaluation of the "merits and demerits of the economic system which crumbled as a result of the Civil War."[28]

Edward Drinker Cope, scion of a wealthy Philadelphia Quaker family and Professor of Zoology and Comparative Anatomy in the University of Pennsylvania, spent most of his life winning fame for his research in vertebrate paleontology. However, in the 1890s he digressed to apply his great learning to prove the inferiority of Negroes and to warn against the danger of miscegenation in the South, an event that would destroy "a large portion of the finest race upon the earth, the Whites of the South." His specific solution was the total deportation of the black population regardless of cost.[29] According to Hilary A. Herbert, a leading student of the race problem who presided over the Race Conference in Montgomery in 1900, "Professor Cope tells us that the sutures of the skull which promote growth and expansion, usually grow up, as they do not in the white man's at about the age of 14 years." Thus blacks were perpetually arrested in early adolescence.[30]

REBECCA LATIMER FELTON: THOUGHT AND ACTION

Scholars such as these lent sophistication, credibility, and intellectual integrity to Radical thought, but most important was the thinking and action of those Radicals who were engaged in the front lines, in the trenches as it were, of interracial combat. As previously noted, Radicalism was an uneven and complex terrain that can only be imperfectly mapped. But let us attempt to survey that ground and, additionally, get some bearing upon how and why people were Radicalized by looking closely at the lives and works of three leading activists in the Radical movement. Rebecca Latimer Felton illustrates well the case of a woman who became a Radical. Benjamin Ryan Tillman offers the example of a Radical in politics. And Thomas Dixon, Jr., illustrates a mass leader as Radical.

Rebecca Latimer Felton (1835–1930), journalist, politician, feminist, prohibitionist, lay leader among Southern Methodists, and the first woman to become a United States Senator (in 1922 by appointment upon the death of incumbent Tom Watson), was one of the most interesting women the South ever produced. Her father, Charles Latimer, had been brought to central Georgia as a child. In Maryland, his family had been eminent planters on lands just across the Potomac River from Mount Vernon. They were, in fact, related to the Washingtons and the Fairfaxes. In Georgia, Charles married into a locally prominent family of planters. He "married" slaves, he inherited slaves, and he bought slaves and land. In addition, he opened a store and tavern near what was to become Atlanta. Charles Latimer was a very successful businessman and by the time Rebecca was five, he could afford to organize a local school, taught, interestingly, by the uncle of Atticus Haygood. When Rebecca's education had progressed sufficiently, Charles bought a house in Decatur and established a household there for the purpose of allowing his daughter to continue her studies at "an academy of high grade." At fifteen, Rebecca enrolled in the Methodist Female College in Madison, and there she acquired one of the best educations available to a Georgia girl at that time. She completed her studies in 1852 at "sharp seventeen," married the commencement speaker, Dr.

William H. Felton, at eighteen, and gave birth to her first child at nineteen. Dr. Felton settled with his bride on a plantation near Cartersville, a village on the rail line between Atlanta and Chattanooga. Working closely with his widowed father, he prospered as a planter. In 1860, between them, they owned fifty slaves, twenty-eight of whom were "prime hands," that is, they were extraordinarily productive and very valuable. Because of ill health, Dr. Felton had given up the practice of medicine, but he did devote much of his time to service as a Methodist minister.[31]

In the secession crisis the Feltons were not fire-eaters, but during the war they were loyal Confederates. At Cartersville their plantation lay alongside the railroad that supplied the Confederate Army facing the Union forces in Chattanooga. After the extremely bloody battle of Chickamauga in September 1863, Rebecca Felton did hard service tending the wounded and dying as they streamed back toward Atlanta on the trains. Young men who had gone whooping off to war, now returned, packed into car after car, lying on the floor—bloody, bleeding, and dying. When the trains paused at Cartersville to take on water and fuel, she and other women went among the men, cleaning them, swabbing feverish throats, ministering and comforting as best they could. In one car she found a young Texan, shot through the body. She wanted to take him home and care for him. He shook his head and would not go. He began to call for his mother, and Rebecca Felton felt his hand grasp hers. He was dying. She wept bitterly—and never forgave the men who made the war.[32]

Anticipating Sherman's assault upon Atlanta, the Feltons took refuge on a farm near Macon in the spring of 1864. Atlanta fell in September, and Sherman turned his army toward Savannah. In Macon, the Feltons experienced the effects of Sherman's "March to the Sea." Rebecca Felton herself soon had dramatic evidence that not all who suffered horribly were Southerners. During one cold and rainy night in December 1864, while she was trying to escape by train from Sherman's advancing forces, she passed a line of flatcars on a siding. The open platforms were loaded with prisoners of war being transferred from infamous Andersonville to some prison more remote from Sherman's line of march. She saw the skeletal bodies and haggard faces of the Union soldiers. She later recalled that by the flickering light of torches she "could look into their faces within a few feet of the train." She noted their Confederate Army guards, posted at intervals, muskets ready. On the station platform, she saw the body of a Negro shot minutes before by one of the guards for alleged impudence; "the quivers of dying flesh had hardly subsided." "I became an eyewitness," she said in regard to the Union soliders, "to their enforced degradation, filth, and utter destitution and the sight never could be forgotten." Rebecca Felton feared throughout the war the death of her only brother, nineteen and a captain at the end of the struggle, and she did suffer the death from disease of two of her children during her enforced exile. She came to appreciate the lesson Sherman had set out to teach the South—war was hell . . . hell on both sides and both sexes, and it was death to young men. She came to despise the men who had so eagerly made a war in which other men died.[33]

After the war, back on their plantation near Cartersville, the Feltons began again, almost literally, from scratch. Within a few years, they were safely beyond poverty. But by 1873, Rebecca at age thirty-eight had lost four of her five children. She bore no more, and she turned to enter public life with a verve unique among Southern women of her day. Before 1919 women in America did not vote except in scattered and special instances; but women were nevertheless in politics, sometimes through their husbands, sometimes as suffragettes and crusaders for women's rights. Rebecca Felton began politics with her husband, but she soon became herself a politician. Almost certainly she was able to perform as she did because of the unusual qualities of the men in her life. Her father had obviously taken great pains to educate his girls in a time when Southern girls were not often very well educated. At eighteen she had married a man of thirty-five. In an age in which women were to be seen and not much heard outside of the home, in a state where husbands might legally whip their wives and sell their property, each of these men was uniquely sympathetic toward Rebecca Felton's rise in public life.

In 1874, Dr. Felton, always a reformer, ran as an independent for Congress and won. During the next six years while he was a Congressman, Rebecca was always at his side, spurring on his campaigns, and writing for the press in his behalf. She lived with him in a Washington hotel filled with Congressmen, including Alexander Stephens, lately the vice president of the Confederacy. Stephens was another older man whose protégé she became. She mixed with people easily and freely, and she learned the ropes of national power. At various times, the Feltons were out-of-party Democrats, Greenbackers, proto-Populists, para-Populists, and friends and allies of Tom Watson. Rebecca actively promoted her husband's political career, and as he came to be better known, so too did she. Soon, she began to construct a public life of her own. She published often in the Georgia press, eventually generating an ardent following and her own regular column in Hoke Smith's Atlanta *Journal*. First and foremost, she fought for women's rights. But often that transcendent passion led her into other reform movements—prohibition; improved treatment of convicts, including women; the industrial education of young white women, particularly in the mountainous region of Georgia; and access for women to the pulpit of the Southern Methodist Church. In a sense, she was also a New Southite; she supported industrialization in northeastern Georgia, and herself bought successfully into mining interests there.[34]

By 1890 Rebecca Felton was well known in national circles, in part because of her close association with the political work of her husband. In that year she was appointed one of the Southern representatives on the board of "Lady

Managers" of the Chicago World's Fair, to be held in 1893. Her intelligence, seemingly endless energy, and extraordinarily high organizational abilities soon earned her a significant influence in the selection and arrangement of exhibits. As a Southerner she was offended by a display in honor of Harriet Beecher Stowe, including a bust of the woman and pictures of Uncle Tom. To counter such Yankee propaganda, Mrs. Felton arranged an exhibit from the South featuring "real colored folks," doing real things like weaving mats and baskets, spinning and carding cotton, and playing the banjo, showing, as Mrs. Felton said, "the actual life of the slave—not the Uncle Tom sort." The editor of the Atlanta *Constitution,* Clark Howell, agreed to raise the money neces- sary to finance the exhibit, and Mrs. Felton proceeded to recruit two elderly "sober and well behaved" Negroes she knew, Aunt Jinny and Uncle Jack, to serve as the living antidote to Uncle Tom. The whole purpose, as Mrs. Felton explained to her husband, was "to show the *ignorant* contented darkey—as distinguished from Mrs. Stowe's monstrosities—to illustrate the slave days of the republic."[35]

After her return to Georgia, Felton became increasingly concerned with blacks and especially with the rising threat of the black savage to white wom- anhood. Her interest attracted correspondence from others of like mind. "I have Kept Steadily up with the Negro procession," wrote Leonidas F. Scott from Conyers, Georgia, in 1894, "and it will alarm any thoughtful mind to notice the awful extent of these most awful of all crimes, and notice that they excite only a 'news special' from the community where the crime is commit- ted. If the brute is caught, if the Victim has many friends, he is lynched, if a poor white woman or girl, the law is allowed in some instances 'to take its course,' and the Sheriff complimented by the reigning governor for maintain- ing 'law and order' when the land is full of murder, outrage, and arson and all sorts of crime." Freed from the restraints of slavery, Scott continued, the Negro had become a curse aggravated by idleness, by "free schools with the Boston social equality attachment," and by a religion that "only affects the head." Deeply appalling was the fact, as it appeared to Scott, that "white peo- ple appear to be reasonably well satisfied to have these brutes around, leaving every home in the South, with mother, wife, sister and daughters subject every hour in the day to these brutal outrages, and this crime is alarmingly on the increase whereever [sic] the negro lives." "In his own home county of Rock- dale, the Negroes seemed a peaceable "Set," but, Scott cautioned, every day "they are inching towards the danger line and the teachers and preachers and negro women are so immoral that they exert no good influence over the more uneducated." The South must be alerted to the danger. "The white people seem to have forgotten that all the Old Uncles and Aunties are gone, and do not know how to figure the possibilities of the new issue. I thought that pos- sibly you might get a chance to hit the subject a lick at some opportune time.

The people of the South had better become emancipated from the negro, and practice and not preach White Supremacy."[36]

One might be tempted to think that Leonidas Scott was a lonely man living some harmless and colorful fantasy off in the piney woods by himself. Actually, he was highly active as a Baptist layman who, in 1904, became the secretary of the Home Missionary Board. In that office, he succeeded William J. Northen, the "reigning governor" who had excited his ire in 1894 by vigorously opposing lynching. The Board represented the entire Southern Baptist Church and had been headquartered in Atlanta since 1882. Thus, after 1904, the very man who was most responsible for coordinating the labors of the church among blacks thought that blacks were rapidly and inevitably deteriorating into savagery.

In the summer of 1897, Rebecca Felton was given an excellent opportunity to "hit the subject a lick," and she struck a devastating blow. She had been invited by the State Agricultural Society of Georgia (the largest, wealthiest, and most influential organization of farmers in the state) to address its annual meeting on Tybee Island, a resort near the mouth of the Savannah River. She chose to speak on ways to improve farm life and one suggestion was that farmers ought to afford more security for their women. "I warned those representative men," she recalled a year later, "of the terrible effects that were already seen in the corruption of the negro vote, their venality, the use of whiskey, the debasement of the ignorant and incitement of evil passion in the vicious. That week there were seven lynchings in Georgia from the fearful crime of rape. I told them that these crimes had grown and increased by reason of the corruption and debasement of the right of suffrage; that it would grow and increase with every election where white men equalized themselves at the polls with an inferior race and controlled their votes by bribery and whiskey. A crime nearly unknown before and during the war had become an almost daily occurrence and mob law had also become omnipotent. . . ." She called upon good men to do their duty. " . . . if it takes lynching to protect woman's dearest possession from drunken, ravening human beasts," she cried, "then I say lynch a thousand a week if it becomes necessary."[37]

To our minds, educated away from this peculiar mode of licensed lawlessness, Felton's words are shocking. But to many Southern minds, besieged by the great fear of those times, they seemed the gospel truth. In part because her words were picked up by the Northern press and she answered their attacks with her usual headlong, full-throated vigor, Felton's speech received national publicity. With wonted extravagance she concluded a exchange with the editor of the Boston *Transcript* with the charge that people such as he were inciting the "new Negro" to rape, and "that the black fiend who lays unholy and lustful hands on a white woman in the state of Georgia shall surely die!"[38]

Rebecca Felton knew whereof she spoke. She, herself, had already heard the rush of a lynch mob as it swept past her country home near Cartersville.

It is ironic that Rebecca Felton had thus sown the wind in an almost incidental fashion. Actually, she had dealt with the black threat only as a part of the larger effort to improve the quality of life for farm people. But that seed, cast upon a soil fertile and already well prepared to give it nourishment, grew rapidly and prodigiously. Georgia was already moving into a Radical revolution in race, and Felton served eagerly to give it focus and effect. On Tybee Island, she recalled in an interview a year later, hundreds of "good, true men cheered me to the echo. . . ."[39]

Rebecca Felton struck heartily responsive chords in Southern hearts, but she also evoked a surprisingly large and sympathetic response from the North. A Chicagoan confessed to her that in regard to lynching he had "long thought *fear* to be the controlling factor in cases of the kind so often occurring" in the South, "and hence largely justifiable." The best solution, he suggested, was to "let" the Negroes lynch their own culprits.[40] One Northern woman who had lived in Florida for ten years admitted that she "was never free from fear of the negro one moment." The contemplation of death, she asserted, she could endure, but "the thought of outrage is worse than that of a thousand deaths." The last sentence in her letter could have been an echo to Felton's constant cry: "It is the duty of white men to those whom God has given them, their greatest blessing, to put a *stop* to this awful state of terror and danger in which ample evidence proves we live."[41]

After her Tybee Island speech, Rebecca Felton, much encouraged by her friends John Temple Graves and Tom Watson, took to the lecture platform to crusade for the salvation of white women from the black beast rapist. In addition, she wrote regularly for the Atlanta *Journal* on the subject.[42] After the turn of the century she wrote a speech in which she offered her thinking on the race problem at length. She postulated a "racial antipathy—natural to the Caucasian in every age and country." In the South that antipathy was rapidly leading to an irrepressible conflict. Thirty years of educating black people had not prevented a recent rise in the number of rapes and attempted rapes to a level of "appalling frequency." This horrendous occurrence necessitated keeping all Negroes away from the polls because white men equalizing themselves with black men in voting persuaded black men to presume that they could claim equality in other places—most dangerously with white women. In the crisis, the North was exacerbating the problem by appointing Negroes to federal offices and posting black troops in the South. "The promoters of Negro equality," she charged, were responsible for an impending "revolutionary uprising" that "will either exterminate the blacks or force the white citizens to leave the country." Felton had no doubt that the whites would remain, regardless of cost.[43]

Rebecca Felton was in the vanguard of a Radical element that revolution-ized popular white thought in the South about black people during the turn of the century decades. For her the fact that black men could outrage white women at such a high rate was primarily but another evidence of the abuse of white women by white men. Felton was keenly alert to the violations of her sex, and she, like many other thoughtful Southern women, came to lay the blame on the heads of the leading men of the South. Her blows hit Southern men at their very roots, in their sense of themselves. The protected charged their self-styled protectors with failure at the crucial juncture.

BENJAMIN RYAN TILLMAN

In the early 1890s Benjamin Ryan Tillman (1847–1918), the governor of South Carolina, also joined the Radical vanguard. For Tillman in the 1890s the trans-lation from thoughts to acts was nearly perfect. In South Carolina in that dec-ade, if Tillman was not the glory, he was most decidedly the power, and his thoughts had weight. From 1890 to 1894 he was the governor, and afterward he took Wade Hampton's seat in the United States Senate, where he continued to be a highly effective political force until his death in 1918. Ben Tillman is worthy of close attention. For students of race relations, he exhibits both the making of a racial Radical and what a Radical might do with political power. For historians of politics, and particularly of politics in a populist style, he is a prime example of a much neglected type—the agrarian rebel who captured the Democratic party in his state instead of leaving it to begin another.[44]

The Tillman movement in South Carolina was, essentially, a rebellion in the usual Southern style. It was a division among the leadership rather than a surge up from the lower levels of society. Tillman and most of his lieutentants were not plain farmers and had never been such, even though in the 1880s and 1890s it was expedient to assume that guise. Like the leaders they opposed, they had participated in the "Redshirt" campaign of 1876 and 1877 that redeemed the state for home rule and founded the new establishment. How-ever, in the 1880s they awoke with intense resentment to the fact that a clique among the Redeemer leadership had seized control of South Carolina and of the Democratic party. The ruling clique, they felt, had stolen the fruits of the victory won by them all and sold out to the business interests in the state and nation. Sometimes called "Bourbons," more often called "conservatives," the ruling ring was dominated by ex-Confederate generals Wade Hampton and Mathew C. Butler. The conservatives were, in truth, very much under the influence of commercial, banking, and industrial interests and the lawyer ser-vants, local and national, of those interests. In South Carolina, this meant that the conservatives were deeply entrenched in Charleston and Columbia and intimately associated with cotton, railroads, and banks, and with the fertilizer and textile industries.

As the 1880s wore on, Southern agrarians of all classes found themselves trapped and relentlessly squeezed in a contracting economy. Distressed and at first unfocused, farm elements in South Carolina soon discovered a strong voice in Ben Tillman and effective organization under his leadership. The Tillman movement was, in part, a revolt of the "red necks," that is of the renters and small farmers who bore the brunt of a vast agricultural depression. But the overwhelming majority of white men in South Carolina were farmers in that style, and any political movement that succeeded—including that of the Bourbons—required their votes.

Beginning in 1885, Tillman set out to capture the machinery of the Democratic party and with it the governor's office. As the Tillman movement gained strength, the Bourbons grew increasingly anxious about their power, their offices, and the material security these afforded. Ever since Reconstruction, whenever dissidents had reared their unsightly heads, Bourbons readily, and not always honestly, met them with a plea for Southern pride and for party loyalty against the threat of the reawakened black voter. Conservatives always raised, as one of Tillman's supporters said, "the old war cry of 76 and nigger rule for all its worth."[45] When the Tillmanites lauched their effort to capture the Democratic convention in 1890, they declared explicitly that they planned to wage their campaign within the all-white Democratic party. True to their promise, the Tillmanites never sought to bring black people to political life again in South Carolina—even in so worthy a cause as the overthrow of the do-nothing Bourbons.

Tillman's opponent for the gubernatorial nomination in 1890 was Joseph H. Earle. Earle, like a number of Bourbons, was not to the manner born, but rather began as a poor boy and ended a rich lawyer. Tillman, after a bitter contest, won control of the convention and collected the nomination. Since the Republican opposition was all but nonexistent in state-wide elections, the Democratic nomination, ordinarily, was tantamount to election and control of the state. Most conservatives, including Earle, took their defeat with fair grace. But extreme conservatives followed Alexander C. Haskell of Columbia in walking out of the convention and forming another party that nominated Haskell for governor. Haskell then began a campaign to defeat Tillman in the general elections in November 1890. Haskell himself was a Bourbon in the classic aristocratic model. He had graduated from the University of South Carolina shortly before the war, lost an eye as a dashing young officer in the Confederate cavalry in Hampton's famous Legion, and ended the war as a colonel. Afterward, he became a very successful lawyer in Columbia, a banker, and one of Hampton's leading lieutenants in the Redemption. Even though Haskell was a Bourbon and a conservative of the highest order, in 1890 he committed the classic—and alway disastrous—maneuver associated with Southern radicals: he left his father's house, the Democratic party, only to enter the house of his father's enemies. He wooed the Negro Republican vote.

It has been traditionally held that Tillman virtually single-handedly disfranchised blacks in South Carolina in 1895 by dictating a new constitution, and that he did so because of the support they had given to the Bourbon Haskellite bolters in 1890 and might give again to other such factions in the future. A close reading of Tillman's voluminous papers confirms that Tillman was indeed the prime mover for the constitutional convention that met in 1895 and that his first goal was the removal of blacks from politics. But it appears that he himself was not frightened by the threat of the Negro vote during the contest of 1890, and that disfranchisement was effected more for social and especially racial reasons rather than political or economic. His almost obsessive passion for disfranchising blacks came well after the election of 1890 and probably during the summer of 1892. At that time he was driven by the conviction that Negro retrogression was fully under way, manifested most awfully in the outrage of white women by the black beast. In sum, when Tillman took the lead in disfranchising black men, it was not primarily as an agrarian rebel that he acted. It was, rather, as a racial Radical.

In South Carolina in 1890, there was in fact a *possibility* that the "black snake" of the Negro in politics might be warmed to life and his vote used against Tillman. In heavily black districts in South Carolina after 1877, blacks had voted and sometimes elected blacks to Congressional and local offices. Tillman knew full well that the Haskellites could and would play for the Negro vote.[46] However, far from being frightened, Tillman had good reason to think that the response would not be significant.[47]

In his inaugural address in December 1890, Tillman gave every indication of remaining totally unpanicked by the race question. On the contrary, he was clearly optimistic about the future of the Negro in the state, and he was distinctly friendly in his attitude toward blacks. He alluded only lightly to Haskell's folly in appealing to the Negro vote, making political hay in the process by painting the Haskellites as villains who would attempt to mislead virtuous blacks. Furthermore, he lauded the evident wisdom of Negroes. "Our colored fellow citizens," he noted, "absolutely refused to be led to the polls by their bosses." Not only did they leave the conduct of the election largely to the whites, but many of those Negroes who voted "cast their ballots for the regular Democratic ticket, and the consequence is, that today there is less race prejudice and race feeling between the white men and black men of South Carolina than has existed at any time since 1868."[48]

The new governor glimpsed the dawn of a new and happier day in race relations. "When it is clearly shown that a majority of our colored voters are no longer imbued with the Republican idea, the vexed negro problem will be solved," he declared, "and the nightmare of a return to negro domination will haunt us no more." Tillman continued his address by urging fairness to blacks. While he denied that all men were created equal, he affirmed that all men deserved an equal opportunity for life, liberty, and the pursuit of happiness. In this vein, he asked for the power to remove sheriffs who failed to protect prisoners from lynch lawlessness. Negroes were no threat to the political life of the state, he argued. Whites were and would be in control, and the suffrage was "as yet beyond the capacity of the vast majority of colored men."[49]

The portion of Tillman's inaugural that dealt with race relations was political, almost blandly Conservative, and could have been written by Wade Hampton himself. But sometime between December 1890 and the summer of 1892 Tillman turned into the channel of Radical thinking. One evidence of his conversion to Radicalism lay in his attitude toward lynching for the crime of rape. As late as September 1891, he congratulated a sheriff who had saved a Negro prisoner from a mob and declared that "lynch law will not be tolerated."[50] However, during the gubernatorial campaign in the summer of 1892, he evinced a distinct reversal in his attitude. "There is only one crime that warrants lynching," he declared to an Aiken audience, "and Governor as I am, I would lead a mob to lynch the negro who ravishes a white woman."[51]

By the spring of 1893, Tillman was quietly encouraging lynching. In Barnwell County a Negro man was at large who was accused of having attempted to rape a fourteen-year-old white girl. The governor was asked to offer a reward, and he telegraphed to say publicly that he would do so if no lynching followed the arrest. Then he instructed his secretary to write privately that, while the "villain deserves lynching and he has been hoping to hear that you had caught and lynched him, you must understand he would not consider it right to have a man caught by process of law and through the instrumentality of the State, simply to break the law by killing him." Apparently lynching before arrest was something less than breaking the law, and a desirable consummation. In the governor's view, capture would be awkward for two reasons. "If caught he feels sure that a Barnwell jury will do its duty promptly, but the trouble would be to restrain the people till trial could be had. Then the punishment for attempt to ravish is inadequate for a case of this kind. It ought to be death." The solution was obvious. "If anything is done of this character it ought to be before the officers of the law get possession of him."[52] The law did catch the fugitive. For a time he lived under the protection of the governor. Then he was delivered to the Barnwell sheriff, from whom he was taken by a mob and lynched.[53]

At the same time that he was shifting his position on lynching, Tillman also revealed a rising Radicalism in his successful opposition to a law intended to keep black males in the state. In December 1891 the large landowners of South Carolina secured passage of an act that levied a prohibitory tax on labor recruiters from other states. Tillman, noting the alarming proportion of blacks to whites in the state, came out strongly for the repeal of the act in *Cotton Plant,* the newspaper of the Farmers' Alliance. He was appalled, he said, by the willingness of selfish planters to support this "iniquitous legislation" that "clung to Negro labor," dammed up the Negro population, and raised "the risk which the white women of the black belt took" in the presence of the "black brute." In the next session of the legislature, Tillman managed the repeal of the act.[54]

People seldom do any large thing for a single reason. Doubtless, Tillman's motives and the motives of those who supported him in effecting the disfranchisement of black men in South Carolina by constitutional means were various. Tillman did have political reasons for his actions in this case. He relished the practical termination of Negro registration and voting by legal devices. In addition he was happy to save white men from the necessity of committing fraud and violence in stealing elections. But there were also other reasons for his behavior, and primary among these was his desire to impress firmly upon the black man his inequality with the white man. The lesson of inequality applied immediately at the polls, but its application was also general, and especially did it apply to the embrace of white women. When Tillman took the lead in disfranchising black men, he probably did so more for racial than political reasons. He was driven by the conviction that Negro retrogression was under way, manifested most awfully in the outrage of white women by the black beast rapist. Like Rebecca Felton in Georgia, he did not invent the idea. Rather he moved with a climate of opinion that swept over the state like a storm. The number of lynchings of South Carolina rose from one in 1891, to five in 1892, and to eleven in 1893.[55] Nor was Tillman the only intelligent and responsible person to succumb to the hysteria. In the convention itself Tillman was much aided by his erstwhile enemies, the conservatives. John Pendleton Kennedy Bryan, a prominent Charleston lawyer, did more than any other man to perfect the legal language of the disfranchising provisions. In the end, only two out of the some thirty conservatives in the convention voted against the new constitution.[56]

When Tillman, the agrarian rebel, went to the United States Senate in 1895, he carried the Radical brief with him. As was his nature, he eagerly and frankly argued the case in vivid language to his often horrified colleagues. Since emancipation, Tillman told the Senate again and again, far from progressing the Negro had actually retrograded. The fall had been so great that the Negro could never recover the virtues he had acquired as a slave. The best Negroes, the most valuable ones, were those who retained the traits instilled in them by slavery. The bad ones were those who aspired to the full realization of white civilization because of the false teachings of Reconstruction and of the North, a folly especially of young blacks. Tillman understood perfectly the dangerous power of great expectations freely encouraged. "Over Education," he urged, simply resulted in frustration and crime. Rape was the act of a Negro excited by the idea of equality but meeting with the universal rejection of white women. It was a drive, perhaps, by the black men to save himself by merging with the great white race. "So the poor African has become a fiend, a wild beast, seeking whom he may devour, filling our penitentiaries and our jails, lurking around to see if some helpless white women can be murdered or brutalized. Yet he can read and write. He has a little of the veneer of education and civilization, according to New England ideas."[57] Tillman urged Congress to do its duty by lowering the expectations of blacks. He himself struggled toward that end and, on a personal level, in his own relations with blacks, he was dramatically successful.

Tillman clearly linked the black man's expectations of political parity with his hopes for social elevation. Consequently, he urged the political reduction of the Negro at every opportunity. He opposed the appointment of Negroes to the most minor of Federal offices because in the South "we realize what it means to us to allow ever so little a trickle of race equality to break through the dam."[58] He was brutally candid in relating what South Carolina had done to Negroes in Redemption, and, by implication, what they would do again if necessary. "We took the government away," he boasted. "We stuffed ballot boxes. We shot them. We are not ashamed of it."[59] Speaking in Baltimore, in a state that had failed to disfranchise its blacks by legal means, he openly recommended a disfranchising device, the understanding clause, as "the most charming piece of mechanism ever invented." By this clause, white judges could qualify an otherwise ineligible voter by an oral examination to test his understanding. Negroes were simply asked difficult questions, he explained, and whites easy ones.[60] He repeatedly warned his colleagues in the Senate that the black peril was fully upon the nation. If encouraged only slightly, the rash young Negroes would drive for full power in regions where blacks were in the majority. Young whites would rise to face them. The inevitable result would be a war of races and, inexorably, the virtual end of the blacks. The South, he said, teetered "on the edge of a volcano."[61] In 1912, two decades after he himself had awakened to the threat of the "black brute," Tillman was still urging whites to stand to their arms. [62]

It is difficult, indeed, to say precisely why Tillman came to embrace the Radical mentality. A psychologist would be tempted to make much out of his childhood, a unique story, extravangantly violent, almost outlandish.

Ben Tillman was born the last child in a family of seven sons and three daughters. The Tillmans should have meshed well with Edgefield County society; seemingly they had all the necessary parts. On the eve of the war, his

widowed mother had owned some 3500 acres and 86 slaves, certainly enough
property of the right kind to place the family in the local aristocracy. In the
1880s Tillman was himself a prosperous landowner. The Tillmans were not
poor white, "red neck," or even middle class in the local order of things. They
were and had been of the planter, slaveholding aristocracy. It might have been
the fruit of his own calculating rhetoric that Ben Tillman was remembered as
a "fighting farmer" rather than as a large landowner, and it might have com-
forted those he defeated to persuade themselves that Tillman was a low-class,
uneducated, rabble-rousing demagogue. Still, no lack of landed wealth or
slaves excluded the Tillmans from Edgefield society, nor did their lineage. The
Tillman family was one of the first in Virginia, and they were pioneer settlers
in the backcountry of South Carolina. One of Tillman's brothers attended
South Carolina College, a solid path of advancement for those who aspired to
become leaders in state affairs. Ben himself was preparing for entrance into
that flourishing institution when one of his eyes became infected. At fifteen,
he lost the eye, and as a result of the infection he almost lost his life. Thereafter, he discontinued his formal education, but the evidences of his academic
achievements in view of his later image as a plain farmer are no less than
astounding. He knew some Latin and Greek, he read exhaustively in literature
and history, and, by the time he entered politics, he could quote the classics
with the ease of a professor and the eloquence of a minister. Tillman did know
very well how to speak to the masses, to the "wool-hat" and "one-gallus" boys,
and he did a great deal of that with obvious pleasure. But he was at no disadvantage with his worst enemies when challenged on grounds of learning, intelligence, wealth, and antiquity of American lineage.

It seems as if the Tillmans deliberately opted not to accept a comfortable
integration into Edgefield society. Ben's father chose to be a Universalist in a
community where nearly everyone was a Baptist or a Methodist, and few had
any idea at all of what a Universalist was. In Tillman's lifetime South Carolina
was an extremely violent society, and Edgefield stood out in violence even
among the violent. It was no mere happenstance that Congressman Preston S.
Brooks, the man who rained blows upon the head of Charles Sumner in 1856,
was an Edgefieldian. Even in Edgefield, where threats flowed freely and blood
followed closely behind, the men of the Tillman household stood out as
extravagantly violent people.

Ben was born in 1847 of a mother who only nine days before had lost her
eldest son, a wild and turbulent young man, in the fighting in Mexico. He had
served under Captain Preston Brooks, the later Congressman. In the same year
in Edgefield, his father killed a man and was tried for murder. Something of a
dandy, perhaps a snob in matters of intellect, and an inveterate gambler, his
father pursued an eventful life until he died of typhoid fever in 1849. George
Dionysius Tillman, the second son and twenty-one years older than Ben, was

marked by brilliance and marred by a lack of discipline. He entered Harvard but quit before the end of his first semester, complaining that the bells of the college interrupted his concentration. Returning to Edgefield, he was soon admitted to the bar. Like his father, he engaged in "numerous personal encounters." He shot a militia brigadier during one affray, wounded another man, shortly afterward and did physical combat with the ubiquitously violent Preston Brooks. George served one term in the legislature and was about to stand for re-election in 1856 when he flew into a rage over a faro game, drew his pistol, and fired at a fellow player. He missed his target, but hit and killed a bystander. George fled to California, and then to Nicaragua to filibuster with William Walker. When he returned home in 1858, he found John, the third son, still in his teens—bright, bookish, "handsome as an adonis"—"lording it over" his widowed mother, three sisters, and three younger brothers. George challenged the tyrant. Tillman later recalled the scene vividly: "When George took him to task about it, he threatened to kill him, and went and got his pistol. George tore his shirt open and said, 'Shoot, you damned coward. You are afraid to shoot, for no brave man ever treated a widow and orphans as you have done.' After waiting for a minute with his bared bosom open, he turned and walked upstairs, and John slunk off." In May 1860, at the age of seventeen, John was killed by brothers whose family honor he has impugned. In December still another brother was killed in Florida "during a quarrel over a domestic difficulty." Meanwhile another son had died of typhoid.

When the war began, George kept his two younger brothers from rushing to the colors, saying that "three of our family have been food for bullets." Nevertheless, a year later George and the sixth brother, James, were in the service and only Ben was left at home, a lad of fifteen with one good eye and three older sisters and his mother to protect. James, barely twenty-one, soon became the captain of his company and was wounded in the fighting in front of Atlanta in the spring of 1864. Ben and his mother anxiously searched through the crowded hospitals around the city before they finally found him. They carried him home and nursed him back to health. James returned to his regiment and soon was cited for gallantry in the battle of Franklin, Tennessee, in November 1864. After the war James returned home, both arms shattered by gunfire and his health broken. Within the year, he died of a disease contracted in the service. Tillman had three brothers killed in their youth, another brother and his father had each killed at least one man and still another brother was a war hero. Ben Tillman, it could be said, had been reared in a family and in a community where a mark of manhood was a readiness for violence.[63]

Tillman had many unique experiences, but one of the most striking was that he was one of the few Southerners in the 1890s who had lived, in his youth, in prolonged and intimate contact with a large number of native Africans. During the Civil War he had been a child on a slave plantation with his mother, his three unmarried sisters, and thirty African aborigines. In 1858 his frugal mother had bought that many of the smuggled cargo of the infamous *Wanderer,* one of the last slave ships to land its dark burden on Southern shores. As a Radical, Tillman did not have to imagine what the American Negro reverting to natal savagery would become. He knew from his own experience in those trying times of adolescence. Forty years later his impressions were still vivid. He remembered those original Africans as "the most miserable lot of human beings—the nearest of the missing link with the monkey—I have ever put my eyes on." The American Negro—ignorant, debased, and debauched as he was—was a veritable god compared with the "satyr" from Africa whose record was one of "barbarism, savagery, cannibalism and everything which is low and degrading."[64] Tillman was on guard against the black savage, and he gave him no encouragement. He was brusque, contemptuous, and profane among Negro slaves. His one area of softness, even then, was with older slaves, who sometimes served as skilled laborers, and sometimes as fellow hunters in the chase of the "possum," as he said.[65]

Tillman, then, might easily have associated the immediate presence of the savage black, invasion by the alien Yankee, and the exposure of women to violation and outrage with these terrifying years before and during the Civil War. At the very time when he was coming into maturity he had every inducement, and a clear opportunity, to identify his role as one of extravagant manliness in the protection of white women. All of his life, Tillman professed a profound respect for womanhood. As governor he explicitly refused to give the women the vote, but the denial, he insisted, was to protect them from the crudity of politics. Neither would he allow them divorces, but only—he said— to keep men as husbands true to their duties when they were prone to dissolution.

Tillman's early life probably added one other important trait to his personality. His mother had lost three sons to early and violent deaths. She was a stern disciplinarian to this youngest son. In his view, his mother was "a very Juno," who managed his father's estate brilliantly. Perhaps, she wanted to save this last and youngest son from the fate of his father and brothers, and perhaps what he learned was an ultimate self-restraint. In his later life, Tillman was known for his courage, for his fierce, combative rhetoric, for moving up boldly to the very edge of bloody violence. But he did not give way to that final urge. He was famous in the United States Senate for couching his scathing attacks in humor and double entendres that afforded room for honorable retreats. He was a raging storm contained. If Tillman was to protect womanhood from the black beast, he had to be ready for the most awful violence. But he had also to save physical combat as the ultimate weapon, and to maximize the chances of his own survival. A dead man was a poor protector. That courageous and blatant combativeness combined with a carefully calculated restraint were precisely the tools that gave him high power in South Carolina politics in the 1890s. It delighted the masses and defeated the Bourbons.

Why Tillman emerged as a protector of women from the ravaging black beast precisely in 1892 is problematical. In 1876–77 he had been a Redshirt captain, and his violence against black men had no discernible sexual implications. In the 1880s he had been simply a family man and a large landowner, a progressive agriculturalist, and then a reforming politician, still with no special concern about blacks and sex. But in 1892 he was deeply disturbed about both. By that time, of course, he had grown daughters himself. He would have said, as in effect he did say, that anyone who knew the realities of life in the black belt would have agreed with him, that his conclusions were simply the fruit of observation and common sense. Further, if Tillman believed that blacks were retrogressing, it might have been easy for him to revert to the behavior of that earlier time in life when he had held, at least in his own mind, the aboriginal African at bay for the preservation of Southern white womanhood as the Yankees marauded about.

Ben Tillman was reared to manly violence and the protection of white womanhood. It seems inevitable that he would become the Radical champion, first in South Carolina and then as a Senator in the nation's capital, using his considerable political power as a broad sword in a crusade to reduce the self-esteem of black people.

CHAPTER V

Tom Dixon and *The Leopard's Spots*

As suggested above, there was no collective *Summa Theologica* of either the Conservative or the Radical mentality. It is probably significant that the one work nearest to a codification of the Radical dogma came not at all in a scholarly form, but in a novel. That book was *The Leopard's Spots,* written by Thomas Dixon, Jr., in 1902.[1] Immediately it was a best seller, and Dixon soon produced another, *The Clansman,* in the same vein. In 1905, he fused the two into a dramatic production, *The Clansman,* also a popular and lasting success. The novel *The Clansman,* finally, supplied the basic story for the film, *The Birth of a Nation* (1915). Plots, scenes, and characters changed superficially, but the racial message remained the same in all Dixon's works. Somehow the Negro had caused the Civil War, and the failure of the North during Reconstruction to recognize the rising reversion of free blacks to bestiality had continued to divide the nation. But Southern Anglo-Saxon blood had mustered its will to dominance and had redeemed itself from Reconstruction. Further by 1900 it was rapidly educating the North to the true nature of the Negro in freedom. Thus tested and tempered by the awful fires of civil war and Reconstruction, North and South were reuniting, joining together the material genius of the North and the spiritual genius of the South to realize the promise that God had given his chosen people, white Americans, for all mankind. "The future of the world depends on the future of this Republic," one of Dixon's characters declares in an echo of Lincoln's Gettysburg Address.[2]

Dixon probably did more to shape the lives of modern Americans than have some Presidents. Yet, his work and Dixon himself have been all but lost to historians. His work and his fame might have been saved by students of literature but for the fact that his writing was generally judged as bad art— and sometimes as no art at all. In truth, his fiction descended almost to dime-novel story-telling, unashamedly melodramatic, undisciplined, and oppressively didactic. By the 1920s Dixon's extravagant romanticism, so popular and acceptable in the turn of the century decades, had become a subject for snickers, and his extremism in race relations an embarrassment to a South that had passed over into an age of genteel racism. Sophisticated Southerners preferred—indeed, had a clear need—not to study Dixon, or his writings, or to give countenance to the ideas embodied in those writings.

Nevertheless, during those early years of the twentieth century, Dixon reached millions of people through his novels, plays, and the film *The Birth of a Nation.* He was so very effective because his work said in a total way what his audience had been thinking in fragments. His grand themes educed precisely what a vast number of people were instinctively and passionately certain was true. In Dixon's work they saw their own genius ratified, and further, glorified. Moreover, it was done and redone in forms that were forceful and exciting. Whatever the form, all of Dixon's later work on race relations merely recapitulated the statement made initially in *The Leopard's Spots.* That book, so worthy of historical notice, is virtually an encyclopedia of Radicalism, catching the movement during its apogee and weaving together into a single and simple piece nearly all of the various and complex strains of the Radical mentality.

THE LEOPARD'S SPOTS AS THE RADICAL MESSAGE

There are two grand themes in *The Leopard's Spots:* national unity and the retrogression of the American Negro. The two are deeply interwoven. American national unity, ultimately, depended upon a full recognition of the rising bestiality of the Negro, first by the South and especially the young men of the South, and then by the North. The novel centers on Hambright, a village in the foothills of North Carolina, between 1865 and 1900. The central character in the story is Charles Gaston, eight years old at the end of the war. Charles's father, colonel of the Confederate regiment mustered in that community, is killed in one of the last, forlorn charges of the war. In the opening chapter, Nelse, the "faithful slave" who has been the colonel's body servant, comes home to convey his master's sword, last words, and news of his master's death to Mrs. Gaston and Charles. In particular, Charles is to receive the sword and be reminded that his great grandfather used it in the War of the Revolution, his grandfather in the Battle of New Orleans, and his father drew it not in defense of slavery, but in defense of "My home and my people." Charles is assured that he will live to see the sword and the flag joined again in a country reunited. Awed by his task, Nelse enlists the aid of the Reverend John Durham, the local Baptist minister. Mrs. Gaston first took the news quietly. However, during the small hours of the night, "a wild peal of laughter rang from her feverish lips," and she collapses, delirious (pp. 6–14). Thereafter, young Charles Gaston takes turns with others nursing his afflicted mother, assuming the watch himself from midnight until two in the morning. Again and again in the dead of night she awakes. Sometimes, she imagines that Charles is his father and talks to him as if he were her lover. At other times she recognizes Charles as her son and, quite herself, tells him to go to bed. Then, again, she lapses into an amorous reverie. Distressed, and overwhelmed, the child cries, embraces her, kisses her, and begs her to acknowledge him as her "little boy." When she falls asleep at last, he is frightened at the stillness, and later, at strange noises in the darkened house (pp. 30–31).

Some nights, other sounds come loudly and all too distinctly to Charles's ears as newly freed blacks, drunk and firing off their weapons, pass the Gaston house. "Burn the rebel's house down!" they cry. "It's our turn now!" The Reverend Durham, pre-eminently the prophet of white supremacy, is the first to realize the true significance of such behavior. He comes to understand that the menace of the freed black "overshadowed the poverty, the hunger, the sorrows and the devastation of the South, throwing the blight of its shadow over future generations, a veritable Black Death for the land and its people" (pp. 32–33). Throughout the novel, Durham's mission is to educate young Charles Gaston to the awful truth about blackness and to make him into an instrument for the salvation of the white race. Most of the story is concerned with tracing out and illustrating dramatically the rapid degeneration of the Negro and its effects upon white society. Black life generally is disintegrating, black people are becoming promiscuous in every way, but centrally, Negro men are increasingly turning their lascivious eyes upon the white maidens of the South.

The transmutation of Negroes from slaves to beasts begins with Reconstruction when victorious but misguided Yankees come South with promises of equality. In a revolution of expectations, ignorant, animalistic blacks take liberty for license. Dixon makes the point horribly vivid by having a squad of black soldiers, led by a "big negro trooper," invade the wedding party of a sixteen-year-old girl, Annie, the daughter of Tom Camp. Tom is poor and white, plain of mind and pure of heart, superbly loyal to the aristocracy, instinctively hating blacks. "Yes, Preacher, God forgive me, I hate 'em!" he admits to the Reverend Durham. "I can't help it any more than I can the color of my skin or my hair" (p. 29). Tom, as a soldier in Colonel Gaston's regiment, had lost a leg in the service of the South. Afterward, he struggles desperately to preserve his small family. A happy day arrives when he marries Annie to Hose, a vigorous young man from the nearby mountains. During the celebration, however, a squad of black troopers pushes roughly into the Camp house on the pretext of searching for arms. After a brief struggle, the leader of the blacks seizes Annie in his arms and the soldiers drag the virgin bride screaming out of her father's house. They flee with her toward the woods "laughing and yelling," their intentions obvious. The young men of the party rush out in hot pursuit, pistols drawn.

"What shall we do, Tom?" they cry. "If we shoot we may kill Annie." Without a pause, Tom replies, "Shoot, men! My God, shoot! There are things worse than death!" And shoot they did, killing two of the soldiers instantly, mortally wounding another, and three crawl away bleeding. But the girl is among the casualties.

The young men crowd around Tom, their faces stained with tears, expressing their regrets. "It's all right, boys," he replies, "you've saved my little gal. I want to shake hands with you and thank you. If you hadn't been here—my God, I can't think of what would 'a happened! Now it's all right. She's safe in God's hands."

On the next day Tom confesses to the Reverend Durham the pain he felt in ordering the shooting. "But, Preacher," he declares, "I'd a killed her with my own hand if I couldn't a saved her no other way. I'd do it over again a thousand times if I had to." The minister hastens to reassure the father. "I don't blame you," he declares, "I'd have done the same thing" (pp. 122–28).

In another episode, Dixon elaborately illustrates the even more dangerous implications, sexual and otherwise, of allowing talented and educated Negroes to participate in the politics of Reconstruction. His exhibit is Tim Shelby, a "full blooded negro" who had escaped slavery in Kentucky and fled to Canada. Having "wit" and "native eloquence," he completes a college curriculum with private tutoring by sympathetic professors. Tim follows the army southward, settles in Hambright, and is highly successful in organizing the blacks as voters. His purpose is to claim for the black man the place of the white man in the South, to seize not only his property, but also his wives and daughters. "Our proud white aristocrats of the South are in a panic, it seems," he scoffs during a speech in Hambright. "They fear the coming power of the Negro. They fear their Desdemonas may be fascinated again by an Othello! Well, Othello's day has come at last." Shortly afterward there is an unseasonable snowfall, and the snow is strangely reddish. "On examination it was found that every snow drop had in it a tiny red spot that looked like a drop of blood!"[8] (pp. 88, 96). An augury, no doubt, a sign from Heaven of the outrage of purity, both personal and societal, that is to follow.

As a member of the first radical Republican legislature Tim introduces a bill, "on which he had spent months in secret study," declaring that all Confederates were felons, dissolving the marriage bonds of felons, and prohibiting their future marriage. His plan is to force white women perpetually into the arms of black men. Intelligent white Republicans rush to squelch the measure, only to see the military governor a few weeks later proclaim virtually the same rule as the law for the state. In Dixon's words, the proclamation "apparently commanded intermarriage, and ordered the military to enforce the command at the point of the bayonet" (pp. 113, 89, 145–46).

Tim hastens to implement Reconstruction in Hambright for his own benefit. He uses his political power to levy exorbitant taxes upon certain property. When the property is forced onto the market, he buys it at scandalously low prices. He covets the Gaston family mansion, the most elegant in the village, for his own residence. When it becomes clear that there was no way for Mrs. Gaston to save her home, she collapses. Upon her deathbed, she charges Charles with his mission in life. "You will fight this battle out," she declares, "and win back our home and bring your own bride here in the far away days of sunshine and success I see for you. She will love you, and the flowers will blossom on the lawn again. But I am tired. Kiss me—I must go." When his mother dies, Mrs. Durham, the wife of the Baptist minister, comes for him. She lifts Charles from his mother's bedside, kisses him tenderly, and leads him away. "You are going to live with me now," she says, "and let me love you and be your mother" (pp. 117–19, 128–40). Within the week, Tim is living in the Gaston house, using the family furniture as if it were his own. He intends also to win for his new home a white mistress. "I expect to lead a fair white bride into my house before another year and have poor white aristocrats to tend my lawn," he boasts to a scalawag friend (pp. 145–46).

Another property seized by Shelby is the house in which young Miss Mollie Graham, her blind and widowed mother, and four small brothers and sisters live. Shelby allows them to remain for a rental of ten dollars a month. Destitute, the very pretty and aristocratic Miss Graham is forced to call on Tim in his parlor to be interviewed for a teaching position in the Negro school. This is precisely the kind of Reconstruction planned by the black leadership—a social as well as an economic and political restructuring of the Southern world. However, Tim much aroused, overplays his hand and makes the move that brings about the beginning of the end of Reconstruction in Hambright and in North Carolina. Alone with Miss Graham in his parlor, Tim addresses himself to the young lady:

> Well, now you know it depends really altogether on my fancy. I'll tell you what I'll do. You're still full of silly prejudices. I can see that. But if you will overcome them enough to do one thing for me as a test, that will cost you nothing and of which the world will never be the wiser, I'll give you the place and more, I'll remit the ten dollars a month rent you're now paying. Will you do it?
>
> What is it? the girl asked with pale quivering lips.
>
> Let me kiss you—once! he whispered.
>
> With a scream, she sprang past him out of the door, ran like a deer across the lawn, and fell sobbing in her mother's arms when she reached her home. (pp. 147–49).

The Ku Klux Klan rides the next night, silently, mysteriously. The following morning Tim is found dead, hung from the balcony of the courthouse. "His thick lips had been split with a sharp knife," and suspended by a string laced through his teeth is a placard that warned others against his crime. Shortly afterward the white manhood of the state combines to redeem their government and save their civilization (pp. 149–50).

Meanwhile, however, black retrogression moves on inexorably. The degeneration of the freedman is most evident in the sexual realm, but it manifests itself in every phase of Negro life. "The spirit of anarchy was in the tainted air," Dixon declared. "The bonds that held society were loosened." Family ties fall away. A black mother burns the remains of an unwanted child "in a drunken orgie with dissolute companions." A black man very nearly severed the head from the shoulders of his paramour's young son with a blow from an ax over an absurd disagreement. But, as the child tells Charles Gaston, the hero of the novel, "de doctor sewed me head back, en hit grow's" (pp. 93, 98).

This lad, Dick, is taken into the Durham household where he is reared side by side with the orphaned Charles Gaston. Dick represents the "new Negro," that signal Radical term defining the black who has not had the civilizing support of slavery. As Dixon described Dick's essence in a prefatory list of characters, he is "An unsolved riddle." Much of the novel was concerned with solving the riddle. Dick, himself, is soon seen to be as brutal as the act that put the horrible scar upon his neck. He is an animal, with something of the loyalty of a puppy for Charles, but unfeeling in the presence of human suffering. He is lazy, malignant, dangerously ingenuously violent (164, 176–84). Like the "Raven" in Poe's poem, Dick in Dixon's prose symbolizes the great mass of hovering blacks, a dark nemesis over Southern civilization. Dick himself soon disappears, but as we shall see, he returns as a young man.

Meanwhile, among blacks at large, promiscuity becomes rampant; epidemics become plagues; and idleness virtually cuts them away from white contacts. Blacks murder one another frequently, callously, and stupidly, without cause. Now and again they slaughter entire families of whites caught alone on the farms (p. 101 *et seq.*). Freedmen were losing the veneer of civilization acquired in slavery. The few good Negroes of the older generation were simply dying away, often at the hands of their own race. Nelse, the faithful Gaston family retainer—huge, protective, intuitively right, sublimely loyal, the man who had brought Colonel Gaston's sword and last words home from the battlefield—dies defending the Widow Gaston and her son against the rising black brutes. He is simply outnumbered and worn away in fight after fight.

The Reverend Durham now refuses to preach in the black Baptist church as he had in the days of slavery because both the congregation and its pastor have degenerated beyond recall. To Durham's imperative that he throw all the sinners out of his church, the Negro minister replies, "Den we ain't got no chu'ch, en de shepherd ain't got no flock ter tend, er to shear." Durham confronts the black minister with his own transgressions, "suddenly darting a piercing look straight into his face." The black man falters guiltily, and Durham bluntly reads him out of Christianity. " . . . I can't afford to go into the pulpit with you anymore," he declares. "In the old slavery days you were taught the religion of Christ. It didn't mean crime, and lust, and lying and drinking, whatever it meant. Your religion has come to be a stench. You are getting lower and lower. You will be governed by no one. I can't use force. I leave you alone. You have gone beyond me" (pp. 306–8).

Eighteen years after Reconstruction a new generation of whites and blacks has matured in Hambright and in North Carolina. The population of the village has doubled, not because of any commercial or industrial development, but because "the country people had moved into the town, seeking refuge from a new terror that was growing of late more and more a menace to a country home, the roving criminal negro." Fathers grew immediately anxious at the birth of a female child, "and when the baby looked up into his face one day with the soft light of a maiden, he gave up his farm and moved to town." The most important change is the "complete alienation of the white and black races as compared with the old familiar trust of domestic life." Reconstruction had created the division, and now the chasm is set firmly in the bedrock of society. The black "had his separate schools, churches, preachers, and teachers, and his political leaders were the beneficiaries of Legree's legacies." Blacks are falling into "habits more insolent." But young white men have only an inadequate appreciation of the black menace. They tend to see only the obvious portion of the threat, the political and social portion, because, now, they seldom came into contact with blacks outside of the position of trifling menials (pp. 200–201).

Actually, the Durhams are the only people who fully understand the signals of Negro degeneration. Mrs. Durham, personifying the aristocratic, slaveholding South, instinctively recognizes and constantly reiterates the danger from blackness. She thinks that any Negro education is only cruelty. "When I see these young negro men and women coming out of their schools and colleges well dressed, with their shallow veneer of an imitation culture, I feel like crying over the farce," she declares. They are being educated to suffer and rebellions will follow. The whites will crush the rebels, but "the numbers who dare the grave and the prison cell daily increase. The South is kinder to the Negro when he is kept in his place" (p. 263).

The Reverend Durham represents the timeless spiritual values of the South. His message, constantly urged upon Charles Gaston, and repeated in italics in the novel five times, is essentially that the future American must be either an Anglo-Saxon or a Mulatto (pp. 159, 198, 242, 333, 383). The immediate problem, Durham tells Charles, is that young white men such as he do not recognize the danger. Racial instinct is our life, and it could be all too easily lost by a failure of understanding or a loss of will. "One drop of negro blood makes a negro," Durham declares. "It kinks the hair, flattens the nose, thickens the lip, puts out the light of intellect, and lights the fires of brutal passions. The beginning of Negro equality as a vital fact is the beginning of the end of this nation's life. There is enough negro blood here to make mulatto the whole Republic." Gaston stubbornly declines to be seriously alarmed. "Ah! there's the tragedy," cries the minister. "You younger men are growing careless and indifferent to this terrible problem. It's the one unsolved and unsolvable riddle of the coming century. *Can you build, in a Democracy, a nation inside a nation of two hostile races?"* You cannot, Durham insists, because in a democracy you have to seek the Negro's vote. Inevitably you have to cross the race line and invite him into your home. Sooner or later, the Negro would be invited to dinner. "And if you seat him at your table, he has the right to ask your daughter's hand in marriage," he concludes. His protégé is still not convinced. "It seems to me a far cry to that," demurs young Gaston (p. 242).

In the early 1890s, in the North Carolina that Dixon depicted, unscrupulous native Republicans had roused the Negro vote, effected a combination with the rising Farmers' Alliance, and seized control of the state government. The Reverend Durham persuades Charles Gaston, now a young lawyer and orator of wide reputation, to take the lead in reviving the Democracy. The party has fallen into the too complacent hands of the old guard. The old guard includes General Worth, the commander of the brigade in which Gaston's father served during the war and the father of Sallie, the object of Charles's very knightly and courtly passion. General Worth is the New South. He has pioneered in the development of the textile industry in the South. The General's own mills are near Independence, a thinly disguised Charlotte, and Dixon probably imagined them to be in Gastonia. The General woos the North for its financial resources, and he worships its values. Charles charges him with evading the race problem by simply excluding blacks from his mills, leaving the problem to politics. Worth replies that he scorns politics and politicians. But Charles retorts, in a fair if simple translation of early-nineteenth-century Germanic idealism, that the Government is the divine institution on earth, the "organized virtue of the community," and that "politics is religion in action" (pp. 280–81).

Charles, at first, has no success in his effort to save the state. The whites in the Farmers' Alliance dupe themselves into pursuing the panacea of a sub-treasury plan that would use "pumpkin leaves for money." Led by a totally earthy and opportunistic "scalawag," Allan McLeod, Republicans muster the black and white farmer vote to triumph at the polls. The farmers win offices enough to flatter and soothe them, even though they are disappointed on the "sub-treasury and other socialistic schemes." But Gaston has, in his own words, "an inflexible will" and on he goes. Before the next election he watches "with thrilling interest" as blacks demand a pure democracy and take "charge in short order" of the offices in "the great rich counties in the Black Belt." Young Negroes begin to push whites off the sidewalks and whites fight back (pp. 349, 284, 350).

Meanwhile, Tom Camp, the poor white, peg-legged veteran, has sired a second daughter, and the beautiful blonde child is eleven years old. Gaston is visiting Tom's home one day when Tom suddenly cries, "Where's Flora?" Gaston replies that he saw her at the spring minutes before. "Tom sprang up and began to hop and jump down the path toward the spring with incredible rapidity." Just as he arrives, he sees Flora at the spring and catches a glimpse of a black man disappearing over the hill beyond. "Was you talkin' with that nigger, Flora?" he demands. The child admits she was. "Didn't I tell you to run every time you seed a nigger unless I was with you!" Only Gaston's intervention saves Flora from a whipping. Tom later explains, "Lord, there's so many trifling niggers loafin' round the country now stealing and doin' all sorts of devilment, I'm scared to death about that child." Turning to Flora, he says, gently now, "But, baby don't you dare go nigh er nigger, or let one get nigh you no more 'n you would a rattlesnake!" Blithely the child replies, "I won't Pappy!"

Two days later Flora is missing. Within minutes, a thousand white men are searching. The next morning they find her, nearly dead, not far from the spring. "Flora lay on the ground with her clothes torn to shreds and stained with blood. Her beautiful yellow curls are matted across her forehead in a dark red lump beside a wound where her skull had been crushed." The jagged stone lies by her side. "It was too plain, the terrible crime that had been committed." The child is brought home, her wounds cleaned, and a broken artery tied. The physician thinks that she might live if kept very quiet. But, when Flora wakes, she goes immediately into a "convulsion, clinching her little fists, screaming and calling to her father for help!" The best physicians are called in, they too make repairs and think she will survive, but as soon as she regains consciousness, Flora again goes into convulsions, tears open the artery, and bleeds to death (pp. 365–71, 373, 374–75). The sad message is that there are indeed fates worse than death, that all of the skill of white men could not save the girl from the awful remembrance of her ordeal.

White men could not protect, nor could they heal; they could only take revenge. Bloodhounds lead the mob, "a thousand legged beast," to the brute. "It was Dick!" Dick protests his innocence and Gaston pushes into the crowd calling for a fair trial. They take Dick to the place where Flora had been found, a hundred men rushing, swaying with Dick and Gaston in their midst. "A crowd that hurries and does not shout is a fearful thing. There is something inhuman in its uncanny silence." Dick is tied to a tree. A great heap of dead wood is piled around him and saturated with oil. Gaston goes from man to man in the crowd, trying to get one person to stand with him against the mob. "Not only was no negro in the crowd, but there was not a cabin in all that county that would not have given shelter to the brute, though they knew him guilty of the crime charged against him. This was the one terrible fact that paralyzed Gaston's efforts." Gaston is tied and held, and the match put to the wood at Dick's feet. Gaston "bowed his head and burst into tears." Then he looks up at the silent crowd. "Under the glare of the light and the tears the crowd seemed to melt into a great crawling swaying creature, half reptile half beast, half dragon half man, with a thousand legs, and a thousand eyes, and ten thousand gleaming teeth and with no ear to hear and no heart to pity!"

With this event, "insistent and personal," Charles Gaston sees the basic truth that the Reverend Durham has been trying to teach him since childhood. After radical Republicans had drawn the color line in Reconstruction, the races had drifted apart. Now the chasm is unbridgeable. Since the recent Republican triumph "such crimes had increased with alarming rapidity." Negroes were gaining offices and "the insolence of a class of young negro men was becoming more and more intolerable." Inevitably "culture and wealth" would give the black man strength to answer "that soul piercing shriek of his kindred for help, and that other thousand-legged beast, now crouching in the shadows, would meet thousand-legged beast around the beacon fire of Godless revenge!" More and more Gaston realizes that the two races could not and would not live together in America (pp. 381–82). Then in 1898 comes war with Spain and with it comes national unity. Americans, it soon becomes clear, are not simply money grubbers; they are patriots. Catholic regiments come eagerly forward as well as Protestant, while rich and poor, North and South, all join in the common cause. North and South had each passed through the tempering fire of civil war. In the war with Spain, the South now passes the test of "Fire and blood" along with the North, and they emerge the new nation. The guns of the battleship *Oregon* had "proclaimed the advent of a giant democracy that struck terror to the hearts of titled snobs," Dixon exalted. "And, most marvellous of all, this hundred days of war had re-united the Anglo-Saxon race." It had "confirmed the Anglo-Saxon in his title to the primacy of racial sway." There remains only the question of the black American (pp. 407–9).

And yet, as surely as blood runs downhill, events are moving irresistibly to solve that problem too. In North Carolina, as Dixon traced the story in his novel, the process begins with the stationing of black soldiers near Independence. During the Spanish-American War, black regulars performed well enough under white officers, Dixon asserted, but volunteers created only riots. In Independence a black trooper roughly jostles a girl on the sidewalk. Her escort "knocked him down instantly and beat him to death." The Republican-Farmer legislature had used its power to reorganize the city government and throw it into the hands of rogues and Negroes. Criminality was rampant. "Burglary and highway robbery were almost daily occurrences.... Negro insolence reached a height that made it impossible for ladies to walk the streets without an armed escort, and white children were waylaid and beaten on their way to the public schools." Further, "the incendiary organ of the negroes," a black newspaper, "had published an editorial defaming the virtue of the white women of the community." Driven to extremes, Gaston organizes the whites to demand the resignation of the scabious government. After a riot in which the blacks in Independence are quickly routed, the spirit of white supremacy sweeps through the state, and whites organize themselves into military bands called the "Red Shirts" (pp. 410–15).

In the Democratic convention, Gaston serves on the platform committee. The majority report is for a "rehash of the old platform," while Gaston and "a daring young politician from the heart of the Black Belt sign the minority report." On the convention floor Gaston begins, "in ringing tones like the call of a bugle to battle," to read his report to a hushed, expectant audience: "Whereas, it is impossible to build a state inside a state of two antagonistic races.... And whereas, the future North Carolinian must therefore be an Anglo-Saxon or a Mulatto...." In a speech following his resolutions, Gaston declares that "God has raised up our race, as he ordained Israel of old, in this world-crisis to establish and maintain for weaker races, as a trust for civilization, the principles of civil and religious Liberty and the forms of Constitutional Government." But that dominance is not inevitable; it depends upon the conscious, willful assertion of their supremacy by whites (pp. 432–38).

Gaston wins not only the platform fight, but the gubernatorial nomination as well. Later he emerges victorious from the hard-fought white supremacy campaign. Gaston plans, in his inaugural address, to recommend the disfranchisement of blacks. But stubbornly, he has not yet learned the full Radical lesson. He advocates industrial education for blacks "along the lines of the new movement of their more sober leaders," taking the idea, no doubt, from Tuskegee and Booker T. Washington. "It's a mistake," the Reverend Durham insists during a private rehearsal of the address. "If the Negro is made master of the industries of the South he will become the master of the South. Sooner than allow him to take the bread from their mouths, the white men will kill him here as they do in the North, when the struggle for bread becomes as tragic. The Negro must ultimately leave this continent. You might as well begin to prepare for it."

This is a rather disturbing passage for the reader. One would have expected by then that Gaston had been thoroughly drilled in the full potential of the black menace. Yet, he is the governor-elect of North Carolina, the novel is about to end, and he is still not the total Radical that he ought to be. This apparent flaw may have reflected Dixon's concern that his home state in 1902 had not, after all, been as restrictive against black education as it should have been. Gaston attempts to argue with the Reverend Durham and to preserve agricultural education for Negroes and at least a place for them on the farms of America. "So much the worse, I tell you," lectures his anxious and unyielding mentor. "Make the Negro a scientific and successful farmer, and let him plant his feet deep in your soil, and it will mean a race war." The master finally grows tired of the persistent obtuseness of his pupil. "Even you are still labouring under the delusions of 'Reconstruction',," he charges. "The Ethiopian can not change his skin, or the leopard his spots. Those who think it possible will always tell you that the place to work this miracle is in the South." But there is no way out, even in miscegenation. "The Negro is the human donkey. You can train him, but you can't make of him a horse. Mate him with a horse, you lose the horse, and get a large donkey called a mule, incapable of preserving his species. What is called our race prejudice is simply God's first law of nature—the instinct of self-preservation" (pp. 458–60). Dixon does not tell us that Gaston ever learned his last lesson correctly. But history does.

THOMAS DIXON, JR., A BIOGRAPHY

The Leopard's Spots is useful in the study of black-white relations in the South because it so thoroughly captures the key elements of the Radical mentality. Dixon himself is worthy of study because he offers some understanding of how the deeply personal and largely secret psychic needs of an individual might impel that person to extreme racism.

Racism is, in its essence, a psychological—even a psychiatric—phenomenon. Racists need devils, or they need gods, and often they need both. They need these manifested in tangible human forms that can be maneuvered so as to make their own lives seem legitimate. The ideology and the institutions (economic, political, educational, penal, etc.) involved in a given racist set are the paraphernalia in a play, the costumes and scenery designed to promote the illusion, to make other people seem to be what the racists need them to be. Racists use other people as tools, and thus racism is tied directly to power and the lack thereof. Racists have power, and they use that power to enforce upon other persons an appearance that is not real. The most awful consequence of racism is that it violates the personal integrity of the individual, the right to be whoever he or she would be, to establish a satisfying identity. Racism is essentially a mental condition, a disorder of the mind in which internal problems are projected upon external persons. The cure begins with self-awareness, with a recognition by individual racists of the patterns they run, and, if possible, to progress to a consciousness of the source of destructive feelings within themselves and their consequent behavior.

Tom Dixon had very deep psychic needs of which he seemed unaware. He needed devils, and he needed gods. Or, rather, in his case, he needed goddesses. He found both of these outside of himself, devils in black people, goddesses in white women. He used the great power that he had as a highly talented, well placed, and superbly energetic white male in attempts to impose those roles upon those persons. In his fantasy world, he enjoyed a striking success in that effort. As students of racism in America, we are fortunate to have in Dixon a person who was exceedingly influential in the Radical movement. We also have a person who left a clear array of evidences of the psychic plight that made him a racial Radical, and that condition is representative of the psychic plight of several million contemporary white Southerners.

Thomas Dixon was conceived and born in very unusual circumstances, circumstances that were indeed linked to the death of the Confederacy and the birth of a nation. That fact, as he later asserted, deeply influenced his life. In the fall and winter of 1863, even while George Cable was riding and fighting in northern Mississippi and Alabama, while Atticus Haygood and Rebecca Felton were ministering to the stricken soldiers who had fallen defending Atlanta, and while young Ben Tillman and his mother waited anxiously on the plantation in Edgefield for news of the fate of Captain James Tillman on the front, Thomas Dixon was nearby, but still unborn. During those very bloody months, Tom, as a child in his mother's womb, crossed that same torn and worried ground upon which the two armies struggled. He was carried by an extremely anxious mother. Amanda Dixon at twenty-nine was understandably concerned about her pregnancy. She had been married at thirteen and gave birth to her only surviving child at twenty. Before the war, she and her preacher husband had taken their slaves, adventurously, to join relatives on new land in central Arkansas. Soon came the war with all its troubles, and, then, the conception of still another child. Amanda grew afraid, so far from home.[2] The Dixons packed their things into a single wagon, took their animals and their thirty-two slaves, and began the trek homeward toward Shelby, high in the foothills of North Carolina. "This covered wagon passed between the line of Sherman & Hood's armies & was 3 months in the journey," Dixon wrote in 1927 to the widow of his elder brother Clarence. "Clarence was 9 years old. They brought their slaves with them & my Father Told me he always slept with his hand on his gun expecting to be killed by bandits or deserters every night he lay down. I was their only child born during the Civil War & it has always exercised a profound influence on my character."[3]

Tom was born early in 1864 in a farmhouse near Shelby, a village in Cleveland County, North Carolina. In that community he spent his first years, a child of prominent families through both parents. His mother's people were

large planters and slaveholders in neighboring York County in South Carolina. One of his mother's brothers was LeRoy McAfee, who won first honors
in his graduating class at the University of North Carolina in 1859, rose to a
colonelcy in the Confederate Army at twenty-five, and died of tuberculosis
during Reconstruction. After the war McAfee was a lawyer in Shelby, a prime
leader in the Ku Klux Klan in Cleveland County, and young Tom's idol. Tom's
parents had met in the "social life" of York County, and they had married in
1848. His father was a descendant of the first white settlers in western Carolina
and the grandson of one of the leaders of the patriot forces in the battle of
King's Mountain. Tom's father, Thomas Dixon, Sr., through his marriage to
Amanda McAfee added substantial wealth to an excellent, if only local, reputation as a Baptist minister. At the end of the war, "Elder" Dixon freed his
slaves, retaining in the household only one aged "mammy." Afterward, he
managed to make a living by combining farming and the ministry. A significant part of Tom's early life was spent in tiresome and, as he saw it, dulling
farm labor.[4]

During Reconstruction, the Dixons like so many others in the South were
poor in the goods of this world, but they were very rich in spirit. They claimed
much of the intensely immediate and personal communion with God that was
the great coin of status in that very Baptist realm in western North Carolina.
Most of all, the Dixons had grit, and with grit, all things were possible. Tom's
father vowed that his children would have the education of which his own
father's drinking and early death had deprived him. At great sacrifice, the family sent Clarence first to Wake Forest College, where he finished at the head
of his class, then through the Southern Baptist Theological Seminary, which
was then in Greenville, South Carolina. Clarence next filled a succession of
prestigious pulpits. One of his first was that of the Baptist church in Chapel
Hill, where he baptized, among others, two young students in the university,
Charles B. Aycock and Locke Craig, each of whom was to become governor
of the state in the early years of the twentiety century. In June 1883, when
Tom graduated from Wake Forest with the most honors ever earned by any
student there, including his brother Clarence, he could feel proud and secure
in his own reputation and that of his family.[5]

Dixon's brilliant record at Wake Forest earned him a graduate scholarship
at the Johns Hopkins University in Baltimore. In the 1880s Johns Hopkins
was deliberately structured to be a congenial environment for Southern scholars, and it was to be expected that Dixon would be happy there. He chose to
work with Herbert Baxter Adams, whose seminar in history and political science was patterned on the German model. The teaching methods were Germanic, and so too were the assumptions of what lay at the roots of the subjects
they studied. One assumption, often called "germ theory," was that each people had a genius, some God-given seed that in time would mature and flower

to enrich the world. For instance, the genius of Teutonic peoples was a capacity for cultivating self-government.

In going to Johns Hopkins, Dixon was traveling a path that many other young Southerners, soon to find national and international fame, followed after the university opened in 1876. Walter Hines Page, later publisher and diplomat, had already come and gone; John Spencer Bassett, the historian, would soon arrive. On his right hand in the very first seminar that Dixon attended, as he later recalled, sat a student only freshly arrived from Asheville, North Carolina, a young man who would become the next Southern-born President of the United States—Woodrow Wilson. Wilson was a very mature twenty-seven, Dixon only nineteen, but the two became friends. They shared a passion for the theater, and Wilson helped his youthful friend win a place writing reviews of theatrical performances for a Baltimore newspaper.[6]

Within four months, Dixon withdrew from the university and hastened to New York to study acting. Mollie Faison Dixon, Clarence's first wife, deplored her brother-in-law's fall. She had rather see Tom in the poor house, she declared, than associated "with such wicked men and women."[7] Tom soon bought his way into a traveling company that a trade paper labeled worse than a burlesque, and took to the road. While Dixon's troupe was touring through upstate New York doing Shakespeare and doing it badly, the manager absconded with the company funds. On borrowed money, Tom returned to New York and attempted still again to penetrate the world of the theater. Standing six feet three inches tall and weighing 150 pounds, so obviously youthful, it was inevitable that he would have difficulty becoming the serious actor that he wanted to be. Finally, a director whom Dixon respected convinced him that he could not then succeed as an actor, and he came home to Shelby.[8]

Warmly welcomed, the prodigal son soon redeemed himself. Dixon began to read law and, following his father's advice, sought election to the legislature even before he was old enough to vote. The forensic skills he had developed at Wake Forest, plus his tendency toward the theatrical enthralled Cleveland County voters and won him the seat over two veteran contestants. Before the assembly met, Dixon was already running for the office of speaker of the house. Only at the last moment did the older members of the legislature awaken to the danger and combine to defeat the startlingly aggressive young man. In the legislature in 1885, Dixon took an active part in pressing for progressive legislation for education and won credit for promoting the first state law for the pensioning of Confederate veterans. However, by the end of the session he was disgusted with the venality of politicians and what he considered to be the failure of his colleagues as leaders. He returned home, vowing never to partake of politics again, and continued the study of law.[9]

In 1885 Dixon went to New Orleans for Mardi Gras. There he met Harriet Bussey of Columbus, Georgia. At first accepted as a gentleman by Harriet's father and then rejected by him as a prospective son-in-law (precisely as was Charles Gaston by General Worth in *The Leopard's Spots*), Dixon returned to Shelby. For a time he concentrated upon his law practice. Still he could not forget the attractive Georgian. Finally he could stand it no longer. In a fever he rushed to Harriet's side, defying her father's wishes. He proposed "late one afternoon at the falls of the Chattahooche River," was accepted, "and we drove home in the twilight" (again, precisely as Charles Gaston wooed Sallie Worth in Dixon's first novel). The couple eloped, married, and settled in Shelby.[10]

Even as he flourished as a lawyer, Dixon grew disillusioned with the legal profession. He won the cases he should have lost, he felt, and he lost those he should have won. Decisions, he concluded, depended too much upon the lawyer and too little upon justice. The end of that career came when he worked very hard to send a man to prison for twenty years for arson, only to become convinced soon afterward of the man's innocence. Within a few weeks, he had persuaded the governor to pardon the victim of his earlier zeal. Frustrated, depressed, he journeyed to Wrightsville Beach, near Wilmington, to meditate. For more than an hour he stood high on the dunes looking out over the ocean where a storm was brewing, fixed by the beauty and power of giant waves rolling in to crash against the shore. In such a glorious display of nature he saw God and felt himself at "one with it all." Dixon then knew that he was called to the ministry. He stumbled down from the dunes a changed man. "I breathed deeply," he later wrote, "and took a new hold on life."[11]

After a brief period of study, Dixon was ordained in 1886 and took his first church in Goldsboro. Then, in April 1887 he was called to the Second Baptist Church in Raleigh. In the capital city Dixon joined a remarkable coterie of young Carolinians, including the lawyer Charles Brantly Aycock who was elected governor in 1900; Walter Hines Page the publisher; and Josephus Daniels, soon to become the state's most influential editor and publisher and later Woodrow Wilson's Secretary of the Navy. Within another six months Dixon had left the South and was in the pulpit of the Dudley Street Church in Boston. Soon after his arrival, he attended a lecture on the "southern problem" at Tremont Temple. When the speaker depicted the South as a continuing menace to the nation, Dixon sprang to his feet, denounced the accusation and its source, and very nearly caused a riot. From that time forward, he later asserted, he studied the Civil War and its aftermath with the view, someday, of telling the true story of the South. Far from casting him out for this public display of temper, Dixon's Yankee congregation relished their fiery young minister. When a call came from the Twenty-third Street Baptist Church in New York in the summer of 1888, they offered to double his salary if he would remain.[12]

In New York, Dixon worked hard in his ministry and on his sermons. Thinking his audiences overly populated with women, he strove to make his messages intellectual and relevant to the special concerns of young men of the time. Soon his sermons came to bear directly upon the problems of the new urban environment. In this way Dixon became a pioneer in preaching the social gospel, in bringing Christianity to the new economic and social order of America. He was a highly effective evangelist. Tall, "weirdly gaunt," closely shaven, with "plentiful coal-black hair," a "strong, almost cadaverous jaw," and "black, deepset, and scintillant eyes," Dixon was impressive in the pulpit. His carefully rehearsed, controlled delivery had "an almost hypnotic effect" upon his audiences. Within a few weeks, he became tremendously popular and had to move his meetings to the auditorium of a nearby YMCA to accommodate the multitudes who came. Among those who attended was fellow Baptist John D. Rockefeller. Rockefeller began by inviting the twenty-four-year-old minister to dinner, and he ended by offering to pay for half of a one-million-dollar "temple" in the middle of Manhattan. Dixon found he was unable to raise the other half, and the project failed. Still, the imperious young Carolinian continued to preach freely and vigorously on all issues—and he prospered.[13]

Increasingly, however, Dixon chafed at the restraints of a denominational ministry. In 1895, amid a storm of criticism, he resigned from his church to create one that, he claimed, rose above the sectarian. "I believe," he announced, "it is more important to lift many men out of the ditch than to spend my time making a few men Baptists."[14] In spite of his desire to include men in his audiences, Dixon was always sympathetic to the recognition of women and he ruled that half of the Board of Deacons of his new church would be women. The "Church of the People" actually had no building, but met in the auditorium of a music academy.[15]

Sunday after Sunday, Dixon sermonized to overflow crowds upon every social issue that crossed his sights. It was as if the restlessness that had marked his life before had now found focused release. He denounced Tammany Hall. He thought that free silver and Bryan were a "bunko-steering business." He supported the vigorous and youthful reformer Theodore Roosevelt for the governorship. Soon, his new church became an American headquarters for Cuban liberation from Spain.[16] Typical of his activism was his appeal to Populist Senator Marion Butler to use his power in Congress to secure recognition of Cuban independence and to end Spanish attempts to crush the rebels in "this war on the white flag of a hospital. . . ." To delay, he warned, was "to cover our history with ignominy and hand down to our children the legacy of Cowardice, stupidity & infamy." Dixon, now thirty-two, pointed the way. "Why don't you younger men who represent the new nation get together [and] answer this cry of Humanity?" he urged.[17] His church also became a forum for social justice oratory. He brought the Populist Mary Ellen Lease, the "Kansas Pythoness," to speak; and he heaped encouragement upon Butler, a young Southerner with ambitions equal to Dixon's own and already the chairman of the national executive committee of the People's party.[18]

Before the Spanish-American War, Dixon had been ardent for Cuban liberation from Spain. But in 1898, he was an eager imperialist for the United States. He urged Butler to shift his position in the Senate to endorse the annexation of Hawaii. "Hawaii will be annexed," he predicted, "every inch of soil over which the flag is lifted as conquered territory will be held." He hoped that Butler would rise to the challenge and grasp the opportunity. "I write this to you simply from my deep regard & admiration for your talents as a Young Southerner," he confessed. "I had dreamed of the day your opportunity might come to try your fortunes for the White House."[19]

Meanwhile Dixon himself had returned to the South in a significant way. Late in 1893 on the eve of his thirtieth birthday, he developed a serious but ill-defined malady. For weeks he could not stand noises or light and lay in his bed fearing insanity and death. His physician advised a move away from the city, and the Dixons soon found a retreat in Virginia. In 1897 Dixon bought and grandly restored Elmington Manor, a fine old plantation house in Gloucester County, Virginia. At one time the estate had belonged to the aristocratic Dabneys. Dixon's lands bordered on Cape Charles, and he pursued his developing interest in boating. Finally he himself supervised the construction of one of the prides of his life, an ocean-going yacht that he named "Dixie." All of this was financed, not primarily by his New York church, but by his growing reputation after 1894 as a star on the lecture circuits. Dixon was a master orator, and he perfected a series of lectures on topics with such titles as "Backbone," "The New Woman," and "Fools." These appealed unerringly to his audiences. By the turn of the century he was much in demand and earning a thousand dollars for a night's performance. He developed a pattern of preaching in New York on Sunday, retreating to Elmington Manor until midweek, then lecturing at night and traveling by day until he needed to return to New York for his Sunday service.[20] The fact that he could range far out into the Midwest in his circuit was a comment on the rising efficiency of the American railroad passenger system of the day. Finally, in 1899, he gave up his New York church and never took another.[21] Popular, affluent, connected with important persons, with a beautiful wife, three children, and an elegant Virginia estate, Thomas Dixon, Jr., was living, it would seen, an idyllic life.

Early in 1901, while he was on a lecture tour, Dixon happened to attend a stage production of *Uncle Tom's Cabin*, the 1852 antislavery story that won such an amazingly long life in America. Incensed at the libel against the South (as he had been by the lecture at Tremont Temple in Boston more than a decade before), he resolved at once to write a reply in the form of a novel. All during that year, while he continued to tour the lecture circuits, he put together a thousand or so pages of notes he had gathered on Reconstruction and planned out the novel. Then, in sixty days of intensive writing, he produced *The Leopard's Spots*. Without revision, he mailed it off to an old friend from his Raleigh days, Walter Hines Page. Page had recently joined in the formation of Doubleday, Page, and Company and was rapidly becoming one of the most creative, influential, and successful American publishers of his time. Page began to read Dixon's manuscript at breakfast one morning. He was so fascinated by the story that he continued to read as he walked down Fifth Avenue toward his office. Absorbed, he was knocked down at an intersection by a passing cab. Retrieving the crumpled and soiled manuscript, he continued to read as he walked to his office. When he finished, he sent an enthusiastic telegram to Dixon, inviting him to come to New York to sign the contract. Dixon did so, and in March 1902, the book appeared. Within a few months, it had sold over 100,000 copies. Eventually, nearly a million copies were printed—roughly one copy for every eight Americans.[22]

THOMAS DIXON'S COMPLAINT

Dixon became a Radical and wrote *The Leopard's Spots* because he had a very deep emotional problem. Rightly or wrongly, Dixon's complaint was that his mother had been sexually violated as a child, and he was not able to cope with that thought. This is evident in a letter he wrote to his sister-in-law, Helen C. Dixon, in 1927 when he was sixty-three years old. Helen was the second wife of his older brother, Clarence. She was gathering information on the family history for a biography of Clarence, who had died in 1925. Arguing mildly with Helen over his mother's age, Dixon pled a case for a specially intimate relationship between himself and his mother. In Dixon's mind, that intimacy was closely associated with a certain period in his life. "I know I am right about mother's age," he insisted. "She and I were perhaps more intimate *friends* than any other group in the family. When her nervous system collapsed during her change of life, the burden of the house fell on my boy shoulders. Clarence was at College. During this period of tragic Shadow *I* Kept the house, made the beds, swept & Kept it clean & my father & I sat up all night with her for many pitiful months—he sat up till 1 o'clock and I from 1 till dawn. I was a very little boy but 8 years old at first and the most vivid & terrible memories of my life are the black hours outstretched by her bedside. When in her delirium she would say terrible things I would put my hand on her mouth, cry & beg her to not talk. She would often awake into calmness— herself quite—& tell me to go to bed—which of course, I couldn't do. In one of those vivid times of mental upheaval she repeated a scene with her own mother (long since dead) which could only have been from memory in which she bitterly upbraided grandmother for marrying her—taking her out of school & forcing her into marriage before her *mensus* had appeared—and She repeated again & again the fact that she was barely 13 years old. I have always been sure that this premature marriage was the underlying physical cause of her pitiful collapse in her menopause." Dixon went on to explain that his mother's failure came "after 4 months of menstrual flooding which the doctor was unable to stop." In the same letter, he described the trying times that his mother and the family had endured in the months before his birth, their trip in the winter of 1863–64, across the dark and bloody ground between Arkansas and North Carolina, and the imminent danger of violence from brigands and deserters. The circumstances of his birth, he was certain, had "always exercised a profound influence on my character."[23]

Helen Dixon soon discovered that Tom had not been "a very little boy but 8 years old" at the time of his mother's collapse. He had been twelve. She challenged him on that fact. He conceded but went on to make the point that his mother's illness followed closely after the birth of his youngest sister, Addie. "She was 52 years old when Addie was born & eighteen when the first baby came—which she told me was *five* years after her marriage."[24] After further research, Helen found Tom once more in error. His mother was in fact forty-one at the time of the birth of her last child and subsequent breakdown. Challenged again, Tom replied defensively. Frustrated, seemingly exasperated, he stressed what he obviously thought were the essential truths in the matter. "My mother was married 10 years before her first children [were] born & three children died, I think before Clarence was born." He admitted that he might have been mistaken about his mother's age at the time of her collapse, and closed the correspondence with a very revealing spurt of words. "Of one thing I am absolutely sure—She married my father in her 13th year," he declared. He heavily penciled over the "3" again and again. "She told me this so many times—and reported it so often in her delirious hours I couldnt be mistaken. Why not leave out the attempt to fixed calendar dates? It never seemed to me of any importance. . . . Frankly I think they cumber a Story & make it less interesting. If I were you, I would omit the dates & get the Spirit of the story in your own mind into the *heart* of the reader.[25]

Clearly, in Dixon's mind there was the conviction that his mother had been ill-used by a premature marriage and early attempts at childbearing. Dixon's impressions are supported by the facts evident in the family history. In 1847, Amanda at thirteen was married to Thomas, Sr., at twenty-seven. She then suffered a succession of miscarriages or infant deaths, perhaps three, before Clarence survived in 1854. It was usual in that time for healthy women of childbearing capacity to deliver a child every two years. Some nine years after the birth of Clarence, in the very eye of the storm of war, Tom was conceived and born to a highly apprehensive mother. He was delivered on January 11, 1864. Two years later on February 9, 1866, his brother Frank was born, followed by sister Delia in 1872, sister Addie in 1876, and a collapse. Indeed, it does seem that his mother had been married prematurely, and subsequently had suffered an unusually painful history in the birth of her children. This impression is strengthened by other facts. According to Helen in her biography of Clarence, the aunt of the child-bride lived with the couple "for some years at the beginning of their life together" and managed the household. Further, young Mrs. Dixon spent so much of her time by herself devouring romantic novels that her husband was forced to express his disapproval. Nevertheless, so thoroughly romantic was she, that she named her first surviving child Clarence, not after her husband or some respected kin, but after one of her fictional heroes. It remained for the second son to inherit the name of his father. Helen Dixon, in her book, did not give Amanda's age at the date of the marriage. "Girls of the sunny South are apt to mature early," she said brightly, rushing past the fact of Amanda's youth. As if in extenuation of the still unconfessed truth, she described Amanda as "tall," "handsome," "much overgrown for her age," and "brimming over with the spirit of romance" while "in her teens."[26] It was true that women in the antebellum South did often marry young. It was not uncommon for girls of seventeen and sixteen to marry. But fifteen-year-old brides were rare, fourteen remarkable, and thirteen even then, as now, a curiosity.

Tom Dixon seemed unable to suppress in his own mind the knowledge that the youthful innocence of his mother had been violated. Nor was he able to forget what appeared to be the awful consequences of that violation. But who was the violator? Who was the guilty party in the assault upon his mother? Was it the mother who pulled the girl unwilling and unready out of school and pressed her into the embrace of a man fully matured before she had become a woman? In his letter to Helen, Tom quickly dismissed the grandmother as "long since dead" at the time of Amanda's collapse. Was it Tom's father, the man who over those first years had inspired perhaps as many as three dangerous and painful disasters in his child-bride before an infant finally survived? Clearly, Tom Dixon was a child of the Victorian age when society and religion combined to insist that fathers knew best and must be honored by their offspring. In Tom there was no sign of remarkable hostility toward his father. There was a rather ordinary resentment that, on one occasion, his father had whipped him too severely for procuring whiskey for his paternal grandmother against the explicit orders of his father. And there was a show of independence made in Tom's scandalous infatuation with the stage. Far from attacking his father, Tom overtly revered the man. On the other side, it appears that he never quite won the kind of approval from his father that he wanted. By entering the ministry, he finally did precisely what his father had done, what his older brother had done, what his younger brother did later, and what his father had wanted him to do. With that step, he recalled, "I breathed deeply and took a new hold on life.[27]

On the other hand, Tom was distinctly hostile to his brother Clarence. That hostility exceeded the usual sibling rivalry and stood in contrast to his highly protective attitude toward his younger brother and two sisters. Possibly Tom made a scapegoat of his older brother because, first Clarence was the only living child born before himself and hence a convenient physical symbol of the abuse of his mother in her early marriage, and, second, because Clarence was away when he was most needed both by his mother and by Tom during her collapse. If Clarence, then twenty-one, had come home, the keeping of the house and the night watch over his mother might not have fallen so heavily upon his "boy shoulders." Later in life, Tom apparently competed with Clarence, embarrassed him sorely, and outrightly assaulted him verbally. At Wake Forest, the college that his father had wanted to attend but could not because his own father drank to excess, Clarence had won the highest honors in his class. Tom followed Clarence to Wake Forest and won more honors than anyone else up to that time. Signally, he won the Orator's Medal while still a freshman, whereas Clarence had won it only as a senior.[28] When Tom went off to Johns Hopkins in the fall of 1883, it happened that Clarence had just moved to Baltimore to take his first metropolitan pulpit. Clarence was already a striking success in life. He was well on his way to a progression of celebrated pulpits and a national reputation as a staunch defender of religious conservatism. Indeed, he would become the founding editor of *The Fundamentals,* a series of publications from which the twentieth-century fundamentalist movement gets its name. Tom not only went to Baltimore, he also moved into the house with Clarence and his wife Mollie. Almost immediately he began to embarrass them by attending the theater and writing about it in the newspapers. Then he deserted not only Southern Baptist orthodoxy but respectability and morality as well by quitting school and striking out for New York and the sinful stage. In the 1890s, in New York as a minister of the social gospel preaching that the church must go to the people where they are, he finally descended to attacking his brother in the public press for his theological and social conservatism. It was, perhaps, not entirely coincidental that at that time Clarence was minister to a prestigious congregation in nearby Brooklyn.

Tom's attacks on Clarence were unfair and vicious. In his own mind, Tom excluded Clarence entirely from caring for their mother while she was passing through those very dangerous straits of the change of life. He and his father each alone, were the nurses, he insisted. Actually, according to Helen Dixon, it was decided that Amanda's illness was not serious enough for Clarence, a seminary student in Greenville, South Carolina, at the time, to make the short trip home. Further, Tom exaggerated the time span of the illness and, by implication, the seriousness of Clarence's defection. Tom said it lasted "many painful months," whereas Helen found that it lasted only a few weeks.[29] Somehow, he failed to mention that there were three younger children in the house at this point, as if he were her only child. In later life he was usually highly supportive of and deeply paternal toward his junior siblings. He tried very hard to find Frank a good pulpit, and he encouraged him to final success on the lecture circuits. He was very helpful to Delia in her long and ultimately successful struggle to become a physician, the first woman in North Carolina to do so. As late in life as 1927, Dixon was still unwilling to give his older brother much credit with his mother in a biography to be penned by a fond and intelligent widow. Instead, her inquiries brought forth a rush of bitter and rather sanguinary thoughts—fantasies—lives that were never lived.

Ironically, it seems that Dixon ultimately blamed himself more than anyone else for his mother's plight. At one level it was almost as if his guilt derived simply from being born, of having jeopardized his mother's life merely to possess his own. More speculatively, perhaps it sprang from some minor fact and some major fantasy in the child's mind related to his mother's collapse. Perhaps he blamed himself for some failing in his mother's sickroom in the midst of night when she raged in fever and delirium and he was a child of twelve, frightened, frustrated by his inadequacy in the emergency, and alone. Perhaps, the child simply could not cope with the specific nature of his mother's illness. He associated her physical condition with her delirious raving about being married too early in life. He sought thereafter to protect her, not only in the present and in the future, but in retrospect as well. At another level, perhaps he even went so far as to project himself into his father's place as his mother's lover because if he were his mother's lover he would have saved her from all that. In his mind, eventually, his mother became all white womanhood, and to protect her from attack was to protect all women from attack upon their sex. If defenses failed, and there were violators, then the violators must be punished —including even himself.

In the very curious play of his mother's and his own ages at the time of her breakdown, Dixon was, perhaps, attempting to escape his fate. The effect of what he did was to assert that he was four years younger and his mother eleven years older at this second critical juncture in their lives, the first having been the time of his birth. One would expect Dixon, a highly aware, very intelligent man in his sixties, to know the simple facts of his own and his mother's ages. However, if his imagined ages had been true, he would have been less able to care for his mother during her collapse, and she would have married much later in life than she did. If he were, indeed, only eight at the time of his mother's illness instead of twelve, then considerably less could have been expected of him, less to be carried by those "boy shoulders" in taking care of his mother in the darkest hours of the night. A child of eight is clearly a child, a child of twelve might experience alarming alternations between youth and maturity. Further, if Tom were only eight, Clarence's absence at school during his mother's crisis seems all the more selfish and reprehensible, a moral transgression not erased by Clarence's later great achievements as a Baptist divine. Thus Tom's later aggressions against his older brother might seem justified by Clarence's neglect of their mother.

Most revealing of all in this fantasy of ages was what it said about how Dixon wanted to see his own mother in her marital and maternal life. If he had succeeded in making a reality out of the myth in his mind, then his mother would have been spared "this premature marriage," three stillbirths, and the consequent "pitiful collapse in her menopause." Amanda would have married at twenty-four rather than at thirteen. Twenty-four, Dixon apparently thought, was a very safe and proper age for a woman's marriage and first sex. In his fanciful world in *The Leopard's Spots,* Dixon created Mrs. Durham as the ideal mother. At a point very deep in the book, he has Mrs. Durham declare, in a passage that does little to move the story forward, that a woman should marry "at the proper age of twenty-four." That age is best, she explained, because then the "maternal life" of the woman coincided with the twenty-one year-"infancy of one child."[30] For a man who so scorned the counting of years, it was no less than amazing how easily Dixon came to imagine his mother's age precisely to fit this ideal. One can hardly avoid taking the next logical step. That is, if the mother suffers a collapse at the end of her "maternal life," the son (presuming that the child is a son) would be twenty-one, a man, and could handle the crisis in a mature fashion.

Dixon's imaginary chronology tended to make a world in which there had been no abuse of his mother in her sexual and maternal life. Still, the hard, hot, never-totally-to-be-forgotten facts were that his mother had suffered an awful history of sex, conception, and birth over the sixteen years previous to his arrival. He felt that his mother had given him birth at tremendous hazard to herself. The child thus born was later deeply grateful, and he loved his mother dearly. But her giving him life was a debt he would find difficult to repay. With her collapse, a surcharge of guilt was added. Somehow, he had let his mother down, try as he might, in the most dreadful hours of her life. He had neither saved her from violation, nor punished her violator.

For whatever reason, Dixon definitely did punish himself. All of his life he repeated a pattern of striving to achieve and then throwing away, almost with an impulsive, yet deliberate turn of the hand, his achievements. No thing was ever enough. At Wake Forest he was the stellar student of his time, won the most coveted honors and a scholarship to Johns Hopkins University, only to cast academics aside for the stage. He did not succeed as an actor, but he certainly punished himself severely before returning to his mother and father in Shelby. He then won credit as a legislator, a lawyer, and as a minister in a sequence of pulpits, only to turn away from each dissatisfied. Finally, in the late 1890s, he virtually deserted the church for lecturing and manorial life in Virginia. Still lecturing was not enough, and he went on to writing novels and plays. In his life he made three separate fortunes and lost each of them in speculative ventures.

In addition, Dixon taxed himself heavily to resist becoming the minister his father was. It is almost as if he spent the first twenty years of his life not becoming a minister, the next twenty years being a dissident and maverick minister, and the last twenty years fleeing from the ministry. In resisting a rather clear and strong paternal male model, Dixon no doubt suffered great pain. His antagonism toward Clarence might have sprung, in part, from the fact that Clarence did easily accept the role modeled by his father and succeeded in it so grandly, eventually becoming, practically the Southern Baptist apostle to Great Britain. In attacking Clarence, Tom was able, perhaps, to make a subtle attack on his father.

As an event in the life of Thomas Dixon, *The Leopard's Spots* was an attempt by him to achieve a psychic cure. As an event in race relations in the South, the book represented a great leap forward in the popular promotion of Radicalism. The conjunction was fortuitous. Dixon was a person who needed a devil, and Radicalism gave him that devil ready made. It remained only for him to turn the instrument to the special purpose of his own salvation.

In 1902 when Dixon sat down in his log cabin study behind Elmington Manor to write out his novel, Radicalism was gaining popularity and power. Indeed, at the very time that Dixon began writing, a constitutional convention was meeting in Richmond to decide whether or not to disfranchise the Negro. The delegates from the east, where Dixon lived, were vigorously, almost violently, in favor of the total disfranchisement of blacks, and that position reflected the racial feelings of their white constituents. Eastern Virginia in 1902 had fallen into the Radical hysteria.

By 1902 Dixon himself had come to something of an impasse in his life. He was thirty-eight, and he had not yet found himself. Outwardly, he was a highly successful man, but so were many others. His chance of making his special mark on the world, of doing something truly and historically grand was slipping away. He had searched in vain for a key to greatness. He had played at national and international politics, but had found no place to stand in order to move the world. Now his life was closing down to the comparatively little worlds of a shadow ministry, the lecture circuit, and the lord of Elmington Manor. Others might have relished life in those realms, but Tom Dixon was a driven man. Becoming a novelist was a way of breaking out yet again, of not closing down his chances for greatness in life, of keeping the game going, and of keeping what was probably a truly Napoleonic ambition alive.

The Leopard's Spots is Thomas Dixon. It is his life as seen by himself looking backward from the high ground of Radicalism in 1902. It is an impressionistic story, quickly and loosely drawn, very imperfect in historical detail, a mixture of fact and fancy, told very much like a patient on the psychiatric couch, trying for the first time to put his life into a single frame. The author was strangely ambivalent about his finished manuscript. He vacillated a few days and then impulsively mailed it to his friend Walter Hines Page in New York. He was obviously anxious about it, elated by its acceptance for publication, and deeply distressed by the first cover, which he saw only after publication. Rather than the tobacco plant he had wanted, it featured a hangman's noose. Dixon reacted instantly. He telegraphed his publishers to withdraw all copies at his expense. They dissuaded him, changed the cover, and Dixon, elated, entered his new career.

WHY THOMAS DIXON WROTE
THE LEOPARD'S SPOTS AND ITS SEQUELS

For Thomas Dixon, writing *The Leopard's Spots* was a sort of attenuated ink blot test. The image held up was the South in the nation after the Civil War. Into his interpretation of that image, Dixon poured a lifetime of emotion, and at least a dozen years of travel, observation, and brooding about himself and his society. Through it all, the characters are rearranged and moved to suit Dixon's own psychic needs. It was his fantasy life, his dream life, the life he felt he should have been living all along. The actual writing was a way of reliving his life as in retrospect he would have it.

Central to this psycho-play was the setting of himself aright in relation to his mother. Simultaneously, however, he set himself aright with the South. Under the circumstances, it is perfectly understandable that Dixon should have been distrubed by the unfortunate sex and child-bearing life of his mother and frustrated because social convention prevented his expressing his feelings against his father and grandmother as the persons most responsible. *The Leopard's Spots* functioned as a vehicle by which Dixon discharged a great store of aggressive potential, partially resolved his feelings of guilt, and repaid in some measure an imagined debt to his mother. As an attempt at psychic self-cure, it was a brilliant, disingenuous performance in which, in brief, Southern white maidenhood substituted for his mother, the black beast rapist was a surrogate for her never named violator, and the violator in the person of the black beast was horribly punished.

In the novel Dixon himself was primarily the young hero, Charles Gaston, but he was a part of other characters as well. Both he and his father merged to form the Reverend John Durham. There was no Clarence, and, indeed no brothers and sisters. The protagonist was an only child and, moreover, was quickly orphaned. There may be a Freudian slip of the pen in Dixon's creation of Allan McLeod, the white villian of the plot. Dixon seems also to have written himself, inadvertently, into this rather diabolical character, this black soul lurking within a white body. Finally, there are indications that Dixon identified himself sympathetically with Nelse, the faithful slave and servant of Charles's father, and, paradoxically, even with Dick, the black villain in the story. There is a special symmetry to the cast of five characters closest to Dixon himself. Two are white and two are black, and one was, in the language of the day, a "white nigger," a white person with black morals.[31]

Charles Gaston, the hero, is the single character most precisely Dixon himself. Charles's father is already dead when the novel began. It is left to Nelse, the faithful slave and servant to his father and living link with him to make interpretations of Colonel Gaston to the reader. It is the black man who brings home the "sword" of the father to be passed on to Charles by his mother. Once home, again it is Nelse who physically defends the family from marauding blacks. Nelse, having been the father's man, replaces the missing father in part, assisted by Charles. On one occasion Mrs. Gaston actually places the sword in his hand with instructions to use it to protect the family.[32]

Mrs. Gaston collapses at the news of her husband's death. Dixon makes Charles eight years old at that point, the same age Dixon makes himself in his fantasies about his mother's collapse. The sickroom scenes are pulled squarely from Dixon's experience with his mother. Young Charles nurses Mrs. Gaston exactly as Tom had nursed his mother—in the middle of the night. In real life Tom's father took the first watch, and Tom the second. In the novel Nelse would have taken the first watch but for Tom Camp's decision to stand that watch alone, and Charles takes the second. Each mother had periods of lucidity in which she told her son to go to bed. Also each mother suffered fits of delirium, but offered profoundly different performances. Mrs. Dixon complained bitterly about having been married to Tom's father before she became a woman.[33] At precisely the parallel point in the novel, Mrs. Gaston imagines that young Charles is his father and speaks to him as if he were her lover. "Dearie, I knew you would come," she murmurs. "How brown the sun has tanned your face, but it is just as handsome. I think handsomer than ever. And how like you is little Charles!" Where there had been resentment and hatred in real life, in fiction there is love.[34] In the fantasy within the fantasy, the son displaces his father and becomes the mother's true and gentle lover. He would do her no violence, of course, and, more, he would protect her from violence.

Charles's mother dies four years later, in part out of grief over the loss of his father, but in greater part because of the rising black menace. Mrs. Durham leads Charles tenderly away from the bedside. "She's done with suffering, Charles," she says. "You are going to live with me now, and let me love you and be your mother."[35] The orphan is then taken warmly into the home of the Reverend and Mrs. Durham who shape the man, the almost totally admirable man that is to be Charles Gaston. Mrs. Durham is a *childless* mother, having lost her only child, a son, during the war. Immediately after the birth of that child she had told her husband, "I didn't mind the pain, John, though I couldn't help the cries."[36] A mother ready-made, an over-flowing reservoir of maternal affection, a beautiful woman, and a flower of the Southern aristocracy, she lavishes attention upon this chosen son. Innately a noble lad, fully worthy of her loving care, Charles flourishes and blooms into a veritable Sir Galahad. In her wealthy slaveholding background Mrs. Durham was clearly modeled on the author's own mother. Thus, by this peculiar carnage of characters—Colonel Gaston, Mrs. Gaston, and the young son of Mrs. Durham—Dixon managed to give Charles Gaston a mother without that mother ever having to bear him. It was a weirdly immaculate conception, strangely needed.

Charles's adopted father, the Reverend Durham, a local Baptist minister like Dixon's real father, passes up a grand pulpit in Boston. Almost Christ-like he "throws his life away," as Dixon phrases it, to save his people in the South from blacks and Yankees. The Reverend Durham represents the spirit of the South, while Mrs. Durham represents its body, its flesh—a curious reversal of the Victorian order in which men are specially materialist and women are specially idealist. She bitterly resents the loss of her land and slaves in the war. Dixon, himself, had not sacrificed his life upon the altar of a Southern ministry, or had his brother Clarence. On the contrary, both opted for prestigious and well paying Northern pulpits. They had, in a sense, "sold out" to the North. However, Dixon lived through the Reverend Durham an idealized ministerial life for himself. Further, in real life, Dixon did redeem himself as a son of the South. In restoring Elmington Manor, in carrying to the nation the truth about the Negro, even in naming his beloved yacht "Dixie," Dixon was, in various ways, picking up the Southern cross again.

After the war, the Reverend Durham becomes so involved with caring for his flock and his community in the travail of Reconstruction that he neglects his wife. Mrs. Durham, partly in compensation, concentrated her energies upon improving the Christian qualities of the older boys in the neighborhood. "You know, I love boys," she reminds a friend.[37] Her special object becomes the white villain of the novel, Allan McLeod. Allan is a totally unprincipled opportunist, and a significant portion of his opportunism lies in the erotic realm. He is in 1865 a sturdy Southern country lad, intelligent, creative, and energetic, with superb powers of organization and leadership. Being totally without honor, as a man he becomes a Republican and in the 1890s uses the corrupt blacks and stupid Populists to seize control of the state. He is steadily opposed by his arch enemy the Reverend Durham who always works behind the political scenes, but with terrific moral power. Allan unsuccessfully woos

the heroine Sallie Worth, daughter of the general, but in the process of pressing his case with her he successfully slanders his rival for her favor, Charles
Gaston, with her father. Reacting to the rejection by Sallie, he attempts to
seduce the perfect mother, Mrs. Durham, a project he long had in mind. When
he was fifteen, and receiving much needed religious training at Mrs. Durham's
knee, Allan thought that the minister's wife had kissed him with a fervor that
was more than maternal. Dixon described one scene between the fifteen-year-
old boy and the thirty-two-year-old woman. "As they started toward the
door," he wrote, she gently slipped one arm around him, put her hand under
his chin and kissed him."[38] Years later, when Allan boldly attempts to seduce
her, she confesses her past temptation. But now she cooly rejects him. She has
seen "scientific" evidence that there are a number of men in the world whose
certain chemistry would draw her powerfully to them in a physical way. Realizing that sexual attraction was purely animal, she finds strength to refuse
Allan and shows him the door.[39]

Apparently Dixon was distrubed by the behavior of Allan McLeod and
found it necessary to explain his lack of morals. How could a Southern lad
like Allan, so attractive in so many ways, fall so far? The answer, said Dixon,
lay in a basic failure of the blood. Allan had a drunkard for a father, who
nevertheless, dies as a loyal soldier in General Worth's brigade, leaving his son
to the care of the general. More vitally, he had a slattern for a mother, a
woman who sprang from a band of outlaws, renegades, and half-breeds in
Robeson County, North Carolina. Dixon never made the point in his novel,
but Robeson County was widely known as the home of the Lumbee Indians.
The Lumbees were native Americans said to have intermarried with both
whites and blacks, sometimes free and sometimes runaway slaves. Thus, there
was a faint suggestion that Allan came from a people who suffered the most
fatal of flaws, a drop of black blood in the veins. That heritage revealed itself
in his behavior, political and sexual. Clearly the author did not intend that
Allan be taken as genetically black, but he did want the aura of blackness to
hover about him and it explained Allan's unbridled sensuality. Allan was, in
brief, a "white nigger."

It is possible that Allan represented Dixon's most physical—and sexual—
self, the self he fought to repress. Dixon's paternal grandfather drank to
excess, and because of it his father could not attend college. Conceivably
Dixon feared, either consciously or subconsciously, that he had inherited a
vital weakness that might lead him too to yield to passions of the flesh—in his
case not to drink, but to lust. Allan at fifteen is patterned upon the real life
"Hose" (for Hosea) Norman, a strapping, large, and earthy lad with whom
Dixon grew up on the farm in Cleveland County. When Dixon was eleven, he
went with Hose to visit two sisters, daughters of a tenant on his father's farm.
While Hose took each sister to bed, young Tom sat by the fire and talked crops

with the other.[40] If Allan is an imaginary construct for Dixon's more lusty self, the effect was a rather neat solution to Dixon's problems relating to his mother. Allan was the equal in talent and ambition of Charles and yet the opposite in virtue. Charles was morally white; Allan was morally black. Together they made a whole, a universe of good and evil that contained Tom Dixon. Through Allan, Dixon went all the way over to live vicariously on the other side of the moral spectrum. Allan attempts to make love to Mrs. Durham, the surrogate mother. Allan is the "white nigger," black in behavior if not in blood. Mrs. Durham understands the realities and rejects Allan. By undoing and defeating Allan in the story, Dixon symbolically undid and defeated the evil, the lust, that he sensed and greatly feared in himself. That feat seems to be overtly expressed in his second novel, *The One Woman* (1903). In that story Dixon has a flaming young Brooklyn Baptist minister (himself, perhaps in his brother's pulpit) seduced away from his family and his faith by an attractive, wealthy, socialist socialite. The seductress in this instance is a woman in her mid thirties, physically much like Mrs. Durham. The Brooklyn minister eventually rejects the flesh and regains his soul.[41] So too, after the reduction of Allan McLeod, there remained the beautiful, almost perfect person, Charles Gaston.

It was also possible that Dixon projected the lusty side of himself upon the black beast imagined by Radicalism. If Allan is blackness masked, then Dick is blackness unmasked and bluntly brutal. The affinity of Dixon for Dick is clear. The real-life Dick was adopted into the Dixon family when he was eight years old, after having been attacked by his father with an ax.[42] In the novel both Dick and Charles are eight when the war ends, and both are adopted by the Durhams. Didactically, the lesson ought to be that each had the same fine familial exposures, but that Dick turned out horribly. What the novel actually conveyed, however, was that Dick was not all bad. He has intelligence, a sense of self-respect, and most of all, the virtue of loyalty to Charles. That loyalty is returned. Even after Dick outrages little Flora, Charles tries desperately to save him from lynching. When they lynch Dick, in effect they lynch Charles too, and, by extension, Dixon. But, at another level, by the literary lynching of the black brute, Dixon destroys the would-be rapist of his mother. Symbolically, he has not deserted her or his duty, or the South.

Most of all what Dixon did in writing *The Leopard's Spots* was to get right with womanhood generally and with his mother specifically. Amanda (1834–1902) was precisely of that first generation in the South born to Romanticism, and she reared in Tom a perfect product of that age. A willing and eager son of the Victorian order, overtly he pedestalized women and worshipped at their feet. Like other Victorian men, Dixon needed to externalize good. Whatever they accomplished, they owed it to mothers and wives, to the women in their lives. Dixon came to lay a terrific burden upon women, especially Southern white women. He would make of them earthly goddesses. In one impassioned speech, Charles confesses: "Every woman is something divine to me. I think of God as a woman, not a man—a great loving Mother of all Life. If I ever saw the face of God it was in my mother's face."[43] In this way his service to God as a minister might have been equated with service to woman. His drift away from the ministry after about 1895 and toward lecturing and the making of money might have increased the need to do something for womanhood and to stand for a higher morality than the formal church allowed.

With the rise of the Radical mentality to feverish intensity in the late 1890s, it must have come to him that there was a new and important mission to be performed on earth, both for God and for woman. White women must be saved from the Negro beast. As white women were the angels of God on earth, black men were the terrestrial minions of the devil. Decent white men approach the pedestal slowly, bowing and dancing through the labyrinthian maze of Victorian language and etiquette that makes the eventual union legitimate. Black men, being savage and animal, attracted by the dazzling purity of white maidenhood, crash dumbly through the barriers, and, in seeking to possess the flower, crush and kill it. There was, indeed, a grand social task to be accomplished, a crusade to be fought to save a holy land. At this changing time of his life, Dixon needed a great cause. Southern white ladyhood at bay before the black beast gave him a cause, and Radicalism gave him an army.

In the novel, Charles Gaston finally won control of the state, with a single speech, a burst of oratorical brilliance that brought two thousand men to their feet, "screaming, shouting, cheering, shaking each other's hands, crying and laughing." Like the knight victorious in the tournament, he laid it all at the feet of his lady, Sallie, recently become his bride in spite of her father's opposition.

> "My love, my king!" she cried impulsively as he clasped her in his arms.
> "Your eyes kindled the fire in my soul and gave me the power to mould that
> crowd to my will!" he softly told her.
> "It is sweet to hear you say that!"

The dialogue was a perfectly Victorian play between the sexes. She charged him with mastery. He ascribed all power to her. She then affirmed his goodness in imputing primal power to her. Within a few minutes Charles concluded his part of the dialogue by doing what might be labeled the king-slave bit: "I may be the Governor," he declared with a cavalier flourish, "but I shall always be the slave of a beautiful woman"—namely Sallie.[44] At that moment in his life Charles Gaston came through for the South and thereby the nation, for the beast-besieged white women of the South, and for mother. Actually, the triumph was rather tardy. Charles was by then forty-three, a fact that Dixon, with his usual sublime and willful neglect of calendrical progression, did not

mention. Furthermore, the novel ended with the marriage still not consummated. Dixon had contrived to have the couple secretly wed while Charles was
unjustly lodged in jail, and the bride, of course, had to be spirited away immediately after the ceremony. To the very end, his favorite brides were saved
from sex—even with their husbands on their wedding nights.

Dixon was programmed for Radicalism. He was pre-set to see and eagerly
to use the black beast rapist for his own salvation, to make himself whole and
well-placed in the moral universe. He might have found other scapegoats,
other devils, He might have become violent against the new immigrants, Catholics, drink, or goldbugs. In later times he might have seen the devil in anti-
Semitism, or in Fascism or Communism. In still later times, he might even
have seen the beast in white racism and become, ironically, a liberal idolizing
blacks and damning Southern whites as devils incarnate. In emotional terms,
Tom Dixon was a loaded gun, cocked, and ready to fire in any direction. But
popular Radicalism offered him precisely the devil he needed when he needed
it, the black satyr, the beast with cloven hoof, a scape*goat,* and Dixon quickly
embraced the idea and made it his own.

As Flora's outrage gave Charles new insight into the problems and prospects of black retrogression, so too did the mass outrages and lynchings in the
turn-of-the-century South give Dixon his ultimate personal enlightenment.
Symbolically, Annie Camp represented those women, and she was also Dixon's
mother on the eve of her marriage to his father. Annie was saved from rape
by a squad of black soldiers only by being shot to death by the men in her life.
Moreover, she was saved from sex altogether. Indeed, her body was taken
directly to the very nuptial couch upon which the marriage was to have been
consummated that evening. "Just where the blue veins crossed in her delicate
temple there was a round hole from which a scarlet stream was running down
her white throat." Tom consoled his wife, "Don't cry so Annie! It might have
been worse. Let us thank God she was saved from them brutes." Incidentally,
Tom might have added, she was saved from sex with her husband. If Annie
was mother, then mother remained a virgin until death. The child bride never
had sexual relations, and therefore could never have been outraged. "There
are," indeed, "things worse than death!"[45]

Flora Camp might also be Dixon's mother as a child, and this second incar-
nation *was* violated. It was almost as if Dixon could not bring himself to the
atrocity committed at the first attempt, even in fiction. He preferred having
the character killed by her friends. But the outrage, when it finally came, as
come it must, was of the most horrible kind. Annie has been sixteen and a
woman, Flora was only eleven and clearly a child. It was very significant that
Flora's profuse bleeding from a broken artery was in the temple where Dick
had struck Flora with a stone. Dixon related the broken artery to the sexual
assault. "Flooding," it will be remembered, had caused his mother's collapse.

It was bleeding that "the doctor was unable to stop."[46] In the novel local physicians are, at first, more effective. Charles Gaston, himself, eagerly donates his blood for a transfusion to save Flora's life[47] Ultimately, Flora bleeds to death, but clearly Gaston is blameless. She dies, not because the physicians could not save her, nor even because the men in her life fail her, but because she could not escape the memory of her violation. It is the black beast rapist who kills Flora, and not by the physical abuse of the assault, awful as it is, but rather by the spiritual violation, the violation of her purity. To live with that ineluctable memory is a fate worse then death.

Thomas Dixon's mother was out of the plantation aristocracy in upcountry South Carolina. She was a Presbyterian, and, presumably, thirteen years old when she first experienced sex. Annie and Flora did not share that history with Amanda Dixon. They were "poor whites" from North Carolina, Baptists, and sixteen and eleven at the crucial moment. In his literary productions over the next three years, Dixon moved closer and closer to his mother in characterizing the girls who would either suffer outrage by the black beast or avoid it by achieving death first. *The Clansman,* his second novel on Reconstruction, replayed the same grand themes exhibited in the *The Leopard's Spots.* He wrote the manuscript in thirty days in 1905 after sifting through more than five thousand books and pamphlets. Within a few months *The Clansman* sold more than a million copies.[48]

Annie and Flora in *The Leopard's Spots* became, in *The Clansman,* Marian Lenoir, a sixteen-year-old beauty rapidly ripening into ideal womanhood. Marian, identically with Dixon's mother, is born of a well-to-do slaveholding family in piedmont South Carolina. Marian, again like Dixon's mother, is a Presbyterian. One night in the very depths of the Reconstruction era, four Negro militiamen burst into the house, tie Marian's mother, Jeannie, to the bedpost, and assault Marian. At three in the morning, the girl recovers consciousness and revives her mother. They agree that suicide is the only honorable way out. They put the house in perfect order, attempting to destroy every trace of the crime and protect Marian's reputation for purity. As dawn approaches, they hasten to "lover's leap," hand in hand. The mother hesitates, saying that they might flee to a strange land and make a new life. "We could not escape ourselves!" responds the young woman. "The thought of life is torture. Only those who hate me could wish that I live. The grave will be soft and cool, the light of day a burning shame." Again, we are told that there are some things worse than death. The mother assents to this pristine wisdom and, still hand in hand, just at the first light of dawn, the two women hurl themselves over the cliff to their deaths.[49] Ben Cameron, the hero, finds the bodies. Marian's "fair blonde head lay in a crimson circle sharply defined in the white sand." But the culprits are discovered. One of Dixon's heroes, whom he describes as a true Southern scholar of science, has learned that dead people hold upon their retinae the last image vividly seen in life. The girl, he discoveres was too young to have developed the force necessary to hold the image. But Jeannie, at thirty-seven, "the full-blown perfection of womanhood with every vital force at its highest tension," captured her last strong impression and held it through death. Looking into his microscope, the doctor sees what she last saw. He describes the picture to Ben. "The bestial figure of a negro—his huge black hand plainly defined—the upper part of the face is dim as if obscured by a gray mist of dawn—but the massive jaws and lips are clear—merciful God!—yes!—it's Gus!" As one might guess, Gus is lynched.[50]

Dixon reworked *The Clansman* into a play in the same year, 1905, in which it was published. In the stage version, Marian Lenoir becomes Flora Cameron. Flora is a piedmont South Carolinian of the planter aristocracy, presumably a Presbyterian, and—at last!—thirteen years of age. Flora Cameron filled perfectly the profile of Amanda McAfee at the time of her marriage. In the play, Flora is killed indirectly by Gus. Fleeing through the woods from his relentless pursuit and finally cornered, she leaps over a cliff to her death rather than suffer outrage. Once again, Dixon's heroine chooses death before dishonor. Perhaps, this comparatively quiet exit for Flora in the play was a concession by Dixon to the delicacy of audiences as yet unaccustomed to rape scenes on the stage. Or, perhaps Flora Cameron was too close to Amanda McAfee, and the author too involved with this character to bring her to the awful end. In either event, the play ended with a typically Dixonian supermelodramatic catharsis. The Klan lynches Gus, drags his body across the stage, and then gathers silently—hoods, live horses, and all—around an actually flaming cross, local fire departments to the contrary notwithstanding.[51]

It would make a neatly happy ending if we could say that Dixon emerged from this literary slaughterhouse fully cured. In truth, it does seem that he was more at ease with himself for a time after 1902. He seemed to "take a new hold on life," much as he had when he first decided to join the ministry. Inevitably, the very creation of *The Leopard's Spots* pressed the author to define himself. In brief, in creating his book, Dixon brought himself together again for a time, and he did so in a way that gave value to himself in his own mind. Ironically, Amanda died within a year after *The Leopard's Spots* was published. Dixon, busy on the lecture circuits in the southwest and with the success of his first novel, could not attend the funeral. Instead, his wife represented him on that occasion.[52] It was almost as if Dixon could now feel sufficiently free to let Amanda gracefully go. In 1903 he published *The One Woman* and dedicated the book to his mother, "to whose Scotch love of romantic literature I owe the heritage of eternal youth."[53] Thereafter, it is increasingly difficult to find the real Dixon in his novels. It was almost as if the characters in his early work had had lives of their own and would do what they would do once put in motion; later characters were Dixon's creatures to command.

In 1905 the play *The Clansman* had its premiere in Norfolk, Virginia. Dixon joined the first road tour of the play to offer, from the stage at the conclusion of each performance, a talk explaining his work. In Norfolk, in the heart of black belt Virginia, the play and the speech were enthusiastically received. At the next performance, in Richmond, it was also loudly applauded, but conservative newspapers were critical of its extreme racism. The company performed throughout Southern and Midwestern America and, while it drew conservative fire rather steadily, it was clearly a popular success. Toward the end of the year Dixon returned to New York to organize another company to play *The Clansman*. Early in 1906 he brought his play home to Shelby, where, of course, it received a tremendous ovation. However, there was at least one dissenter. His father thought that "once or twice you bore down a little too hard on the Negro. He wasn't to blame for the Reconstruction." Tom answered that he had tried to make that point, but the elder Dixon responded, "I wish you had made it a little plainer. You couldn't make it too strong."[54] That probably was the cruelest cut of all. When Clarence had written very critically of the inflammatory quality of *The Leopard's Spots* four years before, Tom had answered with verve and heavy sarcasm. "I assure you I cherish no hard feelings toward you," he began, "I've quite made up my mind always to love you as my 'big brother' in spite of your hideous theology." However, he admitted that he was a bit hurt by Clarence's accusation that he wrote the thing for money. He did do it for money, he said, but only in the sense that Clarence preached for money. To a charge from his brother that he had been neglecting family prayers, he replied that "I don't have family prayers." "I confess," he continued, "that as I grow older, those things bore me more and more—all *formalism* does."[55]

Both companies of *The Clansman* continued to circulate through America during the next several years, and Dixon came to the idea that he might after all succeed in the world of the theater, one of his first great passions. In 1907 he turned *The One Woman* into a successful play, as he did two of his later books, *The Traitor* (1907) and *The Sins of the Father*. The last opened in Wilmington, North Carolina, in 1910. After the performance, the cast decided to go bathing at Wrightsville Beach, the scene of Tom's earlier enlightenment, with the result that a passing shark chanced to eat the leading man. Who then was to play the part of the hero suddenly vacated by the collision of the unfortunate actor and hungry fish? Tom Dixon, of course. Thus it was that Dixon's great ambition to be an actor was fulfilled. During the next forty weeks he traveled and acted the hero in his own play, and then, tiring of the provinces, he returned to New York for more ambitious roles.[56]

Meanwhile, in 1905 Dixon had moved his home from Elmington Manor back to New York to a mansion on Riverside Drive. Over the next several years he worked as a novelist, producer, playwright, director, sometimes actor, and financier. He lost a fortune speculating in cotton futures and in the stock market crash of 1907. However, he quickly amassed another fortune through a steady large stream of productivity.[57]

In 1912 Dixon attempted to translate *The Clansman* into a motion picture but failed. In 1913 he sold the film rights to a company in which David W. Griffith proved to be the cinematic genius. The price was 25 percent of whatever profits the company might make. In a few weeks of intensive labor, Dixon helped produce a script that Griffith took, with other materials, to Los Angeles to make the film. The story in the movie was basically that of the novel, with touches added from other pieces of his fiction. The magnificent artistry of the film is clearly Griffith's but, no less clearly the story is essentially Thomas Dixon's.

In February 1915, Dixon went to a theater in New York to preview the film version of *The Clansman*. Before that production, moving pictures in America had been short and rarely rose above the burlesque. Griffith not only made the first lengthy film developing a full story line, he was also the first to use the montage, the iris (circular) frame, the dissolve, and the close-up. He also made full and imaginative use of music. Performed by an orchestra in each theater where the production was shown, some of the music for the motion picture was adapted from black folksongs, but much of it was Wagnerian, taken from *Die Walküre* and *Rienzi,* as well as Bellini's *Norma.* In one dramatic sequence, the Klan rode to the super-masculine pounding of "In the Hall of Mountain King."

The experts had predicted failure for the film, and the showing in New York was a desperate attempt to enlist the support of the few score influential theater people invited. Dixon, fearing the worst, retreated to the balcony with the intention of slipping quietly away afterward.

After the showing, with grave misgivings as to the reactions of the others, Dixon came cautiously down the stairs. In the lobby, he found an excited, bubbling enthusiastic crowd. Suddenly elated, he saw Griffith across the room. "This is bigger than *The Clansman,*" he shouted to the director. It deserved a better name! The better name was *The Birth of a Nation.*[58] It was not merely superb showmanship that led to that better name. In Dixon's mind, birth, sex, and blood, life, soul, and nation were all intimately and intricately linked, and that rather sanguinary net held the core of being. The birth of a nation was the very heart of what Dixon had been talking about since 1902, and, more, it was his life. Up in the balcony, he had again just saved a larger than life American white woman from the monstrous black beast. He had saved a whole nation of people from division and racial damnation and given them life. With all of that, he had redeemed himself anew. He was transported, ecstatic. It is ironic that *The Birth of a Nation,* a film that did make history, was, in its origin, simply the birth of Tom Dixon.

Using his personal friendship with Woodrow Wilson, Dixon arranged, early in 1915, for *The Birth of a Nation* to be viewed by the President, his cabinet and their families in the East Room of the White House. Afterward, President Wilson made the totally apt remark that the film "was like writing history with lightning." Unfortunately, he added his opinion that "it is all so terribly true."[59] On the very next evening, Dixon set up a special showing for the justices of the Supreme Court and invited members of Congress, Chief Justice Edward Douglass White having been a Klansman in his youth. The film had been under heavy fire for its racist content, but with these seeming endorsements arranged by Dixon it entered a very vigorous early life.

In 1915 Dixon moved to Los Angeles where he established his own film company. As a film-maker, however, he realized no striking success. Five years later he returned to New York and continued his career as a writer. By now both his ideas and his style were dated, and his popularity quickly faded. Even so, during the 1920s he was still a wealthy man. Late in the decade he conceived the idea of developing an elaborate resort near Asheville, North Carolina. He had begun construction and was heavily invested when the crash of 1929 destroyed the project and with it the last of Dixon's fortunes. In the 1930s his health broke, and, after a lingering illness, he died in 1946.[60]

Dixon died, but *The Birth of a Nation* lived on, a monument without inscription. Never without opposition, it was nevertheless tremendously popular. In attendance, it was not surpassed until the film *Gone with the Wind* appeared in 1939. In recent times, very few Americans recognize the name of Thomas Dixon. On the other hand, very few would not recognize at least vaguely the title *The Birth of a Nation,* and many would know something of its racial meaning. Moreover, the film has experienced recurrent revivals, lamentably in part because those revivals mirror the fact that Dixon's world is not yet dead in America. It seems apparent that whatever Dixon did for himself in creating the story in the film, he gave a significant portion of white America precisely what it wanted. Unwittingly, he told a story deeper than he ever imagined, a story about sex and race.

OTHER RADICAL LEADERS

Even today it remains difficult to imagine that a vast part of the leadership in the turn-of-the-century South could actually have embraced the Radical mentality. Contemporary Conservatives tried to ignore Radicalism, hoping that with time it would go away. Later, Southern liberals and historians tried to dismiss manifestations of Radicalism as aberrations, extravagances incidental to economic and political machinations and unworthy in themselves of serious attention. Along with the studied neglect of Radicalism and its effects there went a studied neglect of those who espoused the doctrine. For years the tendency has been to dismiss Radicalism as the work of a scattering of mavericks, maniacs, and demagogues of lowly origins and to recognize the Radical ideas of some otherwise admirable leading men and women with the apology that they were odd in that single way, or that years of frustration in the good causes finally drove them forgivably mad. But the truly surprising thing is that Radicals and Radicalism can be found in every Southern state, and that, far from being mavericks, madmen, and malefactors drawn from the dregs of society, the leaders of the Radical movement were the ordinary leaders in their communities and, as such, largely representative of the hearts and minds of their people.

Liberal Northerners, who were much more keenly aware of these people during those turn-of-the-century years than we have since been, easily identified Ben Tillman, Rebecca Felton, Thomas Dixon, and James K. Vardaman as Radicals. But the list may be expanded to include other highly respectable persons. In Virginia, as we have seen, Philip Alexander Bruce was a pioneer Radical. One might also point to Paul B. Barringer, from 1896 to 1903 eminent as chairman of the faculty of the University of Virginia, and afterward a founding president of Virginia Polytechnic Institute; Alfred P. Thom, a highly successful Norfolk railroad attorney, represented Radicalism in the disfranchising convention of 1901–1902; and John Skelton Williams, founder of the Seaboard Air Line Railway.

In North Carolina, the Radicals included such eminent persons as Furnifold M. Simmons of New Bern. Simmons master-minded the machine that ran the Democratic party through the white supremacy campaigns of 1898 and 1900. He inherited all the power and prestige that accrued to the party by those campaigns, and became a very senior United States Senator and co-sponsor of the Underwood-Simmons Tariff Act of 1913. Also a leading Radical was Alfred Moore Waddell, a direct descendant of three Revolutionary War generals, an 1853 graduate of the University of North Carolina, publisher of the *Wilmington Herald,* a Whig, a unionist, a congressman, and, for a time, Lieutenant Colonel of the 41st N.C. Regiment. Francis D. Winston, a lawyer and district attorney from Windsor, was typical of the local aristocrat as Radical. During the campaign of 1898, he organized "White Supremacy" clubs in the black counties and made "incendiary" speeches. Also from Windsor was George Tayloe Winston, one of the minor theorists of Radicalism. He was successively the president of the University of North Carolina, the University of Texas, and, after 1899, the North Carolina College of Agricultural and Mechanic Arts in Raleigh (North Carolina State University). His brother,

Robert Watson Winston, wrote a praiseful biography of President Andrew Johnson, another native North Carolinian with strong and adverse opinions about black people.

In South Carolina, most of Tillman's lieutenants were Radicals, including significantly his successors as governor, John Gary Evans and Cole Blease. The latter became a bitter rival of Tillman and in later years an extravagant racist. In Georgia, Rebecca Felton was joined by a veritable host of state leaders. Two of the most eminent were the Atlanta journalists John Temple Graves and James R. Gray. During the campaign of 1906, Hoke Smith, Thomas Watson, and Clark Howell vied with one another for highest marks in racial extremism. In the affairs of the Baptist church, Leonidas F. Scott was a leading Radical and, after 1905, the chairman of the Board of Domestic Missions for the Southern Baptists. In Alabama, Radicalism embraced such diverse types as "Bourbon" Senator John Tyler Morgan and the recently risen Senator Tom Heflin. In Mississippi, Vardaman came into power late but, before he died, his state was thoroughly and deeply Radicalized, perhaps more so than any other. When he assumed the governor's chair in 1904, he declared that the Negro was "one-third more criminal in 1890 than he was in 1880." Neatly, he encapsulated the matured Radical view of race relations: "You can scarcely pick up a newspaper whose pages are not blackened with the account of an unmentionable crime committed by a negro brute, and this crime, I want to impress upon you, is but the manifestation of the negro's aspiration for social equality, encouraged largely by the character of free education in vogue."[61] In every Southern state there were greater or lesser reflections of that thinking among eminent persons.

In addition to these leaders, who might be called persisting Radicals, there were others who fell for a time, usually during some state-wide rage of Radicalism, out of the Conservative bottom and into the Radical range. These temporary Radicals were relatively few in number and usually resided in the upper South. Thomas Nelson Page, the most popular (and the most successful—financially, socially, and influentially) of Virginia's postwar novelists, exemplified the process. During most of his life Page was the personification as well as the propagandist of the image of the white man as patrician and paternalist. Yet by 1904 he had deserted the concept of the Negro as a devoted child so often illustrated in his novels, and acknowledged him as the ravishing beast. Page added nothing new to the thinking of Radicalism, but he certainly enhanced its respectability by adding to it his own, and he gave it broad dissemination by his articles, which, as always, were widely read and commented upon. "Time was when the crime of assault was unknown throughout the South," he wrote in his usual even and elegant style. Then Reconstruction began. "This was followed by a number of cases where members of the negro militia ravished white women; in some instances in the presence of their families." As the "New Issue" of blacks matured, the rapists dared more and more. The white resort to lynching was the only effective alternative, he insisted, and it was perfectly natural in the circumstances.[62]

Interestingly, both Page's and Dixon's impressions that "members of the negro militia ravished white women; in some instances in the presence of their families" apparently arose from two events that occurred in Arkansas during Reconstruction. In one case a black militiaman assaulted a white woman while his companions robbed her house, and in another case two white women were assaulted by four militiamen. Both of these happened during the so-called "Brooks–Baxter War" in which the Republican state administration used the militia, white and black, to crush the Klan. During the mid-1890s many Southerners were reminded of the "War" by John M. Harrell's book, *The Brooks and Baxter War: A History of the Reconstruction Period in Arkansas,* published in 1893. Later accounts omitted the highly significant fact that all five men were convicted by courts-martial and shot, the latter four by an all-black firing squad. Yet, even the most severe critic of the black militia at the time of its existence, the Memphis *Appeal,* in its coverage of the case, did not mention rape as being one of the offenses committed. Instead it reported the crimes as those of murder and robbery.[63]

Not all Radical leaders found it wise to announce their personal eschatology of things racial. If one believed that blacks were rapidly retrogressing and becoming beasts, if one thought that now and again race war would be necessary, that eventually there would be no place in America for the black man, and that he was bound to dissolve and disappear, then it might be best not to alert Negroes to the awful end of coming events and better not to drive them to desperation. In fact, some of the more cautious or sensitive Radicals probably dissembled in the face of black people, like the young man who assures the octogenarian that he looks well and will live forever. But the unguarded utterances and actions of some public figures imply that, at least for a time in their lives, they turned into the path of Radicalism. Among these were: Albert Sydney Burleson, Wilson's Postmaster General; David F. Houston, his Secretary of Agriculture; and Josephus Daniels, owner and editor of the Raleigh *News and Observer,* the journalistic strongback in the white supremacy campaigns in North Carolina, and later Secretary of the Navy under Wilson.

Radicals, then, were not mavericks and Radicalism not an aberration. In spite of the horror with which we might now view those racial beliefs, they were an understandable and integral part of Southern culture in the turn-of-the-century years. To dismiss these people or that aspect of their lives as atypical is to miss a necessary key to understanding race relations in twentieth-century America. Unless we understand their feelings and behavior in this phase we can never understand their children, or ourselves.

CHAPTER VI

In Violence Veritas

Thus far we have talked about Radicalism in terms of leadership. Now let us begin to consider Radicalism at the popular level. There were an infinite number of ways in which Radicalism manifested its presence among the white masses, but easily the most visible was the syndrome of violence. In these encounters whites revealed their racial feelings with a fullness and a veracity that they did not always exhibit otherwise. Often in life the Latin phrase "in vino veritas" is apt; in race relations in the South "in violence veritas" is more than apt.

POPULAR RADICALISM

Radicalism was, of course, politics, economics, religion, and everything else, but it was in a major way a phenomenon in social psychology. For instance, it was not primarily for political, economic, religious, class, geographic, or philosophical reasons that Thomas Dixon became a Radical and wrote the deeply racist diatribe that is *The Leopard's Spots*. It was rather because his own personal psychology required that act—or some such act. The array of human qualities that drove Dixon so forcibly toward Radicalism doubtlessly thrust thousands of other white Southerners with similar psychological needs into the same path. Many of these men and women had been children during the Civil War when great numbers of fathers left home for the war and many never returned, when starvation became a real possibility, and powerlessness in the face of a despicable enemy was risingly the rule. Moreover, these people, like Tom Dixon, were the children of a Reconstruction in which all of these things persisted in some degree, and to which was added the menace of the freed slave, presumably ready for a vengeance that matched the cruelty suffered in slavery. In retrospect, it seems not so strange that the adult of later life should be forced to pay some tax for the sad plight of himself as a child, and that these children as adults should seek and find around 1900 a long-needed fulfillment in imagining a North that no longer threatened from abroad and in the discovery of a formidable enemy at home who, by an exercise of will, could be lynched and killed. In 1900 Southern whites of the middle generation might well feel that they had regained, at last a power over their lives and persons that their fathers and mothers had lost.

At the mass level, it was as if Radicalism were a current of thinking joining with currents of Conservatism and Liberalism to form a large stream of racial thinking flowing like a river through time in the composite mind of the white South. With a great rush and turbulence, Radicalism, after 1889, pressed down into the mainstream, swelling its volume and speeding its flow. During its high time, between 1897 and 1907, Radicalism was a very broad current in the whole of white racial thought in the South, and it stood out in sharp distinction from the remainder of that stream. If one could quantify popular thinking, if one could somehow weigh for duration and intensity every thought about blacks that passed through every white mind in the South between 1897 and 1907, most of those thoughts would have reflected the Radical mentality, and hence Radicalism would have outweighed Conservatism. Possibly those dates might be extended backward into 1889 and forward into 1915 without tipping the scales in the opposite direction. After 1907, however, the current of Radicalism began to lose its distinctive color as it mixed and flowed with the whole stream. By the end of 1915 it was lost from sight. It ceased to be a separate current, and Radicalism as a mentality, as a thought-set, died. The river was now again essentially Conservative, flowing smooth and wide, the father of Southern racial waters. Subsequently, Radicalism was all but forgotten. Still, its parts had mixed thoroughly with the whole stream, giving it a new complexion and a different constitution from any that had gone before. Radicalism changed the nature of race relations in the South in a physical way. But even more important it changed them in a ideational way. Finally, it was, as we shall see, a vital part of a drastic change in the whole broad course of Southern culture.

As popular thought, Radicalism was distinctly a black belt phenomenon. Its major geographical outlines can be described accurately enough in terms of racial ratios. Whites in areas one-third or more black tended to be Radicalized. When the proportion of blacks rose above the two-thirds mark, Radicalism continued to prevail as thought, and perhaps, even became more intense, but it seemed in these areas to be slightly less vociferous, less physical, and less overtly violent in its manifestations.

Radicalism was also marked by the way in which state boundaries fell across the black belts. In 1890 in South Carolina, Georgia, Alabama, Mississippi, and Louisiana, blacks outnumbered whites 3,528,000 to 3,377,000. In these five contiguous lower South states, where the proportion of Negroes to whites ran highest, Radicalism tended to dominate white thinking throughout each state. Radicalism, then, prevailed in the hill counties where whites might outnumber blacks ten to one, and it also ruled racial matters in the lower, "piney woods," swampy, and "wiregrass" counties where blacks were not numerous. Official and unofficial institutions in these states—educational, judicial, penal, political, economic, and religious—came to be informed by the Radical persuasion. To be a Mississippian or a South Carolinian was ipso facto to be a Radical or else to be alone in one's racial views. In the deep South, where the power lines of traditional statehood encompassed the great mass of black Americans, lay the heartland of Radicalism.

There were also Radical areas in what might be called the "white-belt" states, those lying generally north and west of the deep South. These areas contained a high proportion of blacks in the population. As might be expected, it was in these areas that slaves had been most numerous in the antebellum period. These included eastern Texas, eastern Arkansas, western Tennessee, and, in Kentucky, regions centering on Louisville and Lexington (the bluegrass country). In the east, Radicalism also prevailed in northern Florida, in the eastern portions of North Carolina, Virginia, and Maryland, and up into southern Delaware. Oklahoma, with its mixture of Indians, Negroes, Kansas Yankees, and deep South Southerners, was a special case. But there too Radicalism was rampant in the "little Dixie" section in the southeastern part of the state.

The habitats of racial mentalities coincided with racial ratios, but one might also think of race relations in this time in ecological terms. In the 1880s there was a relative stability in the interracial environment, both in the actual physical relationships between blacks and whites and in the thoughts that persons of each color had about the other. The balance was only slightly distrubed by the Liberal revolt. In and after 1889, a new organism, Radicalism, appeared. Whenever white encountered black, in body or in mind, Radicalism strove to dominate that contact, to feed upon it. As Radicalism grew rapidly stronger it engrossed the available food supply. Every thought, every act in race relations tended to become Radical. Other organisms, other patterns of interracial thought, conservative or liberal, deprived of food, withered and wasted away. Once Radicalism won dominance in the social ecosphere, it jealously denied the breath of life to any alternative. Thus, the racial ecologies of the black belts of the South were profoundly altered. Where Radicalism lived, it throve; and it ruled with force and fire. But it did need a special kind of food to survive—the vision of the menacing black male. When that image was lost to white minds, Radicalism perished.

For Radicals, the "Negro problem" was how to control the blacks as they passed through bestiality and into extinction. Radicals often saw the solution as a two-sided effort in education. Negroes must be throughly educated to the rule of white supremacy, and the great mass of whites must be brought to an active understanding of the true nature of racial affairs. All too often blacks could only learn by force. That, after all, was the nature of the beast. The ultimate test of racial intelligence among the mass of whites, then, was their readiness to do violence upon black men—to do with deliberate speed the swift and certain violence of rushing the black monsters to their awful end whenever needed. In the Radical years, white violence assumed two essentially new and highly significant styles: lynching and rioting.

LYNCHING

The lynching of Negroes by whites in the South has indeed had a strange career. During slavery, Negroes had been lynched, especially after about 1830. But, even then, it was not at all common, and lynching was by no means reserved for blacks. In Reconstruction there were assaults by gangs of whites upon Negroes as individuals, but the pattern differed from what came later. These early attacks were often in response to trivial abuses—an alleged breach of contract, a verbal insult, a push on the sidewalk, or the display of weapons—and rape or the threat of rape played no extraordinary role. Further, white vengeance, even at the height of Ku Klux activities, was often satisfied with whippings that were graded in severity more or less to match the seriousness of the alleged offense. Atrocious as such punishments were, they stopped short of murder. Negroes were killed by whites in Reconstruction, but when this happened, they were usually shot to death instantly, without torture, without ceremony, and because they happened to be black, not because of some alleged individual transgression. It is interesting that the ubiquitous punishment of slavery, whipping, persisted through Reconstruction. It was almost as if white men reared under the peculiar institution were incapable of innovation in doing physical harm to blacks. The ultimate in studied violence against black people, death by lynching, had to wait for a new generation of young whites to grow to adulthood. Like the "new Negro," perhaps the "new whites" had not enjoyed the "civilizing" effects of slavery. Radicals did not feature blacks as children, of course, and certainly not as their children. In Radical eyes, whipping for blacks was not the ultimate punishment.

For a generation after the Civil War, Southern whites seemed to have no greater fear of black men as rapists than they had of white men committing the same crime. What they did fear, and feared immensely during the first few years after emancipation, was black insurrection, a massive and horrendous upheaval in which vast numbers of whites—men, women, and children—would suffer and die from the black rage.[1] With the rise of Radicalism came the new fear, the fear of the Negro as rapist. With both came interracial violence in a distinctly different mode from any that had gone before. Whites began the practice of lynching as a reaction against the presumed threat of the black beast to white womanhood, but it soon became an appalling habit, applicable to a wide range of offenses, real or imagined.

One of the most striking aspects about the lynching phenomenon was, as we have seen, the suddenness of its appearance in and after 1889 as a distinctly interracial happening in the South. In 1888 there was little indication that in the following year the hysteria would be sweeping through the black belts of the South. Witness, for example, the personal transformation of Marion Butler. Butler, as mentioned before, became the chairman of the national executive committee of the Populist party in the 1890s. In 1889 he was a recent graduate of the University of North Carolina and had become the editor of the Clinton (Sampson County) *Caucasian.* Sampson County was significantly black, with more than one-third of its population Negro. The *Caucasian* itself, as its name suggested and its banner line candidly declared, was devoted to the cause of white supremacy. But the white supremacy to which it referred was that special style that ended Reconstruction. By 1889 that style of racism was rapidly becoming antique, like the Bourbons who represented it in the nation's capital. However, in Sampson County in that crucial year, Butler's own editorials began to add a sharp new cutting edge to the traditional racial sword. In September, he recommended to his readers Nathaniel S. Shaler's thinking on the Negro. "Prof. Shaler (of 'Cambridge')," he said, "considered that the negro was elevated under the conditions of slavery and he [is] losing that elevation under the experiment of citizenship—sinking back to the conditions of barbaric Africa. Prof. Shaler is the author of the new and probably correct theory for explaining the unprogressivism of the negro, namely that his animal nature so preponderates over his intellectual and moral natures, that in the age of puberty, when the animal nature developes, that the moral and intellectual qualities are clouded by the animal instinct and not only cease to develop but really retrograde."[2] A month later Butler was still able to respond to a lynching in a piedmont county by asking for action "to prevent further taking of human life in the barbarous manner in our State. . . ."[3] But two years afterward, an alleged rape by a Negro man of a fifty-five-year-old white woman in his own county brought on what was by then the all too usual lynching and a radically different response from Butler. "This is the first lynching that has occurred in Sampson County within our remembrance," declared the thirty-one-year-old editor, "and though a dangerous precedent, is justified by public sentiment, if not by law. A more fiendish deed has not been attempted in our community in many years."[4]

It is astounding how quickly respectable, intelligent, educated, and leading Southerners turned to support lynching on the basis of the Radical rationale.

Butler, whose origins and education would seem to predict an orthodox, conservative view of blacks, executed a perfect about-face within two years. Governor Tillman, as we have seen, turned from a pronouncement in September 1891 that lynching would not be tolerated to a promise in the summer of 1892 that he would himself lead a mob to lynch a rapist.

As Radicalism seized the leaders, so, too, did it seize the masses. In the 1890s in fourteen Southern states, an average of 138 persons was lynched each year and roughly 75 percent of the victims were black. From 1900 to 1909, the number of lynchings declined by half, but Negroes were 90 percent of those lynched and the lower South remained its special scene. Between 1885 and 1907 there were more persons lynched in the United States than were legally executed, and in the year 1892 twice as many.

Still the statistics reflect only imperfectly the intense heat of white sentiment on the subject. Frederick Hoffman's account (1896) of the wave of lynching was one of the first that presumed to thoroughness and scholarly objectivity. His work was widely cited, but, as he candidly admitted, it was drawn from popular sources and was not nearly all inclusive.[5]

The cold statistics hardly begin to capture the emotional heat generated by the crisis of sex and race in the South in the early 1890s. If rapes had risen in the last few years from practically none to some fearsome number over a hundred each month, as some well-informed contemporaries thought, what was to be expected in the future? If intelligent and informed persons could believe these things, what could minds less sophisticated believe? Clearly, something drastic would have to be done, and done soon.

It is small wonder, then, that lynching increased in the South and very shortly became a regional ritual. By 1893 lynch mobs were already performing much as if their members had attended formal schools on procedures. Witness the ritual in the burning of Henry Smith in February of that year in Paris, Texas, a small town in the richly agricultural northeastern portion of the state. Smith had been accused of having raped, "with demonical cruelty," little Myrtle Vance, aged three years, eight months, and a day. By Bishop Haygood's account, after the sexual assault, the monster took the child by the heels and literally tore her asunder "in the wantonness of gorilla ferocity."[6]

Horrible was the crime, and horrible would be the punishment. For four days 2,000 men combed the countryside in search of the alleged murderer. Finally, law officers apprehended Smith in a neighboring county, and he was brought back to Paris by train. As he stepped down from the cars, thousands of waiting people cheered. By prearrangement, a "cotton float," a huge platform wagon used for hauling cotton, was brought up. Upon it was a large box, and upon the box was fixed a chair. Smith was tied to the chair. The wagon was driven to Paris, where it circled the square in the center of town so that a great crowd of people could observe the monster. Then it moved out into the open country to a place where a platform had been erected some ten feet above the ground. There, about 10,000 people had gathered. Special trains had brought in hundreds of spectators and, according to one informant, "Fathers, men of social and business standing, took their children to teach them how to dispose of negro criminals. Mothers were there too, even women whose culture entitles them to be among the social and intellectual leaders of the town."

The father of the murdered child mounted the platform and asked for quiet while he took his revenge. He promised that when he had finished he would surrender the fiend to any who cared to punish him further. The wagon arrived and Smith was hoisted to the platform. He was bound securely to a stake that ran from the ground, through the platform, and head-high above. "A tinner's furnace was brought on filled with irons heated white. Taking one, Vance thrust it under first one then the other side of the victim's feet, who helpless, writhed, and the flesh seared and peeled from the bones. . . . By turns Smith screamed, prayed, begged, and cursed his torturer. When his face was reached, his tongue was silenced by fire, and henceforth he only moaned, or gave a cry that echoed over the prairie like the wail of a wild animal. Then his eyes were put out, and not a finger's breadth of his body being unscathed, his executioners gave way." From time to time, Vance had been relieved from his grisly labors by his brothers-in-law and his fifteen-year-old son. Now they stepped down and "combustibles" were piled around the entire platform. Smith was soaked with oil, as were his clothes and the entire platform. Then the whole was fired.[7] The Paris lynching not only provided a spectacle, it also provided lasting mementoes of the event. An enterprising photographer took a series of pictures of the occurrence, and it was said that a "graphophone record" of the whole proceeding—including the cries of the victim—was made. On the day after the burning, the ashes were raked as people took out buttons, bones, and teeth for relics.[8]

In the early 1890s there emerged a pattern of lynching. There were definite seasons for the act—July being the most favored month. There were also favored places. Lynching tended to reoccur in the areas where a lynching had happened before. Also they tended to occur in areas undergoing rapid economic changes or in counties where murders had been frequent and murderers rarely punished. There was a general distrust in the latter of the surety of justice in the courts and the integrity of lawyers, particularly when the offended parties were poor. Again Dixon, himself a defector from the legal profession, caught the mood perfectly in the response of the lynch mob to Gaston's plea to let the law take its course.

> "That's a lawyer talkin' now!" said a man in the crowd. "We know that tune. The lawyers has things their own way in a court house." A murmur of assent mingled with oaths ran through the crowd.[9]

It was a common attitude, with more than a grain of truth at its base. But even if the courts had been perfect, a public trial in cases of rape was seen to be more of an ordeal for the woman than for the criminal—since she must testify and, in that sense, relive the assault (a fate worse than death). Usually the mobs worked up a degree of enthusiasm before the lynching, often running through days of conversations, impromptu meetings, and rhetoric. Typically, too, the crime was seen to be part of a larger interracial conflict. White society was endangered. Negroes were becoming "uppity," presumptuous, bumptious. Strangely, whites seem to have recurrent manias about blacks' "bumping" whites, especially white women, off the sidewalks. Sometimes the whites suspected some monstrous secret organization among the blacks and feared a grand uprising. Thus, symbolically, the lynching was often seen as an act against the whole black community and not merely the execution of one or more criminals. In 1908 Albert Bushnell Hart, Harvard University historian, captured the feeling neatly in an interview with a young Mississippian. "You don't understand how we feel down here," the young man explained bluntly; "when there is a row, we feel like killing a nigger whether he has done anything or not."[10]

The physical process in the ritual of lynching was carried out by an active core, perhaps several score men, moving with considerable discipline under the direction of one or a few leaders. Often they took the victim (or, in some cases, victims) quietly. If he had been arrested and the officers resisted, the officers were usually outmaneuvered and overpowered without harm. Occasionally officers saved their prisoner, sometimes they saved him only to lose him later. Ordinarily, there were hundreds and sometimes thousands of spectators. It was not uncommon for railroads to run special "excursion" trains to the site. The mass of whites not only signified their assent to the proceedings by their presence, but also exhibited an active sympathy with the execution. To be sure, some of the interest arose from ghoulish curiosity, but apparently much more of it sprang from an eagerness to see the black fiend get his just deserts. Lynchers saw lynching as "justice." The platform upon which Henry Smith was tortured bore that single word conspicuously displayed in large printed letters. A usual part of the process was the private identification of the assailant by the offended woman, if possible. Later, when lynching had come to be applied to a wide range of offenses, the offended party or, in cases of murder, a relative would confront the accused in some way with the charge. Occasionally, the lynchers would decide that some associate of the accused was not guilty enough for execution in that style and be turned over to the care of the local jailer. Usually there was some effort to elicit a public confession from the accused, and before his death the executioners were almost always satisfied that they had found their man (or, in a few instances, their woman).

The way of death in a lynching generally bore a direct relation to the crime. Often the punishment came within sight of the scene of the crime, or, if convenience permitted, on the very spot. Torture was reserved for the most heinous of offenses. Sometimes the victims were hung without having their necks broken by a fall so that they slowly strangled to death. Usually in such cases, after the bodies had hung for several minutes they would be riddled with bullets. In that process, sometimes, armed men would be organized like soldiers into a firing order—some in front on the ground, another rank kneeling behind, and a third tier standing. The way would be cleared, and at the command hundreds would fire into the body or bodies. Now and again the lynchers would halt their proceedings and pose with their victim so that photographs could be taken or, sometimes, stand aside so that the victim could be photographed alone. Such discipline suggested recognized leadership, understood procedures, and concerted purpose. Lynchers knew what they were doing. Hanging with a quick breaking of the neck, hanging with strangulation, shooting, hanging and shooting, burning, slow burning, dragging, and cutting were all used to kill. Increasingly, simple hanging was thought to be too noble an end for such a wretch. Rumor had it that blacks regarded the hanging of one of their race by lynchers as a martyrdom. Burning, riddling with bullets, mutilation, and exhibition were used both before and after death to demean the victims. Rapists ordinarily suffered the loss of sexual organs. Bodies were always left in plain sight for some time after death, a deterrent to those who might be deterred. Fingers, toes, ears, teeth, and bones were common souvenirs. A pro-lynching governor of South Carolina, Cole Blese, received the finger of a lynched black in the mail and planted it in the gubernatorial garden. A staunchly anti-lynching governor of Georgia in the early 1890s, William J. Northern, frequently received pictures and fragments of victims to remind him of where the power of life and death in that state ultimately lay. In 1906, in Salisbury, North Carolina, several Negroes were hanged and their bodies riddled with bullets, allegedly for committing a set of horribly brutal ax murders. There is a story that the next day, a thoughtful friend brought a female relative, the person of the "little old lady" image, in his car to see the remains and, doubtless, to relish the sweets of revenge. The woman descended from the vehicle, gazed up for a time at the still swinging bodies, opened her purse, took out a knife and cut a finger from the hand of one of the victims. She put the knife and the finger in her purse, closed, it, climbed into the car again and was driven away.

After a lynching, anti-black lawlessness usually worked itself out in sporadic beatings and whippings until the white community as a whole grew irritated by such disturbances. Then the assaults would stop. The tendency was for the white community to ascribe the actual lynching to boys and men of the lower class, but also to say that the victim fully deserved his fate. It seems strange that the active executioners were seen clearly enough to establish that they did not represent the quality of the community, being merely large boys and barroom toughs, but they were seldon seen clearly enough to be convicted in the courts of murder or any other serious charge. Indeed, probably the first lynchers ever to be sent to jail for murdering blacks were two of the leaders in the Salisbury case, a railroad engineer and his fireman. The lynching, most often, was accomplished by "persons unknown." Even though some of the local intelligentsia might well deplore a lynching some distance away in another county or another state, one in their own community was almost always excused if not applauded. When the crime of the lynched person was acknowledged to be anything other than rape, the argument was offered that this lynching could not be condemned for fear of rendering this ultimate tool of justice unavailable when the awful crime did occur. Not only was the person executed guilty in the opinion of the white public, he was often also somehow seen as an alien in that society. He was a drifter or an incorrigible criminal; he was feeble-minded, or he was insane. And, always, he got what he deserved; he reaped as he had sown. During the 1890s numerous leading Southerners were caught up in the Radical mentality and turned not only to excuse lynching but, as with Rebecca Felton and Ben Tillman, actually to crusade for it. At the end of the decade they were receiving the ghastly tokens of their success in a parade of horrific lynchings that made the Paris lynching of 1893 seem ordinary fare. Finally, in the close detail in which lynchings were reported and in the wide dissemination that the reports received, Radicals everywhere shared the effect of each event. In the Radical era, a little lynching went a long way.

RIOTING

With the Wilmington riot in November 1898, the South entered yet another phase of heightened violence, a phase that reached its tragic climax in Atlanta in September 1906. Like lynching, the riot in the South in this era was essentially a new tool for the control of blacks in a Radical racial environment. However, unlike lynching, which singled out individual Negroes for punishment, in the riots white marauders broadened their sights to include any and all blacks. Further, the riots of the Radical era differed significantly from those of Reconstruction and before. During Reconstruction, Negroes in the black belts typically won such fights in the sense that they inflicted more pain upon the whites than they themselves suffered. In those affrays, the side that had the most men and the best weapons was the side that won. In the Radical period, on the other hand, the whites seemed to have the capacity to punish the blacks almost at will, in any area, and as severely as they wanted—indeed, until they exhausted themselves in the effort if they so chose. Riots in Reconstruction seemed to happen more spontaneously, with less preliminary agitation, and yet both whites and blacks seemed not greatly surprised when the fighting began. Typically both sides had their arms ready at hand, people shot and were shot at. In the Radical era, the riot was usually preceded by a long period of agitation on the white side. Radical rhetoric rang to the skies, and blacks did not respond in any effective way. Indeed, blacks appear to have been caught practically unawares in these bursts of violence. They were at first unready and unarmed, even though tensions on the white side had been building for weeks and months before the event and were clearly evident.

Essentially, riots and near-riots, which were much more numerous, were simply symptoms of the prevalence of the Radical disease. However, several of the early outbreaks and threatened outbreaks were triggered by the elevation of Negroes to relatively important political offices. Particularly, many of these were associated with the appointment in the South in and after 1897 by the Republican administration of Negroes to certain federal offices, especially to positions as postmasters, particularly in the black belts. The confluence of these events—the rise of Radicalism and the development by the Republican party of a new Southern strategy dependent in part upon the appointment of blacks to important federal offices—opened a gaping wound in the social body of the South.

The first of these eruptions, the Lake City riot of 1898, occurred after the McKinley administration saw fit to appoint a young politician named Frazier B. Baker postmaster in that South Carolina village. Whites in the area objected that Baker was a Negro and, further, had not previously been a resident of the county. Soon, they petitioned the Postmaster-General to remove him. Before the petition was acted upon, on the night of February 21, several hundred persons surrounded Baker's home. The house was set afire. Three of his children were wounded, shot down as they fled from the burning building. While his wife was running out of the house and away from the flames, she was shot through the arm. The same bullet killed the year-old baby she was carrying. Baker himself was killed by bullets fired into the house. A local newspaperman who witnessed the scene wrote that "the postoffice authorities in Washington are largely responsible for the death of Frazier B. Baker."[11] A startling pronouncement. Yet, in the Radical mind, an obvious truth in that officials had not responded to clear warnings of impending crisis.

The appointment of Baker to the Lake City post office was only one of a large number of such acts in and after 1897. The dust had hardly settled from the hustings of 1896 before the McKinley administration began to tender temporary appointments to hundreds of Negroes in the black belts of the South, primarily postmasterships. Probably these were simply the "spoils of office" promised in 1895 and 1896 for black support for McKinley in securing the

Republican nomination for the presidency. Black Republicans in North Carolina were especially prominent in the process because blacks functioning through the Republican party had fused with Populists in 1896 and seized control of the state. Recognition of that power came in the form of scores of blacks being named to postmasterships in the eastern counties where Negroes were numerous, most conspicuously in what was called the "Black Second." A Congressional district in the northeastern part of the state where the Negro population was solidly in the majority. In 1888 it had elected a black Congressman, and then in 1896 it again did so in the person of George H. White. White was not only very intelligent and superbly well organized, he was also millitant. He made it his special business to press aggressively for the appointment of blacks to postmasterships in his district, patronage traditionally attached to his office, and to concern himself with the appointment of blacks to federal offices generally in North Carolina. Thus it was that the hamlets, villages, and towns of eastern North Carolina, an extraordinarily large number of such commissions were given, and the blacks were, indeed, "rising." These appointments, made on a temporary basis by the President in the spring of 1897 while Congress was recessed, had to be confirmed by the Senate in order to become permanent. Immediately incumbents began to press for confirmation, and native whites began to respond.

What bothered the whites, of course, was the fact that their womenfolk were forced to do business with black postmasters and clerks, often enough with their political cronies hanging about inside the post office. It was in the nature of politics that some of the same blacks who were most influential in the elections ran saloons, bars, or dives of various sorts, that some of these had reputations for living with women to whom they were not married, and, occasionally, of having scars and sores suggestive of veneral disease. Black officeholding at any and all levels, harmless as it might later seem, was viewed by Radicals with distress. Physical contact through the mutual handling of mails and monies was bad enough, but even more awful was the prospect that black men in office would make all black men assume themselves more powerful and be led to approach white women sexually. When rejected, some black men would naturally fall over the edge of civilization and into a *furor sexualis*. The local post office, then, was becoming an institution in which a heedless and heartless federal government was casting white women into the very den of the Minotaur. The objections sent by citizens in eastern North Carolina to post office authorities in Washington became increasingly strident, and eventually they appealed to Populist Senator Marion Butler, who happened to be on the Senate Post Office Committee, to block the appointments. Ironically, most leaders in these towns were staunchly Democratic, and Butler was their bitter enemy, but he was also their last desperate hope in a struggle that was beginning to transcend politics.

Typical was the experience of Scotland Neck, a village in the black belt in eastern North Carolina. In the spring of 1898 the Cleveland postmaster was still in office there, but Congressman White had named and the Senate was asked to confirm the appointment of his political friend, Colin P. Anthony, a black man. Anthony was a successful businessman and one of the five county commissioners, along with two Democrats and two Populists. He had developed a reputation for cooperation with the Populists, but in the spring his Populist friends began to see his elevation to the postmastership as a liability to the People's party. For one thing, he was identified as "the Proprietor of the colored bar in Scotland Neck."[12] The conflict very soon became less one of politics than of protecting Southern white women from exposure to the potential black beast. A local physician entreated Butler to stop the appointment. "I make this request," he pled, "in behalf of my Mother, her Daughters and Grand Daughters that receive their mail at that Post Office. I have no one to recommend, but if you will use your influence to keep the negro out you will greatly oblige."[13] W. A. Dunn, a local lawyer, labored diligently to destroy Anthony's candidacy. He sent Butler a petition and explained why a Negro postmaster was so much worse than, for instance, a Negro customs officer, policeman, magistrate, or even a legislator or congressman. "There are no places where the Negro is so objectionable as in the post offices," he urged. "He cannot or does not understand that the office is a place where loafers ought not to be permitted and it is made the loafing place of his political friends. If the Administration deliberately sought to insult our people, it could not better succeed than by making these appointments, and if it was the purpose to create race prejudice and set back the Negro it could not better succeed than by placing him where he is regarded as an insult to our people."[14]

Anthony's opponents next turned their efforts toward gathering evidence of his sexual misbehavior, a kind of evidence that seemed to them the ultimate disqualification in these circumstances. Lawyer Dunn, after numerous attempts, confessed himself unable to find a Negro who would sign an affadavit documenting the immoral behavior of the liquor dealer. Unfortunately for Dunn's objects, Anthony lived about three miles from town and not a single white person lived in his neighborhood. "You know the nature of a negro," he complained bitterly, "he does not regard such acts as Anthony is guilty of as unfitting him to hold office. . . ."[15] But then, at last, they got what they had been seeking in a single sentence affadavit: "That C. P. Anthony did seduce and get upon one Maggy Toodles a bastard baby."[16] Anthony's appointment was rejected by the Senate. Nevertheless, Congressman White persisted and achieved his basic purpose. He secured the appointment of "Thomas Shields (colored)" as postmaster. Shields had agreed to make Anthony his chief clerk and Anthony's father-in-law agreed to go bond for Shields for the office. Thus Anthony was made virtually the postmaster after all.[17]

The experience of eastern North Carolina was repeated throughout the black belts of the South wherever the Republican administration appointed blacks as postmasters. In 1903, Senator Ben Tillman even objected to naming a Negro *woman* to head the post office in Indianola, Mississippi. There the office was of such small consequence that it was housed in "Cohen's Brooklyn Bridge Store." In Sunflower County, where Indianola was located and where 6,000 whites faced 18,000 blacks, Radicals were sure that even this token exhibition of black power had dangerously aroused the black beast. Already, as Tillman told the Senate, the presence of the black postmistress had caused an "insulting, infamous proposition and insult from a negro man to a white woman, a poor Jewess who was clerking in the same store."[18] That incident and the continued incumbency of the black woman had brought the white people of Indianola to the brink of riotous violence.

Negro leaders seemed unaware of the real virulence behind white opposition to black postmasters. There was good reason for them not to be aware. They were, after all, simply pursuing and achieving the American dream of personal progress, and they could hardly take seriously white assertions that retrogression to a bestial state was their destiny. Radicalism, of course, was a white disease, and it raged on the white side of the line—not the black. The color line itself was like a firewall, allowing some heat but no light to escape to the other side. Occasionally, however, the wall might crumble locally and blacks who happened to be nearby would suddenly feel the searing flames. Blacks might also be caught unawares because they would remember that only recently the Harrison administration (1889–93) had appointed thousands of blacks to federal positions, not a few of them to postmasterships in eastern North Carolina. The second Cleveland administration (1893–97) had only gradually removed these postmasters. What could be more natural with the advent of another Republican administration than that the black postmasters should return to their places?

As the campaign of 1898 began, black leaders in eastern North Carolina, looking at their recent political victories, had good reason not to be fearful of whites and to feel confident about an increase in their own power. In 1896 the Republican-dominated fusion with the Populists had already floated a host of blacks into state and local offices. In Rocky Mount, for instance, the Harrison postmaster had been a black man named William Lee Pearson. During his tenure as a postmaster Radicalism had not yet acquired the power it was soon to achieve, and Pearson enjoyed his office in relative peace. Moreover in 1898 he had moved up to the state senate and the world must have seemed to him a very fair place indeed. All over eastern North Carolina the prospect was the same, blacks were rising at last to ordinary stations in political life. In the euphoria of immediate victories, black leaders failed to see the awful force that was to bring them so suddenly low.

However, it was precisely in eastern North Carolina that the intense racial heat generated in the "white supremacy" campaign of 1898 first raised white tempers massively to the rioting point. In that area, Republicans had joined Populists in 1896 to win a highly significant number of offices for blacks. As the election of 1898 approached, the signs were that the blacks, who made up the overwhelming majority of the Republican electorate, were going to demand and get offices in proportion closer to their numbers. In brief, blacks were rising and whites were horrified. Beginning early in 1898, elements of the Democratic leadership recognized that danger and moved to translate it into a political issue. At precisely the same time, elements of Populist leadership saw the same danger and the same political potential. However, the undisputed leader of the Populists was Marion Butler, and he refused to substitute racial goals for the economic goals he had long espoused.

The case of James Hunter Young illustrates well how the Democrats responded by placing the race issue—and the sex issue—at the center of their campaign. Young was a middle-aged mulatto legislator from Wake County (Raleigh). In 1897 he was named one of the directors of the state's Deaf, Dumb, and Blind Institutions. Probably no legislator in the 1890s had been more effective in improving these important and theretofore depleted facilities and more deserved the appointment. Nevertheless, in the campaign of 1898, white supremacists cartooned Young inspecting the separated living quarters of the blind white girls, and the Democratic party's handbook of that year concluded the matter by asking "How do you like such white slavery to a negro master in Raleigh? . . . Jim Young is a hard man to satisfy."[19] Whether the Democratic leaders really believed the pictures they drew, or whether they were merely creating campaign propaganda, the effect was the same. Whites in eastern North Carolina had been thoroughly Radicalized. They were bound to hear, to believe, and to act violently upon such thoughts. In the summer and fall of 1898 very respectable young Democratic politicians such as Charles Brantley Aycock, Locke Craig, and Robert Glenn, all to be governors of the state early in the twentiety century, went there to fan the flames and beat the Radical drum.

Even so, it was not a world they ever made. If white supremacy politicians in some shape had not existed in North Carolina in 1898, they would have been created by the Radical hysteria. And they would have been molded from any clay—Democratic, Populist, or even Republican. Each of these parties had a very large and important lily-white faction, and each was poised for a flight into Radicalism. In North Carolina, the Democrats took flight first. For a time they grounded the rest, in part simply because whatever a Democrat was, a Populist or a Republican ought not be. The young Democrats who opted for Radicalism chose to ride the wave of the future. They thus assured themselves of possessing high power in their state in the formative decades of the twentieth century, and, incidentally, of gubernatorial, senatorial, and congressional seats as well.

THE WILMINGTON RIOT

The Wilmington riot of November 10, 1898, was the first in a series of outbreaks in which large numbers of blacks were killed, still larger numbers hurt, and hundreds of Negro families driven forever from their homes. Wilmington, in southeastern North Carolina, was the great port city for the state and the commercial center for a vast agricultural hinterland in and about the Cape Fear River basin. The city itself was more black than white, and the county in which it was located, New Hanover, had 14,000 blacks in a total population of 24,000.

The primary cause of the riot was Radicalism. Its rise to feverish intensity in the 1898 campaign had the effect in Wilmington, and in eastern North Carolina generally, of breaking down political lines and erecting in their stead a single line—the race line. Increasingly, white people were forced to choose not between parties but between colors. "The situation here," reported a Wilmington Populist to Marion Butler in October, "derived from the pronounced negro office-holding and their consequent insolence, has produced an issue rather of race assertiveness than of questions of political economy. So ominous is this condition that partisan affiliation is divided and but one question irresistible possesses the attention of our citizens—that of race supremacy."[20] Equivocation brought threats of horrendous violence. As the summer wore on into fall, individual white Populists and Republicans published advertisements in the newspapers announcing their withdrawal as candidates for office. In addition, they often proclaimed their endorsement of the white supremacy crusade. "I have always been and still am for anglo Saxon [*sic*] Supremacy in all things pertaining to State as well as national affairs," declared one retired Populist candidate in Wilmington. "I have always tried to make this plain to fair minded people."[21] In the heat of racial conflict, Populist and Republican leaders lost control of their parties, and so, too, did the Democrats. Democrats chose the right issue upon which to ride back into power. But they did not create the Radical hysteria, nor did they control it. It would be much more accurate to say that in North Carolina Radicalism, for a time, seized and shaped a willing Democracy.

Given the extravagance of the white supremacy campaign, it is remarkable that the Wilmington riot occurred two days after the election rather than during the turbulent weeks that preceded the balloting. Yet, race not politics ruled, and it seems inevitable that interracial violence would have erupted somewhere. The riot that happened in Wilmington could have happened in a

score of eastern North Carolina towns, and it very nearly did. For instance, it
almost occurred in Wilson where, again, the McKinley administration had
appointed another Negro postmaster. In Wilson, on the day after the election,
it was rumored that some two hundred Negroes had gathered at a baseball
field nearby and were marching on the town. The white population, in a
frenzy, armed itself (primarily with Winchester repeating rifles) and hastily
organized for the onslaught, which, of course, never came.[22] Once the riot had
actually occurred in Wilmington, there was no need for it to happen
elsewhere.

There were, of course, a multiplicity of local and immediate causes of the
riot. There were Democratic politicians who had been displaced—largely by
black and white Republicans—in the fusionist upsurge and who did, in fact,
return to offices by dint of racial fears and violence—fears they shared with
their white neighbors generally, and a violence they promoted but did not
create. In the economic realm, laboring class whites did sometimes find themselves in competition with black labor. This was particularly true of those
more recently arrived from abroad and, more particularly still, of the late-
coming Irish. Further, established white artisans were embattled by blacks
moving into their trades. Lower-class whites generally had been gerrymandered into voting districts with blacks so as to be overwhelmed by the blacks
and thus rendered powerless politically. Land and business values were
depressed and falling because of Republican dominance in city and county
governments and prolonged political unrest. Thus, better-to-do Wilmingtonians grew more desperate. Finally, the fusionist legislature had altered the
charter of Wilmington, as it did with a number of black belt towns, to throw
the city into the hands of blacks and Republicans by extending its borders.
Still the evidence is great that, ultimately, the effective ingredient in the riot
came from that unnamed hysteria that swept through the white communities
in the black belts of the South in the 1890s. Whites in the port city saw a
rapidly rising rate of crime among blacks. Black presumptuousness
approached aggressiveness, and often whites feared that blacks were arming
themselves and secretely organizing for a general insurrection. Finally, Wilmington whites assumed that there was a widespread lusting among black men
for white women.

Fortunately, for students of history George Rountree, a leading Wilmington lawyer and a Democrat, left an excellent eye-witness account, not only of
the riot but of its coming as well. Rountree was an intelligent, highly sensitive
man and, by the definitions used here, a racial Conservative.[23]

As Rountree later recalled, "Aycock and Craig had made a wonderful
impression by making White Supremacy speeches at Laurinburg" early in the
summer of 1898. Shortly afterward, a campaign committee organized in Wilmington and "it was determined that this city and county should be

redeemed. . . ." In August, Rountree remembered, "each issue of the paper spoke of burglary which had been committed and lawlessness was rife, and especially were there references to disorderly conduct on the part of irresponsible negroes." Radicals believed that rising Negro criminality, particularly the criminal behavior of unattached Negroes, indicated the massive resurgence of the black savage. The peak of that criminality was represented as a hankering after white women. "I believe, though I am not sure," recalled Rountree, "that it was during this month that the negro paper, edited by one Manly, published a statement impugning the character of white women, and there was a account of a riotous assemble, which apparently quieted down."

The Manly episode that Rountree passed over thus lightly was signally important in Radical minds and in the story of what actually happened. Alex Manly was a rather handsome young mulatto who edited the Wilmington *Record*. A full year after Mrs. Felton had made her Tybee Island speech, Manly chose to editorialize upon that speech in his paper. He readily agreed with Mrs. Felton that the poorer class of farmers failed to take care of their women, and that the quality of life for them was lamentably low. They were, in fact, left by themselves upon the scattered and isolated farms of the South. Actually Mrs. Felton had not singled out the poorer classes explicitly. She had referred to the daughters of Confederate soldiers, many of whom, no doubt, were orphans and impoverished. Leonidas Scott, in writing to Mrs. Felton in 1894, had made the point that the less affluent farm women who fell victim to the black beast rapist went unavenged, and Dixon, in 1902, wrote Annie and Flora into the poor white class. That rural women of the underclass were the special victims of rape by blacks was an idea afloat in the popular mind in the 1890s, and the press read a statement to that effect into Mrs. Felton's speech. Manly's great offense was that he went on, in a rather knowing tone, to suggest that Mrs. Felton ought to look deeper for the cause of the great number of lynchings that were occurring. After all, he told his readers, it was awfully lonesome out there in the piney woods, and there were some very handsome Negro men readily at hand. Lynching, he implied, was the result not of black men assaulting white women, but of white women caught with their black lovers and crying rape to save their reputations.[24]

The Manly editorial might not have received such great attention had not the Democratic press picked it up and repeated it broadcast. For instance, Josephus Daniels, the owner and editor of the Raleigh *News and Observer*, reprinted some 300,000 copies in leaflet form and distributed them over the state. In late August and afterward, the Manly editorial became a *cause célèbre* in the white supremacy campaign and in its power to whip up the Radical hysteria ranked with images of black postmasters abusing white female patrons and Jim Young dominating blind white girls. In early 1902 when Tom Dixon sat down in his study at Elmington Manor to write *The Leopard's*

Spots, he had only to replay what the great mass of white people had been thinking and saying some three years earlier in nearby eastern North Carolina. To them, Tim Shelby was very real.

In retrospect, it is almost incomprehensible that anyone as intelligent as Alex Manly could have lived in the midst of the Radical rage and been surprised by the consequences of his words. One is appalled by his lack of awareness, by the cavalier, almost careless manner in which he published such an essay. Probably, he was influenced by a feeling that black power was indeed rapidly rising in eastern North Carolina and in Wilmington, and that it was safe enough to speak what he thought was the simple truth. That a dangerous mass of white people could actually believe in retrogression and imagine that bestial black men roamed the earth in search of white female prey plainly never entered his calculations. Interviewed after the riot in New Jersey, where he had taken refuge with relatives, Manly explained that he had written the editorial to defend the "defamed colored men." Seemingly still careless of the white hot heat generated by such statements, he declared that "women of that race are not more particular in the matter of clandestine meetings with colored men than are the white men with colored women."[25]

One might be inclined to think less of Manly's powers of perception were it not for the fact that so many Conservative whites, with all of the facilities of interracial communication at their disposal, were almost equally lacking in awareness. Witness again the response of this very astute Wilmingtonian, George Rountree.

Shortly after the Manly article appeared in August, Rountree came down to Wilmington from his summer retreat in the mountains. His intention was to pick up leadership in what he had come to think was a bungled and foundering Democratic campaign in his home county. To his dismay, he found events galloping on ahead. Though he scampered in pursuit and altered slightly the course of affairs here and there, he never mastered the situation, nor apparently, quite understood what was happening. He grossly underestimated the extremism of the Radicals. As he later reported, "White supremacy clubs were formed in the town and unless I am mistaken, Frank Winston came down and helped to organize these clubs—which by this time—in October—were spread all over the State. Personally I had little or nothing to do with any of these clubs, but remember making a speech in one of them in which I started to endeavor to inflame the white men's sentiment, and discovered that they were already willing to kill all of the office holders and all the negroes, and so I immediately reacted and became a pacificist."

Still, Rountree shared with other whites an apprehension of violence from blacks. "The committee was informed that the negroes were getting arms," he wrote, "and at the suggestion of Mr. John R. Kenly, President of the A.C.L.R.R Co. [the Atlantic Coast Line Railroad], whom we four men went to see, we employed detectives, and a negro detective at that—to ascertain and let us know what the purpose of the negroes was and what they were doing, and we ascertained, I believe, that they were doing practically nothing."

In spite of the information that the blacks were not arming themselves for rebellion, whites in the city proceeded to organize themselves militarily as if race war were imminent. Not only were Republican leaders intimidated to such an extent that they were dissuaded from speaking, Republican and fusionist candidates publicly retired from the electoral campaign and virtually endorsed white supremacy. More and more, the contest became purely a local one, focusing upon the city and county rather than the state. More and more, too, the confrontation became one between black and white rather than between Democrats and the rest. A good illustration of the decline of politics as a factor in the riot came when Furnifold M. Simmons, the state chairman of the Democratic party and a thorough Radical, became suspicious at the total collapse of the local Republican opposition. Fearing that Wilmington's white leadership had made some large secret concessions to the enemy in order to achieve such perfect command of the field, he sent an agent to set the Wilmington people straight. Rountree himself told the agent that "Simmons might go to H__, as we were going to run the campaign to suit ourselves down here." In truth, Wilmington Democrats had generally agreed that no one on either side should make speeches, so Simmons might well have been suspicious. But while the Democrats enforced the rule on the opposition, they freely violated it themselves. Rountree himself heard the leader of the Radical faction, Col. Alfred Moore Waddell, speak in the Opera House. " ... and I remember that he used some rather violent language about choking the Cape Fear River with the bodies of negroes." Shortly, the Democratic leadership found affairs slipping out of its control. "The campaign committee found that the temper of the community was hot enough and needed quieting down rather than heating up," Rountree recalled. "By this time the conditions in Wilmington had been advertised throughout the State. The negro office holders were in a state of sullenness. ..."

On November 8, the white Democracy of Wilmington and New Hanover won overwhelmingly the elections for city, county, and legislative offices. The next morning a grand meeting in the Opera House heard a resolution offered to expel immediately from their positions the Republican-Fusionist officers of the city. Rountree, reacting conservatively, tried to turn his friends away from such a blatantly illegal action. He shrewdly offered a substitute motion to name a resolutions committee. The motion carried and Rountree was made a member of the committee. That body, under the influence of the moderates, reported and the meeting accepted a resolution that the Negro editor Manly and his paper be expelled from the city. Thus, it would seem that the expulsion of Manly was the symbol to substitute for the ouster of all the city officers and to relieve the pressure of accumulated hatred in the white community. A committee, led by Waddell, then negotiated with a committee of Negro leaders to effect Manley's ejection. Rountree recounted the sequel:

> I knew nothing further of the matter until I was going home after dark and I met one of the most prominent negroes and he told me that everything was all right; that they had seen Manly, and he was going to leave town at once; that a young negro, Scott, had been deputed to take the answer to Colonel Waddell's Committee. It appears that Colonel Waddell's committee had told the committee of negroes, with whom they had had a conference, that they must have an answer by 7 o'clock [the following morning] at the Light Infantry Armory, and I learned that instead of the negro carrying the information there, like a fool, he put it in the post office and Waddell did not get his mail of course until it was too late and after the devilment was done. The Committee and a large number of people met at the Armory and no answer having been received by the committee, the crowd, or mob, proceeded up the street to the office of the negro paper shooting off guns and proceeded to demolish it. In some way this office caught on fire and there was shouting and great amount of noise, which of course frightened the negro women in that neighborhood a good deal.

Rountree went by the post office that morning just as the row at Manly's newspaper office was subsiding. The Republican postmaster, a white man, working behind a bank of postal boxes, heard Rountree talking and came out. He offered to secure the resignation of the city officers if Rountree would get the businessmen of the city to select replacements. Rountree agreed. As unrest continued, he went home, got his Winchester rifle, and walked to the corner of Front Street, "with my gun on my shoulder, feeling very much like a fool. . . ." Embarrassed, he took his rifle home and came out again. At the corner, he found a large crowd of about 100 Negroes. These men were laborers at Sprunt's cotton compress who had been called out of the yard by their frightened wives. Rountree and other white men went among them, urging them to disperse.

> In the meantime the white people had gotten wind of this gathering and I observed a good many people coming down with guns on their shoulders. In fact, as I recall, I myself telephoned to the Armory for the rapid firing gun, which was a fool thing to do, but which I did so as to have it convenient for use if necessary. Mr. Junius Davis, Mr. Sprunt, Colonel Roger Moore and I went among the negroes and begged them to disband, and some of them looking at the white people with guns, said: what have we done, what have we done? I had no answer, they had done nothing. Soon the white people became impatient, and sent word to us who were in the midst of the negroes, that they were going to shoot unless the negroes dispersed at once (I merely tell you this to show you the frame of mind they were in).

Rountree and a deputy sheriff read the riot act, the Negroes began to disperse, and the whites began to relax. Then they heard firing from Nixon and Fourth Streets. Rountree again returned home, got his Winchester and proceeded to the scene with several others.

... before we got there I received two telegrams one from Darlington and one from Goldsboro, offering military assistance. When I went over the Bridge I saw several negroes lying on the street dead and a good many white people about with arms—few, if any, negroes. I remember immediately investigating the matter so as to be prepared for an investigation by the U.S. Government, if necessary. And I remember taking affidavits to the effect that negroes had congregated at Nixon and Fourth Streets something like they had near Sprunts Compress, but not in such great numbers, and that there were several white men over there with guns, but not a great many; that there had been some talk, but a half grown negro boy fired the first shot, when there was a fusilade of shots from the white people, which dropped four or five negroes."

After that the military company was called out. "My personal opinion is that there were not over six or seven negroes killed at the outside."

The Waddell committee then met and Rountree transmitted the offer of the Republican officeholders to resign. The postmaster brought the Republicans to meet the committee at City Hall. "There was some delay in getting the colored brethren, but we insisted on getting them all there. . . ." Then, one after another, individuals stood and resigned their posts and new officers were selected "until the mayor and board of aldermen and all the city officers had been replaced by the white people." Thus ended the Wilmington riot.

The ambivalence of the moderate Rountree in the sequence of events was typical of that of Conservatives in the face of Radical violence. He was obviously torn by a sense of duty toward both Negroes and Radicalized whites. Above all, he was for law and order. He was disturbed by the rising criminality of unattached Negroes, and, while he did not believe that black males were about to become a race of raging satyrs, he was offended by the Manly article. Rountree returned from the mountains in the late summer ready to whip up a little Bourbon style racism in a good cause, but found race feelings already too extreme. He coolly defied the extremist Democratic party chairman, and he worked hard to moderate local Radicalism; but then he smoothly took advantage of the fright of the Republicans to expel them totally from office. He constantly endeavored, at considerable peril to his own life and limb, to get the Negroes to disperse, yet on two occasions he went to get his gun and he did summon the "rapid firing" (Gatling) gun—all of which he seemed to rue. Finally, the bodies of the first victims were still warm when he began to collect affidavits that he felt would exonerate the whites in the eyes of federal investigators, the nation, and people like himself.

THE ROBERT CHARLES RIOT IN NEW ORLEANS

Two years later, in 1900 in New Orleans one of the most serious outbreaks of racial violence since Reconstruction occurred. At the center of the conflict was a remarkable man, until recently perhaps one of the most neglected historical figures in American race relations.[26] His name was Robert Charles, and possibly he was the first fully self-conscious black militant in the United States. Not only was Charles, apparently, a black nationalist in the intellectual and rhetorical sense, he was also an activist, and, as he soon proved, unique in that he maintained his militancy until death.

Charles came to New Orleans in 1894 after experiencing some difficulty with the authorities in Copiah County, Mississippi, involving the illicit sale of whiskey. In terms of age, he was precisely the most adult issue possible of the "new Negro" of Radical myth, having just barely escaped the "benefits" of slavery. In fact, Robert Charles was conceived in slavery and born in freedon in late 1865 or early 1866. His father and mother were sharecroppers in Copiah County, some thirty miles southeast of Vicksburg, and Robert was the fourth in a line of ten brothers and sisters. He was like many young black folks, who left the tenant farms to seek more lucrative jobs in the modernizing South. In his case, he became first a day laborer on the railroads. Some time in the 1890s, probably in 1894, in the midst of the great depression, Robert Charles came to New Orleans. In New Orleans and elsewhere, he valued his family and his friends from Copiah, and maintained his connection with them until the very end of his life. In the year of the riot, Robert was thirty-four and unmarried, a sturdy dark brown man some six feet in height and weighing about 185 pounds. He was literate and, indeed, rather studious over the newspapers and textbooks he saved. In addition, he kept notebooks in which he wrote from time to time. There was no indication that he was a church member, belonged to any fraternal order, or was an intimate in any other enclave in black life. He drank moderately, affected a droopy mustache, and dressed well, rather stylishly, favoring a brown derby. Charles worked as a laborer in a succession of jobs, finally in June 1900 losing his job stacking lumber at the Pelican Sawmill Company. He moved frequently, living in perhaps a dozen places after his arrival in the city before he came to share a room on Fourth Street with nineteen-year-old Lenard Pierce, another black man out of work. Charles had different jobs and addresses, he also had different names. Sometimes he was Curtis Robertson, and sometimes he was Robert Charles. Having two names was a way of dealing with the white world and the white man's law, but Charles saw to it that each name had integrity. Indeed, when Curtis Robertson got arrested and convicted for selling whiskey in Copiah County, fled, and somehow avoided serving his sentence, he managed some two years later to return and set the matter straight. Finally, Robert Charles liked women. At the time of the riot he had been special friends for some three years with Virginia Banks, "a young brown-skinned woman . . . possessed of more than average intelligence" and probably employed in the city as a domestic servant. The New Orleans riot began on Monday, July 23, 1900, while Robert was waiting for Virginia.

That afternoon about sunset Lenard had come home from a day of searching for work to find Charles writing at a small desk in their room. He was dressed to go out—dark striped trousers, white shirt, black coat, and brown derby. Lenard knew that the bulge in Charles's coat was the .38 Colt revolver he usually carried. Charles asked Lenard if he would like to go with him to meet two women. Lenard asked if there was "anything in it." Charles assured him there was, and Lenard washed and dressed, thrusting his own .38 Colt into his waistband before they went out. Charles was going to see Virginia, and he probably invited Lenard along to meet her roommate, Ernestine Goldstein. Charles understood that Virginia and Ernestine had taken an excursion trip to Baton Rouge that day and would not return until later in the evening. Meanwhile, he took Lenard to visit another young woman. Almost certainly the young woman was his married sister, Alice. Leaving Alice's residence, the two men approached the house in which Virginia and Ernestine lived about 10:00 p.m. They waited for a half-hour at a streetcorner nearby, perhaps assuming that the women had not yet returned home, or, perhaps, waiting for Virginia to fetch them when her landlady had gone to sleep. Pierce grew nervous about the police, and about 10:30 they moved closer to the house, seating themselves on a step in front of the house of a white neighbor. Once or twice they walked down to check Virginia's house and returned to sit on the step.

About 11:00 police Sergeant Jules C. Aucoin, in charge of the night shift in the precinct, encountered a black man who told him that "two suspicious looking negroes" were sitting on the doorstep of a house nearby. The sergeant gathered two of his patrolmen and confronted the two men, demanding to know what they were doing there. The men responded vaguely about having been in town only three days and working for someone. One of them added that "they were waiting for a friend." Charles rose, and one of the policemen, taking the move as a threat, grabbed him. They scuffled. The policeman began to beat Charles with his billy club, then drew his pistol. Charles did the same, and both opened fire. The policeman was struck in the thigh, and so too was Charles, who nevertheless escaped, running zigzag down the street as two of the officers fired at him. Meanwhile, Sergeant Aucoin was holding a gun at Lenard Pierce's head. The policemen took Pierce to the station house where he was questioned by Captain John T. Day. Captain Day was one of the real heroes of the New Orleans Police Department, in 1894 having rescued fourteen people from a fire in the St. Charles Hotel. Large and handsome in the portly style of the time, John Day at thirty-seven was the pride of the NOPD. By 2:30 a.m. he had "sweated out" of the unfortunate Pierce the name Curtis Robertson and the Fourth Street address. He emerged from the station to join a squad of policemen saying, "I know where I can get the nigger now." Warned to be careful, Day replied casually, "Oh pshaw, I'll go and take that nigger myself."

Meanwhile, Charles had returned to his room on Fourth Street, probably to get his Winchester, a lever-action, rapid-firing rifle. It happened that Captain Day arrived with his men just as Charles was about to leave his room. The room had a single door, opening onto an alleyway running perpendicular to the street. The Captain stationed three of his men on the street while he led Sergeant Aucoin, Corporal Trenchard, and Patrolman Lamb down the alley toward Charles's room. With them was a citizen volunteer named Schmidt, who carried a lantern. As they approached the door Trenchard ordered in a loud voice, "Open up there!" Charles suddenly flung open the door and fired a bullet straight through the Captain's heart. Day wheeled, made "an awful cry," and fell dead. Schmidt dropped the lantern and ran. The policemen were frozen in disbelief. "My God, Corporal," said Sergeant Aucoin, "our Captain has been killed. Look at what that negro has done." As if in answer, Charles then fired several more shots into the fallen body. Two of the policemen were now up against the wall of the house by the door. As they began to talk to one another, Charles shouted at them, "You _____ I will give you all some!" Thereupon he fired from the doorway, sending a bullet through Patrolman Lamb's right eye and out the back of his skull. An elderly black woman living down the alley then called to the two remaining officers to slip into her room. They did, and hid there in the darkness for two hours. Charles stalked about in the alley looking for the policeman, cursing them, and daring them to come out. The three policemen on the street declined to enter the dark alley. Finally, about 4:30, Charles came to the street and fired at one of the policemen. At seventy-five yards, in the semi-darkness, he grazed the officer's cap with his bullet. Finally, then, the officers called for assistance, which arrived at 5:00 only to find that Charles had fled.

What drove Robert Charles to defy the police, knowing that the odds of his survival in such an affray were virtually nil? Distinctly, at least three things moved him. Since 1896 he had been an active and earnest advocate of the emigration of American blacks to Liberia. In that year he joined the International Migration Society, an organization that promised transportation to Liberia and three months' supplies to members who would pay the society a dollar a month for forty months. In 1899 Charles had also become, at his own request, a subscription agent for the *Voice of Missions,* a paper published by Bishop Henry M. Turner of the AMEC. Turner was then unrivaled among black leaders in urging Negroes to return to Africa. Among Charles's effects, police later found a great amount of literature advocating emigration to Africa.

Charles was also moved by one of the most horrible lynchings that had yet occurred in the South. In 1899, near Newnan, Georgia, Sam Hose, a black man, reputedly killed a farmer and raped the farmer's wife on the bloody kitchen floor next to the still warm body. Hose was tortured, burned, and then his body reclaimed from the fire and slices taken from his heart and liver. One of the lynchers journeyed to Atlanta in an attempt to deliver a slice of Hose'e heart to the governor. News of the Hose lynching threw Charles into a rage. His acquaintances said they had never seen him so totally angry. As one observed, Charles was "beside himself with fury." Shortly thereafter, he asked to become one of Turner's agents.

Finally, Louisiana had just moved in 1898 to disfranchise black men, and the election of 1900 was approaching. Some Democratic leaders had indicated their willingness to count out the Republicans and their Populist allies even if they were fortunate enough to win the now rigged elections. An opposition spokesman voiced a very hot reply to this threat, suggesting that his partisans "*oil up their Winchesters* and prepare to fight," if need be, to seat their candidates. Later police discovered that Charles was carrying a two-column newspaper account of that speech with him when he died.

Clearly, Robert Charles was giving up on America. When the policeman began to hit him with the billy club and drew his pistol, Charles was ready for war.

Early Tuesday morning the police realized that Charles had again escaped and they mounted a vast search. As the hunt proceeded, the mobs rose. Just as Manly had been an excuse for riot in Wilmington, Charles became an excuse for riot in New Orleans. As in Wilmington there were many causes of the riot, underneath which Radicalism beat like a steady pulse. Black people had been crowding working-class whites for jobs during the depression-ridden 1890s. Further, there had been a move in the state legislature to segregate more strictly the streetcars in New Orleans, a move that was popular in the state at large and was defeated by interested parties only by quietly burying the measure in the state senate. Finally, each of the four major newspapers in the city moved toward radical extremism, and two of these attained that end. Both the press and the police in June and July noticed that young blacks were misbehaving in the city's parks. These young men, it was reported, would "lie in the grass, evidently waiting for the young maidens to pass them," and they would make "questionable if not indecent remakrs." In the same months a New Orleans physician, Gustav Keitz, published a series of articles in the *Times-Democrat* in which he claimed that his medical friends were "agreed that the number of negroes should be reduced, and have discussed asexualization, a measure which should be practiced at the earliest possible period of life." Finally, many blacks, especially young men, did not hide their approval of Charles's actions. White people claimed to have heard remarks praising Charles and his "war on the whites."

On Tuesday, groups of white men, almost totally unchecked by police, began to range through the city, attacking blacks. Indeed, the mobs, allegedly made up exclusively of young men, boys and habitual hoodlums, apparently thought of themselves as the allies of the police. While the police did not share that view, they handled the situation by arresting blacks who seemed too assertive and too approving of Charles. On the third day, Wednesday, the mobs became stronger and increasingly unruly, and it seemed as if the city might plunge into anarchy. The acting mayor issued a proclamation calling for law and order. On the other side, all four newspapers clamored for Charles's apprehension, two of these indirectly urging mob action. A rally was held at the site of Robert E. Lee's monument on Wednesday evening, and it was decided that Pierce would be lynched. A mob of 3,000 marched to the parish prison, only to find it too strongly defended. They then moved on to Storyville, the vice district, intending to attack the black establishments there. Again they were thwarted. Black Storyville was locked up tight and deserted. The mob was reduced to attacking the few as yet unaware and hapless blacks caught on the darkened streets. During the night three black people were killed, and six were seriously injured. Fifty blacks were beaten badly enough to be treated for injuries at the city hospital. Additionally, the mob accidentally shot two white people and beat three streetcar employees who fought to keep the mobs off their cars. On Thursday, the mayor of New Orleans, who had been ill and out of town, returned. He enlisted a volunteer police force of 1500 men, and the governor sent him militia. These were stationed at strategic places, and officials began to gain control of the city again. Even so, three more black people were killed on Thursday, and fifteen were shot or severely beaten. Then, on Friday, the fifth day, a black man informed the police that Charles was hidden in a house on Saratoga Street, only fourteen blocks from his room on Fourth.

Precisely as the press and the populace had charged, Charles had been hidden by his own people. The black "criminal" was given refuge in the New Orleans home of friends from Copiah County. It fell to one of the most respected men on the force, Sergeant Gabriel Porteous, to check out this latest report on Charles's whereabouts. He took with him a corporal and two officers arriving at the address a bit after 3:00 p.m. Porteous stationed the two patrolmen on the street while he and the corporal entered the house. Charles had established his retreat, perhaps for the whole three days he had been missing, in the closet under the stairs in the two-story dwelling. He had spent some of his time making bullets out of lead pipe and reloading cartridges with tools that he had brought with him. He knew that the officers were coming. As Porteous approached the closet, Charles stuck his Winchester through the slightly opened door and fired, killing Porteous instantly with a bullet through the heart. Rapidly working the lever of his Winchester, he then shot the corporal through the stomach. The corporal collapsed, and Charles ran upstairs.

Hearing the shots, one of the officers from the street came in. He sent for a priest who came and administered last rites to the dying corporal. No one guessed that Charles was upstairs. A crowd was gathering in the yard when Charles leaned out a window and opened fire. He shot a young man, apparently chosen at random, first in the hip and then quickly, as the man tried to escape through the heart. By this time a melange of police, volunteers, and militia were arriving and returned the fire. By 4:00 there were a thousand men with guns around the building, and within an hour some ten to twenty thousand men had rushed into the area. This small army sprayed the flimsy structure with bullets. Later, the curious would estimate that some five thousand bullets struck the building during the hour-long siege. Every minute or so Charles would create a distraction at one window, then suddenly pop up at another and fire. Observers estimated that Charles fired about fifty times during the fight. With those shots, he killed two more men, a jailer and a visiting Mississippian, and wounded nineteen others, seven of them seriously. None of the other shots failed to stir the air disturbingly close to their targets. Robert Charles was an uncanny marksman.

Finally, the whites attempted to smoke Charles out by igniting a mattress on the stairs. The mattress, however, set fire to the house. Charles, who must have been hit several times by then, came down the stairs and out the door. He still wore his derby hat, set low over his eyes, and he carried his rifle raised to fire, elbows poised. He dashed across twenty feet of yard toward the entrance of a facing house. He was hit, at last, by a rifle bullet from the room he was about to enter. He paused, his arms weakened and sagged. Then he gathered himself again pulled up the rifle, and crashed into the room. There were eight men in the room, three of them police detectives. But it was a young medical student from Tulane University, a volunteer policeman, who fired the first shot, the bullet that brought Robert Charles down. The black man fell within two feet of his executioner, Charles A. Noiret. Charles tried to move, and Noiret shot him three more times.

Then everybody in the room began shooting into the body, some cursing, some howling. More men rushed into the room and did the same. They dragged the body into the street and fired into it again and again. Corporal Trenchard, who was later dismissed from the force for cowardice in the first confrontation, pointed a double-barreled shotgun at the body. "Now who says I am a coward," he cried and fired both barrels. The mob allowed the son of one of the slain policemen to stomp on the face of the corpse. Finally, officers brought up a police wagon. They flung Charles's body onto the floor between the seats, leaving his head hanging over the end. As the wagon rattled down the street toward the morgue, the battered head, flattened, almost unrecognizable now, jerked crazily about.

On the same day, after Charles's death, the mobs broke loose again, burning down a large school building for blacks, killing three more black people, and beating many others. Finally on the next day, Saturday, the violence subsided, and hundreds of people filed past Charles's body on view at the morgue. The mobs had killed at least a dozen black people and injured scores of others.

On the other side, Charles had killed seven white people, four of them officers of the law; seriously wounded eight others, three of them officers; and marked for life with his bullets twelve more.

New Orleans hardly knew how to cope with the memory of Robert Charles. Many people believed that he drew his courage and his coolness from cocaine. Journalists claimed that evidences of that substance had been found in his room. The Republican paper explained him away as a man driven to desperation, presumably by the Democrats, but it, too, hinted that cocaine had been involved. The conservative Democratic press blamed the affair upon incitement by the liberal North and pronounced Charles the worst and last example of that rare type—the "bad nigger," as if in killing him the danger had passed forever. Paradoxically, one of the most virulent racists in the city, the owner and editor of the *States,* Henry J. Hearsey, the very man who had been most rabid in advocating the quick destruction of Robert Charles and scornful of the cowardice of the police, was the one public person who gave him the most respect. He could not, he declared, "help feeling for him a sort of admiration prompted by his wild and ferocious courage." Never had one man stood off so many for so long. It was, he said, "the courage of the brute[,] the lion or the tiger." Just as Charles Gaston in fiction had a strange affinity for Dick, so too did Hearsey respond to Robert Charles.

On Sunday, the seventh day, the authorities took Charles's body to the city's potter's field—under military guard, secretely, and before dawn. The final earth was shovelled onto his grave just as the eastern sky began to brighten. The plain cross marker bore no name, and New Orleans hastened to erase his memory as they erased his grave. *L'Abeille (The Bee),* the French language newspaper of New Orleans, probably summed up accurately enough the sentiment both of its neighbors and itself when it closed the Robert Charles story with the declaration that he was a black fanatic, in revolt against society.[27] He was crazy, and hence dismissable. Charles and the riot were soon all but lost to the memory of New Orleans, gaining less than three pages in the two thousand-page history of the city that appeared in 1922. He was also lost to history at large, neither he nor the riot gaining more than a few lines in histories before the "Soul Movement" got well underway in the late 1960s.

Black people, especially some black people, had more difficulty forgetting Robert Charles. A black man in Chicago became mentally unhinged when he heard about the New Orleans affair and began to pray in the streets for protection. Questioned about his behavior, he answered that he was "afraid of snakes and white folks." In southwestern Louisiana, a Negro man riding a train, suffered illusions about himself being lynched, grabbing over his head at an imaginary rope. When the conductor approached, the man shot him. At the next station, he was taken off the train and lynched. In Battle Creek, Michigan, a black man walked into the police station and fired a pistol at the chief of police as an act of sympathy for Charles. In New Orleans, five Sundays after the burial of Charles, Lewis Forstall, a black man living on South Rampart Street, walked across the street to where his neighbor, Fred Clark, also black, was seated in a chair reading. Forstall was known to be an admirer of Robert Charles and had brooded about his death. He pulled out a revolver, put it to Clark's head, and pulled the trigger. The gun misfired. He pulled the trigger again. This time the gun fired, killing Clark. Fred Clark was the man who had told the police where to find Charles on the day he died.[28]

THE CAUSES OF THE ATLANTA RIOT

The high tide of Radicalism came during the riot that raged through Atlanta for four days beginning on September 22, 1906.[29] The all-pervasive cause of the Atlanta riot was racial Radicalism. However, that violent eruption had its immediate cause in the confluence of Radicalism and several reform movements, each of which had been seeking, for a decade or more, to achieve its special goal in Georgia. Especially important were four varieties of reformers: prohibitionists, feminists, urban "progressives" and rural "progressives."

Georgia prohibitionists had long recognized their state, wet as it was, as a missionary field of magnificent possibilities. However, during the summer of 1906 the movement assumed a revivalistic fervor much as if the millennium were at hand. In the city of Atlanta, the dry finger of righteous reform pointed quite properly to Decatur Street. That street offered such a plenitude of saloons and other sinful diversions (some for whites only, others for "colored only") that "Decatur-Street-dive" had practically become a single word, and a bad one. In Atlanta, the prohibition effort was spearheaded by the ministry. Conspicuously in the advance was the Reverend "Sam" P. Jones, an evangelist of national renown. During the summer, the Reverend Jones preached sermon after sermon attacking the Decatur Street dives, depicting all manner of debaucheries there and rousing his audiences to frenzies. As the prohibition campaign approached a climax, it came to rest heavily upon the evils of drink among black men. Whites generally thought that black men were specially excited by alcohol, and that their excitement was most especially erotic. They came to believe that pictures of undraped white women were blatantly displayed in the dives frequented by black men. Further, the bottle in which a certain popular gin was dispensed supposedly bore the embossed image of a nude white woman. The idea of the fair figure under the scrutiny of black men and roughly caressed by the dark fingers even as its contents inflamed their passions was almost too much to bear for minds infused with Radicalism. Finally, many whites assumed that blacks liberally laced their drinks with cocaine, thus freeing themselves from whatever shreds of inhibition might have survived the alcohol. It was during these early years of the twentieth century, in fact, that Southern whites first experienced a great apprehension about the use of drugs. For decades, they had themselves freely used a wide variety of narcotics for relief from minor discomforts as well as major pains. Now there began to appear newspaper stories of black men here and there taking "dope," usually cocaine, and running murderously amuck. Southerners, inspired by the black menace, began to think fondly of laws, even federal laws, to regulate the use of drugs. Senator Ben Tillman, for instance, in 1913 was led to explain his position to a constituent who was a physician. Tillman asserted that the Congress did not want to tax doctors of medicine, but cocaine, opium, he said, "are causing so much trouble among the negroes." By way of immediate illustration, he added, "I suppose you saw in the papers some days ago where the two mulatto boys in Harriston, Mississippi, got crazed on cocaine and went on the war path with the result that eight people were killed and a large number wounded.[30]

In Atlanta, in 1906, whites thus thought that blacks were slipping away upon a flood of alcohol and drugs. As white Atlantans looked at Decatur Street, they saw hundreds of wandering vagrant black men daily steeping themselves in corruption, drowning in a carnal sea. The runaway black male of slave times, the "nigger in the woods," had come to town in the modern South. The immediate presence of the Negro beast gave instant urgency to the prohibitionist cause. Georgia drys reminded their more liquid neighbors that the federal government had found it necessary to deny "fire water" to the American Indian. Now they called upon their fellow Georgians to deny drink to themselves, not only for their own salvation, but for the preservation of the purity of their mothers, wives, and daughters, and to save the black man from a "relapse into animalism." Before 1906, Georgia prohibitionists had rejected active participation in the movement to disfranchise blacks, fearing that it would confuse the pursuit of their favored reform. In 1906, they reversed themselves and concluded that the disfranchisement of blacks was a necessary prelude to prohibition. The liquor interests would corrupt the black man and steal his vote to keep Georgia wet. Prohibition, the path of progress, lay directly across the prostrate form of the political Negro. Unhesitatingly, they put their foot upon that path.

Feminist reformers, too, saw black men as roadblocks on the way to reform and eagerly fanned the Radical flames. Rebecca Felton, after all, had long been saying that white men in equating themselves with black men at the polls were encouraging the latter to assert their equality elsewhere. More broadly, Georgia women could easily see their interest in prohibition. Women at large had always known who, ultimately, paid the bar bills. Clearly, the disfranchisement of black men was a move in the right direction.

The riot was also promoted by politicians shaped in the new urban progressive mold. In Georgia, pre-eminent among these was Hoke Smith. Smith had lived most of his young years in Chapel Hill, where his father was Professor of Modern Languages at the University of North Carolina. During Reconstruction, the family moved to Atlanta where Smith read law and was admitted to the bar at the age of seventeen. After years of assiduous application, he arrived, Horatio Alger fashion, at the pinnacle of his profession. In the 1880s he was reputed to be the most effective lawyer in Georgia for suits against corporations and especially suits against railroads. Quite literally, he capitalized upon an increasing popular irritation with the arrogance of railroad management that produced favorable juries, and an imperfect technology that produced a steady stream of accidents for which the railroads could be sued. Smith claimed that by the 1890s his practice paid at least $200 a day and often $500. It was accurately reflective of his character that he made such a statement. He soon bought controlling interest in the Atlanta *Journal,* and in 1892 he used that paper to campaign against the tariff and for Cleveland. As a reward, President Cleveland appointed him to his cabinet as Secretary of Interior. In Cleveland's service (1893–97) he showed himself to be an ardent gold-bug and a stalwart enemy of the liberal, Bryanite, silver wing of the Democracy.[31] However, after the turn of the century, Smith emerged as a progressive Democrat in the urban style.

By 1905 Hoke Smith was ambitious to sit in the governor's chair in Georgia. In the pursuit of that end, he allied himself with the more liberal, agrarian Populistic forces dominated by his old enemy Tom Watson. The price of support of the Watson element was the disfranchisement of the Negro. Behind the scenes in arranging this odd marriage between gold and silver and all that each stood for was, first, James R. Gray, who had followed Smith as the dominant force on the Atlanta *Journal.* Subsequently, Congressman Thomas W. Hardwick, one of the most Radical of Southern politicians, took up the management of the alliance. Hardwick pled for a holiday from partisanship among white men for the necessary end of achieving the complete disfranchisement of the black. The alliance was made, and in one of the most strenuous and prolonged gubernatorial campaigns ever waged in the South, from mid-1905 through the summer of 1906, Smith sought the Democratic nomination for the governorship of Georgia. By this time, the Democratic party of the state nominated its candidate for governor in a primary election preceding the general election. Because the Democratic party was all white, the primary was all white. Because the Democratic party was overwhelmingly the majority party, winning the primary was tantamount to winning the election. Of necessity, then, the campaign was one for the minds of the white masses and newspapers were vitally important to success. Journalistic efforts in the campaign soon descended into the "yellow" style.[32]

On the campaign trail, Smith ripped like a fury unleashed into both the evils of the corporations and the race issue.[33] In Atlanta, where the racial fever centered and where the two candidates lived, he concentrated his rhetoric increasingly upon the black menace and the necessity of controlling the blacks. Reputedly, he announced his willingness to "imitate" the example of Wilmington if necessary. His principal opponent, Clark Howell, the editor of the usually calm Atlanta *Constitution,* strove only to prove that he was whiter than Smith. He did not support disfranchisement, he apologized, only because blacks were already disfranchised.[34] In Atlanta in 1906, as in Wilmington in 1898, the campaign came very close to transcending politics, party, and even personalities. It was a vast social movement in which all the whites were on one side and all the blacks—unaware, unwittingly, and not by their own efforts—were on the other. It was an intense bipolarization with, paradoxically, one pole missing.

All during the long, hot summer of 1906 both sides beat the war drums to the chant of Negro beast. Rival newspapers vied with one another in whipping the populace into a frenzy. Speaking for Smith, the Atlanta *Journal* indicted ruling politicians for having permitted any Negroes at all to vote, and it was furious in pointing out the results of such libertarianism. Allowing black men to participate equally with white men at the polls promoted black presumptuousness in the social realm, the *Journal* insisted.[35]

In addition to politics, there were many other elements contributing to the deterioration of race relations in Atlanta. As we have seen, young blacks, like young whites, were streaming into the city as the marginal farms of Georgia collapsed. Young whites could go into the cotton mills (which reached the crest of a building boom in 1906), into the factories, and into the stores and offices of the city. Black women could find places as domestics in the homes of the rapidly growing white bourgeoisie. But there were relatively few places that black men could go in the new economic order, and those few were typically the places of low-paid menials and roustabouts. The result was that many young black men who came to Atlanta in the turn-of-the-century years did not work steadily; they did in fact often become floaters. Many took their money wherever they could find it and often came to depend on black women working for whites and "toting," that is, bringing home food from the white family's table every evening.

In Atlanta and in cities all over the South, there grew up among urban black males a streetcorner society of pool halls, juke joints, and women. It was a counterculture in which Victorian values were up-ended, and in which the hero was too smart to work and too highly sexed to be satisfied by one woman. Young black men who had been born on the farm and reared to work a full day six days a week and go to church on Sunday came to the city to cultivate the hipster-trickster role, to have a succession of addresses, a number of names, no lasting job, no wife, and no child to call his own. Young black women reared to be wives and mothers on the farm and to stay at home found themselves working in white people's kitchens and minding white people's children. In this new economic order, black women became, per force, the wage earners, the providers for the family, supporting not only their children but, sporadically, the fathers of their children as well.

Thus black culture in Atlanta (and elsewhere in the industrializing, commercializing, progressive South) entered the twentieth century with something distinctly new added. The Victorian order of the peasant past might have sometimes seemed stultifying, but the new roles were not all that gratifying, neither for males nor females. Probably the secular music of these people, the plain black people, told their story best. If the "blues" was not born in the South in the few years around 1905, it should have been. It was then that young black men and women, people like Robert Charles and his woman friend Virginia Banks in New Orleans, found themselves in a world that would not allow them to sustain the values to which they had been born and reared. The early blues was the cry of the cast-out black, ultimately alone and lonely, after one world was lost and before another was found. Small wonder that they bewailed their plight ... and cursed the people who had brought them to this low estate.

White Atlanta, of course, could not even begin to understand what had happened. In their minds, black men willfully persisted in idleness at the very time when there was a scarcity of labor. Seemingly black men were dissipating their days in Decatur Street dives while the city hungered for labor. There was bitter resentment in boomer Atlanta, and a great amount of it, against black men who seemingly refused to work. Shortly before the riot, concerned citizens counted hundreds of black men idling away working hours in Decatur Street dives.

Closely related to white views of black idleness was a rising crime rate and the convict lease system. Judged by the ratio of arrests to population, Atlanta was the most criminal city in America. In 1905, out of about 80,000 whites and 50,000 blacks living in the city, Atlanta police made 17,000 arrests. Roughly 10,000 of those arrested were black men. Among those arrested, convictions ran high. Many of the convicts were leased out to the lumber companies, brickyards, and plantations around Atlanta, all of which were contributing to the city's prosperity. Attrition by death among the convicts was about 10 percent a year. Thus, in reality, black men were serving Atlanta very well indeed.

The seeming idleness, criminality, physicality, and super-sexuality of the young black male in the counterculture fitted snugly into Radical imagery. When Tom Dixon brought his play *The Clansman* to Atlanta in the fall of 1905, white audiences readily recognized its certain truth. At the first performance, the audience responded with loud enthusiasm and kept the author standing before the final curtain for several minutes of applause.[36]

Almost every area of interracial contact contributed to the deterioration of race relations in Atlanta. The streetcars in the city had long been segregated, blacks to the back and whites to the front. During the summer of 1906, however, even the limited proximity then allowed often brought on irritation and sometimes physical assault. In September the traction company moved to enforce a more rigid separation, and conductors became increasingly abusive to black patrons. John Temple Graves, the man who replaced Henry Grady as editor of the *Constitution* and ever the apostle of *apartheid,* urged the company to attach a trailer to each car for the use of the blacks, thus separating the races beyond the chance of contact.

Ultimately, of course, at the very heart of the riot lay the Radical mentality. Fed by the prohibition and political campaigns, racial Radicalism reached a new and dangerous plateau in Atlanta during the summer of 1906. Early in August, Graves and Charles Daniel, the editor of the Atlanta *News,* discovered the existence of a veritable epidemic of rapes—a "torrid wave of black lust and fiendishness" as one journalist soon labeled it. The racial apocalypse, long predicted by the Radicals, had arrived. Black men were spilling pell mell and massively over the rim of civilization into "lust and animal insanity."

The desperation of the Radicals was apparent in the multitude of detailed and appalling remedies they offered. Daniel proposed a law prohibiting white ladies from riding in the front seat of hacks with black drivers because a mere "touching of the garments" was enough to incite the beast to immediate and wanton sexuality. Any white woman "who failed to demand absolute immunity from familiarity," he warned, "invites sudden outrage." Daniel offered a reward of $1,000 for the lynching of a rapist. Graves shortly concluded that lynching was not deterrent enough, in part because satanic black ministers made martyrs of the lynched. He proposed that castration and branding an "R" on each cheek of the transgressor might be more effective. Later, he suggested that the rapist, in full view of the assembled black population, be required to ascend a tower and "pass over a slender bridge into a dark chamber where in utter darkness he perished by a terrible means never known to Negroes." Other people presented a host of suggestions in that racially fateful summer. Women should be armed and trained in shooting schools. Any white female of any age who shot and killed a would-be assailant should get a $10,000 reward. A long-term, but eventually perfect, cure was offered in the proposal to sterilize all black females. Finally, John Temple Graves raised the whole quest for sexual salvation to a new high plane by suggesting use of the ordinary scientific method and the un-ordinary use of current disease theory to meet the crisis. Postulating that there was a "germ of the rapist" much like there was germ for pneumonia, malaria, or typhoid, he proposed a grand scientific effort, the creation of a research foundation, to isolate and identify the germ. Them, presumably, they could destroy the germ and eradicate rape. Perhaps, by mass inoculations.

By mid-August white Atlanta felt trapped in an "intolerable epidemic of rape." Ray Stannard Baker, a nationally famous journalist, came to the city several weeks after the riot and hired investigators to search out the truth in regard to the fifteen rapes or attempts at rape alleged to have occurred in the six months before the day the riot began. He found that three of these had actually been committed by white men. These three received little notice in the press, even though one was a most awful and murderous affair. On the other hand, the twelve cases involving black men were played up in the press tremendously. Two of these attacks went beyond simple brutality, one of the women suffering an eye gouged out. Three other cases were "aggravated attempts" (probably meaning that some kind of assault did occur), and three more might have been attempts. Finally, three were definitely imagined and one was an attempted suicide that the woman tried to mask by making a false charge.[37]

Given the rough and rapid growth of Atlanta in the previous decade and the relative inefficiency of the city administration, it is not surprising that there should have been perhaps as many as eight cases of assault by blacks upon white females in six months. What is surprising (and revealing) is that the white community from top to bottom and across all spectrums had been so thoroughly Radicalized as to lose all perspective on the subject. Baker himself, a highly sensitive, close, and careful investigator of social happenings, perceived at once how greatly the fear of rape worked upon white minds. "I was astonished in travelling in the South to discover how widely prevalent this dread has become," he asserted. Still, the best precautions failed, and the white man's awful revenge spread a terror through the black community that whites rarely even saw—much less understood. "And yet every Negro I met voiced in some way that fear," Baker reported. "It is difficult here in the North for us to understand what such a condition means: a whole community namelessly afraid!"[38] Perhaps in any community fear can not go endlessly on. In Atlanta, they ended it with violence.

THE ATLANTA RIOT

Atlanta was ready for riot; and late in the afternoon of Saturday, September 22, it came. The wagonyards in the city were filled with farmers in from the country for a day of buying and, perhaps of drinking. It was sultry and hot. All day long the saloons on Decatur Street had been filled. About five o'clock newsboys ran through the streets selling papers reporting an attempted assault by a black man upon a white woman. Within four hours, three additional assaults were reported. Two might have been real, two more were obviously imagined.[39] Each crisis brought forth extras from the presses. Seemingly, no one thought of disbelieving the outrageous reports. The evidence was all too clear, the plague of black bestiality had struck and its victims were falling all around. As evening approached, Atlanta was distressed, distracted, quivering in a heat of anxiety.

Beginning about 6:00 p.m., groups of white men began to congregate at streetcorners to discuss the reported outrages. A massive "Negro uprising" was rumored. Blacks gathered in small groups to discuss the news and to wonder at the agitation of the whites. Blacks, of course, discounted the rumors of rape and rebellion. Some whites on the edge of the crowds began to break away temporarily to harass passing Negroes. By 8:30 stories were being circulated of fights between blacks and whites, probably arising from these streetcorner encounters. Near the intersection of Decatur and Marietta Streets, a man climbed on a platform and began to harangue the crowd. Holding up a copy of an extra advertising "THIRD ASSAULT," he shouted, "Are white men going to stand for this?" The response was loud and quick. "No! Save our Women!" cried the mob. "Kill the niggers!" Now and again, fragments of the crowd would break away to encircle and attack blacks who happened to be passing. Other crowds began to move and became roving mobs. Bands of whites surged through the streets, yelling "Nigger!" whenever they saw a black face and rushing after their prey.

Blacks were slow to comprehend their danger. Many found themselves engulfed by the raging white mass before they knew it, others walked unwittingly into its path, and still others rode streetcars—almost placidly, it seems, like cardboard figures—from the suburbs into tornadoes of violence downtown. Very soon, the mob developed a technique for attacking the cars. The cars traveled upon rails in the streets, getting power for electric motors from a trolley that rode along power lines overhead. Several men would pull the trolley down from the lines, immobilizing the car. Then the mob would surge aboard, beating, kicking, and sometimes stabbing the hapless blacks. Surprisingly, it was late in the evening before the streetcar company ceased to send its vehicles into the maelstrom of downtown Atlanta. On the cars alone, three black men died and thirty-six men and women were injured, six critically. The police force was only sporadically effective, and some policemen actually joined the mobs in their work.

On Peachtree Street, crowds of men, women, and children stood on the sidewalks and cheered while gangs of whites gave one black man after another a five-yard start. Then they raced down the street after the victim, clubbing him to the ground, where he was kicked, beaten, and sliced. Weirdly, the mob gathered the corpses of three of its victims and laid them at the foot of Henry

Grady's monument, a life-like image of the New South prophet standing on a pedestal in the street in front of the offices of the Atlanta *Constitution.* One of the bodies had someone's initials carved on its back. An actor from the North, standing with the crowd watching the races on Peachtree Street, found himself among Atlanta's finest people and noted that some of the men in the mobs of chasers were very well dressed, that some left the sidewalk from time to time to join the action, then returned to watch and converse with their neighbors. When it was seen that the actor was from the North, he was forced by the hostile crowd to express his lack of objection to the proceedings.

There were other signs that the middle and upper classes participated in the riot in one way or another. The record of arrests, such as it was, attests to the fact that not all of the rioters were hoodlums and boys, but rather that among them were a number of men in respectable occupations. In addition, almost certainly some of the young sons of the "quality" were involved. But the police apparently did not often arrest members of the more affluent class. Reporters, who shrewdly took up the duty of answering the phones in the police stations while officers were out, related that numerous calls came in from "ladies" in the suburbs asking for protection because their husbands and sons were gone—doubtless many of them to attend the riot in the inner city.

By 10:30 the mobs ruled Atlanta, their numbers probably exceeding 10,000. They attacked streetcars until, finally, the cars ceased to run. They attacked and destroyed Negro saloons, pool rooms, and restaurants. Eventually, one mob turned into Auburn Avenue, the street occupied by the most respectable black businesses in Atlanta. There it methodically destroyed one establishment after another, building up a momentum, crashing into a shop, almost literally exploding it in a matter of seconds, beating the luckless occupants, and re-forming for the next assault. As always, conspicuous figures arose in the mob. George W. Backstock came in from suburban Oakland, "to hunt niggers," as he declared. He became a tiger of terror to the black shops—organizing, directing, exhorting, leading the attackers. One young white woman took up her station on a wagon bed, screaming encouragement over the heads of the swaying, plunging mass of men.

By about 11:00 nearly all of the blacks had fled the central city or found some hiding place there, often with their employers. The first militia companies arrived from neighboring towns only to dissolve into the mobs. Later, when newly arriving units did hold together, they sided with the mobsters against the blacks. Finally, the mobs were stopped only by their own fatigue. By about 1:00 a.m., men had simply exhausted themselves. At 3:00 a cooling rain fell, people retreated to shelter, and, presumably, to restless sleep.

Sunday was quiet and anxious. Late Monday afternoon, the riot took a new course; it moved to Brownsville. Brownsville was the most affluent black suburb in Atlanta, hardly two miles from the center of the city. It was a community of well-kept homes and no saloons at all; its leadership molding itself with great care in the ideal image cast by the best class of whites. It was the cultural center for blacks in the southeastern United States, counting among its distinguished citizens bishops, lawyers, physicians, businessmen, and professors—including W. E. B. Du Bois (who happened to be away at the time of the riot). Among the schools in Brownsville were Clark and Atlanta Universities and Gammon Theological Seminary, the key training institution for Northern Methodist ministers in the South.

During that weekend, Brownsville was understandably apprehensive. Hundreds of women and children had taken refuge in the Seminary, and black men had armed themselves for the worst if the worst should come. Walter White, then a boy of thirteen and later the chief executive officer of the NAACP, remembered his father sending away the women of the family, boarding up the house, arming himself, and remaining there with Walter through the crisis. During the riot in Atlanta, Brownsville had made an official and futile request for police protection. At dusk on Monday evening, a contingent of county police did arrive. But immediately they began to arrest black men found carrying arms, of whom there were many. Seeing a group of blacks gathered in an alleyway, the officer in charge left a part of his force with the prisoners just arrested and moved with the others toward the group of blacks. The police were unmounted—which was unusual; they were armed with rifles—which was unusual; and they had in their midst white men who were not officers and of course not in uniform. They looked very much like an armed mob. Guns were pointed, someone fired, and so did they all, killing a policeman. The officers charged and soon had arrested about fifty black men. As they marched their captives toward Atlanta, two of the prisoners were shot down, one dying instantly. A pregnant white woman watching the execution dropped dead from sheer horror.

The next morning the police returned to Brownsville with the militia. Houses were entered on the pretext of searching for guns and arresting rioters from the day before. Dr. John W. E. Bowen, the black president of Gammon Theological Seminary, and members of his staff were "lined up," searched, and insulted. One professor was jailed, and it was reported that Dr. Bowen was beaten over the head with the butt of a rifle.[40] Police entered one house where they found a man lying wounded on his bed. While his family stood by, officers opened the man's shirt, pressed the muzzles of their pistols to his chest and fired. Miraculously, the man survived both the multiple wounds and the horror of the event.[41] In the Brownsville phase of the riot, four blacks were killed: a prosperous but notoriously outspoken storeowner, a seventy-year-old Union Army veteran and patron of the store who was found knifed to death behind the building, a brick mason whose respectability was signified by the fact that he earned $4 a day, and a carpenter on his way to work Tuesday morning who was shot from ambush.[42] These people were obviously of the better sort. In fact, none of the blacks killed in the riot was a vagrant, nor were any of the more numerous persons who were seriously wounded.

An excellent insight into the Radical mentality as it operated upon Atlanta was provided by Ernest Sevier Cox. Cox was a descendant of the Tennessee pioneer leader John Sevier, and he had been reared on a farm in the rich bottomland near Knoxville. At the time of the riot, he was twenty-six years old and a graduate student in the University of Chicago, then the leading school in America for students of race relations. His sister, six years his senior and married, was living in Atlanta. Cox was eager to join the mob in Atlanta. "Had my financial condition been a little better I would certainly have come and so also would some of my friends," he wrote. "No warfare ever waged was more righteous than this defence of home, family and posterity. There is nothing half so important to my people as the disposal of the negro. . . ." Neither in the Revolution nor in the Civil War, he insisted, "was civilization threatened or the permanency of the home a question involved. The negroes killed in Atlanta was the result of an effort to protect those whom God has ordained that we must protect, an effort that cannot be legally justified but has its ground and justification in a law that is higher than laws made by men." For Cox, violence was overdue. "The Conditions are intolerable and there is but one way of escape, Vengeance must have her fullest satiation until our white brethren the world over will aid us in deporting this black savage again to his native jungle." Like a number of other Radicals, Cox was a colonizationist. The jungle was the proper environment for the brute, and it was the only alternative to race war.[43]

A Conservative response to the Atlanta riot was reflected in a letter written by a mother to her son shortly after the event. "I suppose you saw in the paper about our riot," she wrote.

> Well we had a genuine *one*. While I heard the yelling Saturday night I did not know what it was till next morning when I saw the papers [.] while the city generally was very much excited *our* square & part of town was *very* quiet *we* had none of the excitement. I did [not] even see a police on our block nor a soldier except *on* the cars on their way to Brownsville, where they went by the *car* load. Carrie [the maid of the writer] went Sunday night & spent the night with her brother on Peters St & got in the midst of it but came back Monday morning uningered [*sic*] but scared to *death* & ready to pull out for *Greenville that day*. Jim Hearnshaw the waiter I brought from Porter [Porter Springs, a resort area in which her husband ran a hotel] with us to take the place of Uncle Thomas was also scared to death & ready to go to Gainesville, so that *day* I felt as though I were living over the crator of a volcano, on my "P's & Q's," to hold my help. Monday night was the night Janie was so frightened & came over to spend the night & Tuesday night Fannie Carrie[']s sister & children were run out of their home & came here to stay all night for protection. I

fix[ed] them up in the atic [*sic*] & that was the first time they had undressed & gone to bed since Friday night. *We* really had no fears for ourselves but there was no telling when it would break out next nor where, & while I had *no* feeling of *fear* we all had such a sickening feeling I hope we may never have another but unless the negroes turn over a new leaf & *behave* we certainly will have more of it. We can see in a great many cases much more *marked* respect than before. I do hope they have learned some thing.[44]

Like so many whites who were racially Conservative, this Atlanta house-wife protected "her" black servants but still blamed the blacks generally for the murderous outbreaks. Also like so many Conservatives, while she deplored violence, after it had occurred she was not unappreciative of the results. She liked her servants respectful and welcomed that fruit of the riot. Just as Roun-tree in Wilmington used the violent behavior of others for the end of restoring a proper government to the city and expelling a troublesome black journalist, so too would the Atlanta woman use the riot to restore her household to its proper order. Time and again in the South, racial Conservatives have recog-nized the value of a measure of anti-Negro violence and shown themselves willing and able to use it—even at the same time that they held themselves above such methods.

AFTERMATH

Atlanta has been described as "Janus-faced." Indeed, the two-masked symbol of the dramatic arts, one happy and smiling backed against the other sad and tragic, representing the universe of comedy and tragedy, does seem appropri-ate. The city has been at once radical and reactionary, forward and backward, progressive and regressive, sophisticated and savage, raw and refined, and urban-bodied while it has remained country-minded. So, too, in race relations has this paragon of New South cities been both Conservative and Radical. During the summer of 1906, as Radicalism seized the city, the smiling Con-servative face was almost lost in race relations. Like a tightrope walker on a suddenly elastic line, Atlanta swung distressingly low and almost lost its bal-ance. But when the riot was over, when the disaster had run nearly as far as physical and mental endurance would allow, and a black man of eminence and obvious merit said, in essence, to a meeting of the most influential Atlan-tans, "What, for God's sake, do you want us to do?", the rope grew taut again. There was, embarrassingly, no answer. The great mass of blacks in Atlanta had been doing precisely what the whites told them to do—working, church-ing, and quietly managing their own affairs. They had been doing what Booker T. Washington had advised all blacks to do in that much celebrated speech in the city more than a decade before. They had cast down their buckets where they were, and now the water came up salty, bitter, and foul.

After the riot, there was clearly a Thermidorian reaction among whites. The Radical face receded as the Conservative mask rotated to the fore. With strong, bold, deft strokes of the trowel, Conservative Atlanta quickly mortared over the large and unsightly cracks left by the racial earthquake. Almost a fourth of the police force was fired and its administration reorganized. Courts that had sent so many blacks to the chain gangs now sent to jail some of the white mobsters—including the young woman who had stood on the wagon bed and urged on the Auburn Street crowd. Far from being praised, members of the mobs were frankly labeled murderers. The streetcar companies rearranged their vehicles for a clearer separation of the races and ordered better treatment of blacks by their employees. The fact that mob action and lynching did not deter the potential rapist was recognized and publicly advertised. The grand jury censured the newspapers, and the *News* in particular, for their indulgence in sensationalism before and during the riot. Most journals vowed to do better. A Civil League of leading whites and blacks was organized to promote interracial harmony. Many influential whites began again to beat the happy racial rhythm and sing out the sweet song of how the best whites take care of the best Negroes . . . their "nigras." When they paused to listen, they seemed to hear the black voices responding harmoniously from the other side, uniting with their own.

Two-faced? Precisely. But all of this was better than what had gone before. A white lie, even a very large one, is better than murder. Further, if the Conservative face did not speak the whole truth, it did speak its own truth. It was real. When Atlanta was playing the conservative role, it was Conservative. It was not dissembling to appease the North, and it certainly was not dissembling to appeal to the blacks. Radical Atlanta had, itself, scared Atlanta straight, and Conservatism came to the fore. The city had become Conservative because it could not see itself in its ideal image and continue in violence. Atlanta, in its own eye, was progressive, it was rational, generous, and genteel. Ray Stannard Baker arrived in the city as the Conservative face of Janus was rapidly turning the Radical face to the rear, and he took the Conservative face for the true face, which it then was. Had Baker come two months before, he would have seen another face, and one no less true. As violence came, white fear receded; as violence receded, so too did the desire for violence. Law and order became the great goal, and even the memory of violence faded rapidly away from white minds. Shortly after the riot, Ernest Cox thought that forty blacks had perished in the fray, an estimate commonly accepted. Some weeks later Baker reported ten blacks and two whites dead and sixty blacks and ten whites wounded. A 1969 study counted twenty-five blacks and one white dead and one hundred and fifty persons seriously wounded. The very count of the black dead reflected public consciousness of Radicalism's existence. It moved down from forty to ten to nothing as the riot was forgotten, and rediscovery only occurred late in the Civil Rights movement. The Atlanta riot, like the Robert Charles riot in New Orleans, was practically erased from popular memory and was generally refound by historians only in the late 1960s.

After the riot, whites in Atlanta were more careful in race relations, and blacks became very quiet. Blacks acquired a new caution, both with whites and with each other. Blackness became a serious liability and promiscuous association with other blacks a dangerous matter. They had learned, from bitter experience, to distrust the ability of the friendly face of Janus to control the hate face. Violence could come again. Blacks searched for a modus vivendi in a traditionally cautious style, by withdrawing. Sometimes they left Atlanta, and often they left Georgia, often by the hundreds and sometimes by the thousands. But, mostly, the black world retreated into itself.

The risingly Conservative leadership of white Atlanta worked hard to blame the riot on the lower and ragged fringes of the city's population. It was, so the rhetoric ran, the vagrant and criminal Negro who committed the exciting acts that gave the kernel of truth to the great fear of rape. It was the "white trash" who made up the mobs that stupidly punished all blacks. This lower order consisted of white bodies existing beyond the reach of society and without class. They were pariahs, untouchables, soulless white flesh, "skins," in the language of the day. Worst of all, they punished the best of the blacks for the sins of the worthless few. White trash hated Negroes, while their late masters loved them—in their places,—and jealousy led the lower order to hate the best of the colored people with double strength. Behind it all lay the saloons, and lawless men of both colors. Upper-class whites bore the original sin of not being properly vigilant before the riot. But now, they were ready, and they were redeemed. They were engaged, as Baker so elegantly phrased it, in an "extraordinary reconstructive work" to abolish saloons, vagrancy, and ignorance. Drink had corrupted the flesh, both black and white. Prohibition would begin to effect the cure and compulsory public education would carry it forward. Baker caught the new mood perfectly and, indeed, shared it heartily. His apologia for upper-class white Atlanta was contained in his article "Following the Color Line," which appeared in *The American Magazine* in April 1907, and was read nation-wide.[45]

Within a decade the black beast rapist practically disappeared as an image in the mind's eye of white Atlanta. But so too did the Washingtonian image of the black as progressive—working, saving, building, proudly earning his way into the world. In their stead came a resurgence of the image of the black as child, as neo-Sambo, appealing and appalling again, but most of all needing the helping hand of patrician and paternal whites to hold a place in the society.

What was true in Atlanta was true in the South generally. Black people who did not fit the stereotype of neo-Sambo had no presence in the eyes of whites. Black man as a man became "Invisible Man." The bad image of the black as beast went underground and re-emerged to be applied not to blacks, but to aliens. In the Frank case in Atlanta in 1913, as we shall see later, the beast became a Northern Jew with a German name, a college bred, opera-going urbanite, a wealthy factory master who would grind our girls into dust for gold. Sometimes the beast would be the alien Jew, but often he would take on other guises: he would be alien and Catholic; in both World Wars he would be German; and after the Russian revolution in 1917, he was most often Communist and eager to disturb our otherwise good black people and use them as tools against us. By the 1930s, the black beast of Radicalism had come to be, most often, the Commie-Jew-labor-organizer. It was no more coincidence that in the 1950s during the Cold War and the rage for McCarthyism that deep-South Southerners, the very sons of secession, became the most loyal of Americans, the foremost of America firsters, totally undeceived by, as FBI Director J. Edgar Hoover called the communists, the "Masters of deceit."

CHAPTER VII

Depoliticalization and the Separation of the Races

Violence and the great threat of violence was one way in which Radicals sought to lower the self-esteem of blacks and thus render them more controllable on the way to their demise. But there were other, more subtle means to effect that end. We could never catalogue and describe, nor even count all of these instruments of discrimination. Indeed, the process can not be caught in words that must follow one upon the other. White people talking to blacks in the Radical mood, for instance, was not only a matter of choosing specific words to fall in sequence; it was also a matter of speech inflections, pauses, rises and falls in pitch and volume, of body postures and relative positions, of movements of eyes and hands, all simultaneous and beyond words. It was also more. It was a matter of dress and costume, of naming and titles of address, of place and setting, money in the bank, and talking down from the porch to the yard.

Two of the tools used to reduce and, hence, to manage blacks were disfranchisement and segregation. These tools were often the subject of laws and legalities, verbally expressed. Perhaps it was precisely because these laws and legalities were so amenable to the kind of verbal reduction traditionally favored by scholars, who always deal in words, that they have been so much emphasized by students of race relations. Even so, remembering that we are talking about only a small and not totally representative portion of reality, it is worthwhile to examine those laws and how they came to be as a way of getting at the larger subject.

Radicalism had a special motive in its effort to pass laws to disfranchise black men and to separate the races in public places, one that was distinctly different from the special motive of Conservatism in the same process. The Radical motive was to depress the expectations of blacks, especially black men, to make them less secure and ultimately less aggressive, to lead them to follow with minimal resistance the inevitable path to racial extinction. Radicals readily recognized, as Clark Howell said about disfranchisement in Georgia, that blacks were already practically disfranchised and segregated, but to Radicals the laws were useful in showing explicitly and blatantly the power of whites. They were tokens of hard and present truths and signs of things to come—of the surety of white supremacy and the futility of black resistance. Robert Charles read the signs perfectly in Louisiana in 1900, and his death seemed to confirm the truth of his understanding.

Conservatives did respond to aggressive Radical actions. They responded to lynching, rioting, and the push to enact severe measures of disfranchisement and segregation. But the response of the Conservatives was always muted by the special character of Conservatism. Conservatives were never spectacular. They were not gladiators who descended into the arena to do combat with the barbarian, to do and die. Rather, they were willing to make a test, and to make a true test. But if they did not win that test, they would retire and wait. Conservatism knows that in the end it will win, and it knows that winning is a matter of action, but Conservatism also understands that winning ultimately is a matter of waiting for the right time, the right place, and the right issue. God is in his Heaven always, and in the end all things will come right on earth. The response of Convervatism to the Radical upsurge, then, was a generally soft reaction. It was executed by people possessed of a terrific patience that renders them very nearly unbeatable.

DISFRANCHISEMENT

The movement to disfranchise blacks by legal and constitutional means that swept through the South in the generation after 1890 was only a part of a larger and longer process that might be called the depoliticalization of the Negro. To focus upon legal and formal disfranchisement is to run the risk of neglecting the broad and much more important occurrence. Substantially the depoliticalization of the Negro had been achieved with the close of Reconstruction, especially in the deep South where blacks were most numerous and where they had been most active in the politics of Reconstruction. There, indeed, the political reduction of black people—by persuasion if possible, by fraud and intimidation if necessary—was precisely the central process of Redemption. The effort had its practical side in relieving Negroes of offices and removing ballots from black hands, but it also had a psychological aspect. A major part of Redemption involved enforcing upon Negroes the conviction that significant political power would never be theirs again. Most blacks, it seems, learned that lesson well. They simply retired from practical political activity. During this great emotional recession after Reconstruction, blacks moved downward from a practical inability to vote, to an inability to register to vote, to an inability even to participate in Democratic party activities and the Democratic primary (which, in effect, soon became the real election), and, finally, to an inability to maintain their undisputed representation in national Republican conventions, and, hence, from that, by the 1920s, to a loss of federal patronage.

But when one has said that blacks had already been largely removed from politics by Redemption, one must also hasten to say, "but not quite." Indeed, never quite. Somewhere in the South, blacks always voted, and somewhere in the North there was always sentiment that it should be so. The struggle of black people in the South to maintain a political life for themselves after Reconstruction was most striking in three forms: a persisting activism in certain enclaves heavily populated by blacks where Redemption had not thoroughly penetrated, a rather curious phenomenon that might be labelled the "echo Reconstruction" that occurred in the states of the upper South in the 1880s and 1890s after Reconstruction had definitely died in the lower South in 1877, and various upsurges of blacks in politics as allies of white splinter movements. These forms were not mutually exclusive, and now and again all three combined in one movement.

Paradoxically, one area of the deepest, longest-running, and most powerful participation by blacks in politics in the South after Reconstruction came out of compromises made in the black belts by Redemption itself. In some states in the early years of Redemption, the process of expelling Negroes entirely from politics appeared so vast an undertaking as to seem impossible. Therefore, Redeemers frequently resorted to programs of "containment." They gerrymandered black strength into restricted areas and conceded certain offices to blacks in return for other offices for whites. The South Carolina Democracy, for instance, yielded some offices and functions in the counties around Beaufort and Georgetown where the black majorities were no less than massive. Black political dominance in those areas eroded only gradually as local whites pressed, with aid from a state government firmly in the hands of whites, for more and more control. The gerrymandered black belt Congressional district in South Carolina seated a black Congressman, George Washington Murray, as late as 1896 and a black state representative as late as 1900. All-black militia companies, unarmed, persisted until 1905, and a black man remained as the Collector of the Port of Beaufort until ousted by Ben Tillman early in the Wilson administration in 1913.[1] In North Carolina, the Redeemers created the "Black Second" Congressional District, previously mentioned, to absorb a great portion of the black votes in the state. In 1888 the Black Second elected the state's first Negro Congressman, Henry Cheatham. Beginning with the enclave of the Black Second and thriving under a fusion arrangement with the Populists, Negroes in eastern North Carolina in the mid-1890s generated a

growing, strengthening, grass roots variety of black power that was killed ultimately only by the white power that it, itself, unwittingly engendered in a state
that was 75 percent white.

There was a rather striking persistence of black activism in politics in the
upper South generally. In fact, it is possible to contend that in the upper South
in the 1880s and 1890s there was a second Reconstruction, followed by still
another Redemption. It was, in a sense, an "echo Reconstruction" that has, as
a whole thing, gone largely unnoticed. When we generalize about Reconstruction in the South, we are often referring to Reconstruction in the deep South
where blacks were most numerous and where the process ran its course fully
and deeply before the end of 1877. In the upper South, the first Reconstruction
was not only much more short-lived, it was also milder. This was true, perhaps, because blacks were few enough and native white Republicans were
numerous enough to reduce substantially the strength of race as an issue and
to make the first Reconstruction a milder thing—more of a conflict between
white men and less of a contest between white and black, and therefore relatively less heated.

Tennessee affords a good example of an early Reconstruction and Redemption and a later recurrence of the process. The first Reconstruction in Tennessee began under the leadership of native whites in 1864 and was so far accomplished by 1867 that the radical Congress exempted it from the military rule
established in that year in the other ten ex-Confederate states. The ease with
which Tennessee passed through that first phase had much to do with the fact
that unionism was very high in the state before and during the war (especially
in the mountainous eastern portions), and the Republican party was able to
muster into its ranks after the war a solid phalanx of native whites. Soon, the
Democrats reclaimed the state, but in 1880 they lost the governor's chair to a
still vital Republican party. In the 1880s, the as yet unchastened blacks of Tennessee were encouraged to attempt to move more fully into political life, first
as followers within the resurgent Republican party and then, more assertively,
as leaders willing to cooperate with white Democratic reformers against their
own erstwhile white Republican bosses. The rebellion entered a critical phase
as black leaders, such as John C. Napier, George W. Cable's Nashville friend,
moved to claim offices for themselves and urge legislation favorable to blacks.
Soon, the rebellion came to an abrupt end, brought up sharply against a risingly popular and lethal lily-whiteism among Republicans in the state. Finally,
Democrats used the racial division among Republicans to reduce black political participation in Tennessee to a minimum.

In 1888 Tennessee Democrats pushed through a law that required citizens
to establish their eligibility to vote by registering during a specified interval
well before elections and then closed the books to additional registrations for
some time before elections were actually held. Drawing out the process and

making it complicated had the effect of discouraging the less well informed and determined among potential electors. Most of all, registration allowed political managers to go far toward molding the electorate into the exact shape that they desired and to monitor its performance.

In the same year, the "Volunteer State" was the first in the South to introduce the Australian ballot. This ballot simply listed all of the candidates for each office on a single slip of paper, indicating the party of each candidate and providing some means for the voter to mark his preference in the secrecy of the voting booth. Previously separate ballots for each party had been supplied, usually by the party itself. The voter had only to appear at the polls, ask for the ballot of the party of his choice, and place it in the box. This system lent itself to frauds of many kinds. For instance, voters could "stuff" a ballot box by carrying in a number of counterfeit ballots and covertly casting them into the box along with their legitimate votes. Under the Australian system, widely hailed as a progressive reform, there was but a single ballot and the voter claimed his ballot from the election officials at the polls. He then went into a closed place, and there, in private, marked his choices before placing his ballot in the box. Under the old system, any watcher could learn how a man voted. Under the Australian system, the voter's preference was his secret, and political bosses were thus presumably foiled. Use of the Australian system obviously required more than bare literacy on the part of the voter. The Australian ballot doubtlessly did promote honesty in voting in the South, but it also effectually disfranchised vast numbers of illiterates and near illiterates, black and white. It was, in essence, a moderate literacy test and was sustained as such by the Supreme Court in 1893.

In 1890 Tennessee improved upon the already remarkable results of its registration and balloting laws by adding a poll tax requirement for voting. Thereafter, the state seemed substantially relieved of concern about black voting, even though the black population comprised a quarter of the total and western counties were heavily Negro. Tennessee did go Republican in 1910 and 1912, but it was not because of black votes. The state had long nurtured a very strong white Republican element in its eastern, mountainous portions. A Republican Tennessee, then and since, does not at all imply a black Tennessee.[2]

What happened in Tennessee happened in other states of the upper South as well, but with less clarity. Possibly, there was an "echo Reconstruction" in the upper South in part because the first had not sufficiently raised the race issue, and, consequently, Redemption had not sufficiently downed it. The first Redemption had not "taken," and another, stronger innoculation was required to immunize those states from the ambitions of Negroes in politics. Thus, blacks in the upper South were substantially removed from politics only after the deep South Redemption in 1877.

There was a third form in which blacks re-entered politics after Redemption, and this phenomenon occurred in both the lower South and the upper. White splinter movements rebelling against conservative Democratic domination sometimes turned to appeal to potential black voters. In Virginia, in 1879, ex-Confederate General William "Billy" Mahone used black votes in his successful bid to gain control of the state. For a time he elevated himself to the United States Senate, and, as a by-product of his revolt, he raised the specter of blacks in politics again and absolutely horrified many of his fellow white Virginians.[3] In South Carolina, the Greenbackers did much the same, as did various elements of the warring Democracy in Georgia (in which, ironically, the Feltons were leaders) and Louisiana. In the 1890s Populists all over the South appealed to blacks for their support. In North Carolina, as we have seen, Populists and Republicans made the most successful fusion arrangement, one that held control of the state for four years after 1894, a control powered essentially by black votes. Spectacular as they sometimes were, these threats from white splinters were all evanescent, fading especially quickly in the deep South where blacks existed in relatively great numbers and where black Reconstruction had been most real. There, the very gathering of black power quickly—almost automatically—generated a counter-gathering of white power that ultimately prevailed.

Thus, during the post-Reconstruction era and on into the early years of the twentieth century, when Southern whites undertook to disfranchise black men further by legal and constitutional means, there was a real object in view. In every Southern state some black men did vote in some elections, and always there was a possibility that others might do so.

And yet those threats were limited. In the South at large, the great mass of blacks had not voted since Reconstruction. After Reconstruction black voting never threatened white supremacy in the South as a whole, nor was it ever an active threat in a given state for very long. The threat of black voting was spotty, and it was sporadic. When it arose, white politicians dealt with it locally and relatively quickly.

Why then, did Southern whites pass laws to accomplish what had, in substance, already been accomplished? They did so, it seems, for varying combinations of three basic reasons: reform, politics, and race.

Disfranchisers of all persuasions clearly felt that they were acting in the spirit of reform. The fact was that previous disfranchisement had been achieved and was maintained by corruption, fraud, and intimidation, conditions that steadily tested the tolerance of the North and strained morality at home. The laws passed in and after 1890 sought to obtain the same end by legal means. The laws would purify the process, they would also purify the electorate. As the disfranchisers thought, legal disfranchisement would permanently remove corruptible voters from participation in the body politic—

be they real or potential, major or minor, black or white. To them, the disfranchised were precisely the morally infirm, the ignorant, those who could be bought by the selfish interests or duped by demagogues.

Disfranchisement was also motivated by raw political partisanship. Parties in power do tend to attempt to load the electoral dice to reduce the potential of their opponents. This was true of Republicans, Populists, and independents as well as Democrats, and it was true in the North and West as well as in the South. Politically, the motivation of Massachusetts Republicans in attempting to disfranchise the newly arrived Irish who became Democrats was not vastly different from that of the Southern Democrats who attempted to disfranchise the newly emancipated blacks who became Republicans. Republicans in Reconstruction had disfranchised Democrats, and the Populists in power in the legislature in North Carolina in the 1890s were not at all above attempting to rewrite the charters of towns and alter town limits to throw those usually Democratic strongholds into the hands of Populists.

It happened, of course, that the Democrats were generally in power in the South in and after 1877. They sought, therefore, to disfranchise Republicans, Populists, and independents. Democrats did, in fact, pass laws that took the vote from the hands of hundreds of thousands of Republicans. But it also happened that the great majority of Republicans were black. To disfranchise a Republican was most often to disfranchise a black person. This raises a problem in ascertaining by the results which, between politics and race, was the primary motive? On the other hand, it hardly seems very necessary to establish a primary motive—both motives operated, and both operated powerfully. White Democrats were much gratified at the reduction of a Republican whether white or black, and to hit both with one shot would be especially gratifying. When Ben Tillman disfranchised the black man in South Carolina in 1895, he did not discount the income that would accrue to his party.

Finally the disfranchisers were also motivated by racism. More accurately, disfranchisers were motivated by two forms of racism—Radicalism and Conservatism—and each form had its special set of motivations, its preferences as to ways and means, and its concept of objectives.

Radicals disfranchised black men because, as Mrs. Felton declared, white men equalizing themselves with black men at the polls had the effect of leading black men to think that they could equalize themselves with white men elsewhere—particularly with white women. To Radicals, disfranchisement was a device to promote political and social—even psychological and sexual—purity. It was a way of removing the black voter from the path of progress, and also it was a tool for turning down black self-esteem. Radicals did see themselves as reformers, of course, but when Radicals disfranchised, race was the prime motivation, with partisan politics playing a strong secondary role.

Conservatives, far from thinking of disfranchisement as a way of ruling Negroes out of society, thought of it as a way of keeping them in, of protecting them and preserving them in their place. By relieving the incompetent black man of his vote, one relieved him of the power of abusing himself and others—and, consequently, one relieved whites of the necessity of abusing blacks by fraud and violence before and at the ballot boxes. Partisanship was present in Conservative disfranchisement, of course, but it was probably the least of three motives. On the other side, reform placed a very strong second, if indeed with many Conservatives, it did not place first.

Often, both Radical and Conservative disfranchisement used combinations of the same devices to effect their distinctly different ends, and thus it has been easy to assume a unity of motives among the disfranchisers that did not, in fact, exist. There was a profound division between Radical and Conservative disfranchisement, and that division was reflected subtly in the means preferred, if not always used, by each.

Like a golden thread running through an often confused weave, Conservative disfranchisement was marked by a willingness to leave the best of the blacks enfranchised and, conversely, to disfranchise the worst of the whites. For instance, in Virginia, where the Conservative mentality ultimately prevailed, the disfranchisement provisions in the 1902 Constitution resulted in leaving some 30,000 black voters on the registration books and removing some 60,000 whites. Conservatives, then, would nod approvingly at an aracial application of legal disfranchisement. On the other side, Radicals drove to disfranchise all black men and enfranchise all white men. Moreover, Radicals would never give more than lip service to a racially impartial application of the disfranchising process, and that was given for the benefit of a justifiably suspicious North. Seldom would the Radical yield even that. Like Ben Tillman, he much preferred to advertise loudly that all Negroes, regardless of merit, were going to be disfranchised, blatantly and in the greatest possible numbers and that the South was a white man's country.

Radicals also soon came to distinguish themselves from Conservatives by their preference for the "understanding clause" as a loophole device for letting in white voters and excluding black, while the latter came to prefer the "grandfather clause." These devices grew up in the 1890s as states rewrote their constitutions to meet the new times.

In eight Southern states, disfranchisement was sought by either amending or rewriting the constitution of the state. It will occasion no surprise that all five states that formed the Radical heartland (South Carolina, Georgia, Alabama, Mississippi, and Louisiana) were among the eight that wrote their actions into their fundamental law. Additionally, Virginia, North Carolina, and Oklahoma did so. In those eight states, disfranchisers of both persuasions typically set up standard qualifications of property, education, and good citi-

zenship for voters. The reforming fathers then added a clause allowing prospective voters to by-pass those strict requirements by meeting some other special test. Soon, two alternative tests came to be the most favored: the
"understanding clause" and the "grandfather clause."

The understanding clause permitted a citizen who could not qualify as a
voter under the ordinary standards to do so by explaining a section of the state
constitution read to him by an election official. Usually, three election officials
judged the performance. Ideally, the understanding clause was a test of civic
intelligence. Ultimately, however, it reflected in its results the intentions of the
officials managing the election. Originally, the understanding clause was introduced in Mississippi in 1890 as an attempt to purify the electorate by constitutional means. Mississippi later became one of the most Radical of Southern
states, but in 1890 it was still decidedly Conservative, and disfranchisement
there was first sought in a spirit of racial Conservatism. Constitutional disfranchisement, the leadership thought, would save whites from the necessity
of corrupting themselves in the election process, and it would also allow
blacks to find their proper place in the body social.

Conservative Mississippi invented the understanding clause, but Ben Tillman in South Carolina was the first to turn it to Radical ends. Endorsing its
use to disfranchise Negroes in a flagrantly discriminatory way, Tillman argued
that "some poisons in small doses are very salutary and valuable medicines."
In 1895, in drafting a new constitution for his state, Tillman got what he
wanted. Briefly, the new constitution established adult male suffrage based on
residence and poll tax requirements, plus an absence of convictions for certain
crimes. Until January 1, 1898, anyone who met these qualifications and could
read a section of the constitution (a literary test) or explain it when read to
him (the understanding clause) would be registered for life. After that time, in
order to register, an applicant must be able to read and write a section of the
Constitution (a more stringent literacy test), or pay taxes on property assessed
at $300. The administration of the understanding clause in the "Palmetto
State" produced exactly the kind of disfranchisement sought by Radicals. Virtually no white man who seriously wanted the vote was denied, and practically
no Negroes were allowed the privilege. Indicative was the fact that there were
six black delegates in the constitutional convention itself. They were without
any power save that of speech and a minority vote, both of which they used
adroitly. Nevertheless, within ten years, South Carolina, a state in which a
majority of the adult males were black, had no blacks in the legislature or any
other significant state or local office, a condition that would prevail for more
than half a century.

The understanding clause appealed to Radicals by the very fact that it
allowed election officials to enroll whomever they chose as voters and to
exclude all others. Conservatives grew to dislike it for precisely the same fact.

Shortly, Conservatives came to prefer the so-called "grandfather clause," first developed in the Louisiana Constitution in 1898, as a means of purifying the electorate. Grandfather clauses used a variety of specific techniques, but all rested upon the basic idea that the voter who failed to qualify by other means might do so if either he or one of his ancestors had performed some certain act. Thus, the voter or an ancestor might have voted in some previous year (1867 was a favored year because blacks were not then generally allowed by the states to vote in state elections), or had performed some significant military service for the state or nation (in the Civil War, for instance). The great appeal of the grandfather clause to Conservatives was that qualification relied upon proof of some prior fact rather than the personal impressions of registration officials. A prospective voter or one of his ancestors either had or had not voted in 1867, either he or one of his ancestors had or had not served in the military. Cases thus were lifted out of the realm of personal impression into the realm of legally establishable fact. Law and order prone Conservatives relished this approach to disfranchisement. Not only did it secure the ends they desired, it also re-established rule of law in the stead of rule of men. Without rule of law, they thought, a society could not long survive.

Conservative disfranchisement was also marked by a preference for a short time interval in which the "loophole" device, be it either the understanding clause or the grandfather clause, was to be operative. Initially, both instruments were designed to function only for a limited period during which a new registration would be effected. Thereafter, theoretically, everyone, white as well as black, would have to meet the much more stringent requirements of literacy, property holding, or tax payments. Both Conservatives and Radicals seemed to assume that the few years of grace for white supremacy thus ensured would see whites sufficiently educated and wealthy to perpetuate their predominance. Behind that was the further assumption that whites were innately superior to blacks and would dominate in these areas in a free society.

At first, legal minds among the disfranchisers thought that a short life was essential to standing the test in the courts. However, as Radical politicians gathered experience in disfranchisement, they also gathered the courage to press for allowing the loophole clauses to run for longer intervals. Ultimately, some Radicals would give them life everlasting as a symbol of their intention that theirs would forever be a white man's country. In 1898, when the grandfather clause was first used in Louisiana, its operation was limited to some three months. North Carolina Radicals ultimately compromised for a constitutional amendment, passed in 1900, that allowed registration under a grandfather clause up to December 1, 1908. Virginia, in the end dominated by racial Conservatives, followed with a new constitution in 1902 that allowed its white supremacy clause to run only about a year and a half. Georgia in 1908 adopted disfranchisement with escape devices that included both understanding and grandfather clauses. The life of the grandfather clause would terminate in 1915, but the understanding clause, under Radical pressure, was made a *permanent* feature. In Georgia the line was clearly drawn: white men would vote in perpetuity as long as other white men so chose, and black men would not. Radicalism could hardly have displayed its power more arrogantly.

At the state level, disfranchisement was the first issue upon which Conservatives organized themselves to face the Radical onslaught effectively. In the deep South, Conservatives were usually easily over-run. For example, in Alabama, in a constitutional convention called in 1901 explicitly to effect disfranchisement, ex-governor William C. Oates led the Conservatives unsuccessfully against such vigorous Radicals as young J. Thomas Heflin. On the floor of the convention, Heflin predicted the coming race war and announced his intention to disarm the Negro politically and educationally prior to the fray. "I do not believe it is incumbent upon us to lift him up and educate him and put him on an equal footing that he may be armed and equipped when the combat comes," declared Heflin.[4] In the upper South, however, Conservatism fought and won. In Virginia and North Carolina especially, the Conservative response to the Radical challenge was clearly present in the struggle over disfranchisement, and the process in each state revealed much about the nature of racial Conservatism there and elsewhere.

DISFRANCHISEMENT IN VIRGINIA

In Virginia, disfranchisement was enacted quietly by an oligarchy working in closed sessions during the meeting of a constitutional convention from November 1901 into the following spring. Yet, if one looks inside the convention, he sees that the leadership was deeply—almost desperately—divided on the issue of disfranchisement. The line of division fell between a Radicalized, black belt low-country, led, apparently, by Alfred B. Thom of the Norfolk delegation, and a steadfastly Conservative upcountry. In between, always striving for a quick compromise and a return to business as usual, were the professional politicians. It was also clear that the black belt delegates wanted an understanding clause to let in all of the whites and exclude all the blacks, and they wanted that clause to operate permanently. Law and order Conservatives strenuously opposed adoption of the understanding clause and an extended life for it if used. Finally, Virginia Conservatives were willing to see some blacks enfranchised and some whites disenfranchised, whereas Radicals wanted to exclude all of one and include all of the other.

It has often been said that reformers in the South at the turn of the century were reluctant to call constitutional conventions because they were afraid that the Negro question would break out. Ironically, in Virginia, the opposite occurred. The convention was called specifically to handle the Negro question, but the reform issue burst forth. In fact, the convention spent less than a fifth of its time on the problem of disfranchisement. Instead, after the opening week, that body turned to deal with a host of other reforms. Most especially did it turn its energies into a long and acrimonious fight over the corporations—particularly the railroad corporations. Phrases such as "typical of railroad oppression" were frequently voiced, and the whole tone of the attack would have seemed very Populistic and, indeed, radical were it not for the fact that the words were spoken by men who were devoted Democrats, judicious, and whose whole manner was thoroughly conservative. What they saw and despised was a Virginia that had fallen into the hands of the Philistines. Super-selfish, money-powered corporations were corrupting and exploiting the partial ignorance of the electorate to create a political machine that served its masters with slavish loyalty. Disfranchisement of the corruptible element—white as well as black—was important in the cure. Equally important, if not more important, was a reform program in which the Virginia patriciate would use state government, restructured to include appropriate administrative devices, to bring the venal corporations to heel and to protect all of the people of the Commonwealth from insidious combinations. Possibly, virtuous Virginia gentlemen were even more concerned about protecting their state from cancerous corporate influence than they were about saving it from black voters.

Alexander Caperton Braxton, a delegate to the convention from Staunton, was representative of the Conservative mentality in that assembly.[5] Before he was elected to the convention in April 1901, Braxton had spent twenty years of hard labor as a lawyer in Staunton, a storybook village nestled in the valley of the Shenandoah. His practice provided his only income, which was modest. His private papers indicate that much of his work was "public service," managing a widow's property to provide her with some income, settling small disputes between farmers, and so on. His records, his accounts, his legal papers, and his correspondence all show him to be an intelligent, orderly, and highly capable person. Also he was modest. To a journalist writing an article on the members of the convention, he described himself as a small-town lawyer of no distinction. Almost unmentioned were the facts that his father's father had been a general in the American Revolution and that his mother's father had been a United States Senator. Braxton himself had eschewed politics and public notice. Before he became a delegate to the convention, he had never been active in politics, nor had he held political office. He hardly knew Thomas Martin, the boss of the Democratic machine in the state, or lesser lieutenants such as Daniel, Jones, Flood, or Byrd. But in 1901 when Virginia was in peril, Braxton, like Cincinnatus, the patrician republican of ancient Rome, left his simple plow and entered the fray as a general. He offered himself as a candidate for a seat in the convention, and, in a carefully organized campaign, he defeated three other contestants to win his place.[6]

Before the convention met, Braxton prepared himself thoroughly. He wrote to Louisiana for advice on the grandfather clause. He queried various governors about the effect of the poll tax upon the suffrage in their states. He established contact with Booker T. Washington to get the black viewpoint. In addition, he studied, wrote, and spoke about the legal aspects of suffrage requirements. In the convention, in spite of the fact that he was previously virtually unknown in Virginia politics, he immediately emerged as one of the best-informed and most effective delegates. Consequently, he was made a member of the committee on suffrage and earned the chairmanship of the committee on corporations. Out of the latter, he pulled a constitutional provision for a railroad commission to regulate those most flagrant of arbitrary corporations. After the convention, he continued the battle by fighting to fill that commission with good men who would bring the corporations firmly to heel. Thereafter, he retired to private life and never again stood for public office. To men of Braxton's mind, the revolution of 1900, like the Jeffersonian revolution of 1800, was a revolution of virtue over power. Braxton was as close to the ideal Virginia gentlemen as flesh ever comes. He was noble and modest, talented and unselfish, aristocratic but not arrogant; he was decent, unpretentious, and quietly committed to the public good. He was not a wealthy man, but had he been, he would not have shown it. In Virginia, patrician leadership listened to the people, and then they told the people what they heard. They gave back the word neatly set in the form of sermons, in editorials, in speeches and articles, and in the lessons of the classroom and courtroom. Occasionally, they encapsulated the essence of popular intelligence in laws and constitutions. Virginia leadership was never very far from its followers. Patricians knew that the distance between what the people wanted and what the elite offered as the ideal could never be very great. "As you know," cautioned Braxton in advising a friend not to stand for female suffrage, "the laws should never be too much in advance of public sentiment, for otherwise they can never be successfully enforced, whatever may be their intrinsic merit."[7] The Virginia style of leadership stands out in bold relief against that other Southern mode that might be called the South Carolina (or Deep South) style. In the latter, the patricians speak, the people listen, and the words have no necessary relation to what the people want.

In Virginia, this small distance between what the people wanted and what the aristocracy wanted them to accept was the limited area in which Conservative leadership worked. It worked within those limits with relative contentment because it believed that the *status quo* was mostly right. Time and persuasion, for Virginia patricians, were the great solvents to leach impurities out of the social structure. Change was expected to be a constant necessity; but always around the edges and never in the center. In Virginia (and perhaps in many parts of the South) progressivism was conservatism, and there was no paradox in the fact. The Southern conservative mind could earnestly and honestly embrace the new even as it venerated the old. Thus, Southern progressivism could march surefootedly into the future, as it did, with its eyes fixed confidently upon the past, as they were.

Racial Conservatism used the medium of projected images in channeling society into new forms. The new image, the image of the way things were supposed to be, was worked out by the elite, often secretly, among themselves. Patricians might disagree actively and vociferously; but they also agreed that such divisions ought not to be public. When they had found a practical rendition of that ideal shape, they would offer it to the people as the only one possible. A public division of the leadership would confuse the masses and bring on the most horrible of horribles—a breakdown in the consensus, dissolution, anarchy, and social chaos. A new way had to be "talked up" to the masses by the leadership through its myriad channels of communication as the only way until there was massive acceptance; until the public mind took it as only natural, and dissent seemed unnatural if not, indeed, immoral. When a happy level of general virtue was thus attained, individual Virginians would be their own governors, carrying within themselves a perception and an appreciation of what was right for the whole community, and they would behave themselves accordingly. In such a society, rigid rules give way to sliding rules, every action is measured and fitted to the situation—almost intuitively—by the actor. Everybody does right, and formal government yields its power to its responsible citizens, each reclaiming the self-government that is, innately, his own.

The perpetual duty of the patrician is to bless the good publicly, and to disapprove of the bad, to smile upon conformity to social ideals and to frown upon its lack. The patriciate then becomes a secular priesthood, defining the civil theology, observing and leading the rituals, administering the sacraments at graduations, at militia musters, county fairs, in the courts, at balls and teas, at official and social functions, in the schools, churches, and newspapers, and in their parlors, at their dining tables, and in the streets. Individuals were the bricks, institutions were the mortar, and patricians were masons who brought them skillfully together into the stout building of the church social, the only shelter under which civilization could survive.

In the Virginia model, patricians were to lead by persuasion and by the soft strength of example. Individual aristocrats should strive to be moral. But Virginia gentlemen were not overly burdened with a sense of original sin. They accepted—one might even say they relished—the minor lapses of the flesh, and they awaited, as one waits for birth and death, the one-time peccadillo that seemed to befall each man and woman. But in the church social of

Virginia, there were no Donatists; an imperfect priest could yet administer a valid sacrament. As with the Christian church in its formative years, the latter was a doctrine that worked powerfully for the survival of the institution—gave it, indeed, a life and purity that was beyond and above the sum of its parts. Gentlemen would sometimes fail, but they must strive for perfection. Good works did count; a person could atone for his social sins, venal and cardinal, by laying public service and good intentions upon the other side of the balance. Repentance also counted; the civil sinner should rue his act and vow to go and sin no more. Finally, and perhaps most interestingly, patricians should act upon the principle that "wishing will make it so." If they could not be perfectly moral, then they were duty-bound to seem to be moral. Ultimately, plebeians would follow the true evangel as preached and projected rather than as actually practiced. Ultimately again, plebeians, given and grasping the proper images, would render a less than perfect governor as a perfect government—or nearly so. But, of course, in reality noble Virginians seldom fell very far from grace, and plebeians pursued faithfully their primary duty of emulating the idealized example projected by their betters. In Virginia, seeming was never very far from being.

Thus it was that in the Old Dominion patricians always preached, and, often enough, they practiced; and the plebeians did follow. By the projection of idealized images as present and real, Virginia largely achieved that proper consensus that was the key to its contentment. The Commonwealth might well have made its motto: "Seeming Is Being."

This concept of consensus leadership marked the men who dominated the Virginia constitutional convention of 1901–02. Fortunately, A. C. Braxton, representing Augusta County (Staunton) in the convention, left in his papers a fairly complete record of how the process worked on this occasion.

True to the harmonies of law and order, Braxton was at first strongly attracted to a legally plausible device for removing the Negro from politics. Recurrently, other Southerners had thought of the idea that he soon came to champion, specifically that the Fifteenth Amendment had conferred upon Negroes the right to vote, but it had not conferred the right to hold office. Therefore, Negroes might vote, but only for white men. In June and July of 1901, he worked to construct a brief for that case and read a paper before the Virginia Bar Association urging experimentation in that direction.[8] In the convention, he attempted to offer a provision that a white voter might hold office "provided, that no person having less than three-fourths white blood shall be regarded as a white person in the meaning of this section. . . ." The convention, however, did not respond to the idea.

Once appointed to the committee on suffrage, Braxton made detailed inquiries concerning programs used in other Southern states. Significantly, he did not correspond with the "understanding clause" states of Mississippi and

South Carolina. He had a mild interest in the Louisiana "grandfather clause" and in the results of the disfranchising efforts of the Alabama convention that was closing even as that of Virginia was beginning.[9] By mid-November, however, Braxton was convinced that the poll tax alone, paid some six months prior to elections, "will practically settle the negro question."[10]

Strenuously opposed by the Conservatives in the convention was a plan relying heavily upon an understanding clause. That plan was strongly supported by a Radicalized black belt Virginia. The understanding clause soon came to be championed by Alfred P. Thom, a highly successful railroad lawyer representing the heavily Negro district of Norfolk. The so-called "Thom plan" would have given great powers to local election officials in deciding just who should and who should not vote. The use of the understanding clause in Virginia would be an overkill. The total potential electorate in the state already was about three-quarters white, and the Walton Law of 1894 had already largely disfranchised blacks under what amounted to a literacy test. Conservatives simply could not brook the blatant illegality of that demonstration of power. "Damn what the few fanatics in the black belt want," wrote a Conservative friend to Braxton. "Rather let the negro have all that country, than to take away the rights of a single man to vote. . . . "[11]

Braxton opened his own attack against the understanding clause on November 20, 1901, in a meeting of the Committee on Suffrage. He began by suggesting that the decision of the Supreme Court in 1898 in the case of *Williams* v. *Mississippi* left the use of the understanding clause still subject to review. If evidence of uniform discrimination was produced, the plan would be invalidated. The clause was not necessarily a magic wand for disfranchisement. The Staunton lawyer then turned to the task of putting the whole question into a proper perspective. He rejected the Jeffersonian idea that self-government was a natural form. God gave whites the intelligence and courage to govern themselves and the duty to "govern & protect" Negroes. Blacks were "the undeveloped children among races—to turn them over to their own devices would be cruel." However, in meeting the issue of Negro suffrage, white Virginians were in danger of debasing and debauching themselves. The task of the convention was to save whites as well as blacks, Braxton insisted, and he rued that some delegates had pledged not to disfranchise white men in the pursuit of those ends.[12]

The disfranchisement of white men was a fire through which Conservatives had to pass, and they usually emerged on the cool side with the conviction that some blacks would have to stay as voters and some whites would have to go. One gentleman was unwontedly blunt for his class. He advised scrapping both the proposed understanding and grandfather clauses entirely for a poll tax paid six months in advance and a property qualification, exempting, of course, old soldiers. Do this, he urged, "& you have a plan that will disfranchise ¾ of the negroes & the worthless whites too. Do not be 'demagogues' about the 'poor white man'—"[13]

Demagogues were not conspicuous in the Virginia convention, but Braxton was alive to the deeper threats of an understanding clause to white men. "Will the Understanding Clause either Keep out fraud or Keep in white men?" he asked his colleagues on the Suffrage Committee. Certainly not, it was fraud itself. "It is not merely the *danger* of there [sic] *being fraudulently administered—they are intended to be so*," he asserted. Furthermore, that device might be easily turned against whites with the result that machine politics would rule, and "the hopeless apathy of political death would Settle upon us, as in Miss. where only 40,000 out of nearly 150,000 white men still go through the form of voting!" Soberly, he suggested that it might be better to allow fraudulent politics to continue in certain limited areas of the state if the convention could not offer an honest program. It was typical of Southern consensus leadership to opt for no change at all if the great majority could not agree on what the change was going to be. In committee, on the next day Braxton moved cautiously to support a temporary grandfather clause.[14]

After November, the convention abandoned discussion of the suffrage issue until the middle of March. In the interim, it took on the corporations. Only in its last days did the assembly turn again to what was, ostensibly, its primary purpose for being. As Braxton wrote confidentially to a friend, the issue created "pandemonium." "I do not believe," he said, that "any two members entertain the same views on the question of suffrage." He feared that the convention would either do nothing "or else that the unspeakable horrible understanding clause be fastened upon us indefinitely, to the lasting disgrace of our Convention and the humiliation of the State, which I believe will be at once relegated to the status of Mississippi and South Carolina."[15]

The Committee on Suffrage finally recommended to the convention a permanent understanding clause. Conservatives fought desperately to make the clause temporary and very short-lived. With professional politicians in the middle, a compromise was finally effected in which an understanding clause was inserted into the constitution, but its application was reduced to a matter of months. Afterward, Virginia would be virginal again.

When the convention had finished its work, Braxton was proud of it. He and many of his colleagues were ready to proclaim the good news to the state as finished and accepted fact without submitting it for popular ratification. Shortly the convention did precisely that. Braxton was disturbed to hear that a movement was afoot to protest the convention's failure to offer the new constitution to the judgment of the people as had been promised. He and others argued that the integrity, the talent, and the good intentions of the delegates gave the new constitution its authority. Braxton as much as said that such defects as it possessed would be rendered nugatory by the surface acceptance of the whole thing. Ninety of the one hundred members of the convention favored it, he argued confidentially to other members of the convention, why court anarchy?[16] In the end, aristocratic Virginia did simply proclaim the constitution in effect, and the Commonwealth, as was its wont, accepted.

DISFRANCHISEMENT IN OKLAHOMA AND ELSEWHERE

The framework within which constitutional disfranchisement occurred was constantly changing. Not only was it different in different states and in different regions within different states, it also changed over time. What seemed bold in Mississippi in 1890, or in South Carolina in 1895, or even in Louisiana in 1898, had become quite ordinary within a decade. By the end of 1902, six Southern states had passed disfranchising amendments to their constitutions, and Georgia, in 1908, was encouraged to follow. Oklahoma, in 1910, was the last state to incorporate disfranchising provisions into its constitution.

Oklahoma is, in many ways, the most curious of Southern states in race relations. In some aspects of racial activities, it is also the most revealing precisely because of its peculiarities. One obvious cause of Oklahoma's difference has been the presence there of a highly significant number of original Americans, the Indians, who have added a complicating third dimension to the bi-racial pattern usual in other states in the South. In addition, the northern and western counties in Oklahoma were populated by Yankees of a distinctly anti-slavery tradition. Many of these people filtered down from what had been in the 1850s "bleeding Kansas," bringing with them, if not a pro-Negro attitude, all of the special sensitivity about national democratic values and blacks that had marked that state in its birth. Oklahoma was a Southern state with a large Yankee colony. Finally, Oklahoma was the last in time of the Southern states to join the union. It became a Southern state, however, only after having been administered for a number of years by federal agents in a notably Northern and often Republican style. Government in the Territory of Oklahoma was Northern and officially aracial even though most of its population was Southern and white, many of these having come from Mississippi, Arkansas, and Texas. Because Oklahoma was thus ruled by the federal power between 1889 when it was first opened for settlement and 1907 when it gained statehood, it could be said that, in a sense, Oklahoma was the last of the Southern states to be redeemed from Reconstruction. The lateness with which Oklahomans gained self-rule allowed them to make up an official position on race relations out of materials already formed, to utilize the ready-made fabric that painful experience had woven in states east and south of them. Oklahoma had only to cut and sew, and then slip smoothly into its racial garments. In 1907, white

Oklahoma had simply to decide whether it would opt for the Conservative dress or the Radical. At successive times, it would wear each.

Negroes had come into Oklahoma first as slaves, brought there by their Indian masters during the great removal from the southeast in the 1830s. In a peculiar variant, slavery had thrived in the Indian territory. Indeed, in all of the United States, slavery lived longest in Oklahoma. In the Indian Territory of Oklahoma, the Constitution and laws of the United States did not prevail. Relations between the United States and the Indians (described legally as "domestic dependent Nations") were carried on through diplomacy. Thus, the Emancipation Proclamation of 1863 freed no slaves in Oklahoma, nor did the passage of the Thirteenth Amendment in 1865. Slavery in the Indian Territory was ended by treaty, and only in 1866, a full year after emancipation elsewhere. Nor was this the end of the peculiar treatment of the slaves and ex-slaves of Indians. In the 1880s, when the federal government decided to divide tribal lands among individuals, the administration ruled that this special class of freedmen should be treated as members of the tribe of their late masters. Thus belatedly the Oklahoma freedman in the Indian nations actually received a homestead of, not the forty acres promised in the earlier Reconstruction, but eighty-eight acres.

In the decades after 1865, a large number of blacks migrated into Oklahoma. In 1907, when the territory passed into statehood, the black population was 120,000 or roughly 10 percent of that of the whites. Some of these had moved down from Kansas, others had participated in the so-called "run of 1889." Before 1889 settlement in Oklahoma by ordinary citizens, white and black, was illegal. Nevertheless, many frontiersmen had pushed into land supposedly reserved for Indians. The "run" occurred when the government finally capitulated to pressure and opened the eastern portion of Oklahoma to settlement. At 12:00 noon on April 22, 1889, at a signal from a cannon, thousands of hopeful settlers raced from the boundary line to claim their homesteads.

Those who evaded the authorities and entered the territory before the firing of the cannon were called "Sooners." In smiling recognition of this ambitious chicanery, Oklahoma has since called itself the "Sooner State." Among the fleet-footed, would-be farmers, were a number of blacks. For example, De Leslain R. Dawes, who had been born a slave in Georgetown County, South Carolina in 1860, was one of two Negroes who joined the race for land in Canadian County on that remarkable day.[17]

During its reign in the Oklahoma Territory, the federal government was conscientious in protecting the rights of black citizens. Particularly was this true during the Harrison administration (1889–93), at the very time in which Radical anti-Negro sentiment and lynching was on the rise elsewhere in the South. During these years and afterward, thousands of Southern Negroes moved into the Territory, where soon there were some twenty-seven all-black towns and one rural colony. These included Langston, named in honor of John Mercer Langston, the first Negro Congressman from Virginia and once the president of Virginia State College; McCabe, named for a leading black come-outer; and another town whose name was politicly changed to Taft in 1908. Existing into 1907 in a relatively free federal enclave, Oklahoma blacks seemed to have generated a strong sense of self-worth that they brought into statehood after 1908. When the racial push came, Sooner State blacks pushed back. They did not always win, but neither did they always lose, and race relations in Oklahoma were always a bit different and a bit better than in most of the South.

Even so, Oklahoma was no paradise for black people. Generally whites and Indians were not sympathetic to their darker neighbors. In some communities in the turn-of-the-century years, "Whitecappers" appeared, attempting by the use of white hoods, threats, and violence to drive blacks away. On the urban scene in Oklahoma in 1902, inter-racial warfare flared in Lawton and Shawnee as if in echo to that of Wilmington and New Orleans.

As statehood approached, the position of Negroes in Oklahoma became more precarious. In 1904–05, a lily-white faction emerged even within the Republican party in the state. Still, the official attitude of the party—influenced especially by the racially liberal Kansas wing in the north and west—was very much for equal rights. Under the Roosevelt governor, Frank Franz, a Montanan who had been a Rough Rider with Teddy in Cuba, the Territory was carefully prepared both for statehood and a Republican ascendancy. In 1907, on the eve of the meeting of a convention called to draft a constitution, the Republicans stoutly declared that they stood on a platform of "equal rights to all persons regardless of race, creed, color, or locality."[18]

It soon became obvious, however, that Southern Democrats were most numerous in the territory and would dominate the convention. The overall tendency of the meeting was decidedly anti-Negro and veered toward the Radical. A suffragette, on the scene lobbying assiduously for her cause, tried to enlist the prestige of Radical Ben Tillman under the banner of women's rights. Indulging in truthful flattery, she wrote to the South Carolina Senator that he was "personally greatly admired by the state, where one of the new counties had just been named Tillman."[19] In spite of its Radical proclivities, the convention produced a constitution that was only mildly anti-Negro. Charles N. Haskell, the floor leader of the Democrats, very shrewdly guessed that President Theodore Roosevelt would veto a constitution that was blatantly discriminatory against Negroes. He therefore overrode his chief rival in the party, Lee Cruce, one of several "die-hard segregationists," to write a constitution that was at least acceptable to the federal government. In November 1907, Roosevelt proclaimed the Territory of Oklahoma and its adjunct, the Indian Territory, a state.

In the gubernatorial contest that followed, Haskell for the Democrats faced Franz for the Republicans. Blacks, of course, supported Franz. The Democrats, who were most numerous in the southeastern portion of the state—an area that was Southern enough to earn the title "little Dixie"—strenuously opposed him. Haskell easily won the governor's chair, and the voters elected an inaugural legislature that was heavily Democratic and virulently anti-Negro. A wave of Jim Crow legislation came out of the very first session of the legislative assembly, immediately belying the moderation formerly exhibited in the constitution. Disfranchisement, however, had to wait until 1910 when Oklahoma had its own "white supremacy" campaign.

In the campaign of 1910, the question was not whether the black man was to be equal at the polls. It was, rather, what would be the form of discrimination against him. Lee Cruce, the Radical segregationist, ran against William H. ("Alfalfa Bill") Murray in the primary for the Democratic nomination for governor. Cruce's platform featured a white man's government and an end to "Negro domination"—in some minds, apparently, an imminent possibility in Oklahoma. Compared with Cruce, Murray was conservative. His wife was the daughter of an Indian chief, and he had come to control vast areas of land through his marriage. A progressive farmer, he was so ardent an advocate of alfalfa as a conservation crop that the sobriquet "Alfalfa Bill" remained with him throughout his life. Not only did Murray gain economically by his marriage to an Indian woman, he also gained politically. In some parts of Oklahoma, Indians had wealth, power, and status. In Oklahoma, rather obviously, the right kind of miscegenation was an asset, not a liability. "Alfalfa Bill" liked red, and also he was not consumed with hatred for black. He himself simply assumed that Negroes were innately inferior; hence he was not especially concerned about legislating their subordination. He had mildly supported the Jim Crow laws passed by the 1908 legislature, but he had at first opposed the addition of a grandfather clause to the constitution.[20] Cruce won the election, and the constitution was amended to include a literacy requirement for the suffrage with a grandfather device as a loophole.

Oklahoma was the last state to use the grandfather clause, but the Oklahoma provision was the first to be struck down by the courts. In June 1915 the United States Supreme Court ruled the Oklahoma clause unconstitutional. Governor Robert L. Williams began to sound out the party leadership on calling a special session of the legislature to offer substitute remedies. His respondents reflected well the sentiments of the Oklahoma Democracy on the subject. Among those who answered the governor's inquiry was Oklahoma's blind Senator Thomas P. Gore. Gore was a Mississippian by birth, a Texas Populist by adoption, and finally a Democrat in the Sooner State. Gore thought that there should be an early meeting of the legislature to pass an amendment to the constitution that would give the legislature full and unspecified power in the matter of suffrage. However, one provision would deny any intention of evading the Fifteenth Amendment and another would rule out property qualifications—a sop to the numerous "home-grown" socialists whose presence added to Oklahoma's uniqueness. "My own judgment," said Gore, "is after looking over the field pretty well that Mississippi had devised the best solution of this problem." The understanding clause, he thought, could not be reviewed judicially.[21]

Most members of the legislature were in favor of vigorous action to take the vote out of black hands. A member from Idabel thought that "an election law to preserve white supremacy is the paramount question in southeast Oklahoma."[22] A representative from Washita County thought that the legislature had to save the ballot from "the ignorant and irrisponsible [sic] negro," while a member from Delaware County felt that "we must do something with these Niggers."[23]

Shortly, the governor proceeded to call a special meeting of the legislature, which came to be known as "the Jim Crow session." It passed a law that opened up the registration books for a brief period during which whites were simply welcomed to the rolls and blacks discouraged. Apparently, the process was sufficiently effective until it was challenged in the courts in 1934.[24]

In Florida, Arkansas, Texas, and Kentucky, as in Tennessee, disfranchisement was achieved by means less drastic than constitutional amendment. In these states, many white leaders concluded that a poll tax requirement for registration and voting combined with the Australian ballot was the easy way to relieve themselves of black voters. In four of these states the black population was only a quarter of the total, and in Kentucky it was only a tenth. Hence, these people might well feel more in control of their situations than those in states where the potential black electorate exceeded or came near to the white.

In West Virginia, Maryland, and Delaware, the disfranchisement movement met its Waterloo. In those states, attempts to reduce the black electorate encountered stern opposition both from blacks and sympathetic whites. After sharp contests, the disfranchisers failed. Further North, in New York for instance, there was sentiment for the disfranchisement of blacks, and for the disfranchisement of the new immigrants as well. But, generally speaking, the sentiment produced no significant results in restricting the suffrage. In the North and in the border states, black men—and later women—did vote; and their votes worked to make them free. In 1912, some black leaders had sufficient strength to bargain with Woodrow Wilson before giving him their support for the presidency. It was no mere coincidence that the last black to come to Congress in the first black revolution came from the South, and that the first black to come to Congress in the second black revolution was Oscar de Priest, who came to Capitol Hill from black Chicago in 1929.

Southern Radical leadership never felt perfectly safe from Negro voting. Long after blacks had ceased to be an active threat to white political supremacy, they worked to hold tight the ranks against black intrusion. For instance, in 1914 Ben Tillman wrote an irate letter to a potential maverick in his home state. "To vote the Republican ticket, which you threaten to do, would carry with it your forgetting the great number of negroes in South Carolina who are watching and praying for a division among the white people," he admonished. "We have perhaps forty or fifty thousand who are eligible to register under our own laws, but they are now quiet and doing nothing in a political way. Do you want to wake them up and have a return of the years of 'good stealing'."[25]

Southern white leadership at large was also persistently fearful of Northern interference in Southern race relations. There were always some Northern white liberals who were not willing to let the Negro go, and these always had a measure of power within the Republican party. The result was that, not only did Northern Republicans continue to face the "Southern question," but Southern Democrats never lost sight of the "Northern question"—namely, the possibility of another Reconstruction of their homeland under the not-so-tender auspices of the federal government.

In these circumstances, it is hardly surprising that the white leadership in the South began to gaze fondly toward the repeal of the Fifteenth Amendment. Conservatives saw in repeal a return to law and order and the safe restoration of power to the local, socially responsible leadership where it belonged. Alone and without distorting outside influences, the organic society would re-establish itself.

Radicals saw the repeal of the amendment as the *coup de grâce* to black political aspirations. It seems to have been a trend in those decades that reform efforts at the state level soon rose to the national. Even where Radical reformers won and enacted their programs much as they liked at the state level—as did Ben Tillman in South Carolina and James K. Vardaman in Mississippi—apparently their eyes soon lifted to the national arena. It was almost as if they had come to understand by experience the truth that in an industrializing, centralizing, nationalizing America, local problems were inextricably intertwined with national problems. Local and state solutions could only be piecemeal, and near satisfaction could only be achieved in the national arena. Interestingly, historians of Populism seem to have arrived at the same conclusion concerning the subjects of their study. Populists in power—as distinguished from Populists in rhetoric—were strangely slow and astoundingly moderate in the reforms they actually effected. It was as if their new power imposed upon them a realization of how powerless they actually were.

Many Radical leaders in politics did eventually find their way to Washington, and they carried in their luggage the fond dream of repealing the Fifteenth

Amendment. Thomas W. Hardwick long represented that sentiment as a Congressman from Georgia. James K. Vardaman brought it to the Senate from Mississippi in 1913. Ben Tillman, of course, also relished the idea. But Tillman had been in Washington since 1895. He was wise to the delicacy of the task and sought to school his Radical colleagues. "It will take persistent and long agitation to educate the country and especially the politicians in it up to the point of openly and boldly advocating the repeal of the 15th Amendment," he warned his newly arrived and junior colleague from Mississippi. A step in the right direction, he thought, would have been the insertion of such a plank in the Democratic platform in 1912. He suspected that many Northern politicians were waiting for the day when they could vote for the repeal of the Fifteenth Amendment, and he prayed for the time when he could join in that effort. But, he cautioned, the time was not yet.[26]

Other Radicals arriving in Washington soon learned the lesson that Tillman taught. Several years after the Wilsonians had moved to Washington, Rebecca Felton rued the fact that "not a single Democratic Congressman" had offered a bill to disfranchise the black man nationally. "The South has long expected relief from the negro's ballot privilege if a Democratic Administration succeeded to the control of the Government," she declared. Still, she admitted that repeal would have been frosting on a very large cake already possessed by the Radicals. "It is a fact that the negro has no ballot privilege in the Solid South," she conceded. "Effectually hampered by registration laws, they are effectually disfranchised by white primary elections."[27]

EMOTIONAL DISFRANCHISEMENT

Ultimately, it was not the myriad and ingenious legal stratagems of Southern white leadership that disfranchised and depoliticalized Negroes in the South after Reconstruction. This is true in spite of the fact that literally thousands of books, articles, pamphlets, theses, dissertations, treatises, and lectures have been expended upon those intricate cleverosities. Certainly laws were important to the process, but probably they were even more important as symbols than they were in positively denying the ballot to black hands. Shrewd old Ben Tillman's estimate was accurate: if white solidarity were broken, state election laws would provide only a poor defense. More vitally important than the laws were the economic, the physical, and especially the social and psychological sanctions imposed upon blacks to keep them from voting and participating in politics. In the end, it was white power and white solidarity in the desire to exclude the great mass of Negroes from political life that effected the political reduction of black people. Behind it all, in politics as well as in everything else, it was white unanimity against blackness, molded rigid in a white culture, monolithic, total, and tight, that put the black man either down or out. The exclusion of blacks from politics both drew upon and contributed to the exclusion of blacks everywhere. The Democratic party, the white primary, the numerous legal techniques, and the white men who monopolized the election machinery were but the cutting edge of a determination, deep and wide, already achieved.

Still, responsibility for the depoliticalization of blacks does not lie totally upon the white side of the color line. Blacks, too, contributed to their own reduction by withdrawing from the battle. In the quick snaps of violent Redemption and legal disfranchisement, Negroes in the South began to lose their will to vote. Even in Radical South Carolina, as Ben Tillman noted, the door was not always so tightly closed that it could not be reopened. In Conservative states, such as Virginia, where the laws were looser, black voting declined because blacks were not willing to assert their rights and pay the price, and whites took courage to promote a more perfect exclusion. Ultimately, and in the most conclusive degree, blacks were disfranchised not by law but, rather, by their not appearing at the polls. This is not to say that Negroes did not struggle, nor that they did not show terrific courage in the fray. But the odds were seemingly overwhelming. Faced with the apparent certainty of failure, blacks over the years lost heart for the fight. Overall and in the mass, blacks were concluding—understandably and accurately—that politics ultimately had won them but little, either from Democrats, Populists, or Republicans. It was not at all that blacks were apathetic, nor even that they were unwilling to suffer for the right. It was, rather, that they were unwilling to suffer for nothing.

Initially, whites had little faith in the permanency of black withdrawal. As the years slipped by, however, they began to take the non-participation of Negroes in politics as another sign of black acceptance of white superiority. What had begun as artifice ended as natural. There was much in the palpable world that seemed to certify white superiority and justify the political subordination of black people. By the 1930s, the white electorate, itself greatly reduced, was super-satisfied with its world. The exclusion of blacks from politics was not even thought about; it was accepted simply as the natural order of things.

The "American dilemma" between the ideal of democracy and the way Negroes were treated in the United States that Gunnar Myrdal discovered in the late 1930s and advertised in 1944 was purely academic. What was so very clear from the aracial heights of Sweden was all but invisible in the biracial bogs of the South. Ideally, neatly logically, there should have been a dilemma. In the real and conscious mind of the white South there was none. It did not even occur to the great mass of Southern whites in the 1930s that blacks ought to be in politics; Negroes had nothing to do with democracy. If idealized research could have looked into the hearts of its Southern white subjects in those years, it would have found them bleeding hardly one drop for the oppressed blacks. Instead, they would have seen hearts stoutly thumping with assurance that they beat in rhythm with heavenly drums. In fact, Southerners felt that blacks were in their appointed place, and that they, the Southern whites themselves, were the most democratic of Americans. In every primary election in the democratic, one-party South, every citizen could be a candidate for office, and the best man could win. It was an open game, and any number could play.

When white Southerners eventually discovered a dilemma in race relations, it was not in the realm of politics. Rather was it in the Kingdom of Christ. The evangelist in this Great Awakening was almost the opposite of the Scandinavian scholar in both philosophical and physical terms. He was a Christian spititualist not a social scientist, he was black, and he was truly a native son, one of the deep South's own. He was, of course, Martin Luther King, Jr. In the end it was the power of their own idealized vision of themselves as Christians, transcended into blackness, personified in King and his seemingly loving and non-violent host, that shook them to the roots of self. King's power was, precisely, that he was so Southern. And when they smote him—as they inevitably must—they hurt themselves. Somewhere the whites had taught the blacks all too well, and the whites themselves had somehow learned to value blacks as a spiritual people too much. Through the blacks they became their own accusers, and their guilt was all too clear. Christ would not do what they had done. That knowledge—dim or clear—shook the Southern mind at its moral foundations; and it sent white souls, frayed and frightened, scurrying across the emotional landscape in search of a new peace.

THE SEPARATION OF THE RACES

It is fully appropriate that legal disfranchisement and legal segregation be linked. While legal disfranchisement generally ran its course between about 1890 and 1915, legal segregation generally ran its course between about 1889 and 1915. Also, just as disfranchisement was part of a much larger process that might be called the de-politicalization of the Negro, legal segregation was part of a larger process that might be called the separation of the races. The mental and physical separation of the races practically began, of course, with the beginning of British America. Black people were early distinguished from whites—if not simply by color, then surely by their being non-Christian and non-English—and the distinction soon came to be firmly institutionalized in slavery. Paradoxically, slavery enforced a profound mental separation of the races even as it compelled a physical proximity, a peculiar integration, between master and slave. Not all blacks in the American South were slaves, however, and in the last generation of slavery whites in power moved to bring the quarter-million free blacks under more stringent control. By the time of the Civil War, these people were, indeed, "slaves without masters," and one of the devices by which they were controlled was a more careful legal and physical separation.[28]

With emancipation came a great increase in the separation of the races. In quantitative terms, probably the most significant area was economics. Domestic servants in freedom fled the households of the white elite; but, more important, the demise of slavery meant the demise of the plantation as it had been both in fact and in mind. With certain crops and in certain areas, as with sugar in Louisiana and with rice in Carolina, plantations did remain intact as economic units, owned or leased and managed by one person with a work force of black people under his direct supervision. However, the vast majority of plantations, especially among those that had produced cotton or tobacco as their staple, broke down into so many farms. This occurred, as we have noticed above, because black people—not white people—would have it so. Blacks wanted their own farms, and they wanted their own family and no others on their farms. Whether by somehow buying land, renting for cash, or, as was massively the case, by share-cropping, this was their desire. It was a desire that went stubbornly against the strongly expressed wishes of the landed gentry. Landowners, with good reason, did not trust either the capacity or the willingness of tenants to take care of their lands under year-by-year contracts. Moreover, in late slavery, plantations were thought to be relatively efficient economic units. There were, indeed, economies of scale in running a plantation under skilled managers that individual small farmers could never attain. Even so, because the freedmen simply refused to work in gangs as they had in slavery, their desire to break up the plantations into small farms was, for the most part, realized. Whereas black people in slavery had lived together in the very faces of the whites, they were now scattered over the countryside as separate families, relatively removed from the eyes of the whites. This was, in effect, a residential separation of a high order. The very place in which blacks had been proximate to whites before—in their work on the plantations—was now marked by a high level of separation, a separation upon which blacks themselves insisted.

Ordinarily, black people labored on their farms during the week, and on the seventh day they went to church. Here again the pattern went from whatever mixing there might have been in the churching of whites and slaves to a profound separation. Just as black people pulled away from white control on the plantations, so too did they move to pull out of white control in the churches. In the last generation of slavery, several hundred thousand slaves had been enrolled in white churches. Many hundreds of thousands more were supervised in one way or another by white churchmen in separated services. In emancipation, the white connection ended with amazing rapidity as black members withdrew from white churches and established their own. Black churches that had been physically separated but under white supervision also established their independence. In addition many blacks who had never been churched in slavery became so in freedom. Indeed, several hundred thousand black people joined the two great all-black churches, the African Methodist Episcopal Church and the African Methodist Episcopal Church Zion, both of which had often been excluded from the South in the previous generation. The whole process of withdrawal began with emancipation and by 1868 was practically completed. Certainly one could still find a black member in a white church hither and yon, even into the twentieth century, but a close look at those members would reveal that they were usually sextons, custodians, and servants in the parish parsonage. Even as it grew prodigiously in the first flush of freedom, the black church took on the separated character that would lead people a hundred years later to say with perfect accuracy that eleven o'clock Sunday morning is the most segregated hour in America.

In freedom, there were two areas in which the two races came physically together most often. The first was as domestics, and the second was in the towns and cities and in the public carriers that joined those towns and cities. In the first relation, mixing was very tolerable to whites because the relative condition of each race was clearly fixed. There could be no misunderstanding the fact that the servant was the servant of the master or mistress. Domestic service was tolerable to blacks as a way to earn a living, and they could always move on to another household if need be. Contact in the growing towns and cities where impersonal relations were on the rise was, indeed, a racial frontier. There were not many blacks in urban areas compared with those who remained on the land, but those city dwellers were riding the wave of the future. With federal guarantees of civil rights for all citizens embodied first in the Civil Rights Act of 1866 and then in the Fourteenth Amendment in 1868, urban blacks presumed themselves to have equal rights as citizens, including equal rights to public accommodations. The black codes enacted in the South by the Johnson state governments soon after the war were outlawed, as were a scattering of specifically segregative measures. Very generally, first the military governments and then the Republican governments in the various Southern states in and after 1868 made rules and laws that positively opened all public accommodations to all people. Finally, in the twilight of Reconstruction the federal government enacted the Civil Rights Act of 1875. These acts ruled that streetcars, trains, steam passenger boats, restaurants, theaters, hotels, and all such facilities were open to all persons regardless of race. Even so, the federal and state governments did not make violations of these laws criminal offenses; they were, rather, civil offenses for which the offended party might bring a civil suit and collect damages.

Numerous black leaders asserted their rights under these laws. Apparently, they were often denied in spite of the laws. When they pressed their cases to the end, they usually won. However, the litigation was long and costly, and often damages were awarded in such trivial amounts as to constitute an opinion of the lack of seriousness of these violations. In brief, even in Reconstruction, antisegregation laws were not well enforced, and after Reconstruction were effectually vitiated by the courts.[29]

During Reconstruction the great mass of blacks simply did not seek admission to white-dominated facilities. Even when they did so and won, some form of physical separation customarily prevailed. The fundamental fact was that during Reconstruction and for some years thereafter, the essential pattern of life of the great mass of black people precluded any significant mixing of the races. The vast majority of black people were rural and comparatively poor. They had neither access to nor money to afford public accommodations as did whites. Generally, they did not have the experience that would have led them to want to do what the whites wanted to do, and their way of life itself did not give them opportunity to try. In and for some time after Reconstruction, when one is talking about the mixing of the races in public places, one is talking about some of the most affluent blacks some of the time.

The one area in which integration in Reconstruction might have taken a great step forward was in the public schools. All over the South a mark of Republican Reconstruction regimes was to put in place legislation for compulsory education, and in every state some progress was made in the realization of that ideal. Yet, only in New Orleans were the schools integrated in some significant measure. Here and there elsewhere, black children and white children went to school under the same roof, but even in these circumstances some sort of separation usually prevailed. Even the integration that occurred in New Orleans was seriously impaired by mob action in 1874.[30]

The failure to integrate public schools in Reconstruction, potentially an area of recurrent and intimate association between blacks and whites, was a great loss to the nation. It was an opportunity to bring up a new generation—a New Negro and a New White—that had at least had contact with one another in formative situations in which the authorities were ostensibly committed to equality. The separation of the races in the schools not only perpetuated a separation of cultures, it promoted the cultivation, the enrichment of each to the exclusion of the other. The failure to integrate was based on a conviction among many black leaders and most influential whites in education that if they integrated the public schools, the whites would stay away and thus cripple the whole effort. Black leadership in South Carolina, for instance, argued the point carefully in a constitutional convention in 1868 and decided for allowing a voluntary separation on the understanding that in time white people in their own schools would be educated up to an acceptance of the civil equality of black people.[31] At the national level, ironically, some of the people who were most effective in promoting both white and black education— indeed, the real leaders in promoting public education in America—took the initiative in deliberately taking the schools out of the bill that was to become the Civil Rights Act of 1875.

Active in this connection was Barnas G. Sears, the primary agent of the Peabody Fund for disbursing educational money in the South. In the summer of 1870 he rued that "South Carolina, like Louisiana, is all afflicted with the curse of trying to have mixed schools."[32] Once that issue was cleared and the various states went for separation, the Peabody Fund moved ahead with alacrity to support separated systems. As the Civil Rights bill worked its tortured way through Congress, Sears took alarm that a provision calling for mixed schools would cause all of the white children to be withdrawn from the public schools and lobbied for its defeat.[33] Racially integrated education was not, of course, made a part of the act as finally passed.

The 1880s witnessed a rapid erosion in the legal claims of Negroes to equality of access to public accommodations. In 1883 the Supreme Court vitiated the Civil Rights Act of 1875 in all places except such federal enclaves as the territories, the District of Columbia, and aboard American vessels on the high seas. Beginning with Tennessee in 1882, the various states began to pass laws mandating segregation. In the famous case of *Plessy* v. *Ferguson* in 1896 the Supreme Court ruled constitutional a Louisiana law of 1890 separating the races on most railroads provided that equal accommodations were accorded to Negroes and whites. This "separate and equal rule" would guide the courts in such cases for the next sixty years.

The advent of Radicalism ushered in another era in the separation of the races. It was an era in which separation was legalized. Whereas in Reconstruction there had been laws against segregation, in and after 1889 there were waves of laws passed actually requiring segregation. This change represented no great revolution in physical arrangements because blacks had not been using these facilities in any large numbers anyway. It was a revolution, however, in declarations of intent by governments and the white constituencies they represented. These laws came in three waves: 1889–93, 1897–1907, and 1913–15; and they related to specific areas. The first two waves primarily affected public accommodations, especially common carriers, namely, trains, streetcars, and passenger boats. The third wave related to new industrial and urban situations. Specifically, it segregated facilities in factories, particularly toilets, and set up schemes designed to achieve block-by-block segregation in urban housing. That something new was happening in the separation of the races was indicated by the fact that a new word was required for such occasions. The word "segregation" apparently was not much used before 1899, and when it was used it had no special racial connotations. In and after that time, it was used frequently to refer to the separation of the races, and it seemed to carry with it the idea that the separation referred to was effected by law. The nationalization of the word seemed to occur in 1913 and 1914 with the attention that was focused on the attempt to segregate facilities in Washington, D.C.

Just as there were two essentially different kinds of disfranchisement, so too were there two different kinds of segregation. The laws in each set looked much alike, but they were applied to differing physical situations, they sprang from different motives, and they were designed to and did achieve different results.

Racial segregation as executed by Radicals was a deep South and a black belt phenomenon; the motivation there was to save the white people at the expense of blacks. Segregation was a walling out of black people to minimize the damage they might do to whites on their way to their demise. It was also a device for putting down feelings of self-esteem among black people, first by exclusion and then by relegation to inferior accommodations. Thus, while the Supreme Court had declared that separated facilities were to be equal, they were not so in fact. Often railroad companies argued that they used the very same cars on different runs for both races, but yet somehow black people kept getting the impression that their cars were older, dirtier, and more unsafe than those used by whites. In truth, Radicals wanted black people to have clearly inferior accommodations and to know that they were inferior. Like arbitrary disfranchisement, arbitrary relegation to always inferior facilities was a sign of where the power actually lay, and where it was likely to lie in the future. On trains, steamboats, and streetcars, an extra fillip was that segregation legislation made provision for the servants of white people to ride in the white cars if the white employers so chose. Obviously, the whites made the rules, and they could alter them at will to suit their convenience.

Segregation as executed by Conservatives was for a purpose quite different from that of the Radicals. Conservatives sought segregation in public accommodations to protect black people in their persons and in their dignity. For Conservatives, segregation meant giving the black person a very special place in which he would be protected. Far from putting down the self-esteem of black people, Conservative segregation was designed to preserve and encourage it. Conservatives also segregated for the purpose of saving whites from abusing themselves by abusing black people in public accommodations. White men lowered themselves by making suggestive remarks to black women in the second-class cars on the trains. Often black men resented those remarks, and fights broke out. If disorderly white men were removed from proximity to black people, then this kind of disturbance would cease.

As in disfranchisement, Virginia offers a good example of Conservatism in segregation. There had been precisely such troubles on the trains in Virginia in the 1890s. When the reformers got firmly in control for a time after 1900, they passed a segregation law. It set aside facilities for black people, a place where black people could ride by themselves and have dignity as well as comfort. In true Virginia style, it also divided white facilities. Trains that made sufficiently long runs were required to provide not only a separate car for blacks, but also first- and second-class cars for whites. The second-class white car was for the less genteel sort, the people who wanted to do what they used to do in the second-class car, plus those who chose not to or could not afford to pay first-class fare. The first-class car, of course, was for ladies and gentlemen. Just as Virginia reformers were willing to leave some black men enfranchised and were not at all unwilling to disfranchise some white men, so too would they make a place for black people on the trains and segregate less worthy whites in second-class facilities. In segregation, as in disfranchisement, Conservatism moved in a mood distinctly different from that of Radicalism.[34]

By far the most vigorous acts of segregation came in the first two waves. The third wave, in 1913–15, was clearly feeble. Indeed, it was then that segregation was turned back at the borders of the South. Ordinances for effecting residential segregation block-by-block were reversed or failed to pass in Baltimore and Oklahoma City. In Wilmington, Delaware, a move to establish separate windows for black and white citizens to do business with the city was defeated. In the North, attempts to pass legislation based on Radical premises also failed. In 1907, for instance, a proposal by the future mayor of New York City, Jimmy Walker, to pass a law against miscegenation was defeated in the state legislature. Geographically, by 1915, Radicalism had reached its high water marks somewhere south of Wilmington and east of Oklahoma City.

After 1915 the era of legal separation expired. Obviously, segregation laws were passed in considerable numbers thereafter; but they were passed sporadically, spottily, and in a makeshift fashion. Often they came in response to new technology or new institutions. Thus, laws concerning elevators, airplanes, and buses appeared. Here and there laws required that textbooks that had been used in black schools could not be used in white, and separate Bibles were required in the courtrooms upon which to touch and swear.

Unlike laws disfranchising blacks, which at least were well-thought-out and internally consistent within each state, segregation laws within each state were passed over a long period of time, related to different areas, varied widely from state to state, and varied even more widely within each state as towns, cities, villages, and other local communities made their own laws. The results were rather chaotic, especially for a black person traveling. In 1892 a young black man from Raleigh, North Carolina, on his way to enroll in Meharry Medical School in Nashville, Tennessee, came to appreciate that fact. He had just been in railroad stations during his trip in which the drinking fountains were not segregated. Arriving in Chattanooga, he was bending down to drink at the fountain when he sensed some movement behind him. He turned just in time to see a policeman poised to bring his billy club down on his head. He was able to explain to the policeman that he did not know the local law or custom and escape beating and arrest.[35] Again the Radical point was vividly made. White people made the rules, and they could make them as arbitrarily as they pleased. If black people did not understand the rules, it was but another sign of their non-belonging in a white man's country.

THE SEPARATION OF CULTURES

The deep and peculiar separation of races that came to the South in the twentieth century was a matter of minds as well as bodies, and it had its roots in the separation of black and white cultures. There had always been separation, of course, but sometimes the distance between the races was greater than at others. Slavery bred its own curious brand of physical integration. Physically, of course, slavery required that blacks and whites be touching close day by day. Moreover, in its last generation the peculiar institution worked diligently to press a limited but smooth integration of the mass of black people into a culture ruled by whites. In Reconstruction, cultural integration continued, altered now to substitute Northern white ideals for Southern, as Northerners streamed into the South. However, even as Northerners in the South urged blacks, at least rhetorically, to join the mainstream of Northern white culture, Southern blacks were withdrawing physically—in religion, in education, and on the land. Paradoxically, even as black people were getting "whiter" in the cultural sense, they were retreating physically into enclaves that were increasingly black. With the exodus of Northerners after 1877, the process of disengagement accelerated rapidly, and the vision of white culture was practically lost to the immediate view of black folk.

The process of cultural separation was long in the making, but it was in full flux precisely as the passage of segregating legislation reached a crescendo between 1897 and 1907. In that decade, those multifarious black enclaves that emerged during and after Reconstruction were coming rapidly under the unifying aegis of Booker T. Washington, and in their many parts they carried within them the hard core of black culture for the twentieth-century South. Washington's leadership had many failings, but it did at least raise a flag under which the great mass of black people could rally as distinctly black. However arrived at, the South—and the nation—would soon have a black world on one side and a white world on the other.[36]

The growing separation of cultures in the postwar South was evident in many ways. One clear manifestation was in music. Blues was long considered "race" music; that is, for blacks only. As such, it was often denigrated by jazz musicians of both races. Unalloyed Bluesmen, such as B. B. King, found little audience for their talent outside of the "chitlin circuit," as the round of black clubs and theaters was called.

Cultural separation was also manifested in a separation of language. Black and white language evolved away from each other, and that process was succinctly illustrated, as mentioned before, in naming practices. In slavery, black people had typically taken names from four sources. In early slavery, African names, such as Sambo, meaning second son, persisted. As creolization occurred, and Africans in America began to generate a new world culture fitted to their lives on this side of the Atlantic, African names sometimes shifted into American variations. Negro children in America in the fifth, sixth, and seventh generations continued to receive African names or variants thereof, not in veneration of Africa, but rather in honor of some older American-born relatives who bore those names. In slavery blacks had also taken Biblical names such as Gabriel, Joshua, and Rachel, classical names such as Bacchus, Scipio, and Phoebe, and British names such as George, Charles, and Mary. In freedom, African-derived and classical names tended to disappear while Biblical and British names remained. Toward the end of the nineteenth century, however, black people began to invent given names that were not at all in the language of whites.[37] For examples, Robert Charles's youngest sister was named Floril, and a younger brother Aliac. Another brother, born in 1869, was named John Wesley, while three older brothers born in slavery were named George, Henry, and Charles.[38] In the twentieth century the tendency became even more pronounced, and one encounters Countee Cullen, Eartha Kitt, Wynonie Harris, and Leontyne Price. Beautiful, euphonious, and close-fitting names, but distinctly not white.

Given two cultures, the issue became not a matter of whether or not there would be separation. It was, rather, a matter of what would be the process and form of separation. There would be prejudice and discrimination on both sides, and there would be responses on both. There would be a white country and a black country, and the frontier would find itself wherever the balance between the needs and power of white people and the needs and power of black people was struck. How was the balance struck? Historically in the South it has been found in a process probably best described as the "etiquette" of race relations. That process has never been a matter primarily of either laws or no laws, and de facto separation is a rather clumsy term, hobbled specially by the fact that it has come to be reflexively juxtaposed to legal separation. Legal separation was embodied in the whole matrix and had no opposite.

In a very real sense, there was no single or unitary race line in the South either before, during, or after the era of segregative legislation. Probably, only a Northerner like the journalist Ray Stannard Baker, who wrote a book on the subject, could imagine that he was following a color line, and he, perhaps, was led to do so by his origins in a North that in 1908 was being flooded to overflowing by ghettoizing immigrants from Southern and Eastern Europe.[39] Just as the attempt to apply class lines derived from European culture does not work well in the homogeneous Old Settled South—indeed does more to confound understanding than it does to promote it—so too with race lines. Race relations in the South have been worked out very much like white relations have been worked out—each case, each event, each meeting between one and another as it occurred. When black met white, the nature of the exchange was negotiated according to the time, the place, and the individuals involved—with sensitivity to generally understood customs. There were guidelines to behavior, but what was to be done in a specific situation was what was most comfortable to the parties concerned. In a specific situation one could err in judgment and act beyond the tolerances of custom, as Cable perhaps did in having dinner with the Napiers at their table in Nashville in 1889. But etiquette itself required forgiveness of the avowedly contrite transgressor. It was always a matter of individual responsibility. The two cultures evolved words to say, gestures to make—a language in which individuals might negotiate interracial encounters; but each situation was unique, and the solution in each situation personal and creative. There was a black country and a white country, and the frontier between them was not clearly marked and was ever-shifting as if in some undeclared and usually quiet war. The location and nature of the frontier were much more a function of mind than of matter, of white minds and black minds rather than white bodies and black bodies.

CHAPTER VIII

The Conservative Response to Radicalism

Conservatives responded to face Radicalism across the frontiers of disfranchisement and segregation, but even more clearly they joined battle upon the issue of lynching. Conservatism stood firmly and openly upon the ground of law and order. In its judicious mind, it could never yield to the idea that there was a higher law that made legitimate the violation of order. Hence it was that Conservatives sometimes met Radicals in quick and vicious firefights concerning lynching. Two Conservatives stood out in this combat: Andrew Sledd, who lost his fight in Georgia in 1902, and John Spencer Bassett, who won his in North Carolina a year later. There were a few Conservatives who continued the battle openly and with great verve, but the great majority made one sharp thrust against Radicalism and, when that proved unrewarding, retired to certain enclaves and turned their energies to working among their white brothers and sisters rather than among blacks. By about 1915 Radicalism as a whole operating system had, indeed, died, and Conservatism emerged from its strongholds to control a new set in race relations. In the new set the black as beast was lost to sight, and the black as child was very much to the fore.

THE SLEDD CASE

In July 1902 there appeared in *The Atlantic Monthly* an article entitled "The Negro: Another View." The author was Andrew H. Sledd, a thirty-two-year-old Virginian who had taken a bachelor's degree at Randolph-Macon and a master's at Harvard, and who had come to Emory College to teach Latin and Greek. Sledd was a racial Conservative and his article bore the essence of that creed. It asserted that the Negro belonged to an "inferior race," but that he was human and did have "inalienable rights." Sledd then lacerated Radicals without mercy, labeling the supporters of lynching "blatant demagogues, political shysters, courting favor with the mob; news sheets, flattering the prejudices, and pandering to the passions of their constituency; ignorant youths and loud-voiced men who receive their information at second hand, and either do not or cannot see." Next came the words that probably did most to outrage the Radicals. First, Sledd insisted that lynching was not used as a specific weapon against the black rapist. On the contrary, only "a very small proportion" of the 1700 victims in the previous decade were even accused of rape. Second, he asserted that "our lynchings are the work of our lower and lowest classes." This was tantamount to saying that Radicals were the dregs of Southern society, which was certainly not true. He dwelt upon the savagery of the mob. The lyncher used the license given him by Radical leadership "to gratify the brute in his own soul, which the thin veneer of his elemental civilization has not been able effectually to conceal." On the occasion of a recent well-advertised lynching, one of Georgia's leading railroads ran two special trains on excursions to the scene. "And two train-loads of men and boys, crowding from cow-catcher to the tops of the coaches, were found to go to see the indescribable and sickening torture and writhing of a fellow human being. And souvenirs of such scenes are sought,—knee caps, and finger bones, and bloody ears. It is the purest savagery." Lynchers, he concluded flatly, are murderers.[1]

Relatively few Southerners read the Boston-based *Atlantic Monthly,* and it took some weeks for the reaction to Sledd's article to gather force. Late in July, a fellow Georgian wrote from Washington urging Rebecca Felton to make a reply. She did so by sending a scathing letter to the Atlanta *Constitution.* Felton clearly did not know Sledd's true identity. She noted that he was a Southerner and simply fell back upon the stock charge that here was another traitor to the South willing to sell out his people for a fat job in the North.[2] Immediately, there was a rush to enlighten her. A Covington, Georgia, resident wrote at the request of the "good men of our City to let you Know who A Sledd is[.]"[3] Shortly, a chorus of writers echoed Mrs. Felton's reaction. Radical rhetoric dominated the field, and if moderation dared to raise its head, it was immediately blasted.

Flooded in a sea of vitriol, Sledd sent in his resignation to the President of Emory College, James E. Dickey. "I want to get away; I feel alien and wronged," the young man complained to his father-in-law. "I am cramped and stunted by the atmosphere that prevails. I had thought to be able to bring about a better state of things; but the people and the College will have none of it. Emory College needs regeneration. I had hoped its time had come. But I now believe that I was wrong in such hope."[4] The Sledd case was made more interesting and revealing by the fact that Sledd's father-in-law was Warren A. Candler, the leading bishop in the Southern Methodist Church, and, in a large measure, the organizational and spiritual heir to Atticus G. Haygood. Bishop

Candler, like Haygood, had been a president of Emory and had saved it from imminent financial disaster, in part by calling upon the benevolence of his brother, Asa, soon to achieve fame and fortune—especially fortune—as the founding genius of the Coca-Cola Company. The ever resourceful bishop quickly thought of a perfect accommodation. The board would accept Sledd's resignation. But they would also vote him an adjustment in pay that Sledd would then use to continue his graduate studies at Yale University. Shortly, there was a very strange meeting of the Emory College board of trustees in which a young professor was sent away in disgrace to complete his doctorate at Yale with a $1000 "adjustment" in pay to finance the venture.[5]

Not every Georgia Methodist was blind to the violence done to academic freedom in these proceedings. One member of the Education Board tried to reopen the case, arguing that otherwise "every good man will come to believe" that "the College is contemptible."[6] The bishop himself shortly entered the field again seeking some better arrangement for Sledd, only to find President Dickey unwilling to retreat. The bishop flew into a rage and accused his erstwhile friend Dickey of acting too hastily. "You let the enemies of the college lynch a capable professor and banish my child from Georgia," he charged and curtly closed the correspondence.[7]

In September 1903, Candler himself spoke out in a newspaper article against, as one grateful black correspondent phrased it, "mob violence and lynch law."[8] Immediately John Temple Graves, thinking himself accused in the article, attacked Candler. Among other unkind things, the Atlanta journalist painted Candler as smug, self-satisfied, and a "fat Bishop." Candler wrote to Graves, an old friend, explaining that his newspaper piece had been directed against the Chautauqua activities of Ben Tillman and not against Graves's lectures at that famous meeting place in New York. Graves responded in kind, expressing regret for his intemperate words.[9] Apparently, the bishop had made his last public pronouncement on racial extremism, but, privately, he was not yet finished with the subject.

THE BASSETT CASE

In spite of all the power that his kinship by marriage to Candler gave him, Sledd was routed by Radicalism and totally lost his battle in Georgia. But Candler soon won a measure of revenge by playing a small part in preventing the dismissal of John Spencer Bassett from the faculty of Trinity College. Trinity was a small, but very prestigious, liberal arts college in Durham, North Carolina. In time, heavily endowed with funds by Benjamin N. Duke, the founder of the American Tobacco Company, it would become Duke University. In 1903 Trinity College was, like Emory, a Methodist institution. Bassett was a native Carolinian, having been born in Wayne County in eastern North Carolina in 1867. When he arrived at a proper age, his parents sent him to the public high school in Goldsboro, the county seat. Interestingly the schools in Goldsboro were superior and thus attractive to parents ambitious for their children because they had recently come under the influence of a coterie of young men about to make North Carolina one of the leaders in public education in the South. On the board of education was a young lawyer, Charles Brantley Aycock, later to be the "education" governor of North Carolina. One of John Bassett's teachers was Edwin A. Alderman, soon to become the first Professor of Education in the University of North Carolina, then the president of that institution, then of Tulane University, and, finally, the head of the University of Virginia. (In the same era, Goldsboro acquired a new and highly energetic young Baptist minister, Thomas Dixon, Jr.) After high school, Bassett went on to Trinity College and, subsequently, in 1891, to Johns Hopkins University. At Hopkins he, too, sat at the feet of Herbert Baxter Adams, earned his degree, and returned to Trinity as a professor in 1893.[10] Like many young scholars in the South who pursued a professorial career in the liberal arts, he emerged in the 1890s as a staunch Conservative in race relations.

In the fall of 1903 Bassett published in the *South Atlantic Quarterly Review* an article entitled "Stirring up the Fires of Racial Antipathy." In the article, he said, in brief, that Southern journalists and politicans had needlessly stirred up racial antipathies for political advantage. Having found the tool so useful, they were reluctant to give it up, and, instead, turned it to their own selfish ends. As an example, he pointed to the furor that had recently been created by the press when Booker T. Washington and a party of friends, traveling through the state by rail, arranged—with typical Tuskegee forehandedness—to dine at a certain lodging house along the way. Unexpectedly, several white travelers had wanted to dine there also, but they had to wait for a time because no provisions had been made for them. Eventually they were served in segregated quarters, while the Tuskegee party occupied the main dining hall. Almost incidentally in his essay, Bassett opined that Booker T. Washington was the second greatest man, after Robert E. Lee, to appear in the South since the Revolutionary era. Near the end of the article, Bassett asserted that the black man at large was being bludgeoned out of his cowardice and that there would be a great struggle in which the blacks would win their equality.[11]

As he soon admitted, Bassett had deliberately set out to provoke the South into thought and words, and perhaps into action, on the race issue. He himself had founded the *South Atlantic Quarterly* in 1901 as an instrument to promote free thought and the discussion of Southern problems—precisely in the spirit of Cable's Open Letter Club. Implicitly, he, like so many other leading Southerners, assumed that introspection and full public discussion would eventuate in proper behavior. Previously, he had made tentative gambits in that direction without getting the sort of full response he sought. Finally he decided, as he later said, "to take them up" in the "Antipathy" article.[12] Thus Bassett's extravagant language was cooly calculated.

However, the young professor did not expect to reap a whirlwind from so slight a sowing. Indeed, he created a storm that very nearly consumed him. In the vanguard of those who attacked Bassett was Josephus Daniels, the owner and editor of the highly influential Raleigh *News and Observer* and the key propagandist of white supremacy in the North Carolina campaigns of 1898 and 1900. Quite rightly, Daniels assumed that he was one of the prime targets at whom the article had been aimed, and, with characteristic verve, he rushed to war. He went unerringly for the two most vulnerable passages in the article: Bassett's ranking of Booker T. Washington above a multitude of notable white men, and the assertion that a dire struggle between the races would result in equality. Bassett had insulted a host of Southern statesmen, Daniels charged, from Lamar and Vance to Aycock and Simmons. He was unfit, the tar-heel editor declared, to write about politics and race "from the standpoint of a Southern man."[13] Far from feeling abashed at the increase in the lynching of blacks in the South, Daniels vigorously and proudly defended the practice. "What Prof. Bassett enumerates as an evidence of hostility is the growing glory of Southern manhood and Southern chivalry," he asserted, and went on to equate integration with miscegenation. For a month, Daniels kept up a ferocious barrage of invective, including, for example, a yellow journalistic trick of repeatedly printing Bassett's name as "bASSett."

Behind Daniels's hostility to Bassett lay the fact that Trinity College had received very generous support from Benjamin Duke, the founder of the American Tobacco Company, which, at that time, had established virtually a monopoly, a trust, over the "slow burn." Daniels was a "progressive" Democrat and against the trusts. Also involved was the fact that Duke was one of the strong backs in the Republican party in North Carolina, and that the Democrats had only recently redeemed the state from the Republican economic royalists and their radical Populist allies after a bitter struggle. It was clear enough to Daniels that Bassett's defiance of the popular will and flagrant irresponsibility were directly related to a divine right of rule assumed by his masters, the Republican industrial monarchy. "The pathway of free and untrammeled thought in the Department of History at Trinity," he charged, "is lit by the steady glow of the trust cigarette."[14]

If Daniels was in the vanguard, other critics were not far behind. In close support was nearly the whole of eastern North Carolina. One of the striking, and most revealing, facets of the Bassett case was that those who viewed it as a vital matter were divided into two groups according to geography. Almost to a man, people who demanded his dismissal did so vehemently and were from eastern North Carolina, where lived the great majority of the state's

black population. Those who insisted upon his retention were from the relatively white western portion. Further, it is very clear that what motivated the
easterners was the Radical mentality. They felt that the fires of racial antipathy
had not been stirred nearly enough on the white side, and that on the black
side Bassett himself, the ivory-towered professor, arrogantly aloof from the
real world, was carelessly pushing the black beast perilously close to the edge
of sexual rampage.

Shortly, the east answered the clear call to battle. The entire congregation
of the Smithfield Methodist Church resolved for Bassett's dismissal upon the
ground that "such statements are unjust to our southern institutions, and
southern sentiment, and are compromising and humiliating to southern
Anglo-Saxon manhood and womanhood."[15] An intelligent and eloquent statement of the eastern attitude soon came from John F. Bruton, a member of
Trinity's board of trustees. Bruton was a banker in Wilson. His father had
been a minister and presiding elder in the Methodist Church South. Bruton
had taught school in Wilson before attending law school in the University of
North Carolina in Chapel Hill. He was a conservative in all matters except
race; and while he was a Radical in that respect, he was by nature far from
hysterical. "It has occurred to me that possibly our folks in and about Durham
are hardly aware of the true conditions throughout the east," he wrote to the
chairman of the board of trustees two weeks after Daniels had opened his
attack.

> They do not know what we have gone through in the recent past. The dangers
> which have threatened our homes on account of the negro are not relegated to
> forgetfulness by any means—every published declaration like those of Dr. Bas-
> sett quickens the pulse of the black man which is observable by their demeanor
> on our streets and in other public places. Our women are afraid to be left alone
> even in the day time in sparsely settled communities and in towns they dread
> to be left alone at night. It requires superior finesse to avoid trouble with the
> negroes in our eastern towns day in and day out—and following a period like
> the one established by the publication of Dr. Bassett's article, white men must
> be more than careful to avoid ruptures. Labor becomes disorganized, and the
> spirit of arrogance and a reckless indifference to consequences becomes almost
> unbearable.

A duty to the college as "sacred as the virtue of our wives and daughters," he
concluded, demanded Bassett's removal.[16]

But of course the rub was that Bassett was well aware of conditions in the
east; he simply perceived them differently from Bruton. He viewed the race
problem from the Conservative standpoint. As Bassett saw it, the Negro had
not been a threat politically, even in 1898 and 1900; there was a subordinate
place for him in the American South, and it was inconceivable that black males
were on the verge of becoming raving, raping beasts. Bassett's failing, like that

of many other Conservatives, was that he sadly misunderstood the Radical mentality. Bruton and people like him were both mistaken and honest in their Radicalism; they deeply believed what they said and should have been understood as they represented themselves. It was a lamentable irony that many Conservatives, so judicious by their very nature, did not allow Radicals the same degree of integrity that they claimed for themselves. So certain were they of their own clear moral correctness, that they could only impute dishonesty and self-interest to the opposition. Disfranchisement was, according to Bassett, "an enamelled lie," and the threat of black domination a myth. Walter Hines Page phrased the Conservative appraisal of the opposition succinctly when he wrote to Benjamin Duke encouraging him to stand firmly behind Bassett. The forces of repression had crudely seized upon a false issue to work their will in the state. "It is simply the cry of prejudice," he declared, "a blind howl by those who think that they can rule North Carolina and do gross injustice to men who differ with them—by simply howling 'Nigger.' Now if this crowd can have their way and drive men from our institutions and from the State in this way, then there can be no free thought and no free action in North Carolina." Page reminded the tobacco magnate of the Sledd case and concluded, "Well, Emory College is now held in pity and contempt at all the great institutions in the land."[17]

The west was as ardent in Bassett's support as was the east against him. A Greensboro lawyer ridiculed the attack and reminded James H. Southgate, the chairman of Trinity's board of trustees, that fifty years before "a man could not say publically, that he favored the emancipation of the slaves."[18] Trinity alumni at Columbia University sent down resolutions urging the board of trustees to retain Bassett, and his colleagues on the faculty issued a statement of support. Warren A. Candler apparently took great pleasure in answering Southgate's request for advice by urging him to let his trustees know that the faculties of their schools did not "hold office at the will of irritable and inflammatory people who too easily join in any hue and cry that may be raised."[19]

John C. Kilgo, the president of Trinity, handled the case masterfully. In the crisis he did everything right that the administration at Emory had done wrong. First, he had a private and official interview with Bassett in which the professor was able to explain fully what he meant in his article. In that interview, every provocative sentence and word was reduced to seeming harmlessness. In regard to his assertion that blacks would inevitably advance to equality, Bassett explained: "I mean merely this, that the time will come when the negro race will have a due proportion of wealthy, educated, prosperous and civilized individuals, just as the other people of the world have. . . . This does not mean, nor did I intend that it should mean that there will be social mingling of the races." Queried as to how long this might be, Bassett answered: "O, I don't know; not less than two hundred years; perhaps it may take five hundred years. Social changes move very slowly. I don't think any of us will live to see it, do you?" Asked if his use of the word equality meant social equality, he replied: "Not by any means. It was not in my thought. I do not think that anyone who knows me would believe that I meant to advocate anything of the kind. Between the two races is a wide gulf, and I should be the last man to try to bridge it. I had no thought of social equality in mind. I was thinking only of the industrial and civic outlook of the negro race." Finally, when asked about the highly inflamatory sentence linking Robert E. Lee and Booker T. Washington, Bassett explained that he had only been talking in terms of overcoming obstacles. Lee had fought against tremendous odds, and Washington's struggle was made great by the very fact of tremendous Negro inferiority. To say that Washington's accomplishment was great was only to emphasize the depth of black inferiority. Bassett now thought it would have been more accurate to describe Washington's achievement as "most remarkable" rather than great.[20]

Ultimately, the board of trustees of the college met to decide Bassett's fate. Both side came to the meeting fully prepared to do battle. The twenty-five trustees convened in the college library in closed session. Nevertheless, anxious and inventive students listened at the windows, through the transom over a door, and even stole into the basement and listened through the cracks in the floor. One of the last group recorded the proceedings in his diary. In his opening remarks Dr. Kilgo pictured Trinity as a virgin about to be despoiled. "I stand here tonight to plead for the virtue of Trinity," he declared, "as I would plead for the chastity of my mother and the purity of my wife!" Brilliant imagery to a Radical mind. He read some of Josephus Daniels's editorials of a year before in which Daniels defended Sledd's right to speak, asserting that "a college professor ought to have the liberty to think, speak, and write as he chose without fear of persecution." Then the Reverend F. A. Bishop "got up and in his deep drawling voice said that these trustees did not understand how the people down East thought about this thing. He had talked with Brother Carter on the train and with Brother Jones in the factory, etc., and all condemned Bassett. One preacher told him there was not a man in his parish that did not demand Bassett's removal." Senator Furnifold M. Simmons, another trustee, asserted that there was a dead line in a church and a dead line in society beyond which free speech might not go. Liberty, he said, did not license folly.

On the other side, Kilgo explained that Bassett's article had been grossly misrepresented, that his views were actually those presented in the formal interview. Southgate then made a speech arguing as Candler had advised—let Trinity stand for freedom. Kilgo again took up the debate. During his six years at Trinity, he had found that the faculty felt an "affection and admiration" for the Negro. In time, the professors thought, blacks would make for themselves "a sure and worthy place in our American life." They came as savages, but soon had acquired "much of our culture, and have produced outstanding scientists, literary men, industrialists and leaders in social and religious movements." The student diarist, listening at his post in the basement, concluded that President Kilgo did not approve of "social mingling" and certainly not of miscegenation. "But he looked forward to a time when all economic and political barriers would be broken."[21] In the balloting that followed the debate, eighteen trustees opted to retain Bassett and seven voted for his dismissal. Bruton of Wilson and Simmons of New Bern joined with five black belt ministers to cast the seven negative votes.[22]

Once the commitment was made, the great majority of persons concerned thought that Trinity had made a good decision. "I never was much on Trinity College," a Burlington man wrote to Southgate, "but from this on I will always feel like taking off my hat to that institution." Trinity had declared "in language that cannot be misunderstood that freedom of conscience must and shall have full sway in the 'old North State!'"[23] Similarly, a trustee who had returned home wrote to assure Benjamin Duke that they had acted wisely in standing against the "vaporing of the senseless rabble," and that "the *West is solid.*"[24] And, again, a Greensboro lawyer came very close to the truth when he indicated that the Negro was more under the white man's control than ever and that "social equality" was a term of a generation past and gone. "No fool, white or black," he said, "with sense enough to dodge a street car or brains enough to ring a doorbell, can entertain a dream of the possibility suggested by this obsolete term.... The white manhood of the south has settled and pigeonholed that question for all time. The white manhood of the north has recognized and approved the wisdom of its solution."[25] Even a Statesville pastor who had demanded Bassett's removal wrote to reverse his stand.[26]

One of the interesting aspects of the Bassett case is that among those who saved him, not a single person endorsed what he had said. The trustees, even as they voted for his retention, declared their disagreement with Bassett's opinions and asserted that "it clearly appears that the faculty and the students disagree with certain of Professor Bassett's opinions—so far as we can ascertain, unanimously."[27] Indeed, his colleagues on the faculty seemed to relish their dissent from Bassett's views. As they saw it, their dissent rendered them "exceptionally free to devote ourselves to the great and general principle involved," that is, to promote free speech in the South.[28] After the decision was made, numerous letters of support came to Bassett's defenders, and all grasped the great point that freedom of "speech," "conscience," and "thought" had been preserved in the South. Thus they rested their case precisely upon the grounds that Bassett himself had been building at Trinity for half a dozen years—namely, that freedom of thought and expression was essential to social, and Southern, salvation.

THE ALIENATION OF THE CONSERVATIVE ACTIVIST

Like hundreds of other Conservative and Liberal Southerners, Bassett's alienation from the South began when he set out simply—almost naïvely—to tell
the truth about race relations upon his native soil. It was not, of course, that
he was sentimental in his sympathies with blacks. At the personal, emotional
level he never attained the plateau that Cable apparently reached where he was
able to consider blacks as people very much like himself. "I have never been
able to divest myself entirely of the inborn Southern feeling that a negro is not
to be treated as a white man," he wrote in 1911.[29] On the other hand, when
Bassett read Dixon's *The Leopard's Spots* in 1902, he had no difficulty at all
in coming quickly to a conclusion diametrically opposed to that of the author:
"that the negro has absolutely no place in American life."[30] As with other
racial Conservatives, for Bassett the mission had long been to find the
"place"of the Negro. Characteristically for his time, he devoted his abilities as
a scholar and social scientist to the task of finding that place and leading black
folk to it. Very soon after he returned to Trinity from Johns Hopkins, Ph.D.
in hand, a young professor schooled in the most recent methods of social science, he turned a major part of his professional interests in that direction. He
was probably the first trained scholar in the South to undertake black studies,
and the profession has forgotten how far he had progressed before the Trinity
episode. As he wrote to his mentor at Hopkins, Herbert Baxter Adams, well
after he was into his work on black history, "I desire to find out what there is
in the negro, what he has done, and what he can and will do."[31]

In 1895, young Dr. Bassett was already in the field, testing the Negro historically. He spent the summer in the archives in Raleigh, collecting material
on constitutional history and on "The Negro in N.C." He voiced the complaint about source material that his colleagues three generations later would
reiterate—"The negro matter is not so rich." Particularly, he anticipated difficulty with black religion and outlined a persisting problem of black religious
history. "It is going to be rather hard to tell how much he had, where he got
it, how fast he got it, & just what kind it is."[32] Apparently, Bassett put a great
amount of labor into his black studies. He promised again and again to make
an end to them and to give the results in a series of lectures on the subject at
Johns Hopkins. But in 1900 he was still striving to organize his materials. In
a nearly perfect prelude to what became the standard order in Afro-American
studies seven decades later, he found that his project fell into three segments—
the Negro in Africa, in slavery, and in freedom. Again like more recent historians, even though he attempted "to make the treatment historical rather
than sociological," he discovered that "it will not be possible to avoid a mention of problems of today."[33] In his "Johns Hopkins Negro Lectures" Bassett
was perhaps the first Southern white scholar to raise the possibility that black

Reconstruction may not have been all bad. "The negro seems to have gained through political life" in Reconstruction, he said, and a number "have contributed to the progress of their people and of the nation [as] governors, senators, congressmen." He thought that it would have been far worse to have turned the Negro over to the care of the Southern states, "in which case he would not have been entirely free."[34] In the late 1890s, Bassett seemed to grow more and more involved with the race question in the South. He participated in a series of lectures offered by Trinity scholars to blacks in Durham; he spoke to black groups elsewhere in the state; and he reviewed books concerning blacks in journals.[35] As editor of the *South Atlantic Quarterly,* he published numerous reviews and articles concerning the Negro and race relations.

Bassett's interests included blacks, but, beyond that, he was deeply concerned with the South and its history. Almost from the first, his prime objective as a professional historian was to turn the best of the Old South into the New South. Inevitably, this meant that a major portion of his labor would lie on the white side of the color line. Again, Bassett presaged his professional fellows by three generations. After the second Reconstruction, white historians who dealt with black history and matters of race in America would also come under fire and increasingly turn their efforts away from the black experience and to the white. They, like Bassett, would indicate by their actions that their ultimate calling was the education of their fellow whites. Bassett thought that the education of the South in that time ought to extend into many areas. The region was changing and ought to change, all of which necessitated freedom of inquiry, thought, and expression. He himself undertook to lighten the corner where he was. "I am trying to put a new spirit into the historical work of the South—so far as my influence extends," he wrote to his mentor in 1897. "Last night I made a talk on our historical ideal. I spoke of the freedom of thought in the history department of this College and of the obligation laid on us for a revival of ideas. I appealed to the boys to let it be so that our society would be at least one place in all the South in which man could present his opinion of our history and get a respectful hearing. At this point they cheered. I think we are making progress."[36] Bassett did believe in the progress of the New South, and he sought to preserve all that was good in the old to leaven the new. He was for industrial development, against populistic legislation (even when proposed by Democrats), and he certainly had no objection to the Dukes or to the American Tobacco Company. As the white supremacy campaigns of 1898 and 1900 whipped up Radical racist fevers in North Carolina, he did not take to the field. Instead, he confined his expressions to writing and lecturing. He did so, in part, upon the advice of Adams.[37]

Even so, as the Spanish-American War got under way, Bassett thought that the South might now be sufficiently tolerant for him to do a study of the Ku Klux Klan. "I have an idea that one result of the war is going to make it easier to publish scientific & critical history in the South."[38] Perhaps encouraged by a high spirit for national unity exhibited in the South during and after the war, Bassett took increasingly larger liberties in his inquiries and in publicizing them. He conceived and, in 1901, began to publish the *South Atlantic Quarterly* both as a training ground for Southerners in public expression and exchange and as a device to promote freedom of thought and discussion in the South. In the magazine he deliberately arranged things to excite attention and invite debate. His "Antipathy" article was actually the third in a series increasingly critical of Radical tendencies in race relations. He wrote it in a deliberately provocative way, trying, as he phrased it, "to take them up."[39] But he hardly expected the violent reaction that came to his "Antipathy" article. When the furor had passed, he resolved to be more careful.

More significantly, there crept into Bassett's thinking an idea that marked, and marred, the writing of Southern history for decades afterward. That idea was that a wave of democracy had flooded the South in and after the 1830s and closed out freedom of thought. Rising Jacksonian democracy had empowered popular racism in the prewar South, as he saw it, and the ignorant masses had stifled intellectual inquiry and dissent. Thus it was that a species of "mob" rule had strapped slavery upon a noble people, when freedom of thought and expression would have wiped it away—and thus saved the nation the blood and treasure consumed in the Civil War. And now, with the new democracy of Populists like Marion Butler or Democrats like William Jennings Bryan there came a new racism, and freedom of thought and expression was again in danger of strangulation. It occurred to Bassett that the most recent wave of popular politics sweeping through the South in and after the 1890s was associated with the mob spirit behind lynching, and carried with it the danger of yet another submersion of freedom of thought and expression.[40]

Actually, Bassett need not have worried. His opponents delighted in a very open expression of opinions, and they felt sure of their power to destroy their enemies in verbal combat. On his home ground of Trinity College, in 1904, two teams of student debaters did forensic battle on the proposition that the new suffrage amendment in North Carolina and laws in the Southern states should exclude both blacks and whites without "discrimination." The victory, as one observer noted, was "Won *by the Negative*," meaning that blacks should be discriminated against.[41] The problem, ultimately, was not that freedom of thought and expression were denied. It was rather that whites were generating a new consensus on the nature of Negro inferiority—an inferiority that would put the Negro down but not out.

In 1906, Bassett was offered an appointment to the faculty of Smith College in Northampton, Massachusetts. "The thing in my profession which I like best is the writing of history," he confessed to Walter Hines Page, "certainly the quiet and stimulus of the New England town are the best calculated to promote it."[42] Within the year, Bassett had settled in Northampton. There he lived next door to that venerable Southern expatriate who had preceded him twenty years before, George Washington Cable. Of both, and of scores of others before and after, it might be fairly asked: Did he jump ... or, was he pushed?

THE RETREATS OF CONSERVATISM: EDUCATION

Very generally, Conservatives in the South responded to rejection by simply withdrawing from combat. They did not withdraw to die, but rather to preserve their strength and wait for the day when they could sally forth again.

It is clear that as individual Conservative leaders found themselves unable to make progress across the race line without bringing down upon their heads a hail of public scorn, they turned their paternalism, heretofore expended upon blacks, into labors among their white brothers and sisters. There were a dozen areas and sub-areas in which the effects of this effort were evident. Persisting Conservatives were highly visible in universities and colleges that favored work in the liberal arts. Closely associated with their involvement in universities and colleges was their labor in public education and in the academization of medicine. In religion they threw themselves into mission movements, especially into stretching out denominational arms to embrace again whites who had somehow become unchurched in the movement of America from the farms to the cities and industrial villages, and to those in the mountains and swamps of the Southland who had somehow hitherto escaped the focused interest of the churches. In this redirection of the missionary effort of organized Southern Christianity, the churches also picked up again their work in foreign missions. If they could not carry the light to blacks at home as they had in the past, they would carry it to the benighted "colored" peoples of the world. Conservatives also spent their paternalism in "progressive" politics and business, either in or outside of the South. Progressive to them meant enterprises pursued primarily for social as opposed to personal gain. Finally, Conservatives persisted as literary people—often as the steadfastly sensible editors of newspapers large and small, and sometimes as novelists, poets, and folklorists tacitly calling for a return in some fashion to what they perceived to be traditional values of moderation and equity.

Higher education in the South before the 1890s had been very much a seamless web. There was a great circulation of people between the leading schools, present professors taught future professors, and all joined together in endless communion precisely as they do in higher education in any Western academic society. In the 1890s and afterward, however, there was a decided tendency for higher education in the South to split into two circles. The divi-

sion occurred as technical education began to splinter away from the older
trunk that had stressed the liberal arts—followed by professional pursuits in
law, medicine, and graduate studies. Those who led in shaping the character
of technical education had passed the same way as had their late colleagues
who continued to evolve in the liberal arts tradition. Just as Populists were
splinters of the Democracy, and just as Radical racists were splinters from
Conservative racism, so too were the leaders in technical education splinters
reared in the classical tradition. It is striking that in higher education in the
South in and after the 1890s there was a conjunction between technical education and Radical racism and between classical education and a persisting
Conservative racism.

In the public universities, the line of division between those schools that
exhibited a Conservative bias and those that became Radical is quite clear.
Generally speaking, those older state universities that continued to emphasize
the liberal arts in undergraduate training (sometimes with professional schools
of law, medicine, and graduate studies added) became centers of Conservatism.
Conspicuous as hard core centers of Conservatism were the Universities of
Virginia, North Carolina, and South Carolina. Softer cores existed in Alabama, Mississippi, Tennessee, and probably Texas. On the other hand, the
newly formed technical schools tended to be Radical. These included Virginia
Polytechnical Institute, the North Carolina Agricultural and Technical Institute, and Clemson College in South Carolina. The last was virtually the single-
handed creation of Ben Tillman, who saw to it that the board of governors
was given the power to fill its own vacancies so that no black person would
ever be allowed to sit as a member of that body. Probably inclined in the same
direction were the Georgia Technical Institute and deep South technical
schools generally. Some of the older state universities had technical schools
tacked onto their traditional structure. Where this occurred, as in Georgia and
Louisiana, there seems to have been an ambivalence on the race issue. They
were at the same time populated by Conservatives and Radicals.

The spirit of Conservatism also seemed to retreat and maintain its strength
in certain private schools. Johns Hopkins was obviously a key center of Conservatism. Out of the Hopkins came such notable Conservatives as Walter
Hines Page, Woodrow Wilson, John Spencer Bassett, and three other scholars
not previously mentioned, Stephen B. Weeks, William P. Trent, and Broadus
Mitchell. Johns Hopkins was the great secular private school in the South;
among the denominationally affiliated institutions there were a dozen others
that exhibited strong Conservative tendencies in matters of race. Very important were the "big four" Southern Methodist schools, each of which suddenly
expanded about the turn of the century from relatively small, limited colleges
into fairly large universities with offerings not only in the liberal arts but in
medicine, law, and graduate studies as well. With Trinity (Duke) in North

Carolina, Emory near Atlanta, Tulane in New Orleans, and Vanderbilt in Nashville, these four effectively covered the South. Moreover, each was situated to take advantage of New South boomerism. Indeed, each benefited vastly from donations from the quickly gotten gains of late nineteenth-century tycoons. Duke sprang from tobacco and utilities, Emory from Coca-Cola, Tulane sat happily at the very mouth of the great Mississippi Valley, and Vanderbilt, of course, drew its first great fortune from the iron rails of transportation. Baptist schools, too, participated in the Conservative holdout, most notably the University of Richmond, Wake Forest University, and the Southern Baptist Theological Seminary, located first at Greenville, South Carolina, and later in Louisville, Kentucky. Additionally, there were smaller Baptist schools, such as Georgetown College in Kentucky, that kept the faith. The Episcopalians, of course, maintained the University of the South at Sewanee, in the high mountains just west of Chattanooga. In these Conservative strongholds, public and private, the Radical hysteria was met and repulsed. They became enclaves in which scholars could think and talk about black people much as they chose, if they chose.

In these schools, of course, the faculty, students, and administration were all white, and matters of race were always tangential to their major concerns. Hundreds and thousands of students passed through with never a deep thought about race. Doubtlessly, many students came as Radicals and left as Radicals. But many others came and absorbed, consciously or unconsciously, an education that was informed by the Conservative bias. When they did think about race, they were pre-set to think in a Conservative direction. They were also pre-set to be gentle persuaders initially, willing to work and wait for the time when their influence would be effective. In the first half of the twentieth century, these schools poured forth studies on various aspects of Southern life and history. Indeed, probably the first course in Southern History to be offered in America was given at Trinity College in 1907. Inevitably, students of Southern culture came to consider such problems as convict leasing, the lien system, and peonage, and these things brought them squarely to the close study of the black experience and a reconsideration of the equity of the *status quo* in race relations. In the 1960s, when the time came to move outside the ivy covered walls and into the streets, these were precisely the schools in the South that furnished white activist leadership. Indeed, in this phase of racial history in the South, they ventured forth with a verve that was much more reminiscent of their Radical uncles and aunts, the Ben Tillmans, Becky Feltons, and, even, the Tom Dixons, than of their Conservative fathers and mothers. For a time, the Southern Conservative-*cum*-liberal could be very aggressive and very physical, as well as very spiritual.

As the universities of the South divided in and after the 1890s between Conservatism and Radicalism so too did administrators and faculty. Johns

Hopkins, of course, was a wellspring of Conservatism that supplied a steady flow of professors and educational administrators to the South. Walter Hines Page and Woodrow Wilson soon chose to go north, but just as Wilson left Baltimore, William P. Trent arrived. Trent was a young Richmond native and a graduate of the University of Virginia. He took his Ph.D. in 1888, and went on to become Professor of English in the University of the South until 1900. Trent established a solid interest in Southern literature at Sewanee, appropriately enough becoming the first scholarly biographer of William Gilmore Simms (1892) and of Robert E. Lee (1899). Close behind Trent at Johns Hopkins came Stephen B. Weeks and John Spencer Bassett, both of whom came from North Carolina and soon returned to teach at Trinity. During his trials at Trinity, Bassett was strongly supported by Edwin Mims, an Arkansas native who took two degrees at Vanderbilt, in 1892 and 1893, and a doctorate at Cornell. Not only did Mims stand firmly behind Bassett during his fight with the Radicals, he also assumed a share of the editorship of *The South Atlantic Quarterly* when Bassett left for Smith College. In 1909, Mims moved across New Hope Swamp to Chapel Hill, before moving still further west to Vanderbilt in 1912. At his *alma mater* he became the head of the English Department and presided, somewhat uneasily, over the doings of the Nashville Agrarians in the 1920s. Before Mims came to Vanderbilt, Williams S. Baskervill had already built a large interest in Southern literature there. Baskervill's literary interest prompted his alliance with George Washington Cable in the Open Letter Club, an operation under way even while Mims was a Vanderbilt undergraduate.

One of the most interesting and important schoolmen in this process of maintaining Southern ideals, including Conservative racial ideals, was Edwin A. Alderman, the head of the University of Virginia during the first quarter of the twentieth century. Alderman took a degree at the University of North Carolina in 1882 and shortly became one of a dynamic group of young men who undertook to revitalize public education in the state. Among other things, as we have noted, he taught John Spencer Bassett in high school in Goldsboro. Alderman soon became an evangelist for public education, touring the state offering workshops for teachers in their home counties. In 1893 he became the first professor of education in the University in Chapel Hill, and in 1896 he became the president of the University. In 1900 he moved on to head up Tulane. While he was in New Orleans, Alderman engaged with Booker T. Washington in an attempt to work out some plan of interracial accord looking to the education of black people. Also, he began seriously to work up the concept of Southern idealism as the basic value system that would save the nation. In 1904, when the call came to take the helm at the University of Virginia, he accepted, in large part because it gave him a more effective position from which to urge that favored cause.

It is highly significant that Alderman replaced Paul B. Barringer, who became one of the founding presidents of Virginia Polytechnic Institute. Barringer was one of the most extravagant Radicals in higher education in the South. While he was head of the university, from 1896 to 1903, he became famous for his Radical speeches and writings on black people and race relations. It was, indeed, incongruous that such extreme racism should have been expressed by the head of Mr. Jefferson's University, by a man who was himself a graduate of that institution. It was fitting that he was followed in that office by a man dedicated to the celebration of Southern values. Similarly, George T. Winston, also a Radical, was the president of the University of North Carolina before Alderman and passed over to lead North Carolina's agricultural and technical college from 1899 until 1908. And again, David F. Houston, who eventually became Woodrow Wilson's Secretary of Agriculture, was one of the founding presidents of the Texas Institute of Technology. He was born in North Carolina in 1866, was educated at the University of South Carolina and Harvard, and rose through the academic ranks as a political scientist to become the president of the University of Texas.

Alderman, of course, was closely associated with the development of public school systems in the South. So, too, was a young professor of chemistry who taught at the University of North Carolina while Alderman was a student there, Charles W. Dabney. Dabney was the son of Robert L. Dabney, the biographer of Stonewall Jackson, Presbyterian minister, and philosopher of the Old South persisting in the New. Charles took his Ph.D. in chemistry from the University of Göttingen in 1880 at the age of twenty-five and became a professor in the University of North Carolina. He soon emerged a leading expert in agricultural chemistry and participated in the development of scientific agriculture within the state. In 1887 he was elected president of the University of Tennessee, and, at the turn of the century, began to involve that institution heavily in the public education movement. Joining with "schoolmen" all over the South, he worked to channel funds into Southern public schools. He made his campus, in Knoxville, near the center of southern Appalachia, a headquarters for numerous summer institutes for teachers. In his very important book, *Universal Education in the South,* Dabney argued for a place for the Negro and urged a system for his education.

With leadership from such Southerners as Dabney and Alderman, public education in the region moved into the modern age. Before the Civil War only North Carolina had made progress in building a system of common schools, education generally being a private matter. Reconstruction regimes established programs in the various states, but the execution of those programs was ragged and thin. Generally, when schools were available, they ran for only a few months each year, offered only a few years of elementary instruction, and the qualifications demanded of teachers were not high. Outside the towns, the availability of a common school education to the children was spotty and often sporadic. In the 1890s, however, there were stirrings, and the first decade of the twentieth century saw the schools of the South, at last, become roughly comparable with those in the rest of the nation. Those schools were organized, managed, and largely staffed by the "gentry." Quite clearly, these people were committed to bringing the great mass of white children in the South up to the standards to which they themselves had been born.

Conservative patricians also turned their energies into public medicine. The practice of medicine in the nineteenth-century South was a various thing. Some physicians were trained on the job, virtually as apprentices to established physicians. Others attended medical schools in the South, and an impressively large number attended the best medical schools in the North. Many of the latter were the sons of planters who returned to the plantation to practice medicine among great numbers of slaves. Because of the value of the slave, the health care system attached to slavery was often well financed and fine tuned. With emancipation, health care became an individual matter, and probably the level of care declined considerably.

At the turn of the century, there was clearly a revival and reorganization in the study and practice of medicine in the South, and the orientation of that new organization was distinctly white. Medicine was made academic, scientific, and professionally rigorous. At the heart of this move toward what might be called "patrician medicine" were the big four Methodist schools (Emory, Tulane, Vanderbilt, and Trinity, soon to become Duke), Johns Hopkins, and the University of Virginia. Sewanee surrendered its medical department, but probably the most eminent Southern-bred physician of the early twentieth century, a paragon of the patrician as physician, was William C. Gorgas, who had attended the University of the South while his father was provost there and moved on to do pioneering labor in fighting malaria, first with the army in Cuba and later as consultant to various public health activities in the South. Where the Episcopalians had dropped out of medical education, the Baptists moved in, and in the 1920s established Bowman-Gray Medical School in Winston-Salem, North Carolina. Young men emerged from these schools to serve not the blacks nearly so much as their own Southern white fellows, and these not only in contact with individual patients, but in the great public health crusades that swept the South in those early years of the twentieth century. It was this generation that led mass campaigns for improved sanitation on the farms and in the homes, for better nutrition, and against the very common and highly debilitating diseases of hookworm and pellegra.

THE RETREATS OF CONSERVATISM: RELIGION

Conservatives also retreated into religious missionary work, first among black people at home and, finally, as that grew more difficult, transferring much of their missionary effort to "colored" people elsewhere in the world and to whites. To work among black Southerners was very much a revival of the interest and effort that had marked the immediate prewar decades. As we have seen, Bishop Haygood had been a pioneer in that labor in the 1880s, as his mentor Bishop Pierce had been in the prewar years. During the period in which the Radicals gained strength in the South, every major Southern church was active in missionary labors among Negroes. Because of the great secession of black people from white-dominated churches immediately after emancipation and the ardent recruitment thereafter of new members by the all-black churches, the number of black people involved in these connections was minuscule. In missionary work, as in disfranchisement and segregation, the activities of whites with blacks were much more a matter of qualities than of quantities. Nevertheless, the manner in which whites touched blacks in religion closely reflected the whole nature of race relations in the South in these transitional years.

No one denomination stands clearly first in the ardor with which it sought to make that connection. In each denomination there were Christians who felt strongly a call to duty with black people, some who felt no such call, and still others who were passionately against maintaining any relations at all. Speaking generally, however, those who were most ardent and most persistent in preaching the duty of white Christianity to blacks were professional churchmen. They were priests, ministers, and bishops who, ideally, lived for, as well as by, their religion. It is easiest to see the history of that work in the Episcopal Church, the most hierarchical of the four major denominations in the South. At the same time, the basic history of the Episcopalians in this regard was shared by the other denominations.

It was probably in recognition of his concern for blacks and his quiet, genial effectiveness that the Episcopal church selected Thomas Underwood Dudley, the Bishop of Kentucky, to head its Board of Domestic and Foreign missions. Dudley was a Virginian, educated at the University of Virginia, where, in fact, he remained for a time after his graduation in 1858 as a professor in Latin and Greek. During the Civil War he served as a commissary officer. Afterward he entered the church, becoming the Bishop of Kentucky in 1884 and then, in 1901, was elected chairman of the House of Bishops. The primary function of the Board of Missions was to distribute funds raised in the dioceses of the church nationwide. These funds were large, in part, because the Episcopal church, unlike the Methodists, Baptists, and Presbyterians, reunited north and south immediately upon the close of the war. Taking funds from the Board, each bishop then had broad powers within his diocese to shape his missionary efforts among blacks, whites, and Indians as he saw fit. Thus there was a wide range of performance in various dioceses. Even so, a general pattern emerged in which the effort among blacks rose in the early 1890s, crested about 1904–05, and then declined but never entirely disappeared. As the decline proceeded, interest in missions among colored peoples abroad increased, as did interest in missionary work among whites at home.

In some of its dioceses, the Episcopal church was remarkably successful in maintaining and increasing its effectiveness among blacks, though it must be remembered that the numbers were always small. In these areas success seems to have been related to the personal attitude and special talents of the presiding bishop and to the willingness of some churchmen to commit their lives to the labor. William Crane Gray, the missionary bishop of southern Florida, was one of these. Bishop Gray personified the continuation of the antebellum concern of the church. He had had Negroes in his own church before the war and continued the work after emancipation. A portion of Gray's success may have arisen from the fact that many blacks came into his diocese from the West Indies, where the Church of England had long maintained a large and successful missionary effort. The Negro archdeacon for northern Florida, who also served the black parish in Jacksonville, noted the West Indian presence in complaining of the lack of a church school there. Many West Indian Negroes coming in, he explained, had been well trained in the islands and expected care and schools, which they had had in the islands in an excellent degree. His own children, he lamented, were forced to attend a public school with 1400 other students, "some packed to over one hundred children in unsanitary rooms."[43]

Generally, the Episcopal church was most successful in its mission to black people in the upper South, and it was least successful in the lower South, where vast numbers of Negroes seemed to drive bishops to despair. Even so, in 1909 a Virginia bishop lamented that "the great difficulty about getting our people to do anything now is the alienation of a great part of the race from the whites and the loss by the negroes of the sense of their actual position in the scale of civilization." Out of the alienation came an inability of whites to establish real communication with blacks. "After twenty-odd years of experience in dealing with the colored people," wrote the bishop of northern Florida, "I know the colored man is not going to tell the white man the whole truth about his people."[44]

Beginning with a meeting of Southern Bishops at Sewanee in 1905 and proceeding over the next few years, the Episcopal church undertook to find a rational solution to the problem of missions to Negroes.[45] Generally three plans were devised to meet the issue, and each of them relied upon a black intermediary. At first, most bishops used a black archdeacon, and the trend was to turn almost every function over to him. Vigorously rejected by the bishops was a plan for a black field secretary to be under the control of the Board, and, hence, not of themselves. The third plan was to have a completely separated organization under a black bishop. Soon the church did create a "Suffragan" bishop to oversee the black portion of the church. This officer, a black man, was aside from and somewhat below the regular bishops, with no power to vote in their councils. It was, in effect, yet another demonstration of separate and unequal.

Separation was never total. Some churchmen never surrendered what they considered to be their God-given responsibility to care for an inferior race. Bishop Gibson of Virginia confessed in 1909 that he thought blacks were "incapable in every department" of rising to the level of white people, most of all in matters of conscience, even as he continued to encourage mission work in his diocese. "They know about honors and distinctions and high places and insignia," he declared. "These things they understand and are reaching for them constantly, but they have no sense of responsibility commensurate with the places they seek. . . . I have never seen the development in any of them of higher moral qualities than could be found in a bright white boy of fourteen years of age, and most of them, in these qualities, never get beyond the age of seven or eight." He welcomed black schools in the South because their graduates often left the South. "To show you my feeling about this situation," he confessed, "I say to you what I have not often said, that when a negro goes North, I never want him to come back." He thought the very best that could be done was to keep black people in contact with the best whites.[46]

There were such whites, and they did persist in their labors. In Virginia the Reverend Robert William Patton, grandson of a lieutenant-governor of the state, son of a colonel who had served under Jackson, and between 1896 and 1900 himself rector of Christ Church in Roanoke, served as the secretary of the Department of Sewanee during most of his life. In that position he "revolutionized the attitude of church members toward the missionary work of the church" and saw gifts for missionary labors in general triple. He himself possessed a special proclivity for work among blacks. "From boyhood he was much interested in the welfare of the Negro," reported his biographer. "His mother had conducted a school for Negroes on the family plantation and he himself opened a school for colored children before he was ten years of age." In 1914 he became the director of the American Church Institute for Negroes, an institution established to provide a quality of education for black children that the public schools were not providing. Under Patton's direction, the Institute came to operate nine schools with 4500 full time and 10,000 part-time students.[47]

If one was moved to missionary work among the colored people, there were darker races abroad upon whom the willing might lavish their lives without hindrance from Southern whites of the Radical persuasion, and indeed with a great deal of support from the mass of their fellow whites. Episcopal churchmen had gone out into the world missions before racial extremism rose in the South, of course. Yet, it seems clear enough that after the rise of the

Radicals many young Southern churchmen spent abroad the coin that they could no longer spend at home.

The outreach of the Southern episcopacy to foreign parts was vastly assisted by a rising American imperialism. The church moved into the Philippines with the army in 1898 and very soon established a large operation there under a missionary bishop. In the Caribbean, where they found themselves confronting the well established and formidable Church of England, progress was more difficult. The opposition of the C. of E. was made even more formidable by the fact that so many of its priests were of mixed blood and so much more effective among the local people than white Americans.

At home, as it became more difficult for whites in the South to continue missionary labors with blacks, they turned their efforts to reaching out to unchurched whites. Much of this energy was spent in simply evangelizing the white masses wherever they happened to be. A part of that labor, of course, lay in the growing cities and towns, and in the industrial villages across the Southland. A relevant and highly interesting part was spent in reaching those whites who somehow for generations had been passed by and left alone in the mountains, swamps, and pine barrens. As labor with blacks became more difficult, it was inevitable that the white alternative would manifest itself to the missionaries. A Virginian, hard at work among the blacks in northern Florida in 1900, wrote to the Missions Board his "own deliberate opinion ... that there is no more prolific field of labor today for the Church than among the so-called common white people of the Southern States."[48]

Each of the other major denominations exhibited much the same array of responses to the black presence as did the Episcopal church. As we have seen, the Methodist Episcopal Church, South, almost from its beginning, supported a tradition of protective paternalism toward blacks and sought actively to carry its mission to them. Bishop Pierce, a founding father of the Southern church, has passed the flame on to Bishop Haygood who carried it nobly, having barely decided not to pursue missionary labors in China in the 1850s. Haygood's protégé in turn was Warren A. Candler, by 1900 himself the most eminent bishop in the Southern Methodist Church. The interests of these three men illustrate neatly the transition of white religious interests in blacks in the South. Pierce belonged to that very powerful first generation of paternalists, Haygood to the next very embattled generation, and, finally, Candler turned away from an active paternalism toward black people at home and toward a very vigorous paternalism among "colored" people abroad. Candler had refused on one occasion to head up Haygood's Paine College in Augusta, created by Haygood to produce black ministers for the black work. While Candler was steadfastly Conservative, as we saw in the Sledd case, he was not willing to give much substance to that paternalism. Instead, he soon threw himself into the work abroad.

With the Spanish-American War, Candler became the bishop not only of Texas and Florida, but of Cuba as well, an odd diocese more likely to have been designed by John C. Calhoun than by St. Peter. Candler brought his church into Cuba upon the very heels of the United States Army. He worked closely with the natives, turning previous organizations to his own advantage. In one instance, he converted a Catholic priest to Southern Methodism and set him to the task of making other converts among Cuban Catholics. A forceful man who liked to chain-smoke cigars during three- or four-day church conferences, Candler was candid in claiming the Pearl of the Antilles for the Southern church. The bishop resented editorials in the Northern papers that implied that the Southern church was unable to deal with the race question in Cuba. "In view of the great work we have done for the negroes in the United States and the work we are still trying to do, in view of the results we have already achieved in Cuba; and especially in the view of the Color line drawn by your annual Conference organizations these editorials seem to be only pretexts to defend an unfraternal purpose."[49] Candler soon indicated his willingness to return the "unfraternity" of the Northern Methodists by visiting their supposedly exclusive domain in Puerto Rico. Apparently, the bishop could easily contemplate turning the Caribbean into a Southern Methodist sea.

Increasingly, however, Candler's interest shifted to the Orient. At various times he visited Japan, Korea, and China. Indeed, at the time of the Atlanta riot, he was traveling in China, visiting missions and Methodist colleges there.[50]

Among Southern Baptists, racial separatism at the popular level came easily immediately after emancipation because separatism per se came easily to Baptists. To the Baptists, the congregation was the church, and if the congregation wills itself to become two, then so be it. Hundreds of thousands of Southern Negroes had become Baptists before the war, some formally within the white churches, many more in congregations on the plantations that were overseen by whites. With emancipation, black Baptists separated themselves from the whites and coalesced into loose associations. Not all white Baptists, however, surrendered their concern about black people. Especially in the early 1890s there was a revival of the prewar interest in carrying the mission to blacks. In 1886, for instance, Southern Baptists had twenty-two ministers in the black work; in 1889 they had forty-one; in 1890, fifty (forty-five of whom were black); and in 1891 fifty-one. In the latter year, the Home Missionary Board asked for $50,000 yearly for ten years, as it optimistically declared, to "settle this race question forever." In 1895 the Board came to support the "New Era Plan" that called for the establishment of training institutes for black ministers and for traveling agents. The Board supported the plan for about thirty years, but only the states of Missouri and Virginia participated fully.[51]

As with Episcopalians and Methodists, Baptists found the work of recruiting blacks most difficult in the lower South. In this experience Alabama was typical. Alabama Baptists divided between those who remained Conservative and those who went Radical. During the early 1890s Conservatives appear to have surged forward, weakened in the late 1890s, and largely lost to Radical extremism about 1906. After 1906 Radicalism continued strong, but was only sporadically effective.[52] The hysteria about the black beast as rapist seems to have risen in Alabama in 1906 much as it did in Georgia in the same year. Alabama Baptists, like Georgians in Atlanta, tended to associate the evil with drink. The Atlanta riot justified precisely what Alabama drys had been saying all along and intensified the move for temperance there, at least for blacks. The necessity was made pointed by an outbreak in Mobile shortly after the Atlanta riot. Several Negroes were killed in a bloody outbreak caused by "negro dives," the rape of two white women by "the negro brute," the slowness of justice, and by white men living openly with Negro women as their wives (especially one Mobile official).[53] As in Georgia, it seems that when Alabamians had gone to an extreme in violence, they began to swing back. Radicalism persisted but tended to lose focus.

As Radicalism rose, Southern Baptists lost the ability to condemn racial injustice. One student perused the minutes of 1,003 district association meetings between 1910 and 1935 and found that only nine of these discussed lynching or mob violence. Much more revealingly, he searched the minutes of 117 association meetings where 134 lynchings had occurred within the boundaries of the association within four months prior to the meeting. In the 134 events, a total of 206 persons were lynched, including eight women (one pregnant), a ninety-six-year-old man, a sixteen-year-old boy, one man for "poisoning a mule," another for "writing an insulting note to a white girl," and still another for "trying to act like a white man." In only one meeting, that of the Rankin County Baptists in 1934, did the association denounce a lynching. In this case, a man had been killed for "talking disrespectfully."[54]

Southern Baptists never totally lost the faith. It persisted, for example, in such individuals as B. F. Riley, the president of Howard (now Samford) University in Birmingham, who published a book, *The White Man's Burden*, in 1910 calling for black education and denouncing the claim that blacks were after social equality as a "phantom born in the brain of the racial hater."[55] It also persisted in institutions such as the Southern Baptist Theological Seminary in Louisville, where the faculty maintained something of a shadow school to teach black ministers who could not, of course, officially enroll in the seminary, and from which there emerged in the 1930s and 1940s a great wave of very impressive and liberally biased studies of black people in Southern religion.

Southern Presbyterians at large were like the Episcopal hierarchy in that they took the matter of race very seriously, and they persisted in their attempts to wrestle with the problem of maintaining the mission across the race line. Also like the Episcopalians they believed in the necessity of establishing schools along with their churches. They were unlike the Methodists and Baptists in that there were not many of them, both white and black, even though the influence and power that they generated was very large.

THE RETREATS OF CONSERVATISM: CONCLUSION

Conservatives also moved to help their white brothers and sisters in "progressive" politics and business. Political Conservatism produced such lasting characters as John Sharp Williams of Mississippi and Oscar Underwood of Alabama, both of whom had long and distinguished histories as members of Congress. These were people who never yielded to simple showmanship, race-baiting electoral rhetoric, and the cruder tastes of elements of their constituencies. Some Conservatives left the South, as did Woodrow Wilson. William Gibbs McAdoo, originally from Chattanooga, also went north, where he managed to combine both business and politics. He became a lawyer and eventually settled in New York. There legal business led him into railroading, and he masterminded the completion of the first railroad tunnel under the Hudson River to connect New York City with the Jersey shore. Later McAdoo became Wilson's Secretary of the Treasury, his son-in-law, and, in 1924, the Democratic candidate for the Presidency. Other Southerners of the Conservative persuasion, such as Virginius Dabney and Jonathan Daniels (son of Josephus), became editors who turned their efforts toward calling white Southerners back to what they thought to be the true values of the South. Finally, there were racial Conservatives in literature who addressed their messages primarily to whites, messages that called for racial sanity and for a return of the South to its traditional spirit and ideals. Some of these people were folklorists, some were poets, and some were novelists, the latter stretching in a rich and continuous line from Ellen Glasgow in Virginia in the first quarter of the century to William Faulkner in Mississippi in the second, and on to Walker Percy in more recent times.

Conservatives retreated only in the sense that they did not continue to do public combat for what was, in their view, equity for black people. In a broader sense, what they did was simply redeploy their energies to spend them on the white side of the line. By this profound alteration of direction in the flow of their energy, Conservative patricians effected a revolution in the style of life in the South. As in the last generation of slavery, the black presence had again worked to alter the essential nature of Southern culture. As in that earlier generation, a large body of white people in this generation—the Radicals—had come to perceive black people in a style distinctly different from what had gone before. Radicals strove to adjust the social order to meet what they perceived to be the new realities. Conservatives met the Radical onslaught, and, ultimately, defeated it. But in this struggle, black people were reduced and the white world was taken apart and reconstituted yet again. The new set is the set that still prevails.

CHAPTER IX

The Crucible of Race

Thus far we have focused very narrowly upon what white people, the dominant racial group, thought and did about black people up through the turn-
of-the-century years. Out of this approach has emerged a tripartite separation
between Conservatism, Liberalism, and Radicalism. Conservatism downed
Liberalism easily in the 1880s only to turn and find itself battling for its life
against a new and vastly more powerful challenger, Radicalism. During the
next generation the contest between the two raged. To understand the nature
of that contest, it seems useful now to pause, to raise our eyes beyond the racial
horizon, and to define in particular terms the relative positions of Radicalism
and Conservatism within the broad perspective of Southern and American history, to place them, indeed, as they must be placed in the larger universe of
Western civilization. We can begin that effort best, perhaps, first by looking
at the leaders of the two principal elements and focusing closely upon what
characteristics distinguished one group from the other, and, then, to seek further light by focusing closely upon the characteristics they shared.

THE PHILOSOPHICAL DICHOTOMY

At the most fundamental level, philosophically, there was a broad and profound difference between Radical and Conservative leaders. Very generally,
Radicals tended to be realists in the classical Aristotelian sense. Without denying the truth of the idea of the thing, Radicals were inclined to give primacy
to the reality extant in the thing itself. They saw life as affording practical
alternatives among which one must make rational choices. Radicals were
intolerant of disjunctions in their lives, and they worked to gain power to
manage the immediate world in which they lived. Conservatives, on the other

285

hand, tended to be idealists in the classical Platonic sense. Reality for them lay in the idea of the thing rather than in the thing itself. They viewed the world that we seem to see about us as a dim reflection, a shadow of the higher, truer, and ideal world toward which mankind was progressing, slowly, unevenly, and over the generations. Radicals were very much of this world, and they were, compared with Conservatives, relatively casual about the next one. Conservatives, on their side, carried a steady consciousness of the next world about with them. Their constant effort was to divine God's will for them in their specific time and place, and to hold up the image of what was His will for all to see. "Being" was important to the Conservatives, but "seeming"—images of what was to be—was even more so.

Progress for Conservatives was necessarily slow but by God's will inevitable; for Radicals it might be rapid, but it was not at all inevitable. Radicals could envision the absolute retrogression of American life, on the white side as well as the black. Radicals, therefore, tended to be presentists and activists. They also tended to see immediate crises and the necessity of being aggressively combative. They were prone to use the power of government vigorously as a tool to manage race relations. At first, they used the power of local and state governments, but they soon passed on to think that national problems might be more effectually managed by national power. Still, it was not government in the Hamiltonian sense that they admired. Indeed, they hated the idea of inherited aristocracy, exclusiveness, insiderism, and the closed alliance of business and government. They were close to the theoretical Jefferson in thinking that power corrupts and absolute power corrupts absolutely, but they added with the practical Jefferson that power was all right in their own good hands. In Radical hands, power was an instrument for reform, for rooting out corruption and letting the dead past wither away, devoid of artificial nourishment. The allusion to Thomas Jefferson is more than merely coincidental. There was, in fact, a minor Jeffersonian revival among Radicals; this occurred after the sage of Monticello had been in eclipse in the South for three generations. It was no mere chance that Tom Watson published a well-received biography of the great Virginian and in 1906 chose to rename his magazine *Watson's Jeffersonian Weekly.*[1]

Conservatives were idealists and Radicals were realists, but we ought to qualify the generalization by adding that each Conservative and each Radical carried within himself or herself the potential of the opposite. Idealists never surrendered their consciousness of realism, and realists never surrendered their consciousness of idealism. It was a matter of emphasis, of individuals over a long span of time chosing to give primacy to one style over the other without ever surrendering a potential for sliding to the alternative. The difference in basic philosophy between Conservatives and Radicals manifested itself in many ways. One very important area was in character of leadership.

THE ONE-SHOT STYLE OF SOUTHERN LEADERSHIP—WITH
WILLIAM J. NORTHEN AS AN EXCEPTION

While the Sledd and Bassett cases were the most spectacular, they were only two in a series of tests to which freedom of thought and expression on race in the South was put during the turn-of-the-century decades. Out of the series, there emerged a pattern of response and a style of leadership that marked the racial Conservatives and distinguished them from the Radicals. With only slight exaggeration the Conservative mode might be called the "one-shot style of Southern leadership." Conservatives seemed driven to speak out at least once in a public way upon the subject of racial injustice. This was the case with Sledd, and then with Bishop Candler, and later with Bassett and Bishop Kilgo. It was more or less the case with Lewis Harvie Blair of Richmond in 1889 and Issac DuBose Seabrook of Charleston in 1895, each of whom wrote lengthy manuscripts calling for fairness to the Negro. Seabrook never published his manuscript. Blair published his as a book and repeated the argument in a paper read at the Chicago World's Fair in 1893 and printed in *Arena,* a national magazine. Within a few years, however, he too fell silent. Still another example was Quincy Ewing, an Episcopal priest in Louisiana who published a single article in the *Atlantic Monthly* in 1909 that set him conspicuously upon record as opposing lynching and the Radical racial establishment.[2] In a sense, the entire body of Conservatives in the Virginia constitutional convention of 1901–02 did the same thing. They came out in force one time, some like A. C. Braxton out of their very private lives, to save racial sanity and the old values in Virginia. In the Virginia case, the Conservatives won. And when they were done, they quietly retired. If the Conservatives lost, which they did in Radical states, usually drowned under a great hue and cry of personal condemnation, they subsided and were not heard from upon the subject again.

The aristocrat as moralist ought not to attempt to persuade the masses by an endless reiteration of the emerging truth. Because God had planted the seed of all truth in the hearts of men, when His time came for the seed to grow, one single ray of God-given light would warm it to life. One flash of the clear image, one effort at transmission was the end of their duty. In race relations, Conservative leaders understood that they, themselves, lived outside of the sin of an improper discrimination against blacks. It was their task to point out sin to their brothers, including that of whites against blacks. But, also, the last stone might be cast with the first. If the flesh-encrusted and sinful world chose to go wrong after the Word had been said, then racial Conservatives would neither pray nor plead, nor lower themselves in any way to save the masses from the bitter fruits of their willful ignorance. A failure of the masses to follow in this matter simply meant that God was not yet ready to reveal His will to the people at large. Only with pain and suffering and the mortification of the flesh would they eventually rise to sufficient purity to receive His message. Until then, Conservatives must find other fields of His choosing for earthly labor—public education, public health, the abolition of child labor, foreign missions, and so on, endlessly.

To term the Conservative style of leadership "one-shot" is a slight exaggeration both because it refers to their public rather than their private efforts, and because there were a few Conservatives who were highly persistent in their public expressions of dissatisfaction with the manner in which blacks were being treated. Interestingly, most consistently and avidly engaged were those Conservatives who, on the one hand, came very close to the Liberal stance in seeing their role as one of picking up again the paternalistic burden conceived in slavery, and those who, on the other, shared with the Radicals a fear of black degeneration. One person who exemplified the persisting Conservative was William J. Northen, Democratic governor of Georgia from 1890 to 1894, leading Baptist layman, and peripatetic friend of black people.

Northen was born into the planting gentry of Georgia in 1835. "I had thirty years' experience with slave service on the part of negroes before the civil war," he recalled late in his life. "An old negro Mammy nursed me in my babyhood; I grew up with negro slaves in the fields; negroes in the home and negroes all about me."[3] After completing his studies at Mercer College in 1853, Northen became first a teacher in and then the principal of an academy, Mt. Zion. When the war broke out he enlisted in the Confederate army as a private, serving in a company of which his father was captain. After the war, he returned to teaching until his health, damaged in the service, failed. He retired to farming, where his restless intelligence turned to the plight of the Sourthern farmer. He experimented with the diversification of crops and the production of milk with a high butterfat content. He entered politics and served in the Georgia house and senate and, in 1886, was elected to the presidency of the Georgia State Agricultural Society. In 1890 he stood for governor with support both from the Society and the Farmers' Alliance. In 1892, when the Populist party was formed and offered a candidate for the governorship, he was reelected as the regular Democratic nominee. An intensely Christian, and a humane and generous person, he suffered for the masses, black and white, as the depression deepened after 1893.

Simultaneously, Northen pursued still another career, and a significantly influential one, as a Baptist layman. For three years, he was the president of the Southern Baptist Convention and, for several years before 1890, he was the president of the Home Mission Board. During these early years, Northen turned his face resolutely against the rising Radical hysteria. He became governor in the same year that Tillman assumed that office in South Carolina. But unlike Tillman, who soon turned to support lynching for "the awful crime,"

Northen vigorously, openly, and persistently opposed it. All during his tenure as governor he stood against lynching, even though he complained in 1892 that "quite a number of the colored people of Georgia saw fit to take position and do active work against me and for the success of a party not at all committed to the interests of the colored people."[4]

As the decade of the 1890s wore on, Northen became thoroughly alarmed at the racial prospects. In the early nineties, he had been distressed by the barbarism of white people in the lynch mobs. Toward the end of the decade, he became increasingly distressed by the barbarism of blacks. In Boston, in the spring of 1899, he made a nationally celebrated speech on race relations in which he soundly berated Northerners, Southerners, and blacks each for their faults. A part of the speech related the details of the "Sam Hose affair," the rape and lynching that had so deeply disturbed Robert Charles.

Northen was by nature a hopeful, progressive person, but even he was temporarily shocked out of his perennial optimism by the rising frequency of alleged attacks and subsequent lynchings. "Since I returned from Boston," he reported privately to a friend in that city, "there have been more than five assaults, in this State, and practically, in the neighborhood, so to speak, of the fearful and horrible burning that occurred some little time ago. These things amaze me and are not to be accounted for upon any theory with which I have been familiar heretofore. It behooves us all to seriously consider a proper solution of the difficulties that surround us."[5]

Corresponding with Walter Francis Willcox, the Cornell statistician and census expert who predicted the demise of blacks in America, Northen repeated his indictment of the Eastern press for inflaming the racial situation in the South. If, indeed, blacks did die out in America, he charged, it would be the fault of demagogic Northern journalism.[6] Willcox, on his side, preferred to believe that eventually most blacks would be squeezed out of existence by industrial competition with whites and that the remainder would be absorbed by the much more numerous lower classes of whites.[7]

In the person of Northen the activist, high Conservatism bent down to touch the Radical bottom, thus forming a curious circle out of the Conservative-Radical continuum. Middling Conservatives had faith, albeit a limited faith, in intelligent and vigorous leadership. Northen at times sounded like a Radical because he was so keenly aware of the capacity of both whites and blacks to misunderstand and mishandle racial problems. A race war might possibly occur, not because it was in the nature of Negroes to regress, but because Northern whites might mislead gullible blacks to rash action, and, hence, Southern whites to make great and false issues out of their erroneous impressions of Negroes.[8]

For Georgia, the "trouble in the land" came to a violent head in Atlanta in 1906, and it was, as Northen had predicted, a culmination of "disaster, slaughter and blood." Northen went to work immediately after the riot with his usual show of courage. Initially sponsored by the "Business Men's Gospel Union," he began to travel through the rural regions of Georgia, crusading against crime and lawlessness.[9] In every community he gave an address in which he deplored the rise of the criminal Negro and denounced the prevalence of lynch law. Following every talk he asked for a show of hands in support of expressions of opposition. After one junket of forty-nine counties, he reported, with his usual optimism, "my endeavors were heartily and unanimously endorsed, except by ten adverse votes out of all the multitudes of people I had the honor to address. The ten votes included the mayor of a town, who said he endorsed Tillman's views—"using Tillman's language." In each county, Northen organized a committee of businessmen to aid the authorities in suppressing the twin evils of Negro criminality and lynching. "At every place I have spoken, I pronounced criminal assaults the most villainous iniquity known to the catalogue of crime and I urged the people to remove, as far as may be within their power, the conditions that make such outrages possible." His committees obligated themselves to supply the local sheriff with men to form a posse to pursue the rapist "and to see that the lawless element of the community is entirely excluded from such pursuit." After visiting eighty-five counties, Northen concluded that "public opinion on law & order is rapidly changing for the better." [10]

In addition to his civic effort, Northen launched a moral crusade. As a leading Baptist layman, he continued to call upon the church to do its duty. In 1909, speaking to the Georgia Baptist Convention, he charged the denomination with neglecting its mission to blacks. He indicated that 3600 new members had been added to the convention and not a single convert was a Negro. When another Baptist leader replied that the blacks did not need the ministrations of the church, Northen responded that care for the souls of black folks was "a duty put upon him by God," and that "he would rather see a million negroes in the South soundly converted than to see the conversion of two million Chinese, Japanese, or savages from some remote island."[11]

In 1911, Northen was seventy-six. After twenty years of campaigning for fairness to the Negro in Georgia, in the church, and in the South, he was nearly ready to lay his burden down. Ironically, in his fatigue, his optimistic faith weakened, and he caught a glimpse of the Radical apocalypse. On the one side, he was depressed by the seeming physical and moral degeneration of the Negro. He cited the belief of a Macon physician that "they have added to their freedom an almost universal infection from venereal diseases and tuberculosis." Towns, he found, were infested with professional black prostitutes. "The conditions of the race are pitiable to us of the old South, who can appreciate what the negro had been. His rapid degeneration, physically, mentally, and morally and his reversion to barbaric tendencies with all of the added vices of civilization, is appalling."[12]

On the other side, Northen was even more appalled by what he saw among whites. Again and again, he crashed rudely against the wall of the Radical hysteria. Even when he appeared in Boston's Tremont Temple in 1899 to defend the South on the race issue, he drew criticism from Georgia because he agreed to sit on the platform with a black spokesman.[13]

After the Atlanta riot, Northen had begun his county-by-county work under the auspices of the Business Men's Gospel Union. He had been president of that organization for some years, but discovered, as he later admitted, a stubborn opposition to his work against lynching even among these highly respected persons. "I found before I had advanced very far that some of the members of my Committee were not in sympathy with my work, but were in sympathy with the attack made on me by the Atlanta Journal." Since June 1907, he admitted, "I have been practically upon my own resources."[14]

Further, by 1911, Northen found Radicalism so strong and pervasive that he was ready to retire from the struggle. "During my recent canvass over the state, in the interest of law and order I was amazed to find scores and hundreds of men who believed the negro to be a brute, without responsibility to God, and his slaughter nothing more than the killing of a dog," he declared sadly.[15] Within a few weeks, he declined to do an article for a Baptist home mission journal, asserting that he thought it best "to be silent from this time on." He confessed he was tired. "My nature is sensitive and I have groaned under the burdens I have carried. I now feel I have done my duty and I shall retire. I do not think I ought to write any more and I shall decline to make any more speeches ... I deeply deplore the conditions, but I feel that my skirts are clear."[16] He had kept the faith, he had endured, and he had fought the good fight—virtually alone.

It was in the nature of Conservatives that they, like Northen, should hold up the image of what ought to be as if it were already present, that they should "whistle in the dark." It behooved them to say that things were getting better, and that all would be right in the end. Thus, as late as 1907, Northen was stoutly declaring in public that honorable Georgia was with him. When he capitulated in 1911, it had become disastrously clear that Georgia was not with him and had not been with him in matters racial for at least a dozen years. It was but a part of the Conservative style of leadership that he should begin by chanting: "We're winning, we're winning, we're winning," and end, abruptly, by admitting: "We lost."

THE GRIT THESIS:
A CLASS INTERPRETATION OF EXTREME RACISM

It would be fortunate if we could simply say that all of those Conservatives who failed to strike fire in the hearts of the white masses for racial justice did, indeed, simply wash their hands and go on to other things. They did go on to other things. But some of them bitterly resented that the masses had resisted their light, and they sought explanations for why that was so. The cause, some concluded, lay not in their stars, nor even in themselves, but in others. They found devils, in this instance, ironically, white devils.

Specifically, some disillusioned Conservatives found the root of evil in the ignorant white mass, the "grits," led by unscrupulous politicians and journalists. These Conservatives were among the leading intellectuals in the South, and they tended to see organized ignorance in the region as smothering the sort of free inquiry and discussion that George Washington Cable and John Spencer Bassett had advocated. Thus was generated in its modern form a persisting myth, a "grit thesis" that popular democracy in the South was at war with freedom of thought and speech, and, further, in race relations, that the lower classes were racial extremists while the upper classes were not. If the masses would simply heed the advice of the elite, the South would have happier, if not, indeed, totally happy race relations. Manifestations of racial extremism such as lynching and rioting, so the myth ran, were born of the lower classes and ran counter to the wishes of the elite. The horrid state of race relations that came to the South in the early twentieth century was fixed upon the South about the turn of the century by demagogues, a new breed of power-seeking politicians and journalists, leading the newly risen mass of "red neck," "cracker," "lint head," "wool hat," and "one gallus" boys in a conspiracy to smother liberal and conservative expressions on race under a mass of white opinion and Democratic votes. This was the beginning of a persisting class interpretation of race relations in the South. It was pervasive, but it began amid the thinking of a relatively small element in the Conservative elite, an element drawn from the more active Conservatives—those who had tried hard and failed.

Of course, there were fragments of truth in the grit thesis. In the antebellum period nonslaveholding whites often recognized that slavery and slaves were inimical to their interests, and some of them were led into bitter denunciations of both the peculiar institution and black people. When slavery ended, so too did slaveholding. There were no slave owners in Reconstruction, and hence no locally controlling force to set and hold the bounds of racism. Thrown into direct contact and competition with blacks without solidly entrenched institutions to give them an edge, whites of all classes were very likely to use racism to gain and maintain an advantage. In the turn-of-the-century South, there was indeed a rhetoric in the air suggestive of a new, more popular democracy—one that improved upon the less than totally successful effort of the Jacksonian era. Democrat Ben Tillman advertised himself as a man of the people opposed to the Bourbons, as did Tom Watson, the Populist, and both eventually became conspicuous in their advocacy of the total reduction of black people. Further, both Sledd and Bassett in their one-shot articles had clearly and accurately indicted politicians and journalists as racial extremists. When the replies came to Sledd and Bassett, they came in their most vicious mode from those very quarters, and they were devastating to sensitive egos.

Understandably, some Conservatives might see a racial universe in which aristocratic whites tried to stand for sanity against the great unwashed and failed. They tended to press that universe into unreal extremes. In their minds the South came to be populated exclusively by two kinds of people, aristocrats on the one side and poor whites on the other, the cultured and the uncultured, and the bifurcation was pushed backward through history to populate the antebellum world with the same two classes translated into slaveholders and nonslaveholders. There was a distinct tendency in the first half of the twentieth century to lose sight of the fact that the great majority of Southerners before the Civil War had been neither aristocrats nor poor whites, but were rather of the yeoman and middling class.

By 1906 the written version of the grit thesis was already under way. In 1906, for instance, John Spencer Bassett took an opportunity to review Moncure Conway's just-published autobiography in the *South Atlantic Quarterly*. Conway was a Virginian born squarely into the aristocratic tradition. As a young man in the 1850s he had become an abolitionist and insisted upon being publicly verbal about his persuasion. The result was his expulsion from his native state, not by the authorities, but by popular pressure. In his review essay Bassett took the line that patricians such as Conway might have led the South out of slavery without the necessity of a terrible civil war had they not been squelched by public opinion licensed and given power by the newly rising Jacksonian democracy. As Bassett saw it, he began the *South Atlantic Quarterly* specially to keep freedom of thought and discussion alive in the South and to avoid such disastrous aberrations as the masses had forced upon the leadership in 1860–61.[17] In Atlanta, in the aftermath of the riot in 1906, when the ruling heads of the city needed to excuse themselves from blame and get on with the task of rebuilding harmonious race relations, the grit thesis was already on the ground and ready for practical deployment. They picked it up, as we have seen, and promulgated it with great effect. The lower classes, white and black, had caused the violence, they announced, and proceeded to discipline those people by drying up Georgia, by disfranchising black men, and by compelling all the children of both races to attend the public schools, presumably there to be socialized out of such savage behavior.

Thus promoted, the grit thesis sank into the academic mind and has not yet dissolved. In 1932, the very influential South Carolina editor and scholar William Watts Ball published his book, *The State That Forgot: South Carolina's Surrender to Democracy,* a vigorous and candid indictment of popular

politics and its consequences. *Vox populi* was the voice of mediocrity and corruption, Ball insisted. Men like Wade Hampton, "men on horseback," who
had the capacity to crush the corrupt would not lower themselves to the judgment of the all-white primary. The result was that "democracy (note the small
d) is ascendent, triumphant, and democracy is epidemic and pestilential. It has
deadened South Carolina."[18] In 1940 when North Carolina-born historian
Clement Eaton looked for where the South had erred in the antebellum period,
he put his finger precisely upon the spot of Jacksonian democracy. In his monumental book *Freedom of Thought in the Old South* he held that slavery and
racism might have been manageable had popular rule not so seized the South.
Before the Jacksonian era, political leaders had not to "scramble for votes by
low appeals to the prejudices of the electorate." However, the admission of
"large numbers of illiterate or semi-literate men in Southern elections tended
to intensify intolerance and sectional animosity," and politics was reduced to
"slogans, political workers, and demagogic appeals." Freedom of thought and
expression by the elite was squelched and the peaceful end of slavery rendered
impossible.[19]

In the popular as well as in the scholarly mind of the South and of America
at large, the grit thesis of the origins of segregation, disfranchisement, black
proscription, and extreme racism generally has had a long and a strong life.
During the civil-rights movement of the 1960s when the most elegant drawls
in America were pleading for the closing of schools and defiance of Supreme
Court decisions, the myth was seriously embattled. But in more recent years
the thesis has shown a capacity for life anew. The resurgence is dangerous
because it is no more true today than it was true then. Upper-class Southern
whites are still no more specially sympathetic to black people than are lower-
class whites. There is and there has been a difference between the racism of
upper-class Southern whites and that of the lower orders. But the difference is
not one in essential assumptions and consequent attitudes. The upper class is
more sophisticated in its statement of those assumptions and attitudes, but the
significant difference between the upper and lower elements is the style in
which these are manifested in action. Lower-class prejudice toward blacks (and
toward other objects of fear—communists, labor organizers, Jews, and Catholics) is often translated into overt physical violence that compels attention
and easily gets it. It is highly newsworthy. Upper-class racial prejudice, on the
other hand, is often manifested in more subtle forms of economic, social, psychological, educational, and judicial manipulation. Yet ownership of the land,
control of money and credit, of schools and courts, and domination of the
marketplace can be just as violent, if not, indeed, more violent than guns,
whips, and bombs. Among upper-class Southerners there was an idea that they
understood the Negro best, that they knew how to talk to him, how to manage
him as no one else did. On a personal level they were often quite cordial with

individual blacks, and at the material level they were often unconscious of what they were doing and of how deeply effective their manipulations actually were. At their worst and most unaware, they thought that somebody else did it. In effect upper- and lower-class whites have actually worked in tandem on the racial front. They have functioned, not against each other, but both against the Negro, the intermittent, sporadic, open violence of one complementing the steady, pervasive, quiet violence of the other.

It is also useful to remember that upper-class Southern whites can be physically violent if they want to be, both in and outside of the racial context. Not all of the whipping of slaves on the plantations was done by overseers, pictured in the popular mind as having sprung from the poorer class. Masters and mistresses did a share of the mayhem that was done against black slaves, and in return they sometimes suffered the blows of rebellion. Emancipation did not alter that pattern. The Ku Klux Klan of the Reconstruction era was at first organized and headed by upper-class whites, and studied terror and violence were its chosen instruments. Turn-of-the-century mobs of lynchers and rioters also included "respectable" persons sometimes as participants and ordinarily as spectators. When the physical subjection of the black man was achieved, when he was down and out and seemingly promised to stay there, the necessity for violence decreased, and upper-class Southerners could very well afford to see themselves as the even-minded children of light and peace. The whole idea of a specially vicious attitude toward blacks prevalent among lower-class whites is an upper-class myth. It was primarily a technique that the elite used to divorce itself from unflattering deeds no longer productive, and thus to arm itself to take the lead in peacefully putting things in a lasting order with itself at the top.

OTHER RADICAL-CONSERVATIVE DICHOTOMIES

The very great majority of Conservatives, the moderates who were only mildly anxious about the future of black people in America, looked upon the mass of their fellow white Southerners more kindly than did these latter who had been more or less burned and scarred in the racial wars. Conservatives in general were relatively optimistic about the innate goodness of mankind. If they firmly believed in original sin, they also had faith in the ultimately redemptive capacity of Christianity, of the spark of divinity within each individual. Radical leaders, on the other hand, tended to have a low estimate of their fellow man. They seemed to think him a highly fallible creature, given to rushing extremes of emotion and depravity. The black savage, for example, would inevitably bring out the white savage in the form of the lynch mob. What saved society, the Radical leaders seemed to say, was the will of the special few in shaping the behavior of their people. Heightened interest in the importance of will was general in Western thought in the late nineteenth century. Nietzsche represented a revealing extreme in the movement: there are supermen in each society and the society is doomed to mediocrity and dissolution if the supermen do not drive the masses to proper action. Radicals were strong and unsmiling leaders, and they seemed to think that the masses must be more or less driven in the right direction. Tom Watson, for instance, railed against the indifference of "an ignorant, inappreciative people." "What discourages the reformer most," he complained to Rebecca Felton, "is the indifference of the masses of the people. On six days of the week they swallow without winking what the subsidized daily papers preach to them; on the seventh day of the week they swallow without blinking what a caste-bound priest-hood chooses to hand out from the pulpit."[20] It was no coincidence that Watson took time in a busy life to write a biography of Napoleon. Dixon, too, was deeply immersed in the current cult of will. He was impressed with the necessity of a few good men reaching out, catching up the people, and setting them right. He urged his brother Clarence to take the offer of a Boston church for "your personality is a force they would recognize and appreciate." The church, he argued, was not an end, rather was it a vehicle "for your full power." His own method of influence was to seize the people with commanding oratory, to rouse them up with a sort of furious energy and animal magnetism, and to save them in spite of themselves by the strength of his own imperious will. Like Watson, he was a great admirer of Napoleon, having delivered his prize-winning oration at Wake Forest on that imperial leader.[21]

Conservatives were not totally untouched by the interest in "will" that marked Western philosophy in the late nineteenth century. But compared with the Radicals, their interest seemed relatively cool and academic. Andrew Sledd, for instance, studying the classics in New Haven in November 1902, took the trouble to mail his father-in-law, Bishop Candler, a book on the subject he had discovered and promised to look for others. However, he warned, he was not working much in philosophy in those days.[22] Radicals stressed the will of man in effecting change. Conservatives stressed the will of God, in His own good time inevitably made evident to man. As Edgar Gardner Murphy, a leading Conservative intellectual, phrased it, the old aristocracy in the New South knew "that artificial conditions would sag and fall by their own weight, and that thereafter the real landmarks of a sound social organization would appear. . . ."[23] A Conservative would say that we must always be searching for the issue of the hour, but we could make neither the issue nor the hour.

The entire tone of the Radical campaign was vastly different from that of the Conservatives. Radical leadership offered an immediate and great crisis, requiring quick, dramatic, and valiant action. The effect was electric, and especially appealing to men who felt threatened by terrific and unseen forces.

Whites who had won honor in war might recapture that glorious feeling by joining in the Radical crusade to lynch and riot. Young white men who had had no chance at war might rise by this struggle into the peerage of the courageous. Whites who had been too young to have charged at Gettysburg, or, like Tom Dixon, were still unborn on the day the Confederacy reached high tide, could perform courageously in this new battle. Those who had been too young or too old to dash up San Juan Hill with Teddy Roosevelt still had a chance to exhibit their manliness in heroic acts. And we can truthfully use the term "heroic" because, however much appalled we might be in looking back at this phenomenon, the people who were involved in the action did see a real and great crisis in which they were defending home and hearth, their mothers, wives, sisters, and daughters. In the Radical mind, lynching and rioting were grand Southern social necessities, and appeared just as important in their time as the charge at Gettysburg had been in its time.

Compared with the fire and dash of the Radicals, Conservatives seemed pale and effete. All they offered was a still developing problem and a long and difficult solution. Conservatism was by its very nature an elite movement. There was no room in its program for vigorously physical action by the masses, for tearing down one's fears by running, shouting, and shooting. Their action would be most tedious, it would have no end, and its heroes—like William J. Northen—were liable to go unsung. Northen fought the issue as bravely and as long as anyone could, and he died with less reputation than he had when he began. Young men in the Radical era were not likely to emulate his example.

Radical leaders were also persistently combative. Indeed, once they had found the truth, they evinced a crusader's willingness to campaign again and again, and, if need be, to die in the unceasing cause. In contrast, only a few Conservatives, such as Northen, fought long and hard, and even he did not die, so to speak, with his racial boots on. Most, like Sledd at Emory and Bassett at Trinity, spoke only once in a public way and never spoke again. Radicals were marauding cavalry, while Conservatives manned the coastal artillery. Radicals dashed about with pistols and sabers and plumes in their hats. Conservatives sat in their forts and fired ponderously in a nearly fixed direction.

It was not Radical racists who caused freedom of thought and expression in race relations to cease to exist in the South, if, in fact, it did cease to exist. On the contrary, Radicals seemed to spoil for public statements of opinion by their adversaries so that they might relish the open combat that would follow. In this they were very much unlike the slaveholding class in that previous era. Indeed, in the realm of free thought and expression, the Radicals themselves had been more sinned against than sinning. Many of them were the original dissidents and had been denied a measure of freedom of expression by being barred from equal access to the established presses and pulpits by the very people who are here called Conservatives. Tillman constantly charged, and with perfect truth, that very nearly the whole of the South Carolina press denied him a fair showing. Rebecca Felton attacked the hierarchy of the Southern Baptist and Methodist churches (especially Bishop Candler) for denying the use of the pulpit to women even as speakers while some Northern churches not only opened their churches to feminine orators but admitted them into their clergy as well. The demise of freedom of thought in the New South on racial matters—insofar as freedom of thought had existed and insofar as it did die—was most certainly not the result of an upsurge of democracy, nor even of any intent on the part of the Radical leadership to still the voices of their opponents. Radicals were very sure of themselves and of their rightness, and they welcomed the combat as a way of making stronger the backbones of their not always disciplined soldiery. The silence of the Conservatives, as we have seen, was very largely self-imposed. Vicious verbal fire-fights in public were simply not in their style. The end truth was that in certain areas Radicalism so totally possessed the popular mind that Conservativism had no audience.

The popularity of Radicalism had something to do with its penchant for simplicity. At least by the time of the American Revolution, revolutionaries had learned that catch phrases were highly effective in promoting the success of a movement among the masses. "No taxation without representation," "Give me liberty or give me death," and so on were phrases that reduced complex thoughts and associations to simple symbols. Liberals and Conservatives had no such simple slogans. They preferred, on the contrary, to argue their cases in thought-laden essays and books, treatises that would engage the classes but hardly the masses. Radicals, on their side, offered the public a simple problem and a simple solution. They were able to evoke all the response they needed by raising up the image of the "Nigger Beast," and to reduce their whole program to the neat slogan "White Supremacy." Radicals had no need to enter into elaborate philosophical discussions in print. On the contrary they preferred the short argument and the personal encounter—from the pulpit, the stump, and the stage. The message was preached warmly, vividly, humanly, and, it must be said, entertainingly. Tillman, Graves, Dixon, Felton, and Vardaman were great showmen, and they made businesses of traveling and spreading the evangel of Radicalism on the lecture platforms. When they wrote their message, they wrote with a verve, a dash that Conservative language never rivaled.

Radical leaders seemed to value and very much need popular acclaim. There was a passion among them for contact—almost intimacy—with the people. Tillman obviously loved the lecture platform, the political stump, and the floor of the United States Senate because he stood upon them on every possible occasion and orated. Further he relished opposition and delighted in an aggressive challenge and his own quick and demolishing retort before an appreciative audience. Radical leaders were enraged by other leaders who seemed to hold themselves above the people, above rough and tumble combat in the public forum, and above the consequent judgment of the masses.

In this same vein, leading Radicals seemed to delight in catching pompous individuals off their social bases, exposing them, and getting the umpire of public opinion to rule them out of the game with hoots, cat-calls, and laughter. Graves did that to Candler when the Bishop presumed to attack the lynch mobs. Graves and Candler made up, but the notoriously self-appreciative bishop was brought down a notch. Josephus Daniels attempted the same thing when he repeatedly rendered Professor John Spencer Bassett's name in the most influential newspaper in the state as "bASSett." Ben Tillman took on the whole aristocratic population of Charleston, and Rebecca Felton carried on a decade-long vendetta with Senator John B. Gordon. Gordon was an ex-Confederate general who had lost an arm in the war. By the 1890s he was a Georgia Senator, a paragon of the gentlemanly ideal, a professional veteran, and a placeman for the business interests. After years of plaguing the hapless Gordon, she finally caught the often impecunious Senator profiteering in a minor railroad scandal. At the same time, Felton was steadily friendly with the ever-popular Senator Joseph Newton Brown, whose capacity for turning unbridled political opportunism into material advantage has hardly been matched since in a state not devoid of striking performances in that process. It was as if Gordon's very image of gentlemanly perfection made him a target for her special vituperation.[24]

Conservatives, on their side, were not specially anxious to put themselves before the public eye, or to win approval from the masses. When Conservatives attacked, the target was usually a thing. They seldom singled out an individual to charge by name, or libeled his character. They argued against lynching as a practice, for instance, rather than against this or that specific person who participated in the evil or defended the practice. They spoke in code. Radicals in combat tended to be personal, Conservatives abstract.

Radicals also seemed somewhat greedy. Each of them had a keen eye for earning a dollar and investing it wisely. For instance, Tillman earned large sums on the lecture circuits, turned some of his considerable acreage in South Carolina to truck farming, and invested in western lands through a Texas banker. Rebecca Felton, taking advice from Joe Brown, invested successfully in mining operations in northern Georgia. A goodly number of Radical leaders made considerable amounts of money by writing or lecturing on the race problem itself. Dixon, of course, made a fortune at it. On the other side, Conservatives actually spent money and lost money in their efforts in the racial arena. William J. Northen practically beggared himself trying to save Georgia from racial extremism.

Interestingly and revealingly, Radicals emerged as strong nationalists in comparison with Conservatives. Radical nationalism was not without its qualifications. Not all Radicals, for instance, were eager to undertake the white man's burden that American imperialism entailed. Some saw brown people abroad as no more easily manageable than black people at home. But, by and large, as long as the nation allowed the South home rule in matters of race, Radicals could be among the most ardent of Americans and strong in the ranks of those who wanted to see the nation respected as a leading world power. Ben Tillman, for example, served on the naval committee in the Senate and soon became its chairman. As such he was one of the prime movers in building up the "Great White Fleet" that Teddy Roosevelt ordered to sail around the world to signal the arrival of the United States as a global power. Conservatives, on the other hand, seemed to invest primary loyalty in their local communities. They matched the Radicals in loyalty to home states, but seemed to exceed them somewhat in loyalty to the Old South. Finally, Conservatives were sufficiently American, but they also often appeared to be international in their interests and outlook in a degree not shared by the Radicals.

Radicals also shared several other characteristics that set them at variance with Conservatives, but with diminished intensity. Radical leaders exhibited some tendency toward being practical, "progressive" agrarians, much given to improving, living, and celebrating the rural way of life. Hardly a one did not have a farm, even if he himself had to live in the city. Dixon retreated to Elmington Manor while he earned his money in the urban world and, like Tillman, experimented with truck farming for the Northern market. Conservatives might be progressive farmers, too, but many of them seemed quite capable of removing themselves totally from the land to dwell contentedly in the towns and cities.

WHY SOME LEADERS BECAME RADICALS

A most revealing thing about white leadership in race relations during this generation is that they all—Liberals, Conservatives, and Radicals—shared certain characteristics. All these people were concerned about black people, and some were no less than obsessed by the subject. Not all white leaders in the South were so deeply concerned. One can read correspondence maintained by some whites while they lived in the midst of a sea of black people and find no mention of the other race. On the other hand, one encounters some diaries and chains of correspondence of whites that report minutely on the prosaic comings and going of blacks—preachers and politicians, workers, servants, and children. It is a fact that some whites have been very sensitive to the black presence, and others, relatively speaking, have not. The concern might manifest itself concretely in pro-black activities, as with Liberals or high Conservatives, or it might surface as Ku Klux terrorism. Some, clearly, are touched, and others are not.

Foremost among the traits common to all leaders in the three groups was that they were Southern "aristocrats," which is to say that they had been themselves or were the heirs of substantial slaveholders and relatively large landholders, were considered "well-to-do," at least in their home communities, and were well-educated, if only self-educated. From the beginning and on through the Radical era, no one who had any large influence on race relations was poor white, or came from a background that might be described as such. Moreover, none were even "plain folk," yeoman farmers, or urban middle class, or born of such parental stock. Of the many people who gained sufficient prominence to be mentioned as leaders thus far, only one, Edgar Gardner Murphy, was not born to the patrician life. As we shall see, by the time he became an adult, he was himself a superb example of a Southern gentleman, and as such he would never have been so ungracious as to mention that anyone of proper manners and spirit had been born poor.

Poor boys—and poor girls too—have made it in the South, but they did not seem to make it in the age of Radicalism. Our cohort of Radical leaders all had a headstart in life by dint of being born to those certain parents. They were leaders at large at first, leaders in race relations later, and they all began as Conservatives. Exactly why some made the shift to Radicalism and others did not remains a difficult question to answer. At the mass level, I have suggested that it had much to do with psychological images of self, generated out of Victorian ideas and internalized in Southern culture in the years before the Civil War. In the agricultural depression in the late 1880s and through the 1890s, white men lost power in a new and frightening way. They found themselves disadvantaged and locked into a rapidly changing national and international economics that they were powerless to control. At the same time that the material pie was shrinking, blacks were becoming increasingly competitive with whites. Attempting to regain some measure of control through political action quickly proved abortive. The result was that Southern whites in the mass were unable to play the role of protector-as-breadwinner with the satisfaction to which they always aspired and had sometimes achieved. Embattled, white men picked up and emphasized another part of that role, the protector-as-defender of the purity of their women, in this instance against the imagined threat from the black beast rapist. Lynching and rioting, total disfranchisement, and blatant segregation formed satisfying displays of power in one area of their lives when they could no longer display power in another. Such displays were most gratifying in precisely the regions where they were most needed—in the black belts where the power of black men in Reconstruction had been most striking and their potential for displacing white men was now greatest.

One common thread that tied Radical leaders to followers and separated them from their Conservative neighbors lay in the realm not of economics or politics but of psychology. Some men and women among the Southern white elite seemed more susceptible to the Radical hysteria than others simply by dint of entering the era with psyches ready-made. Some needed devils, and Radicalism supplied the need with the full sanction of society and seeming truth. Thomas Dixon, for example, did not feel that he was being victimized materially. Indeed, he was rich and getting richer, but that was not enough. What he really needed was a victim to lay upon the altar of his mother's suffering, and the "black beast rapist" appeared as if by providence to supply that end. Ben Tillman was relatively rich, twice governor of his state, and a United States Senator when he led the disfranchising movement in South Carolina; yet he needed to see himself as the great protector of womanhood, and Radicalism allowed him to skip rather gloriously into that role. These two men were not only caught up in Radicalism, they moved to lead it as they moved to lead, if they could, whatever they were in. As leaders, they were tremendously effective in broadcasting its ideas and institutionalizing it in public life. In the whole of the white population of the South, they found millions of kindred spirits.

In that same Southern white population, there were people whose psyches sought angels, and they found these in such various places as in "woman," in churchly missions to their unspoiled Anglo-Saxon brothers and sisters at home, or the as yet untouched and un-Christian masses abroad. In the 1880s it was still possible for some whites to see blacks as innocents, as children of God. In the minds of the whites that image was never totally lost, and was most strongly held in the camp of the Conservatives. But even the most stringent Radicals were often rapt in their praise of the old-time Negro, the few long-lived Aunt Jennys and Uncle Neds whom they treasured. The slide from a Conservative to a Radical posture in race, from a need to see the Negro as angel to a need to see the Negro as devil, was deeply grooved and well lubricated. Atticus Haygood phrased it beautifully when he chided some fellow whites for having conceived of the black person as "an angel in ebony." When they found that black people could not live up to the expectations imposed upon them, he charged, the whites were sorely disappointed and reversed themselves. The Devil is, after all, a fallen angel, and, as Haygood suggested, the tendency of some of the disappointed was to race to the opposite extreme. Seeing the Negro as angelic child carried, built-in, the threat of seeing him as demonic adult. Moreover, as Radicalism carried the Negro down, it carried white women up, and it highlighted each at opposite extremes. Finally, Radical leadership was possessed of a curious tendency to externalize both good and evil, to see the source of each as emanating not from themselves, but from these visible bodies outside of themselves.

Rebecca Felton, too, had her special needs. What was she lacking that Radicalism provided? Woman's role was not that of breadwinner. As a "lady," she had only to stand upon the pedestal and offer images of piety, purity, domesticity, and submissiveness. Yet it seems that in 1873, at age thirty-eight, she decided to stop having children after four of her five children had died. Almost immediately thereafter she attempted to come down from the pedestal and to be something other than what the role prescribed—to enter active politics via her husband. No one would challenge Rebecca Felton's piety and purity, but, after 1873, her domesticity and submissiveness were seriously suspect. She later declared that for eight or ten years she hardly got outside her gate during that early period of child-bearing and rearing.[25] Any image of piety that she might have previously sustained was severely damaged by her flagrant social agnosticism, and her submissiveness soon evaporated entirely. In the 1890s she was "no lady," but she was highly effective as a critic of her society. Like her fictive fellow Georgian Scarlett O'Hara and many other Southern women in and after Reconstruction, and especially in the seemingly never-ending depression of the 1890s, she had found herself in the difficult position of attempting to scrub the floor from the heights of the pedestal. Those women, perhaps, were conscious of the unfairness of being trapped between expectations and realities, and it would not have been unreasonable for them to assume that it was upper-class white men who had created that dissonant world. These men had indeed run Southern society through the Civil War, Reconstruction, and into the great depression of the 1890s, and they had made a mess of it—cumulatively. Felton's devils were men, not all men, but especially some men such as the *"poseur"* John B. Gordon on the white side and the black beast rapist on the other.

In the 1890s it was as if Rebecca Felton wanted to explode the world on the chance that when the pieces fell and came together again, the arrangement would be better. For her, Radicalism in 1897 was a splendidly clever bomb that she rolled boldly and squarely into the grand gathering on Tybee Island of the richest and most gentlemanly of Georgia farmers, and detonated. Rebecca Felton blew them away. She hoisted them by their own Victorian petards. Even if they did succeed as breadwinners, even if they lynched the thousand black men a week that she demanded, they could never save every single white woman in the South from violation by a black rapist. Given the retrogressing Negro male, white men could never be perfect in their role as white women could be in theirs, and, hence, they could never deliver as promised and never give satisfaction to the Rebecca Feltons of the South who called them repeatedly and firmly to their duty.

Radical leaders, like Radicals at large, seemed to be people specially affected by a sense of powerlessness, people who strove valiantly to develop power and exercise it to counter that feeling of vulnerability. Of course, managing black people in an arrogant and arbitrary manner was a satisfying exercise for such people, but there was another nemesis to be dealt with, and a very real one—the North. The North had crushed the South by raw force, and it was painfully evident to the postwar generations that the North was the victor. The North clearly had power over the South, and it could do with the South as it chose. In the 1880s and 1890s, it had chosen to do nothing in the South racially, nor to intervene politically, as long as the South in effect submitted to colonial status. The South obtained its first significant chance of redeeming itself in the nation by participating wholeheartedly in the Spanish-American War. Dixon, quite appropriately, made national reunion one of the two interwoven themes in *The Leopard's Spots,* (a pattern he repeated in *The Clansman* and carried into *The Birth of a Nation*), and he marked the beginning of success in that movement with the "splendid little war," as Theodore Roosevelt's Secretary of State, John Hay, called the Spanish conflict. At the same time, Ben Tillman was promoting the Great White Fleet, even if it meant doling out giant contracts to the much hated steel trust. By the end of World War I, the allegiance of the South to the nation had passed from the suspect to the assured. Southerners paid dearly in material terms for that confidence, but it seems that they paid willingly, and even eagerly.

The complexity of why some Southern leaders became Radicals while others did not is also related to the Janus-faced image I have raised before. It is in the nature of Western culture to see things in dichotomies—hot-cold, him-her, up-down, heaven-hell, angel-devil, love-hate, and so on *ad infinitum,* dividing every facet of life in two and stretching it out to either extreme. In that Southern world of human affairs there were many dichotomies and two faces for each. There was a face that looked politics, others, economics, religion, or race, and so on through a vast array of categories and sub-categories. Behind every face there was its opposite, and the opposites were joined in continuums. Every white Southerner, for instance, contained within himself a potential to see the black person either as child or as beast, joined together at the point at which the child becomes the beast. Each individual at a given time would come down on the scale at a given point, but he would show only a single face, or, briefly with the edge, none. In the same fashion, everyone carried within himself as a part of his culture a potential to go relatively Aristotelian or Platonic. If one got outside the South and outside Western Civilization, he might move out beyond the continuum and break it, but given the time and place the continuum contained the limits of possibility. In the South, then, every Conservative carried within himself the seed of Radicalism. Within the same universe in the white mind, the black child angel could shift across the scale to become the adult devil always there. With some Conservatives the shift occurred and the Radical potential took life in or after 1889. It grew and came to rule the person in racial matters. In others the shift never happened. In these, the Radical potential was arrested and held in check by the other, the Conservative self.

Radical leaders were people who came to stand high on the extreme end of certain scales, and who came together to agree upon a common perception of the nature of black people, and, hence, of the proper course of race relations. In the white leadership cadre of a black belt area there were people whose bias was already high as philosophical realists, who were willful, crisis-oriented, combative, simplex, prone to seek popularity, and who were always moved by basic feelings of insecurity that led them into hard drives for power, drives for a capability to rearrange and order the disjunctive world in which they lived. There were also among these people some who needed devils. In the late 1880s and afterward, as unrest—economic, political, and cultural—swept through the land, their previous attitude toward black people came unfixed and slipped across the mid-point to fill that need for devils. The child became the beast, and ideas about race began to fuse with ideas about other things—the nature of man, economics, politics—to form a world-view. As unreast continued and, indeed, raged in the 1890s, these people came to the fore and they fixed, from time to time, upon the retrograding black as the great evil. It was not, ultimately, that Radicalism was created in and after 1889, it was rather that a potential always latent had come into power in the black belts of the South.

Those among the elite who did not resonate to ideas of the retrogressing black, people such as John Spencer Bassett, Andrew W. Sledd, William J. Northen, or Warren A. Candler, lost out as leaders of the masses in racial matters. Racial Conservatives simply had no constituency if they happened to live in Radical areas, even though they might well retain great and even ruling influence in other realms. Leaders whose personal proclivities were idealistic, who saw a complex world and did not feel the need of adulation from the masses, who felt relatively well satisfied with themselves and did not need devils, and who held to the more tenable idea of Negro as child were simply by-passed in matters of race.

Thus many things combined at a particular time to give a tremendous thrust to Radicalism. Had there been no great world depression in and after 1893, had the material pie not been drastically reduced, people might have felt fulfilled in their images of themselves, and there would have been no Radical revolt. Had there been no industrial revolution, there would certainly have still been exploitation and there would have been racism, but it might never have achieved the vicious fillip that it attained in the turn-of-the-century years. Even more centrally, had there been no Victorian era in the South with exaggerated roles assigned by gender, had white men not seen themselves bound by God to the comfortable material support of their families and the domestication of their women, there probably would have been no Radical rage.

AN UNREAL WORLD:
RACE AND SEX IN THE MODERN SOUTH

But, of course, the industrial revolution did happen, and out of it spun Victorianism and, in the 1890s, a horrendous, seemingly unending depression. The special conjunction of two vastly powerful currents in the society, the one unreal (exaggerated sex roles) and the other all too real (the loss of material security as the economic depression lengthened), bore this strange, this peculiar and bitter fruit. Given the limits of its understanding of itself, given the acceptance of certain ideas of individualism, freedom, and laissez-faire economics, there was no way in which the society in the South could cope with the real problem. Unable ultimately to deal with the real world, Radical leadership opted to create in the life of the mind an unreal one. It was almost inevitable that they would use black people in this effort as they had used them before. Most signally, of course, they picked up on the idea of the retrogressing black. That idea finally expired of its own weighty untruth and fell by the wayside. But in the psychological realm the damage had already been done. Radicals had worked effectively to unplug the South from the real world at large by generating an unreal racial world. While they failed, finally, in bringing their racial image to earth in a new order, they nevertheless promoted a loss by Southerners of their grasp on reality. It is a great and terrible paradox that the Radicals, so realistic in every other way, should misperceive black people so grossly and thereby contribute to the generation of a twentieth-century set of race relations that was fundamentally unreal.

It was almost as if the Radical era were a rehearsal for the unreality that marked the South in the twentieth century. That rehearsal had as many aspects as did the play itself. But probably nowhere was the unreality so widely divorced from the reality as in the specific image of the black beast rapist. That mythical being, so totally the creature of the white male imagination, has labored for white people in and after the Radical era probably as no real black person has ever done. If we can understand how he came to be and how he functioned, we will understand much of the history of the Southern white male mind, and, indeed, of Southern culture. It is a case of unreality, *in extremis.*

By the time of the Radical era, Southern white men had painted themselves into a sexual corner. In the antebellum era they had pedestalized white women in their minds. In so doing they had violated the equal humanity of women and removed them, in some degree, from possibilities of real intimacy with themselves. The Victorian complex that they so eagerly embraced spun out the curious idea that men were more sexual than women and, more importantly, that women (in the South, white women only) did not enjoy sex, that sexual relations were painful to them and allowed only out of a sense of love and duty. In the circumstances, men who pressed their attentions upon their wives violated them. They were beasts who, brutish and totally physical, satiated themselves at the expense of the very persons whom they has sworn before God to protect.[26] It seems unlikely that white men, in fact, much denied themselves sexual pleasure with their wives or with white women in general. However, if they did deny themselves, they felt tension; but if they did not, Victorian mores led them to feel tension of another sort, namely, guilt. Whatever they did, they were caught in a trap of their own making.

In the antebellum period, if men of the white elite denied themselves sex with their wives, they did have other resorts, and the signs are abundant that there were many who used those resorts. Indeed, in the Old South, if a man had money and was unfeeling enough, he could buy a woman for life and use her pretty much as he chose with no fear of the law and little fear of his neighbors. If he had enough money he could buy a very desirable woman. In slavery, slave owners had full access to slave women, at least mentally, whatever they might or might not have done with them in the body. The myth arose that Negro women were especially lusty creatures, perhaps precisely because white men needed to think of them in that way. With emancipation, however, white men's access to black women virtually ended. Miscegenation, contemporary observers agreed, practically stopped. Mulatto women and black went with their husbands, and dark Victoria was no longer easily available in either body or imagination to upper-class white men. Furthermore, black men, now free, denied white men access to the heretofore ultimately satisfying alternative, black women, while white men continued to see black women as superbly sexual creatures, uninhibited, unlimited in venereal appetites and potential satisfactions. Black men were now mates to the sexual earth mothers. In Radical eyes in the 1890s, black men came to be not at all the Sambo of antebellum myth, but rather the insatiable satyr, specially built both physically and mentally for the libidinal women they served. The satyr sought all women, and at his most outrageous he sought especially the white woman heretofore denied him. The white man in the black belts found himself alone and often lonely—his women angelic above him, the black male (fully supported by black women) below—and he strapped with the largely unrewarding task of holding the two apart. Of course, it was a task where success went unnoticed and unrewarded, and his inevitable failure from time to time was conspicuously marked and condemned. One careless moment and another black man crashed through the white lines, plunged into the interior and devoured another fair maiden. The black beast rapist was the only man on earth who had sex with Southern white women without inhibition, to the exhaustion of desire, and, *mirable dictu,* without guilt. Black men had achieved what white men, in the Victorian infatuation, had lost—"no-fault" sex. Simple death, clearly, was too good for them.

Black leaders who explained the alleged epidemic of rape in the South as the work of white men disguising themselves as Negroes with burnt cork in order to achieve sexual satisfaction and yet escape punishment were not, after all, very far wrong. There was a beast abroad in the land, but he lived in white minds rather than black. White men were projecting upon black men extravagant sexual behavior because they were, at varying levels, denying ordinary sexual behavior to themselves. Southern white men, and most especially Southern white men of the upper class, used Southern black men much as the fictional Dorian Gray used the canvas in his attic to draw the portrait of his ugliness even as he showed himself beautiful to the world. To paint the black as ugly and then to destroy him was to destroy the evil within themselves. To punish the black was to punish themselves, without hurting themselves, a rare and pleasurable power. Excessive punishment of the sin constituted high penance and ensured re-entry into the communion. If black men were, in essence, having sex with angels while white men abstained, then the punishment of black men must be as awful as the white man's guilt in contemplating himself in the same act, compounded by his frustration in abstaining. Never before had white men in the South elevated white women so high on the pedestal as did this first generation of boys born to Victorian mothers, and never before had they punished any men, white or black, as horrendously as they punished some black men in those years. The lynching of Henry Smith in Texas in 1893 and of Sam Hose in Georgia in 1899 were and have remained unmatched in horror in the history of such events in the region. Something was indeed new on the Southern landscape.

Thus black men were lynched for having achieved, seemingly, a sexual liberation that white men wanted but could not achieve without great feelings of guilt. In their frustration white men projected their own worst thoughts upon black men, imagined them acted out in some specific incident, and symbolically killed those thoughts by lynching a hapless black man. Almost any vulnerable black man would do. In effect, the black man lynched was the worst part of themselves. A function of lynching, if not indeed the primary function, was to offer up a sacrificial lamb for the sins of white men. Only about a third of the lynchings had anything at all to do with rape. Yet for more than a decade Southern white men insisted that lynching was especially for that crime, and they became blindly furious when Sledd and others charged otherwise. White men needed to count every lynching against the awful crime because they needed every such performance they could get to quiet the boiling seas of emotion within themselves. There could hardly be enough of lynching; and, to get the most out of each, lynchings should be reported widely and in the closest detail as to what the black man did to the victim and what the lynchers did to him. The lynchers, active and passive, needed constant assurance that the evil had been destroyed, precisely because it had not. Castration was an ordinary part of the lynching ritual as applied to alleged rapists, and genital dismemberment was not unheard of. That symbol worked to declare that the evil was abolished permanently from the earth. William Faulkner, with his usual unflagging instinct for truth about the South, caught the image perfectly in the lynching of Joe Christmas in his novel *Light in August* (1932). Percy Grimm, at twenty-five a bachelor, a totally sterile young man, and a captain in the Mississippi national guard who had missed his true calling by having been born too late to have fought in World War I, chases Joe down relentlessly and shoots him. Before Joe dies, Grimm grabs a butcher knife and cuts away Joe's genitals. Flinging away the bloody knife, he declares, "Now you'll let white women alone, even in hell."[27] Percy Grimm himself certainly let white women alone in the body all of his life, but God only knows at what cost or what he did with women in his mind.

It is small wonder that observers noted a generalized restlessness before the alleged crime that brought on the lynching; noted, too, the purposeful, judicial, and most of all, the weirdly silent proceeding of the mob; counted the hundreds and even thousands of onlookers, often including women and children and sometimes brought in by special trains; saw the feeling of satisfaction, of peace, that followed the event, and, finally, the fact that if a community had done it once they were likely to do it again.

In the myth of the black beast rapist, the Radicals joined race and sex together in a way that would be momentous for twentieth-century America. Within the South, particularly the black belt states of the deep South, the power of the whites over blacks locally was tremendous. With the further defection of the North in things racial, it grew even stronger. The people who held that power imputed, implicitly and explicitly, great sexual potency to black people, and especially to black men. Radicals came to be obsessed by the possibility of sexual relations between black men and white women. Radicalism died, but the institutions it bred, formal and informal (including the etiquette of race relations), spoke out the message with exceeding clarity—that black men were to be kept away from white women, precisely because black men were super sexual creatures. As time passed, many black men would hear that message from the dominant whites. Some of these came to divest it of bad connotations, to believe it, to weave it into a counter-cultural system of values, and to act upon it.

Radicalism was a rehearsal for unreality in the twentieth-century South. The black beast rapist did not exist and neither did retrogression. Southern whites had had a rehearsal for unreality even before the Civil War in the creation of the Negro as the stereotypical child. In the 1890s they again set out upon a Yellow Brick Road of race, seeking a Wizard of Oz who would supply their missing parts—courage, heart, a manageable universe—and make them whole. They were spurred forward in that quest by having almost totally lost control of their material and mental worlds. It was perfectly symbolic of their fall that most Presidents before the Civil War had been slaveholding Southern planters, while no dyed-in-the cotton Southerner was President for a century afterward. The loss of economic, political, and psychological power was simply the price of having gambled and lost, fair enough in the world of *Realpolitik*. But it was, nevertheless, a hard fate to go so suddenly from high to low. In the quick snap, Southerners tended to lose their grasp on this world, racial and otherwise, but, almost measure for measure, as they lost this world they tended to improve their grasp upon the next.

THE BIBLE BELT

There was a rhythm in the life of Radicalism that fits well with the psychological principle of cognitive dissonance. That principle holds that dissonance arises when people perceive a disjunction between their ideas of what ought to be and what is. Relief from dissonance is sought in new behavior. In the South, from 1887 into 1915, Southern white men passed through three cycles in their attempts to fulfill their assigned roles as the protectors of white women, both materially as providers and physically. In each cycle they attempted at first to deal with the real economic problems that had severely reduced their capacity to provide for the material support of their women and other dependents. In the first cycle they attempted to achieve economic reform by economic action. In the last two cycles they resorted to political action to achieve economic reform. However, each of these efforts failed, and they then sought and achieved some measure of relief by raising the idea of the black beast as a physical threat to their women and acting to deal with him. Ultimately, economic, racial, and political actions all failed to restore to Southern men a satisfactory sense of self. By the end of 1915 they had ceased their struggles to build new structures in these areas and turned their minds in a significant degree away from the things of this world in favor of contemplating the next.

The theory of cognitive dissonance also holds that when people have made a choice between two ideas, they tend to love the choice they made and hate the choice they rejected. This concept helps to explain the astonishing extremes in love and hate that appeared in race and politics in the South in those years, extremes that have deeply marked Southern culture in the twentieth century.

In the late 1880s the South was moving into an agricultural recession. Something was distressingly wrong in the economic realm, and Southerners who were most affected generated farmers' alliances, initially economic institutions, as an attempt to deal directly with the problem. By 1889 that movement was proving to be not very satisfying, and farmers were thinking in terms of political action to achieve economic ends. Still there was not much one could do politically in 1889. In fact, on March 4, 1889, the Republicans under Benjamin Harrison had taken office, having swept the nation the previous November on a platform more menacing than helpful to farming interests in the South. There would not be another election until 1890, and even that would not include a presidential choice. The result was that many people opted for race as the area of activity. If the road lay not with economic or political action, perhaps it lay with race. Cognitive dissonance would say that they would love the choice they made, that they would embrace and promote their choice with extraordinary, indeed, with unreasonable fervor. Racial extremism matched in magnitude the extreme dissonance of their era. Race was hot precisely because Southern society was hot.

Rather clearly, Radicalism experienced three periods of heightened activity, and each followed a period of vigorous economic or political activity— the political activity in each case having a large economic input. Radicalism ran very hot from 1889 to about 1893, with a sudden swell of lynchings and a first wave of disfranchising and segregating legislation. Between 1893 and 1897 it cooled and was less active, as was evident in declining lynchings and the relative absence of new segregating and disfranchising legislation. It was as if racial extremism had not been very satisfying after all, and the political alternative resurged in attractiveness, especially among Democrats of a liberal persuasion but particularly with the appearance of a distinct body of dissidents in the form of the People's or Populist party in 1892. Populist rhetoric, contrary to what Populists actually thought and felt, was, indeed, famously and revealingly non-racist. Populists at first, like both Democrats and Republicans, would certainly have welcomed black votes for themselves and consequently did not often advertise their racism. The record of events suggests that if Populist leaders felt that they could win their rebellion with Negroes voting, they would smile; if they could win with no Negroes voting, they would smile still, and more broadly. Politics reached one of its hottest times in the whole of United States history between 1892 and 1897. This is, in fact, the only time since the 1850s when it has seemed likely that a third party might gain viability and replace one of the two dominant parties. However, that political thrust cooled rapidly after 1896. In the sequel, racism surged up again and ran with unprecedented fury from 1897 through 1906. This most torrid phase of Radicalism was marked by a racist rhetoric never equaled in virulence in America and a new high state of violence, rioting, distinguished from lynching by the fact that any black, not a specific black, sufficed as a target. It was also marked by the passage of a great wave of disfranchising and segregating legislation—again probably the greatest such yet seen in America. It was as if racial extremism offered the kind of satisfaction that extreme politics had proved incapable of affording.

By the early twentieth century a pattern had been established in which Radical leaders responded to the disorder in their lives in either one of two primary ways—either politically by attacking the great corporations as the authors of evil, or racially by attacking the retrogressing black. It is highly significant that Ben Tillman in those years concocted only two speeches for the lecture circuits upon which he so frequently and profitably appeared. One of his talks was "The Race Question," and the other was "Railroads, Trusts, Monopolies." Each of these, as one would guess, was extravagant and engaging. Tillman always allowed the audience to choose on the spot, and, as he later reported, his race lecture was by far the most popular. In Georgia, in 1906, Hoke Smith, too, soon found that on the hustings his race speech outran his "monopolies" speech in popularity. Even so, race faded after 1906. Preluded by the progressive politics of Republicans Roosevelt and Taft, from about 1911 through Wilson's election in November 1912, politics-as-economic-reform took stage center again. Between 1913 and 1915 Radical racism had a mild resurgence, especially in the nation's capital as Radical leaders moved to segregate further the federal service and in legislation in the South designed to effect a more perfect segregation in newly rising industrial and urban situations. Thereafter, with the exception of a brief flare-up in and after World War I, neither race nor politics ran very hot for more than a generation. Indeed, it seems that a little success and a great deal of frustration on both those fronts promoted the choice by the South, after 1915, of still a third way, religion, at the expense of both race and reform politics. (See pp. 314–15.)

The South has been particularly, and accurately, marked in twentieth-century America as the distinctly religious region—"the Bible belt." By this, people seem to mean that the South is given to Biblical fundamentalism, a sustained religious enthusiasm, and a high level of active church membership. Tom Dixon, in *The Leopard's Spots,* probably caught the essence of the fundamentalist South in a description of the ministry of the Reverend Durham. The Reverend Durham, he said, had a profound mastery of the Bible and could "speak pages of discourse in its very language." It was "a divine alphabet," from which all things could be spelled. The minister and the Bible were one.

As a preacher he spoke with authority. He was narrow and dogmatic in his interpretations of the Bible, but his very narrowness and dogmatism were of his flesh and blood, elements of his power. He never stooped to controversy. He simply announced the Truth. The wise received it. The fools rejected it and were damned. That was all there was to it.[28]

The idea of the South as "the Bible belt" was new. No one talked about the South as a Bible belt before the Civil War. Indeed, when one thought of red-hot religious fervor in those years, he thought of the "Burnt-over district" in upstate New York, an area that had been so repeatedly swept by the fires of Christian evangelism as to suggest a burned-over forest. During the Civil War both the North and the South went through very strong religious revivals; but the South, after the war, generally fell away from religion. By the turn of the century, however, an all-white Protestantism was clearly on the rise, and it tended toward fundamentalism, evangelism, and other-worldliness. Increasingly, the Southern church absolved itself from responsibility for judging race, economics, politics, or the social order.

Tom Dixon, again with his usual sensitivity to what was going on in popular feelings, caught this withdrawal well in a passage in *The Leopard's Spots*. In the novel he paints his alter ego, the Reverend Durham, as preaching in his church the purely spiritual message that transcends events in the outside world:

The Preacher never touched on politics, no matter what the event under whose world import his people gathered. War was declared, and fought for four terrible years. Lee surrendered, the slaves were freed, and society was torn from the foundations of centuries, but you would never have known it from the lips of the Rev. John Durham in his pulpit. These things were but passing events. He spoke of God, of Truth, of Righteousness, of Judgment, the same yesterday, to-day and forever.[29]

In this passage, of course, Dixon depicted his father's ministry and not his own. He operated in precisely the opposite fashion and, accordingly, soon found for himself no place in the Southern church. His father was a fundamentalist, and Tom knew the style well. As a child he had probably gone with the senior Dixon to service country churches around Shelby. His father was known as "Preaching Dixon," and tradition has it that whenever he came to lead a meeting he always swung down from his horse singing a hymn. As he marched into the church still singing the congregation would take up the song with him, and from there on it was pure gospel.[30] One of the hymns that the Reverend Dixon might have sung was a Southern favorite that captured the mood perfectly. "This world is not my home," it declares, "I have no mansions here...." After the turn of the century, the other-worldliness always latent in Christianity came powerfully to the fore in Southern Protestantism.

The transformation of the South into the Bible belt was not unlike the Roman reaction to the fifth-century invasions in which the city of Rome itself was sacked repeatedly, almost at will, by the barbarians. The final response of

PERIOD	IDEA	VS	IDEA	NEW BEHAVIOR	DISSONANCE, RELIEF
1887–89	True men protect women		Not doing so materially against economic monopolies	Farmer's Alliance	D
1889–93	"		Trying so physically against the black beast	Lynching, segregation, disfranchisement, proscription	R
1893–97	"		Not doing so materially against economic monopolies	Political action for economic reform, as in the People's party	D
1897–1907	"		Trying so physically against the black beast	Lynching, rioting, segregation, disfranchisement, proscription	R
1907–13	"		Not doing so materially against economic monopolies	Progressive politics with Republicans TR and Taft, Democrat Wilson	D
1913–15	"		Trying so physically against the black beast, but finally, 1915, with no great success	Segregation in urban and industrial situations, and in the federal service	R

1915–		Consonance
Nothing to protect against in regard to women	Acceptance of economic colonization	
	No farmer's alliance	
Nothing to protect in regard to women	No reform economics	
	No unions of workers	
Piety and purity protected, in part, by ministers and evangelists	Paternalistic economics	
	Acceptance of political colonization	
Rise of otherworldly, spiritual emphasis in Southern thinking	Decline in meaningful political activity	
	No reform politics	
	Dixie demagogues	
	Decline of race as an issue	
	Decline in lynching	
	Decline in riots	
	Decline in new segregation legislation	
	Decline in new disfranchising measures	
	Decline in new proscription practices	
	Rise of the Bible Belt	

the Romans was encapsulated in St. Augustine's book *The City of God* (525 A.D.). The real city, he said, was not this earthly vanity called Rome. The real city was in heaven. The lesson is that when the earthly city becomes untenable, when we can no longer live in this world as we were wont to do, we retreat to the heavenly City of God. So, too, in the South.

The modern retreat of the South into the City of God might have had its beginnings on the bloody battlefields of the Civil War. That war brought Southerners from high to low very suddenly, so suddenly, perhaps, that they are as yet unable fully to absorb the fact of their defeat. Faulkner was probably right again when in his novels he went back to hang up Southern white youth upon that afternoon of July 3, 1863, just before Pickett's charge at Gettysburg. If one had to choose a specific point in time and a specific place when Southern white culture altered course, that was close enough.

The retreat of the South from reality might have been furthered by the seizure by the Yankee barbarians and the black defectors of the bodies of the Southern states during Reconstruction. The hard material realities of Reconstruction and the depression of the 1890s might have reinforced and exaggerated that alienation by unfreezing religion, as it unfroze race and politics, to produce a shift toward other-worldliness and Biblical fundamentalism.

When Southern life recrystallized again after 1915, religion was at stage center. By that time the experience both in politics and race had been, at once, satisfying enough and frustrating enough to open the way for the primacy of religion. Just as the South had previously sought relief from dissonance in extremes of politics and racism, it now sought—and found—relief in an extreme of religion. Southern white ideas and behavior, true to the model, changed profoundly. Both politics and race remained severe problems in the South, but Southerners developed and maintained in their retreat a capacity to see neither. Outsiders were more perceptive of the obvious. Even the Knickerbocker and thoroughly Northeastern President Franklin D. Roosevelt recognized in the 1930s that the South was the nation's number one economic problem. Ironically, Southern patricians were the least able among America's leaders to recognize that fact. And, of course, in race, the Negro problem in the Radical vision was totally lost. Women were protected, or, more pointedly, there was nothing really to protect against. By the end of the 1920s there was *no* Negro problem at all in the South if outsiders would simply leave Southern blacks alone. The retreat, the withdrawal of Southern culture into otherworldliness was virtually measured—inch, foot, and mile—in the so-called "Monkey Trial" in Dayton, Tennessee, in 1924. In that trial, the court upheld a state statute banning the teaching of Darwin's theory of the origin of species in the public schools. The South held firmly to its cloud, and it would not come down to earth. Neither the whole subjects of science, economics, politics, or race would hold even half the charm for them as a whole people that several dozen evangelists would hold. Further, at least in regard to these men, piety and purity had become a male province, while domesticity and submissiveness was certainly left totally to women. Southerners had, in a sense, shuffled off this mortal coil, and they lived, really lived (and by their own lights thrived) in that other world. Southern strength in national councils in the twentieth century might, in part, be precisely a function of that talent. The Southerner is, in a sense, the other American distinguished from the real, body-built, getting-ahead-in-this-world American. The Southerner is the idealistic American as personified, for instance, in Billy Graham, Sam Ervin, and Jimmy Carter, men who perceive Truth as transcendental. When our armies are defeated on the frontiers, when the crops are burning in the fields, when the barbarians sit steaming, bloody, and furious at the gate, it is Southerners who sometimes seem to offer the ultimate haven, the world of the spirit where no hard and violent hand can touch.

THE CENTRAL THEME OF SOUTHERN HISTORY

The first lastingly famous scholar of Southern history was the Georgian Ulrich B. Phillips (1877–1934). In 1928 Phillips passed over political and economic explanations to declare that the "central theme of Southern history" was the resolve of white men that the South "shall be and remain a white man's country."[31] Phillips had come to maturity in that earlier Georgia, the Georgia of Rebecca Felton, John Temple Graves, Tom Watson, Thomas Hardwick, Hoke Smith, and the rage of lynching. He was himself a racial Conservative, but he knew the Radical mind and presence, and race to him was indeed wide, deep, and long-lived. But what he published in 1928 would have been much more comprehensible in his natal Georgia in 1906. Indeed, by 1928 the idea might not have been all that real in daily life and speech, and even in the facts of recent history it might not have been all that true. What is basically misleading about the idea as an interpretative device is that after Reconstruction white men *were* supreme by any general definition of the word, and the South *was* a white man's country. White supremacy was never thereafter successfully challenged for a long time or over a broad geography. While white men might have been resolved to maintain white supremacy, they were not often required to act upon that resolve. Thus the behavior of white men in the South after 1877 is not totally explicable in terms of race and the corollary of white male domination.

It might be well to amplify the Phillips thesis as an interpretation of Southern history for the half-century after Reconstruction by saying that white supremacy was central in that it touched everything, not in that it everywhere and always ruled everything. In some places for some times, for instance in eastern North Carolina from 1898 through 1900 and in Atlanta through the riot in 1906, race did rule everything, and the prime issue was indeed the resolve that this particular area would be a white man's country. It was these "runs" of Radicalism that gave form to the centrality of race in Southern life in the twentieth century. But in these runs, the question was not, ultimately, white domination versus black domination. The hard reality was that whites in America outnumbered blacks ten to one, in the South roughly two to one, and even in the blackest of belts the whites possessed the vast majority of material wealth and controlled practically all of the ruling local institutions—including the police, the courts, and the military. With hindsight, we feel safe in saying that, finally, white America at large stood behind the white South for white supremacy, and there was little chance that white supremacy would fail.

The real historical question was not whether whites would rule. It was how much it would cost them to maintain their ascendancy. And, further, what would be the nature of the costs? How much would they have to change their schools, their police, judicial and penal systems, their ideas about Christianity, their ideas about men and women, class, and so on infinitely in order to keep black people in their place? In brief, how much would white society have to change itself and white Southerners change themselves in order to keep black people down? When they were through with the Radical era, there was hardly a facet of life in the South in which the whites had failed to respond to the black presence, and the nature of that response gave Southern white culture in the twentieth century its basic shape.

I have argued here that the Negro was a scapegoat in the turn-of-the century South, that whites were having difficulty coping with a burgeoning industrial-commercial-political order as it impacted upon a social-psychological-sexual order earlier generated, and that in that crisis they used the Negro in constructing an illusion that they were indeed managing their lives in important ways. My argument assumes that race is, in fact, not a real problem, that any person of any race is not barred by any physical difference from belonging to any culture. Race, in brief, is a problem of the mind and not of the body. It also assumes that, overall, white people have the power to make scapegoats of black people, to manage them sufficiently to create the illusion that they want to see. Actually I have selected out only certain areas of scapegoating to explore. The uses to which white power put black people in this fashion were virtually limitless. Once the game started, the Negro could be made the scapegoat for any number of ills, either of the body or of the mind. Indeed, from the white point of view, one might say that the Negro-as-scapegoat has been one of the nation's most valuable renewable resources. He can be used again and again and yet again, and never wear out. Lynching soon developed sophisticated variations. One could lynch just as effectively by genteel means as crudely by rope and faggot. Negroes could be lynched by account books. And they could be lynched by written history. They could be blamed retroactively for the Civil War and for the alleged excesses of Reconstruction. The reduction of the Negro opened the way for an honorable reunion of North and South. The Negro had been wrong simply by being there, and North and South had both been right.

I have advanced a scapegoat thesis in which the controllers acted unconsciously. There is another scapegoat thesis that argues that in the turn-of-the-century South special interests of various sorts consciously used the racism always latent in the white masses for their selfish ends. A variant of the latter depicts the racial extremist as the reformer who has been counted out by the political Conservatives and, in his frustration, gone understandably mad.

There are elements of truth in each of these latter scenarios, but as generalizations with wide applicability, they do not hold. Conservative leaders could not simply wave the flag of white supremacy and drive reform issues away. The scapegoat thesis does not work at all well when applied to big business. The masses were not duped into attacking the Negro instead of the monopolies by the arrogant powers of big business working through its lawyers and political placemen. Big business was arrogant, and it did have legal and political minions that sought avidly to do its bidding. Further, they were certainly not above using race, the Confederate cause, or practically anything else to achieve their goals. But their efforts in this relation were not famously successful. Indeed, business in matters of race has been a paper tiger, seemingly all powerful and voracious, but actually following the dictates of its society, respectfully, often even meekly, and at a foot-dragging distance. Only when the *status quo* deteriorates beyond recall, and business sees the promise of peace, good order, and predictability on the other side, does it flex its rather strong muscles and move with seeming strength and self-assurance to cross over. The response in understandable. Business exists to make money. Segregated facilities were more expensive than unsegregated facilities so that businesses with unsegregated facilities resisted oncoming segregation. But disorder and violence destroy business altogether. If the violence was to be ended by segregation, business readily adapted and passed the cost along. Once segregation was in place, and the machine running smoothly again, business wanted the machine to continue to run without disruption. It supported segregation, and the racial establishment generally, until violence and disorder threatened again. In the 1960s when it saw order and predictability on the side of desegregation, it moved for that end. Business has never been a self-conscious prime mover in race relations in America; rather it has always responded to the obvious necessities of its own interests.

Largely arising out of the "grit thesis," there is also the idea that racism was a scapegoat used by unscrupulous politicians to secure offices and power for themselves. These people allegedly went about raising racial fevers where temperatures had been normal before. If demagoguery suggests a measure of deception, of leaders saying things they do not believe, this allegation is totally unfounded as applied to the Radical era. The Radical leaders that we have talked about thus far were not at all dishonest. Indeed, it is difficult to imagine anyone being more candid, almost brutally so, than Ben Tillman, Rebecca Felton, James K. Vardaman, and their cohorts. Radicals were, in fact, probably more candid than were the Conservatives, such as William J. Northen, who raised images of what ought to be as if they already existed. Radical leadership really believed that the Negro was retrogressing. They did not dissemble, and they moved, by their own lights, in a highly responsible way to meet the challenge. There have been a vast number of demagogues in the South, and race has been the favored vehicle upon which they rode, but they came later and basically only after Radicalism as a mentality ceased to be.

There is an elaboration of the scapegoat thesis that asserts that the racial demagogue in the early twentieth century was the honest reformer gone mad. He had fought the good fight and lost unfairly, by violence and fraud at the polls perpetrated by Conservative politicians. In his frustration the reformer lost his mind and turned aggressively upon the Negro. There is in the broad history of the Radical era a shifting between race and politics that gives verisimilitude to this theory. When politics was not working, race was. But yet, in the main, it seems that a given leader, such as Marion Butler, either was Radicalized or not early on, and circumstances sooner or later caused his Radicalism to manifest itself. Consequently, it was not that the given leader was racially Conservative, encountered frustration, and then became a Radical. It was rather that he was consistently Radical but found it politically expedient to closet his Radicalism for a time.

But once I have said that, yes, the whites unconsciously made the Negro a scapegoat for the unmanageable evils of the industrial Leviathan and for certain personal and social psychological difficulties, I must also say more. I must say that in certain places during certain times, white people in the main—high, low, and in between—saw the Negro in retrogression as the clearest and most present danger there was. In that sense, at the living level, the Negro was not a scapegoat at all. Regardless of the absolute reality that might seem clear to us in retrospect, the reality that they perceived was the one by which they moved and made history. There were no consciously bad motives in the rise of Radicalism, no dishonesty in seeing one thing and saying another. Radicals were horribly wrong, but they were not cheats. What they did is inexcusable, but it is comprehensible. These people took certain materials that were within themselves, they looked at the world about them, and, moved by a whole complex of motives, they brought themselves together again far over on the Radical side of the racial scale. The Radical possibility had long been there. In

1865 it was freed with the freeing of the slaves, and after 1889 it realized very nearly its worst potential.

During the Radical era, racial thought and act became as extreme as they ever became in the South or in America. Black people were murdered horribly and in great numbers, and the quality of black life was deliberately and cruelly reduced. For blacks, the promise of American life grew small and dim even as it grew bright and large for white Americans. The physical abuse was terrible, but the real revolution in the South in the 1890s was not one of the relative placement of bodies. It was a revolution of minds—first of white minds and then of black. Radicalism was at the very core of the process. It flashed a message to Robert Charles in New Orleans and to W. E. B. DuBois at Atlanta University that there was no place for black people in white America. The response of each was that somehow black people were going to have to "come out" of white America and build for themselves a black life. Radicalism was extremely effective in throwing both white and black cultures into high flux, but, ironically, Radicalism as a mentality—as a system for thinking about black people—died after about 1915, and as a system it was virtually forgotten. Afterward, it was very easy, very convenient, and perhaps even seemingly necessary to lose sight of the depth of racism in those turn-of-the-century years, and to assume that racism in the South had always been steady, monolithic, and mild.

We found when we later rediscovered the Radical era that things had not always been the same. It was a highly valuable discovery. If racism in the South is and has been immutable, if it has always been unchanged and unchangeable, then there is little hope of betterment. If there were turn-times when race relations improved or grew worse, then, perhaps, turns can be managed. In the same vein, if there were varieties of racism, then some are likely to be more tolerant than others. One can favor the best and disfavor the rest. The 1890s was a turn-time in race relations, and the turn was toward the worst variety. We have tended to think of that turn-time and the racial extremism that occurred then as a "burst effect," a one-time aberration, built upon misunderstanding. And so it was. But, lamentably, the misunderstanding was not engineered by exterior devils. And the cure, hence, was not so easy as identifying the malefactors and erasing them. The mass of white people who became Radicals were not duped in any ordinary sense of the term. There were no barkers at carnival side shows, though that certainly came later. The Radicals were mistaken in their perceptions as all people are liable to be mistaken in their perceptions, and to do horrible things in consequence. The rise of Radicalism attests to the fact that racism does evolve, but it also attests to the fact that it is deep and broad, more deep, more pervasive, perhaps, than we as a nation are yet willing to recognize. Radicalism also attests to the fact that there are different kinds of racism in America, and the differences are vital. But no kind of racism has ever been benevolent, and none are now. Racially speaking, every white person has a picture of Dorian Gray in the attic, and each would do well, very well, to put him in the parlor.

CONSEQUENCES

What came out of the combat between Conservatism and Radicalism in the generation after 1889 was that in the deep South, particulary in the five black belt states of the deep South (South Carolina, Georgia, Alabama, Mississippi, and Louisiana), Radicalism gained absolute ascendancy and ruled for a time. It had its special perception of the Negro, and, consequently, in power it moved strongly to build and to alter institutions and psychologies to conform to that perception. That process affected social structure, economics, politics, religion, education, medicine, and judicial, police, and penal systems, and both white minds and black. The result was that in whole states, indeed, in a solid block of five contiguous states, black people were deliberately and carefully reduced materially and spiritually. Moreover, there was a spill-over effect from the Radical heartland, so that adjoining black belt areas in the South tended to fellow-travel with the Radical core. Eastern North Carolina, Virginia, and Maryland, southern Delaware, northern Florida, western Tennessee, eastern Arkansas and Texas, and southeastern Oklahoma all shared strength with the Radical heartland. It was a vast, pervasive system, and it did have a devastating effect upon black people and upon race relations in America.

In the upper South, on the other hand, in North Carolina and Tennessee and states north and west of these, Conservatism eventually won the struggle. Radicalism had its impact in the upper South, especially in the black belts within the various states, but it did not rule those states, and it did not have a controlling hand in shaping public institutions. After 1915, even in the five black belt states, Radicalism as a mentality died of its own inadequacies. Nevertheless, it had prevailed for a time, and the material and mental reduction of the Negro continued as perpetuated by the institutions that Radicalism had set in motion. After about 1915 Conservatism did resurge in the black belts all over the South, but when it did so, it tended by its very nature to license what it found. If black people had been reduced because Radicalism had once ruled race relations in a given place, resurgent Conservatism worked to freeze them in that lowly place. The freeze would last approximately half a century, and it functioned to press black people down, not only in the black belts, but wherever they were.

Race has happened all along and virtually everywhere in America, between whites, Indians, blacks, and Orientals. But specially it happened in the South in the turn-of-the-century generation. What happened there is the crucible of twentieth-century race relations in America. In that time and place the disengagement and alienation of black people from white people, signally begun in Reconstruction, was practically completed and the crystallization of a separated and viable black culture begun. In the 1890s, a distinct acceleration of the outmigration of blacks from the South set in. What began as a trickle became a flood between 1916 and 1930. In the decade before 1920 nearly a quarter of a million blacks left the five states of the Radical heartland for the North and West. In the next decade the number doubled.[32] In the diaspora, Southern blacks met Northern blacks, and, in the 1920s, in Harlem and elsewhere, black culture evolved into a phase of greater strength and conscious celebration. The outmigration ensued, in some measure, precisely because the North allowed the South greater freedom in ruling its own race relations, and those relations deteriorated. The North got at last what many Northerners had always feared would be the result of the death of slavery—an exodus of blacks to the North. The Southern race problem of the nineteenth century became the national race problem of the twentieth, in part precisely because of the abandonment by the North of the Negro in the South.

PART THREE

The North and the Negro, 1889–1915

CHAPTER X

The North and the Negro in the South

During the turn-of-the-century decades there was a steep decline in the commitment of the North to blacks in the South. From the beginning, the liberality of the North to the Negro had been chained by its own racism. Led out by American ideals of equality, the North was always liable to be jerked back from its liberal posture by the shortened chain of its own prejudice. Tentatively and briefly committed to ideals of equal citizenship in Reconstruction, it soon tired and abandoned that effort. In the 1880s and 1890s, the North grew increasingly more concerned about problems at home, and as it did so it became less concerned about the Negro in the South. The rise of giant combinations of economic power and an influx of immigrants bringing "Rum and Romanism" threatened to drown the American image of the country as pure and Protestant. "Rebellion" now came to signify not only the past Southern penchant for rule or ruin, but rather the future threat from the left, from organized and violent labor, and an array of frightening ideologies ranging through socialism and anarchism. In and after the panic of 1893, the anxieties of the preceding decade were heightened and reinforced. Rather clearly, the North began to think that it had problems at home more deserving of its attention than the racial situation in the South.

NORTHERN SUPPORT OF BLACK SCHOOLS IN THE SOUTH

A fair index of the changing attitude of the North was exhibited in its behavior in regard to support of black schools in the South. The experience of Atlanta University, a liberal arts school founded in Reconstruction and staffed by an excellent and predominantly New England-bred faculty, provides a handy case in point.

Atlanta University had always depended for its support upon numerous private and very personal gifts from individuals, churches and clubs, mostly in New England and the Northeast. Sometimes the gift was a scholarship for a specific student for a year (worth about $40), sometimes it was a barrel of clothing, seldom was it a gift of more than $100. While that giving was often unselfish, noble, and Christian, it was not always so. At its worst, it represented the same sort of paternalistic exploitation with which the South was charged. Indeed, it was sometimes difficult to know who gave more in these exchanges, those Northern whites who gave or those Southern blacks who, ostensibly, received. An extreme example of the latter occurred in 1893. "If you have a young unpromising young girl (Col) who has had no opportunities—but has expressed a desire to attend your school—and will adopt the name of *Priscilla Livermore,* and is willing to leave off one of her given names, so that the whole name would not sound burdensome, I think a Scholarship for such an one might be raised for her but in these troublesome times for no one else," offered a letter from Boston. The university was not above undertaking the assignment. "I have to say that I think I can find a colored girl unpromising enough to satisfy the most critical," responded a member of the staff. "A girl of this description recently applied here for entrance, and if she can be induced by your offer to change her name it will read thus, when signed at the bottom of a letter: 'Lena Priscilla Livermore Jones[']. The initials, L. P. L. J., 'put out in good shape,' are quite pretty, I think."[1]

As the depression deepened, embattled Atlanta University strove harder to raise funds in the North. It encountered a rising inclination to support industrial education. One women's group hestitated about financing a scholarship in the University, "preferring," as the spokeswoman said, "to help a poorer school and an industrial one. . . ."[2] Often the friends of Atlanta found that the Wizard of Tuskegee or his minions had preceded them and laid claim to all available resources. "I am interested in the Atlanta University and wish it well, but I am also preempted [*sic*] in my sympathies for Tuskegee and Hampton," wrote the rector of All Souls Church, Chicago. Thomas Van Ness, the minister of the Second Congregational Church in Boston, declined for his parish, primarily because "I found we are already pledged to Robert T. Taylor the Agent of the Tuskegee School, who speaks in our church next Sunday."[3]

Possibly, as the North was turning away from higher education and toward industrial education, it was, in effect, diminishing its commitment to blacks in the South. The industrial education that it preferred was terminal. When boys or girls had learned their skill, they would be put out into the world to make their own way—presumably never to be heard from again in the way of charity. Under the hegemony of Booker T. Washington and the "Tuskegee Idea," black education also became blacker and, hence, relieved whites of responsibility. Black principals and black teachers tended to fill black schools and exclude whites totally—including Northern whites theretofore active. On the other hand, when one sponsored a black for higher education as a teacher, doctor, or minister, one undertook an unending commitment. To raise up their race, black teachers would need schools, black doctors hospitals, and black ministers churches. The appeals for aid would be endless. What the North wanted for the Negro seemed to be changing in the 1890s, and it was turning downward. By 1900 the defection of the North was clear. In that year, the president of Atlanta University rued "the great tide of disapproval of higher education of the Negroes which seems to be sweeping over the country now."[4]

In the North, personal interest in Negro education in the South simply lessened. What remained changed direction, but also it was displaced to some extent by a rising concern with matters at home. For instance, for several years Class No. 15 of the Sunday school of a church in Worcester, Massachusetts, financed a student in Atlanta University. Taught by a man, the class was made up of working girls who "have to earn all of the money they get (as teachers, book-keepers, Stenographers, etc.)" "During the last year or two," the teacher wrote in 1897, "there has grown up a feeling among some of the members of my class, that we were neglecting very important work at home in order to perform our work in Atlanta." Many of his students wanted to terminate their scholarship so that "we could be free to take up work at home which has seemed to appeal to us very strongly, and which we are forced to neglect as long as we continue our Atlanta Scholarship." It was not, he urged, that "we love Atlanta less, but because we feel a very heavy responsibility for other work as well."[5]

In the North, the sentiment that distracted the friends, and the potential friends, of black education in the South was the same mix of fears and aspirations that led Jane Addams and her fellow workers to go down into the slums of Chicago and open Hull House, which led Lillian Wald to venture into Henry Street on the seamy side of New York, and later prompted Eleanor Roosevelt and Harry Hopkins to join other pioneers in social work there. The North was more and more frightened by local threats to its own cultural integrity. Jane Addams argued explicitly and with great effect that it was better to meet the masses in the bottoms before they swarmed over the heights. Ironically, a part of Northern interest in blacks in the South had always been to keep them there and away from the North. By the 1890s the urban and largely alien poor of the North were surpassing the black poor of the South as threats to high culture in America.

When the depression passed and Northern aid for black schools in the South took solid form again, the shape had changed so much as to constitute a change in quality. After the turn of the century, assistance to black education in the South moved from numerous small and very private gifts offered through Northern white missionaries to relatively large grants made by foundations established by the philanthropy of a few very rich individuals and channeled through agents in their employ either to black leaders such as Booker Washington or through the black minions of white governments in the South. Further, the target of giving shifted from higher education to elementary. Of special interest to Southern blacks was the Rosenwald Fund, established in 1912 by Julius Rosenwald, an executive in the Sears Roebuck Company. In the first twenty years of its life, the Rosenwald Fund stimulated the building of more than five thousand elementary schools for blacks throughout the South. Thus, Northern philanthropy toward blacks in the South followed the path of American life from local and personal in the nineteenth century to national and impersonal in the twentieth. The human effect was to divorce Northern whites as individuals from a need to concern themselves about the men and brothers they had freed from slavery.

SOUTHERN RACIAL MISSIONARIES TO THE NORTH

The North abandoned the Negro in the South to the South not only because of its concern for itself but also because Southerners themselves labored diligently to effect that end. There was a virtual crusade in which the South undertook to explain itself to the North. It was a two-step progression. First, Conservatives evangelized the North. Then, while Conservatives were still engaged in the field and fighting on the front lines, Radicals erupted out of the South, burst through salients already established by Conservatives, and spilled into the racial territory of the North.

Conservatives were central to the process by which the North yielded, for a time, control of the race question in the South to the South. Conservatives had long been at this task, and with considerable success. Even before the war, they had been actively engaged in a propaganda effort to convince the North, and themselves, that the Negro was happy in slavery and that he could be safely left in their tender care. During Reconstruction and after, Southern Conservatives such as Wade Hampton and Lucius Quintus Cincinnatus Lamar of Mississippi argued to the North that Southerners understood best how to deal with Negroes and that the great mass of Negroes would remain in the South if the mangement of race relations were left in their hands. The Negro problem was essentially a Southern problem, they declared, and Southerners would solve it to the satisfaction of all.

Northern travelers in the South were often converted, but probably the conversion rate among Northern residents in the South was even higher. Southern society was structured to enforce conformity in racial etiquette upon whites as well as blacks. Northern whites could hardly survive congenially in the South without accepting the racial manners of their white neighbors—or at least seeming to do so. Many simply capitulated, and even those with the hardest shells and greatest sympathy for blacks found themselves straining to maintain their equilibrium. Not only had they to withstand the slings and arrows of their seemingly outrageous white neighbors, they also had to resist being demoralized by a black world that they saw as afflicted by extreme poverty, isolation, and cultural deprivation. Mary E. Putney was a "Yankee" who lived in black belt Georgia for twenty-five years before 1913. In that year, she forgot to pay her annual subscription to Atlanta University. "The negro don't grow better in morals," she complained to the president of the school. "It seems as if they were going the other way. I help them, and wish for a better state of affairs." She continued to contribute to two black schools, she said, "but O, I know so much of the impure lives and 'no-account' manner of living."[6]

No doubt many Northerners were converted by Southern visits in which they enjoyed personal contacts with well-educated, intelligent, humane, and humanistic Southerners, but many others were affected by what amounted to Conservative crusades among the racial heathen in the North. Probably the first signal and still the most widely commented upon appearance of this sort was made by Henry Grady before the New England Society of New York in 1886, but after him there flowed a continuous stream of visiting evangelists, all preaching "trust us."[7] Sometimes race relations was the prime theme, more often it was tacked onto another effort. Thus William J. Northen preached the message of the businessman, Barnas Sears, J. L. M. Curry, Charles W. Dabney, and Edwin A. Alderman spoke for education, and a host of ministers represented the church. The very quantity of Conservative spokesmen was imposing, but it was perhaps the quality of individual Conservatives that converted the most thoughtful and influential Northerners. For example, the Episcopal priest Edgar Gardner Murphy was a man of splendid sentiments, talents, and attainments who became, in the first decade of the twentieth century, in effect the ambassador of Conservative Southern white civilization to the intellectual North. Murphy's arguments were so convincing as virtually to shatter the racial sets of some leaders in Northern thought and to make them rethink and adjust their pro-Negro biases in such a way as to favor the white South. Murphy wrote as well as he spoke, and his messages were easily broadcast. In 1906, Lyman Abbott, a young abolitionist who subsequently became a prominent editor of national journals and was at that time editor of *The Outlook*, congratulated Murphy on an article in the *Sewanee Review*. "I have just returned from nearly a three weeks trip in the South, speaking in colleges in North and South Carolina, and have come back with a new sense of the difficulty of the problem which Southern leaders have to face, but also with a new sense of the wisdom and courage with which at least some of them are facing it," he confessed. "Your article is a splendid reflection of the best thought of the South."[8] Joseph H. Choate, philanthropist, friend of the Negro, and Ambassador to Great Britain, was no less impressed by Murphy's first book and undertook to recommend it far and wide. "I have read it with interest and satisfaction, and now for the first time I understand our Negro question," he declared. "I liked it so much that in speaking on Wednesday night to our great Tuskegee meeting in Carnegie Hall—packed to the ceiling, I advised everybody present to read it, and am by tomorrow's steamer sending copies of it to Mr. Balfour, Lord May, Sir Ralph Littler, and Sir Charles Dalrymple, all friends of mine in England to answer the question Englishman are always asking 'What about the negro problem? What are you going to do about it?'" Choate was unreserved in his praise. "I congratulate you very much on having written a book that exactly meets the needs of the times."[9]

Racial Conservatives commenced the labor of converting the North, and Radicals advanced it. Radicals came into the field after the turn of the century, a bit late in the campaign. But when they came, they brought fire to the fight. A key forum was the Congress, with its ready-made national audience. Tillman was, of course, the Radical pioneer in the nation's capital, but he was soon joined by others, including the long-time political leader of Alabama, J. Thomas Heflin. "We can and must educate the North on this question," Heflin urged his Mississippi colleague, James K. Vardaman, in 1906. "At the last Session of Congress I introduced an amendment to the rate bill to prevent negroes and white people from riding in the same sleeping cars. I also introduced a bill requiring the street car companies of Washington to furnish separate cars for the negroes and whites for the District of Columbia."[10]

Even as they were winning in the deep South, a number of Radicals were taking to the lecture platforms of the North. It was the last great age of non-electronic oratory, of the speaker pure and virtually unadorned. Any town with any pretensions at all had its lecture hall or theater, offering an almost continuous program of entertainment and education, including such speakers as Mark Twain, George Washington Cable, "Sockless" Jerry Simpson, William Jennings Bryan, and the outrageous and intriguing atheist Robert G. Ingersoll. It was a time when people still went to the great watering places for their vacations—the Hot Springs in Virginia and Saratoga Springs in New York. Often a part of the entertainment in such places was a program of lectures. The Chautauqua series was the most famous of these and drew its name from Lake Chautauqua, a summer spa in upstate New York. Tom Dixon, as we have seen, took up this highly lucrative profession, speaking, he later claimed, to five million people between 1899 and 1903. His talks treated such favorite subjects as "Backbone," "The New Woman," and his most popular, "Fools." Audiences, thus, were readily available. Radicals had only to set their trains upon the tracks and shovel coal. And they were very good at pouring it on. John Temple Graves, for instance, took occasion at Lake Chautauqua itself in 1903 to impress his Radical views upon an eminent assembly of Northerners. The Atlanta editor urged the method upon Rebecca Felton, Tom Watson engaged in it sporadically, and James K. Vardaman entered the field in 1908. Vardaman called his single platform offering "The Impending Crisis," and in it he warned against the black beast rapist. "Ambition in the negro is concreted in lust," he declared to audiences throughout middle America.[11] Probably the most influential of all the Radicals in converting the North on the lecture circuits, however, was Ben Tillman.

Tillman first seriously entered the lecturing profession in 1901 with, as we noted before, two prepared speeches: "The Race Question" and "Railroads, Trusts, Monopolies." "From the demonstration of approval and satisfaction at the three places where I have delivered the lecture on 'The Race Question' I am satisfied that be the most popular work that I can engage in," he wrote to his agent. Ever the showman, and now the apostle for the propagation of Radicalism in foreign parts, he could hardly wait to attack the enemy in his very citadels. "I want to get into New England and talk on the Race Question," he urged his agent, "and I hope you will push matters in that field."[12] By 1903 Tillman was making tours of six and ten days, speaking in different towns night after night, in Minneapolis, Saginaw, Madison, Mason City, Iowa; Big Stone City, South Dakota; and Cawker City, Kansas. In 1906 his fee was $150 a night if the agent could book him for six nights or more in a row; for lesser runs his fee was $200. Now and again he insisted upon a $500 fee. In August and September 1906 he undertook one tour that carried him to speak in nineteen places in Minnesota, Nebraska, Iowa, Illinois, Indiana, Kentucky, and Missouri.

Tillman had a tremendous impact wherever he went. He always excited interest in the race problem, and he did make converts. On several occasions his speeches nearly created riots, and he came to seek guarantees before he appeared in dangerous places. "I know the negroes in Indianapolis are very impudent and you have a very large criminal class there," he warned a gentleman of the town who invited him to come. "I believe that in the not distant future you will have a bloody race riot and nothing else will straighten out the miserable conditions in which you find yourself."[13] Tillman won enduring attention and a great amount of admiration by his speeches, as his later correspondence testifies. A judge of the superior court of Washington State living in Seattle, remembered a typical Tillmanesque encounter. "I recall you very well," he wrote, "and perhaps you may recall me as being the presiding officer the night you lectured here, and there is one incident you will certainly recall, and that is that you were interrupted during the course of your remarks by a man, whereupon you ceased and said—'I think, sir, you are an octoroon, are you not'? to which he replied, 'Yes, sir.' Thereupon your retort brought down the house, and your interrupter was quieted."[14]

Southerners resident in the North were also highly effective in securing freedom for the South in race relations. In business, in law, in publishing and literature, in the military, as professors and students in colleges and universities, in every walk of life, they defended the South and propagated the racial faith. Usually they were Conservatives. Many Southerners such as George Foster Peabody of Georgia went north to make their fortunes. Later, in proper paternal tradition, they plowed their wealth back into the soil of Southern humanity in the form of various philanthropic enterprises for both blacks and whites. Edgar Gardner Murphy spent much of the last ten years of his life in New York and New Haven, dealing out monies to the South on behalf of wealthy Northerners. Still-rooted Southerners were in the North, and they were there in surprising numbers and influence. It almost amounted, as one contemporary observed, to a Southern invasion of the North. Occasionally the invaders were even organized, as they were in the Southern Society of New York. In 1905 Edwin A. Alderman, the president of the University of Virginia, addressed some 500 members of that organization. The South had values but not enough social inventiveness, he charged. Southern leadership had not had the training for "social awakening, of social imagination, and of social and political initiative in the things that can strengthen and really enrichen our common life."[15] Implicitly, he was calling for leaders in higher education in the South to join the progressive movement.

Persisting Southerners in the North served as perpetual brokers in the intersectional exchange of ideas—philanthropic, progressive, and racial. They did not close the gap, but they did measure the distance, describe the nearest edges, and build bridges. In 1909, Charles W. Eliot, the president of Harvard University, responded to the comment of an "old grad" from Alabama that Southerners felt "held off" at Harvard by the lack of a color line. "It is really impossible for Harvard University to draw a color line," he declared, "and yet we know that a color line against the African is drawn, and must be drawn, in education institutions throughout the south." It was all very understandable. "This diversity of practice and opinion is of course due to the fact that the proportion of students of African blood that can arrive at Harvard University is so small as to be negligible."[16]

The very manner in which Southerners divided on the race question tended to reduce Northern resistance to surrendering the Negro problem to the South. Beginning particularly in the 1890s, Southern Conservative representation to the North tended to break up the severe threat of a revival of Reconstruction represented by such measures as the Lodge Bill. Conservativism, by its certain nature—moderate, sane, slow—was a good parry to the neo-abolitionist thrust. Patrician, cultivated, thoroughly responsible, Conservatives enjoyed high creditability among their influential peers in the North. Conservatives made racial converts there that Radicals could never hope to touch. At the same time, however, they opened the ears of the North to the South and made possible the entrance of the Radical plea. Once on Northern ground, Radicalism doubtlessly touched masses of people suited to respond to its special argument. Conservatives had opened the beachheads that allowed the Radicals to land. Both were shock troops in this latter-day battle of Gettysburg in which the Northern line was broken and the North invaded. The fruit of the racial campaign was not so much to conquer the North, as it was to free the South.

The relationship between Radicals and Conservatives was, in part, direct and functional. Seemingly instinctively, Conservatives interposed themselves between their Radical brothers and Northern criticism. Even as they denounced lynching in the South, they mitigated that crime to Northern audiences by alluding to its spontaneous nature, to the awful provocation of rape, and blamed both the provocation and the lynching upon Northern insistence that the Fifteenth Amendment be honored. In the Wilmington and Atlanta riots, the blood had hardly dried in the streets before Conservatives were gathering evidence tending to minimize the crime. Recurrently, Conservatives sheltered Radicalism from exposure and criticism in the North; and, in effect, they prevented the punishment of criminals. Their Southern loyalty must have been very rich to pay such a tax.

Conservatives, most of all, wanted a unitary harmonious society, and they would sacrifice lesser things to achieve that end—even perfect candor. They did not want a social world at war with itself, and hence they were reluctant to draw a hard and fast line in all things between themselves and their Radical opponents. They would not close the Radicals out; they would not deny them the breath of life. Rather, they sought constantly to bring their Radical brothers in, to reduce the heresy and arrogate the late heretics into their own ranks.

It seems obvious that an erosion of concern for the Southern Negro by the white North, accelerated by Conservatives in the turn-of-the-century years, became a landslide applauded by Radicals during the early years of the twentieth century. Such vigilance as there was in the North on behalf of Negroes was check-mated by the activism of Conservative and Radical evangelists. The process involved politics, but by the early twentieth century it had become, as well, a great social question that frightened politicians and left politics powerless. Losing power, politicians also lost interest. Early in Reconstruction, the white North turned and began to walk away from its commitments, implicit and explicit, to black Americans. In the early twentieth century, the walk became a run. The runners sometimes looked south, but they almost never looked back.

RACE AND REUNION

The abandonment by the white North of the black South was a complex affair
that was related to the whole process of the reunion of North and South.
Thomas Dixon, Jr., exhibited his usual quicksilver brilliance when he joined
the black problem to re-union and saw the beginning of the birth of a nation
in the Spanish-American War. The Negro, in symbol and in reality, had been
an obstacle to the joining together again of North and South. Working against
the obstacle was the desire for a more perfect nationhood rising in America.
As in so many things, Americans were merely taking a slice from the pie of
Western civilization when they embraced supernationalism at the turn of the
century. What many people missed, then and later, was that Southerners too
caught the disease of nationalism then rampant in the world. No less than
Germans, French, British, and Serbians, they too wanted the status inherent in
belonging to an exclusive and powerful club. It was no simple coincidence that
Theodore Roosevelt came in 1912 to tie up his program under the label "New
Nationalism," a nationalism that included the South and neglected the Negro.
The working out of the details of reunion took time, roughly half a century
from 1865. In that process, the Northern actor and the Southern actor played
their parts, while the black actor was shuffled from stage-center to the wings.

In fiction, literary people rather consciously promoted the reunion of
North and South. Thomas Nelson Page, probably the most often read and
best-selling Southern author in the last quarter of the nineteenth century, candidly confessed that his literary formula was to take one Southern belle and
add a handsome Yankee, let love blossom, introduce an obstacle between
them, and overcome the difficulty to effect in the end the promise of everlasting bliss. The Southern woman was beautiful and impoverished by the war,
yet her spirit was far from broken. The Yankee was handsome, well educated,
and rich. The symbolism of a spiritual South joining with a materialistic North
was heavy-handed, but the logic of each bringing to each what was so desperately needed was rather compelling. Thomas Wentworth Higginson, the Uni-
tarian minister who had supported John Brown and commanded the first permanent regiment of black troops raised in the war, himself in 1879 published
a novel that followed the formula precisely. Appropriately enough, he entitled
his novel *The Bloody Chasm,* and he might have added the subtitle: *Crossing
Same.* It remained for Thomas Dixon, with usual dramatic extravagance, to
do the formula in doubles. In the *Clansman,* play as well as book, he married
two sets of brothers and sisters, one Southern and one Northern. The theme
went on to achieve terrific cinematic success in *The Birth of a Nation*—with
Lillian Gish as one of the Southern belles. Divorces were then rare, and the
double marriages effected at the end of the stories provided a reassuring double
bond against disunion.

Southerners also adjusted their history to facilitate the reunion. Slavery in retrospect became a school of civilization that raised blacks up to the point where it was possible for the North to liberate them without danger. Thus South and North had operated in unwitting concert, in tandem, in seeming conflict but actually in harmony to work out God's plan for blacks in America. Slavery was an idea whose time had died. Similarly, the Confederacy had its brief and noble hour and passed. The Confederacy as a potential separate nation was an embarrassment to reunion. History came to the rescue by stressing the inevitability of Confederate defeat, and hence the fact that its existence was not really a threat to the nation. The cult of Jefferson Davis, which bloomed only after the Yankees had made the mistake of incarcerating him in a dungeon in irons, gave way in the 1890s, as we will see, to the cult of Robert E. Lee. Lee represented the transcendent values of man, timeless, in history but above it, ideals to which the North as well as the South might aspire. Calhoun went into eclipse as the premier intellectual; and Jefferson, the sun-king of Southern political thought, re-emerged.

The heightened imperialism of the 1890s had an effect upon the posture of the North vis à vis both Southern whites and blacks. Most significantly, it produced the "splendid little war" with the Spanish. In that war, the whole-hearted rush to the colors by Southerners was not only a cause of reunion; it was a perfect license for it. It was almost as if Southerners now shedding their blood for the expansion of the nation abroad could atone for the blood they had exacted from the North in attempting to destroy the union at home a generation before. The heat of war, brief and relatively small as it was, was nevertheless hot enough to melt further the parts of the nation into one.

Imperialism united North and South, but it also separated Southern blacks from Northern whites. If the North accepted the South, it must accept more or less the whole South and—to make a useful pun—give the South *carte blanche* in matters of race.

Further, a direct result of the war was to bring the North face to face with the necessity of deciding what was its attitude toward the colored peoples of the world. If the nation would annex the Philippines, Puerto Rico, and various other islands, then it would have to decide where it stood on the issue of race. Ultimately it opted for annexation, and it decided that these peoples would not be treated as equals, but as children to be tutored in the American way. The practice of paternalism abroad would sanction paternalism at home. If the depth of that sentiment eventually proved rather shallow abroad and its energies largely misdirected, so too at home. Ironically, one great cry against imperialism came from the Radicals in Congress. They recognized the depth of racism in America and its inability to relate well to the darker peoples of the earth.

Imperialism had its generalized effect upon race in America, but one incidental effect of imperialism had an immediate and very tangible impact. The
Spanish-American War brought the black military to the fore again. Early in
Reconstruction it had been decided that black troops in the South were more
likely to cause a war than to keep the peace. Consequently, the army disbanded
its regiments of black volunteers in 1866. Shortly, however, it created four
regiments, two of infantry and two of cavalry, to contain, under white officers,
virtually all of the blacks in the regular army. During some thirty years the
black regiments were stationed in the West. There, they did their fair share of
holding down the first Americans with their guns even as they held down
hundreds of frontier bars with their elbows. It took the Spanish-American
War to bring the black troops east again, en route to Cuba, and, by the fortunes of war, into the Southeast, the heartland of Radicalism. In 1898, as the
regulars flowed into Florida and waited for the assault ships to load, they went
into the towns seeking refreshments and other diversions. In town they often
insisted upon being treated with more respect than the native whites would
allow. The result was violence. In Tampa, for instance, a bloody riot erupted.
Soldiers of the Twenty-fourth and Twenty-fifth Infantry regiments invaded
the town after Ohio soldiers had abused a Negro child. They fired pistols
freely, wrecked saloons and cafes that had refused them service, and crashed
into a white brothel. Finally the riot was quelled by Georgia troops, but
twenty-seven blacks and several white soldiers were seriously wounded.[17] In
Macon, Georgia, and elsewhere the racial order was shaken as black men in
the volunteer regiments made the same demand for liquid services, were
refused, and waxed militant.

Black leaders had hoped that their participation in the war would win for
them a new high level of acceptance in the nation. The result was quite the
opposite. Theodore Roosevelt, himself, who had good cause to be grateful to
the black regulars for their help at San Juan Hill, cast aspersions not only upon
their fighting skill, but even upon their courage. After the war, black troops
were again posted to the frontiers, including the Philippines—helping to fight
the rather awful civil war in process there.

However valiantly they might serve, the days of the black regiments were
numbered as sentiment rose against them. "I see the 10th cavalry has returned
from the P.I. [the Philippine Islands] & have gone to Elten Fort in Vt.,"
observed Dr. C. P. Purvis in 1909. A black leader in Reconstruction South
Carolina, Purvis practiced medicine in Brookline, Massachusetts, and was then
vacationing in the White Mountains of New Hampshire. "I hope they will
not commit any overt acts," he declared, "'Jim Crow Cars' are recommended
for them already."[18] In World War I the men in the four regiments were scattered to serve as instant non-coms for the mass of black recruits mustered in
for the war. Those troops, for the most part, served in "labor batallions," i.e.,

performing hard labor. Then and later, whites chose to believe that blacks did not make good combat soldiers.

THE NORTHERN CAPITULATION TO RACISM

In the quest for social justice in America, there seems to be such a phenomenon as battle fatigue. The social body tires of laboring at a given problem, and especially so if there is less than striking progress toward its solution. No doubt there were many humane, generous, and concerned Northerners in this period who were quite willing to hear and believe that they could safely lay down their burden of race. They were probably highly receptive to the argument that most Negroes were in the South, would remain in the South, and that it was in the South, ultimately, that the problem would be met. The North capitulated for a bundle of reasons and in a variety of ways. And in the turn-of-the-century years, evidences of the capitulation were increasingly apparent.

Reflective of the general desertion by the North of the Negro was a tendency among leading national magazines to turn away from the race question. In 1899, Joel Chandler Harris, the Georgia author of Uncle Remus fame, thought he might like to do some social polemics for the *Saturday Evening Post*. "With regard to editorials," the editor warned, "we do not care to run up against religion and race matters, or partisan politics, but outside of these barb-wire fenced subjects the whole range is open to you."[19] Similarly, *The Youth's Companion* was willing to entertain an editorial on the late Robert C. Ogden by a Southern writer provided, as the editor warned, "the negro question doesn't enter into it too much."[20] Even the Boston-based and arch-abolitionist journal, the *Independent,* tacked somewhat away from race in asking William Garrott Brown to report on "the more progressive movements undertaken by the Southern white people." Chafing under criticism that it gave too much space to race, the managers felt that "if we had someone to keep us in touch with the progressive Southern developments that have nothing to do with the race issue it would obviate the charge against us that we are unfair to the Southern white people." He added that "we can attend to the race issue here ourselves in the office. . . ."[21]

In the early years of the twentieth century the North had not only surrendered any serious idea of interfering with race relations as they were developing in the South; it was also coming to a rather open acceptance of its own racism vis à vis black Americans. "The plain fact is," Ray Stannard Baker told the Sagamore Sociological Conference in 1909 after extensive research on the problem, "most of us in the north do not believe in any real democracy as between white and colored men."[22] Southern blacks who went north had ample opportunity to test Northern attitudes on race as compared with Southern. An Atlanta University student who worked for a banker in Bridgeport, Connecticut, made it his business to study the difference during one summer. Prejudice in the North was milder, he observed, but the real result was the same. "I came to the conclusion," he wrote to his friends in Georgia, "that the luke-warm or mild race preduce [*sic*] in the large cities of the North works quite successfully against absolute *equality* of opportunity for all members of the Negro race with those of white people."[23] It was the early perception of this truth that led some blacks in the North to pioneer in the organization of the Afro-American League in the 1890s, the Urban League in 1911, and the NAACP following the Niagara Movement of 1905–09.

Ultimately, the critical factor in the capitulation of the North was its own racism. In truth the Southern assault upon the North, first by the Conservatives and then by the Radicals, was an assault upon a hard thin shell. Once inside the walls, the invaders found little resistance. Still the prejudice of the North was more latent than manifest; its practical effects were scattered and relatively mild. Basically, the difference between the North and the South in racial attitudes was that the North had not yet discovered what its prejudices were. It had not done so because the number of blacks in the North was not yet great enough to force that region to a confrontation with its racial self. It was only in the latter third of the twentieth century, when half of the black people in America would live in the North and West, that the depth of the commitment of the North to racial equality at home would be hard tested—and found wanting. What the South got from the North by about 1915 was not so much an open and conscious acceptance of Southern racial attitudes (though the North had traveled far in that direction), as it was an acceptance of the South itself, including its racial attitudes, whatever they might be.

CHAPTER XI

Northern Republicans and Southern Race Relations, 1895–1912

As early as 1868 Northern people had begun to turn decisively away from a concern with the Negro and race relations in the South. Politics followed, as it usually does in these matters, at a respectful distance and on a parallel course. Curiously, politics in the North was always more concerned about the Negro in the South than were the people at large in the North. That was because there were always blacks who voted in significant numbers somewhere, and those voters had to be included in political calculations. Democrats paid attention to black voters mostly by attempting to disfranchise them. The Republican political problem concerning blacks was much more complicated.

On the one hand, there were always lily-white tendencies within the Republican party, either overt or latent. On the other hand, the party had depended heavily upon black voters in Reconstruction, and had profited by them. After Reconstruction, the Republican party as a whole never said a final farewell to its Southern allies, and Republican politicoes at the top never ceased to face the Southern question or to generate Southern strategies and programs. If nothing else, Southern Republicans, both black and white, were perennially important because they sent voting delegations to the national nominating conventions. Broadly speaking, Republican leadership moved back and forth between an emphasis upon exclusion of blacks from the party at one extreme and their full acceptance on the other. In the 1880s in several places in the South, black leadership found it best from time to time to step back and yield prominence in the party to white Republican leaders. But as they moved into the 1890s, blacks were still in the Republican party, and the wisest Republicans insisted upon keeping them there.[1]

HANNA AND McKINLEY DISCOVER SEPARATE AND EQUAL

A new departure began with the presidential aspirations of William McKinley—or, perhaps more precisely, with the presidential aspirations of Marcus A. Hanna for William McKinley. Hanna, after making a fortune in the iron and steel business in Cleveland, Ohio, turned his energies into the management of the political careers of other men. In that business he proved himself superbly talented. In January 1895 he came to take a large house in Thomasville, Georgia, near the Florida border. In the 1890s Thomasville was a winter resort for wealthy Northerners. Indeed, Hanna's own brother owned an estate there. Soon, a procession of political guests came to call at Hanna's house, blacks and whites, sometimes singly, sometimes in pairs, sometimes in groups. They came from the various Southern states, and they came to plan ways and means of controlling the state Republican conventions that would assemble in the following year. Those conventions would name delegates to the national Republican convention, which, in turn, would nominate a President. Without doubt, Hanna knew, as Henry Cabot Lodge later expressed it, "what southern delegates are good for," namely, to nominate a President—not to elect him. With characteristic political acuity, Hanna worked upon this highly significant number of delegates before the opposition even awoke to the new intensity in the game. Two months after he arrived, Hanna was visited, unsurprisingly enough, by his friend William and Mrs. McKinley. The best of Southern society in Thomasville made a distinction between well-to-do Yankee visitors and those not so well-to-do. Those who came with money, particularly in these depression-ridden years, were warmly received. Just then, McKinley was the governor of Ohio, and when he arrived Thomasville turned out five hundred strong in a rather genteel reception to show their hospitality. On that occasion McKinley was welcomed in a gracious address by a prominent local lawyer, a Democrat. The Governor responded, in his usually banal manner, with a few words about hospitality and made some happy observations about a country reunited. The only blacks at the reception were servants.

Behind this soft social setting a hard political game was being played. En route to Thomasville, McKinley had stopped in Atlanta at the home of Colonel Alfred H. Buck. Buck, once a public school principal in Maine, had ended the war in command of two regiments of black troops. Afterward, he became an iron manufacturer in Mobile and a Republican Congressman from Alabama. He moved to Atlanta and, after 1882, was virtually the "boss" of the Republican party in Georgia. McKinley, apparently, received several leading Republican gentleman at the Buck home on the day of his arrival, and in the evening he was taken to the Aragon Hotel, where many of the best people of the city called to see him. Some of these were friends he had made while visiting the city to make a pro-tariff speech during the presidential campaign in

1888. They were all, perhaps, convinced that the nation should be organized around and in support of the business interests they represented.

From Thomasville, the McKinleys made a brief visit to Jacksonville, the seat of Republican strength in Florida. It was noted that during the Jacksonville stay no meeting was arranged with Negro leaders, and that an invitation to meet with black Republicans was politely declined. Turning northward, the McKinleys proceeded to Savannah. There, after a tour of the city and an informal reception at the Commercial Club, all white, the Ohio governor managed to squeeze in a meeting with some fifty black ministers in a black church. One of the ministers offered a welcoming address. McKinley responded briefly with a gracious acknowledgment of their hospitality and a few happy phrases, as was his style, about the educational and material progress of the race. The manner in which McKinley and Hanna set blacks carefully aside and gave them measured consideration was reflected elsewhere in national political circles in the rising image of separate and equal.[2]

During the spring of 1894, while Hanna and McKinley were still working out their Southern strategy, Booker T. Washington appeared before a Congressional committee to urge an appropriation in support of a proposed Cotton States Exposition in Atlanta a year later. The appropriation was made, and Washington, whose appeal to the committee had been strikingly eloquent, was invited to make one of the opening addresses. On that occasion, in September 1895, speaking to a largely Southern white audience, Washington offered what has been well called "the Atlanta Compromise." He said, in essence, that blacks would give up all claims to preferred places in the South in return for a fair recognition of earned places. He promised that blacks would eschew agitation for social equality, that they would till the land, and happily supply the labor necessary for progress. Washington also included subtle hints that when sufficiently elevated, blacks would expect full equality with whites. But, by and large, Southern whites did not note, and perhaps they did not even hear these hints. Instead Conservative whites heard that Booker T. Washington, rapidly rising to become the recognized spokesman of his race, had accepted for his people the offer of place that the Conservative mentality would have accorded them.[3] It was perfectly symbolic that one of the first persons to shake the speaker's hand amidst the joyful cheers of the audience was Governor William J. Northen—ex-slaveholder and Confederate veteran—who rushed across the stage to do so.

If Washington understood that race relations in the South were rapidly deteriorating in the Radical direction, then compromising with the Conservatives, with men like William J. Northen on the basis of separate and equal was excellent strategy. With black bodies swinging from trees and burning at stakes, with one-eyed Ben Tillman next door in South Carolina even then raging like some racist Cyclops for the disfranchisement of black men, it hardly seems possible that Washington could have been unaware of the deterioration. If men of Northen's ilk could be pitted against the Tillmans at the cost of conceding formally things that blacks did not in fact have anyway; if, for instance, Georgia could be saved even while South Carolina was being lost, then Washingtonian accommodationism might seem like a good move. And such it was—in 1895. The Exposition was itself a model of separate and equal. It included a "Negro" building designed by "Negroes, constructed by Negroes, and for Negro exhibits. Washington's speech was taken by whites to mean the perpetual acceptance of such separation. As one of Washington's biographers has asserted, "most significantly, the Atlanta speech helped to establish the 'separate but equal' principle as the yardstick in American race relations for half a century or more."[4]

A few months after Washington had spoken the compromise, the United States Supreme Court, overwhelmingly a Republican body, ruled in the case of *Plessy* v. *Ferguson* that public carriers might afford separate and equal accommodations to the races without in any way violating the legal or constitutional rights of any persons. One might doubt that their honors the justices were aware that separation already prevailed widely in public accommodations in the South, and that when it prevailed blacks did not get equal return for their money. But such was the case and, whether the justices realized their liberality or not (perhaps some did), the Plessy decision, far from being one that cast the Negro out and down, was in reality a progressive decision. If facilities for blacks were already separate and unequal, saying that they must be equal represented, at least in the wordy reality of the legal world, an improvement in the condition of black people. But it was also a compromise. Surrendered was the ideal of unseparated facilities, and gained, assuming that laws did indeed change realities, was an equality of accommodations in public places, something that blacks had previously sorely lacked.

Mark Hanna and Bill McKinley, the Gold Dust twins of *fin de siècle* American politics, were out to make a President in 1895 and 1896. They did that, but in the South they also put a new bottom on the boat of interracial Republican politics. It would not be accurate to say that they introduced "lily-white" Republicanism in the South. Indeed, that tendency had been there from the first and had already flowered conspicuously in some states. On the other hand, "black-and-tan," that is, racially mixed, Republicanism continued strong during McKinley's administration and after his demise. What they did do was to license the separation of black and white in the Southern wing of the party and accord black Republicans thus separated equal treatment with white Republicans. In so doing, McKinley and Hanna found a device for avoiding the penalties of having to choose between a lily-white or a black-and-tan Republican organization in a given state. This strategy flowed smoothly into the idea of separate and equal already abroad in the land, one that the Supreme

Court and Booker T. Washington were simultaneously espousing, and to which the interests each represented would remain married for half a century. The effective message of the new Southern strategy was to advertise that a white man could be a Republican without reference to his feelings about blacks. At the same time, they advertised that there was a place for black voters and black leadership in the party. They soon made evident the fact that those places could be very comfortable, and, indeed, highly remunerative. The McKinley administration appointed an unprecedentedly large number of Negroes to conspicuous and profitable offices. Still, those places were separated. The very manner in which McKinley met whites in one place and blacks in another, if he met them at all, suggested a full endorsement of the racially separated pattern in the South. At the same time, Hanna and McKinley, acting for the Republican party, surrendered the "bloody shirt." An aggressive posture finally melted into one of compromise. What they hoped for in return was an acceptance of the full golden line by conservative white Southerners under the lead of white Republican organizations in various Southern states.

Lily-whiteism in the Republican party in the South, like lily-whiteism in the Democratic and Populist parties grew fully as much from social as from political sources. The inclination toward separation was always there, and it intensified in the 1890s. McKinley's Southern strategy allowed the structural division within his party to deepen. After 1900, the peculiar freedom that aspirants for the presidential nomination gave to racial jealousies brought lily-whiteism in the Republican party out in a new and virulent form. Division ultimately resulted in the relative exclusion of Negroes. The broad outline of what happened to Southern Republicanism in Congress is neatly revealing. The last black Congressman elected in the South in this age won in North Carolina in 1898. Yet, no less than twelve Republican Congressmen were elected in the South in 1910. Not one of these was black.

THEODORE ROOSEVELT AND SOUTHERN POLITICS

Those who specialize in the lore of Theodore Roosevelt have long disagreed as to his personal attitude toward blacks and what his policy toward them as President was. By the end of his administration, many and probably most blacks thought that Roosevelt was, on balance, against them. They had begun, in 1902 and 1903, by thinking quite the opposite. Southern whites, conversely, began by thinking that the President was too sympathetic to Negroes and ended rather well pleased with his performance. Looking backward, progressive period historians and biographers of Roosevelt have thought that the TR policy toward blacks fit the pattern of his apparent policy in so many other areas: that is, first to pull one way and then the other so as to maintain a general equilibrium between contending forces. Others have suggested that the key was political expediency; that Roosevelt merely played upon the racial situation in each state to gain maximum returns. If one peruses his words and his actions, they are consistent with principles that held that in the mass blacks were inherently inferior to whites in the mass and hence no threat to white supremacy; but that blacks were citizens of the Republic and, like all other citizens, had basic rights and privileges that must be equally honored. Thus publicly, he could make black appointments and support them with a rhetoric of civil equality that won black votes, while privately he could assure whites that white supremacy would inevitably reign.

There is more than a glimmer of evidence to suggest that, even as Roosevelt reluctantly became the Vice-President of the United States in the spring of 1901, he was thinking of ways to seize the Republican presidential nomination in 1904. In the South, his ambition would lead him to fish in the troubled waters of racial politics, and, indeed, to trouble them himself. In states where the McKinley organization was relatively black, TR would need to be relatively white, and, of course, vice versa. Inevitably, he would be a rebel, unsettling the separate and equal compromise that had worked so handily for Hanna and McKinley. When McKinley was shot by an assassin in September 1901 and died in October, Roosevent suddenly found himself in possession of the presidency and, along with it, those smoothly functioning McKinley machines in the Southern states. Until he secured the presidency under his own banner in 1904, a wise Roosevelt would do in the South as McKinley had done, and an ambitious Roosevelt would do it better. After that, if he chose, he could afford a change.

There seems to be no "typical" Southern state in Republican politics, but one in which Roosevelt and the racial division can be seen, and revealingly seen, is Arkansas. There the Republican machine of the Reconstruction period built up by Governor Powell Clayton, a onetime general in the Union Army, persisted through the turn of the century with the General at its head. From the first, the Clayton organization depended heavily upon black voters from the eastern counties along the Mississippi River, while not excluding white Unionist voters from the Ozark Mountains to the west. This separate harnessing of blacks and whites served Clayton well for forty years and was not even seriously disturbed by a Democratically inspired secret ballot law passed in 1891, a poll tax law passed in 1892, and a subsequent reduction in the turnout of black voters in general elections from some 72 percent to 24 percent of the total potential.[5] By including both blacks and whites smoothly in his organization, Clayton was able to ally himself with Hanna and McKinley. His personal reward after victory was the ministership to Mexico.

The Clayton machine ran comfortably along, and the fuel upon which it fed was, of course, federal patronage. Winning elections at the state level had little to do with federal patronage in the South. Indeed, it was unlikely that Arkansas Republicans of any shade or flavor were going to win much in the way of elections, either local or national, though Clayton's men never quit trying. Patronage had more to do with supporting the right man for the party's nomination for the presidency every four years, and a lot of civil service time paid for by federal monies was spent in trying to discern in advance just who the winner was going to be. But even here, going into the convention with a loser did not mean that one could not come out with the winner. Furthermore, there was always plenty of time between the nomination and the election to exhibit sufficient loyalty to the winner, an opportunity which the Clayton forces never neglected. Republican leaders in the South, even if they earned their living otherwise, were ever and always professional Republicans.

The key to retaining control of federal patronage was a united front by the "ins." Simply being able to make up a neat package labeled "Arkansas" (or the Republican part of it anyway) and leaving it on the doorstep at 1600 Pennsylvania Avenue in Washington, D.C., with your card was a valuable gift to offer any president. And any President who had ever tried to organize such a package, or even witnessed such an attempt, or knew anything at all about the South and blacks and Republicans there, would appreciate the effort. A truly wise President would put the gift gingerly on a shelf in his closet while looking away and never go in there again without first turning out the lights.

Powell Clayton recognized the value of unity, and he enforced a rigid discipline upon his followers. "Arkansas has accomplished a great deal by reason of its solid front," he wrote to one of his lieutenants in 1897. "Do not let us ever permit it to fall into the condition of Mississippi, Texas and some other Southern states I might name."[6] The game, as Clayton saw it, was always the same. "The outs will naturally organize against the ins, which makes it essential for the latter to stand together," he warned, "and the old stratagem of dividing and conquering is as effective in politics as it is in war."[7]

In Arkansas, the Clayton machine always kept the Negro prominently within the Republican organization, and there was little room to divide the "ins" by appealing to blacks. It was inevitable, then, that the "outs" should gravitate toward playing upon the racial exclusiveness of the white Republican mass concentrated in the western and more mountainous portion of the state. In Arkansas the "outs" were actually lesser "ins," that is, they were subordinate figures in the party who wanted to displace those above them. The lesser ins organized around the ambitions of a man named A. S. Fowler and his ally, W. S. Hold, the secretary of the state Republican party. In 1899, while Clayton was away serving as McKinley's minister to Mexico, the Fowler faction made a strong bid to use the color line as a lever to oust the Claytons and seize control of the party. Clayton's first lieutenant in charge was Harmon L. Remmel, a New Yorker who had come to the state in 1876 to become a very successful and highly respected businessman. Remmel reported the move by the rebels to Clayton. He related in particular the attempt by Fowler to use the nomination of a Negro to an office by the machine to overturn the established leadership. Following orders from Washington, Remmel had nominated for appointment to a federal pension board one white Democratic physician along with a white Republican and a Negro Republican named Hayman. After some agitation, the white Democrat refused to serve on the board with a Negro. Finally, after great trouble, an all-white board was named. Fowler and the Democrats had done much to create the furor, and now Fowler tried to use Remmel's promotion of the Negro candidate against him and the Clayton hierarchy. "He criticises Auten and me for having sustained the darkey," Remmel complained to Clayton, "but this was the choice of the entire committee. He does not seem to realize that the colored man is a very important factor in the Republican organization of this State, and that the chickens may come home to roost before he can even get an entering wedge in the movement which he perhaps openly and his friend Holt silently may be trying to instigate."[8] Old fox that he was, Clayton had no difficulty devising tactics to meet the rebels. "As to Fowler," he advised, "the best way is to let the colored man know that he is responsible for the defeat of Mayman [Hayman]. This should be worked for all it is worth. Let it be understood that he did it through the G.A.R. organization, not through any influence that he had at Washington." Make no open breach, he warned, but "let colored men be appraised quietly of the fact."[9]

Clayton and Remmel had been early supporters of the Hanna-McKinley machine, and they had received their rewards. In 1900, they were still solidly in the camp of the glittering Ohioans. In that year, for instance, Hanna wrote to the head of the New York-based life insurance company of which Remmel was the regional agent, urging the company to give Remmel leave to run for governor of the state.[10] Theodore Roosevelt, however, soon emerged as a menace to the Clayton machine in Arkansas. The Rough Rider had hardly been inaugurated as Vice President in March 1901 before his cause and that of the outs in Arkansas began to coalesce. Particularly was the connection strong between the aspirations of Roosevelt and the western part of the state where the whites were in a decided majority. In 1901, when Remmel and Clayton found their nominee for postmaster in Huntsville in northwestern Arkansas being blocked, Clayton instructed Remmel to inform Hanna that the opposition was a part of the Roosevelt movement, and that they wanted to hold the state solidly for McKinley and company. "I think we may expect the opposition in Arkansas to rally around the Roosevelt standard," he wrote in the summer of 1901, looking forward to the presidential campaign of 1904. "My idea is that we should hold our forces together and work with the original McKinley men in the convention." The boss was much perturbed by having received a letter from a Republican in Camden that concluded with the line, "Hurrah for Theodore Roosevelt for the next President."[11]

Of course, Roosevelt may have taken no active hand in stirring up such enthusiasm, and the hapless hack who so blundered might simply have been thinking that all Presidents retired after a second term. But it is almost inconceivable that the astute Teddy in the summer of 1901 was not already contriving ways of winning the nomination in 1904. An obvious step in that direction was the winning of the Southern delegates. If the "ins" were mostly white-led black-and-tan coalitions that Hanna and McKinley had made, then TR and the "outs" might gather strength by raising the lily-white banner. In September of that year, a single shot from an anarchist's pistol dictated a reversal of that strategy—almost before it had set. With that shot, Roosevelt found himself in command of the very troops he had set out to fight. As always, he took command readily, only a little surprised at his good luck. Immediately, the signals went out that Hanna-McKinley machines would remain in place. Clayton felt much complimented by the fact that the new President quickly confirmed him in his office as minister to Mexico. "It was especially gratifying," he wrote from Mexico City in a letter that seemed to drip with honey for a generous Teddy, "as I had no personal claims on President Roosevelt and from the fact that we were generally in different political camps inside of the Republican party."[12]

If Roosevelt had, indeed, been moving in the lily-white direction in the summer of 1901, it behooved him that fall to make some move in the black-and-tan direction. Until after the nominating convention in 1904, the President concentrated upon checking attempts by the persisting Hanna faction to grab the delegates of the Southern states. Mostly that involved the President's upholding and working with split-level organizations that somehow included both blacks and whites, the very organizations, ironically, that Hanna himself had labored to construct.

The machinery through which Roosevelt operated in the South was called the "referee system." Under this system, he named a man in each state to settle matters within the party and to make recommendations concerning appointments. The referee came to be, as one might imagine, a very important person. He was the man who laid the package on the White House steps. In some states, the referee tended toward lily-white, and in those states the party tended to lose its color in spite of the President's policies. But the conspicuous thrust of the first Roosevelt administration was to continue the black-and-tan leadership, demonstrated most poignantly by the continued appointment of blacks to conspicuous and sometimes significant federal offices in the South.

Further, it soon became common knowledge that Roosevelt was taking advice from two very influential pro-black sources. His key white adviser in Southern racial matters was James S. Clarkson, the Iowa publisher and editor who had labored with ultimate success to get Benjamin Harrison to recognize Southern black leadership in 1889. Clarkson had supported Senator William B. Allison for the nomination in 1896 and lost influence until Roosevelt's elevation. Most significantly, Roosevelt also sought advice from the nearly undisputed leader of Southern blacks, Booker T. Washington. At Roosevelt's explicit invitation, the sage of Tuskegee came to the White House to discuss Southern appointments on October 16, 1901. Out of this meeting came the famous incident in which Booker T. Washington was the man who came to dinner. That occasion created a terrific furor in the white South, but it also advertised clearly that Roosevelt intended to allow the black constituency a new high level of consideration.

The effect in the North of the Booker T. Washington dinner was negligible. Among blacks nationwide, the result was probably to enhance Washington's already large dominance. The white South was furious. Radicals, of course, anxiously anticipated a new outbreak of attacks on white women by black men. Conservatives expected a new wave of insubordination from Negroes, and they resented the tax thus carelessly levied upon them. William Garrott Brown, a Harvard-trained Alabamian, later assessed the perceptions of Southern whites accurately. "It is not that intelligent Southerners any longer fear that 'social equality' will be, or ever can be, forced upon them," he explained to Charles W. Eliot, the president of Harvard. "It is that they Know from experience the effect on the negroes of such utterances, & of such incidents as President Roosevelt's dining with Booker Washington at the White House. These effects are apparent in the criminal courts, in the behavior of domestic servants, & in other very disagreeable ways; & it would be hard to name any countervailing good effects."[13]

It was most unlike Booker T. Washington to be caught in such an embarrassing scrape. One can only speculate as to why he accepted the invitation. First, he probably did not expect any great reaction. He had dined with prominent Northerners before, sometimes at public dinners, and there had been only minor repercussions. Second, the practical gains to be won by quickly closing with the new President were worth the possible cost. If he could win a promise of security for black officeholders, press for the appointment of more blacks to office, and win some influence over which white men were going to be appointed to important federal places in the South, his power in the black community would be no less than awesome. He would be, truly, a wizard. This was but another step in the typical Washington ploy of getting in at the top and thus flanking all opposition. Finally, dinner at the White House represented more food for the ego of the ever aspiring Washington. It was arrival at the summit. After the event, Washington did not respond to the criticism, perhaps thinking to lessen the cost of the venture and still to collect dividends from the investment. Wisely, his first concern was Roosevelt's reaction.[14]

Theodore Roosevelt's response was mixed. On the one side, he was angry and said that he would invite Washington to the White House "to dine just as often as I please." On the other side, Washington understood that he was "too busy to give it more than a passing notice."[15] TR made no public response to the outcry, and that was good politics. Later, he reportedly asserted that there had been no dinner and the Roosevelt ladies had not sat at table with Washington. Actually, the meal was a luncheon, taken from trays in the President's office while the two men talked business. As such, it represented little more than a farmer and his hired hand eating lunch in the shade of the same tree beside a half-plowed field.[16] Eventually, Roosevelt put it among what he called his "blunders." In spite of his bumptious assertion that he would have whomever he pleased for dinner at the White House, it never pleased him to have the Principal of Tuskegee to dinner again. He rued his lack of judgment in allowing the incident to occur, and he deeply resented the presumption of Southerners in attempting to dictate to him in such a matter. Subsequently, he found that Southern whites never totally forgave him the error. He came to wish that it had not happened. His lily-white politics needed that it not have happened. In time, perhaps, he persuaded himself that it really had not.

Whatever the realities of the dinner might have been, in 1901 the new President quickly assured Washington of his good intentions. "The last time I talked to the President," Booker T. Washington reported to Whitefield McKinlay, his agent in the capital, early in 1902, "I went over the matter of Negroes in office very carefully and he told me that it was going to be his general policy to either keep the present men in office or wherever he thought it necessary to remove them to put other colored men in their places if decent colored men could be found." Very soon, TR gave tangible proof of his intentions. "This policy had been pursued in Alabama," Washington indicated, specifying the President's actions.[17] Later in the year, Roosevelt welcomed a chance to make a black appointment in that state as "a fitting rebuke to a certain portion of the Republicans of Alabama who are attempting to form a party based on color."[18]

In the next two years Roosevelt further evidenced his good faith by standing firmly by two Negro appointees in two of the blackest states in the South. In South Carolina, he appointed Dr. William D. Crum, a mulatto physician, as collector of customs for the port of Charleston. Ben Tillman immediately rose in the Senate to filibuster until confirmation was denied. Yet, Roosevelt continued to give Crum interim appointments for the next seven years, and Crum continued to occupy the office in spite of Tillman's verbal violence. Roosevelt had appointed Crum after having visited Charleston and having been assured by many of the best citizens that Crum was a man of the highest type. It was not, Roosevelt answered one protester, that he wanted to offend the wishes of the people, "but I can not consent to take the position that the door of hope—the door of opportunity—is to be shut upon any man, no matter how worthy, purely upon the grounds of race or color. Such an attitude would, according to my conviction, be fundamentally wrong."[19]

Soon after taking office, Roosevelt also defended the Negro postmistress of Indianola, Mississippi, in her appointment. This was the appointment mentioned earlier that so exercized Ben Tillman. Yielding to what amounted to mob pressure, the postmistress sent in her resignation. After an investigation, Roosevelt refused to accept it. When the agitation continued, he simply closed the post office without dismissing the postmistress. The residents then had to get their mail at a neighboring town. "They sent to the next town for theirs," Kermit Roosevelt told Dawson, "and for this task they selected a *Negro*." When the term of the postmistress did end, and she chose to step down, the President gave the office to the white man who had been most conspicuous in his attempts to defend her.[20]

Roosevelt's demonstrations were very convincing to black leadership in the South. The very astute George Washington Murray, South Carolina's last black Congressman, praised TR on the eve of the convention of 1904 for "proving himself such a stalwart friend of ours."[21] Booker T. Washington's man in Washington, Whitefield McKinlay, was profoundly impressed by the Roosevelt demonstrations. "Hurrah for Teddy!" he wrote from Saratoga Springs in the summer of 1903 in reaction to one of TR's missives. "If I was not an ardent and uncompromising supporter of the President this letter would make me one."[22] McKinlay, along with a few others, never lost his enthusiasm for Teddy. Even in 1913, after Roosevelt had revealed clay feet of startling friability, he remained an ardent supporter.[23]

A close look at Roosevelt's treatment of blacks in this first administration brings one to the conclusion that something like a shell game was progress. The President began by clearly putting the pea under the black shell; indeed, he did so dramatically and with a flourish, as in the Crum affair. Then he slid the shells around with grace and ease, meanwhile keeping up a steady flow of language suggesting that the pea was still under the black shell. Yet, if he stopped the game as early as 1903, and we pointed to the black shell, we would have been wrong. Actually, Roosevelt was making many white and very few black appointments in the South. In South Carolina, for instance, even at the time that he was standing steadfast by the Crum appointment, he named a notorious lily white, John B. Capers, as his "referee." In 1902, Capers secured the appointment of "one of the original 'Lilly Whites'" in the state as United States Marshal, and in 1903 was said to be cooperating with Republican Senator Jeter Pritchard of North Carolina in a general move "to oust the Colored man."[24] As Roosevelt himself acknowledged in 1906, Crum's was the "only original Colored appointment" he made in South Carolina where he made scores of new white appointments.[25]

Southern whites were not totally imperceptive, even when Roosevelt's pro-black demonstrations were at their height. "If you ever get the ear of the President," wrote a Mississippi planter-merchant to one of the President's friends in January 1904, "tell him that we are with him, that we are not blind, and 'know a good thing when we see it,' and believe in him and trust him."[26]

Apparently, black leadership was slow to realize that Roosevelt's affection was barely skin deep. They supported him solidly for the nomination in 1904 and in the election that followed. After the election, however, he seemed to care little about continuing the game and moved overtly in the pro-white direction. In the spring of 1905, shortly after his inauguration, he chose to make a speech dealing with race relations to the Iroquois Club of Chicago, significantly a Democratic organization. In drafting that speech he drew freely upon the counsel of Jacob McGavock Dickinson, a Nashville lawyer with impeccable Southern credentials. Dickinson (1851–1928) was the great grandson of Felix Grundy, one of the founding fathers of Tennessee. He was the scion of large slaveholders, educated in the best American and German universities, and in the 1890s had been a state supreme court justice and Cleveland's Assistant Attorney General. Dickinson had prospered as a lawyer for the giant Louisville and Nashville Railroad, and in 1907 he became the president of the American Bar Association. Politically, he was an anti-Bryan Democrat. Racially, he was a Conservative.[27]

Dickinson was well known to the President, their intimacy reaching back to a hunting trip in the wilderness around the Sunflower River in Mississippi. "A week of camp life is worth a year of intercourse amid the surroundings of our complicated civilization for learning a man's character and ideals," he wrote to Roosevelt. The President had put the mind of the Nashville lawyer at ease on the race question, perhaps as they hunkered down over the campfire late of an evening, much like characters out of a Faulkner hunt story. "I have never felt at liberty to repeat some of the things you said to me on the negro question," Dickinson declared, but he had assured his Southern colleagues that they would ultimately find in Roosevelt their true friend.[28] After they had worked together on the speech for a time, Roosevelt responded to Dickinson's statement. "You do not know how you please me in what you say of the effects of my attitude on the negro question," he wrote. "Really, so far as I have any theory in the matter at all, my theory is to get hold of southerners with your ideas and then back them up as heartily but as unobtrusively as possible."[29] Very soon this special alliance was cemented further by the appointment of J. C. McReynolds, a close friend of Dickinson's and also a Nashville lawyer and Vanderbilt University trustee, as Assistant Attorney General.

Shortly, Roosevelt was able to display conspicuously just where his sympathies lay. Near midnight on August 13, 1906, a dozen or so men moved through the village of Brownsville, Texas, firing high-powered rifles into the buildings. One person was wounded and one killed in the melee. Brownsville, on the Gulf near the Mexican border, was the site of Fort Brown. Recently the garrison of the fort had been relieved by a battalion of the all-black Twenty-fifth United States Infantry Regiment. The regiment had fought well in Cuba and in the Phillippines. It had just spent four tedious years in Nebraska. On the great plains, race as related to blacks was not highly significant. In Brownsville, however, the black soldiers faced not only segregation but a degree of racial hostility to which they were not accustomed. Signs of Radicalism were clearly present among the whites, and shortly the story of an alleged attempted rape hit the press:

INFAMOUS OUTRAGE

Negro Soldier Invaded Private Premises
Last Night and Attempted To Seize
A White Lady

The facts of the incident are not clear. The woman assaulted lived in the "tenderloin" district, but had a good reputation. At the worst, she had been seized by a black soldier at her back door and thrown to the ground. When she raised a cry, her assailant fled. At the best, a large black man passing by her fence put his hand on her head and said, "Hello pet," or some such words, and walked on. The aroused citizens made representations at the garrison, and that night the ten-minute raid occurred. The townspeople were certain that the raiders were soldiers from the garrison.[30]

The Inspector General of the Army was ordered to Brownsville to investigate. Shortly he found that a number of soldiers had slipped out of the barracks that evening and assaulted the town. Their identities could not be fixed because all of the men in the three companies professed not to know who was responsible. He recommended, therefore, that all 167 of the soldiers be dismissed from the service "without honor." This would surely punish those who sheltered the culprits by their silence as well as the rioters. Included were five men who had won the Congressional Medal of Honor and whose dismissal would mean the loss of their pensions. At this point, Booker T. Washington, employing his usual *entre-nous* tone, wrote personally and confidentially to the President suggesting that he had important information bearing on the case. He seemed to expect the President to give him an audience where he would educe the material that would allow Roosevelt to do justice to the black soldiers. Washington found not only his secrets scorned by the President, but himself rather rudely rejected. There would be no information passed under the table in this case. On the very day on which the President handed down his decision, November 5, 1906, he brought Washington up short. "You can not have any information to give me privately to which I could pay heed, my dear Mr. Washington," he replied with some asperity, "because the information on which I act is that which came out in the investigation itself."[31] Washington proved immune to either insult or rebuff; within the month he was attempting, still secretly, to influence the President's State of the Union message as it related to race riots in the South.

Roosevelt acted impulsively in the Brownsville affair. Yet he also acted consistently with his steady advice to the South on interracial violence. He had always said to black people that they must not harbor their criminals, which he and many others insisted that they did. And he had always said to the whites of the South that they must punish the lynchers. In Brownsville, the black troops who rioted were, in effect, lynchers who took the law into their own hands, Thus, in this case, both the harborers and the lynchers were punished. But it was peculiar in that both elements in this event were black, they were largely defenseless, and the incident revealed Roosevelt in the lily-white light that his politics then required. It was significant that Roosevelt ordered the dismissal on November 5, but the news was not released until the evening of Tuesday, November 6, 1906, election day. On that date, New York had elected a Republican governor, and the nation had returned a thoroughly Republican Congress, including Roosevelt's own son-in-law whose Ohio constituency included 3200 black voters.[32] With no intention of running for reelection in 1908, TR was now free to pursue the golden fleece that had so long eluded Republican leadership—a fully respectable white Republican party in the South. In the next few years, Republicanism in the South would go lily white with a rush.

While Roosevelt never totally lost his black following, the Brownsville matter largely alienated him from the great mass of Negro Americans. Politically, however, it cost him little, no more, in fact, than he seemed very willing to pay. He had chosen as his successor, William Howard Taft, his Secretary of War. He shortly announced that Brownsville was his own affair and not that of the genial, rotund Taft, as indeed it was not. Divorced from Brownsville and having the full power of presidential patronage at his command through Roosevelt, Taft was able to organize the black delegates for himself in the convention in 1908. In that meeting, he received 261 of the 279 voting Southern delegates, or roughly a third of the total votes in the convention.[33] Once elected, Taft largely ignored black Republicans and moved openly to convert upper-class, conservative Southern whites to the Republican party.

TAFT AND THE LILY-WHITE SOUTH

Between the two Reconstructions, probably no Republican President was more successful at the task of enlisting elite, educated, professional, and business-minded men in the South in the Republican cause than Willian Howard Taft. In various parts of the South, so-called Taft Clubs formed quite aside from pre-existing Republican organizations. With remarkable frequency those who supported Taft in such clubs or otherwise, either publicly or privately, were racially Conservative. In the presidential election in November 1908, the Republican vote in the South increased 122,000 over that of 1904. Most of the increase probably came from whites of the "better sort." In 1906, five Republican Congressmen were elected in the South; in 1908, nine were elected; and in 1910 an even dozen. Among these, John Motley Morehead of North Carolina represented a new kind of Southern Republican. Morehead was the very wealthy son of the pioneer railroad magnate in his state, and he was an enterprising businessman in his own right. In North Carolina, the new Republicanism was supported not only by old-line professional Republicans, but by such newcomers as the Dukes of the American Tobacco Company. In addition they gained recruits from among goldbugs such as Morehead and Daniel Augustus Tompkins (pre-eminent in textiles in the South), those disaffected by Bryanism in the Democratic party, and from among ex-Populists whose core of life was a hatred of the Democracy.[34]

Very soon, the new President gave substance to his sympathy with high-toned Southerners by appointing TR's friend Jacob McGavock Dickinson his Secretary of War. That eminent Mississippi-born Nashville lawyer was the perfect magnet to draw the kind of Southern support suited in every way to Taft's temperament and political needs. One of those so drawn was Thomas Nelson Page, the Virginia novelist. "I feel as if it were a Southerner who had been elected," confessed Page, ever the well-oiled weathervane of Southern Conservative sentiment, "and that means that I have been broadened." During the fall of 1909, Taft made a grand tour of the South from El Paso, Texas, to Alexandria, Virginia. He urged Dickinson to accompany him. "Your selection has given throughout the South a belief in the sincerity of my declared friendship for and interest in the welfare of that section. . . . ," he wrote. "I want to go to your home at Columbia, Mississippi, and I want to go through the South with you; and I want to say some things about you to the southern people."[35]

Taft's Southern strategy worked beautifully. Dickinson was inundated with letters of congratulation and significant elements of the press applauded.[36] Much of the applause was in the tone of a Birmingham gentleman who said that Taft "understands our conditions as no other man who has been in the White House since the War has understood them." The South, he thought, "ought to meet him fully half way."[37]

Up and down the line, Taft's patronage program emerged with increasing clarity. He appointed blacks to jobs in the West, North, and in Washington, D.C., but he stripped them of Southern places. In addition he relieved of their positions a number of Republican hacks and purely professional party men, men of no standing and little property. In marrying himself to such people as Dickinson, Taft identified himself with racial Conservativism. "I have studied the question and thought more about it than any other question and always with the deepest anxiety for the future of the South," Dickinson wrote to the President.[38] Dickinson himself helped to set the moderate racial tone of the new administration by securing the appointment of his fellow townsman James C. Napier as Register of the Treasury in Washington.[39] Napier was a well-to-do lawyer, long the leader of the black community in Nashville, and a man who had endeared himself to Conservatives of Dickinson's stamp in the mid-1880s when he had led blacks to join in a successful movement to reform the city government. The appointee whom Napier relieved was a professional Republican from Georgia, also black.

Taft swept through the South like some white tornado, uprooting black officeholders, and some white, and tossing them aside. In Virginia the last two Negroes to hold presidential appointments were displaced, and in North Carolina a leading Conservative Democrat who had recently led in drafting the disfranchising measure for the state was appointed to a federal judgeship while both lily-white and black Republicans went begging.[40] In South Carolina, where fourteen of the eighteen delegates in the 1908 convention had supported his nomination, Taft removed the last four blacks holding presidential appointments.[41] Black Georgians, who had suffered at Roosevelt's hands the loss of their last black member on the Republican National Committee, now lost their last major position in the federal service in the state when Taft fired Henry A. Rucker, the Collector of Internal Revenue. In Alabama, the President bypassed the referee system and Booker T. Washington as well to appoint to a federal judgeship a friend his son Horace had made while a student at Yale. In Mississippi, the black postmaster of Port Gibson was removed because, as Taft said, "the presence of a number of female schools there seems to increase the friction due to his remaining." In this instance, however, the judicious Taft gave the man an equally good position in Washington. In Louisiana, Walter Cohen had long headed one of the most effective of the black-and-tan factions. In January 1911 he too was dispatched, signalizing the rise of the lilies in the Pelican state. Finally, the referee in Texas, Cecil Lyon, a Rough Rider and a Roosevelt appointee, rapidly erased Negro influence in the 5000 federal posts in the state, removing the last of three important black officers in September 1909.[42]

Taft was not a man to play the shell game, and black leaders responded to his open assault with bitterness. Richard T. Greener, Harvard graduate, black intellectual of the Reconstruction era, lately TR's consul to Vladivostok, was refused even a hearing by President Taft. He looked back over what he saw to be forty years of Republican perfidy and found the climax in TR and Taft. TR, he decided, was a "montebank" who always had "his eye on the gallery" and "copy ready for the reporter." Taft was worse, for "the South owns him body and soul, and he accepts as truth, all its *dicta* about the race relations." Some blacks were moving toward open rebellion, and Greener was "looking to see what that Walters-Waldren-Trotter-Sinclair-Grimke, Dubois, et al., fierce, strenuous Independents were going to do at Atlantic City Aug 4."[43] In the crisis some black leaders were tending independent, and some were even beginning a flirtation with the Democracy. Others, including Booker T. Washington and the superb politician Robert W. Anderson of New York, began again to think fondly of TR. "The African Hunter will be the next President or the next occupant of the White House will be a democrat," threatened one rebel.[44]

In mid-1910 Taft trimmed his white sails slightly to catch a bit of extra wind for the November elections. He did so primarily by playing with offices that were outside the South and traditionally filled with black appointees. Dr. Crum was now made minister to Liberia, Whitefield McKinlay was named Collector of the Port of Georgetown (high on the Potomac above Washington and little used), P. B. S. Pinchback (once acting governor of Louisiana) was given a lucrative place with Anderson in the New York customs, William T. Vernon was made Supervisor of Indian and Negro Schools on the reservation in Oklahoma, and, in an exchange of no real consequence, John C. Dancy replaced Henry Lincoln Johnson as Register of Deeds in the District of Columbia.[45]

Taft's romance with the Conservative white South was renewed after the elections of 1910, and it flowered beautifully until the summer of 1911. Then, perhaps motivated in part by his determination to hold the Republican party fast against the Progressive usurpers, he opted to sacrifice some of his credits with Southern white Conservatives in favor of holding black support for the nomination and election. When he made manifest his decision, Southern whites who had followed his lead felt betrayed. Unwittingly Taft created a need in the South that Woodrow Wilson filled nearly perfectly. Wilson had always been there, waiting and not simply waiting at the same time.

Woodrow Wilson (1856–1924) was himself a personification of the interpenetration of North and South. Born in Staunton, Virginia, of two long lines of Presbyterian ministers, he had grown into adolescence in Reconstruction Columbia, South Carolina, lived for a time in Wilmington, North Carolina, attended Davidson College, practiced law briefly in Atlanta, and took his doctorate at Johns Hopkins. He was a professor in and then president of Princeton, and after 1911 the popular and progressive governor of New Jersey.

How the South came to transfer its saddle from Taft to Wilson can be neatly seen through the eyes of William Garrott Brown. Brown, too, was a Southerner who had invaded the North. The first wave of Southern collegiates had gotten as far as Baltimore and Johns Hopkins. Brown had been among the first of the second wave to push on to Harvard and to open a channel in which others would follow. They went North not to become Yankees, but to be better Southerners. They were already good, and they wanted to be the best. Their ambition was quietly great, and they were distinctly heard from after they left that New England Oxford. Brown finished Harvard College *summa cum laude* in 1891, took his master's degree in 1892, and remained on as a librarian. A gentleman, an Episcopalian, an attractive, perfectly mannered bachelor, he found favor in the highest circles. Prevented by deafness from pursuing a career in politics, he soon won success as a political and social commentator. In 1902 he published *The Lower South in American History,* a book that earned him national eminence as a Southern historian.[46] Soon after, Brown developed tuberculosis, and by 1908 he had retreated to Asheville, in the mountains of North Carolina, seeking relief.

In Asheville, Brown came to be good friends with Thomas Settle, a native white politician with a long Republican history. "I took him with me as my guest to attend several political conventions and committee meetings," Settle later wrote to Brown's biographer, "took him on the floor of the convention, seated him next to me with our delegation so that he could get the inside of the proceedings." Brown, the Harvard don, and Settle, one of the original spring bottom boys of Republican politics in North Carolina, "colaborated [sic] in political matters."[47] In 1908 Brown wrote much of the Republican platform for the Tarheel state, and in 1910 he did even more. "About everything in it is mine," he confessed to a friend.[48]

What moved Brown and others into the seeming apostasy of taking a Republican posture was actually a deep loyalty to the South—not merely to its racial establishment but to the whole thing of Southern culture. What Brown and others wanted was to break the solid South so that the South would again be a force in the nation. By bringing down the Democratic South, the solid South, they would build up another and a better one. By the fall of 1910, Brown's writing on Southern and national politics had attracted the attention of Charles Dyer Norton, a secretary to President Taft. The liaison was very soon effected. The key to success for both sides, Brown thought, was a fully respectable Southern Republicanism. That, in turn, depended upon throwing some of the rascals out and "the practical acquiescence of the Republicans therein." There were several positive steps Republicans could take to promote the process. One was to appeal, as the Democrats had not, to the "national sentiment" rising in the South. Another was to offer more encouragement to Republicanism outside of the mountainous areas of the South. Roosevelt had done that, Brown noted, "but the effect of it was largely marred by the Crum appointment, the Booker Washington dinner, and the Indianola incident." Taft "so far has made no such mistakes." He advised the President, however, to speak more to the emotions of the South: " . . .Southerners being an extraordinarily sentimental people, the oftener he strikes the higher note, the note of feeling, the better." Finally, Brown found no fault with the administration on the race question. He wanted Negroes mostly out of politics for the good of all, except that "a few good negroes" might be put, with the *consent* of their communities, into inconspicuous places *which would* not bring them objectionably in contact with whites."[49]

Norton brought Brown's talents to the attention of the President. Soon, the two men were discussing Brown's views favorably while the President planned a Charleston speech.[50] Shortly, Taft wrote personally to Brown letters full of praise and agreement. The President hoped that the vote would be restored to Negroes "after the division of the white vote at a time when they should become really eligible under proper qualifications to exercise the franchise, in such small numbers, however, as not to threaten control by the baser element of the community." Further, the President admitted that "in my inaugural address I attempted to foreshadow a policy of not making Southern appointments from negroes." He did it, he said, because offensive officers cannot perform their duties efficiently and because it was a disservice to blacks themselves.[51]

The honeymoon was not to last. Indeed, one lover proved very demanding. Late in May 1911, Brown asked Taft to make a statement on Southern policy in which he would denounce the use of federal offices for political purposes. He enlisted Henry Cabot Lodge and an old Harvard friend, A. Piatt Andrew, then Assistant Secretary of the Treasuty, to help him bring the President around.[52] Even at the moment when Brown was pressing Taft thusly, the President was organizing to do the opposite. Charles D. Hilles was now his right-hand man for Southern affairs. Hilles was working with Booker Washington and the black politicoes to secure the nomination for Taft. Of course, that meant black appointments. Hilles tried to hold Brown delicately at arm's length, assuring him that the President was studying his proposal. But he would not act impulsively "for it contemplates a revolution in a venerable system which operates in fourteen or fifteen States."[53]

The impatient lover was not long held at bay. In October, Brown addressed himself to Woodrow Wilson, then governor of New Jersey, confessing that he had been wanting to write to him for more than a year and had been secretly helping even longer: "I believe I now speak for thousands of sincere men to whom your rise and your party renascence has seemed to offer their first chance in many years—their first opportunity to take the aggressive for their political faith and ideals."[54] As one might expect, the new suitor for Southern affections needed a little grooming to qualify, and Brown was not long in bringing the proper tonsorial artist to the fore. He urged Piatt Andrew, his friend in the Treasury, to join Nelson W. Aldrich, the great protectionist Senator from Rhode Island, in talking to Wilson on finance "because his ignorant out-givings on this subject are making it hard for me to support him."[55] By mid-December, Andrew had progressed far in educating the Democrats on the money question, including among his students Brown's old friend from Alabama, Congressman Oscar Underwood. The availability of such excellent students, he acknowledged, was totally due to Brown.

By now Brown was an ardent Wilsonian. When "Colonel" George Harvey, prime mover both for *Harper's Weekly* and Wilson's presidency, grew anxious about Brown's loyalty to one so ignorant in finance, Brown assured him that a personal letter from Wilson "has simply made me his'n, and if the Colonel gets discouraged he'll find me on his back if I have to hire the *Outlook* to do it with!"[56] Concerning what was a rather ordinary letter, one that stood pale beside the flattery the Republican President customarily lavished upon him, Brown said to his friend Andrew, "You never saw a franker, manlier letter."[57] Beauty is often in the eye of the beholder, but the beholder often performs no less beautifully for all of that. Brown launched into a great effort to "expose" the sordid machine system of the Republicans in the South.[58] He also was willing to advise Wilson's campaign manager on just who in the South might head their efforts in the various states.[59]

Wilson had to be spruced up for the South, but Brown was not at all unwilling to spruce up the South a bit for Wilson when needed. Particularly he undertook to enlighten Virginia on the initiative, referendum, and recall, those popular democratic devices that had grown up in the West and were now having some appeal in the East. These were devices that Wilson himself seemed to like. When Brown's friend J. Stewart Bassett, editor of the Richmond *News Leader,* indicated that the people of Virginia were very suspicious of the progressive governor because of his pursuit of such "false gods," Brown hastened to explain "how deeply students of our government, state & national, have been impressed with the failure of the representative feature of our government." Thus, "the most serious & candid minds have, therefore, been long pondering how to remedy this weakness, how to make our legislatures' legislation truly representative, Wilson's among them." He felt from an after-dinner conversation at Colonel House's that Wilson would not want such provisions everywhere, he assured, but only as a safeguard in special places to be used, as Wilson said, as a "gun behind the door." "Remember, too, that yours is a *very* conservative community—hardly second to S. Carolina, & comparatively exempt from the worst abuses of the representative principle, your effective electorate being relatively very English & decidedly not aggressively progressive. That your people don't want or don't pressingly need the new schemes proves nothing as to the great number of states."[60] Virginia capitulated, and went for their native son as the proper moderate between radical socialism on the one side and brittle conservatism on the other.[61]

All during the campaign Brown, by then bedridden, continued the good fight for Wilson, writing often and effectively for *Harper's Weekly.* Immediately after the victory he welcomed the idea that "the South is going to have great power in our common government." That fact would result in national good. "Southerners," he wrote, "because they *are* Southerners, ought now to feel an especial call and consecration to the service and guardianship of the whole nation."[62]

THE DEMISE OF BLACK REPUBLICANISM IN THE SOUTH

By the middle of 1911, Roosevelt had returned from Africa, denounced Taft for deserting "my policies," and taken leadership in the progressive wing of the party. Soon a bitter contest for the nomination in 1912 was underway. Taft, who had continued the reduction of black Republicanism in the South after the elections of 1910, now began a subtle shift to pick up black delegates in the coming convention. He appointed a personal secretary, Charles D. Hilles, who worked with Booker T. Washington to woo Southern delegates. He made it known that he favored higher education for Negro leaders and stood against lynching. In several states the black and tans were encouraged yet again, though lily-whites were by no means alienated. Overall, the black presence in the federal service had been so thoroughly reduced that a little restoration was hardly significant. [63]

On the other side, Roosevelt again discovered that his racial views coincided with his political ambitions. He made little effort to enlist black delegates, made no special play for black votes, and, finally, actually excluded blacks from formal participation in the "Bull Moose Party" he formed after walking out of the Republican national convention. Still some blacks persisted in their loyalty to the Rough Rider. "Lincoln made a great mistake when he freed the mass of niggers," wrote Pinchback from New York in the summer of 1912. "Quite a number of them up this way are still shouting for Roosevelt. *They smell boodle.*"[64]

Ultimately, conventional political wisdon prevailed among black Republican leaders, and they went with the man currently on top, President Taft. In the convention, 223 Southern delegates voted to swell the Taft majority to 561 as against 107 total for Roosevelt. Of the 62 Negro delegates in the convention, 54 voted for Taft. Almost immediately after the convention, Taft reversed his posture toward color in the South still again, frowning upon blacks while he sometimes smiled at the lilies and always favored Conservative native whites. In October 1912 he struck a hard blow at both black and white Republican politicoes in the South by putting fourth-class postmasters (about 16,000 of them in the nation) under civil service. Probably no single move could have more damaged patronage-consuming Republican politics in the South.[65]

Increasingly disillusioned with the Republican party, stymied by a split in party leadership in which the pot seemed as white as the kettle, a significant splinter of black leadership moved openly to support Democrat Woodrow Wilson for the presidency. The threat to the Republican party was not, potentially, an idle one. There were important minorities of black voters in such vital electoral states as New York and Illinois. Further, as indicated previously, black votes in the upper South were still considerable. In 1915, Democratic Senator Thomas P. Gore of Oklahoma quantified their significance rather precisely. "Delaware had a colored vote of 9000 and the Democracy generally loses it by 1000," he indicated. "Maryland has a colored vote of 64,000 and we carried it the other day by less than 4,000. Kentucky has a colored vote of more than 75,000 and we carried it by about 300. Tennesee has a colored vote of 119,000 and we lost it in 1910 and 1912."[66] The movement toward Wilson was led by Bishop Alexander M. Walters of the African Methodist Episcopal Church Zion. Bishop Walters felt he had assurances of fair treatment for black people from the Democratic candidate. The attraction was great, and some who had their fingers on the black pulse sensed life and strength. "I very much fear that a large number of Negroes will vote for Wilson, which I think exceedingly wrong on their part," observed Whitefield McKinlay.[67] Ultimately Walters proved to be a sort of political Moses who began to lead his people out of Republican bondage toward the promised land of the Democratic party where, in the twentieth century, they would find themselves more comfortably settled.

Apparently, a considerable number of blacks voted for the victorious Wilson, and the Republican party moved to restructure its convention system. In 1916 and thereafter representation in conventions depended mostly upon the vote delivered in the previous national election. For several decades Southern delegations, white or black, would have little or no importance in Republican conventions. For a few months in the election of 1928, Republicanism in the South became important, but the issue was not race nearly so much as it was the "wetness" and the Catholicism of the Democratic candidate, Alfred E. Smith of New York. Thereafter, a Republican revival in the South would have to await a second Reconstruction, a move most often supported at the national level, ironically, by Democrats and most often resisted by Republicans. The new Republicanism in the South would be conservative not liberal, officered initially by professional politicians, not men of means, and persistently more racist than not.

CHAPTER XII

Radical Swan Song: Radicalism and Conservatism in Washington under Woodrow Wilson

The Wilson administration brought the South to power in Washington; it also brought Southern solutions to the race problem to the nation's capital. The story of race relations in Washington during Wilson's two administrations was a replay on a small scale of the broad history of race relations in the South during the preceding generation. From Wilson's inauguration in 1913 into 1915, Southern Conservatives and Radicals in the government struggled with each other over race at the same time that they wrestled with others over the great social issues of tariffs, currency, and the regulation of national industries. Northern white liberals also entered the racial fray, as did black militants and accommodationists. Throughout the play there was much misunderstanding by each element of the motives and goals, the points of view of other elements, and of the real situation. Overall, the pattern was a nearly perfect repeat of a whole generation of Southern interracial history. Initially a vigorous Radicalism attacked a rather complacent Conservatism; Conservatism withdrew until circumstances allowed its resurgence with strength; the counterattack regained some ground, but for the most part it fixed and legitimated the physical segregation that Radicals had achieved. Whatever was was right. As in the South, thereafter Conservatism drifted—with neither anchor nor direction, and in effect rudderless.

Racial discrimination in the federal service and in the government offices in Washington was not, of course, new with Wilson's administration. It had existed in Reconstruction, and, with the appointment in the Harrison administration of thousands of blacks to jobs in the civil service, the occasions in which discrimination could occur increased vastly. Even so, observers generally agreed that the whip of prejudice cracked more sharply after Theodore Roosevelt's election to the presidency in 1904, and that his successor Taft allowed abuses, including segregation, to continue.[1]

THE WILSONIAN RACIAL SOLUTION

Wilson came to Washington with commitments to blacks already outstanding against him. During the campaign in 1912 when he knew he needed every vote he could get, a delegation of Negro leaders came to him led by Bishop Alexander Walters of the African Methodist Church. In return for their support, Wilson assured them that his regime would be no less kind than the Cleveland administrations. Two years later, accused by an irate Mississippi Senator of having been too generous to blacks in appointments, Wilson explained that "while I was a candidate for the Presidency I had an interview with some very straight-forward and honorable negroes whom I knew, to whom I felt constrained to say that I should feel myself morally bound to see to it that they were not put to any greater political disadvantage than they had suffered under previous administrations. This, I am sure, they interpreted as a promise that I would not willingly take away from them the minor offices they had so long occupied in the District. I see no escape from this promise on this inference, and I hope with all my heart that my course will be understood and supported at the Capital."[2] The sort of assurance that Walters won for the Negro in politics, Oswald Garrison Villard—the grandson of the abolitionist, the chairman of the board of the NAACP, and an early friend of Wilson's presidency—apparently won for the interests of the race at large in the summer of 1912.[3]

After the election Negro Democrats were not laggard in pressing for places in the new administration. A man who advertised himself as "the oldest Negro Democrat in the country" wrote from Mississippi to stake his claim.[4] A black friend of John Sharp Williams, the senior Senator from Mississippi, tried to relieve that classic Southern gentleman of criticism from black Democrats. P. S. Golden, the "Grand High Priest of Royal Arch Freemasonary State of Mississippi," found that a lot of the "Democratic brethren" of Granada were "back biting" the Senator and "trying to array the Negroes, dogs, cats and snakes all against" him. Central among the charges was that the newly elected junior Senator, James K. Vardaman, "has just got to Washington only a few days ago, and have [*sic*] secured a position for a white man and a Negro too," whereas "John Sharp Williams, has never done such a thing; and never wilt [*sic*]." While denying that he was looking for a job, Golden nevertheless managed to convey the idea that he was willing to take an appointment and thus help relieve Williams of at least half of his embarrassment.[5]

Actually, little urging was needed to get the Wilsonians moving in the matter of removing black Republicans. In all, there were tens of thousands of removals and new appointments to be made, but the new regime was moving zealously enough on all fronts. Fred R. Moore, Taft's minister to Liberia, had actually switched his newspaper, the New York *Age,* to support Wilson, Bishop Walters, and the Democratic campaign, but a bit too late to escape the axe.[6] Inevitably, incumbents dreamed of being retained. Whitefield McKinlay, collector of customs at Georgetown, pinned his hope upon the probability that he was the last Negro collector in the country and, hence, would be retained as a token. After three feverish months, he too was shaken from the patronage tree like some over-ripe plum by a curt note from the Secretary of the Treasury, William Gibbs McAdoo, asking for his resignation.[7]

One of the most prized appointments traditionally awarded to blacks was that of the Register of the Treasury, from which J. C. Napier of Nashville was being relieved. Upon the request of the famous blind Senator from Oklahoma, Thomas P. Gore, the administration sent the name of Adam E. Patterson to the Senate for confirmation for the position. Patterson was black and an "Okie" from Muskogee. Ironically, Gore had called upon McAdoo soon after the inauguration to urge that an Indian rather than a black man get the post. It happened that the staff of the Registry included some 150 white women, many of them relatively young. Several months later, when Gore was under heavy fire at home for having endorsed a black boss over white girls, he secured from the Secretary a statement as to what happened. "The facts are," McAdoo asserted, "that you first called on me and sought the appointment of an Indian as Register of the Treasury. I explained to you that the President was inclined to the view that a Negro should be appointed to this office, since a Negro had occupied it for the past sixteen years, and the Negroes had come to regard the appointment to this position as being a distinct recognition of their race. I said that I concurred in this view, and believed that it was only just and fair that a Democratic Negro should be appointed; you said you would like to have Patterson considered for the place. . . ." After Gore left, McAdoo looked up Patterson's record, found it good, and he and the President agreed to send the name to the Senate.[8] According to one well-informed black journalist, Bishop Walters, "leaving no stone unturned to see that his brethren share in the loave[s] and fishes that the democracy is about to distribute," approved of Patterson's appointment on the condition that Gore would support the confirmation of the candidates of the Walters faction.[9]

In the Patterson nomination, the administration must have felt that it had gone far toward meeting its commitment to black Democrats. Shortly, that nomination was linked with a new and revolutionary concept of race relations in the federal service. The President and his Cabinet seemed to be in concert on the concept, but it appeared to fall most often to McAdoo to justify it. It would not be inappropriate to call it the McAdoo idea. The concept, to those who pursued it, was beautifully simple: in order to avoid friction between the races in the government service, certain divisions and sections would be set aside that would be all black, from the top to the bottom, from chiefs to clerks to stenographers, messengers, and laborers. Not only would this allay friction between black and white workers and avoid the disturbing prospect of black bosses over white workers, it would set aside a number of relatively high positions to which Negroes might aspire. In short, it allowed for separate and, almost, equal opportunity for black people in the federal service. A fine place to start was in the Registry, already heavily black, where the Negro Nashvillian J. C. Napier then sat as chief, and where Adam E. Patterson was soon expected to command. McAdoo explained the concept to Oswald Garrison Villard in a letter in October 1913. He and the President had decided upon the appointment of Patterson, he said, with the plan of making the Registry all black. This "would give the negroes an opportunity of national dimensions, to prove their fitness to run, unaided by whites, an important bureau of the department."[10]

Racial Conservatives understood the McAdoo idea immediately and rushed to its defense. It was, they maintained, non-discriminatory and fair on all sides. A native Mississippian reacted against criticism of the plan from Villard's *Independent* to ask John Sharp Williams if McAdoo had not acted for the greater comfort of the whites "and for the ultimate advantage of the Negroes who were in danger of being crowded out of the government service all together through direct competition with the whites."[11] "Of course, segregation is not discrimination," the senior Mississippi Senator replied, striking a note that Southern whites would sound for two generations. "Not only does the voice of common sense say that much, but the voice of the Supreme Court of the United States has said it." Negroes, he said, have a weakness for pushing themselves in upon whites and regarding association with those of their own kind with abhorrence. If Negroes are not inferior, he declared in response to the neo-abolitionists of the *Independent,* then segregation is not discrimination. "There are no inalienable human rights nor is there any principle of Democracy involved in the question of having separate rooms and separate desks and separate water closets for the two races."[12] McAdoo himself simply could not understand that his plan was discriminatory. In a letter to Villard, he declared that there was no "segregation issue."[13]

James Calvin Hemphill was a free-lance journalist in Washington who enjoyed a close relationship with the Wilson administration. In the late 1890s he had been editor of the Charleston *News and Courier.* In that capacity he wrote an often quoted essay in which he attempted to oppose the segregation of the races on the railroads by reducing the idea of strict segregation to an absurdity, saying that next it would be Jim Crow jury boxes, docks, and Bibles, until they might as well be done with it at one stroke by establishing two or three Jim Crow counties in the state.[14] Now, however, Hemphill found McAdoo's program of segregation wholly admirable. This was an experiment, he opined, that was well worth making, and a bureau that was already 40 percent black offered excellent material with which to begin.[15]

RADICAL SEGREGATION IN THE WILSON ADMINISTRATION

Woodrow Wilson and James Gibbs McAdoo were racial Conservatives, and they sought segregation in the Conservative spirit. There was Radicalism in the Cabinet, however, and in other high places in the administration. The seeming license that Wilson gave to segregation and the defense that McAdoo offered provided a cover under which all kinds of segregation proceeded—including that which was motivated by Radicalism. Probably most segregation was carried out with the idea that it was legitimate administration policy; probably some of it was a deliberate stretching of policy to cover an extravagant Radicalism. What made it possible for racial extremists to operate within the Wilson administration was that the administration as a whole ultimately did not regard race as a vital matter. Reform—the tariff, money, and taming the economy—was the all-important issue. Race relations was something they handled with the little finger of the left hand—and they preferred to do it quickly, almost summarily. The administration actually did not know what was happening in segregation in the federal service in the summer and fall of 1913. It remained for an outside and largely hostile group, the National Association for the Advancement of Colored People, to find out.

The leadership of the NAACP at this time was not primarily black but white, composed mostly of the descendants of the abolitionist crusade. The organization stood firmly against lynching, disfranchisment, and segregation. The chairman of the board of directors was Oswald Garrison Villard, the grandson of the most famous of the liberators. The officer who had immediate charge of the investigation of segregation in the federal service was a white person, May Childs Nerney, the secretary of the Association. Nerney made a prolonged visit to Washington during the summer of 1913. She talked to a large number of black employees, including members of the NAACP, and to black leadership in the District. When she returned to New York, she received a steady stream of reports from black civil servants, especially from the Treasury and Post Office Departments. In the fall of 1913 probably no one in America was better informed on the subject than she.

One of the first things that the NAACP learned was that the separation of the races in the federal service, was, as one informant neatly worded it, not "a flower of recent origin." He told Villard that "the Republicans are by no means blameless in this matter for during and since the day of the late lamented McKinley, each president has seemed to lean more and more towards the policy of condoning the political offenses of that section of our Country where our race has next to no political recognition. Mr. Taft's declaration that he would not appoint colored men to positions in the Sections that would feel offense at such action has borne abundant fruit in the temper of Departmental Washington towards colored employees and the present administration is merely seconding the motion."[16] What was new, the NAACP concluded, was that separation was now more sweeping, and that it was executed upon official orders.[17]

Particularly, the NAACP found that officials in the Treasury and the Post Office Departments pursued new forms of segregation most vigorously. These were the very departments in which by far the greater number of Negroes in the government served. Much of the action was carried through by officers below the Cabinet level. In the Treasury, for instance, an NAACP informant actually obtained a copy of the order that separated the lavatories in that Department. It was issued to the chief clerk on July 12, not by McAdoo but by the Assistant Secretary of the Treasury, John Skelton Williams, acting in the absence of Secretary McAdoo.[18]

John Skelton Williams was yet another Southerner recently come to the nation's capital. He had been born in Richmond in 1865, the scion of a leading Richmond banking family. As a young man he had organized his own bank and then, before 1899, put together the Seaboard Airline Railway System in the face of bitter opposition from the powerful Morgan interests.[19] Where Williams stood on the scale of racial ideology is not perfectly clear. However, in September it was reported that he fired the assistant chief of a division because he was black. When the man's superior protested that he was the most efficient employee in the office, Williams replied "that it mattered not about his efficiency, the department would not countenance a colored man being over white employees."[20]

Rather clearly, McAdoo had envisioned a pattern of separate and equal facilities in his department. In the execution of the plan, however, something slipped. It was almost as if prejudice were licensed to kill, and latent viciousness rushed to the fore. By no means were all subordinate officials Radical, but some were, and they undertook to execute their assignment with a vengeance.

Segregation in the Treasury Department had wide-reaching effects in spreading segregation in the federal service throughout the nation because the department, through the Office of the Architect, was charged with responsibility for constructing and maintaining federal office buildings in major cities everywhere. These buildings were, of course, local headquarters for many departments and, often, of the United States courts as well. This administrative situation, apparently, gave a wide application to the Williams lavatory order. In mid-September it was reported that "instructions were given to the Architect's office, which is under the Treasury Department, to provide separate toilet rooms in every federal building south of the Mason & Dixon line." With this order, the observer noted, 5,000 Negroes in Washington and perhaps 15,000 elsewhere would feel the thrust of the segregation movement. The damage would not be limited to the South, warned the informant. "With the order to provide for separate toilets in every federal building south of the Mason &

Dixon line a matter of record, it will be but a short time until that order covers federal buildings in the North where colored employees are present to any considerable extent.[21]

In some areas of the Treasury Department, there were signs that the McAdoo idea was implemented in a spirit more in keeping with that of its authors. Nerney thought that "colored clerks" (that is, those who were relatively high in the laboring structure) had been "assembled in the Registry Division" where J. C. Napier had sat as head and Adam E. Patterson had been nominated to sit.[22] In the office of the Auditor of the Post Office, a branch of the Treasury housed in the headquarters building of the Post Office Department, Negro women were taken from the main workroom and transferred to a small anteroom. Negro men in the office were transferred to two smaller rooms, where they worked alone "on the machines." Possibly the men were engaged in some special task not shared by other workers in the office. A portion of that information was transmitted to the NAACP by Moses Walker "who is a clerk in that office and who had the courage to face John Skelton Williams and denounce segregation." Walker was then trying to get a transfer to Chicago.[23]

In the Post Office Department much the same pattern developed as in the Treasury, but with significant variations. There seemed to be more of the Radical spirit in the Post Office Department, and some of it might have sprung from the personal predilections of the new Postmaster General, Albert Sydney Burleson. A Texan, Burleson was a grandson of one of the officers who commanded Houston's center at the battle of San Jacinto and he traced his ancestry back to a signer of *Magna Carta*. For many years he had been a "cotton" Congressman, representing the district of which Austin was the center. In Wilson's Cabinet he was a key man in the distribution of patronage. He was superbly "tough-minded," but famously fair. He believed that society operated by natural laws, and he had faith especially in the law of supply and demand. Upon that basis he ran the Post Office. During the eight years of his administration, he rationalized the transportation of the mails and saved, by his own estimate, some $130,000,000 for the service.[24]

When Burleson came to the Post Office, only seven Negro clerks were among the more than one thousand persons who held what might be called the more responsible positions in the Department's headquarters in Washington. Three of these were in the Dead Letter Office, three in the Bureau of Supplies, and one served in the office of the Chief Post Office Inspector. On the morning of May 31, 1913, when these seven people returned from the Decoration Day holiday, they found that the three men in Supplies had been transferred, symbolically enough, to the Dead Letter Office. In that office a row of lockers "fully ten feet high" was arranged so as to divide the room. The six Negro clerks were established on one side and the white clerks on the other.[25]

One could hardly imagine a more cruel arrangement of Negro clerks than this. "Visitors in Washington go sightseeing in the Post Office Department, and always visit the Dead Letter Office," explained one of the NAACP informants. "I am told by the clerk in the Dead Letter Office that the segregated colored clerks are pointed out to visitors, who often look at them sneeringly and derisively."[26] The seventh clerk, in the Chief Inspector's office, was not moved, but screens were placed around his desk so as to separate him from other employees.[27] By mid-October, orders were issued to transfer sixty clerks from the Department offices to the City Post Office in Washington, six Negro clerks being among those so ordered.[28] The single black clerk remaining among the one thousand white clerks in the headquarters building was probably the man at the desk behind the screens.

Observers agreed that segregation was pressed concertedly only in the Treasury and Post Office Departments, even though various elements of separation prevailed in other departments. "Up to date," reported one NAACP informant on September 6, "Secretary McAdoo and the Postmaster General appear to be the only cabinet officers who have by official "ukase' made the federal government a partner with the peculiar institutions which exist farther South."[29] In other departments there was sometimes an increase in segregation, sometimes no change at all. For instance, one watchful Washingtonian reported that there was "no change" in the Library of Congress and in the Land Office, while in the Census Bureau "conditions are as they were under the Taft administration."[30] One division chief in an unidentified department, Dr. John Keenan, called his Negro employees together to vote on the segregation proposition. Among his subordinates was a Negro who bore the title Professor, suggesting that at least some of these employees held relatively important positions. The vote was unanimously against segregation, and Dr. Keenan declared: "It shall not be while I am your chief."[31] Now and again, white colleagues sympathized with their fellow workers. "I have noticed no change of attitude on the part of the white clerks in this office toward the colored employees," reported a black gentleman who had been a lieutenant in the volunteer army during the Spanish-American War. "They are quite as friendly as formerly and several have declared the lavatory matter infamous. Whether this spirit of friendliness is typical I cannot say, but have heard that it is."[32]

THE BLACK REACTION:
THE NAACP IN THE NATION'S CAPITAL

The National Association for the Advancement of Colored People reacted with amazing swiftness and impressive vigor against the segregation movement that marked the accession of the Wilson administration. As early as May 6, Villard, apparently understanding that the separation envisioned by the railway mail clerks applied to the mail service at large, wrote a letter of protest to Burleson. "We understand," he asserted, "that an effort is being made on the part of white employees in the United States Mail Service to segregate and ultimately to eliminate colored postal employees regardless of their ability or length of service. We feel confident that so undemocratic a movement cannot meet with your approval."[33]

Curiously enough, officials at NAACP headquarters in New York thought that the segregation movement in Washington was the direct result of a recent Supreme Court decision that ruled against a Negro woman who did not buy a first-class ticket on a passenger steamer from Norfolk to Boston, and who was, by company policy, forced to take second-class accommodations occupied exclusively by blacks. Previously the courts had annulled the Civil Rights Act of 1875 as applied to states, but had not done so on the high seas or in the District of Columbia. Consequently, discrimination in public accommodations in these two places, undeniably under federal jurisdiction, had been actually illegal, even though so far as is known, no blacks had ever been able to effect action under the law. Now officials of the NAACP feared that segregation was proceeding in those areas where there was no longer a legal barrier against it.[34]

In mid-August the NAACP sent its formal protest to Wilson. In that letter the Association raised the image of the federal government as a bastion of racial justice. "Never before has the Federal Government discriminated against its civilian employees on the ground of color," it declared. "Every such act heretofore has been that of an individual State. The very presence of the Capitol and of the Federal flag has drawn colored people to the District of Columbia in the belief that living there under the shadow of the National Government itself they were safe from the persecution and discrimination which follow them elsewhere because of their dark skins." With prophetic accuracy it predicted the future of race relations under segregation: "It has set the colored apart as if mere contact with them were contamination. The efficiency of their labor, the principles of scientific management are disregarded, the possibilities of promotion if not now will soon be severely limited. To them is held out only the prospect of mere subordinate routine service without the stimulus of advancement to high office by merit. . . . Behind screens and closed doors they now sit apart as though pariahs. Men and women alike have the badge of inferiority pressed upon them by Government decree. How long will it be before the hateful epithets of nigger and Jim Crow are openly applied to these sections?" Interestingly, the letter closed with an appeal derived from classic Conservative Southern tradition and exhibited an appreciation of the good that Wilson and McAdoo were attempting to achieve: "They ask therefore that you, born of a great section which prides itself upon its chivalry towards the humble and the weak, prevent a gross injustice which is an injustice none the less because it was actuated in some quarters by a genuine desire to aid those now discriminated against."[35]

The organized interest of the NAACP was a warning to the administration that its actions were being monitored. Nerney had three interviews with Secretary McAdoo in late summer.[36] As she indicated to a fellow worker, "the very fact that you and I are hounding the people in Washington for exact data may help our cause more than we know."[37] In October Villard himself journeyed to the capital to represent the case against segregation in a formal interview with the President. When the "Nerney Report" on segregation was issued in November, the NAACP had every reason to believe that they would receive a favorable response.[38]

The NAACP knew that it had friends who would exert themselves in the cause, some of them powerfully. For example, Belle Case La Follette, the daughter of the progressive Wisconsin Senator, turned the pages of her influential Washington journal, *La Follette's Weekly,* to a close and sympathetic coverage of the battle against segregation.[39] And a protest against segregation in the federal service from George Foster Peabody must have been most impressive to the administration. Peabody was a native Georgian, a millionaire philanthropist who resided in the North, a fund-raiser for the Democratic party, and a man with considerable influence with other leading Southerners resident in the North. Inviting his good friend and fellow clubman William G. McAdoo to vacation with him, he took the opportunity to urge the Secretary of Treasury to retain a very efficient black Republican in office. He then let fly some cleverly directed arrows. He knew "of very serious depression of mind on the part of most valuable supporters of President Wilson" because of "the segregation order" and another surrender to Southern Senatorial pressure. "I have, as you know, been through this Negro situation South and North for over thirty years and I really think I understand it. I think nothing is more injurious to the South and its future than to have them successful in their efforts to proscribe the Negro in this fashion. The extreme position taken by Hepborn, Vardaman, Blease and others, has of course its value in causing sensible southerners to stop and think, but the success of such an effort as this segregation policy has an extremely bad effect upon the coming generation and may turn out in connection with the conditions of 1916 or 1920 to be a deciding matter in the Presidential vote. It is not right, which is of course its worst feature."[40]

The NAACP also had help from other quarters. Social worker Florence Kelley unlimbered her guns to let shots fly at Congressman Willian Kent of California, who had recently spoken—to the delight of Ben Tillman—against the invasion of his state by the "yellow race." When Kent admitted to Kelley that he did not know what to do about the race question, the daughter of the pig-iron tariff champion in Congress replied: "I think the complete solution of the Negro problem is to be found in the literal, universal application of the Golden Rule, in every relation, on every occasion."[41]

Not the least among the allies of the NAACP was the liberal Northern press. Rolfe Cobleigh, associate editor of *The Congregationalist and Christian World,* thought that Wilson's performance in his interview with Villard "revealed poor judgment with reference to the beginning of the segregation movement and moral cowardice with reference to the present situation."[42] Shortly a very strong indictment of segregation in the federal service as pursued by the Wilson administration appeared in *The Congregationalist,* ending with urging its readers to "Protest against the wrong; demand justice; keep on demanding it until we win." The article was copied by the *Boston Transcript,* and from an issue of the *Boston Transcript* it was clipped and inserted, among a great mass of clippings on proposals for currency legislation, in a scrapbook that, apparently, officials caused to kept in the Treasury Department.[43]

The NAACP found that it gained strength by engaging in the segregation contest in Washington as if exercising the muscle made it stronger. A decade later one of the Washington informants admonished an official of the Association that "you should know that the NAACP first made itself a power in this community by the great mass meetings which it held opposing segregation."[44] The struggle encouraged the Association to recruit elsewhere in the North. In the heat of the crisis in 1913, Villard urged a Cleveland Negro eager to protest to join with other like-minded Negroes, some of whom he named, and form a local chapter of the NAACP. Villard was also alert to the possibility of using the threat posed by the segregationists to bring black postal workers into the organization en masse. To an active leader among the workers in Cincinnati he pointed out that he had been able to enroll 650 mail men in a large western city and urged him to enlist his fellows in his own city.[45]

The answer of the administration to the prodding of the NAACP was the usual dilatory promise to investigate and consider the matter. Finally frustration blunted the attack. By December, Nerney was upset by the ineffectiveness of the Association. Particularly, she was depressed by the impression that Villard thought that there was nothing more that the organization could do to intensify its campaign. Almost in desperation, it seems, she applied to Joel Spingarn, one of the founders of the Association, to press the issue.[46] The response came in a telegram to the President and the Secretary of the Treasury from the NAACP and signed by Moorfield Storey (the president of the Association), Villard, and Spingarn urging the end of segregation of "colored employees in Federal Departments at Washington."[47] In truth, there was very little more that the Association could do. It would soon appear that Wilson was not then very willing to fulfill his promise to black leadership, that he was stopped for a time by what he considered more vital matters. When those matters were cleared away, he would move vigorously.

THE BLACK RESPONSE IN THE NATION AT LARGE

Beyond the efforts of the NAACP, the local response to segregation in the federal service was disorganized, scattering, and often underground in its nature. "In a subterranean way I have been giving the widest possible publicity to the reactionary policies of Messrs. Burleson and McAdoo and I am delighted with results up to date," one of the most astute of the Washington informants of the NAACP reported in the summer of 1913.[48] Senator James K. Vardaman, one of the most extreme advocates of segregation in the capital, received anonymously a clipping that he presumed had been cut from a Negro newspaper in Washington. In the article it was reported that a white employee asked an elderly Negro worker what he would say to segregation in his office. "I just wouldn't say nothing. I'd just leave it to God," he replied. Then he alluded to the fact that Ben Tillman had suffered a stroke that seriously impaired his speech: "Senator Tillman went up and down the country abusing my people, and when God got tired hearing him abuse us he paralyzed him so he couldn't talk plain. And God's got vengeance He'll wreak out on Vardaman, Hoke Smith and the rest 'fore this year is out, I reckon." Written in at the head of the clipping was the warning: "Vardaman a terrible fate awaits you. Remember Tillman['s] affliction."[49] Within five years Tillman did, indeed, have another stroke and die. Vardaman lost his Senate seat in 1916. In 1922 he ran for the seat vacated by John Sharp Williams. He was running well when he began to miss scheduled appearances. When he finally appeared at one meeting, he spoke so weakly that no one could hear him. After about twenty minutes he stopped suddenly and sat down. Mentally ill, he never made another official public appearance, and in 1930 he died.[50]

Negroes in the civil service in Washington were in delicate circumstances, and one can imagine that they were careful in their relations with other employees and their chiefs. Probably most felt themselves in the same position as Henry E. Baker, a native of Mississippi, who confessed to Villard that "we who are in the Departments making our daily bread through our service there, and working at present in an undeniably unfriendly environment there, cannot, in my opinion, put ourselves on the firing line in this fight, if we wish to keep our positions."[51]

Negroes outside of the civil service and in the North were more outspoken in their critique of Wilsonian segregation. That militancy seemed to have something to do with the distance from Washington and the South and the security that blacks felt in their home territory. On January 6, 1914, there was a meeting in Boston on the occasion of Charles Sumner's birthday. At that meeting the Reverend I. N. Ross urged fellow blacks to stop buying musical instruments and sending their children to dancing schools and start buying guns and giving their children a military education. "Prepare for war in times of peace is the policy of the nation," he shouted. "It should be your policy if you wish to break from the oppression, from the fetters of this era of new slavery." From the audience came applause, a waving of handkerchiefs, and cries of "We are with you!" "That's right!" and "Go on!" In the meeting was Oswald Garrison Villard who "vigorously dissented" and declared that Tillman, Vardaman, and Hoke Smith misrepresented the South. The Reverend Mr. Ross, undaunted, repeated his remarks and was again applauded.[52]

Scattered evidences suggest that Negro employees in the federal service outside of Washington and outside of the South were more active and probably more effective in their efforts against segregation and against their proscription from higher positions in government. Almost as soon as they heard of the move to segregate the railway clerks, the Negro postal clerks of Cincinnati protested the move. But the signal case of success in the movement of blacks to maintain themselves in some prestigious positions in the federal service centered upon Charles W. Anderson, the Collector of Internal Revenue in the Second District of New York.

Charles Anderson was the boss of black Republican politics in the city and state of New York. Realistic politician that he was, Anderson was always very careful to maintain the dignity and integrity of his race. Soon after Wilson's inauguration, he was appalled by the blind rush for office among the black Democracy and its press. "They have all been engaged in a mad scramble for office," he wrote to Booker T. Washington, and they had neglected important concerns. "As a result, Jim-crow car bills, segregation bills and marriage restriction bills have whitened the legislative chambers in almost every state in the union. Here in New York there is a bill before the legislature providing against intermarriage and inflicting dire penalties on those who violate it. The penalty proposed for concubinage between the races is one so horrible that it cannot be expressed in language, even between man and man. . . . The State Boxing Commission here has made a rule against boxing matches between white and colored pugilists and that rule is now in full force. Insofar as it eliminated Johnson, I have no fault to find with it. . . ."[53]

As a Republican officeholder, Anderson was, of course, marked for slaughter. However, the peculiar nature of New York politics soon offered him a chance for survival in office. During the summer of 1913 Democratic leaders in New York City concluded that they wanted to support a fusionist candidate for mayor in yet another of those recurrent movements for municipal reform. They began to woo Anderson to deliver the Negro vote. George Foster Peabody was among the prominent New York Democrats bringing great pressure upon the Wilson administration generally and McAdoo particularly to keep Anderson in his place, presumably in return for that vote. Anderson did support the fusion candidate, and he did so very effectively by concentrating upon the anti-Negro tendencies of the opposition—in this case Tammany Hall officials. Especially did he focus upon the candidacy for re-election of a certain Tammany judge named Zeller who "was formerly counsel for the Brewers Association and since he has been on the bench, has never held a bartender or a proprietor of a hotel, or a restaurant or saloon for refusing to serve colored people." Anderson worked up this aspect of the Zeller case, got the Bar Association to repudiate Zeller, and published a pamphlet spreading the indictment generally across the racial record of the incumbents on the opposing slate.[54] Zeller was defeated, the fusionists were victorious, and Anderson stayed in office under a Democratic administration! Black votes, black leadership, and Democratic need could make a friend indeed.

Behind Anderson's retention, and striking another blow for the good of the race, was the hidden hand of Tuskegee. The person who probably sparked Peabody's initial endorsement of Anderson's retention was Major R. R. Moton, the Commandant of Cadets at Hampton Institute and a stalwart Washingtonian. In writing to Peabody, Moton noted that Anderson's wife had graduated from Hampton, but more importantly he indicated Anderson's astuteness in racial matters. "One of the first changes he made when he went into office was to transfer a white lady stenographer from his office to another, and I think high position, and he placed a graduate of Hampton, colored of course, in her place as his stenographer. As I have said, he has wisely and very tactfully walked around the race situations that might have arisen."[55]

In 1915 Moton would replace the Wizard as the Principal of Tuskegee Institute. He early demonstrated that he possessed the wisdom and the soft strength necessary for the place. Like others, he saw the segregation movement in the federal service as "bringing Negroes together in a way nothing else could have done and we ought to make the most in some way of any strong sentiment for cooperation among colored people." He had spoken on the subject in Washington, but more recently he had had an opportunity to address a group of university professors, including Southerners, who visited the Hampton campus. Here he did the work he was made to do. "I thought I might as well be perfectly frank with them," he reported to Booker Washington. "I told them that what I was saying was in confidence," he began in the typical *entre-nous* Tuskegee style, "but that I would like to tell them what was in the back of my head and I think in the minds of Negroes generally with reference to segregation. I laid before them the fact the Negroes opposed segregation as a principle because back of the promotion of segregation was the idea that the Negro was inferior and back of this inferiority was still a more subtle idea that the Negro was cursed and therefore there was no opportunity for him to rise very high. I made the point that the Negro did not oppose segregation because he wanted to be with the white people, but that we enjoyed being with our friends whether they were black or white, that the white people had the best hotels, best schools, best coaches on the trains, best streets in the cities, best roads in the country along side their farms, as a rule. I said that when we got alongside of white people it was because we wanted to get the best."[56] No more incisive and succinct statement of the case against segregation from the black point of view has been made for the twentieth century. In those few words, Moton caught the essence of the black indictment of segregation for that day, and the days that followed.

RADICALS vs. CONSERVATIVES WITHIN THE WILSON ADMINISTRATION

With a native Virginian in the White House, with Southerners in five of the ten Cabinet seats, and with a Southern-led Democratic majority in both houses of Congress, Southerners after March 4, 1913, understandably felt that the way of change in the nation would be theirs. "You know," Senator Tillman wrote to an Anderson, South Carolina, banker, "that in the constitution of the Senate and the House the South has come to her own."[57] The Southern way would rule in many things, but especially would it reign in the matter of race relations. On the floor of the Senate, John Martin of Virginia explained to his colleagues that only Southern men understood the Negro character, and hence in these matters Northerners would have to trust to the competence of Southern leadership.[58] But it remained for the highly learned Senator from Mississippi, John Sharp Williams, to give a proper lecture to the President. "Washington has always been considered, before the war and after the war, as being south of Mason's and Dixon's line," he told Wilson in rejecting a black nominee for a federal office in the District. "I do not care what is done up in Yankeedom. If they want negroes let them have them; but the people of this District do not want them, and we, who rather peculiarly represent the people of the District are Southerners, do not want them."[59]

Southerners in Washington generally were jubilant over the prospect of racial segregation in the federal service. But when it became evident in the summer of 1913 that Wilson and McAdoo envisioned not only segregation, but the appointment of blacks to significant offices including that of Register of the Treasury, Southern Radicals became livid with rage and Conservatives red with embarrassment. Confirmation of Patterson as Register was up to the Senate in July and, while vociferous opposition was typical among deep South senators, it became the happy lot of James K. Vardaman, the freshman Senator from Mississippi, to lead the attack that included in its vanguard such influential Senators as Ben Tillman of South Carolina and Hoke Smith of Georgia. The point of the attack centered upon the fact that if Negroes were appointed to supervisory positions in the government, as was the case with Patterson, white women employees would often be required to work under them, at least until transferred. Implicit in the words and actions of the Radicals was the idea that Negro bosses acquiring the habit of giving orders to whites in public places would come to presume that they could give orders to white women in private places.

James K. Vardaman was the white knight to save womanhood from the black beast. In the tradition of great Southern Senators he affected an all-white linen suit, white shoes, and a broad-brimmed white hat. He was a large man, barrel-chested, full of face, and with a long flowing mane of silver hair that was always neatly if loosely combed back and hung gracefully over his collar. In an age of great orators, he was among the greatest and shortly took his oratory—like Dixon, Tillman, and John Temple Graves—to the boards on the Chautauqua circuits. There his message was that the repeal of the Fifteenth Amendment and the consequent denial of political equality to blacks would allow the natural order to prevail and cause the Negro to cease to seek social equality. Like other Southern orators of similar mien and with similar messages, he did not go unappreciated in the farthest North. "He was applauded frequently," came one report from Crookston, Minnesota, "and many persons crowded forward to shake his hand after the meeting. Most of these were women."[60]

In Washington as a Senator, Vardaman entered a larger theater than he had ever worked before. In an interview with the Associated Press he avowed himself a friend of the Negro. "But I unhesitatingly assert," he added, "that political equality for the colored race leads to *social equality*. Social equality leads to race amalgamation, and race amalgamation to deterioration and disintegration."[61] Vardaman's solution to the race problem was an American apartheid. "I expect to favor and urge the enactment of laws that will make perfect the social and political segregation of the white and colored races," he declared. "We cannot now follow the idea of Lincoln and send the colored man away to a country of his own. The next best thing, therefore, is to bring about complete segregation."[62]

In the city of Washington itself, the freshman Senator found many of the same appalling conditions he had fought in Mississippi. "The women of the southern states were living today in a state of siege," he reportedly told the Senate and the nation, "with more dread than in the days when the wild man and the wild beast roamed the frontier."[63] In the District of Columbia, in the four days before July 17, 1913, Vardaman claimed to have discovered that no less than seven women had been attacked by Negro men, including the sister-in-law of a Senator, and another woman had been threatened with "bodily harm" by Negro women employed in the office of the black Recorder of Deeds.[64]

Vardaman soon found that the methods he had used to attack such problems in the deep South were also very effective in Washington. On the night of August 6, he spoke to a mass audience in the Masonic Temple. He declared his belief that many of the outrages in Washington had their inception in black men sitting next to white women in the streetcars. Segregation would alleviate that condition. He then called upon Congress to pass a law segregating Negro employees in the federal service and putting them under the supervision of white men. Finally Vardaman addressed himself to the question of the North and the Negro. "The people of the North have great love for the negro—at a distance," he declared. "They love him as a race and hate him as an individual." In concluding, he called for white America to unite. "Let the South and North stop this hating each other," he begged, "for we will need all the love at our command, all the intellect and all the patience and Christian forbearance to save this country from the black race." Hardly had the Senator taken his seat when the meeting passed with a "storm" of yeas a motion to take up a collection to "fight for race segregation here and for the protection of white women from negroes."[65]

Vardaman might have been the most conspicuous of Southern Senators pressing for segregation, but Ben Tillman was probably the most effective. Barely a month after the new administration assumed office, Tillman asked the Assistant Secretary of the Treasury to transfer a white woman to another position because she "really wants to get away from the negro employees in the Bureau of Printing and Engraving and the ill mannered Republican bosses."[66] Three months later Tillman was incensed that the woman had been given a raise but no transfer. "She is a refined Southern woman," he informed the Assistant Secretary, "and unused to her environment; and has only stayed there because of her necessities. The newspapers have told us that there was to be segregation between the negroes and the whites in the Departments. I hope it was not a dream of some reporter with a lurid imagination."[67] Indeed, it was not imagination. On that very day, July 12, Williams issued the order segregating lavatories. Tillman was much gratified by the order, he said, "particularly where women are concerned, because everyone knows the danger of catching contagious diseases."[68]

Radicals in Washington could applaud that part of the Wilsonian racial program that called for segregation, but they could never applaud or, apparently, even understand that part that called for black sections in which Negro officials could rise to positions of trust and honor. For Radicals, elevation of the Negro in any sphere would promote a sense of self-esteem in Negro men everywhere that the precarious balance of sexual relations between black men and white women could hardly withstand. Thus, when Wilson and McAdoo sent Patterson's name into the Senate, they had, ever so innocently it seems, sown the wind. They would reap the whirlwind. Always vigilant in the protection of young white women from blacks, Thomas Dixon wrote to Ben Tillman late in July urging him "with every energy of your body & soul" to "fight the confirmation of Patterson, the Negro, appointed to boss white girls in the Treasury Department! It is inconceivable to me that the President has made this appointment."[69] Of course, it was inconceivable to Wilson and McAdoo that anyone should create such a furor over such a minor and clearly sensible act.

Patterson's candidacy gave Radicals on Capitol Hill the focus that they had previously lacked. Late in July with Tillman, Vardaman, and Hoke Smith in the lead they launched their attack.[70] Vardaman laid bare the ultimate weapon of the Southern Senators. "But this is more than a question of partisan politics or office holding," he insisted. "It is the great race question. This appointment, if confirmed, will create in every negro in the country a hope that he may some day stand on social and political equality with the white man." Wilson desperately needed the votes of the Southerners for his program of economic reform, and he could not ignore the message that followed. "Compared with the tariff and the money question, now occupying the attention of Congress, the race question involved in this appointment is a Pike's Peak to the shrub-covered foothills," Vardaman declared. "I would rather see the tariff and the money legislation defeated than this nomination confirmed."[71]

Tillman himself had little doubt that the Southern Senators would win. Indeed, he knew from personal experience the power of a single Senator to block an appointment if he felt strongly enough to hold fast.[72] Nevertheless, he was pleased that the conflict did not cause a break with the administration. In mid-August the President withdrew the nomination of Patterson and sent in, instead, the name of an Indian from Oklahoma—precisely as Gore had asked in the beginning. "Some of the negro-lovers proclaim the Fatherhood of God and the brotherhood of man," observed a much relieved Tillman, "but we all respect the Indians because they were too brave to ever consent to be made slaves while the negroes have submitted to slavery and seemed to thrive on it. This in itself is explanation enough why Southern Democrats would consent to confirm an Indian and still reject and fight the confirmation of a negro."[73]

Tillman and the Southern Democrats generally were pleased at their victory over the Patterson appointment, but they were much displeased by the snail's pace at which the administration removed Republican officeholders especially black officeholders, and replaced them with Democrats. The loaves and fishes, it seemed to them, ought not to be kept waiting. "The President is not dispensing patronage as rapidly as we think he ought to," Tillman grumbled late in July.[74] Even when the administration's political considerations were met, Tillman found the appointments distressingly faithful to the civil service system. "The rules and regulations are so strict," he protested, "and Woodrow Wilson's administration is so careful in carrying them out, that we Democrats are absolutely disgusted because of our inability to get places for our friends."[75]

"Pitchfork" Ben Tillman was one of the shrewdest politicians in the capital, and he soon found a way to turn the civil service system from a liability into an asset. It happened that a vacancy appeared on the three-person Civil Service Commission, and he urged Wilson to appoint to the post his good friend Charles M. Galloway, a fellow South Carolinian who had served as the private secretary of the junior Senator from the state, Ellison D. ("Cotton Ed") Smith. Tillman apprised John Sharp Williams that he was urging the appointment on Wilson. He was certain that Galloway "would *make good* in every respect" if appointed. "What we want in the office," he said, "is youth, vigor, and ambition to do something for the party and the country rather than for the Republican party."[76] Galloway was appointed, and he did make good. One of his interests, apparently, was the operation of the Efficiency Division of the Commission that, among other things so reformed the methods of the accounting division of the Treasury as to reduce the number of clerks from 184 to 94.[77] "Efficiency," almost certainly, was directly tied to the removal of black employees. Galloway's appointment gave Tillman great flexibility in the war against Negro officeholders and candidates for office. Not only did it give him a very energetic representative on the Commission and one vote out of three on every removal and appointment, through Galloway he might also proceed to terminate a position entirely, change it slightly so as to open it as a new place and make a new appointment, or simply to call for a new examination for the office. With Galloway on the commission it was possible to attack any officeholder anywhere in the federal service in some very effective way.

Galloway soon had an opportunity to assist his patron in a proceeding designed specifically to illustrate to blacks that the South was a white man's country. The case was purely symbolic; it involved the ousting of a Negro Republican whose term in office had less than sixty days to run in any event. The man was Robert Smalls, a sometime Congressman from the Beaufort area of South Carolina. Smalls had leaped into national fame in 1862 when he led his friends to seize the Confederate steamer upon which he was the slave pilot and sailed out of Charleston harbor under the guns of Confederate-held Fort Sumter. During the war, Captain Smalls and his ship, the *Planter,* fought on the Union side. Afterward he was a prime leader in the Reconstruction government of the state. In 1913 Smalls was the Collector of the Port of Beaufort, an office that Taft had, along with many similar small customs offices, ordered abolished as of July 1, 1913. Anticipating an attempt to remove him, Smalls had tried to muster his friends on the Committee of Commerce to act to hold him in place those last few months. "His ambition is to be the last collector of the port at Beaufort," Tillman observed accurately. The Senator was determined that the ambition should not be realized, and that "Robert Smalls, an octoroon" would be ousted.[78]

In spite of the best efforts of "Bob" Smalls, Tillman secured his dismissal and got his own man confirmed by the Senate during the evening of June 2. He hastened to effect the change of command and to move on to get the assistant collector, also black, removed.[79] Actually the Deputy Collector held his place more securely than the Collector because his was a civil service, not a political appointment. Undaunted, Tillman rushed to enlist the aid of two young friends from South Carolina, Civil Service Commissioner Galloway and James F. Byrnes, a low-country Congressman eventually to become a justice of the Supreme Court under Franklin Roosevelt and Secretary of State under Harry Truman. With scarcely a week left for the office to exist in any form with any incumbent, he reminded McAdoo that he had promised to remove the deputy, "and lest you forget, I am writing to you to jog your memory. The deputy's name is J. I. Washington, a gentleman of color."[80]

All of the then considerable power of the southside Democracy had moved to prevent two minor offices from being memorialized by having expired with black incumbents. The lesson was clear enough: Radicals in power would use the cannon to destroy the fly; they would use all of their strength to smash the least of black pride.

Scattered evidence suggests that Tillman also had large success in removing blacks from the postal service. Custodial personnel aside, there were perhaps more blacks in the Post Office Department than in any other. Still, the great mass of these did routine clerical labor.

In the Post Office, as in other places, Tillman found that Taft's acts in his last days in the White House and the civil service idea were both impediments. Four days after Wilson took office, Tillman urged the new President to rescind Taft's order that fourth class post offices go under civil service. The effect would be, he explained, to "open wide the door to negro applicants throughout the South, and nothing but the rigid application of the rules made purposely for the purpose can keep a good many negroes from winning those offices."[81] The hazard of civil service to white supremacy was laid out vividly and with a little gall by Tillman to a white Carolinian who naïvely inquired about white boys replacing Negroes as railway mail clerks on the Georgetown (S.C.) and Western Railroad. Those places were under civil service, the Senator explained, and even then the waiting list was probably all Negro. "A negro knows he had to win it on his merits, while our white boys [*sic*] expects 'pull' to land him, and as a result the negro gets the job."[82]

Even so, Tillman knew that there were many ways to skin an officeholder and the best way was with the help of your powerful friends. One of Tillman's friends was Albert Sydney Burleson. "Since my visit this morning I will never call you 'Mr. Secretary' again," he wrote to the Postmaster General in mid-March, "but will go back to the 'old entitlement,' to use a negro phrase, and stick to it."[83] Several weeks later Senator Tillman pressured Burleson gently in relation to the postal clerks in the South: "There are entirely too many negroes among them, for my use, and I hope you will find some way to weed these out and transfer them to other fields of activity. . . ." He thought it would be well to transfer them to the North. "They love the negro. So let us give them a good dose."[84]

Shortly, the Senator's deft political hand was at work on the problem. Tillman pressed Burleson to promote an especially useful inspector to oversee the work in the Atlanta division of the railway mails. "We want fewer negroes in the Railway Mail Service and Barry may be depended on to get them out wherever possible," he coached the Postmaster General. "Of course this letter is strictly private, although the world knows my views on the negro question. But then we ought not to shout it from the house-tops that we are turning the negroes off just because they are black."[85] The results were significant. A year after the Wilson administration came to power, Tillman declared that Burleson had done more in shipping out Republicans and substituting Democrats than any other department head.[86] No doubt many of those shipped were black.

Southern racial Conservatives were more embarrassed than vocal over Wilson's attempt to appoint Negroes to important offices. For instance, Senator Gore probably suffered more politically from the Patterson nomination than anyone. It was a hapless day for the Senator from Oklahoma when he stepped into McAdoo's office to suggest an Indian for a post that the Secretary, with a great mass of business in hand, needed to find a black man to fill. What began as an ordinary attempt to pick up a patronage token for his Indian constituency led to a great furor, and ended in his serving as a resident whipping boy for the Radicals. If one can believe Gore's opponents, the Oklahoma Senator early tried to stop the avalanche by appealing personally to Vardaman simply to vote against Patterson and not talk about it. This, of course, Vardaman refused to do. In the summer of 1914, when Gore was running for re-election, his enemies in Oklahoma published a broadside that depicted "Senator Gore and His Nigger Friend Patterson" standing outside the gate to the U.S. Treasury. Gore was positioned protectively in front of Adam E. Patterson, who was rather blandly smoking a cigar. Facing Gore with one hand raised in the "halt" position was Vardaman saying, "these white girls shall not be servants of a black negro." Behind Vardaman, strung out between the gate and the temple-like treasury building, were thirteen young women, exhibiting varying degrees of distress, disconsolation, and weeping. One would presume that they faced the prospect of becoming the captive harem of the sensual black man.[87]

Being an honest Radical, Vardaman could speak his mind on the Patterson appointment and win plaudits in the deep South at Gore's expense. Even though he had been born in Mississippi and had been a Mississippi Democrat and a Texas Populist before he was an Oklahoma Democrat, Gore was not allowed a fair hearing in any quarter in this case. In praising Vardaman for his victory in stopping the Patterson appointment, the *Amory* (Mississippi) *Times-Press* thought it "such a pity that poor old Tom Gore didn't have some of his bravery. Certainly Gore was as much opposed to negro appointments, else he wouldn't be an honored son of Webster county, but God Almighty hasn't done as much for him as he has for Vardaman—Vardaman is full of the Patrick Henry stuff. . . ."[88]

Now and again, racial Conservatives did speak out. The Columbia (S.C.) *State,* for instance thought that Vardaman, in putting the Patterson incident above tariff and currency reform, "collapses into a pathetic figure at which his enemies will laugh." The *State* felt that the country was "nearly at one about the negro in politics," and "the chief danger of loss of ground in the work of removing it altogether lies in the impatience and super-heated passions of men like Vardaman—and Vardaman, as we have said, is not incapable, apart from the habit of nursing his anti-negro wrath to the exclusion of other things, of usefulness."[89]

THE WILSONIAN RACIAL SETTLEMENT

The Wilson administration was highly sensitive to criticism both from Southern Senators and from blacks and Northern white liberals. When it encountered opposition to appointing blacks to significant offices, on one side, and to the segregation of workers on the other, it withdrew. The withdrawals were orderly, calculated, and strategic. They were also partial; the astuteness of Wilson, ably seconded by McAdoo, was highly impressive. Clearly, the prime concern was tariff and currency reform, and in that pursuit the administration was willing to sacrifice neither Southern white nor Northern liberal votes over a matter of race.[90] After the passage of the Underwood-Simmons Tariff Act and the Federal Reserve Act late in 1913, the administration stiffened its back against Southern critics on the race issue. During 1914, the cries of pain among both Radicals and the more stolid Southern white Conservatives would be highly audible, but avail naught.

In mid-August 1913, the administration formally withdrew the Patterson nomination and before the end of the month added frosting to the cake by nominating a white Missourian as minister to Haiti. Even before the Cleveland years, the tradition had been to send a black representative to the black republic. Southern Radicals were delighted, not nearly so much at the appointment itself as at the cries of anguish from Negroes and Northern liberals that it evoked.[91] This was a blow against Negroes that not even Vardaman or Tillman had thought to strike. Indeed, Tillman himself had always been willing enough to concede to blacks the ministerships to Haiti and Liberia. Shortly afterward, as the *Washington Post* reported, Wilson advised Northern Democrats pressing for the appointment of Negroes to sound out the Southern Senators to see "to what extent they will go in drawing the color line."[92] If the extremes would fight, the administration was determined not to be caught in the middle.

Even as it was placating Southerners, however, the administration was also withdrawing from a policy of effecting a relatively total and neatly organized segregation of the races in the federal service. The administration was fully aware that blacks in the North had votes and that white liberals had political power well beyond their numbers. If they tended to forget those facts, there was always someone to remind them. The Washington *Star,* a black newspaper, estimated that there were about 600,000 Negro voters in the North, with 20,000 in Massachusetts, 30,000 in New Jersey, and 50,000 in New York, all pivotal states. Some Democratic Congressmen did have Negro constituents in considerable numbers, and those Congressmen pressed the interests of blacks. For instance, the *Star* understood that Representative George of New York was pushing Wilson to appoint more Negro Democrats.[93] The administration wanted to retain such votes as those of Representative George, and it was far from willing to alienate needlessly the Congressional friends of black voters. Consequently, when the first attempt at implementing segregation drew a strong reaction, the administration withdrew from the consistent application of its rule. During the first week of August, 1913, the chief clerks of several departments published on the front page of the *Evening Star* a statement that no formal order had been issued segregating colored people.[94] This false start, incidentally, made it difficult for observers to determine just where and why segregation was being effected.

By the end of September, Secretary McAdoo had decided that it was time for a command decision. "I enclose a letter from Senator *Jones,* of the State of Washington," he wrote to the President, "together with a petition addressed to you and the members of the Cabinet, which I bring to your attention because numerous protests are being received here, and it is evident to my mind that much misunderstanding exists about the alleged 'segregation' in the different departments. I should like very much to discuss this matter with you when I next see you, because I think it is assuming proportions that May make a definite statement or announcement necessary."[95] Shortly, Wilson himself was pressed by liberal Northern leaders such as Villard, Moorefield Storey, and Jane Addams to halt the movement toward segregation. In the fall of 1913 a delegation of liberal whites and Negroes called at the White House and interviewed the President on the issue. Wilson offered to consider the matter. A year later, one of these leaders published the President's version of the result: "He and his cabinet officers had investigated as he promised, and cabinet officers told him the segregation was caused by friction between colored and white clerks, and not done to injure or humiliate the colored clerks, but to avoid friction. Members of the cabinet assured him that the colored clerks would have comfortable conditions, though separated. He had taken their view that the segregation was the best way to meet this situation and that the best thought of the administration has so decided."[96]

In spite of the President's decision in Cabinet to segregate, apparently no explicit, written orders were issued from the White House. Indeed, in mid-December the Washington correspondent of the Boston *Advertiser* was certain that the President had ordered cabinet members to stop segregating workers. Officials, he found, were reluctant to discuss the matter, but he did not doubt that the President had "given the word." What had happened was that the lesser officials who were so inclined had pushed ahead vigorously in the first wave, faltered, and then drifted. "As a general thing," the New York *Evening Post* reported, "it is pointed out, segregation has been the idea and ambition of the minor officials, who took advantage of the fact that their superiors did not show any opposition to it—until overwhelming pressure was brought to bear upon them from outside."[97]

Interestingly, there were people on both sides of the race question who worked to leave Wilson room to maneuver. Celia Parker Woolley, the president of the Frederick Douglass Center in Chicago, wrote to Villard that she was anxious to know Wilson's real convictions. "I can understand how he must move cautiously in that matter, and I think we should be prepared to give him a good deal of time, until he [has put] through tariff and currency reform [and] established himself strongly in the people's trust, before we ask him to be very active on this colored question, sure to arouse so much antagonism among his nearest supporters and the party in general. But just what and how much did he mean by the letter to Bishop Walters. And—Alas if we could keep some of the negroes themselves still, of the Trotter and similar sort. But that is unreasonable."[98] Wilson could not have said it better himself.

On the other side no less a Radical than Ben Tillman counselled caution. "It is very artful and adroit demagogy, as you know," he wrote to a friend after having heard that Cole Blease had made a strong "Negro Speech" on December 1, 1913. "President Wilson cannot do more than he is now doing through his cabinet officers to get rid of the negro. Otherwise he will arouse all the old abolition sentiment through the North and all to no purpose. The race question fight is not up now and the South is wise to let it sleep a while longer until the Republicans and fanatics of the North come to their senses more than they now have, and [a] few more [of] the old ones die off."[99] Again, Wilson himself could not have said it better.

On October 3 the Underwood Tariff became law, and on December 23 Wilson signed the Federal Reserve Act, a measure that put the government very much in the business of managing the currency. The year 1914 would see a continuing stream of important reform legislation, but with these two acts the Wilsonians felt that they had attained the basic goals they set out to achieve. Notes passed about within the administration during that Christmas season fairly exude an air of triumph. Wilson had not forgotten his promises to his black supporters and, perhaps, he still chafed at the buffeting he had suffered at the hands of both Radicals and Conservatives because of his attempts to fulfill his promises. Now with the core of his program achieved, those who were at the extreme on both sides of the race question, North and South, could expect less gentle treatment at his hands. That was precisely what they got. First there came a series of pro-black acts, one after another like machine-gun fire, accompanied by howls of outrage from the Radicals and a few cries from the Conservatives. Later in the year, black extremists would also be punished for their disrespect.

Hardly had the ink dried on the Federal Reserve Act before word leaked out that Wilson and Attorney-General James C. McReynolds expected to nominate Robert H. Terrell, a Negro and a graduate of the Harvard Law School, for re-appointment to the municipal court bench in Washington. The outcry in the South was great. "It is unthinkable to a resident of this section of the country that a white defendant should be tried before a negro judge," declared the Biloxi, Mississippi, *Herald,* "and it is incongruous for a Southern-born Democratic president to make this concession to the demand of the negro in the northern states for political recognition."[100] Vardaman, of course, was not slow in leaping to the attack. Casting a threatening glance at his senior colleague, John Sharp Williams, he indicated that if a Negro was good enough to be a judge, he might be good enough to be a Senator. At home, the Hattiesburg *News* applauded the comment and announced its pride that one Mississippi Senator "was born to lead the fight for the absolute supremacy of the white race in this country."[101]

Conservative leaders responded in anguish. They might or might not accept the kind of appointment that Terrell represented, but Radicals would certainly fry them on the publicity griddle if they did not make strong and often hollow protests against such acts. Senator Williams, for instance, writhed under the punishment meted out by Vardaman, and he took Wilson sharply to task for recommending Terrell. The President replied rather coldly. "I assure you that I could not avoid the nomination of Terrell," he said. "In the first place, there is every reason to believe that he has not only performed his duties excellently, but that he had been the best judge of his rank in the District...." He reminded the Mississippi Senator that before the campaign he had virtually promised Negroes minor offices.[102] Williams would not be assuaged in his distress. "I do not see that the explanation as to the Terrell incident helps me any in my situation," he wrote. "Of course, you might have known beforehand the situation we were in.... It would spell absolutely the political death of any Southern Senator who would agree to the confirmation of one of them in this place." Having opened the wound, he poured in the salt. "I do really think that you might have considered the situation of your friends. Of course, there are men in the Senate who will welcome it as an opportunity to 'flim flam' and demagogue for consumption at home on the negro question. I am not one of them. I and men like me must fall between the upper and nether millstone."[103]

After a rumor flew that Wilson had retired again and rather sheepishly before the Vardaman onslaught, it became clear that actually the contrary was the case. Wilson stood by Terrell, and he was confirmed. Radicals were outraged. In Georgia, Rebecca Felton leapt into the saddle, sword in hand and arm raised. She heaped double blame on Wilson because he was "Southern born and bred" and even accused Tillman of weakly allowing the confirmation to pass in executive session. The Democrats in the South and surely the Democrats in Georgia, she warned, "stand for nothing except the exclusion of Negroes from public affairs."[104]

Even while the Radicals were still ranting, the President sent to the Senate the name of another black man for appointment as Recorder of Deeds for the District of Columbia. Again, this was an office that paid well, involved the supervision of a number of skilled employees, and had been traditionally filled by Negroes. As usual the Radicals raised a cry of protest with Vardaman in the lead. "Senator Vardaman considers it a disgrace to the nation that this important office, where white men and white women are compelled to go to record their deeds, should be filled by a negro," observed a sympathetic correspondent, "and he has demanded of President Wilson the appointment of a white man, pledged to remove all the negro clerks employed there, at the earliest possible moment."[105] Again, Conservatives were caught. Andrew J. McKelway, a native North Carolinian who then headed the national movement for child labor reform, urged the administration to withdraw the nomination at least until after the primaries in South Carolina and Georgia were over. In South Carolina, the rabid Radical Coleman Livingstone Blease was going against Ellison D. "Cotton Ed" Smith for a Senate seat. In Georgia, now thoroughly racist Joseph E. Brown was going against racist but progressive Hoke Smith. Smith had supported the Terrell appointment and did not oppose the appointment of "a worthy negro to office." But both Smiths would have to defend themselves if the administration pushed the appointment before the elections.[106]

Wilson not only dealt the Radicals a severe blow in the District of Columbia, he moved as far south as Tuskegee, Alabama, to do so. Perhaps as one of Burleson's efficiency measures, the federal post office at Tuskegee Institute was marked for extinction. Thereafter the students and the institution would be forced to rely upon the services of the white post office in town. Booker T. Washington dispatched an urgent telegram to Wilson asking that the campus post office be retained. "One of the objects for the separation was to prevent possible trouble by large numbers of colored students going into the Tuskegee town post office," he explained, deploying an argument that would certainly appeal to Wilson. The Wizard of Tuskegee achieved the desired effect. "Here is a matter which seems to me of considerable importance," the President stated on the following day in passing Washington's request on to the Postmaster General. "I think that it would be wise not to disturb the existing arrangement at Tuskegee." George Foster Peabody and Seth Low, both rich benefactors of the Democratic party, also wrote to Burleson and the President favoring the retention of the post office, probably at the instigation of Washington.[107] Needless to say, the post office at Tuskegee Institute survived as a separate and all-black institution.

During 1914 Radicalism seems to have used up most of its strength in the higher reaches of the administration; it had also, apparently, spent its coin in Congress. During the spring of 1914, Radicals made an attempt to push through Congress a bill mandating that the executive departments segregate black and white employees. May Nerney learned on March 6 that the House Civil Service Committee was going to hold a hearing on the matter on the 7th. Hastily she telegraphed a member of the NAACP in Washington to appear and protest.[108] Actually, it was purely accidental that the Negro community was able to offer its case at all. Archibald H. Grimké, an eminent black citizen in the District, learned about the hearings even as they were happening. He rushed up to the Capitol and, as he told Nerney, managed to get in twenty minutes of testimony with good results. He found that Mr. Aswell of Louisiana and Mr. Edwards of Georgia had introduced bills for segregation in the District as well as in the civil service.[109] Again in December 1914, Congressman Vinson of Georgia introduced a bill requiring segregation in the federal service.[110] Neither these nor three score other such bills were passed.

Wilson stiffened his back against Southern Senators in 1914; he also turned a stern face against black militants. His move against the hard-core Radicals had stymied the segregationist thrust. By the fall of 1914, segregation was adrift, moving up a bit here, falling back there, without plan or power. In this situation William Monroe Trotter, a Bostonian and a Harvard-trained lawyer, led a group of black militants in calling on the President in November 1914.

The President told the protesters that the Cabinet had reported that friction between white and black employees necessitated the segregation and "the best thought of the administration has so decided." He then made a statement understandable only in the context of racial Conservativism. "Segregation is not humiliating but a benefit and ought to be so regarded by you gentleman," he insisted. He then argued that they should preach to the Negro community that it was right, and that general acceptance would soon make it right.

The Conservative argument flew by Trotter's ear like a poorly aimed arrow. He replied instead to the President's earlier assertion that friction between employees in the departments caused the separation. Such was not the case, Trotter challenged. Wilson apparently understood that Trotter was calling the President of the United States a liar.

One imagines a stony face and words coming out like dry ice. "If this organization is ever to have another hearing before me," warned the President, "it must have another spokesman. Your manner offends me."

Apparently this shaft, too, flew by Trotter's ear for he continued the attack. "Now we colored leaders are denounced in the colored churches as traitors to our race," he declared.

"What do you mean by traitors?" asked Wilson.

"Because we supported the Democratic ticket in 1912," came the quick reply.

Wild went the temper of the chief executive, and out of the White House as if shot from a gun came William Trotter and his cohort.

Twenty years later, Wilson's Secretary of the Navy, Josephus Daniels, wrote an account of the incident:

> The papers played it up and for several days nothing else was talked about. While the papers were talking about this and the Republican papers generally were denouncing the President, I was over at the White House to see him upon some matter, and I remarked: "Governor, you did not seem to get along very well with our colored friends."
>
> He said: "Daniels, whenever a man loses his temper he loses his judgment. That is what happened to me in the interview. What I should have done was to have listened to what they had to say, asked them to leave their request, and promised to give it consideration. If I had done that the incident would have been a passing incident. As it was, when I lost my temper and unwisely ordered them to leave the executive offices, I lost my advantage and thereby I raised an incident into an issue."
>
> He paused, and, looking out of the window, then said: "I hope this will be a lesson to me and I think you will find it worth while to remember it, that whenever a public man loses his temper, no matter about what, and permits himself to act as foolishly as those he is trying to rebuke, he raises an incident into an issue. Never do it."[111]

Wilson rued the political results of his haste, but it does seem that in the exchange the real racial Wilson revealed himself. Like a parent defied, he sent the cheeky child from the room with the seeming injunction not to return until he had a civil tongue in his head. Furthermore, a specific punishment soon followed. In the immediate aftermath of criticism of his action, Wilson allowed Tom Dixon to premier the film *Birth of a Nation* in the White House. He clearly did not relish the movie, but he made the quotable statement that it was "like writing history with lightning."

After 1914 he concerned himself little with racial affairs generally and in 1916 made no special effort to woo the Negro vote (and neither did the Republicans). Yet, seemingly, there was guilt. He apparently felt that he had not delivered as readily as promised, and his over-reaction to Trotter perhaps owed much to that feeling. In June 1918, when George Creel, in effect the administration's propaganda director for the war, suggested that Wilson receive a delegation of Negro editors, Wilson declined: "I have received several delegations of negroes and I am under the impression that they have gone away dissatisfied. I have never had an opportunity actually to do that which I promised them I would seek an opportunity to do. I think probably it would be best just to carry out the programme without me for the present, until I am able to act in a way that would satisfy them."[112] On the other side, Wilson did pick up support in the South by his stand in the Trotter affair. Perhaps some of the support might not have been warmly welcomed. The secretary of the Chamber of Commerce of Hot Springs, Arkansas, wrote to applaud the administration for the "segregation of the race in Washington," and to declare that "the insulting and uncalled for manner of a gang of negroes to our President is about the last thing in clinching an argument that the more you educate a negro the smarter he thinks he is, and meaner he gets."[113]

To the Wilsonians, as to the rest of the white nation at large, race relations was a minor matter. The race problem was simply not seen as a significant issue by the whole people at any given time. The Wilsonians themselves, in 1915, came to the realization that if they were to win in 1916, they must renew their reform efforts. In that year and the next there came a second wave of legislation that capped earlier efforts. Also, there was the distraction of difficulties along the Mexican border and military action there. Finally, there was the war in Europe.

After the United States entered the conflict in April 1917, war-related installations involving thousands and tens of thousands of people were created out of whole cloth. Preconceived ideas of the proper relationship between blacks and whites were projected onto and ruled these new establishments. Race relations were as much pre-fabbed as were some of the buildings. On the Cumberland River below Andrew Jackson's "Hermitage," the government created a gun powder factory that came to be called the "Old Hickory Works." Eventually, it included about 40,000 workers, of whom over 5,000 were black, some 3,000 of them laborers. "In the early history of the camp, colored labor lived in tents that dotted the hillside," a welfare worker, Lou Cretia Owen, recorded in her diary. Afterward, black families moved into houses that the whites had occupied at first. "Residences are provided for 58 negro families and bachelor quarters for 176 single girls. The negroes here are invaluable. There are fifty-seven janitors employed to look after the different offices and buildings." For the most part, the black community was served by blacks. "We have a colored supervisor of welfare work for Negro women, Mary Keely, a college graduate," reported Owen. "She is a real southern negro and has the interest of the negroes in the plant at heart." During the great influenza epidemic she observed that "Negro doctors for the negro village are rendering a great service and volunteers among the negro[es] are doing splendid work." Segregation was the rule. "The colored Y.W.C.A. opened today," noted Owen. "It is near the colored village [where] the negroes are segregated. It is called the colored camp." The secretary of the Y.W.C.A. was the wife of the black minister. Black and white did come together outside of the plant upon occasion, as the diarist asserted, but under controlled conditions. "We went to a negro rally held at the colored Y.M.C.A. tonight," she wrote. "A large crowd of negroes crowded the auditorium but special seats were arranged for the white guests." The laudation was for the loyal service that blacks had rendered to the war effort.[114]

Charles Hunter, one of the founders of the Negro fair in North Carolina, was employed in the Norfolk Navy Yard during the war. He reported that at Camp Lee near Petersburg the troops were housed in separate but equal facilities. In the Yard at Norfolk he saw no discrimination, with what he considered to be minor exceptions. "Negro women, it seems, have been debarred from employment," he wrote. "There is separate toilet accommodations and separate cups at drinking places. These constitute all the distinctions so far as I have been able to see."[115] In 1918 the Navy Department in Washington divided its clerical workers in the enlisted personnel division along the color line in accord with the McAdoo idea. Negro clerks assumed total responsibility for records in the pre-1885 period, and white clerks for those afterward. Obviously, the earlier records were not very important. In the Veterans' Bureau immediately after the war, a separate "colored" section was established to process papers for the black warriors of World War I. Further, the Bureau created segregated hospitals for afflicted black veterans.

During the war, the military was, of course, separated as before. There were black regiments, and there were white regiments. Most black troops were organized in "labor battalions" and functioned as supporting elements to combat units. The most revolutionary idea came to the Navy Department, where someone suggested a "black battleship" on which all of the enlisted men and some of the officers would be black and where black men could distinguish themselves free of the complications of association with whites.[116]

Most white Americans were already willing to let racial matters lie before the war, but during the struggle many shared, perhaps, the reaction of Walter Hines Page to that tragedy. Page was Wilson's ambassador to Great Britain when the war in Europe began. As the fight dragged on from one bloody slaughter to the next, he was at first stunned, then horrified. He was morally appalled by the seeming indifference of "high society" in London to the murderous excesses of trench warfare on the Continent. By 1915, the plight of the Negro in America, in which he had invested three decades of work and sympathy, seemed not to rank very high in the scale of world horrors. Meanwhile, race relations in America had already suffered a relative de-escalation in attention. Race was not a large concern compared with reform; now it was even smaller compared with the holocaust in Europe. Conservatives had a special capacity for ignoring what they did not want to see and for believing what they wanted to believe. They could imagine that the McAdoo idea had more or less settled race relations in America in the "separate and equal" pattern. It is too much to say that a part of Wilson's plan for postwar peace as embodied in the Fourteen Points was an extension of the "separate and equal" doctrine. Yet there is profit in the thought: "self-determination" of peoples, each ethnic group upon its own ground, functioning in its own way to pursue its destiny under the assumption that ultimately if each is free to find himself all will harmonize in the end, was not unlike the McAdoo idea of "separate and equal." Probably both ideas sprang from the same roots, a diluted version of European romantic nationalism.

During the Harding administration, in spite of the fact that the President had suggested that he would not change the racial pattern, Negro leaders had hoped that the Republicans would return to the *status quo ante* Wilson. That hope was soon dashed. "I further know that conditions of segregation are not different now from what they were under the Wilson administration," wrote a veteran informant of the NAACP in 1923 as he criticized the Association for paying too much attention to lynching and not enough to segregation in the various departments of the national government. NAACP headquarters replied that it was having difficulty getting testimony on the subject.[117] Several months later the executive secretary of the District of Columbia branch of the NAACP submitted a letter detailing "the notable instances where the segregation on account of race and color is open and above board, without any attempt whatever at concealment, and while to a large degree this separation [is] applied to the grouping of the colored employees at work, it more generally applies to the uses of lavatories and wash rooms, and is as a whole hardly without an exception, applicable to the lunch rooms."[118] A later investigator, L. M. Hershaw, thought that segregation in the cafeterias had begun under the Wilson administration by departmental orders. "There is, however," he added, "one exception to the statement and it is to be found in the Navy Department where race distinction was begun in the cafeteria only after the Republicans were returned to office."[119] Altogether, very little new segregation occurred in the 1920s. Such as did exist, however, was rapidly settling into hardened form. "So you see," Hershaw explained to the New York office in 1927, "segregation is becoming crystalized and institutionalized in the Departments here."[120]

Northern interest in race relations in the South has always been severely taxed by its own racism. Even at the height of federally sponsored "Black Reconstruction" in the South, the commitment of the North to civil equality for black people was considerably diluted by the manner in which that effort supported the interest of whites in the North and West. Reconstruction was not over before the defection began, and with Redemption desertion became wholesale. Primarily inspired by Republican leadership, there were revivals of interest in the 1880s, but as the recession of the late 1880s gave way to the great depression of the 1890s, politicians of all parties showed a disposition to use black people when they could and to abandon them when they could not. The election of Roosevelt in 1904 marked the beginning of the end. By 1916 the Republican party had practically severed its relations with black people in the South and ended that phase of its history. Vestiges of the old connection would survive, but they had no strength. By the early 1960s, it would be difficult to find a black person in the South who was a Republican. In the first half of the twentieth century, Northern interest in the Negro in the South would be largely relegated to attempts to effect reforms through the federal government, especially through the federal courts. Meanwhile, there were always Northern whites teaching blacks in the South, even though their numbers were much diminished after Reconstruction. When one searches for truly aracial white Americans, one is likely to find them among these people. At Tougaloo and Tuskegee, at Fisk and Atlanta Universities, and in such lower schools as the Penn School on the Sea Islands in South Carolina, one can barely perceive the continuing sympathetic pulse of Northern white concern about black people in the South.[121]

PART FOUR

Soul Folk

Race relations in America in the twentieth century took its essential form from both black and white reactions to developments during the Radical era. On the black side what emerged was an alternative to the Washingtonian program. Its prime spokesman was W. E. B. Du Bois, and the concept was neatly encapsulated in the title of his book *The Souls of Black Folk,* published in 1903. On the white side there came an amendment to the Conservative mentality that profoundly influenced the nature of Conservatism from that time to the present. That variant amounted almost to another mentality, as we have defined the term, and we might aptly designate it "Volksgeistian Conservativism."

Ironically, both the black movement and the white were built up directly from the same philosophical foundation, and that foundation was a large current in the mainstream of Western civilization. Specifically, they were the direct offspring of the resurgent idealism that appeared in the West as a reaction against the extreme realism of the "Age of Enlightenment," dragooned, as it was, into disgrace by the excesses of the French Revolution and Napoleonic imperialism. In the vanguard of that grand and vigorous revival of idealism was G. W. Friedrich Hegel, a professor of philosophy in the University of Berlin after the Napoleonic era. Hegel's effectiveness as a thinker came to full maturity in the 1820s, and much of what he did found its way into the period that is often called "The Age of Romanticism," an age that cognates very closely with the beginning of what we have heretofore called the Victorian era.

CHAPTER XIII

The Souls of Black Folk

The essay that marked the modern beginnings of the idea of "black soul" in America was published by W. E. B. DuBois in 1897 in the prestigious, Boston-based national magazine *The Atlantic Monthly*. The article was entitled "Strivings of the Negro People." In the same year DuBois published a companion piece expressing the same basic concept under the title *The Conservation of the Races*. In 1903 these came together as the lead and theme-setting essay, entitled "Of Our Spiritual Strivings," in his monumental work *The Souls of Black Folk*. We discussed that work in relation to the Washington program in Chapter II, above. Here we will be concerned first with the philosophical sources upon which it drew, and then, briefly, with manifestations of those ideas in the evolution of black history and race relations in the twentieth century.[1]

DU BOIS ON BLACK SOUL

So often autobiographical in his writings, DuBois began his 1897 essay with the statement of his own racial dilemma. With him, it began with his birth in Great Barrington, Massachusetts, in 1868. Of mulatto ancestry on both sides—and very light—he grew to consciousness in a community in western Massachusetts where blacks were few and far between. During his early life, he was hardly conscious of his darkness. Then, as he later recalled the pointed moment, the children of his crowd, all white and mostly well-to-do, decided to exchange visiting cards as did their elders. It was a happy game and fun, for Will DuBois as for the rest. But, of course, visiting cards were sometimes refused; and a "tall newcomer," a girl who perhaps did not understand the value of this slight, dark boy in the community, chose to play out that part of the role upon him. She refused his offered card, abruptly, "with a glance." With that refusal there dropped the "veil" between the superbly talented and highly sensitive young man and the great white world. Thereafter, for a time, he turned his energies into beating whites in every possible competition. But over the years his haughty contempt faded, and he found that all he wanted was white, all he wanted was theirs and not his. Attraction and repulsion left him floating between white and black. By 1897, when he published his "Strivings" article, he had found a philosophical structure to explain his dilemma, one that also contained a solution for that problem for himself . . . and for his people. In doing so he drew heavily upon the widely accepted concept that each people possessed a unique "Volksgeist," a folk spirit, a germ implanted by God in the beginning to be warmed to life in His own good time to play its part in the evolution of the history of the world. DuBois had discovered "The Souls of Black Folk."

"One ever feels his twoness," he wrote in that exquisite miniature of the black dilemma in a world predominately white, "—an American, a Negro: two thoughts, two unreconciled strivings; two warring ideals in one dark body, whose dogged strength alone keeps it from being torn asunder."

"The history of the American Negro is the history of this strife," he continued, "—this longing to attain self-conscious manhood, to merge his double self into a better and truer self. In this merging he wishes neither of the older selves to be lost. He would not Africanize America, for America has too much to teach the world and Africa. He would not bleach his Negro soul in a flood of white Americanism, for he knows that Negro blood has a message for the world. He simply wishes to make it possible for a man to be both a Negro and an American, without being cursed and spit upon by his fellows, without having the doors of opportunity closed roughly in his face."

"This, then," he concluded, "is the end of his striving: to be a co-worker in the kingdom of culture, to escape both death and isolation, to husband and use his best powers and his latent genius. . . ."

Next DuBois turned to explain how the problem had arisen; how it had happened that the black person in America had not been able to bring his potential genius to share fully in the development of national culture. In Egypt, in Ethiopia, in the careers of certain black men—flashing briefly like falling stars—had appeared the shadow of a great past and of black genius. In America, in the relatively few days that had elapsed since emancipation, the black man's very power had been made to seem like weakness. "And yet it is not weakness,—"asserted DuBois. It was, as he phrased it, "the contradiction of double aims." On the one side, black leaders had been led to drive their people to do white things, to hew wood and draw water in a white man's world. On the other side, black leadership had been able to see the dark genius only dimly. Black artists could not depict the beauty of black soul to whites because whites despised the black race. Black artists could not do white things because they were not white. This conflict of two souls had been devastating. On the one side, there was the soul of blackness; and on the other, the genius of white America. "This waste of double aims," declared Du Bois, "this seeking to satisfy two unreconciled ideals, has wrought sad havoc with the courage and faith and deeds of ten thousand people,—has sent them often wooing false gods and invoking false means of salvation, and at times has even seemed about to make them ashamed of themselves." As Du Bois saw history, blacks in slavery had yearned after the ideal of freedom, in Reconstruction they had turned still again, to follow the ideal of "book-learning." But it was white books and white learning that they sought, so long, so hard, and with so little profit.

And yet, even as they struggled after that last ideal, black people began to generate the solution to their dilemma, to discover the beauty of the souls of black folk as a thing in itself. The effort "changed the child of Emancipation," to use Du Bois's language again, "to the youth with dawning self-conscious-ness, self-realization, self-respect.... He began to have a dim feeling that, to attain his place in the world, he must be himself, and not another." As Du Bois saw it, out of evil came good; out of the very degradation of the Negro came the necessity of adjusting education more closely to real life, of focusing better his understanding of his social duties and of realizing wherein lay real progress for himself. Thus dawned the age of "Sturm und Drang: storm and stress...." Significantly, Du Bois chose to use the Germanic phrase, and to use it in the German language. Freedom, the ballot, book-learning were not false ideals, they were simply incomplete, the "dreams of a credulous race childhood," as he said, or the aspirations of fond whites for blacks. Black folk needed all of these, argued Du Bois as he moved toward the essence of his solution, "not singly but together, not successively but together, each growing and aiding each, and all striving toward that vaster ideal that swims before the Negro people, the ideal of human brotherhood, gained through the unifying ideal of Race; the ideal of fostering and developing the traits and talents of the Negro, not in opposition to or contempt for the other races, but rather in large con-formity to the great ideals of the American Republic, in order that some day on American soil two world-races may give each to each those characteristics both so sadly lack. We the darker ones come even now not altogether empty handed: there are to-day no truer exponents of the pure human spirit of the Declaration of Independence than the American Negroes; there is no true American music but the wild sweet melodies of the Negro slave; the American fairy tales and folklore are Indian and African; and, all in all, we black men seem the sole oasis of simple faith and reverence in a dusty desert of dollars and smartness."

Thus it is that by getting out, by pursuing an exclusive blackness in a portion of their lives, which they must inevitably do, will black people get into the total American life. By looking inward, black people will move outward toward their ultimate destiny, and in that future all things, black and white, will be harmonious.

DuBois's solution to the race problem in America was new, and it was revolutionary. Booker T. Washington could imagine no culture worth having that was not thoroughly laced with white ideals and directed toward a consummation of whiteness. DuBois could boldly envision an evolution that began with a self-propelled withdrawal of black people from the single-minded pursuit of white culture and a plunge into pure blackness with faith that the two would harmoniously join further down the stream of time, without a loss of essential blackness. He did this by appropriating and adapting to the race problem in America late nineteenth-century idealism, especially Hegelianism, and most especially Hegel's philosophy of history.

DU BOISIAN THOUGHT AS HEGELIAN

In what way was DuBois's solution Hegelian? It was not, in fact, purely Hegelian. Significant portions of Hegel's thought were ignored, and had to be ignored. Hegel, who died in 1831, barely allowed subtropical Africans to walk onto his stage of history. Egypt was prominent, but only as an extension of Persia, and the latter functioned primarily as a connector between East and West.[2] Further Hegel saw each people possessing its own geography and their genius as springing from that geography. A poor climate and a poor land would not produce a world historical people. One would not look to the polar areas or the tropics for greatness. "The true theatre of History is therefore the temperate zone"; he declared, "or rather, its northern half, because the earth there presents itself in a continental form, and has a broad breast, as the Greeks say."[3] Hegel did not envision a healthy mixing of races or of world historical peoples. Indeed, each people had its innate genius, and a cultural mixing was essentially impossible. In the Hegelian universe DuBois, as a mulatto, was himself unreal; persons of mixed racial ancestry had no place. DuBois would be forced, ultimately, to amend Hegel.

In this as in other things, DuBois was eclectic. Habitually, he surveyed the field of contemporary knowledge, used what he wanted, and left the remainder to drift. During this early stage of his professional life he seems to have had difficulty constructing tight and long-running rationales to undergird his writing. In 1890, his English instructor at Harvard caught his weakness in this respect precisely. "Unthinking seems to me the word for your style," he wrote. "With a good deal of emotional power, you blaze away pretty much anyhow.

Occasionally, a sentence or paragraph, and sometimes even a whole composition will be fine. Oftener there will be a nebulous, almost sulphorus [sic] indistinctness of outline. As for reserve of power, it is rarely to be found."[4] That was exactly the case with DuBois's "Strivings" essay, with much of his writing, and with much of his life. "Emotional power," not logic, was his greatest strength.

It would be fruitless to search for a one-to-one appropriation of Hegelianism in DuBois's essay. But yet it is fundamentally Hegelian, and it is useful to consider it in that light. First, it is Hegelian in its language. The ten pages are heavily laden with such favored Hegelian words as ideal, consciousness, strife, and self; spirit, soul, and genius; conflict and contradiction; Freedom (three times with a capital "F" as in *Freiheit*), and, of course, folk. Most relevant is his appropriation of the Hegelian view of history. DuBois, like Hegel, sees the history of the world as the spirit of freedom rising to realize itself through specific world historical peoples. Consciousness is not achieved individually and one by one, but rather through the people, each people rising to a consciousness of itself, pursuing its "Volksgeist," its spirit, its soul, its genius. It is as if God implanted in each people a distinct seed, and that essence, that spirit struggles with its opposite (matter) for life. As the spirit struggles, as it exercises its will, it rises and matures, unfolding the full promise always there, pre-formed, latent in the seed. On earth, life is filled with confusion, conflict, and contradiction. But it is all working toward a rising communion of man with the Godhead. All soul, all spirit, all truth and reality ultimately is an emanation of God's mind. In God's mind all is harmonious, all is one, all things are unified, and there are no contradictions. As each people rise to know their true selves, they rise closer to God, and thereby to each other and to true Freedom. Hegelian *Freiheit,* true freedom, consists in knowing one's self through one's people, of sharing the common vision of reality, and, hence, of governing one's self in accordance with the folk spirit. The freedom of the Enlightenment (*liberté*), in contrast, was the absolute freedom gained by rational man in a rational universe. The world and man were governed by certain eternal natural laws, such as the law of gravitation or the law of supply and demand. We had discovered many of these, and by the use of innate reason we would certainly discover the remainder. Man had only to understand the laws and respect them to live in perfect freedom. He might do so with total success as an individual and without reference to others. Hegelian man, on the other hand, must move collectively in the direction of perfect freedom. If we seem so unfree on this earth, if we seem so separated one from another, it is because we do not well know ourselves personally and collectively. That ignorance is the measure of the distance of our separation from God. Painfully, through "Sturm und Drang: storm and stress," we will inevitably know more, and we will know freedom. "The History of the World," declared Hegel, "is none other than the progress of the consciousness of Freedom. . . ."[5]

The Hegelian idea of progress maybe described as moving by a thesis-antithesis-synthesis-thesis model. At a given time a given society is complete within itself and relatively static. Then, as that society slowly matures, it breeds out of its own self a contradiction, an opposite, an antithesis. There will follow a period of conflict, of struggles that will generate a new and transitory phase in which the best of the old, the eternally valuable fruit of the now withered and dying order, is not destroyed but rather is married to the new in a synthesis. In still more time, vestigal contradictions between the two systems peel away, and a new thesis emerges, a new higher stage of culture, closer to God and hence more real, true, and free. Shortly Karl Marx revised Hegel by arguing that material changes created the antithesis, but Hegel emphatically preached that the prime mover was ideas, ideas contrary to the old order grasped out of that very order by "world historical men." New ideas are the engines that move people forward through history toward God. By this program of creating and resolving contradictions, by this so-called "dialectical" process, the world rises cycle after cycle spiraling ever closer to union with the Godhead.

In Hegel's own time, as he saw it, the dialectical process occurred through the agency of nations. It was not in nations in the older monarchical sense, nor in the newer popular sense encouraged by the American and French Revolutions that progress occurred. It was through nations in the cultural sense—that is through a people joined by a common language, common customs, common values, and, most of all, a common history. The state, said Hegel, in referring to this sort of cultural nationalism, "was the divine idea on earth." God worked through the various cultural nations to bring man to truth. The history of a people charted their progress in that journey. Most recently, Hegel contended, the German nations had moved through Christianity to know the truth that man is innately Free, and to point the way toward ultimate salvation.[6]

DuBois neatly pressed the Negro American into the Hegelian model. Hegel traced the World Spirit as having moved forward toward a realization of itself through the successive histories of six world historical peoples: Chinese, Indians, Persians (culminating with the Egyptians), Greeks, Romans, and Germans.[7] DuBois brought on the Negro as "a sort of seventh son, born with a veil, and gifted with second-sight in this American world. . . ."[8] In voodoo belief, the seventh son is the fortunate one and to be born with a veil is to have the gift of prophecy. Hegel had not treated the temperate zone of North America with depth because, as he said, that was the future and he was concerned with History.[9] DuBois stood ready to fill out the story quickly, inserting black folk into North America and drawing out the Hegelian dialectic with a heavy hand. Out of American Negro slavery itself had come black Freedom, he declared. The Freedom that black folk in America came to know was newer and richer than any known before because "few men ever worshipped Freedom with half such unquestioning faith as did the American Negro for two centuries." Out of slavery and out of the later striving of black folk for whiteness in an oppressive white world came a rising sense of black soul. Thus it was that white thesis bred black antithesis, which took the best of white culture and moved it upward toward a new synthesis. The whiteness that was in black Americans—the realization of the ideal of freedom, of civil rights, of white book-learning—was a good thing. It had brought blackness to life and had nurtured it. Du Bois would not erase white learning from black minds. Rather would he mature the new-found blackness both with and against whiteness. Out of the racial dialectic would come an eventual harmony. Thus, what appears to us on earth as conflict and strife—"two souls, ... two ... strivings; two warring ideals—" is but the working out of the Hegelian process. What seems to be a contradiction and an insoluble problem is, in Hegelian dialectics, a solution in progress. One needs to add only faith and will. The move toward self-conscious blackness had begun, and it would run its inevitable course. When black people know their souls, they will know Truth, Beauty, and, the ultimate reality, God. When they know themselves, they will know whiteness too, and they will be at peace with the whiteness that is within them. In America, black and white will finally join together in rising harmony and unity to make a better nation, to form a new thesis in which human brotherhood and human freedom will more perfectly reign.

HOW DU BOIS BECAME A HEGELIAN

How was it that Du Bois became so deeply Hegelian? The answer is by personal commitment and an academic progression.

When Du Bois went to Fisk in the fall of 1885, he was already committed to accepting black folk as his own in spite of his Northernness and his own light skin. From the time that the "tall newcomer" had snubbed him and the veil had dropped, Du Bois cultivated his alienation as a virtue. "I had thereafter no desire to tear down that veil, to creep through; I held all beyond it in common contempt, and lived above it in a region of blue sky and great wandering shadows," he recalled. "The sky was bluest when I could beat my mates at examination-time, or beat them in a foot-race, or even beat their stringy heads."[10] His family and white friends resented the fact that the local whites who sponsored his education were sending him South. But Will Du Bois welcomed the opportunity. He realized that at home he was falling into a "spiritual isolation," and he saw in the South a chance to join his own. At dinner on the night of his arrival at Fisk he was "deliriously happy" to sit across the table from "two of the most beautiful beings God ever revealed to the eyes of 17." One of these was Lena Calhoun, the great aunt of the actress Lena Horne, and, according to Du Bois, "far more beautiful." He gloried in the beauty and strength of his schoolmates, and for two summers he went out to teach black children in rural Tennessee. At Harvard University he continued to accept himself "as a member of a segregated caste."[11]

There were signs that at Fisk Du Bois had already begun to think in Hegelian terms. Philosophy under President Ernest Cravath had been his favored subject. In moving on to Harvard, he recalled, "above all I wanted to study philosophy!" He chose to take a course in ethics with George Herbert Palmer, the chairman of the Department of Philosophy and a popular lecturer.[12] Most of all he was a profound and devoted Hegelian, and famous as one of those scholars who promoted a revived Hegelianism in the United States in the 1880s.[13] Du Bois could hardly avoid meeting Hegelian thought in academic America, and it was a philosophy that was congenial to his nature and his needs. Even so, he always combined, like America at large in his lifetime, a paradoxical teaming of the ideal and the real, the romantic and the pragmatic. At Harvard he further refined and combined each.

It happened that Palmer went on Sabbatical before Du Bois arrived in Cambridge in 1888, and the new student actually took his first philosophy course under William James.[14] James was in the process of developing his "pragmatic philosophy." As yet, he had not so much developed a philosophy as he had an opposition, including a loyal and loving opposition to such idealism as was represented by Palmer's Hegelianism.[15] Du Bois found James intriguing, and James responded. As James's young colleague George Santayana noted, James had a "love of lame ducks and neglected possibilities."[16] Those predilections certainly got Du Bois two votes from his philosophy professor. James invited Du Bois to his home several times, and he became, as Du Bois remembered, "my friend and guide to clear thinking."[17] During his first year at Harvard, Du Bois also counted among his favorite professors Nathaniel Southgate Shaler, protégé of Louis Agassiz and, as we have seen, one of the architects of Radicalism. Shaler was a professor of natural sciences whose class in basic geology attracted hundreds of students.[18] A central theme of Shaler's teaching stressed the great age of the earth and the longevity of man's presence on the earth. He taught that each people had distinctive traits that were deeply grooved in time, pre-set almost before history began. In 1904 he published a book about black people, alleging that they were born with certain traits. Among these he stressed their spiritual and musical natures.[19] Shaler, a Kentuckian by birth and the son of a slaveholder, was also very sympathetic to Du Bois. He expelled a student from his class who objected to sitting next to

DuBois because of his color. The professor explained to DuBois that the expelled scholar "wasn't doing very well, anyway."[20]

In his second year, DuBois studied French and German philosophy with Santayana, then a young instructor fresh from studies at the University of Berlin. In the same year, he earned an "A+" in history from Albert Bushnell Hart, who had himself appropriated from the Germans the seminar method of graduate instruction along with a faith that the scientific study of the institutions of a people would reveal the nature of their fundamental genius. Hart was fascinated by the race problem in America, and he took a special interest in young DuBois.[21] At the end of his senior year, in his commencement oration, DuBois combined philosophy and history. In a tight, neat dialectic, he pitted the arrogant, aristocratic Jefferson Davis as the logical product of antebellum Southern culture against an opposite pole of, as DuBois worded it, "the patient, trustful, submissive African as a type of citizen the world would some day honor."[22]

A graduate student in his third year at Harvard, 1890–91, DuBois adopted an activist method he would long pursue, that of the social science researcher. He would study the Negro scientifically, he resolved, and find the truth beneath the black experience. Even as he continued to refine the idealistic side of his philosophy, DuBois evolved a realistic side. One might spend his life in that, as he phrased it, "lovely but sterile land of philosophic speculation." He had wanted to do just that before he met James and Hart. James convinced him that philosophy paid poorly, and Hart not only opened the way for him to a profession, he also trained him in the social science method, a device that would give substance to his philosophy. " ... after my work with Hart in United States history," he recalled in his autobiography, "I conceived the idea of applying philosophy to an historical interpretation of race relations." At Hart's suggestion, he began that work with his doctoral dissertation on the suppression of the African slave trade to America.[23]

In the fall of 1892, DuBois went abroad to study. In Europe he met racial prejudice, but there were significant times when he seemed able to let his blackness go and to appreciate the fact that "white folk were human."[24] More at ease with whites himself, he was able to see more clearly a black folk independent of whiteness. Europe also seemed to give DuBois an appreciation of the contemporary world. Nationalistic, capitalistic, and industrializing, white Europe was rapidly devouring the colored world, from South Africa to Samoa, from Singapore to Siberia. That great fact did not escape the young scholar.

In Germany, DuBois chose to study in the University of Berlin. Perhaps it was not significant that Berlin was the university where Hegel himself had brought his great career to a close three generations before. It was significant, however, that when DuBois arrived, Berlin was in the midst of a Hegelian revival. Among those under whom DuBois studied in his first semester was

Heinrich von Treitschke, perhaps the most famous of the neo-Hegelians. DuBois was deeply impressed by "the great Teuton." "To me by far the most interesting of the professors is the well-known von Treitschke," he declared in his diary.[25]

On the eve of his twenty-fifth birthday, February 23, 1893, DuBois performed a solitary and singular ceremony that suggested that he had absorbed a large and rather pure dose of Hegelianism. Alone in his room, he made, as he reported in his diary, a "sacrifice to the Zeitgeist." He conjured with candles, wine, oil, song, and prayer, and dedicated his library to his long-dead mother. Finally, he turned to his diary. "I am glad I am living," he wrote, "I rejoice as a strong man to run a race, and I am strong—is it egotism, is it assurance—or is it the silent call of the world spirit that makes me feel that I am royal and that beneath my sceptre a world of kings shall bow." He resolved to live his life to the fullest, declaring: "Its end is its greatest and fullest self—this end is the Good. The Beautiful its attribute—its soul and Truth is its being." Perhaps the candle was still flickering against the iron cold winter night as he resolved to live for the good of his black brothers and sisters, and for the world's good. The latter he could not define. "I therefore," he vowed, "take the work that the Unknown lays in my hands & work for the rise of the Negro people, taking for granted that their best development means the best development of the world." DuBois paused, then he concluded. "These are my plans: to make a name in science, to make a name in literature and thus to raise my race. Or, perhaps to raise a visible empire in Africa thro' England, France, or Germany."[26]

It is possible, then, that by 1893 DuBois saw himself potentially as one of Hegel's world-historical-men, a dark Messiah to lead his people toward salvation. In June 1888 his commencement oration at Fiske had been on Bismarck, a man who, by his own strength and will, "had made a nation out of a mass of bickering peoples."[27] More recently, he had felt the thundering pan-Germanism of von Treitschke. DuBois as a black Bismarck was very conceivable in Hegelian terms, for salvation existed in a new idea, realized by a very special man. As Hegel explained, there are ideas whose times have come. A "*creating* Idea," a truth striving toward a consciousness of itself, will come to light in the personal ambition of a *World Historical Individual*. Hegel had offered the example of Caesar, whose great ambition served his people, even as it served Caesar. "Such are all great historical men," asserted Hegel, "—whose own particular aims involve those large issues which are the will of the World Spirit." Historical men move from an "inner Spirit," he said, "which, impinging on the outer world as on a shell, burst it to pieces, because it is another kernel than that which belonged to the shell in question." These people are Heroes; their visions, their deeds, their words signify the essence of their times; and their fellows listen because they hear and know intuitively that the hero speaks the truth for that epoch. No happy hearts are heroes. A life of strife, of struggle, of essential and profound unhappiness, and then, as Hegel said, "they die early, like Alexander; they are murdered, like Caesar; transported to St. Helena, like Napoleon."[28] It was not the fate of DuBois to suffer the great end, though he courted both suffering and the great end. He did not die early but late; he was not murdered, and would not even be forced into exile. But he could take himself off to Africa at last, as he did; and he could have an ultimately unfulfilled and tragic life-time, and he did that too.

Thus Hegel gave DuBois a philosophy and a purpose in life, both of which he very much needed. Hegel also gave him a formula for working his way out of a difficult situation for himself and for black people. In the real world whites were not accepting blacks into a culture dominated by whites, and the prospects were that they never would. If black life was to have meaning, to have value, it would have to be a separated life. If black people were to find values for themselves, those values would have to be black and tied to a separated black culture. DuBois used Hegelianism to rationalize his way around the white wall, to legitimize its existence, and its exclusiveness, without devaluing himself or his people. In its meanest possibility, DuBois's system was an evasion of reality; it was a way of coping with the outrageous oppression of blacks in American life. Like an earlier evasion of magnificent proportions, it asserted that the City of God was in Heaven rather than Rome. It was at first more a formula for survival than for prosperity. It was a philosophical system constructed to obviate an outrageous reality, a way of dealing mentally with impossible and omnipresent oppression. In its best possibility, on the other hand, it was the salvation of black America.

DU BOISIAN ACTION AS HEGELIAN

What does this presentation of DuBois as an Hegelian add to what we already know? First, it adds something to the picture of DuBois as a black leader. It seems that in 1893 DuBois saw himself as destined for great things as a leader of his race, perhaps even as the world historical man who would lead his people onto the stage to play their destined role in the progress of mankind. This sense of mission shaped his attitude toward other black leaders. In 1891 he alluded to the venerable Frederick Douglas as a "time server."[29] In 1903, at the age of thirty-five and while he was a professor in Atlanta University, he challenged an entrenched Booker T. Washington and the Tuskegee machine. Washington had other opponents; but it was DuBois who took the lead in the opposition, not with a machine, not with an organization, but with an idea— the souls of black folk. DuBois's strength in the combat lay in the breadth of his intellect. He was tremendously sophisticated. He was as complex as the world civilization from which he sprang, and he was superbly well armed to do combat in that world. In philosophy, his idealism encompassed his realism, and it also encompassed Booker Washington and the Tuskegee idea. Du Bois could go as far as Washington, and, also, he could go further. When Washington's program began to fail, Washington had no great alternative. As a realist, he dealt with what was, and the internal dynamics of what was—the rise of Radicalism—worked toward the continuing reduction of black people. As an idealist, Du Bois could deal not only with what was, but with what ought to be. He could absorb reality, and he could transcend it. It was not inevitable that the two men should have differed. Indeed, for several years they did not. It is conceivable that if the Tuskegee idea had worked well enough, if the world had not left it behind, Du Bois would never have raised the idealistic alternative as he did. But increasingly after 1900, as the world moved on, as lynching and riots continued, as legal disfranchisement, segregation and exclusion proceeded, it became clear that Southern Negroes under Washington's leadership were rapidly losing ground, especially in the deep South. For Du Bois the switch to the idealistic alternative was almost automatic.

Philosophically, Booker T. Washington was essentially a realist. He looked to the visible, palpable world for truth and concluded that black culture was separate from white only in that it was denied access to whiteness. There was no separate destiny, no divinely inspired integrity in blackness itself. Du Bois, on the other hand, began as an idealist. For him ultimate truth, ultimate reality existed in the realm of ideas. Once he assumed that color was culture, he permanently separated black from white, in America and in the world. But Du Bois was not without the means of meeting Washington on his own ground. His idealism, like that of many of his contemporaries, was complemented by a host of practical programs, Thus he could whole-heartedly endorse black business, scientific farming, and industrial education for the mass of black youth, and sometimes he seemed himself very Washingtonian.

Further, if one remarks Du Bois's "Messiah complex," one understands his loneliness, his aloofness, and final alienation. The role prescribed such isolation, and Du Bois seemed determined, often perversely, to achieve it. The role also prescribed suffering, and he sought that too. In a smooth mixture of Christian and Hegelian metaphors, he painted himself in *Dusk of Dawn* as being "crucified on the vast wheel of time," while "he flew round and round with the zeitgeist."[30]

Also Hegelianism was easily turned into Marxian socialism. As Karl Marx declared, he found Hegel standing on his head, and he set him aright. Setting him aright consisted of substituting material or economic engines for ideational ones. Du Bois was impressed with the power of economics in determining culture. His pursuit of the "scientific method" in studying the Negro problem inevitably brought him into contact with the pervasive power of economic motivation. He was early attracted to socialism, and it is often asserted that in the 1930s he became a Marxist. Yet he was also repelled by the racism of socialists, and it is not at all clear that his Marxism was not Hegelianism "nebulously, almost sulphorously" rendered. Ultimately, he was probably always more Hegelian than Marxist and distinctly more black than socialist. If Hegel was upside down, then Du Bois seemed quite comfortable in that position.

When seen in the frame of Hegelianism, Du Bois's turn in the 1930s to the "self-segregation" of blacks was not, as critics charged, a giving up of the struggle for equal rights in America or a reversal of previous directions. It was rather a reasonable reaction to black folk losing their souls to whiteness in the despair of depression. It is more of Du Bois's steady idea that only by realizing their own genius can black people share fully in America. It is only by getting out that they can get in.

Always some American blacks had been interested in Africa, but it was Du Bois who grandly rationalized and institutionalized that interest, who gave it international organization in a series of conferences. Black soul led inevitably to black Africa. Blacks all over the world were bound together by blackness, but mother Africa was home. If, as Hegel said, the history of the world is the struggle of the World Spirit through world historical peoples to realize the principle that every one is Free; if, as he suggested, each great people has its special geography; and if, as Du Bois intimated, the black race is the seventh and next world-historical people, then Africa is the place where freedom will reach its next and highest level. "Africa," he wrote in 1924, "is the Spiritual Frontier of human kind."[31] Thus, the preservation and the promotion by all blacks of mother Africa, of Pan-Africanism, became vitally important. Du Bois organized the first Pan-African Conference in London in 1899. He led another in Paris in 1919. Eventually, he would go to Africa and make it his home. In the end, he would die and be buried where blackness began.

Finally, and by far most important, is the fact that Du Bois's Hegelianism led him into generating what appears to be one of the lasting polar positions through which black people in America interpret themselves. Du Bois was the first of the soul brothers, and he was more than that: he was the Christ of the soul movement, the man with the saving idea. Very much as if he were acting out that Messianic complex evinced on the eve of his twenty-fifth birthday, he came forth with the idea that was to save his people. He was the first to provide a large and satisfying philosophy that declared that black is not only present and innate, that black blood means a black culture that is not and never can be white, but that it is also God-given and beautiful. Far from erasing black culture and merging black folk into the white world, he would cultivate black culture and preserve its uniqueness. The Harlem Renaissance in the 1920s went very far precisely in that endeavor.

This brings us back to where we began. Like black people at large in America, DuBois was both black and white, culturally as well as physically. He was at war with himself, in himself, as were black people. To be black and to be American seemed a contradiction because America seemed so totally a white nation. With the concept of black soul he was able to transcend the apparent contradiction. True blackness, when realized, would incorporate the best of the white American experience, and rise to new heights of truth, of reality, of being—without ever ceasing to be black.

The soul movement, so pervasive among black people in America in the 1960s, had its strong beginnings with DuBois. In the early twentieth-century, the movement had its pharisees, and its Herod. It had its heresies and its apostates, and later in the 1920s its Renaissance and its Reformation. Even recently, white America seems to be in the process of granting the soul movement an edict of toleration. It seems highly probable that the Church Black—like the Church White—is here to stay. If we would better understand the Church Black, the cult of soul, we might lay the template of Hegelianism upon it. One can understand the special passion of the soul movement in the late 1960s to include all of the brothers and sisters if he knows that in the Hegelian system souls are not purely single, that each suffers the flesh, that each is liable to be overwhelmed by the world of matter unless it realizes its true life in a spiritual communion with its folk. Black people who do not join the communion are beyond the pale, cut off from the warming light of being, doomed to wander the earth like zombies, as flesh without soul, to suffer not simply isolation and death, but unreality and non-being. Salvation lay only and ultimately in the Church Black, and all without were doomed.

DuBois died in 1963. If he had lived still another decade, he would probably have viewed the progress of events in America with great satisfaction, with, indeed, feelings of vindication. He would have seen black consciousness move up yet another round on the Hegelian spiral. The civil rights movement struggled against white oppression. It made its mark upon the white world, but it made a greater mark on the black world. Out of the very denial of whiteness, out of the denial of American-ness, out of the continuing oppression of neo-slavery came black self assertion. In the stress, in the struggle, in the storm to get into whiteness, black people rediscovered blackness. They found that to melt oneself into whiteness, to be perfectly white American, would have been death and denial. In the storm and stress of trying to get in, black people had learned that they had to get out—that their first duty was to know themselves. In the mid-1960s the song shifted from "We shall overcome" to black is beautiful. Black people struggled, and they rose to a newer and higher awareness of self—an awareness that now could never be denied, never reversed, that would always be a part of what is to come.

DuBois, more than any other person, gave black people in America the concept of soul as a way of organizing their lives. In doing so he gave them a vital and enduring idea that not only gave them a present, it also gave them a past, and a promising future.

CHAPTER XIV

White Soul

DuBois left a great legacy to black people, but he also left something of value to white Americans. If one is white and American, appreciating the idea of black soul is a way of understanding one's white self more fully. Lamentably, white people in the South in the turn-of-the-century decades had no DuBois to call forth so powerfully their better selves in ethnic terms. Their whiteness had focus, but the focus was all too often tragically directed against other races, specifically against blacks by Radicals. Yet, a few thoughtful whites in the early years of the twentieth century did borrow structures from Western idealism to build up a positive image for white Southerners just as DuBois drew materials from the same source to construct a positive image for blacks. These people respected the souls of black folk, and they generated a concept of White Soul, a Church White that paralleled Black Soul and the Church Black. They poured great energies into the effort to propagandize the gospel of whiteness and to realize its genius. The emergence among white people of popular education, popular religion, popular politics, and a warming interest in Appalachian and swampland folklore as deep-freeze depositories of Anglo-Saxon purity were all, in significant measure, conscious attempts to bring forth white soul. What might well be called "Volksgeistian Conservatism" was abroad in the land, and it left deep and lasting marks upon Southern white culture in the twentieth century.

The term Volksgeistian Conservatism describes this thought-set very well because, first, it presumed that God had implanted in Southern white folk a unique and valuable spirit—that is, a "Volksgeist"; second, it was a rather direct translation of Germanic, and particularly Hegelian, idealism into the Southern cultural and racial scene; and, third, it sprang from roots that were indeed squarely within the Southern Conservative tradition. It was no mere coincidence that those who led the Volksgeistians in the propagation of the

414

gospel of whiteness were among those very persons who cared most for the souls of black folk. Often enough, individual Volksgeistians had initially launched efforts to raise the Negro. When those efforts failed, they turned their attention to the elevation of their white brothers and sisters.

Volksgeistian Conservatism, like Radicalism and Liberalism, was a splinter of racial Conservatism. Volksgeistians, like other white Southerners of their time, had all been born Conservatives. During the turn-of-the century years, however, they came to a new, more rarefied philosophical appreciation of the meaning of race. There were not many of them, but they were vastly influential upon people who had power, and, in that sense, Volksgeistian Conservatism was greater than the sum of its parts. It was as if it had a life of its own that transcended and outlived the few people who most clearly articulated it. It colored and moved everything that it touched, and it touched, in some way, everything. The institutions that ruled the South in the twentieth century were, essentially, the creatures of the early years of the century when the Volksgeistians waxed strong. Those institutions were deeply influenced in their inception by the Volksgeistian mood, and they came to rule the modern Southern world, not only in race, but in economics, politics, education, religion, courts of law, prisons, medicine, public health, philanthropy, journalism, folklore, and literature. Ironically, by the 1920s Volksgeistian Conservatism was dead as a system of thought, but the assumptions of the Volksgeistians had marked and continued to mark virtually every aspect of Southern life.

EDGAR GARDNER MURPHY AS A PRIME SPOKESMAN FOR VOLKSGEISTIAN CONSERVATISM

A pioneer exponent of Volksgeistian Conservatism was Edgar Gardner Murphy (1869–1913). Professionally, Murphy was an Episcopal priest. He was born in Fort Smith, Arkansas, in 1869. When Edgar was only five, his father deserted the family, leaving his wife, Janie Gardner Murphy, with two young children and afflicted with tuberculosis. Janie, with the help of her sister, took her children and made the trip by rail, stagecoach, and army ambulance to San Antonio, Texas, where the dry air was considered the best palliative for her disease. In San Antonio, she opened a boarding house. Janie Murphy worked hard and not only recovered her health but also gained a mild prosperity. Her boarding house became something of a social center in the village. Among those attracted was the local Episcopal rector, Walter Richardson. The Reverend Mr. Richardson soon took Edgar into his choir, then into his church, and, finally, in 1885, persuaded the professors at the University of the South to take the young man on scholarship. At Sewanee, Edgar, already determined to enter the ministry, fell eagerly under the influence of William Porcher Du

Bose, the Chaplain of that arch Episcopal institution and the founder of what soon became its School of Theology. From Du Bose, Murphy absorbed a commitment to "living Christianity," that is to a creed that linked the spiritual world with the real world and saw the Christian mission as one that pursued palpable earthly as well as heavenly ends.

Murphy worked diligently throughout his life to advance the cause of social Christianity, first as a lay assistant to the rector in San Antonio, next as an Episcopal priest in Laredo, then for six years as rector of a parish in Chillicothe, Ohio, and for another year at Kingston, New York. Murphy was "high Church," a phrase identifying those more aristocratically inclined Episcopalians who stressed the importance of ritual and hierarchy within the denomination. But he also believed that the Christian church had a duty to care for the bodies as well as the souls of all people—low as well as high. Consequently, wherever he went, he moved with what came to be called the "Social Gospel," establishing missions to the poorer classes, white and black, and clubs for the young. In 1898 he returned to the South to take the rectorship of Trinity Church in Montgomery, Alabama, probably the most influential Episcopal parish in the state.

As Murphy himself later declared, his initial public act concerned the race problem. Like many Conservatives, he was first activated by the monstrous evil of lynching. Early in 1893 he organized a petition in which a number of citizens of Laredo protested the torture-lynching of the "Negro Smith" in Paris, Texas. In the words of that document, written by the twenty-four-year-old priest, there was "no justification of a penalty which made an orgy of torture and a festival of agony." Even though the petition carefully stated that the signers complained only of the manner in which Smith was put to death and not his execution, Murphy was able to persuade barely a score of the men of Laredo to endorse the statement. Further, he suffered the direct opposition of many of the town's leading citizens, including members of his own parish.[1]

Undaunted, Murphy continued to labor for the salvation of blacks. In Laredo, Chillicothe, and Montgomery, he founded missionary churches in the black communities. During 1899, the first year of his renewed residence in the South, lynching seemed to reach a crescendo of horror, particularly in the neighboring state of Georgia. Deeply distressed, Murphy organized a "Southern Society" to study the race problem. Soon, the society planned a grand Race Conference to be held in Montgomery in May 1900. Presided over by the racially moderate and highly respected Hilary A. Herbert, recently Cleveland's Secretary of the Navy, twenty-one carefully selected persons addressed the Conference. Seventeen of these were racially Conservative, four were Radicals. Walter F. Willcox came from Cornell to give a social scientific prospectus for the evaporation of black people from America. Alfred Moore Waddell came fresh from the front lines of inter-racial combat in Wilmington to argue for the inevitable race war. John Temple Graves pled for racial separation, and Paul M. Barringer brought all of the prestige of the Chairman of the Faculty of the University of Virginia to preach, much to Murphy's distress, the gospel of black retrogression and dissolution.[2] After some discussion of the matter, it had been decided that no Negroes would be invited to speak, the leading candidate having been Booker T. Washington. However, on the night of the final session, several hundred blacks were admitted to the galleries.

Murphy's use of the conference was typical of the Conservative style of leadership. He immediately pronounced it a resounding victory for racial Conservatism and spoke as if the whole of the thoughtful South would fall into line. Somehow, he passed over the fact that he himself had loaded the dice and smoothly arranged the final score of seventeen to four.[3] Assuming that the world was ready for reform, Murphy immediately proposed the establishment of a national magazine to be called *Race Problems*. That journal, edited by himself, would serve as a clearing house for ideas on the subject. Further, he suggested the establishment of an advisory board on racial matters to operate at the national level and composed of men who thought along Conservative lines. The Montgomery Conference had been held with the idea that it would be repeated annually. For a time, meetings in other cities in successive years were suggested. After a few months, however, all this faded. No reason was given for the sudden collapse, only a muttering that time would be a better solvent to race problems than discussion.[4]

Murphy himself continued to think and to write on the subject of race relations in the South and in the nation at large. But his thinking and his writing on the matter turned into a new and highly important channel. This emerged most signally in two books: *Problem of the Present South*, which appeared in 1904, and *The Basis of Ascendancy*, which he published in 1910.[5] As an activist organizer, however, he all but deserted the black cause. Instead, he turned his energies into reform efforts for which the people were ripe and the response was—if not totally positive—ultimately gratifying. He turned initially to work on the problem of child labor, first in the textile mills of Montgomery and later in the South generally. Leaving that work in the care of a very able colleague, Andrew J. McKelway, he resigned from the priesthood in 1901 to become the Executive Secretary of the Southern Education Board. There he moved vigorously to meet the vast problem of public education in the South, especially the education of white children. In that effort he found his final and most rewarding call. For several years Murphy worked for the Board in New York and lived in New Haven with his wife and two sons. Soon he became one of the few most trusted brokers in the rapidly rising field of dealing out Northern philanthropy to Southern Education.[6]

From his academic training and out of his experience with the race problem, Edgar Murphy generated a relatively complete set of ideas on race in the

South, a set that he shared with some of his more influential contemporaries. As a thought system that squared neatly with currently observable facts of life, it was a beautiful piece of work and it had, for that reason if no other, great power in its time. Quite clearly, it made a large contribution toward building the "mind of the South" that reached its zenith in the 1920s and 1930s.

At the core of Murphy's racial system and implicit in his life and work was the idea that each people, each racial folk, had a genius, a spirit, a "Volksgeist," that was God-given, distinct, and the key to progress. "The deepest thing about man—next to his humanity itself—is," he declared, "his race."[7] Each people had a moral duty to strive to realize its genius because therein lay the salvation of the race and individuals within the race. The soul was the part of God in every man. By introspection, by knowing thyself, one knew God best, and, thereby one knew his brothers. Ultimately, all things, the seemingly separate genius of each people, and the souls of everyone were joined in God. God was the source of all truth, of all reality, of life, of being, and in his mind all things were one. In God's mind there were no conflicts, no disjunctions, no disharmony. Life on earth seemed contradictory and conflict-ridden only because we were yet so far from God. Salvation lay in each person searching out the essential nature of his own soul, in stripping away the shadows, the unreal husk of appearances to uncover the kernel of truth within. One could hardly begin that quest without establishing a communion with his brothers of like spirit. Truth was collectively rather than individually perceived. Thus each people, black and white, must withdraw from the other in some significant measure, perfect a communion with its inner nature, and rise to a consciousness of its unique genius. One need not be overly concerned about a seeming hostility between blacks and whites in America because there would inevitably come a union in God's being for Americans of all races. Meanwhile, each race had its duty. In the South, there was white soul to be sought on the one side, and the rich earth of blackness to be cultivated on the other. When the white South was true to itself, it would be true to blacks, and to white America at large. Murphy, like Du Bois, had full faith in "the unifying ideal of Race."[8]

By 1904 Murphy was arguing that "social segregation" was "the elementary working hypothesis of civilization in our Southern States." The separation of the black race was a necessary prelude to the raising up of black leadership and the cultivation of qualities of character among black people. Black folk, ultimately, could not be white, and it was a trespass against God's plan to attempt to make them so. There were, indeed, very narrow limits to what white people could do for black people. The real work was the definition and realization of black soul, and only blacks could perform that task. The primary obligation of the whites to the blacks was simply to give them the freedom, the isolation, the independence necessary for them to find themselves, to seek out their genius and to nourish it. White people must honor the efforts of black people. "If any race is to live it must have something to live for," Murphy insisted. "It will hardly cling with pride to its race integrity if its race world is a world wholly synonymous with degeneration, and if the world of the white man is the only generous and honorable world which it knows." America's best hope for progress, then, lay in a benevolent species of apartheid: "For the very reason that the race, in the apartness of its social life, is to work out its destiny as the separate member of a larger group, it must be accorded its own leaders and thinkers, its own scholars, activists, prophets; and while the development of the higher life may come slowly, even blunderingly, it is distinctly to be welcomed. . . ." Therein lies the real reason why America must license "race integrity."[9]

Murphy argued stoutly that segregation was not degradation. It answered the needs of both races. Of Negroes, he insisted, "every tendency of the present seems to be making not toward their disintegration but toward that social and domestic segregation demanded by their own interest as well as by the interest of the stronger race about them." In the Negro's behalf, the South had developed "customs which have protected him from hatred and have made possible his existence and his happiness." It was not at all a matter of separate and equal; it was a matter of separate and incomparable, of apples and oranges. Blacks were a child race and the white race was mature and strong, but neither race was inherently better or worse than the other. They were, simply, different. The desire of the South, he explained, "is not to condemn the negro forever to a lower place but to accord him another place." This was indeed something new in Southern white though about blacks, and it was signalized in the phrase "another place." Potentially, it was revolutionary. In and after the last generation of slavery, Conservatism would have put the black man down in fixed subordination, and in the 1880s Liberalism would have put him up, in the 1890s Radicalism would have put him out, and, now, in the early twentieth century, Volksgeistian Conservatism would have put him, simply, aside. For Volksgeistians, the shoring up of the walls of segregation by legislation was acceptable because it decreased inter-racial friction, marked clearly the perimeters within which each race would find its identity, and promoted the growth of race consciousness. It was, as Murphy declared, but a wise extension of the rule that "good fences make good neighbors."[10] It behooved the white South to continue and to encourage the arrangement in order to allow black folk the freedom in which black soul could rise to self-consciousness unhampered by contact with whites. The alternative was to embrace the awful plight of the ancient mariner, to suffer marriage to a dead and dying thing, to tie the white South to soul-less flesh—the very negation of life.[11]

Race identity was a necessary stage in the advancement of world civilization, Murphy argued. For a time, whites must concentrate upon nurturing their whiteness as blacks must cultivate their darkness. In America, where whites were most numerous and where white soul was already well developed, white assertion would admittedly violate the ideal of democracy because blacks would in some degree be controlled by the stronger whites. But that was a temporary expense. "As a basis for democracy, the conscious unity of race is not wholly adequate," Murphy conceded, "but it is better as a basis of democratic reorganization than the distribution of wealth, or trade, or property, of family, of class."[12] Thus white racial democracy would save us from more egalitarian reorganizations such as socialism or communism. In one sense, antagonism between the races was lamentable. In another, it was natural because the races must hold themselves apart during this transitional stage. Particularly would race enmity be a trait among young persons because, more than their elders, they were empty vessels free to find and take their fill of the new race consciousness. Probably taking his thought from the current term "the new Negro," which was applied by whites to blacks born after 1865, Murphy suggested that Southern whites reared after slavery were also new men. "Between the new negro and the new white man, there is likely to be enmity and there is very sure to be suspicion," he declared.[13] But this seeming curse was actually a blessing. Among other things, it was reducing miscegenation to negligible proportions. The mulatto population, he surmised in an egregious and revealing error, was not the product of recent years, nor even of slavery ("for the old negroes are the black negroes"!). They sprang instead, he declared with astonishing sureness, from the loins of the marching armies at the close of the war when "the lower classes of the Northern army demoralized by idleness" and "the lower class of the Southern army demoralized by defeat" were "thrown into contact with the negro masses at the moment of their greatest helplessness."[14]

Like many white liberals in the late 1960s, Murphy concluded that, ultimately, only blacks could save blacks, and that the true labor of white leaders lay on the white side of the color line. " . . . the white race, in the interest of the efficiency and the happiness of the masses of its own life, must bring its culture still more closely into relation with social needs." The culture of the South, he declared, will find "its supreme and immediate interest" in "the undeveloped force of the stronger race."[15] Murphy's philosophy reflected the facile and graceful turn that he himself had made, swinging his primary effort within a few months from the white man's burden *vis à vis* blacks to one to save white children from the bone-crushing jaws of the industrial Leviathan, and then, within another few months, still again to a very satisfying crusade to bring all white children into the white communion by way of a compulsory public education. God's time may not have arrived to save whites from committing atrocious crimes against blacks. It did so only painfully and slowly for child labor reform. But clearly the *Zeitgeist* favored the public school movement, and Murphy spent the last dozen years of his life in that labor, joyfully and triumphantly.

Edgar Gardner Murphy could thus serenely leave blacks alone because he confidently expected that in the end American democracy would open its arms to embrace all colors. He could easily differ with Booker T. Washington on such issues as the repeal of the Fifteenth Amendment—which he favored, contending that the Amendment was an artificial construction not in harmony with the times—because, as he phrased it, he had faith in the eventual "realization" of ideals, in this case, in the ideal of democracy. One key idea that was bound to rule eventually was the Christian ideal of the brotherhood of man. In the last order, there would be a grand democracy in American life, and "its unity is truer and richer because not run in one color or expressed in monotony of form. Like all vital unities, it is composite."[16]

DEMOCRACY AND EDUCATION IN THE NEW SOUTH

Conservative thought did change from time to time. One of the ways it changed in the late nineteenth and early twentieth century was to come about to accept the arrival of an all-white "democracy." For instance, Walter Hines Page, in "The Forgotten Man," a famous speech given in Greensboro, North Carolina, in 1897, called for the elevation of the plain folk of the South. By 1902 he was hardly less than ecstatic in anticipating that event. The South, he thought, held the promise of evolving a more perfect democracy than any yet seen in America. Southerners, he concluded, "are the purest American stock we have," and it was their destiny to generate "a democratic order of society which will be a rich contribution to the republic that their ancestors took so large a part in establishing."[17] Page was not alone. In contrast to the horror with which men like Charles E. A. Gayarré and Paul Hamilton Hayne had viewed "levelling tendencies" in the 1880s, there was a curious happiness in the acceptance of the "new democracy" by Conservatives at large in the turn-of-the-century years. That shift was probably closely related to the abundant presence of blacks no longer under their control and to the rise of Radicalism, and it was definitely facilitated by the rationales of Volksgeistian Conservatism. If the matter of the race problem was getting out of hand, if blacks were acting independently and whites were outrageous, Volksgeistian thought offered a marvelous retreat that allowed one to say, after making an effort at racial reform and the restoration of social sanity, that there was presently nothing of substance to be done with black people. Furthermore, if a white Conservative found himself powerless to accomplish anything helpful on the black side of the race line, it was consoling to know that he could be highly effective on the white side—and this meant effective among white people of the lower elements. Whatever the reasons for their acceptance of the new political order, whatever the sources from which their rationale was taken, many Conservatives, especially those accustomed to working in intellectual circles, came easily to embrace the "new democracy" and place it firmly in an idealistic setting that was distinctly Germanic.

Implicitly, Murphy applied the Hegelian formula to the South as he saw it in the early twentieth century. The Old South had represented a new and higher stage of society. Most of all the institution of slavery had generated a patrician leadership, conscious of its place, its honors, and its responsibilities to the masses, white as well as black. Paternalistically cared for by the elite, but "outside the essential councils of the South," were two great classes of people, the "non-participants," as Murphy labeled these two classes. The non-participants were the Negroes and "the non-slaveholding white men." As the early twentieth century unfolded, it was evident to him that white society in the South was ready to rise another round on the scale of progress and achieve a flowering on a higher plane. Through the travail of slavery, through the test of fire in civil war, and through the hard moral tribulations of black Reconstruction, the lower elements of white people in the South had suffered and risen to a more refined level of purity, of spirituality, of self-consciousness. Even in the antebellum South while non-slaveholders were sometimes opposed to the thesis of slavery, they were nevertheless absorbing something of the manners, ideas, and values of the slaveholding elite. What followed the dialectical struggle between thesis and anti-thesis was the synthesis that had already occurred in the early twentieth century. The line of division between the old elite and the white mass was still visible, but total fusion was inevitably coming. Even then lower-class whites were being rapidly integrated into Southern life—politically, economically, and socially. Thus it was that "the expanding and enlarging life of democracy has included in the conscious movement of our civilization the most important of the non-participants of the older order." Murphy hailed the transition as a significant event in the progress of the world. "It is," he declared, "one of the far-reaching achievements of a democratic age." One should not be disturbed that it was the whites who rose first. "It was inevitable that the movement of democracy should have included the non-participants of the homogeneous population," he explained.[18] A later stage would embrace the blacks.

In this synthetic phase, the new democracy was not without its dangers, and Murphy hastened to warn the South against itself. Democracy could err, and when it did, there was grave danger that the error would be made to seem not an error but the opposite because in the new age mass sentiment tended to be accepted as morally correct. Thus, it was easily possible to introduce a wrong "into the national life and national spirit" that could not be easily removed. The preventive was a moral and intellectual leadership, a leadership that the masses might cultivate by according "trust and reverence everywhere to the policies of freedom," especially to freedom of thought and expression. Paradoxically, Murphy's concern to save the people from error almost brought him back to deny democracy by giving a license to the authorities to thwart the popular will. Sometimes, he pointed out, probably recalling the Sledd and Bassett cases, "those who have served democracy most truly are those who have saved the people from themselves."[19]

Predictably, Murphy thought that the universities of the South were key centers for the development of the moral and intellectual leadership desired. Here was where the masses must allow a maximum of freedom and tolerance. Here young men would hone themselves to a sharp perception of God's will in this world. In the universities would be generated the diversity of ideas from which would emerge the single ideas, one after another, that would bring the South up through successive stages of progress. A wide range of perceptions, bred in open and intensive inquiry, would prove the saving grace of Southern civilization. It was around this banner of freedom of thought, perhaps more easily than around any other, that racial Conservatives leaders—both Volksgeistian and regular—in the New South could rally. They could readily join in deploring the outcome of the Sledd case at Emory and take great heart in the results of John Spencer Bassett's affray with the Radicals in North Carolina. There were other cases, and out of them came both defeats and victories. In the main, however, Conservatives and their Volksgeistian allies did seize the universities as strongholds and castles. There they slowly and successfully built up the not-always-ivory towers against the repeated onslaughts of the Radicals.

The masses must give latitude to their leaders, Murphy argued, but the leaders had obligations to the masses. The South was particularly fortunate in having an upper class that possessed a high sense of responsibility for the lower orders. Ironically, slavery itself had deepened that sense of *noblesse oblige,* of paternalism. This was, to quote Murphy, "the noble and fruitful gift of the old South to the new, a gift brought out of the conditions of an aristocracy, but responsive and operative under every challenge in the changing condition of the later order." Paternalism, an idea generated directly by a ripened slavery, tried, tested, and found true in the Civil War, was a central value of the old order that would be brought to the new. The idea was brilliantly "personified in Lee." Robert E. Lee was the perfect product of the idealism of the Old South. He had himself shouldered the blame for the defeat at Gettysburg, and when asked why he was so protective of his men, he answered: "Because they are under me." General Lee was the paragon, but Murphy went on to name other, more latter-day saints such as J. L. M. Curry, Lucius Quintus Cincinnatus Lamar, Charles Brantley Aycock, Hilary A. Herbert, and Andrew

Montague (the Virginia governor), men who illustrated that the ideal of paternalism lived on after slavery had died.[20]

The new synthesis would also be effected in culture generally, and specifically in education. The masses, Murphy predicted, would be caught up in the
burgeoning common school system in the South. New England, the North,
and the West had long since established more or less comprehensive systems
of elementary education. The South had been peculiarly laggard in that area.
Almost as if to celebrate the beginning of a new century with the beginning
of a new cultural era, the South after 1900 finally realized the ideal of mass
education that had been preached for two generations.[21] Thus it was that great
flocks of white youth were being ushered into the persisting high culture of
the Old South through the schoolhouse doors. In the schools they found teachers and administrators who were not common folk like themselves, but rather
the vestigal remains of that Old South aristocracy. The schoolhouse was
staffed by the sons and daughters of the Old Regime. And in that place they
brought the lasting values of the Old South to the children of the New.[22]

In his writing Murphy gave pointed recognition to a revolution in public
education in the South that was actually taking place. Compulsory education
laws were forcing into the schools virtually every Southern white child who
was not a fugitive, notwithstanding a measure of opposition from recalcitrant
parents at the lower end of the economic and social scales who were suspicious
of the use the white elite intended to make of their children.

At school, it was especially the daughters of the Old South who ruled the
students. Often, she was without husband. Her father had been a planter, a
slaveholder, and an officer of rank in the Confederate States Army. But she
never—or almost never, certainly never in such a way as to seem to boast—
reminded her pupils of her origins and her social status; to say it herself would
be to destroy it. Others would say it for her as needed, but it was seldom
needed because everyone knew it well enough. She taught her students reading, writing, and arithmentic, but that was only the beginning and the lesser
part of her labors. Most of all, she brought them into the white communion.
As Walter Hines Page well said, "Educational work in these states is . . . something more than the teaching of youth: it is the building of a new social
order."[23]

Specifically, the teacher taught her children to take care of their bodies, to
improve their minds, and to act like, to think like, and eventually to be ladies
and gentlemen. The schoolgirl would be a little lady, and sugar and spice and
everything nice would describe her neatly enough. Girls were important, but
boys were more so, the sexes bearing a relation to one another not unlike
support troops to combat troops. The teacher would fix herself specially on
the bright young men, and if they survived her instruction they would be
gentlemen. If they wanted to go anywhere at all in that Southern world, they

had to absorb her teaching more fully and more totally than any Sambo ever did his tutored role. And if these men were sometimes other things—liars, laggards, drunks, cowards, and cheats—they at least knew their sins and rued them. When they were good, they were very, very good; and when they were bad, of course, they were horrid. In the twentieth century, the Southern male at large was given to a special schizophrenia in which he did, indeed, sometimes have trouble in meeting himself.

Her given name might well be Emily, Ethel, or Minerva, and her family name might well be something like Hampton or Habersham. If it were, say, Minerva, her students and everybody else would call her "Miss Minerva." The odds were that she was without husband, especially as long as she pursued her profession. Her lack of husband, her chastity, her spare spinster body itself announced the fact that she saved herself for this mission so gravely and utterly demanding that it could brook no rival, no drain of energy to husband, much less child, no ounce or pound of extra flesh of body to slow her soul in the pursuit of its goal, only bones, muscles, and tendons visible here and there under taut white skin. She was sometimes over-rouged like a toy soldier, but that seeming sumptuousness only made more vivid the plain purity that lay beneath. Miss Minerva had no visible husband, but she was married. She was married to the Church Social of the Old South. She wore the habit in expensive but sensible shoes, gloves, and often a silly hat that she somehow fancied to be especially feminine. Her cross was a cameo, and her Bible was The Bible, and, sometimes but not necessarily at all, *The Book of Common Prayer*. Her saints were the saints of the South.

Miss Minerva was her name and manners were her game. She knew her manners and so should you. Little girls always did this and never that. Little boys were something else again and much more complex. First she taught the boys respect for women, and when she had done that she might go on to adoration, and, when she could, still further to pedestalization and idolization. But again, that was only a beginning, a commencement, an ordinary process of life like breathing and walking, a necessary function that one did as a matter of course and habit without thinking so that one could free himself to go on and do greater things. The greater end was to teach values, to teach what was important. Featured were: (1) honor (2) courage (3) grace (4) Christian reverence (5) truth (6) loyalty (7) respect for self and others (good manners) (8) public service (9) law and order (10) hard work (11) personal cleanliness, and (12) good health. There was actually no priority in values; one did not come before another. Rather did they all come at once and all together.

Miss Minerva trained her boys well. For years afterward they would say "yes ma'am" and "no ma'am" and feel good about it. The very sound of the words was sweet to their ears, as if by saying the simple sounds they were in harmony with the music of the universe. Miss Minerva had tuned them up to that. The girls became ladies. At least enough girls became ladies to supply the need. Actually, one average Southern lady could easily keep at least three men fully supplied with ladyhood, and a few, the truly professional ladies, so to speak, could manage a score or more. With angelic smiles they anointed the good act, the noble male performance. They smiled a lot, and warmed by that radiant sun, gentlemen ran fast and with grace. Let a lady in a crowded hall head for a door, and half a dozen stout men begin a footrace to beat the fair white hand to the door knob. Let a lady drop a pencil in the post office, and bending male knees pop like a string of firecrackers on the Fourth of July. Let a lady pass down a Southern street of a summer's day, and a succession of seersucker-suited men touch their straw hats with the warm comforting monotony of wheat bowing to a breeze. Like rosary beads, these were things upon which people could count.

Miss Minerva was aware of the world, even sophisticated about it. Given that special Southern slant, she knew where things were. She might even have gone to Paris during one summer in her young adult years, with side trips to Mont-Saint-Michel and Chartres. Appearances to the contrary notwithstanding, she was not really a prude, and she was not at all devoid of humor. At bottom she was intelligent and very warm; she loved her students as she loved her work. Especially, it seems, she loved those little boys.

Little boys became men, and Miss Minerva's men would become gentlemen or else. No snakes, no snails, no puppy-dog tails allowed. Sometimes, frankly, it was matter of a painfully tweaked ear, a knuckle deftly rapped against a seemingly empty skull, and occasionally the twelve-inch ruler resounded against the upturned palm while girls made "O's" of their mouths and every boy but one relished the show. But mostly Miss Minerva bought what she sold, she ruled with what she ruled for—manners. More precisely— manner. Miss Minerva had, to use the vulgar term, style. She had grace, and she also had command. The brightest among her boys were at once the most vulnerable to what she taught and the most apt at learning it. With Jesuitical intelligence, Miss Minerva went for those fellows. And she got them mostly because they sensed that she was into something big, and she was. She had a system. She had a world in which a man could find validity and value for himself, not only a feeling of being, but a feeling of being somebody. It was a world, they somehow concluded, well worth the price of admission, and no man went that way but by Miss Minerva. There was a cost involved in maintaining the order of things beyond submission to the tutelage of that lady. The hidden cost of maintaining that Southern world in which Southern men *seemed* to have substance and power was the effective—but certainly not the rhetorical—subservience of the South to the North. As long as the ransom was paid, the Hun held himself at the gate and left the city to rule itself. But even if Miss Minerva was consciously aware of that hidden cost, she could not have told her boys about it. It was one of those things never discussed, any more than anyone ever talked about trying secession again.

The very poverty of the South, the material poverty of Miss Minerva and her sisters and cousins and aunts, perhaps helped to force these vestal virgins into the pedagogical temples of the New South. Yet, to some people, the poverty and its results seemed providential, more of mysterious ways miracles to perform. Edgar Gardner Murphy saw the poverty as a blessing that had brought these representatives of the highest culture into education, thus supplying "a teaching force of broad abilities, of real culture, and of generous refinement." In this fashion the Old South was "touching through its *best* the life and institutions of tomorrow."[24]

What was happening in a broad way at the base of the educational pyramid was also happening in a more exclusive and more concerted way in the colleges and universities, particularly those of antebellum origins. Miss Minerva's own "talented tenth" would go on to a higher education, in a large measure by her and for her. If the boy was a South Carolinian, for instance, and not already bent toward a technical education, he would probably go to the state university in Columbia rather than to either the technical school at Clemson, the military school in Charleston, or one of the small denominational colleges that dotted the state. If he went to the University in Columbia in or after 1909, he would encounter as his president a masculine counterpart to Miss Minerva, a gentleman who would further complete what she had begun. The president of the University of South Carolina in those years was Samuel Chiles Mitchell.

Mitchell, born in 1864, was out of the slaveholding aristocracy of Mississippi. He had attended Georgetown College in Kentucky and the University of Chicago to earn his degrees and had risen through the academic ranks to become a professor in Richmond College (later the University of Richmond), an eminent institution sponsored by the Virginia Baptists. Mitchell himself had caught the fever of idealism, in a major degree perhaps during his stay at the University of Chicago. He came to South Carolina convinced that the regeneration of the South depended upon a return to the quest for ideas, for ultimate values, as well as a more effective engagement by the University in the things of this world.[25] Under his aegis, the state university turned from a rather pedestrian traditional pursuit of the classics to a quest for the golden fleece. Or, rather, fleeces, the truths of life. The search advanced dialectically, in part, because most of the student body was divided into two debating societies—the Clariosophic and the Euphradian. The debating halls rang with cracked-voice adolescent oratory searching for the eternal verities lying enfolded in such ideas as "loyalty," "courage," "honor," and "love." The fever of idealism was catching, and for a time it seemed as if the south side of Columbia had moved back to pick up where Carolinians had left off in the 1850s when the fleece had definitely been sighted and, it seemed, almost

428   *Soul Folk*

grasped. There in the background was Medea—alias Miss Minerva, alias Southern womanhood.

Mitchell was, in essence, a more secular Edgar Gardner Murphy. He moved with sure foot and great energy to press the University into the living age. He expanded the offerings of the school to include such practical curricula as engineering and business. He inaugurated extension courses and an evening school by which the University reached out to touch palpably South Carolinians, old as well as young, far beyond its walls. He encouraged his professors to speak to the people on every possible occasion. He, himself, became very nearly notorious in that activity, once giving a talk to an audience of textile mill workers in Greenville on "Mirabeau, the Foremost Figure of the French Revolution." Mitchell was ardently for prohibition, child-labor reform, and compulsory education, and he was sympathetic to Negroes. In South Carolina, however, he found it necessary to repress somewhat expressions of his interest in these areas in order to be effective in others.

For four years Mitchell led the University to reach out into the state as never before to bring into the cultural communion all of the white people. Then entered the devil in the form of the Radical racist snake, Governor Coleman L. Blease (called Coley [ko-li] by his many enemies as well as his many friends). In 1913 Coley fired Mitchell amidst a general assault upon the alleged aristocracy of the university and its "diplomatized mollycoddles." The University did not collapse, nor did its idealism evaporate, but when the boys at the University got near the fleece later in the century, it wasn't quite the fleece anymore.[26]

Coley Blease was himself born neither a "redneck" nor a "linthead." Much as Tillman in the late 1880s had won the votes of the farmers by appearing in their wool-hat image, Blease won the votes of the dirt farmers and cotton mill workers by speaking their language, by seeming to be their champion, and by living and dressing in the outlandish style that they themselves would have lived and dressed in had they been governor. Blease's father had been, in fact, a businessman and a leader in Newberry, a small town just above the fall line. The elder Blease owned a hotel and livery stable and served as magistrate of the town. Coley, himself, had been educated at Newberry College, the University of South Carolina (before being expelled for plagiarism), and the law school of Georgetown University. Early on, he had been a Tillman supporter in the legislature and later boasted that he had introduced the first segregation legislation in South Carolina. By 1910 he had split with Tillman and won the gubernatorial chair over the opposition of a Tillman-backed Conservative.[27] Blease inaugurated a new fashion in political leadership in South Carolina— the demagogue, the extravagant, flamboyant, voluble, one-man band, full of sound and fury meaning very nearly naught. Coley's function was, ultimately, to occupy a public office and to entertain. His fulminations against the aristocracy and the University came to nothing. The University mustered its many friends and alumni in the legislature not only to survive, but to prosper as a Conservative stronghold long after Mitchell had been driven from the state. Like so many institutions generated and regenerated in the South in the early twentieth century, it continued to run in the quasi-popular style of its original momentum, even after it forgot why it was doing so.

THE INDUSTRIAL REVOLUTION IN THE SOUTH: FOR WHITES ONLY

By 1900 there was clearly under way a movement toward industrialization in the South. As Murphy and many others understood, this was not a new beginning but the revival of an old one. It was a renaissance and an extension of something that had begun before the Civil War and was on the verge of success in 1861. "It is but one reassertion of the genius of the old South," Murphy insisted. The largest industry in the South by 1910 was textiles—almost wholly cotton textiles. The movement had begun in the antebellum period, revived in the early 1880s, and boomed in the late 1890s. In the South in 1880, there were 161 textile mills employing 17,000 people. In 1900 there were 400 mills with 98,000 workers, and in 1904 the number of mills had swelled to 550. In 1907 there were 600 mills with 125,000 workers. By 1910, South Carolina was second in the nation only to Massachusetts in the number of spindles running, and North Carolina was fourth.[28] The boom in mill building peaked out after 1907 when, apparently, surplus labor had been absorbed. Murphy saw the mills as potentially a great liberating force for the region. In 1904 he maintained that textiles held the promise of effecting an "industrial rescue" from oblivion of a multitude of Southern whites among "the great army of nonparticipants." However, as the mills were then operating, they were not living up to their potential for good, especially in their employment of children. "The factory system, as a system, betrays a tendency to hold its humbler industrial forces in a state of arrested development; which from the broader social standpoint, and in relation to the larger life of democracy, means an arrested participation," he explained. "Here is an eddy in the fuller and freer current of democratic life; here, in the industrial imprisonment of the child, is a contradiction—however temporary—of those positive and deeper forces which are claiming the human possibilities of the individual—however lowly—as elements in the power and happiness of the State."[29] Murphy, himself, was a pioneer in promoting legislation to regulate the labor of children in the textile mills. But his work was not so much against the factories and the owners as it was for the children and the South.

Murphy asserted in an elaborate but abstract way that the South should accept the textile revolution, but Broadus Mitchell, in 1921, was the first to attempt a specific description of what it actually was in the region and to offer an explanation of how it got that way. Mitchell was the son of Samuel Chiles Mitchell. He was a pioneer economic historian, and another of those young scholars who emerged into the academic limelight from the graduate school at the Johns Hopkins University. As Mitchell declared in the preface of his book, *The Rise of the Cotton Mills in the South,* he tried to catch "the spiritual aspects" as well as the material aspects of that phenomenon. In that endeavor, he avowed, he owed most of his interpretation to his father, who held that the region lost the struggle for national eminence because it opted for slavery instead of liberty, state's rights instead of nationality, and for agriculture alone instead of industry smoothly integrated with agriculture. His study, he confessed, was "little more than illustration" of his father's analysis of the Southern experience.[30]

Samuel Chiles Mitchell had been much more than merely an academic observer of the textile manufacturing scene in the South. In 1911, he began an association with one of South Carolina's leading mill men, Thomas F. Parker of Greenville, who, incidentially, was an alumnus of the University. In that year Parker sent Mitchell a pamphlet describing the paternalistic activities of a large German textile operation, the Bodische Company. He wanted, he said, to "illustrate what manufacturing concerns are doing in other nations of the world for their operatives." Parker asked for Mitchell's support and urged him to use the pamphlet to enlist others, "contrasting the condition portrayed by it to those found in our average mill villages." Suggesting that life was indeed lowly in some textile communities, he added, "the worst mill villages of South Carolina are those least accessible and least visited."[31] Parker found that Mitchell's concern coincided with his own, and that the president of the University of South Carolina was fully ready to swing into action. "The Bodische Book I examined with keen interest," Mitchell replied, "and I wish to get it into the hands of Mr. August Kohn of the News and Courier and Mr. W. W. Ball of the State, etc. I feel, however, that the example which you are setting at the Monahan Mills will prove to be the really effective model for this State."[32] The Bodische Company reflected a general tendency in German industry concerning paternalism toward workers. The Bismarckian regime had begun that movement during the 1880s as a deliberate device to counter socialism. If the owners and managers built up a sense of community including themselves and their workers, ran the rationale, there would be little danger of the workers building a community of interests antagonistic to that of capital and management.

Broadus Mitchell's dissertation and first book continued the concerns of his father. The younger Mitchell contended in this work that Southern leadership, imbued with a sense of paternalism, had created the textile mills of the South in order to save the mass of whites from poverty. The movement began with the loss of the presidential election in 1880, he explained. The South had rested all of its hopes upon a Democratic victory in that year. With the defeat came a realization that the future prosperity of the region would have to be found outside politics. Thereafter, the South turned in upon itself, and found there the path of progress. By "conscious teaching" the leadership produced a "social regeneration" in all places during the turn-of-the-century years. "When the South, after 1900, did embark on an educational campaign, the fervor previously given to industry received new expression," he declared. "It was 'Real Reconstruction' reaching another task."[33]

As Broadus Mitchell and most Conservatives saw it, the movement into the mills represented a direct translation into the realities of the New South of the Old South values of *noblesse oblige,* paternalism, loyalty, and service. Before he began to write his book, Mitchell interviewed scores of textile executives, some of them long-lived captains of the Old South who were themselves the very personification of this process of bringing the old into the new. He found that each of the textile pioneers "feels himself in touch with the spirit that was the South's salvation." They were "far-seeing, public-minded, generous—natural leaders because lovers and servers." These men, he insisted, "have proved themselves true patriots."[34] Mitchell argued that "a study of the facts shows how frequent and normal was the philanthropic incentive" in inspiring these men to build mills "to give employment to the necessitous masses of poor whites, for the sake of the people themselves. . . ."[35] In South Carolina, Henry P. Hammett, the president of Piedmont Mill, for a time one of the largest in the world, was one of these patrons of industry. Another patron in the same state was James L. Orr, Jr., who founded Orr Mills in Anderson County in the 1880s. Orr was the son of an antebellum Congressman, a Confederate colonel and senator, and the first elected governor of the state during Reconstruction. Ironically, the father became a fellow-traveling if not indeed a card-carrying Republican and finally President Grant's minister to Russia, but the son first came to eminence as a leader in the Redemption in 1876 and 1877. Daniel Augustus Tompkins, working for the textile revolution in both of the Carolinas, was a man squarely out of plantation slavery in the Old South. Tompkins was born in 1851 near Graniteville, South Carolina, the site of a very successful and highly paternalistic antebellum experiment in textile manufacturing. He was educated in engineering at Rensselaer Polytechnic Institute in upstate New York and worked in the iron industry in the North and in Germany, some of that time with the Bethlehem Iron Works, the progenitor of the modern steel corporation. In 1883 Tompkins returned south to Charlotte to establish his own company. Shortly, he was building cotton seed mills for others and on his own account. In 1892 his company began work on its first textile mill, and by 1907 Tompkins owned three mills himself, one in Charlotte and two in South Carolina, and had built all or part of more than a hundred others. Paradoxically, he was so enamored of the textile mill as the salvation of the South that he personally sparked more than a dozen local communities to build mills that soon competed in the marketplace with his own.[36]

In 1928 Mitchell published another book in which he again depicted the beginning of the textile movement in the antebellum South as associated with the salvation of the lower class of whites by a patrician leadership. This book was a biography of William Gregg, the man who had pioneered before the Civil War in establishing the textile factory at Graniteville, South Carolina. Gregg, according to Mitchell, had a "keen consciousness of the poor white," and he had begun his mill to redeem that class.[37] In his biography of Gregg, Mitchell offered a vivid personal example of Murphy's idea that the textile movement was a revival of Old South idealism rather than a totally new beginning. The concept of uplift through textiles was more than an early seed at the beginning of the Civil War, he insisted, it was virtually an embryo.

Astutely, Mitchell never argued that the mills were begun only for the purpose of saving the poor whites. Indeed, it was abundantly clear to him that there were many incentives, one of which was profits. Early earnings often ran from 30 percent to 75 percent annually of the capital invested. In Gastonia they generally ran about 75 percent in their first phase. However, after the great wave of building new mills between 1900 and 1906, profits settled to about 7 percent, approximately the level earned by New England plants.[38]

After 1900, a new idea was introduced into the doctrine of Southern salvation through textiles. It was that the paternalists had created the textile mills not only to save the lower class of whites from poverty, but also to save them from competition with blacks. In 1902, one manager testified before a Congressional committee that the mills had deliberately passed up black labor, even though it was cheaper, to spare white people from competition with blacks. They had so sacrificed, he said, because "mill life is the only avenue open today to our poor whites, and we have with earnestness and practically without exception kept that avenue open to the white man alone."[39] It was perhaps inevitable that a grand rationale would gradually take form explaining that blacks were simply not built for work in the factories. James L. Orr, Jr., averred in 1901 that experience had proved that "they will go to sleep actually or metaphorically in a very few minutes after they are allowed to stop, hence they have never been worked to any advantage in the cotton mills." Orr felt that "the industry furnished almost the only refuge for the laboring white people of the South from the strong competition of cheap negro labor. . . ." The white worker "would resent most bitterly any intrusion of the negro in cotton mill work, which he now regards as his own. It is all right where men alone work, in the mines, at masonry and all kinds of hard labor, to mix the races, but it is wrong to work negroes in association with white women and children."[40] Since more than half of the workers in Southern mills were women and children, that rule alone would have excluded blacks.

In reality, pioneers in the textile movement had not begun their mills to protect whites from black competition. Indeed, blacks had worked in textile factories throughout the nineteenth century, even though in segregated work places, and some managers had thought that they worked very well. In 1880, twenty-five of the one hundred hands in the Saluda Cotton Factory in South Carolina were black, and a Charleston plant attempted to use black workers exclusively until it found that absenteeism made it expedient to use white hands in two of its departments, "separated, of course, from the negroes upstairs."[41] About the turn of the century, however, the shift occurred. All but the most laborious or menial of the mill tasks became white tasks, and textiles in the South became, practically speaking, all white. Sometimes white workers themselves insisted upon that exclusion. In the great depression after 1893, there was "whitecapping" in the mills just as there was whitecapping on the land. Times were hard, very hard, and both livable land and paying jobs were at a premium. Economic distress did find direct relief in racism. In 1899 a Griffin, Georgia, lawyer, freshly back from soldiering in Cuba, got as his first case the prosecution of some white men "charged with whipping & beating negroes at the factories" in a conspiracy to exclude blacks from jobs in the mills. The lawyer was retained not by the black men, but by the mill owners. The case was lost, however, because "the jury were largely in sympathy with the white [people]."[42] Owners might have preferred Negro labor because it was cheaper, but once white workers took a firm stand against the use of black workers in the mills, owners would fall easily into line. Harmony by way of black exclusion was much less expensive than strife and a possible work stoppage. The pattern was quickly and solidly set, and the *fait accompli* soon rationalized. Edgar Gardner Murphy concluded in 1904 that the omission of blacks from the mills was caused by their innate "inadaptability" to that environment, and by management's desire to favor whites. Since the two races did not work well together, management chose whites for their "teachableness, endurance, and skill." Murphy, himself heartily endorsed management's decision. By 1910 when white workers in the textile mills in the South numbered 200,000, black workers numbered less than 5000.[43]

Broadus Mitchell applied to the textile experience much the same idea of homogeneity that Murphy had adduced in explaining the "new democracy." It was a fact vital to the textile revival, Mitchell argued, that the Southern white population was "homogeneous." They moved with a whole spirit. "No people less homogeneous, less one family, knit together and resolute through sufferings, could have taken instant fire, as did the South, at such appeals." The textile industry throve "within the Southern family. It made for an intimacy which at first rendered impossible and which continued to retard division between factory owners and workers according to economic interest."[44] The mills, then, represented a kind of new economic democracy in which great profits and high wages were not the ruling incentives. Rather was the mill the symbol of the Southern community in harmony with itself and with the real and modern world. Masters, trained to care for slaves on the plantations of the Old South, now brought capital and a kindly management to the white workers in the factories of the New. Less gifted whites brought labor and loyalty. In the mills of the South, management and labor gathered familiarly around the "coke box." The workers called the manager Mr. Frank, or "Cap'n," or Colonel, and he called each by his given name of Will, or Jim, or Carter, and all felt secure. This socially gentle weave of the new economics and traditional hierarchy was the combination that offered, Mitchell implied, high promise for the future of American life.

Whereas slavery had squeezed the less fortunate whites out of society, Volksgeistians now insisted that the textile mills were an instrument for bringing them in again. In the early colonial South, all whites had been very much alike. But increasingly slavery had divided the whites into two distinct classes, and the lower class, the "poor whites," deprived of "participation in the larger life of the section," had become non-participants. As Mitchell interpreted the process, "the pressure of slavery, if it worked to bring a small number of whites to the surface, gave to masses an impulse ever downward." But "when the 'poor whites' entered the mills, they reentered the life of the South." The mills had "opened the way" for the lower orders again to be integrated into an organic and very viable Southern culture.[45] William Garrott Brown reflected the same thinking. He felt that the elimination of slavery opened up among the poor whites "great unutilized industrial reserves." Whites would seize the textile jobs as their own, eliminate the Negro, and thrust the South into the forefront of national life.[46]

Whatever the source of their belief, it is undeniable that textile managers in the turn-of-the-century South were convinced of their own paternalism. There was a feeling among them that they not only protected their white neighbors and cousins from the threat of black labor, but that they also provided them with a life well above the level of bare subsistence. H. P. Hammett of Piedmont Mill declared as early as 1880 that "we give our operatives good wages and take care of their morals."[47] At the turn of the century, James L. Orr insisted that mill owners took especially good care of their workers, providing them with schools and churches as well as fair wages. And Daniel Augustus Tompkins in 1907, when labor was becoming scarce in the South, welcomed that occurrence, in part because it would raise the wages and living standards of white workers.[48]

The public seemed at first to take management as it offered itself. Since most of the workers in the mills were literally women and children, the "paternal" role was not difficult for an all-male management to play—and to enjoy. In the mills, "the use of children was not avarice," Mitchell argued, "but philanthropy; not exploitation, but generosity and cooperation and social-mindedness."[49] Still some Conservatives echoed Murphy's concern that the new mills would not live up to their responsibility. Mitchell himself in 1921 deplored that with a rising technical and commercial atmosphere about the mill "there has been a separation of the economic and humanistic elements so intermixed at its beginning. . . ."[50]

Wilbur Cash was one Southerner who wrote about what might be called the "textile legend," the story that in the South the mills were built paternalistically to save the poor whites. No doubt Cash erred when he decided that one could best talk about one mind of the South rather than many. But there was, indeed, one mind that he did know and could talk about with authority. That was the textile mind, and more specifically the mind of textile management. Cash was himself born the son of a mill superintendent in Gaffney, South Carolina, and he spent many of the forty-one years of his life in another mill town, Boiling Springs, North Carolina, where his father managed a hosiery mill. After graduating from Wake Forest College in 1922, Cash worked as a teacher and journalist for several years. In the late 1920s and into the 1930s, he suffered ill health and lived with his parents. In 1937 he became an editorial writer for the Charlotte *News*.[51] Charlotte was the Manchester of Southern textile culture, and Cash could not escape absorbing a sharp impression of the textile legend. He thought, as he said in *The Mind of the South*, that regional economic progress had been achieved "so completely within the framework of the past that the *plantation* remained the single great basic social and economic pattern of the South. . . ." At bottom, he declared, "that is exactly what the Southern factory almost invariably was: a plantation essentially indistinguishable in organization from the familiar plantation of the cotton fields."[52] The mill, after all, was simply the next stage through which cotton flowed on the way to market.

Indeed, there was a general congruence between the mill village and the plantation. The great house of the owner-superintendent was like the manor house of the planter, and the company store was like the plantation commissary where labor drew its allowances (in both often no real money changed hands). Each company had its chosen color and seemed to take great pride in painting everything in sight in the same tint or hue. The color was seldom appealing; as often as not it was a dirty yellow, a washed-out blue, a dingy gray. In contrast to drab paint, however, the mills and their villages often wore the most appealing and appropriate names—reminiscent of the plantations of old. Avondale, Belmont, Bellevue, Equinox, Lad-Lassie, Twiney, La France, and Oconee often laid a charming and euphonious mantle upon an otherwise gritty and depressing reality. Near the mill, usually within sound of the whirring machinery and always within sound of the whistle, were the look-alike company streets filled with look-alike company houses reminiscent of the "nigger street" and its cabins on the old plantation. But of course there were more workers in a mill usually than there had been slaves on a plantation. There would be many streets numbered and lettered ("F" Street or "G"), ranged in rows and squares over the hillside, crowding the factory itself in the valley, set by a muddy stream, the stream blocked by a concrete dam, making a small lake for the use of the factory and the "mudcats" (catfish) for the fisherman's catch. Sometimes mills would be built on the edge of pre-existing towns, and sometimes they would be built whole, village and all, in the middle of the wilderness like the first plantations. But whether the mills drew upon a town for their social logistics or whether they organized their supplies separately, there were invariably the company ministers (official or unofficial) for the company churches (Preaching what: faithful labor, familial morality, glory in the later life?), company teachers in company schools (Teaching what: faithful labor, personal morality, room at the top?), company police keeping company order, and often even company baseball teams and movies. Sometimes, before the American Medical Association got a firm grip on the supply and made the fee system sacrosanct, there was even a company physician (just as the plantation physician had been as ordinary as the plantation veterinarian) because the human machine needed fixing as often as did the looms. But even where the mill village was not also the town, the town identified with the mill owner. Mayors, businessmen, teachers, preachers, doctors, lawyers all made their obeisances to the lords of the loom, just as they had in the past paid their respects to the masters of the slaves.

Like the labor of slavery, the work in the factory was long, tedious, and often dangerous, but there were differences. Plantation labor had been limited, providentially—if that is the word—"from day clean to dusk," and the length of the day was tied to the seasons. In the factories the electric light lengthened the day of labor for man—and for woman—and for children as well. Electric light revolutionized the night and made it day; and, further, the industrial revolution revolutionized the labor supply. Whereas previously certain strong muscles had been needed to plow, or to wield the hoe, scythe, or machete; now water power, steam power, and finally electric power provided the muscle that gave fantastic power through machines to the hands of almost, one might say, babes. And "babes" is hardly an exaggeration. By the census of 1900, about 25 percent of the workers in the Southern mills were under sixteen. While no one knew how much under sixteen these workers were, Edgar Gardner Murphy himself saw "children of six and seven years who were at labor in our factories, for twelve and thirteen hours a day," and he had seen them "with their little fingers mangled by machinery and their little bodies numb and list-less with exhaustion."[53] North Carolina was the only state to gather statistics on workers below the age of sixteen, and there it was found that 18 percent of the labor force was under fourteen. The industrial revolution did indeed put power into the hands of mere children, and sometimes it took those hands away. What sort of print did a bleeding hand make in the cloth moving swiftly through the looms? Never mind. The light of social justice shone only dimly in those early years of the factory New South, even among the workers themselves.

In truth, textile mills were, at first, very much family and community affairs. They were owned and operated by people who felt themselves an inte-gral part of the local Anglo-Saxon community. Owners and managers were seldom off to socialize in Newport, Rhode Island, or the Virginia springs. They worked hard with their heads, and probably with their hearts too. As people will do, they mixed their material ambition and their hunger for power with a measure of *noblesse oblige,* and their lives were thus made better than bearable. They lived well, and they thought well of themselves and their work. Also, at first, they lived in the community with their people. Uppers were sep-arated from lowers by all the social lines, but not ordinarily by spatial ones. Social differentiation itself was a pleasant dividend for owner and manager. Deference was clearly paid, but it was not the deference of slavery. "Jack" Cash thought that the lords of the loom, more than the masters of the plan-tations, had effected a tight slavery of their workers. But that was a typical Cashian hyperbole. Mill towns were not plantations; it was another age, and the workers were white. Runaway workers were not advertised in the papers, nor branded, nor officially beaten. All in all, the mill worker probably was a freer man than his tenant-farmer cousin. In a sense he was free after every weekly payday, he had a special skill as spinner, weaver, or loom-fixer, and he had no liens and was not tied to a single money crop and worn-out farms year after year. Even Cash conceded that his white slaves of the postwar South never knew that they were slaves, and the workers themselves certainly never confessed to any such thought. Indeed, the wave of strikes that occurred dur-ing the Great Depression attested to the fact that workers held the opposite view of themselves. The giant and telling difference, of course, was that the slaves had been black and the mill workers were white.

In the factory, both the reality and the rhetoric worked to keep white body and white soul somehow together for a remarkably long time. In the imagery of paternalism, the owner-manager was the father of his workers, a role pre-scription easily filled. Sometimes, the manager was in fact in some way the blood kin to some of his workers. Ultimately, all were brothers and sisters, fathers, sons, and daughters in, if not under, the skin. Adult children of respectable farmers fleeing agricultural recession and depression did not scruple at taking cash-paying jobs in the mills. And Southern society had never been so stratified that talent could not crash the class lines, if such they might be called, and old families often willingly accepted new blood . . . especially if it were red and rich.

Not all of the South was rice-country South Carolina or sugar-growing Louisiana where the best lands were limited in quantity, engrossed early, and gave rise to great and exclusive families. Nor was it even Old Virginia, where intermarriage between the great families proceeded so long that eyes crossed, hearing grew faulty, and noses lost their points. Outside of the old settled areas intermarriage ran up and down the scale of land and slaveholding. A pretty figure and a vivacious manner, male or female, coupled with respectability, could occasionally marry slaves and land, and all of his or her kin were then akin to the land and slaves. On the slave frontier (moving as it did through upcountry South Carolina and Georgia, across the great rich middle belt of Alabama, into the delta of Mississippi, and out onto the rich flat lands of Arkansas and Texas) where life and love were not so much settled, if the poor did not marry rich, the respectable middling folks sometimes did. William Faulkner was right again. Thomas Sutpens did appear on the slave frontier; they rose from rags to riches; and they did marry Ellen Coldfields. Consequently, Miss Rosa Coldfield, her sister, was also married to the land and slaves, and no more divisible from them than she was from Henry and Judith, the children of the marriage. White Southern society in 1900, in the mass and spread over the whole geography from ex-slaveholding Delaware to the outer limits of Austin, Texas, was not so much a class society as it was one of twenty million personal dots hierarchically and organically arranged in thousands of community clusters, each person, each dot self-consciously occupying one special place in the array and highly conscious of the other dots and of the particular forces that fixed each in its certain place. It is often convenient, perhaps even necessary for communication, to use the term "class" in talking about the white South, but that society is not even nearly describable by two or more neat lines drawn horizonally across the whole population.

Winners in the marketplace and at the marriage altar did not dissolve family ties. Economic and social elevation was not a license to forget your family, even in its fartherest reaches. On the contrary. Even in the hierarchical ordering, where some whites were distinctly superior to others, there was, nevertheless, a sense of kindredness, a *Gemeinschaft,* among all the whites, just as the Volksgeistians would have it. In 1900, white Southerners were, in essence, very much alike and becoming more so; and clearly they were more like one another than anyone else. The curious fact that academicians attempted to blink away that truth and soon came to assume that mill workers were "poor whites," with overtones of "poor white trash," was but another manifestation of the notorious tendency of the turn-of-the-century intelligentsia to lose sight of the great middle class of yeoman farmers that had existed in the antebellum period and afterward, and to flatter themselves that they as moderns were creating something grand out of what had been, theretofore, merely a remote potentiality. Whatever the myth, the workers in the mills were not, in the main, poor whites. They were the yeoman farmers of the Old South and their children translated into the industrial situation. Metaphorically, they were indeed the loyal men who had ridden around the Yankees with J. E. B. Stuart, charged with Pickett at Gettysburg, and, surrendered with Lee at Appomattox. They were those men and their wives and children translated down through time into the factory. If they were duty-bound to the leadership, they were also duty-due. Deference, after all, is only one side of a two-way street. It has its price, however willingly paid. Southern whites who deferred to their betters got something from their betters in return. Indeed, the stuff they traded, recognition of the alleged personal superiority of the elite, was clearly so valuable, so far beyond mere material price, that they eventually got whatever they thought they wanted . . . which was, in reality, not much. But for our purposes, for the mill towns, let us say simply that the workers, like vassals in the feudal order, got maintenance and protection—including in the latter an ostensible respect for their women.

Thus it was that Southern whites at large in the early twentieth century moved toward a sense of community, a sense of community that seeped sweetly and generally through the South in the 1920s and 1930s. Aristocrats and commoners, men and women, adults and children, were all caught up neatly, happily in a seamless and comfortable web of social orderliness, admittedly often more apparent than real, but nevertheless real in a significant degree. By the ordinary measures of man, they were a happy people because they felt that they knew who they were, where they were, and why they were there. Not many people, in not many cultures, for very long have had that feeling of surety. It marks a people, it marks a person, and one does not easily surrender the feeling.

Playing the role of protector of the common whites did not mean, of course, that either mill owners, regular Conservatives, or Volksgeistian Conservatives were anti-Negro. Indeed, they wanted to conserve the Negro and include him in their systems. "Place" was all important to them, and another true task of leadership was to find the proper place and realm for black people in God's steadily unfolding world. Enlightened textile leaders and their philosophical friends had no difficulty at all in finding the Negro's proper calling and in urging him to take it. His future was in the cotton fields. Again it was almost a divine Providence, as James Orr pointed out in 1901, that the South had been given mills where the white folks could spin and weave the fibers that black farmers would coax from the good earth.[54] This fortunate and natural division of labor was the key to economic progress in a biracial order, a happy prospect that was not lost upon the philosophers, and one they hastened to exhibit to the intelligence of the North. Such was Murphy's message when he spoke in Boston in 1902 at a meeting to raise funds for Hampton Institute in Virginia, a school begun in Reconstruction primarily for the education of freedmen in the trades and agriculture. Murphy was followed by Hollis B. Frissell, a Northerner and the president of Hampton, who very quickly put the Negro in the same slot where Murphy and Orr had put him. The Negro's place is in the country, Frissell insisted, not in the city; it is in the South, not in the North, and this is what Hampton would teach him.[55] Several years later, Broadus Mitchell's father, writing to Frissell, rhapsodized upon how beautiful black people were upon the land: "peculiarly timely is the bearing of Hampton on farming in the South, for farming is the open door to the negro race. To lead him to the land, to enable him to enrich the soil, which is his permanent bank account, to stimulate him to embrace on the farm all the opportunities for thrift, self-reliance, health and sound morals, this is the one thing needful for the negro. In its work for these two lowly races, the Indian and the Negro, Hampton has been led to exemplify in a fruitful way the idea of humanity and the sense of brotherhood."[56]

Blacks for the land, whites for the factories. If the upper side of progress lay with the whites in the factory, that was all right because so too did the upper side of brotherhood lie with the white brother. He was the older, the stronger, the more advanced. But in the Volksgeistian view, between black and white, it was ultimately not really that one was better than the other. It was that they were different. It was not, either, that the sable fellow was being given an inferior place. It was only that he was being given, as Murphy with wonted and succinct elegance phrased it, "another place."

The harmonic beauty of an economic system in which each racial caste had its special function was relished by the Volksgeistians. Whites would come to appreciate blacks who supplied them with raw materials for their own profitable labor in the factory. Blacks would be grateful to whites who allowed them a room of their own in the economic house of the South. Material interdependence would promote a mutual toleration, if not indeed a mutual understanding and affection. Thus, with blacks on the land and whites in the factories, diversities—even apparent contradictions—would move toward an essential unity. In Murphy's view, political democracy would in time expand to include the two races, and economics was already pioneering in that direction.

It seemed very clear to Volksgeistian Conservatives in the South that the factory was the coming idea, the world-moving idea that was driving society forward. It was vastly important that the white people had risen to an awareness of the dynamic idea of the coming age and that they—spontaneously, intuitively—had combined themselves together in what amounted to a spiritual movement to begin the textile mills in the South. As Mitchell described the mood: the very machines were endowed with a spiritual quality.[57] That movement on the part of the white people was very much the result of their racial homogeneity and intercommunication, without which they could never have had the collective perception necessary to begin it. But they had perceived the emerging truth, and now they were in the very vanguard of those moving into futurity.

In a sense, blacks were to fill in the farm places left by whites moving into the factories. But it was not really that the farm was becoming an inferior place. Far from being associated with decline and degradation, the family farm, in Volksgeistian vision, was a place for the cultivation of virtues as well as the cultivation of crops. It was where "thrift, self-reliance, health and sound morals" were cultivated along with cotton and corn. White farmers were moving to the villages, towns, and cities, and blacks were filling their places and inheriting, along with the earth, their previous virtues. The whites were moving out onto a new frontier with new rewards and a new set of hazards to the old values. It must have been in some degree comforting to those who had been born in the country and lived in town to know that someone was back there, holding securely the proven bastion. Back on the farm there was a still solvent bank of virtue, there was a refuge if the brave new world of industrialism did, after all, prove unmanageable. One could always go back and take his stand on the land. Southern whites knew the horror of mistaking the wave of the future, to be eagerly and egregiously wrong, to be out of phase with the realities of the world as they had been in 1861, and to struggle back to being right. And so, it was hoped that the Negro on the land would harvest the old virtues along with the cotton. Whites would buy the white fleece from the black man's bag, but they would leave with him the golden fleece of traditional virtue.

At still another level, there was an economics working mightily to reinforce the seeming rightness of the Volksgeistian conception of the world. In the late 1890s, the international demand for cotton fiber increased, and the price paid for the staple in New York rose quickly from less than 5 cents a pound in 1893 to a high of about 10 cents in 1900. In the next decade it averaged a prosperous 11½ cents. The result was that conditions on the land did improve—and improve significantly. Now and again there was a temporary reverse, but the entry of the United States into World War I in 1917 soon added a happy peak to an already large mountain as cotton prices more than doubled to 17 cents and moved higher.[58] Labor that had been a glut on the market in the desperate times of the mid-nineties came to be highly valued by 1906. Doubtless this history of bust and boom had something to do with the history of Radicalism. Heated anti-black sentiment in the early nineties was related to the fact that black men sought places that white men felt they needed in order to live and support their wives and children. Ironically, the Negro was assaulted for working during the depression when white men needed his job, and he was assaulted for not working during prosperity when white men needed his labor. In 1905 and 1906, in boom-town Atlanta (where textiles were contributing directly to that prosperity), inter-racial tension arose, in part, from the belief that black men were deliberately idle. Where hard laboring rural black men had caused tension in the 1890s, now the perception of non-laboring, urban black men created tensions no less disturbing, and among all classes. After 1907, however, tensions eased. Black men did find places or else they were lost from sight, very often by migration north and west. And Radicalism, too, commenced its decline.

Domestic economy was laboring to lend verisimilitude to the Volksgeistian vision, and so also was the world economy. Almost from the first, Southern mills had produced the cruder threads and cloths, and it was that kind of material that sold best in the South and, more importantly, in markets abroad. As industrial Europe penetrated the economies of the Far East, so did industrial America, and, withal, the industrial South. H. P. Hammett's Piedmont Mill, in South Carolina, reputedly the largest factory under one roof in the South and certainly one of the largest in the world, was famous in China for its three-yard sheetings. Particularly after 1898 were those Far Eastern markets opened. They were vast, they were lucrative, and the South was in the forefront in their exploitation. In the cotton year 1899–1900 the South supplied 60 percent of all the American cotton cloth exported abroad. Roughly half of the entire export came from South Carolina, and China was the special market. In 1903 the total export of cotton cloth was nearly 500 million square yards, of which 273 million went to China alone. In 1906 the value of cotton cloth sold by the United States to China amounted to nearly $30,000,000.[59] The great wave of mill building in the South in the turn-of-the-century years was, in part, a response to opportunities in the international market, and the end fact was that they ran out of labor before they ran out of capital and markets.

The human result was that literally scores of white families with textile capital floated into the affluent elite to join the hundreds of families that had already arrived via slave-owning, landowning, politics, commerce, transportation, and tobacco factories. The founders of these dynasties sometimes came out of the planter class, as was the case with Daniel Augustus Tompkins. Others, like H. P. Hammett, the founder of Piedmont Mills, were poor boys who made good. Still others came out of the merchant class. However, no one entered the business and succeeded signally without some prior close associations with the industry. Hammett had learned the business from his father-in-law, who had, in turn, been taught in New England by Samuel Slater, the very person who brought textile technology from England to America in the 1790s. One thread that tied many and perhaps even most of the early captains of cotton textiles together was a connection with the cotton trade to the north and abroad. Tompkins, for instance, had been involved on the technical side in manufacturing iron bands to secure bales of cotton for shipment, in selling gins, and in building plants to produce cottonseed oil. Probably the majority of these pioneers previously had eagerly sent the fiber away from the South; now they were determined to profit by keeping it at home and turning it into cloth. For a time laboring families in textiles shared a sense of prosperity with owners and managers, and, even though they were less prosperous than their employers, their new circumstances made the 1890s seem like life in a Potter's Field. Probably most white Southerners would have agreed with Walter Hines Page, who saw labor in the mills as a way up for the able and ambitious. The mills, he thought, gave "mobility to social life and opportunity to them that can take it."[60]

The psychological end of such economics was a sense of well-being in the South in the early twentieth century comparable to that which it had enjoyed in the 1850s. Moreover, the discovery of a relatively prosperous economics had the totally unsurprising effect, eventually, of leading people to conclude that they had also discovered a proper morality. Their special perception of the industrial revolution was a unique discovery, they felt, one that only Southerners could make because only they had experienced the travail of a peculiar institution that bred a peculiarly superior people. Elements in the story could easily be slotted into the Hegelian formula: materialism in the form of pre-Civil War, Northern industrialism and commercialism was the antithesis that had destroyed the thesis of agrarianism, represented quintessentially in the Old South. Just as the true, the real, the "soul" portion of the thesis is never destroyed but rather becomes increasingly clear as the unreal, the artificial, the shadow, is burned away in earthly conflict, so too had paternalism as a part of the Southern genius persisted. And finally, just as the antithesis merges with the best elements of the old thesis and forms a new synthesis, which, in turn, becomes a new thesis, so too would the new factory system fuse with paternalism and pass on to a higher order. Out the ashes of slavery—truly now an idea dead and shucked away—rose the saving idea, the ever-living ideal to which God had given light and life through the people near to Him. The leadership ideal of the Old South had not been lost. With steadfast faith, it waited for what it knew would come to pass, namely, as Murphy phrased it, "that artificial conditions would sag and fall by their own weight, and that thereafter the real landmarks of a sound social organization would appear. . . ."[61]

Paternalism would tame the factory system and harness it to Southern progress, but it would also save America, and the world. Volksgeistians saw an industrial system in the North and in Europe that was literally tearing civilization asunder. The rich were getting richer and the poor poorer; there was a dangerously rising alienation between the few of the classes and the many of the masses, between capital and labor. Excessive materialism, impersonality, and inhumanity was the bitter social fruit of the factory system. Hard as steel and fully as unfeeling, the industrial revolution was conquering the world, pressuring itself into every crevice of human existence. The factory system was like a runaway engine pulling a train with all humanity aboard, racing faster and faster toward some sudden and disastrous halt. In Europe, masses of people were frankly embracing class consciousness and hence social divisiveness, swelling socialist numbers into political pluralities in France, Great Britain, and Germany. Even in America, in 1912, Socialist presidential candidate Eugene V. Debs mustered more than a million male votes in his support. Most awful in all of this was the destruction of orderly society and the orderly evolution of society. Strikes, riots, and gutted factories were our promises. Socialism, communism, anarchism, sabotage, and assassination were the ultimate results of the rise of the factory Leviathan unrestrained. It had already begun in America. The bomb in the Haymarket riot in 1886, the general violence in the Homestead and Pullman strikes in 1894, the special violence of the Wobblies (Industrial Workers of the World), and the assassination in 1901 of President McKinley by an anarchist whose very name was unpronounceably alien were all plain forewarnings of an unredeemed America. The politics of "grab" in the post-Civil War era, and the more recent pursuit of a scheme of amoral laissez-faire had not worked, and disaster was in the offing.

In the crisis the South now offered the great saving ideal—paternalism. Paternalism, the key idea that had risen out of the ordeal of slavery, was to be infused into the new industrial order. With a selfless, enlightened leadership at the throttle, the train would be controlled, its progress would be slower, safer, and rendered totally beneficial. The factory system under the captaincy of the paternalists would carry us all smoothly into the happier land of God's promise. The whites first, but all in a train. And all finally together. The South had risen again, ran Volksgeistian thought, not merely to survive as an eddy in the backwater of American life, not as some insignificant and dependent part of a greater whole, but indeed as the very soul and spirit of that progressively rising order that was the new American nation.

OLD SOUTH IDEALISM BROUGHT INTO THE NEW

Volksgeistian Conservatism had its roots in nineteenth-century European idealism and, often, specifically, in Germanic idealism. No doubt, it received much of its impetus from continuing importations across the Atlantic either directly by Southerners visiting the Continent and attending European universities, or indirectly through such institutions as Johns Hopkins. But it was also indebted to the domestic variety of idealism, imported in the antebellum period, turned into a flower of local growth, and still alive, however precariously, during the Reconstruction era and afterward.

The antebellum South's becoming idealistic in this vein represented a profound alteration in its thinking from Revolutionary times. Speaking in the broadest, most general terms, thought in the South in the mid-nineteenth century slipped from a largely realistic, rationalistic world-view to one that was Platonic, idealistic, romantic, and transcendental, but one that included also a subordinate rationalism.[62] The declining world of Thomas Jefferson affords an accurate index to the change. In the South, by the late 1850s, Jefferson and his thought were either ignored, misused, or in outright disrepute among high thinkers. It was perfectly symbolic of the reality that on the eve of the Civil War beautifully rational Monticello was being used by a careless tenant as a hay barn.[63] Before the war, Southern thinking was moving with supple muscularity toward the creation of a philosophy that would organize their peculiar world by including both slavery and race. Southern intellectuals appropriated much of European idealism, and, specifically, much of that was Hegelian. Slavery was an idea and so was race. What mattered in slavery was not the practice of this or that slaveholder so much as the ideal of slavery itself—perceived in its true God-given nature uniquely by Southerners and progressively unfolding. What really mattered in race was not this or that specific Negro so much as it was the idea of "Negro." The two ideas combined neatly, and they were laced into an Hegelian progression to predict the attainment of new heights of freedom. For Negroes in America, perfect slavery was perfect freedom; crimes against Negroes arose only from an imperfect slavery. For whites in the South, perfect mastery was perfect freedom, and crimes arose only from a failure in mastery. If all this was not totally clear in 1861, it seemed surely to be headed in that direction.

The loss of the war damned the philosophy, and it damned no less the philosophers. How could it, and they, have been so wrong? With the end of the war, Southern intellectuality very nearly ceased to be. There was no strong current to swim either with or against. It is a useful hyperbole to say that the great mass of Southern whites in Reconstruction did not think at all. Minds numbed by a bloody civil war and crushing defeat, emotions shocked by alien invasion, occupation, and "black" Reconstruction, Southerners at large seemed incapable of philosophizing deeply about their experience. Anyone reading the literary remains of those people gathered in the archives of the land will be struck—and depressed—by one overwhelming fact: the South was physically and mentally devastated by the war. Southerners were reduced to the material and elemental. Quite literally, they were most concerned with food for their bellies and the bellies of those they loved. Reconstruction for Southern whites was a monstrously physical time, an animal time.

In this respect, Margaret Mitchell in *Gone with the Wind* was profoundly historical. Melanie Wilkes never surrenders the pure values of the Old South, but Melanies after the war were few and far between. Distressingly close to the common experience was that of Scarlett O'Hara. Fleeing a burning Atlanta and returning in the middle of the night to Tara, the once splendid and now ruined plantation, she and her dependents are on the verge of starvation. In the film, Scarlett (played by Vivien Leigh) discovers the remains of a slave garden, scrambles about frantically in the dirt, unearths a radish, and gnaws at it hungrily. She bends over retching, then lifts her face, dirt-stained and tearful. She struggles to her feet amidst the desolation of the plantation, fists clenched, grimly determined, looking to the sky: " . . . as God is my witness," she declares, "the Yankees aren't going to lick me. I'm going to live through this, and when it's over, I'm never going to be hungry again. No, nor any of my folks. If I have to steal or kill—as God is my witness, I'm never going to be hungry again."[64]

Scarlett was a metaphor for the New South that grew directly out of defeat in the war and did not wait for Henry Grady and other later prophets windily to announce its coming. That first New South, reflexively and without thought, put matter over mind and called it good. The roots of the immediately postwar New South ran shallow and visible on the earth of the Old. Those roots were manifested in manias for slaves and land and wealth, and then for more slaves, and more land, and more wealth—palpable things that you could see and touch and count, things that translated easily into earthly pleasure and power. Again, Scarlett illustrates the history well. In April 1861, lounging on the veranda at Tara with her suitors the Tarleton twins, she carries in herself the blood of her mother, "a Coast aristocrat of French descent," and her "florid Irish father." A belle of sixteen, she holds her "small white hands folded in her lap," and she wears twelve yards of fine muslin in her dress, the gift of her father's wealth. "Her manners had been imposed upon her by her mother's gentle admonitions and the sterner disciples of her mammy; her eyes were her own." Those green eyes, in "the carefully sweet face," were "turbulent, willful, lusty with life." They gazed upon the Tarleton twins, nineteen, six-two, lean, hard, sunburned, gay, and arrogant. "They laughed and talked, their long legs, booted to the knee and thick with saddle muscles, crossed negligently." In the yard were their horses, "big animals, red as their masters' hair; and around the horses' legs quarreled the pack of lean, nervous possum hounds." The twins were infinitely more physical than mental, and that quality had just led to their expulsion from the state college in Athens. Previously they had been expelled from the state schools of Virginia, Alabama, and South Carolina. The Tarleton twins were perfectly identical, and "their bodies" were "clothed in identical blue coats and mustard-colored breeches." Each was totally infatuated with Scarlett, and each pursued her ardently. But miraculously, neither was jealous of the other. Scarlett could have them both. She played them as a conductor plays an orchestra, first one, then the other, then both together, and she got what she wanted—two superbly physical male animals, as spirited, as strong, as perfectly obedient to her will as horse and hound, two men for the price of one.[65]

Excessive materialism—the prime sin of the New South—was, of course, plainly evident in the prewar South. There were, as the contemporary writer William R. Hundley labeled the type, "Southern Yankees" before there was any war at all.[66] Yet the war and the defeat did turn Southern Yankees loose as never before. Apparently, there is always an urge among the defeated to take on the imagined winning attributes of the victors, if only to beat them in the struggle next time. It should occasion no surprise that Southerners in defeat became somewhat Yankee, that some became totally Yankee, and that a few became more Yankee than the Yankees themselves. The lesson of the war for that first New South was that quantity (men and matériel) did, after all, beat quality. Scarlett and the great mass of Southerners learned that lesson well, and neither they nor their progeny ever totally forgot it. Scarlett was one of those who learned it early and practiced it to perfection. She began to build her fortune, most successfully by using convict labor, white as well as black, at the cost of ten cents a day, to produce lumber for the rebuilding of Atlanta, Forsaking the ideals of the Old South, Scarlett exploited her white brothers and the advantages of her sex, freely associated with the Yankees for profit, indulged in a soul-less materialism, and wallowed in the pleasures of the flesh with the highly physical Rhett Butler (Clark Gable in the film). Rhett Butler, an aristocratic South Carolinian by birth and breeding, was himself nearly all body, carrying within only a hint, a mere flicker of soul somehow surviving from his low-country Carolina past.

Ultimately Scarlett reaps as she has sown. Her daughter, ironically named Bonnie after the "Bonnie Blue Flag" of the Confederacy, is as beautiful, selfish, physical, and as empty as each of her parents. Bonnie is killed by a beautiful brute, her pony. Bonnie's neck is broken in a fall taken by both animal and mistress when she tries to jump him over a high bar. Rhett brutally kills the pony, in the film with a blast of his shotgun. He then goes away because he is seemingly only the shell of a man, however handsome and attractive the shell, and, frankly, he did not "give a damn," not for Scarlett, or the Confederacy, or the South, or anything else.

The South in Reconstruction, again like Scarlett, did not so much surrender thought as postpone it in favor of eating. Many eminent Southerners—such as James L. Orr, the father of the founder of Orr Mills—were not at all slow about going into business with Yankees in the first years after the war. Later, there would be time to think. "Food! Food!" says Scarlett to herself, "Why does the stomach have a longer memory than the mind?" She acts first to save the body. "I'll think of Mother and Pa and Ashley and all this ruin later—," she decided. "Yes, later when I can stand it." At the very end of the novel, Scarlett is twenty-eight and the year is 1873. Melanie dies and Scarlett at last can marry the man she has always loved, Ashley Wilkes, that masculine remnant of Old South aristocracy. She finds, finally, that she does not want him. "He never really existed at all," she declares, "I loved something I made up. . . ." She now sees in Rhett a flash of the virtue that she had imagined in Ashley. She has images of Tara, of her head against her black mammy's bosom, of getting Rhett back. "I'll think of it all tomorrow, at Tara," she decides in the last lines of the book. "I can stand it then."[67]

There were a few Southerners who thought deeply about the meaning of the war, defeat, occupation, and black Reconstruction even as they lived in the midst of those experiences. Some of these concluded that these scorges were signs from God that they had been wrong in slavery, wrong in the presumption that they had somehow discovered God's plan on earth for His people. The idea of the organic society had been a gross error, mocked in Reconstruction by the inversion of the hierarchy. In the black belts of the South the Yankee victors had put the blacks on top, put hands where heads were supposed to be, and they had made hands of heads. Black men in the state house and white men at the plow was the reality, and in some states and communities there was no end of that new order in sight. The Old South way of life seemed outside the pale after all; it was not the way of God. There was a mood of terrible vacuity among Southern whites after the war. It was worse than if the South had simply died; it was, indeed, as if it had never lived.

Some of the most thoughtful ascribed the fall of the South to the surrender of white men to the sex of black women. Flesh had smothered soul. "It does seem strange that so lovely a climate, and country, with a people in every way superior to the Yankees, should be overrun and destroyed by them," wrote low-country aristocrat William Heyward to a friend in 1868. "But I believe that God has ordered it all, and I am firmly of opinion . . . that it is the judgment of the Almighty because the human and brute blood have mingled to the degree it has in the slave states. Was it not so in the French and British Islands and see what has become of them."[68]

A very few Southerners, a corporal's guard persistently philosophical, explained defeat as simply the turning down of the great wheel of progress in another grand cycle. Defeat was not at all a judgment by God that the Southern people had been wrong. It was, rather, a part of the process of purification of his people for the next surge upward.

Soon after Redemption, and especially in the 1880s, intellectuality in the South began slowly to revive, and with it came the philosophical consideration of the meaning of slavery, the war, and defeat. There was in that decade a rising idea that the South had not, after all, been spiritually wrong, either in the war or in slavery. What had been interpreted as punishment for error was actually God testing and purifying his people. The life and labor of the Old South was not only valid, it was valuable because it had generated the virtues that brought the white people of the South through to the modern South. Clearly, there were men and institutions deeply involved in affording continuity to that process. It had to do with the Charleston intelligentsia, the University of Virginia, the University of the South, and the Johns Hopkins University. It had to do also with the thinking of certain related individuals, how those individuals evolved in their thinking over time, and how this all came directly to bear such fruits as that evinced by Edgar Gardner Murphy in the turn-of-the-century years.

THE WHITE COMMUNION

As described above, it seems apparent that when regular Conservatives could no longer do what they had been bred to do in a paternalistic way with black people they turned their paternalism into labors among their white brothers and sisters. In the early years of the twentieth century, regular Conservatives moved to elevate their fellow whites in virtually every area of Southern life, and Volksgeistian Conservatives lent focus and a rationale to those movements.

In education, the Volksgeistians had an obvious and important role in promoting the communion of whiteness from the lowest to the highest grades and in both public and private schools. The Volksgeistians did not, of course, by themselves alone create the public school systems of the South and revitalize higher education. But they were activists in the front ranks in both movements, and they did give both solid philosophical underpinning. Working with and often through their regular Conservative friends, they were highly effective.

There was also a concern among turn-of-the-century Volksgeistian Conservatives, as we have seen, for creating an economy that took care of white people. In religion too there was an effort to reach the less affluent elements in the white population. Missions were established by the uptown churches in the factory villages. Uptown, for instance, there might have been a fine stone Episcopal church building while in the factory village there was a missionary branch in a small but decent wooden structure, perhaps served by the assistant rector of the parent church. The churches not only began to follow the people into the factory and the new city, they also began to seek out their sisters and brothers in the thinly settled mountainous and swampy lands of the South, heretofore the demographic backwaters of the region. Close behind the churches in this search were the folklorists, seeking out these plain folk of the

Old South, not to carry a message to them, but to bring one back. The assumption was that these people of the Southern outback were aboriginal Anglo-Saxons, providentially transplanted to the New World and hustled into isolation where they remained unspoiled by the distortions of slavery, commercialism, and waves of new immigrants. They were repositories of primal white culture, and if the white South would more perfectly know itself, then it must study them.

One of the most striking manifestations of the concern of the elite for the white masses was in medicine. The great public health campaigns, beginning about 1906, against tuberculosis, yellow fever, hookworm, and pellagra, and for improved sanitation on the farm and in the home, might have been, in part, a sublimation of a drive by the patricians to do their duty to blacks. To be sure these movements had national and international dimensions; but, in their region, Southern Conservatives turned these crusades to their own special ends. Walter Hines Page, for instance, was the key person in the creation of the Rockefeller Sanitary Commission in 1909 with the object of wiping out hookworm in the warm Southern climate where it throve. Hookworm was a microscopic parasite that usually entered the body through the bare feet, worked its way into the intestinal tract and other organs, and produced an anemia that rendered its victims easily tired, listless, and ineffectual. By 1909 the cure was found to be a very simple dosing with epsom salts and a chemical called thymol. Hookworm was specially a rural phenomenon, and it struck the less affluent. Experts estimated that more than two million Southerners were infected with the disease, and the vast majority of these were at the bottom of the social scale. Afflicted blacks were included in the campaign, but clearly, the main interest was in whites, especially poor whites.[69]

Highly organized teams from the Commission moved in on communities like Christian revivalists, advertising their advent well in advance, preaching the prevalence of hookworm much as evangelists preached the prevalence of sin, and offering the cure like salvation. They won converts not only among those infected, but also among the well, and even among local physicians. At first, practicing physicians generally resented the intrusion of the medical crusaders. At the same time, however, they themselves had seldom recognized the symptoms of the disease or treated it. Hookworm victims were usually poor. Physicians, then as later, worked on the fee-for-service system and were not well attuned to the needs of those who could not pay.

By 1912, Page was ecstatic about the social benefits of the anti-hookworm crusade. He declared that every visitation generated a "new community spirit." He saw the movement as introducing a "new epoch" in the region. It was now obvious to him that hookworm was the cause of so much of the South's difficulties hitherto ascribed to the effects and after-effects of slavery on "a large poor-white" element in the region. "The Southern white people are of almost pure English stock," he declared, and thus "it has been hard to explain their backwardness, for they are descended from capable ancestors and inhabit a rich land." Page was led by his zeal for the elevation of the white mass to claim much for the destructive power of the tiny parasite. "The hookworm has probably played a larger part in our Southern history than slavery or wars or any political dogma or economic creed," he opined. "It has, in part, had a strong influence (nobody can say how strong) in shaping political dogmas and economic creeds. If there had been no hookworm victims in our Southern states it is certain that our national history would in some way, perhaps in many ways, have been very different." But then with the victory over the parasite came salvation for the two million Southerners furtherest down, Page exulted, the people who were "wretched and a burden, not by any necessity of heredity or by any wilful defect of character, but because they are sick." The lowest order of non-participants, to use Murphy's term, were being readied for full elevation into the communion of whiteness. The cure of their bodies would free their souls, and a new age in the South would follow. "I predict," one crusader glowed, "that within five years the whole face of this country will be changed and one will see here a new people and new earth."[70]

Simultaneously with the great public health campaigns there grew up something that might well be called "patrician medicine." The practice of medicine in the nineteenth-century South was a various thing. Many sons of planters in the black belts took training in leading Northern medical schools and returned to practice, primarily among blacks in the neighborhoods of their father's plantations. After the war, many of these men remained in the country and continued to work among the freedmen. Compared with what happened to the freedman in the city, those who stayed in the country enjoyed relatively good health and good medical attention. Often enough, both before and after the war, Southern physicians were taught by local physicians for profit, many of whom were themselves haphazardly trained. After the turn of the century all of this changed rapidly with the establishment of a number of medical schools in the South, the primary ideals of which seem to have been public service rather than personal profit. Probably the six schools of medicine most effectively associated with this trend were in universities that we have designated as special retreats of Conservatism, specifically, the "big four" Methodist universities (Emory, Tulane, Vanderbilt, and Trinity, which became Duke), Johns Hopkins, and the University of Virginia. At one point, at least, the Volksgeistian input into the new order was specific. The very large Medical College of Virginia in Richmond was thoroughly reorganized in and after 1913 under the leadership of Samuel Chiles Mitchell. Graduates of these schools emerged from their training oriented to serve their fellow Southern whites, not only in contact with individual patients, but in the great public health crusades that swept the South in those early decades of the twentieth century. These physicians came, like Miss Minerva and her pedagogical cohort, not up from the masses but out of the Conservative elite, and the focus of their practice in the black belts shifted from the black community to the white, from the country to the villages, towns, and cities.[71]

Conservatives were also very active with their white brothers and sisters in other fields. Conservatives who successfully made their fortunes in the North often turned a part of their wealth back into the South to patronize education, health crusades, and the general uplift of their less fortunate kind. Others who did not themselves get rich, like Murphy and Page, became brokers in the process of distributing Northern philanthrophy in the South. The same general paternalism moved into politics in the form of Conservative progressivism. Out of this came institutional reforms, such as the eradication of the convict lease system from the penal systems of the South, and such political personalities as those of John Sharp Williams of Mississippi and Oscar Underwood of Alabama, leaders who did not yield to race-baiting electoral rhetoric, flashy showmanship, and the cruder tastes of some of their fellows representing the region. Two of the finest political flowers growing out of Southern Conservative roots were, of course, Woodrow Wilson and William Gibbs McAdoo. In addition to politicians there were influential editors such as Virginius Dabney and Jonathan Daniels (the son of Josephus), both of whom continued to attempt to serve rather than be served by the people.

In literature, much the same might be said of Southern authors from Ellen Glasgow at the beginning of the twentieth century to William Faulkner at its middle. Both of these writers themselves spoke faith in the essentially good soul of Southern white people in the face of the ravages of the modern world. Moreover, each produced novels that Edgar Gardner Murphy, and Volksgeistian Conservatives generally, would have found highly congenial.

Ellen Glasgow's novel *The Voice of the People* (1900) was a nearly perfect fictional model for the system that Murphy adduced in *Problems of the Present South* four years later. In the novel, the "voice of the people" is Nicholas Burr, the son of a poor white dirt farmer in eastern Virginia. As a young boy Nick is taken in tow, educated, and socialized by a genteel Virginia family, the head of which is Judge Bassett. During the 1870s, with the judge's help, Nick is privately tutored along with the children of the local white elite, who are themselves the continuation of the Old South aristocracy. Again by the judge's hand, he matriculates with the brightest and the best in the University of Virginia and becomes a leading lawyer and politician. Slandered by the degenerate son of another eminent local family, Bernard Battle, he is never able to marry Bernard's sister, Eugenia, his childhood sweetheart and the love of his life. A bachelor in early middle age, with that rough, dogged strength of the plain folk that the Volksgeistians admired so much, he becomes the governor of the state. As such he brings to the highest office in the Old Dominion both the superb sense of values that aristocratic tutoring has imbued within him and the vast potential power of the awakening white mass. In the end, the governor comes to face a lynch mob in his home county. In the mob are the very lads of the common folk with whom he grew up, and they are out to lynch a Negro for the "usual" crime. The raw power of the people misguided is met, in Nicholas Burr, by the raw power of the people educated and imbued with proper values.

Nick falls in with the mob as it sweeps toward the jailhouse door, moves suddenly to the front, and blocks their entrance. It is a moonlit night, and "from the shadow he saw here and there a familiar face—the face of a boy he had played with in childhood. Several were masked, but the others raised bare features to the moonlight—features that were as familiar as his own."

Nick speaks to the crowd. "Men, listen to me. In the name of the Law, I swear to you that justice shall be done—I swear."

"We ain't here to talk," responds one of the men, "you stand aside, and *we'll* show you what we're here for."

The mob presses closer as a black cloud shuts out the moon and darkens the scene. Nick tries to speak again, but a man beside him shouts, "We'll be damned, but we'll get the nigger!"

Ellen Glasgow imagined the sequel:

> ... The words struck him like a blow. He saw red, and the sudden rage upheld him. He knew that he was to fight—a blind fight for he cared not what. The old savage instinct blazed within him—the instinct to do battle to death—to throttle with his single hand the odds that opposed. With a grip of iron he braced himself against the doorway, covering the entrance.
>
> "I'll be damned if you do!" he thundered.
>
> A quick shot rang out sharply. The flash blinded him, and the smoke hung in his face. Then the moon shone and he heard a cry—the cry of a well-known voice.
>
> "By God, it's Nick Burr!" it said. He took a step forward.
>
> "Boys, I am Nick Burr," he cried, and he went down in the arms of the mob.
>
> They raised him up, and he stood erect between the leaders. There was blood on his lips, but a man tore off a mask and wiped it away. "By God, its Nick Burr!" he exclaimed as he did so.
>
> Nicholas recognized his voice and smiled. His face was gray, but his eyes were shining, and as he steadied himself with all his strength, he said with a laugh, "There's no harm done, man." But when they laid him down a moment later he was dead. ...
>
> The sheriff knelt on the ground and raised him in his arms. As he folded his coat about him he looked up and spoke.
>
> "And he died for a damned brute," was what he said.[72]

Presumably the lynching did not occur, and Glasgow ended her novel quickly with the suggestion that, while Nick Burr died, he lived on in those whom he had touched.[73]

William Faulkner took up an even more pure form of Volksgeistianism in his 1948 novel *Intruder in the Dust*. In that story, Faulkner saved the Negro Lucas Beauchamps from the lynch mob by the joint initiative of an uncorrupted youth in the person of Charles "Chick" Mallison and a seventy-year-old unmarried daughter of the antebellum aristocracy in the person of Miss Habersham. These two were aided by Chick's young black friend, Aleck Sander, and seconded, finally, by the active intervention of county attorney Gavin Stevens and the sheriff. In what amounted to a peroration, Faulkner, speaking through Gavin Stevens, entered a plea for saving the South, the white South, from a Northern incursion and a second Reconstruction on the excuse of effecting racial justice. The white South was the hope of the nation, he seemed to say, because of its homogeneity. "We alone in the United States . . . are a homogeneous people," says Gavin. In warding off the North "we are defending not actually our politics or beliefs or even our way of life, but simply our homogeneity from a federal government to which in simple desperation the rest of this country has had to surrender voluntarily more and more of its personal and private liberty in order to continue to afford the United States." Like the Volksgeistians, Faulkner believed that real progress came only from homogeneity. "Only a few of us know that only from homogeneity," continued Faulkner as Gavin Stevens "comes anything of a people or for a people of durable and lasting value—the literature, the art, the science, that minimum of government and police which is the meaning of freedom and liberty, and perhaps most valuable of all a national character worth anything in a crisis—that crisis we shall face someday when we meet an enemy with as many men as we have and as much material as we have and—who knows?—that can even brag and boast as we brag and boast." The South lost a bloody war fought on both sides ultimately to establish "that Sambo is a human being living in a free country and hence must be free." Now the South must insure that the income from the awful sacrifice be achieved by insisting on freeing Sambo itself. That freedom "won't be next Tuesday," he declared. "Yet people in the North believe it can be compelled even into next Monday by the simple ratification by votes of a printed paragraph."

Faulkner exalted white soul, but he had no trouble exalting also the souls of black folk. "And as for Lucas Beauchamp, Sambo, he's a homogeneous man too, except that part of him which is trying to escape not even into the best of the white race but into the second best," that is, into a flashy materialism. DuBois himself could hardly have said it better, nor indicted white America outside the South more effectively than did Faulkner. Sambo, he continued, "has a better homogeneity than we have and proved it by finding himself roots into the land where he had actually to displace white men to put them down, because he had patience even when he didn't have hope, . . . not even just the will but the desire to endure because he loved the old few simple things which no one wanted to take from him. . . ." In fine Hegelian fashion Faulkner looked to a final fusion of black values and white. "We—he and us—should confederate: swap him the rest of the economic and political and cultural privileges which are his right, for the reversion of his capacity to wait and endure and survive." Then the South would rise again. "Then we would prevail; together we would dominate the United States; we would present a front not only impregnable but not even to be threatened by a mass of people who no longer have anything in common save a frantic greed for money and a basic fear of a failure of national character which they hide from one another behind a loud lipservice to a flag."[74]

Faulkner's appeal for confederation of black and white as a way of progress was almost an echo of Murphy, who had predicted a final great synthesis of American life in which "its unity is truer and richer because not run in one color or expressed in monotony of form. Like all vital unities, it is composite."[75] Further, in assessing the basis of the strength of black people and in urging whites to learn from the black experience, the Mississippi author resounded DuBois's words of nearly two generations before: " . . . all in all, we black men seem the sole oasis of a simple faith and reverence in a dusty desert of dollars and smartness. Will America be poorer if she replace her brutal dyspeptic blundering with light-hearted but determined Negro humility?"[76]

THE NEW ORTHODOXY

Volksgeistian Conservatives differed from regular Conservatives in regard to their attitudes toward both blacks and whites. Racially, Volksgeistians sought to put blacks aside upon the assumption that thus freed they would rise within their separated sphere as high and as fast as they should. Regular Conservatives, on the other hand, would hold Negroes within the organic society and keep them in the super-subordinate place where they found them. Conservatives assumed that there was no such thing as God-given "black soul" and hence no black culture that whites needed to respect. Indeed, it was as if black people were white people in arrested development, and black culture at best was but a perpetually imperfect imitation of white culture.

In regard to the white world, the primary difference between Volksgeistians and regular Conservatives was that the Volksgeistians had more faith in the capacity of the mass of whites to rise to the behavioral and moral traditions of the white elite. Volksgeistians seemed to envision an eventual melting upward of the white mass into a total cultural assimilation with a persisting and evolving Old South aristocracy—a *Herrenvolk*—and they seemed to expect in the result something like the arrival of God's chosen people at a new high of earthly attainment. In their view, the paternal energies of the white elite were turning and should turn to raise up the whites of the lower orders. Regular Conservatives did not have such great faith in the capacity of the mass of whites for elevation.

The result of these differences was that the array of institutions generated in the South in the early twentieth century—the institutions that were to rule the South through most of the century—were a curious mix of attitudes that were both inextricably interwoven and contradictory. In race relations, main-line Conservatism evolved to build what might be called the "new orthodoxy." The new orthodoxy retained much of the Volksgeistian emphasis on the ineradicable separateness of black people and set them aside at a great distance from whites. It also retained the extreme reduction of black people that Radicalism had effected. But even as resurgent Conservatism ruled blacks down and out, even as it insisted upon their inferiority and wide separation from the white world, it maintained its faith in the organic society and insisted that black people remain within that society. Congruently, it demanded that blacks strive to attain the whiteness that they would never be allowed to possess. After 1915 Conservatives struck paternal postures as evidence of their sympathy with the efforts of blacks to help themselves, but those postures yielded little of substance to benefit black people.

On the white side of the line, the Volksgeistian legacy took the form of a persisting suggestion that the South supported a superbly refined all-white democracy, both in politics and beyond politics. Even after Volksgeistian Conservatism as a system of thought had rather totally passed away in the 1920s, the institutions that Volksgeistians had helped to create rolled on, for examples, in the public schools and in medicine. These institutions, headed by the elite, continued to do the real work of raising up all white people together that the Volksgeistians had envisioned and to lend the appearance of truth to the suggestion of democracy. In reality, however, regular Conservatives never gave up the idea that theirs was properly an organic society and that leadership was necessarily the work of the elite distinctly separated from the masses. In the twentieth century, in their view, Southern society was a pyramidal hierarchy with blacks lumped rather indiscriminately together on the bottom and whites carefully arrayed on the top. Individual whites found specific places in a functional and harmonic order ranging from the lowest to the highest, and most whites were expected to remain in the places to which they were born. Individuals might move up—or down—by dint of their talents, virtues, and industry, but they did so within the everlasting pyramid. Thus, there was a rhetoric that preached equality of opportunity for whites and there was a measure of truth behind the rhetoric, but power remained decidedly hierarchial.

This transition from one Conservative order to another was not unlike that which occurred in the last generation of slavery. In 1889, as in 1831 after Nat Turner's insurrection, the white elite began to perceive black people as shockingly threatening to themselves. They moved to adjust to the threat with the result that not only did race relations change in essential ways, but so did the structure of white society. The fabric of Southern society un-wove itself. Some of the old threads were lost, others changed color and texture, and some from the world outside the South were imported. After the Atlanta riot the reweaving of Southern society began, and by 1915 the new fabric was visible.

Like the reconstitution of Southern society that had occurred in the last generation of slavery, this new order after 1915 had its hard side and its soft side. The hard side, the fruits of Radicalism, were represented in institutions that kept black people down. The soft side, in part the fruits of Volksgeistian Conservatism, accorded black people in their place a degree of independence and a vague, romantic affection. In a world largely invisible to whites, black people were able to gather the strength to survive in a universe that was at best non-caring and at worst destructive. White people at large simply lost awareness about black people, and in the new orthodoxy there was a passion among whites not to see a race problem. Our blacks are good blacks, so ran the thought, if outsiders would simply leave them alone. As in that earlier reconstitution of Southern society, what had begun as a reaction against blackness ended as an assertion of whiteness. The focus of conscious interest in white minds passed from the black mass to the white mass. In the antebellum order it had been the white elite that counted. In the new order it was white people all together that counted. Blacks stood at the bottom of society, and they all looked alike. Whites stood at the top, and each individual white looked different. Blacks were all right in their place, and white Southerners were beautiful wherever they were.

At one level the Volksgeistian system provided Southern whites with a positive image of themselves; at another it functioned as simply one more Southern philosophical accommodation to existing realities. In the early twentieth century the factory had already come to the South in a significant way, and it was, relative to general economics in the South and the nation at large just them, a tremendous success. Mill owners and managers had already turned their institutions into practically all-white enclaves. At least in their own minds, they did see themselves as the paternalists of legend, and, as yet, workers seemed more respectful and grateful to their employers than otherwise. In race relations, blacks were already separated from whites and were becoming, in the cultural sense, progressively blacker. Separation—and disfranchisement also—was explained by the Volksgeistians as merely another curve in the path

of progress and, hence, totally acceptable. Militant white supremacy was rationalized as but a transitional phase, a necessary discomfort that would fade
away when it had run its course. In one sense the Volksgeistians were arch
accommodationists in a specially sophisticated style. A true soul was duty
bound to oppose the unreal and to struggle for the ideal, and to do so vigorously for a time. But if one did not overcome obstacles, it meant that he battled
for an idea whose time had not yet come. His duty was then to seek another
more satisfying front upon which to spend his energies. Thus, Volksgeistian
Conservatism was a way of absorbing, intellectually, realities that one could
not avoid; it was a lubricant to ease the white South into the twentieth century.

CHAPTER XV

Legacy:
Race Relations in the
Twentieth-Century South

At its worst Volksgeistian Conservatism was a justification, an intellectual legitimation of a sad racial plight. In that it contended that whites could do nothing essential about blacks but must leave them room to find their own genius and salvation, Volksgeistian Conservatism sanctioned a white withdrawal from blackness both in the body and in the mind. A logical result of such thinking was the promotion of the invisibility of black people, the further removal of white people from the possibility of recognizing the equal humanity of blacks, and, finally, the loss of the black problem in the white mind. Volksgeistian Conservatism licensed the turning of the white elite away from its hereditary interest in blacks, and it encouraged them to channel their interest instead toward their white brothers and sisters. The fear and hatred engendered by Radicalism shifted, too, from blacks to the alien enemy—to Jews, Catholics, and the Communist threat from abroad.

The white South in the 1920s and 1930s became, in both its mind and body, what it had been seeking to be since the 1830s, a relatively solid, unitary, most-together place. It was precisely this fact that made it possible for Wilbur Cash, who had been born in 1900 and matured in the 1920s to write such a book as *The Mind of the South* (1941). It was not possible for close students of Southern culture to write such a book earlier, nor to be totally comfortable with that one since. The profound fissures that had existed in the South before those years—between black and white, between the slaveholding elite and the non-slaveholding mass and, subsequently, the social heirs of each, Conservative Democrats and Radical Populists, between racial Conservatives and racial Radicals, and between men and women—were not dissolved, but they were covered over by a heavy plastering of myth, troweled smoothly on by an elite determined to make it seem that there were no cracks in the structure that was their world and never really had been. Out of that labor of mythologizing the past and imagining the present, they brought forth a most peculiar phenomenon. In the South, white leadership adduced a silver age without there ever having been a golden one. They imagined a past that never was.

THE WHITE SOUTH LOSES THE BLACK PROBLEM

The most striking aspect of race relations in the South since the Radical era has been the inability of white people to grab hold of and securely retain an appreciation of the realities of black existence. Of course, the white South had long had difficulty in performing that task, but at some times they came closer to success than at others. Radicalism served to disengage white people from black people with unprecedented totality, practically to finish, in fact, a move toward unreality in race relations that had begun in the last generation of slavery and was signalized by the creation of the Sambo stereotype. It is ironic that, after such a great display of strength, by 1915 Radicalism had lost its hold on race relations and had died as a system of thinking about black-white relations. With that death went the death of the image of the Negro as beast. Of course, various ideas and attitudes of Radicalism persisted and evolved (such as an association of black people and super-sexuality), but Radicalism as a thought-set passed away and was soon lost to living memory. In spite of its short life, Radicalism had possessed great power, especially in the black belts. It had done its work there most effectively, more effectively in fact than its authors ever appreciated. In the black belts, it left black people in a society in which ruling institutions had been reshaped in an ethos that presumed their eventual demise. Those institutions persisted even though that assumption was forgotten by the society as a whole. The result was that black people lived in a world in which powerful forces worked automatically day by day to depress the quality of their lives. Moreover, Radicalism, by its very death, contributed to the continued reduction of black people because, as Radicalism dissolved, its absence induced Conservatism to flow quietly and gently back into the land, to fill young minds, and, in essence, to freeze race relations at the low levels generated by the Radical rage.

Individual Radical leaders lived beyond 1915, of course, and many of them continued to think, talk, and do battle as before. Shaking hoary heads, waving palsied hands, and crying out in reedy voices, like so many aging Cassandras, they warned of the race war to come. Most alarming to them was the apathy of uncommitted youth, and the tendency of these to lose sight of the black menace. Speaking in upcountry South Carolina in 1909, that unhappy and wrinkling warrior Ben Tillman struggled to muster troops for the new fight as he had for the old in 1876. "Under the lead of those editors who were many of them in knee-breeches when we were in the throes of the Reconstruction era," he charged, "the rising generation has been taught that we have no race problem and there is no possible danger from negroes now...."[1] Tillman was undeceived by accommodationist dissembling, and he remained a Radical until he died of a stroke in 1918. So too did other Radical leaders keep the faith. Tom Watson passed away in 1922, having been elected to the United States Senate for the term 1921–27. The governor of Georgia appointed Rebecca Felton to fill the office until a special election could be held. Walter George was elected, and he very graciously allowed the still lively Felton, then aged eighty-eight, to occupy that seat for two days before appearing to take the oath himself. One can only imagine the sense of satisfaction Rebecca Felton must have derived from being the first woman ever to take a seat in the upper house of the highest legislature in the land. She died in 1930, and so too did James K. Vardaman, in his case after nearly a decade of mental illness. Tom Dixon lived on until 1943, but was virtually an invalid during the last ten years of his life. Radical leaders persisted, and often they thrived in the areas of their lives that lay outside of race, but like trees that fall in the deserted woods, their Radicalism tumbled and crashed where there was no ear to hear, no eye to see, and no one to care. They continued to preach a race war, but nobody came.

The very success of the Radicals in their first great effort promoted their failure in this last campaign. Conservatism had been practically muted in the black belts, and there were no whites willing to give vigorous battle. But most of all, Radicalism was defeated by the fact that its basic assumption was grossly in error. Black people were not retrogressing, and they were most definitely not going to disappear. Indeed, as the census of 1900 clearly showed and that of 1910 confirmed, the number of black people, like that of white people, was steadily increasing decade after decade. Intelligent young Southerners, noting those statistics, seeing blacks all around, and not having matured in the world to which the Radical leadership had matured, simply had no faith in the dissolution of black people. Blacks were here to stay, they thought, and, further, that fact did not demand much attention because blacks would stay in their places. The new generation took Booker T. Washington at what they thought to be his word: that he spoke for all Negroes, that all Negroes were happy in their then low estate, that they were content to put down their buckets where they were and work with what they had, and that they were to be, essentially, hewers of wood and drawers of water.

Throughout the South the new generation of white people, the generation that was born about 1900 and came to maturity in the 1920s and 1930s strangely lost the Radical idea of race, but they lived with the fruit of their Radical fathers' thought. Their racial patrimony, however unwillingly bequeathed, dwindled from a Negro dead and dissolved to a Negro felled and fixed in a new low of super-subordination. The base line of the new orthodoxy, the anchor that held it firmly to earth, was the reality of Negro life.

Negroes in the mass in the black belts were undeniably low. To white people in the new order, it seemed that a simple recognition of material and moral realities argued that blacks were indeed what whites assumed them to be. In white minds, the fact supported the idea, and the idea supported the fact. The power of white people in the South was not without limits, but at the local level it had terrific force to press black life downward and outward.

White-hot Radicalism melted white people away from racial realities so thoroughly that they were unable to re-establish relatively effective contact with blacks for some two generations afterward. The image of the black beast had been born suddenly and grew prodigiously. Everywhere was the potential rapist, waiting for the unwary prey—to rape, mutilate, and murder. It was indeed a system to raise emotional fevers and breed insanities. The horror of the black image in the white mind was soon matched, and overmatched, by the real horror that was inflicted upon blacks by whites in riots and lynchings. Ultimately they turned and walked away, and they did not look back. There followed a decade of relative vacuity, a racial hiatus. Whites were certainly not talking much about black people, and, apparently, they were not thinking much about them either.

What came out of the hiatus was still another image, another stereotype of the Negro—the neo-Sambo. Most of all, neo-Sambo was a Negro with whom whites could live happily ever after. He was a relatively stable end to a long process of flux. After 1831, Nat Turner, the black rebel, gave way to the Sambo of late slavery. Beginning during the Civil War and accelerating with Reconstruction, the image of the Negro in Southern white minds traveled rather rapidly and with some confusion. In first freedom, whites continued as they had in slavery to think of blacks as mental children contained in adult bodies. Blacks cut loose from slavery were as dangerous to themselves and, ultimately, to others as five million children left suddenly alone. The child, after all, could become the beast, latently violent, murderous. As Reconstruction proceeded, the image seemed to soften. Blacks were merely ignorant, indolent, and gullible, susceptible to the blandishments of Yankees and scalawags. With Redemption, however, the image of the Negro as docile and loyal to the white elite began slowly to re-emerge. The new image, or more accurately the old image revived and transmuted, oozed to the surface in the 1880s. In the new order Sambo was allowed to grow into a young adult. He and she could survive very well by themselves without immediate white supervision. They could live comfortably, for instance, on a tenant farm. In the 1890s Conservatives, forced to counter the Radical idea of the black beast within in the South and meet a changing world outside the South, built in their minds a better, more serviceable Negro. The Negro was lifted to his feet, modernized, wound-up, and set into motion, driven by the engine of free enterprise much as Booker T. Washington depicted him. This new Negro differed essentially from the old in that he was progressive, not static. He had a life of his own, and a mind, too, to give his life direction in concert with the whole of society. Most of all, he had wise leadership. Specifically, he had Booker T. Washington and all of the lesser Washingtons scattered across the land. He could be as separate as a finger, yet a part of the hand, and a willing help. No threat, no potential rapist, no murderous Nat Turner, no militant and civilly menacing Frederick Douglass, not even a tax upon white energies, he could assist in the building of the new nation. He was "up from slavery" and still rising. Productive at work, at leisure he was as appealing in a folksy way as the Fisk Jubilee Singers or Uncle Remus telling his droll sage tales.

Neo-Sambo, the Negro who appeared in the white Conservative mind in the 1920s and after, was substantially diminished from the 1890s' version. Strangely he had somehow lost his progressive capacity. His engine in the model described by Booker T. Washington had somehow lost power. The sage of Tuskegee had died in 1915, and there was no longer a single conspicuous person who seemed to have a license to speak for blacks or to lead them. Instead there were many lesser leaders and in the South they seemed to voice only fading echoes of Tuskegee. Neo-Sambo did not press forward as a separate finger of the social hand. Indeed, it seemed to whites that he hardly thrust forward at all, but he did continue to be unthreatening. Like the original Sambo, he was docile, subordinate, pliable, conforming, and loyal. What had changed was that blacks, male and female, were allowed to gain a species of adulthood and a measure of independence within a separated world not permitted in the pre-Civil War model. These qualities would be handy to Southern whites if blacks were a permanent presence, and if they were to remain essentially "out there" rather than to be invited "in here." Blacks had learned to survive in the world without the constant and immediate supervision afforded by slavery, and they were marginally useful. They could be released after work on Saturday to do whatever marvelous things it was they did on Saturday night, and usually they could be trusted to show up again Monday morning, if only in jail. In the eyes of white people, blacks did retain some of the qualities of children, but they were child-like young adults rather than the raw children of the Sambo model. They were naïve, physical, easily frightened, sometimes innocently wise, usually harmless, and frequently amusing. They often engaged in "antics," guffaws, knee-slaps, jumps, and turns.

Some few exceptional black people were comfortably mature, much above the common type, and they usually became the local leaders by white designation. Often the local leader was a minister, undertaker, restaurant owner, landlord, storekeeper, or hip-pocket banker. His money came from the hands of black people who worked for the whites, and he drew a measure of insulation and hence of independence from that fact. Whites in the know quoted him as the authority on all things black. Whatever the words, the message was always the same: "He says that black people like it down there, and they always behave that way." The mass of blacks in their separate communities could be safely left to the management of these local leaders who understood them so well and explained them in confidential voices to interested whites.

The black leader had an elevated status only in his local world. If he left home he melted into the black mass. In the eyes of the whites, all Negroes looked alike unless they knew them very personally, and, in the opinion of whites, all could be treated essentially alike. Black people who resisted the neo-Sambo role were either exiled, jailed, killed, or they became, quite simply, "invisible." The new image of black people was suggested accurately enough by characters who appeared in the world of white entertainment—first on the stage, then on the radio, and finally on film. The black person in the abstract often was the singularly talented entertainer, dancer, or musician who, it seemed, had no other life than that of delighting white people. Beloved among whites were such characters as Amos and Andy, the Kingfish, Aunt Jemima, Stepin Fetchit, Buckwheat of "Our Gang" comedies, Scarlett O'Hara's Mammy, and Jack Benny's man Rochester. Among the favorites in a different, more serious vein, was George Washington Carver of peanut butter semi-fame. Credits were given by whites to black talent, but it was always discounted even as it was awarded.

In the 1920s, 1930s, and on into the 1940s, neo-Sambo washed over the black beast in Southern white minds, rendering Marcus Garvey merely pretentious and ridiculous, obscuring W. E. B. DuBois and the NAACP, fading to fleeting shadows the image of the black beast rapist, and totally erasing any active memory of Nat Turner and black men in the Union Army during the Civil War, black rebels against white rebels, double rebels, ready, willing, and able to shoot down white men upon the field of battle. Again in the mid-twentieth century, as in the last generation of slavery, white Southerners were insisting that their Negroes were good Negroes, and there was really no Negro problem at all as long as Negroes remained in the place made for them, and misguided and ill-intentioned whites left them alone.

THE PARANOID STYLE
IN THE TWENTIETH-CENTURY SOUTH

After the end of the Atlanta riot, white Southerners positively needed not to see the black beast rapist anymore. Collectively, they pushed him below the threshold of consciousness, and with him lost the white beast also. With both, they lost the Negro problem and, in the process, very nearly the Negro himself. Certainly the fear of blackness in the South did not die, and could not die. It simply went underground and was displaced. Southerners came to fear hidden blackness, the blackness within seeming whiteness. They began to look with great suspicion upon mulattoes who looked white, white people who behaved as black, and a whole congeries of aliens insidious in their midst who would destroy their happily whole moral universe. The continuous search for invisible blackness, the steady distrust of the alien, and the ready belief in the existence of the enemy hidden within gave rise to a distinctly paranoid style in Southern white culture in the twentieth century.

This paranoid style certainly had roots in the late slave period when Southerners argued that slavery was absolutely right and insisted that it was firmly endorsed by all significant parties, including God. Yet they felt the peculiar institution so peculiar, so grandly different from everything else in the world as to be endangered by anything foreign. The result was that the South closed itself off in vital ways from the outside world, and it persecuted vigorously those suspected of internal subversion. The United States mails, for instance, did not run in the South when they carried abolitionist literature, and more than a few itinerant merchants departed with a tarred skin and a coat of feathers. Southern paranoia had its modern beginnings in late slavery, but its continuous history began with the Radical era. It had its genesis in the Radical mind during the red-hot fights of that age when Radicals drew a clear, firm line between those who were on the right side of the race line and those, white or black, who were on the wrong side. This extreme intolerance of deviation among their white brothers was so strong as to breed a new definition of blackness in the South. Whites who sided too closely with blacks, were, as the phrase went, "white niggers." One could be perfectly white genetically and yet be black morally. Clearly, about the turn of the century, there was a rising frequency in references to the behavior of certain whites as being Negro-like. In North Carolina, in the white supremacy campaigns of 1898 and 1900, for instance, there was a marked upsurge in the tendency to read out of the white community and into blackness those whites who consorted, politically or otherwise, with Negroes. Very often those who drew concerted fire were thought to have committed acts of sexual transgression.

The Robert Hancock affair in North Carolina in 1898 illustrates the point well. Hancock was a native white Republican of some power during the fusion movement in the 1890s. As a reward for his political work, he was made president of the Atlantic and North Carolina Railroad, a line owned by the state. It was charged that he had recruited his wife's niece, Miss Abbott, an unemployed schoolteacher, to serve as his "confidential secretary" and that he had seduced her. Holding her in his power economically in those sorely depressed times, he repeatedly used her sexually. It was, in a word, rape. Not only did Hancock head the railroad, he was also a member of the local school committee. When Miss Abbott's sister, a teacher, objected to the abuse, he used his association with black political leaders to punish her. As one observer reported: "He also got his Negro Committeeman to vote with him & discharged Miss Abbott's sister from the Graded School in New Bern because she became indignant at his treatment of her Sister. The man who voted with him is W. W. Lawrence, the Negro man whom Hancock was pressing [U.S. Senator] Pritchard to have appointed for Collector of Customs at New Bern." The language used in discussing the case effectively declared that this was Negro-like behavior. Indeed, Hancock might be neatly substituted for Tim Shelby in the Mollie Graham episode in Thomas Dixon's *The Leopard's Spots.* Tim offered "Miss Mollie" a teaching position in the public schools in return for a kiss, presumably the prelude to further ardent demands.

Populist partisans recognized the danger of affiliating with such Republicans as Hancock. "By all means let us have a white man—Skin & heart" stand for all places, a black belt Populist leader urged Senator Marion Butler in 1898. "As I before stated we don't want any more Hancocks on our shoulders." But beyond politics, there was an even greater danger posed by Hancock. J. S. Basnight, a James City lumberman, understood it perfectly because he had a daughter of marriageable age. "Such conduct as Mr. Hancock has been guilty of with his Niece, needs especial attention on a moral line, if not on political lines," he insisted. He pictured his own daughter traveling by rail and meeting Hancock. "Suppose my daughter were coming home from college and he came by, talked cordially and sat with her without her knowing of this. What a shame."[2]

Robert Hancock was a "white nigger" in real life in 1898; Allan McLeod was a "white nigger" in fiction four years later in Dixon's *The Leopard's Spots.* In the story, McLeod, like Hancock, is a white Republican leader in the fusion government in the Tarheel state. He might have had the fatal one drop of black blood invisible in his veins, or he might not. The vital point was that he was morally black, and that his blackness was totally hidden under a white skin. He was purely sensual, sexual creature, plotting carefully, virtually for decades, to seduce the perfect Southern woman, Mrs. Durham. If his skin had been dark, he would never have had that opportunity, just as Hancock would never have had the shameful chance of sitting next to Basnight's daughter on the train had his skin betrayed the danger to her.[3]

In the white mind as it functioned in this vein. black political power was associated with the sexual exploitation of white women. As noticed earlier, a special target of the white supremacy campaign in North Carolina in 1898 was James H. Young, a legislator from Raleigh and one of the leading black Republicans in the state. Democratic campaign literature featured the idea that Young, as a member of the board that governed the Deaf, Dumb, and Blind Institute, insisted upon closely inspecting the quarters of the young white women in the school and hinted that he took advantage of their blindness and dependence to create for himself there a captive harem. Young, the Democrats declared, was "a hard man to satisfy."[4] Clearly, such propaganda built upon white assumptions that blacks were extraordinarily sexual creatures and that black men in politics used their power for sexual gratification. In this particular case, a special fillip was the fact that Young's black skin was invisible to the young women involved.

By about 1900 it was possible in the South for one who was biologically pure white to become black by behavior. A white person could cross over to blackness. Blackness and whiteness became a matter not just of color or even blood, but of inner morality reflected by outward performance. Black people could seldom rise near to white values and white culture, but they ought to strive to do so. On the other hand, white people could easily descend into blackness, and some did. In the very midst of the whites, there were unseen "niggers," men with black hearts under white skins who might marry their daughters, who might by that fact quietly, insidiously rape them, and spawn a despicable breed. Increasingly in the early decades of the twentieth century, it was the unseen enemy that Southern whites came specially to fear.

White skin might also hide African ancestry. Southern whites of the Radical persuasion became very fearful of mulattoes passing for white. At this time, the white elite in the lower South were well into a changeover from a view that prevailed among them up to about 1850 that recognized mulattoes, and especially free mulattoes, as a useful group somewhere between black and white to one in which mulattoes and blacks were lumped together in an essentially undifferentiated mass. The "one drop rule" that relegated all to the same caste was rapidly becoming universal. One drop of black blood made anyone all black. In Radical eyes all mulattoes shared fully the bad characteristics ascribed to blacks, even though they possessed certain attributes special to themselves.[5] Tom Dixon in 1912 published a novel on this theme entitled *The Sins of the Father*. Its protagonist is a white journalist who has labored successfully to save his state from Negro rule only to be seduced by a very attractive young woman. It develops that she is actually black and passing for white, but already the corruption is there and running strong, threatening his own adult son.[6] Southern whites became deeply suspicious of dark strangers, sometimes even expelling such a person from their community on the ground that he was attempting to pass for white. Prospective brides and grooms, applicants for admission to schools, fraternities, and sororities, and people in general with whom one's children might come into intimate contact came to have their ancestries closely scrutinized.

By the 1920s Radical frenzy had been replaced by a steady, quiet, yet alert fear that the attack would come not openly and violently from without by people obviously black, but unseen and insidiously from within, by people with apparently white skins. Your very neighbor might be a Negro, they whispered in their minds, your son or daughter might unwittingly marry one. The unseen Negro might be genetically black in some slight degree, or he might be pure white. The phenomenon is delicate and difficult to define, but it left its mark on Southern thought and behavior. It is evident in the vigil that resurgent Conservatism maintained against alien incursions into local affairs. The latter was often manifested in the fact that, when there was a serious disturbance among black people in any locality in the South, whites usually insisted that it arose not from any intrinsic failing in the Southern social order, but rather from the machinations of evil outside forces—the Germans in World Wars I and II, Communists after the Russian Revolution in 1917, and Jews, Catholics, and labor organizers all along. Figuratively, Southerners after 1915 were constantly casting quick glances over their shoulders and nightly passing broomsticks under their beds to detect the hidden enemy. This curious phenomenon, the emergence of the alien rather than the black as the ultimate menace to Southern civilization, appeared powerfully in early form in the case of Leo Frank. The affair began with the murder of a thirteen-year-old girl, Mary Phagan, in Frank's pencil factory in Atlanta in 1913 and ended with his death by lynching in Marietta in 1915.

Leo Frank was Jewish and in 1913 he was twenty-nine, five feet six inches tall, a thin, intense man with protuberant eyeballs behind thick lensed glasses. He had grown up in Brooklyn, graduated from Cornell University as a mechanical engineer, and came south in 1907 to manage the four-storied factory near Five Points in downtown Atlanta. The factory belonged to the National Pencil Company, a venture owned mostly by an uncle who lived in New York. Frank ran the factory efficiently, and the company profited steadily. In 1911 he married Lucile Selig, eight years his junior and the daughter of a settled, well-to-do Jewish family in Atlanta. The Seligs drew their money from making and distributing disinfectants, detergents, and other chemical products. In 1913 Leo and Lucile were living with her parents. Leo was well respected in the Jewish community. He was of German derivation, American-born, and college educated. Soon after he came to Atlanta he was elected president of the local lodge of B'nai B'rith.

Mary Phagan was the very child of the New South. She was born near Marietta, about eighteen miles northwest of Atlanta. Her parents had been tenant farmers, but when the price of cotton dropped to disastrous lows, the Phagans, like many other farmers in the region, were squeezed off the land. One day the parents and their six children simply left Marietta and walked to Bellwood, a mill village on the outskirts of Atlanta. John Phagan, the father, began working in the mill, and so did his older children—at 5 cents an hour. When John died, Mrs. Phagan married another mill worker. By 1913 Mary had a job in the pencil factory in Atlanta, commuting into town from Bellwood on the trolley, and earning 12 cents hourly. For ten hours a day she worked at a machine pressing erasers into brass rings fixed to the tops of pencils. On Saturday morning, April 26, 1913, Mary ate a breakfast of leftover cabbage and bread and took the streetcar downtown. She intended to collect her pay at the factory, knowing that Frank always did his books there on Saturdays. She expected to stay downtown to watch the Confederate Memorial Day parade along Peachtree Street. The widow of General Stonewall Jackson was to review the two hundred veterans of the rebel army who would march in the procession. A working child taking a holiday. Mary was small, four feet ten inches tall, and she weighed 105 pounds. She was an attractive girl. She had filled the role of "Sleeping Beauty" in the church play some two weeks previously, and she was rapidly becoming a young woman. Had she lived, two weeks later she would have been fourteen.

Mary entered the factory building and climbed the stairs to the second floor. She found Frank in his office, a space closed off by partitions from the machinery that filled the room. "I came to get my pay," she said. "I was out Tuesday, but I have Monday coming." Frank found her pay envelope and put $1.20 in it. Mary took the envelope and left. Frank thought he heard a thumping noise. He looked across the factory room, saw nothing, and returned to his books. It was then about 12:00 noon. It would later be established by medical examiners that Mary Phagan had died at 12:30. There were a few workmen servicing machinery on different floors, and some people came and went during the day. Frank went home for lunch about 1:20 and returned at 3:00 to work until 6:00. He left the night watchman on duty. Then he went home again and read, while Lucile, other members of the Selig family, and guests played bridge.

About 3:00 a.m. Sunday, the night watchman at the factory discovered Mary's body. She lay face down on a trash pile in the basement. The watchman telephoned for help, and the police came. Mary had been bitten on the shoulder and neck and beaten, but the cause of death was probably strangulation. Still wrapped around her neck was a cord, so tightly drawn that it had cut the flesh, and Mary had bled profusely. Her tongue protruded. A piece of her underclothing was also wrapped around her neck and partially covered her face. There had been, apparently, an unsuccessful attempt at rape. A door affording a rear exit from the basement stood open, bloody hand prints smeared over it as if the murderer had fled by that way.

The police immediately arrested the night watchman. Shortly after 7:00 Sunday morning the officers went to Frank's house. From the start they were hostile, and within two days they had arrested him for the murder. Frank's trial was probably the most celebrated ever to occur in Georgia. Hugh M. Dorsey, the state's prosecutor, wanted to be governor, and this was his chance.[7]

It was hot in Atlanta when the trial began late in July; the courthouse, near the state capitol, caught the sun from early morning. Daily the temperature hovered at 90°. The doors and windows of the courtroom on the first floor were thrown open. The large blades of an overhead ventilator swung lazily around and palm fans fluttered against the too still air. The courtroom itself, the corridors, and even the yard around the windows were filled with people, men and women, red-faced and perspiring. The air was laden with an angry, violent mood insisting that Frank be convicted. Now and again the crowd shouted, "Hang the Jew, or we'll hang you."[8]

Prosecuting attorney Dorsey was alive to the spirit of the mob and the political advantage of giving them what they wanted. The press, the pulpit, and the politicians had all painted a picture in which an innocent virginal Southern girl had been outraged by an alien Jew. He was college educated, wealthy, and, they suggested, unscrupulous in using his power to abuse sexually the girls and young women held virtually captive in his factory. Dorsey felt certain that he could give the people a conviction. His key witness was a black man, Jim Conley, who worked as the sweeper in the pencil factory. Conley at first told police that he had not been at the factory on Saturday and that he knew nothing. Several days later the police discovered that he had lied. After repeated questioning and some beating, he broke down and confessed more and more of the "true" story. He admitted to previous lying, layer upon layer of it, and finally came to a story that depicted Frank as a man who had engaged in various "crimes against nature" with women in his second-story office while Conley locked and guarded the front door to keep visitors away. Frank was a monster who had performed unspeakable acts of sexual perversion. On at least two occasions, Conley had entered the room while Frank and his lover were still in suggestive positions. He was not, as Conley reported Frank saying of himself, "built like other men." Conley swore that Frank had killed Mary when she resisted his advances and then asked him to help dispose of the body. Together they carried her to the basement. Frank intended at first to have him burn the remains. He also had Conley pencil two notes constructed to look as if Mary had written them just before she died. The notes accused the nightwatchman of the assault. However, Conley refused to attempt to burn Mary's remains without Frank's help. Thus, the body was found hours later in the basement with the notes near by.[9]

In the South in 1913 white people did not believe that black people ordinarily would tell them the truth at first questioning. Black people would lie, and whites would need to break through the lies to get the truth. Dorsey put his star witness on the stand and led him through confessions of his lies. Then the prosecutor had him tell the final story. The defense made the mistake of attacking Conley's credibility by going through the same routine in greater depth. It almost became a litany of lying as Conley confessed to having told one untruth after another. The all-white jury followed the proceeding with seemingly great satisfaction, nodding assent as Conley confessed to each lie and even repeated the performance of hanging his head in shame as he had done when the police had found him out in his mendacity. However, when the defense lawyers came to the crucial element—that Frank was the man who had killed little Mary Phagan—they were surprised to find themselves unable to break his story.[10] He was the chastened Negro, telling the truth at last. Ironically, the more the defense exhibited Conley as a liar, the more thoroughly the jury believed the final, and unbroken, lie. In the white mind, that last story had to be the absolute truth, and a black man's testimony in these circumstances was more valuable than the purest gold.[11] Diogenes had found his man.

Frank was, of course, convicted. He was sent to the state penitentiary in Milledgeville. In prison he was attacked by an inmate who cut his throat. He was saved from bleeding to death by another prisoner who happened to be a physician. In 1915 Governor John Slaton, a lawyer by profession and deeply disturbed by the blatant inequity of the trial, decided to commute Frank's sentence at the risk of ruining his own political future. Word of his intention got out. Several automobiles full of men went from Marietta more than one hundred miles to the prison in Milledgeville. The men broke into the compound, seized Frank, and took him away. They brought him to Marietta, near the site of Mary Phagan's birthplace. They stood him on a table, put a rope around his neck, and kicked the table away. The fall tore the stitches that had closed his neck wound. He bled profusely, and died.[12]

Leo Frank was lynched just as the murderer of Mary Phagan would have been lynched had he been black. But he was lynched upon the testimony of a black man, and that testimony was rendered in such a way as to compel white prejudice to judge it true. The awful irony in this case is that it was probably the black man himself who committed the deed. Conley drank heavily, and on the morning of the murder he had attempted to borrow money for drinks without success. Most likely, he killed Mary simply for the $1.20 she carried in her pay envelope. Neither the money nor the envelope was ever found. Jim Conley's subsequent behavior suggested that he was mentally deranged. Later, in a confused relationship with a woman whose lover he wanted to become, he apparently admitted the crime.[13] In retrospect, it seems clear enough that Frank was innocent.

In the Frank case, white Atlanta, white Georgia, and the white South at large were stoutly and steadfastly determined not to see a black beast rapist when they had one right before their eyes. They were rapidly losing the capacity to cope with the omnipresent threat, and they were determined to substitute menaces more manageable. Leo Frank was killed as a surrogate for the black beast rapist. He was in a sense a scapegoat at least twice removed from the real cause of his death. He stood for the alien menace to the South, and the alien menace stood for blacks. Specifically, in the first connection, Frank represented the penetration of the South by the industrial revolution in a new and frightening way. He was a rich Jew, managing a factory mostly owned by his New York uncle. Little Mary Phagan was Southern, white, and an innocent virgin. She was born in the country and killed in the city, in a Yankee-owned factory, fighting to preserve her purity against a bestial Jew. Such was the menace to the South at large, and the South turned its anger away from blacks and toward those alien forces that seemed most threatening to its essential virtue. The cry thus shifted from "the blacks are raping our women" to "the imperialist mills are raping our women" to "the Jews are raping our women."[14]

It was appropriately symbolic that the film *The Birth of a Nation* was shown in Atlanta during the fall of 1915 after Frank was lynched. It was even more symbolic of things to come that the "second Ku Klux Klan" was organized in Atlanta that same year, and its regeneration was celebrated by burning a huge cross on top of Stone Mountain. However, in personnel and motive, the second KKK was most definitely not a continuation of the first. Indeed, it began primarily as a business venture, and its creators virtually sold it to other, more aggressive entrepreneurs in 1920. Like the original Klan it featured the idea of white brotherhood and relied upon regalia, rituals, and exotic titles for a part of its appeal. The gigantic difference was that the second Ku Klux Klan featured a hatred of Jews and Catholics that obscured its anti-Negro animus. This is not at all to say that black people were left out, but the fact was that in the 1920s the great mass of white people in the South did not think that black people were a problem. Those who looked for devils in the South in the 1920s and after were forced to look elsewhere. They found them in the relatively small and relatively visible Jewish and Catholic populations. The second KKK was not, of course, an exclusively Southern phenomenon. Under the banner of native Americanism, it spread north and west, and gained such power as to influence the elections of one governor and several senators in a number of states, outlaw parochial schools in Oregon, and influence a presidential nomination. Eventually, in the 1920s, the Klan came to claim Indiana as its special stronghold, electing one of its own leaders as lieutenant governor of that state.[15]

The relative decline of blacks as objects of hatred by the second KKK and the taking up of Jewish people as a special target was something new. Before the twentieth century, there was no extraordinary anti-Semitism in the South. There were scattered references to Jews having killed Christ and to the venality of Jewish shopkeepers, but these slurs were more than balanced by numerous friendships and a great deal of respect between Jews and Gentiles, and by a large number of Jewish people (such as Judah P. Benjamin, a member of the Confederate cabinet) who shared fully in the Southern world-view. However, early in the twentieth century the rhetoric of anti-Semitism emerged and in some quarters rose to furious levels, for instance, in Tom Watson's journals. Nevertheless, even after the Frank case and the emergence of the Klan, Southern white Gentiles made a distinction between Jews of Old South and New South origins. The latter were often of the more recent migration from the Slavic countries; the former were British, German, and Sephardic in their ancestry.

New-coming Jews were insidious to the virtue of Southern women, and so too was the Catholic church. Tom Watson, in and after 1907, turned his venom upon Catholics. By 1912 he was accusing priests of using the confession to seduce attractive young women. By his questions, the priest learned which of his penitents were most vulnerable. Watson imagined the scene:

> Remember that the priest is often a powerfully sexed man, who lives on rich food, drinks red wine, and does no manual labor. He is alone with a beautiful, well-shaped young woman who tells him that she is tormented by carnal desire. Her low voice is in his ear; the rustle of her skirts and the scent of her hair kindle flames. She will never tell what he says or does. She believes that he cannot sin. She believes that *he* can forgive her sin. She has been taught that in obeying him, she is serving God.[16]

Another "white nigger," another rape, another secret outrage.

Southerners came to associate the hidden enemy at home with the overt enemy abroad. And they tended to associate both with their otherwise good Negroes. During World War I, the enemy was, of course, the Germans. Sarah Patton Boyle, whose lineage laced neatly back to the First Families of Virginia and whose father was the Episcopal priest in Virginia most conspicuously concerned with missionary work among blacks, was a child during the war. She lived at that time on the family farm in the heart of the black belt relatively near the coast. She heard rumors that the Germans were landing agents from submarines to go among the Negroes and stir up insurrections preparatory to an invasion. Sarah secretly dug a cave in a hillside near her house. She intended to hide there with her family when the blacks insurrected at the instigation of the Germans.[17]

After the Communist revolution in Russia in 1917, the white South had another and very durable unseen enemy to combat. It did not improve their sense of security that the Communist International soon adopted a program for American blacks inspired by their own expert in racial and ethnic affairs, Josef Stalin. After the revolution, Stalin would solve the race problem in America by setting aside certain states in the deep South for exclusive occupation by blacks. In Communist America, as in Communist Russia, the race problem was expected to achieve first a geographical resolution and then a political one. After World War I was over, the Communist menace became the most popular menace in the South just as it did in America at large. Moreover, often enough, the visible Communists happened to be Jewish. Sometimes, almost as a bonus, they might also be labor organizers. When the Scottsboro case broke in 1931 the South had a perfect opportunity to exercise its paranoia. In this affair, nine young black men were accused of raping two white women hoboing on a freight train in northern Alabama. The Communist party in America made a *cause célèbre* of the case. In the Southern mind, the involvement of the Communists and a leading lawyer from New York named Leibowitz, who was Jewish but not a Communist, represented the nightmare come true. The Alabama Department of the American Legion deplored the "horde of Communists" who flooded the state and incited riot among the blacks by their defense of the "negro rapists" in the Scottsboro case. It is virtually certain that the charges were not true, but, as in the Frank affair, that hardly seemed relevant. Eight of the nine young men were convicted immediately and sentenced to death in the electric chair. Prolonged court action saved the lives of all the "Scottsboro boys," but a generation before such a resolution would have been most unlikely.[18]

During World War II, the Germans came to the fore again as the hidden enemy. And again, the white South associated the threat with black insurrection. Curiously, this time it was thought that maids in the white homes of the South were organizing so-called "Eleanor Clubs" in a conspiracy to raise wages and "bump" ladies off the sidewalks of Southern towns. Allegedly, somehow inspired by liberal Eleanor Roosevelt, black women were organizing to walk up and down the sidewalks of the South rudely shouldering against white women as they went about their business. Perhaps the simple desertion by black women of white people's kitchens for well-paying factory jobs inspired these rumors.

Easier to understand was the idea that the Germans had organized "Swastika Clubs" among blacks to insurrect at the right moment to make a Nazi invasion of America successful. "Hitler has told the Negroes he will give them the South for their help," one informant reported to sociologist Howard Odum. Closely associated with the Nazi threat was the "ice pick rumor." Appearing throughout the South was the same basic story that the Negroes were buying up all the ice picks in preparation for an attack on the whites during the first blackout or at some other signal occasion.[19] All of this seems rather ridiculous, but what followed had no humor in it.

When the Cold War came on, Southerners were ready for it. They seemed almost to welcome the combat. With the Russians in possession of transoceanic aircraft, rockets, and atom bombs, it seemed fully possible that the outside enemy might very quickly become an internal one. What had been invisible suddenly became very visible. When the cold war warrior Senator Joseph McCarthy of Wisconsin first appeared, he had hearty approval in the South. The civil-rights movement was already gathering headway. Southern whites were quite ready to believe that any agitation on the part of black people was not the result of local conditions, but rather of alien agents—of whatever color—in the pay of Russian Communists. When F.B.I. Director J. Edgar Hoover published his book *Masters of Deceit,* he merely affirmed something Southern whites already knew. Many Southerners, and perhaps most of them, firmly believed that Martin Luther King and the whole civil-rights movement were instigated and paid for by Communist agents. Without interlopers and provocateurs, their blacks would be good blacks.

THE UNREAL SOUTH

It is ironic that at the turn of the century, just when other Americans were entering an identity crisis, Southern whites were emerging from one. Southerners seemed to undergo a personality collapse in 1865, a slow recovery in the 1880s, and something of a boom in and after the turn-of-the-century years. They emerged in the 1920s and 1930s with their world intact, a world that pleased them, however much it might displease others. Other Americans had not so happy a flight. In 1893 historian Frederick Jackson Turner announced that American national character was primarily democratic. Such, he insisted, was the logical fruit of the marriage between the frontier experience and the American people. In the early decades of the twentieth century the "frontier thesis" had great currency in explaining the course of America toward democracy. But there were disturbances in the nation to upset a tranquil cruise to a democratic end. Not the least of these were massive new waves of immigration that brought in people with ideologies arcane and disturbing in the American setting. It did not help allay the sense of crisis that President McKinley was assassinated in 1901 by an anarchist. The new immigrants largely avoided the South. They made their places, rather, in the urban and industrial North. The numbers swelled and approached a million arrivals each year. The new arrivals were much more Catholic than Protestant, more Slavic than Teutonic and Celtic, and many were Jewish. In the crisis the North moved to redeem native America. In the 1920s legislation reduced the number of new immigrants yearly to a trickle, and intellectuals generated the "melting pot" concept to predict an early and perfect assimilation of these newly arrived Americans.

Meanwhile, even in the first decade of the century, Southerners were coming to very definite conclusions about their own essential nature. They were deciding that they were a specially spiritual people with a high sense of ideals and personal honor. Symptomatic of the South's rising appreciation of itself was the fact that there were now beginning to appear "Southern" textbooks, written in the South, published in the South, and used by Southern students in a growing network of public schools. Professor J. G. de Roulhac Hamilton began to collect manuscript materials relating to Southern history at the University of North Carolina in Chapel Hill, while some ten miles away in Durham in 1907 the first course in Southern history was taught by William K. Boyd in John Spencer Bassett's Trinity College. Southerners were putting themselves together again, and the South was rising—at the very least, in its own eyes.

The white South felt that it was finding itself, and it thought that the rest of America might well profit by its discovery. In an address to a joint meeting of the American Historical Association and the American Economic Association in December 1903, Edwin A. Alderman, then the president of Tulane University and shortly to become one of the great heads of the University of Virginia, declared his belief that:

> America needs this intense idealism of the South, stamped into its life by its sad, strange history. The nation should thank God that it is here, for, after all, it is a spiritual force needed to help combat vulgar strength and coarse power, and a vast indifferentism to finer issues. I have said that industrialism will change this idealism, and so it will, but it is too deep for destruction or submersion. . . . Whenever this vast grip of Southern idealism takes fast hold of the idea of national unity, of national destiny, of national hope, the great Republic that we all love and count it a glory to serve, will feel its buoyant power as men in a valley feel the tonic of upper altitudes. Let the nation then cherish this idealism which it sometimes thinks of as parochialism. It lies in my thought as a benign national asset. . . .[20]

The rise in the Southern sense of self had much to do with the use it made of its past, most especially its Confederate past. One of the most interesting and revealing carriers of the Southern revival was the Kappa Alpha Order. The order was first organized in Washington College in Lexington, Virginia, in 1866 by students, some of whom were Confederate veterans. In its first two generations, it was a highly idealistic activity. It was formed for the purpose of preserving what those young men considered to be the virtues of the Old South. Foremost among these was "honor," followed closely be veneration for Southern ladyhood. Both of these were overlain with a heavy blanket of Christianity. "Order" was precisely the appropriate term to describe the character of this specially Southern fraternity in its first phase. It was built upon a regimen, a strict code for living in society in such a way as to purify the body and refine the spirit. Initially the KAs were not unlike the orders of the medieval church, such as, for example, the Knights Templar. KAs should not curse, drink, or otherwise defile their bodies, and they should pray. The early KAs saw themselves as something very much like Christian knights.

In the 1890s the KAs suffered schisms over several issues. Until that time the fraternity had accepted new chapters only if they were located in Southern schools. The question arose: should the order accept Northern chapters? Could a Northerner naturally possess the virtues that the order required? Did one actually have to be born into the *Volksgeist* of the white South to possess the ideals requisite for membership? Ultimately, the answer was that Yankees could not, indeed, be properly endowed, and the order remained distinctly Southern. The single exception was the West. It was decided that certain Western areas were sufficiently Southern to host the order. In 1895 a chapter was organized at the University of California in Berkeley and another contemplated at Stanford.

Kappa Alphas also split over the proper ranking of Robert E. Lee in the hierarchy of Southern leaders. Actually, Lee himself had been the president of Washington College when the order was founded. The late commander of the Army of Northern Virginia apparently never noticed the order, and the order in return was less than enthusiastic about Lee. Instead, the KAs raised up T. J. "Stonewall" Jackson as their pre-eminent hero. Jackson had died of wounds received in the war, and was famous for his piety. The KAs painted Jackson as a Christian knight martyred fighting for the liberty and honor of the Southern people. By the 1890s Lee too had died, and the order finally decided to elevate him to the sainthood also. The myth arose that Lee had somehow inspired the genesis of the order. In the early twentieth century, young KAs were encouraged to show the same sense of honor and duty, of *noblesse oblige,* in their lives that the great general had shown in the war.[21]

In moving to welcome Lee to the hall of Southern fame, the KAs were only doing what leading Southerners were doing. It is highly significant that Robert E. Lee became the great war hero of the South only in the 1890s. Before that time Jackson and Davis were the idols. Jackson was, of course, a candidate easily elected. His dashing generalship, chalking up victory after victory with his small, tough army corps, his tragic death, shot by his own men while bravely scouting the front lines, and his quiet Christian faith were the very clay of which mythical heroes are made. On the other hand, Davis might not have become so venerated had not the national government seen fit to arrest him immediately after the capitulation and send him in chains to a cell, almost a dungeon, deep in the bowels of Fortress Monroe, Virginia. Davis was not good raw material out of which to fashion a postwar Southern hero, either for Northern or Southern consumption. He was, after all, a great slaveholder, a politician tied to treason against the nation by his position in the Confederate government, and not at all a good symbol for sectional reconciliation. As the war dragged to its conclusion, Davis lost popularity in the South nearly as rapidly as his government lost states to the Union armies. In the end it appeared that he was all too willing to sacrifice slavery itself for the survival of the Confederacy. By April 1865, when he was captured fleeing through south Georgia, allegedly in women's clothes, his stock was very low. With his arrest, however, the much criticized Jefferson Davis became a martyr to his people. By the 1890s, Davis was dead, and, interestingly, as he receded from the public consciousness, Robert E. Lee came to the fore. Lee emerged, even over Jackson, as the personification of all that was great and good in the Civil War. His sense of honor, courage, loyalty, and care for his people were the great spiritual values of the South. Those values were also universal, of course, and they could exist among individuals in the North as well as in the South, KA opinions to the contrary notwithstanding. The two sections could reunite upon those qualities, erase the hatreds of the Civil War, and in union give birth to the new nation. Lee memorialized, in effect, became a bridge upon which North and South could meet again, embrace, and recognize their natural brotherhood. In the turn-of-the-century years, the special elevation of Lee and his association with Jackson, displaced the symbols of slavery, secession, and treason and focused attention on the totally virtuous Army of Northern Virginia.

The whole effort was abetted by the organization of Confederate veterans and their descendants. Veterans of the Confederate army organized themselves soon after the war, and they continued their associations through the decades. Most conspicuous in these organizations were the late soldiers of the Army of Northern Virginia. By the turn of the century, however, their ranks were sadly thinned, and it fell to their sons and daughters to continue the tradition. Associations of sons and daughters of the Confederacy became perpetual in the ensuing decades of the new century, marking the graves of their fallen fathers with maltese crosses, cleaning the grave sites, erecting statuary, and celebrating Lee's birthday every January. For a time after the war, annual memorial services had been held in the graveyards of the valiant dead on the anniversary of the surrender at Appomattox. By 1900 those services had been moved out of the cemeteries to the public parks and squares, and the dates chosen tended to coincide with the first rush of spring in the particular part of the South in which they occurred. Thus, the death of the Confederacy came to be associated with a perpetual rebirth of life, a resurrection. The dead had not died in vain, and the South was, indeed, risen again.[22]

The tragic truth was that, as whites discovered a mythical past for themselves in the 1920s and 1930s, they practically lost all understanding of race as a primary determinant of Southern culture and any real appreciation of the Negro. Tillman's nightmare had come true—the young South went to sleep at the Radical rack and let the Negro get away. The escape of black people from the white mind was amazingly total, and the Negro practically disappeared as anything more than a cipher in Southern white calculations. Negroes, for instance, were almost left out of History. Where they did appear, there were no problems. Slavery was a sort of boarding school for blacks; it was necessary, but it was also for the most part a fortunate connection and an enjoyable experience. Booker T. Washington might get a nod in history schoolbooks written for consumption by Southern whites, but barely more than George Washington Carver got for peanuts. Ulrich B. Phillips did publish his central theme essay in 1928, and historians should have taken that as a cue to keep Negroes and race relations to the fore in writing Southern history, but they did not. In scholarly writing, racial determinism was swept rather quickly and easily aside by other prime movers and particularly by economic determinism employed in varying strengths—up to and including industrial. After World War I, a heavy reliance upon the economic explanation swept through American historical writing like influenza. It was not the presence of the black man that made the South the way it was, ran the interpretation, it was cotton and commerce, railroads and factories, and, finally, greedy men and voracious monopolies. The Negro, much like his white contemporary, was a pawn in the economic game. Nat Turner and Frederick Douglass were all but lost to living memory, and W. E. B. Du Bois was vaguely up North somewhere. The Negro had so lost power in the conscious mind of the South that he could no longer even qualify as a devil.

As Radicalism faded away, a bland Conservatism came to life and power again. The new Conservativism of the 1920s and 1930s was much more complacent than any had ever been before, with the possible exception of a few years in the 1880s. It was tepid rather than warm, tinted rather than colored, and its action was very slight. Paternalism toward neo-Sambo was its heaviest burden, and that burden was light, almost a pleasure to carry, hardly more than a miniature flag on one's lapel. Anybody who thought about black people at all in these years was able to find some black person to patronize—the cook, the laundress, the janitor at the office. Southern whites drifted into a racial dream world in which there really were no problems—that is, if Yankees, Germans, and Communists would simply leave the blacks alone. As Southerners saw it, they were married to their black people, and they took care of them—in sickness and in jail. The new Sambo was built up not only day by day in face to face encounters, but also by an intricate network of persisting beliefs and institutions that tied all tightly together. In a large measure, the image was maintained by the very distance that separated the races and the invisibility of black people to white. But, further, it was sharpened by the sheer power of whites to make visible blacks seem to be what they wanted them to be. In the first half of the twentieth century, Southern whites had great power to hold blacks in place and to enforce upon them prescribed behavior in the presence of white people. It was very clear that white people would use that power just as they wanted. They used it in a series of riots as black soldiers came home from France after World War I, and afterward in scattered violent forays. But they developed a method whereby they could see themselves both as the good parents of blacks and yet do the violence necessary to keep blacks in place. White people proved again and again that they were perfectly capable of descending from the racial dream cloud upon which they preferred to ride, exercising whatever ruthlessness was necessary to repress the imagined outbreak, and then climbing back on the cloud and pretending they had never left. Our Negroes are good Negroes, they would say to one another, it was aliens, outsiders who caused this late unpleasantness. It was an aberration now gone forever, and, hence, in effect it never happened.

Black people were lost from the textbooks; they dropped to the lower rungs of even the Ku Klux Klan's list of devils; and they very nearly evaporated from politics. The one place they did appear prominently was in the rhetoric of a whole genre of politicians who might be called "Dixie demagogues." Extreme racism had been aggressively preached by the Radical politicians, of course, but there was a difference between these people and those who came later. There can be no doubt that Tillman, Felton, Watson, Smith, and Vardaman believed what they preached about black people. The next generation of politicians, however, saved their race-baiting for election day. They raised cries of "Would you want your daughter to marry one," knowing full well that such an event was highly unlikely—in the South impossible by law, and in the North improbable by custom. These people represented a low in Southern politics, probably the lowest ever. They were essentially dishonest and negative. They did nothing socially, and they really did nothing politically. Their prime function, it seems, was simply to be colorful and to entertain. Gene Talmadge, Governor and later Senator from Georgia, was famous for his red galluses (suspenders). Robert Rice Reynolds, Senator from North Carolina, was known for his silver shirt. Ellison D. "Cotton Ed" Smith, for thirty-six years a Senator from South Carolina, had cotton white hair and campaigned from a cotton float drawn by farm mules. Theodore Bilbo, first a Governor of and then a Senator from Mississippi, was best known for his colorful and often profane language. Most of all it seems that the function of the Southern politician in this era was to entertain in a flamboyant manner, and race-baiting was but a familiar, favored, and, most of all, a safe song to sing. Politics in the South in the 1920s and 1930s were simply romantic. They were unreal. The one politician who was real, perhaps all too real, was Huey Long, and he was shot down and killed by his own people heading north and running for national power.

During the 1920s and 1930s, even as they lost their grasp on the real world, it seemed the whole of the white South came together as never before. As they slipped further away from an understanding of blacks, they found themselves as a people separated from the nation. They were bound together very much by a common perception of a past that featured a valiant soldiery and a tragic and honorable end. But also in these decades the Old South rose again. It was as if the Army of Northern Virginia had labored first and made legitimate the resurrection and laudation of the antebellum order. It became permissible, even creditable, to have owned land and slaves, and it was as if in the 1920s and 1930s everyone in the white South somehow retroactively acquired slaves and plantations. The great mass of yeomanry in the Old South, the plain folk, virtually disappeared, and the best efforts of historian Frank L. Owsley of Vanderbilt University and his very capable and energetic students seemed unable to raise them to lasting historical recall. The poor whites, often denominated "poor white trash," were remembered, but they dwindled to an insignificant few, a token few who, it seemed, in some miraculous way, left no descendants at all. White families, rather, remembered their fallen soldiers and faithful black servants. Blacks in the war were loyal to white masters because understanding whites in slavery were kind to blacks. There was no problem with race in slavery, and there was no problem with race in the conscious mind of the white South in the 1920s and 1930s.

Along with identification by the white mass with planters and slaveholders came an identification with the Confederate army. Retroactively, everyone joined that mighty band. The Confederate army of myth was built, of course, upon the reality of Lee's Army of Northern Virginia, and while that army lost physical battles, it won an unbroken series of spiritual victories right up to and including that one at Appomattox. In the early decades of the twentieth century, it seemed that everybody in that Confederate army enjoyed a constant progression of promotions. At the end of the war, there appeared to have been a whole flock of "boy colonels" and not a few generals in their mid-twenties. They seemed a virile, romantic breed, siring a massive progeny. And in the twentieth century, if one could not be lineal descendant of a Confederate colonel or general, he or she could at least sing "Dixie" and verbally endorse the courage and nobility of the men in gray.

The myth of a whole South fused in its finest hour into the Army of Northern Virginia was promoted in formal history. Douglas Southall Freeman, another of those great deans of Virginia journalism, wrote a four-volume biography of General Lee in the war, and then did another three volumes on Lee's lieutenants.[23] The Army of Tennessee was all but forgotten. No one seemed easily to recall that it had retreated not only through and out of Tennessee, but also through Mississippi, Alabama, Georgia, South Carolina, and into North Carolina, finally to surrender so that in the end its very name mocked its failure. It had suffered defeat in Kentucky and never once crossed the Ohio. It came as something of a surprise to young Southerners to learn eventually, that there were other armies of significance in the Confederacy besides that of Northern Virginia and other generals of worth besides Lee and Jackson. It was even more shocking later to learn that there were deserters from the Confederate army, and a mild surprise that behind the armies there had been a Confederate government with a president named Jefferson Davis. It was almost as if the Army of Northern Virginia was out there disembodied, a spirit-fed army, that had no need of a great clanking, faction-ridden, dissident government to give it sustenance. Jefferson Davis, after all, was treason and best forgotten in the effort at reunion, while the Army of Northern Virginia was courage. The very thing that made the war so bad also made it so good. It was terrific courage, a capacity for fighting hard and dying bravely that bound the Union and Southern armies together even in most awful and bloody combat. The soldiers on each side could recognize the virtue of the other and so could their sons and daughters, and finally their grandsons and granddaughters—of spiritual as well as physical descent.

In spite of the boom and bust in world economics and politics, the 1920s and 1930s was a grand era for the South. Southern whites looked backward and somehow felt all together, warm, and secure. The Old South that might have been had been truncated, its heart had stopped in 1865, and then started again. It was as if the South of the twentieth century were a child, an embryo, frozen in its early youth and later warmed to life. In the freezing it had somehow stepped out of time and lost its place in the flow of the larger world. Southerners had lost the beat of time as other Americans knew it, and, by the 1920s, they had largely lost inclination to find it again. From the late 1880s into the 1910s, they had tried economic reform through political activity, alternating through several cycles with racial reform. Neither had worked, and, in the 1920s and 1930s, they tried nothing. Nevertheless, what the South had lost in action, it gained in a sort of contented, even defiant resignation. The South felt that it knew what was important, and it could live in peace throughout its day. It had earned its silver hair with honor, and it could observe its own existence with equanimity. The South might finally die, felled by the material Leviathan, but it would die differently as it had lived differently—safe in its own mind with the idea that it had marked the world with courage and grace. There, in the mind, all was woven together with the smoothness, the sheen, the toughness of silken cloth. The South was a fine spun living dream, and, in the decades of the 1920s and 1930s, the dream waxed rosy, romantic, and unreal.

SOUTHERN WHITE LIBERALS IN THE
TWENTIETH CENTURY

In the preceding chapters we have seen generated a racial world in which blacks were vastly reduced in power, the North withdrew from racial concerns in the South, and white Southerners erased the race problem from serious conscious thought. The next story in the sequence is the opening of the problem again in the Southern white mind.

The recognition of the race problem in the South and moves to do something about it constitute another story and a very complex one. Moreover, it becomes one that cannot be told exclusively in terms of the South because not all, or even the great majority of black people in America were located in the fifteen ex-slaveholding states. In the 1960s perhaps slightly less than 50 percent were so located. In two generations, black people had moved out of the South and spread themselves across the nation from Boston to Chicago to Oakland, California. Particularly did they move into urban and industrial areas, a migration that was strongly promoted by the industrial needs of the military in World Wars I and II. The migrants were for the most part country-born and country-bred, but they lived their mature lives in the city. There, of course, they encountered a radically different environment from any they had known before. But they did meet the old and all too familiar prejudice. Ultimately, they responded to racial prejudice in the North and West as they had responded to it in the South by building up rather solid fortresses in the black community, especially in families, clans, clubs, and churches, wherein they might survive.

The story of race in America in the twentieth century is necessarily a national one, but it is also international. In 1941 the United States found itself locked in a bitter struggle against the fascists in Europe and the Japanese in the Pacific. The help of the Negro tenth of the American population was clearly a necessity. What had begun in World War I was repeated and multiplied in World War II as hundreds of thousands of black people entered war industries all over the nation. Black leadership was alive to the possibilities of the situation. In 1941, on the eve of America's entrance into the war, A. Philip Randolph, president of the Brotherhood of Railroad Sleeping Car Porters, organized a march on Washington to insist upon the opening up of economic opportunities to blacks. President Franklin Roosevelt, fearful of a show of division in the face of the coming war, struck a compromise in which Randolph called off the march in return for the establishment of a Fair Employment Practices Committee that would promote jobs for blacks in war industries.[24] Government contracts, then and thereafter, were a vast part of the national economy, and each contract contained fair employment practices provisions that opened jobs for black workers. Compliance was less than enthusiastic, but the war itself strained the manpower of white America to the limits, and it soon became highly acceptable for blacks, and white women as well, to enter jobs previously denied them. Also women and blacks enlisted in support units of the military in vast numbers, freeing white soldiers and sailors for front-line duty. As the war ground on and the number of casualties rose, black leaders agitated for the deployment of black troops under black officers on the front lines. At the beginning of the war, white America was firmly fixed in the opinion that black men would never make reliable combat soldiers. However, as the fighting took its toll, white soldiers barely eighteen years old were dying on the battlefront, and white men up to the age of forty-five were being drafted. Finally, the military yielded, most conspicuously, perhaps, in

sending the all-black 92nd Division against the Germans in Italy and in transferring the 99th Pursuit Squadron to engage the Luftwaffe over northern
Europe.[25]

The hot war with the Germans and Japanese had hardly ended before the
Cold War with the Russians commenced. That struggle was more totally
global than the earlier one, and it lasted much longer. Even as the Cold War
began, the empires of the old order were breaking up, and out of those empires
new nations emerged. The vast majority of people in the new nations were
non-white. This "Third World" became vital in the struggle as the Russians
attempted to recruit them to their side with the idea that Communism was not
only anti-imperialist but also anti-racist. The United States, offering itself as
both the modern exemplar and the champion of democracy, was faced with
the problem of wooing the non-white people of the Third World into the anti-
Communist camp while racism ran riot at home. It was fortunate that Harry
S Truman, the senator who had been most involved with the FEPC, was then
President. Truman had already in 1946 set up two commissions to study
aspects of race relations in America. One concerned itself with the area of
higher education and the other with civil rights. In 1948 the President proposed to Congress sweeping legislation looking toward racial equality. Also,
as commander-in-chief of the army and navy, he ordered the military to desegregate. In 1951, during the Korean conflict, American forces found themselves
suddenly thrown back from the Yalu River by masses of Chinese troops just
entering the war. The American lines were so thinned by losses that the army
was forced to use black support troops—cooks, stevedores, teamsters—to fill
up the ranks of combat units. They discovered that not only did black troops
fight as well as white troops, but that in the crisis black and white troops on
the front lines fought well together.[26] From that time forward the services
enlisted black men and women with increasing eagerness. While relations
between blacks and whites in the service have often lacked harmony, the number of black people in the armed services has risen progressively, and black
representation in the officer corps has increased dramatically.

Meanwhile, the NAACP was at work pressing toward, among other
things, the end of segregation in the public schools. In 1954 when the Supreme
Court handed down the Brown decision prescribing integration, four other
such cases were pending, and three of the four were backed by the NAACP
through the Legal Defense Fund. An alert and active black leadership and the
real power of international politics were working in tandem to change race
relations in America. The first hard thrust would come in the South, most
especially in the deep South, and from a liberal element among the whites as
well as from a progressive element among the blacks.

From the time of the Montgomery Race Conference in 1900 there persisted among Southern white Conservatives a thin thread of organized interest

in black people. The Conference in dissolving itself resolved to have yearly meetings thereafter. That first meeting was, of course, a practical failure, and the annual meetings anticipated did not materialize. Even so, there was an echo of the idea in the yearly session of the Southern Sociological Congress that began in 1912. These gatherings, made up primarily of university professors, continued to track the problem of race relations in the South. In 1919 a permanent organization was established as the Commission on Interracial Cooperation. The Commission was organized in Atlanta and had some of its roots in the "Reconstruction" work that followed the Atlanta riot of 1906. More immediately, the Commission was a response to a rise in racial tensions and violent outbreaks all over America in 1918 and 1919 as a result of the rapid changes engendered by the war. Under the headship of William W. Alexander, a 1912 graduate of Vanderbilt's divinity school and for some years a practicing minister, the Commission functioned, for the most part, as an organization for investigation, study, and publication in race relations. In the 1930s, however, it took an important step toward activism when it employed Jessie Daniel Ames, a Texas women's rights leader, to organize the Association of Southern Women for the Prevention of Lynching. In that decade, Jessie Ames traveled from state to state, turning women's clubs and women's movements previously successful in the fight for suffrage into anti-lynching organizations. When a crime occurred that might result in lynching, local women would pressure local officials to act vigorously to prevent it. White women in the Association declared pointedly to white men that they did not want protection in this way. Ironically, Ames was a personality much like Rebecca Felton, but she delivered a message to white men that was precisely opposite to that of the fire-eating Georgian. She was a very strong woman who labored to maintain a household and rear three children after her husband's early death, and she was not very respectful toward men as men. She was forceful, a superb organizer, and highly effective. Also active in the Interracial Commission was Willis D. Weatherford. As a young man, Weatherford had been eminent in the YMCA. Even in the first decade of the century, he had worked to create and focus interest in the race question in YMCAs on the campuses of Southern colleges and universities. In 1910 he published a book, *Negro Life in the South,* designed to be used as a basis for discussion by such groups. Because of the work of Weatherford and others, during the first half of the twentieth century, campus YMCAs were one of the few places in the South where organized and liberal discussions of the race question could occur.[27]

In 1944 the Interracial Commission dissolved into the Southern Regional Council, an organization that expanded its interest broadly to include many other concerns of the South. While the Council as such was not an activist group, members often were active as individuals and pressed the organization to take direct action, especially in combatting segregation. In the postwar era, the Council became an important collector and dispenser of material relating to Negroes and race relations in the South and in America.[28]

The New Liberals, the native white Southerners who participated in the breakup of the neo-Conservative order in the middle of the twentieth century, were, for the most part, decidedly not organized. Their rebellions against the rigid racial establishment were mainly individual, scattered, and evolved over the decades. The New Liberals, like the old Liberals of the 1880s, were born Conservatives who somehow came to perceive black people in an image different from that of the mass of their contemporaries. Very often the generation of a new perception began with paternalism in the Conservative mode. For all its evils, paternalism led, at least, to contact with black people, and it sometimes happened that contact led to the racial re-education of white people. Once engaged, some white activists passed beyond paternalism to recognize the full humanity of blacks.

The experience of Harry Ashmore, who became well-known nationally as the editor of the *Arkansas Gazette* during the Little Rock school integration crisis in the late 1950s, illustrates well the pattern of a Conservative who began as a paternalist and ended as a Liberal. Ashmore, by profession a journalist and editor, was born into an extensive family of upcountry South Carolina planters, slaveholders, judges, and Congressmen. Like virtually every Southern gentleman of his generation, he was reared in the paternal tradition. He well remembered, for instance, the customs of some male member of the family taking the black manservant into the kitchen on an appropriate occasion and sharing a celebratory drink with him—somewhat on the sly, away from the eyes of the ladies of the family. In the early 1950s, while still a young man, Harry Ashmore was given the task by a regional group of gathering statistics on educational expenditures in the Southern states. The principal idea behind the survey was typically Conservative—that the Southern establishments were actually spending vast sums of money on black education (perhaps more than the taxes paid by black people justified) and that black people would do well to consider carefully the effect of integration upon their educational opportunities. Separate was being touted as equal, and, all in all, perhaps as even better. Presumably, the Ashmore study would also work to keep the North at bay.[29]

As so often, the South was again deceiving itself. Yet, there was a grain of truth in the idea behind the educational study. South Carolina, for instance, under the leadership of Governor Jimmy Byrnes, had just spent unprecedentedly large sums of black education. Of the $124 million of state aid granted to education in the four years beginning in 1951, two-thirds was spent on black schools when only 40 percent of the population was black. In the Palmetto State, where schools for black children had often been little more than wooden shacks, there now appeared with miraculous rapidity handsome brick edifices.[30] A quick rash of spending, of course, could not erase the effect of the three generations of deprivation since Reconstruction. But if one wanted to believe that separate was equal, new school buildings made the illusion easier. In the end, the overall figures were certain to show a vast gap between the support afforded for the education of black children and that of white. While Ashmore was in the midst of this project, he happened to encounter a wise old political friend who asked what he was doing. Ashmore told him, and the friend understood better than most what was about to occur. "Son," he said, "it sounds to me like you have got yourself in the position of a man running for son of a bitch without opposition." Several years later in Little Rock, Harry Ashmore won the election, as he said, by "acclamation." And all he did was simply tell the truth.[31] In the South in matters of race, the truth does not set one free, it makes one a Liberal and, very often, lonely.

Much of the paternalism that initially motivated New Liberals to make contact across the race line had a decidedly Christian character. For decades the Southern Theological Seminary in Louisville, Kentucky, nourished an underground concern for black people that manifested itself in the covert teaching of young black ministers in something of a shadow school for blacks alongside the apparent one for whites. In addition, in the 1930s and especially in the 1940s, the attitude of the seminary was manifested more openly in a remarkable series of theses and dissertations that dealt very boldly with churchly problems of race in the South. Beyond the seminaries, in virtually every denomination there were professional churchmen who kept up long-running contacts with blacks for the sake of Christ and salvation. Also, there were always laymen who never quite accepted the idea that God had made Christians in two colors for eternal separation and discrimination. There were some other Southern Christians who began with that understanding as it related to earthly life, but finally came to feel that the racial order in the South was wrong. One of these was Sarah Patton Boyle, the person mentioned earlier who, as a girl in eastern Virginia during World War I, had dug a cave in which to hide when the Germans landed.

Sarah Patton Boyle's credentials for membership in the Virginia gentry, and hence for leadership, were impressive. Her great-grandfather had owned 4000 acres and 163 slaves and was, for a time, acting governor of the state. The family had supplied a general in the Revolution, a colonel in the Stonewall Brigade of the Army of Northern Virginia, and another general, George S. Patton, in World War II. Sarah's own father was an Episcopal priest of national eminence. He was known especially for his work in promoting the education of black children through church schools. In the 1930s, Sarah married a junior member of the faculty of the University of Virginia in Charlottesville. In the next decade, she was a painter, a writer, a faculty wife, and the mother of two sons. That highly stable world began to fall apart when in 1950, the University admitted Gregory Swanson, a young black man from Danville, to its school of law. Swanson was the first black person to enter the University as a student in its 125-year history. Sarah Patton Boyle was stirred to write him a letter of welcome. The letter was well-meaning but thoroughly and blatantly paternalistic, and the response was the beginning of her re-education in the nature of race relations in the South. Swanson accepted Boyle's offer of friendship with an eagerness that frightened her. She was, she thought, encouraging him to "FORGET HIS PLACE." When she hastened to retreat, so too did he, much to her distress. Even so, soon she was eager to learn, and that ambition brought her into contact with T. J. Sellers, the editor of the black newspaper in Charlottesville, who schooled her in the facts of racial life as seen by a black man. In the early 1950s she was increasingly active and conspicuous in her advocacy of integration. In November 1954, after the Brown decision, she testified in Richmond before a governor's commission of inquiry that was earnestly segregationist and an audience of some 2000 people that was largely hostile. Finally, in February 1955, she published an article urging the idea that Southern whites were ready and able to accept integration in the public schools. That article was printed in *The Saturday Evening Post,* which, with about 17 million readers, was one of the most widely circulated magazines in the nation. Boyle hoped to encourage a few fair and firm leaders of her own persuasion to step forward and guide the potentially amenable South to an equitable integration. Her expectation was not unlike that of George Washington Cable seventy years before in publishing his essay "The Silent South," and the result was much the same. What she got over the next three years was a torrent of personal abuse, and not all of it from strangers. Indeed, the worst of it came from people in her own circle whom she had thought to be very close friends—and Liberals. She was charged with selling out to the North for money, and, worse, of lusting after the bodies of black men. Ultimately, she experienced the dubious honor of having a cross burned in the front yard of her home. She chose to take the symbol literally, as a testimony of her Christian behavior in race relations. Soon after this experience she published her widely read book, *A Desegregated Heart,* in which she traced her own tortured journey from Conservatism to Liberalism. She, like so many others of that latter stamp, made the journey alone, at her own pace, and by her own particular lights.[32]

Religion sometimes moved Conservatives to racial liberalism, but there was another prime mover that could appropriately be called empathy. It was almost as if some few Southern whites had the sensitivity and imagination necessary to put themselves in the place of black people and to understand something of the burden that color carried in the South. George Washington Cable had that quality; it made him a pioneer prison reformer in New Orleans, the translator of Creole culture for Anglo-Americans, and a champion of racial equity. Perhaps the best example in the twentieth century of one able to make the intuitive leap to a more equitable racial posture was Lillian Smith, the Georgia author. Born in 1897, Smith was the daughter of a prominent Methodist layman. In the early 1920s she had gone to China as a teaching missionary, and later in the decade she ran a summer camp and school for girls at her retreat in the Georgia mountains near Clayton. Progressively, the school came to teach a liberal message, racial and otherwise. In 1936 with the aid of friends, Smith established the *North Georgia Review,* a magazine devoted to literary art, social criticism, and humanism. That journal was bold and aggressive in racial matters, and so was Lillian Smith. In 1944 she published the novel *Strange Fruit,* an indictment of the sexual exploitation of mulatto women by Southern white men of the elite class. The book sold three million copies. It was banned in Boston because of its explicit statements about sex, and it underwent a withering fire in the South. Smith never flinched but rather continued the assault. In 1955 two young men burned down her house. In that fire she lost most of her papers and other personal treasures. Ultimately, her voice was stilled only by death in 1966 after a long and hard-fought battle against cancer.[33]

Finally, scores of academicians emerged from scholarly retreats to urge the restructuring of race relations in the South. Many of these people were moved by paternalism, by a Southern Christian faith, and by a sensitivity that led to sympathy and action, but also many of them seemed to be moved most essentially by a fundamental rationalism—a sort of philosophical intellectualism that put great faith in research and reason while it damned irrationality and illogic. These people did not set out to become Liberals. Rather they were committed to the pursuit of truth through conventional methods of scholarship, and that pursuit led to an appreciation of the racial realities. In the 1920s and 1930s, and on into the 1940s, the Liberal syndrome in this vein touched several disciplines and many schools, but sociologists and historians seemed particularly affected, as did certain schools that emphasized the liberal arts.

It was no accident that, among academicians, the New Liberals initially emerged in such schools as, for example, the Universities of Virginia, North Carolina, and South Carolina rather than in Virginia Polytechnic Institute, North Carolina State University, or Clemson College. New Liberalism in academia came out of the special retreats of racial Conservatism, and, in each state, one of the resorts of Conservatism was the campus of the state university that was devoted more or less intensively to the liberal arts. In terms of race relations, the more technical schools went Radical, and even those schools where the technical and liberal arts curricula were joined tended to have their Liberalism muted. Naturally not everyone who went through racially Conservative schools in the middle decades of the century was much concerned with race. Indeed, probably the great mass of students and most professors hardly gave the matter a scholarly thought. But they did afford environments not deadly hostile to inquiry into racial matters, and the venture came to be made with as much objectivity as faculty and students could muster. Once they began the inquiry, they, like Harry Ashmore, sometimes learned much of the truth; and they were bound to tell it. When they told it, again like Ashmore, they easily won election to a difficult and unfavored office.

Academic Liberals tended to group together, and they flowed through certain channels. One clear, direct current ran from Emory University to the University of North Carolina. Howard Odum, for example, as a young student in Emory College in 1901 and 1902 took Latin at the feet of Andrew Sledd shortly before Sledd's forced departure for having written in the *Atlantic Monthly* that, among other things, lynching was a crime. As a Latinist, Sledd was reputedly partial to that early egalitarian Cicero. Cicero and the writers of his time were much concerned with the "freedmen" of the late Roman Republic. Their writings were full enough of expressions by those lately slaves that they were forever grateful to their erstwhile masters for raising them into civilization, and that they did not want to "marry their daughters." Odum passed on to take a doctorate at Columbia University and later settled himself as a professor in the University of North Carolina. Along with Rupert Vance he created the Institute for Research in the Social Sciences, and together they led in winning international fame for the University as a center for regional studies—their own Southern region being, of course, the pilot and model study of the type. The Institute fostered a host of scholars and sociological studies of Negro life and race relations in the South. Guy B. Johnson, Guion Griffin Johnson, John A. Wooster, and Arthur Raper were among those who made signal contributions in the field. Wooster, for instance, did a deep study of the black people in the Sea Islands of South Carolina, the black population in America culturally closest to Africa. Raper published in 1933 the only close study of lynching that has been done in the last two generations.[34]

Among historians, Fletcher M. Green, long-time professor at Chapel Hill, followed the path that Odum took from Georgia to North Carolina. Green took his bachelor's degree from Emory in 1920 and his doctroate at the University of North Carolina in 1927. He, too, joined the coterie of scholars in the Institute for Research in the Social Sciences. As a professor of history in the university, he directed the work of more than a hundred doctoral students. The dissertations of nearly all of these related to the South, and almost all of those included some consideration of Negroes and of institutions, such as convict leasing and the lien system, that touched black people most intimately. Two of Green's students were among the very first white scholars to begin to put black people back into the mainstream of history as understood by whites. Vernon Lane Wharton, a native of Mississippi, finished his dissertation and published it in 1947 as *The Negro in Mississippi, 1865–1890*. George Brown

Tindall, a native of South Carolina, finished his dissertation in 1949 and published it in 1952 as *The Negro in South Carolina, 1877–1900*. There had been histories of slavery before, and shortly, during the civil rights movement, there would be a flood of such. There had also been histories of Reconstruction that included Negroes in a highly pejorative way, and black historians, of course, had been steadily at work. Generally the work of black historians, like black history and black people themselves, was largely invisible to white scholars. Probably the single great exception to the rule was Du Bois's *Black Reconstruction* (1935), a book that was rather easily dismissed among Southern scholars as a "Marxist view." Wharton's and Tindall's were the first studies by white scholars that depicted the experience of black people in and after Reconstruction realistically, with objectivity, and commanded both the attention and the continuing respect of scholars in the field. The history of black people, virtually lost to white historians after John Spencer Bassett's abortive efforts in the late 1890s and early 1900s, was re-found.

A decade after Fletcher Green, C. Vann Woodward made the same trek. Born and reared in the black belt of Arkansas, Woodward took his first degree at Emory and in 1934 moved on to the University of North Carolina to take his Ph.D. in 1937. His primary scholarly ambition in those years was to write the biography of Tom Watson, the Georgia Populist and 1896 vice-presidential candidate. In his biography of Watson there was the strong suggestion that Watson tried to cope with the real economic problems of the nation in the 1890s but that the interests of big business did him in. Watson was painted as rising above the common posture in racial matters, reaching across the race line to preach to black people that blacks and whites together were held down in the ditch by the forces of big business who used the cry of race to divide, dupe, and control them. Watson was defeated, and in the early twentieth century, driven somewhat mad, became a rabid racist. Woodward seems to have sensed in the 1930s that there was a strong connection between the race problem and the industrial revolution, and that, indeed, something had gone horribly wrong in race relations in the South in the 1890s.[35]

In the fall of 1954, in a series of lectures at the University of Virginia in Charlottesville, Woodward defined rather precisely his conception of what had gone wrong. In the previous spring the Supreme Court had rendered its decision in the Brown case. Early in 1955, those lectures were published as *The Strange Career of Jim Crow*. The author dedicated his work "to Charlottesville, and the hill that looks down upon her, Monticello." Woodward's book became, as Martin Luther King, Jr., called it, the historical Bible of the civil-rights movement. It sold more than half a million copies in the generation after its appearance, and it has been not only read, it has been widely taught in the universities, colleges, and public schools of the land. It is highly pertinent that the book opens with the point that things have not always been the same between blacks and whites in the South, that there has been after all a history of race relations in which things did evolve over time. Moreover, the book makes the signal point that there has not been a single mind of the South in regard to race. Rather there have been several minds, and two in particular stood out in the turn of the century years—Radicalism and Conservatism. Woodward's use of those terms was different from the use made of them in this study. His Radicals were people, like the Populists, who would use political power to achieve economic reform. His Conservatives were those political types, like the conservative Democrats, who could not or would not surrender their *laissez faire* ideals even in the crisis of the great depression in the 1890s. As he interpreted events, each of these two elements offered a system of race relations better than those that came. Radical leaders offered cooperation with black people under the rationale that both races were held "down in the ditch together" by the special interests in order to control and use them. They offered a species of political equality that was, in that place and time, "radical." On the other hand, Conservative leaders offered paternalism, and that was better than the extremism that followed. Facing the prospect of Radical success, the Conservatives lost their heads, counted the Radicals out at the polls, and otherwise employed fraudulent means to defeat them. Populists were frustrated by being robbed of their victory, and Conservatives were frustrated by having to resort to such measures. Frustration of this sort bred aggression, and aggression needed a scapegoat. Black people in the South were the traditional, the ready-made, ready-to-wear scapegoat, allowed to suffer as such in and after the 1890s by a North busily engaged in imperialistic ventures among "colored" peoples abroad. Thus it was that Southerners passed legislation generally segregating, disfranchising, and proscribing black people. Before this interplay occurred, race relations had not been fixed, black people were not always segregated or always disfranchised. Those ends came about by laws, and the laws made the mores.[36]

The Strange Career of Jim Crow was a synthetic work. It drew heavily upon Wharton's and Tindall's books and upon Woodward's own previous studies, especially his biography of Tom Watson (1937) and his extensive and deeply researched *Origins of the New South, 1877–1913* (1951).[37] It also pioneered the field of race relations in American history. Wharton's and Tindall's books were conceived as histories of black people rather than as histories of race relations. In his own previous writing Woodward had treated the history of race relations as some very important half-remembered thing. Then in the fall of 1954, after the Brown decision the preceding spring, it was as if he suddenly recalled what he somehow already knew, that there had been, indeed, a history of race relations in the South, that things had not always been the same. Woodward was the first to grasp firmly the idea that the story of race relations in the South and in America had been diverse and evolutionary, and that it had not frozen with the end of either slavery or Reconstruction into an absolutely monolithic, rigid, and lasting pattern. He opened a new field of study in American history.

More immediately, in the lectures at Charlottesville and in the book, Woodward offered an interpretation of the origins of segregation and the history of race relations in the South that was much needed. He was not alone in his desire to supply psychic relief to the embattled white South. At the same time that he was turning his lectures into the book, Sarah Patton Boyle was in Charlottesville working up the article for *The Saturday Evening Post* that she entitled "We Are Readier Than We Think."[38] What the Woodward thesis of the origins of segregation said to that Virginia audience and later to Southern whites at large was that they could accept the Supreme Court decision and desegregation without violating their Southernness. If a Southerner was heir to the Populistic tradition, he and she had a history that allowed them to reach boldly across the race line to promote the common good. If a Southerner came from the Conservative tradition, he and she had a paternalistic history that made it encumbent upon them to deal with black people with consideration and care. Extreme racism in the South was the result of not coping with the real problems of the 1890s and afterward. It was understandable that the South should have made a scapegoat of the Negro but it was an error that could be corrected by Supreme Court decisions, by laws, and, most of all, by a re-appreciation of true Southern values by Southern whites. It was a hopeful message to a people in emotional distress; it was an invitation to a cool, rational, and humane perspective on desegregation.

THE THREE FACES OF EVE

In the early 1950s, in the very midst of the rising furor on race in the South, an attractive woman of twenty-five entered the office of Corbett H. Thigpen, a psychiatrist on the faculty of the Medical College of Georgia. Eve, as they then chose to call this young woman, was the soul of Southern ladyhood. She was demure, sweet, very responsible, and mannerly. She was married and the mother of a three-year-old daughter, Bonnie. Eve had been suffering from severe and prolonged headaches, fainting spells, and, more recently, blackouts. She was distressed that her marriage was in danger of dissolution; she was Southern Baptist and had reneged on her pre-marital promise to have her child reared in the Catholic faith of her husband. Finally, she sought psychiatric help. Over the months, Eve's condition grew worse. Added to her previous ills, she began to hear voices when no one was there. During one interview she showed signs of extreme pain, alternating with a blank look, and ending with a slight shudder. Then, as Thigpen later reported, "she relaxed easily into an attitude of comfort the physician had never before seen in this patient. A pair of blue eyes popped open. There was a quick reckless smile. In a bright unfamiliar voice that sparkled, the woman said, 'Hi, there Doc!'" The psychiatrist suddenly found himself talking to another person in Eve's body. That person was apparently the polar opposite of the first Eve. She was sexually provocative, an exhibitionist who smoked, drank, and used racy language. She was frankly physical and hedonistic. "I like to live and she don't," she declared of Eve. Marvelously, Thigpen called the first woman Eve White and the second Eve Black. Beneath the extravagant differences, the two women shared an inability to bring sexual relations to a consummation. The doctor concluded that Eve White was "frigid," and Eve Black, in spite of her apparent sensuality, always eluded her would-be lover, if need be finally by dissolving herself and letting a bewildered Eve White emerge to face the persistent male. Eve Black had been with Eve White from early childhood and knew her intimately, but Eve White did not know that Eve Black existed. Even as a child Eve Black would sometimes "come out," as she called it. Occasionally, she would do bad things that Eve White did not recall and for which Eve White's parents would punish her. As therapy proceeded, Eve Black began to come out more frequently, learning that she could harass Eve White, weaken her, and take over the mind and body. She confessed that it was she who had caused Eve White's recent headaches, and the voices that Eve White had heard were hers. By the time she revealed herself to the psychiatrist, she felt that she could emerge almost at will. "I'm getting stronger than she is," Eve Black insisted. "Each time I come out she gets weaker." If that continued, she thought, "then the body will be mine." The struggle for control tended toward all or nothing, and Eve Black was winning—there was no middle ground. Finally, Eve White attempted to slash her wrists with a razor and was stopped only by Eve Black's emergence after a hard struggle. "I think she meant business," declared a thoroughly shaken Eve Black.

After more than two years of treatment, and again during an interview with the psychiatrist, a third person suddenly appeared, one who chose to name herself "Jane." She was superbly balanced, intelligent, responding to every situation with a rationality that was almost uncanny. "All her behavior was constructive and socially acceptable," Thigpen asserted. In a word, Jane was sane. She knew nothing of what had gone before; she thought of herself as having been born the moment she appeared before the psychiatrist. All Jane knew was what the doctor told her plus what she learned from the two Eves as she observed and heard them after her own emergence. She was an avid student of their histories and a fast learner. Soon she developed an extraordinary sophistication and vocabulary, well beyond the capacities of either Eve White or Eve Black. Seemingly Jane's stability was made possible by Eve White's recalling more and more of her childhood. It was finally Jane who, under hypnosis and in yet another, a fourth, voice, recalled the traumatic event some twenty years before that had educed a lasting Eve Black. When she was a little girl, Eve's grandmother had died. Her mother, a person of strong religious convictions, felt that touching the face of the dead was the best way of dealing with grief over the death of a loved one. It was, to her, a way of saying good-by in this world and an expression of faith in reunion in the hereafter. At the funeral, she forced little Eve to touch her grandmother's face. Under hypnosis, Jane recalled the scene: "Mother . . .! Oh, mother . . . Don't make me. . . . Don't. . . . Don't. . . . I can't do it! I can't do it!" Then Jane screamed, as Thigpen reported, like a "banshee." When Jane emerged from this sequence, she had mutated into a fourth personality—still recognizably Jane, but warmer, more comfortable and real. Thus, it was only after more than two years of working to get well and in the process of generating still another personality that the funeral episode was recalled. Eve had repressed the memory of that experience and the memory of her great revulsion against the act her mother had forced her to commit. Behind that episode she recalled other events—her mother gave birth to twin girls several months before the grandmother's death; she had experienced a profound envy over a cousin's new doll and suffered feelings of neglect, and, finally, she had been haunted by the knowledge that a strange man had drowned in a ditch filled with stagnant water near her home.

At first, as Eve Black and Jane One had become stronger, more and more they controlled the body and the conscious mind in which all three personalities existed. Eve Black had very little sympathy for Eve White, but she did not wish her ill. Most of all, Eve Black simply wanted full access to the mind and body so that she might live as she chose. Significantly, Jane One was more fond of Eve Black then she was of Eve White. Finally, both Eve White and Eve Black weakened as Jane Two came to the fore. During this stage Thigpen and his associate in the case, Hervey M. Cleckley, published the story of Eve in a book entitled *The Three Faces of Eve* (1957). The book led to a motion picture in which Georgia-born Joanne Woodward played Eve and Lee J. Cobb played Thigpen. In the film, in a last interview with the psychiatrist, Eve Black, who was so beautiful, and who had been so full of fun and life, fell sad. She knew that she was dying, that she would not be allowed to come out again, and she said goodbye to her friend the physician. It is a unique death scene and one of the most moving sequences in American film. When both Eves had died, Jane Two confessed to missing Eve Black most, and suggested to Thigpen her impression that he shared her sentiment.[39]

The story of Eve is a nearly perfect allegory for the mind of the white South in race relations. There was a time in the youth of the South in which its potentialities for development were various; it might have become many different things. But then it chose to walk a certain path, and that path led eventually to the practice of acts that were unnatural and repulsive to Western civilization, specifically the acts of slavery and its concomitants. In another time or place those acts might have been totally acceptable. But in Western society in the last generation of Southern slavery such was not the case. The South did not cope at all well with the experience of slavery, or with its memory. When slavery had passed, the South quickly repressed the memory of the horrors of that stage of its life, smoothing over the fault line with layer upon layer of the plaster of myth. In the 1880s, the era in which the Bourbon Democracy had ruled politically, Eve White came out in race relations in the South in the form of mild paternalism. The white South in the 1880s was unreal. It was a castle built upon a geological fault line, shatterable by the first strong shock. That shock came in the late 1880s and early 1890s in waves of economic, political, and psychic distress that brought forth Radical racial personalities in the very minds and bodies that had previously housed Conservative personalities. The extravagantly wild and murderous South of the 1890s and early twentieth century, physical, destructive, and sex-ridden, was unreal too, as unreal as Eve Black. Like Eve Black, when the South as Radical began to see the real horror of its acts, when it could no longer sustain the role and carry it to the murderous end implied, it dissolved itself and brought forth its more responsible—almost super-responsible—other self. The Janus face turned. The mind of the South in the 1920s and into the 1950s effectively lost the memory of its Radical personality, and it made slavery seem a beautiful thing. It coped with neither. The saccharine sweet South that showed its face to the world in those decades was Conservative and unreal, fully as unreal as Eve White in the early 1950s. An alert contemporary might have sensed difficulty. There were headaches, fainting spells, blackouts. No one is that good. "Maybe she is too good," was what Eve White's perplexed and desperate husband Ralph had said of her trouble.[40] In the late 1950s and early 1960s when the pressures became too great, when the sober, responsible South-as-Eve-White could not cope, the South-as-Eve-Black was loosed again. One can easily see her in the mad, wildly angry face of a woman in the crowd at Little Rock's Central High School, in the opened jaws and bared fangs of the police dogs set loose in Birmingham, and in the hysterical shooting of three civil rights workers in Mississippi and the mangling of their bones. Again in the later 1960s and on into the 1970s, when the South as "bad" could no longer maintain itself, when it could not live with what it had done and was doing, it dissolved . . . gave way, and the South as good, as "white," cycled to the fore. This time, as before, the South as white gained national approval and applause simply because it had ceased being horrid. Southerners came to dominate the field of Christian evangelism; Southern girls became Misses America; Jimmy Carter became President; and in 1981 the center point of the "Moral

Majority" for all America seemed to find its locus in Lynchburg, Virginia. But no one is that good.

The story of Eve works as an allegory for the South because Eve was herself so very Southern. In her life and in her personality she recapitulated her culture, as, indeed, did her psychiatrist. She was so feminine, almost an exaggeration, a caricature of femininity, and he was so masculine. In the South, the absoluteness of the race role plays directly into the absoluteness of the sex role and roles of good and bad. Eve was wholly white racially, visibly she was thoroughly female, but she had difficulty being totally good. If she could not be totally good, she would be totally bad. In the South, a "good woman" (white) cannot be a little bit bad, or a little bit masculine, anymore than she can be a little bit black. At the other pole of race and sex, a black man is termed, in the lowest parlance, as either a "good nigger" or a "bad nigger." Probably no white Southerner has ever said the sentence: "He is a so-so nigger." Southern culture is deeply purist and intolerant of mixtures; indeed, it abhors a mixture—racial, sexual, or moral. Margaret Mitchell, a Georgia woman born to the generation previous to that of Eve, in the 1930s caught magnificently in fiction the extreme forms of Southern white womanhood encompassed by the two Eves. Scarlett O'Hara was virtually Eve Black. She was a "taker," physical, sensual, sexual, hedonistic, socially irresponsible, and, when the consequences of what she had done began to intrude upon her desires, she dissolved herself with the phrase, "I'll think of it all tomorrow." Melanie Wilkes was Scarlett's opposite. Melanie was a "giver," idealistic, spiritual, and totally responsible. Scarlett, like Eve Black, wanted no children; while Melanie, like Eve White, wanted children and hazarded everything, even her own life, for their lives. Eve White's daughter Bonnie, unlike Scarlett's Bonnie, was at the very center of her life ... and, perhaps, of her death also. At the spiritual level, Scarlett was death and destruction; Melanie was life. But yet, from another perspective, each embodied the seed of the opposite quality; physically, Scarlett was always living, and Melanie was always dying. In the body, Scarlett still lived when Melanie had died, and in life there is hope. Margaret Mitchell left us with a suggestion that Scarlett would follow Rhett to Charleston and through him reclaim the spiritual qualities that were her natural heritage and would make her whole.

The South is a land of extremes, all linked together in tight tension. Extremes of one sort support and maintain extremes of other sorts. Extremes in the same category constitute a whole, and each extreme gains definition and clarity by reference to its opposite. Whites are made white by blacks, men are made men by women, and good is made good by bad. It is totally understandable that Eve should have appeared in the South and been a Southern white woman, that both Eve White and Eve Black should exist in one mind and one body, and that only one side could manifest itself at a time. It is also understandable that Corbett Thigpen chose to call one personality Eve White and the other Eve Black. Finally, there is an instinctive rightness in Jane's affection for Eve Black and her sense that Thigpen too was fond of Eve Black. They were fond of her, probably, in the same way that the South and all America were fond of Scarlett O'Hara. All America remembers, loves, and, indeed, relishes, Scarlett. Not many Americans even remember Melanie Wilkes, and if they do, they merely admire her. They adore Scarlett—perhaps, because she was "bad," and hence more real. She was a bad white woman in an America filled with white women striving to be good, whose society insists with double strength that they be extra good, and who, at the same time, resist not the tendency of the role but the extremity of the role as assigned. "Bad" Rhett Butler, appealing as he is and even as played by Clark Gable in the film, runs a clear second to Scarlett because he is a man. Men do not have to be as good— or, for purposes of negative identity, as bad—as women, and hence Americans did not find him so powerfully useful. Melanie is a good white woman, almost too good, and not nearly so valuable in affording definition as is her opposite. In real life as in fiction, Ashley Wilkes, the good white man, had virtually no use at all because white men do not need to be any better than they are.

The use of *Gone with the Wind* by America is a reflection of the use of the South and its culture by America. America relishes a bad South because it gives definition to a good America. The good South, itself, loves, protects, and will not surrender the bad South because, perhaps, it fears that without the bad South there would be no South at all. The "real" South, the "ought to be South," so to speak, lies somewhere between the good and the bad—in the person of, symbolically, some sane Jane. We sighted Jane in the Liberals in the 1880s, and again in the Southern academy in the 1920s, 1930s, and 1940s. She strove powerfully to come to the fore in the fall and winter of 1954 and 1955. Lamentably Jane represents a balance that the South has not been able to achieve in well over a century of striving.

In the mind of Southern whites for something over six generations, there has been a tendency to look at black people in essentially two ways. Blacks are either children and loved, or beasts and hated. As we have seen, there has been a trend for the mass of white people in the South to oscillate between the two extreme views without any substantial mediation between the two. The charge that Atticus Haygood leveled against his fellow whites in 1895 remains true: that they unrealistically expected the Negro to be "an angel in ebony" and when that proved not to be the case they lost all hope. Extreme racial views in the South are congruent with extreme views of sexuality and of good and bad. Southern white culture, Southern white personality, and Southern white ideas on race, sex, and morality are inextricably intertwined. To change the one is, inevitably, to change the other and, ultimately, the whole structure.

Racial Liberalism, then, involved a threat not only to the racial establishment, but to traditional ideas about sex roles and ideas about good and bad as well.

Thus, when the sons and daughters of Conservatism—when Harry Ashmore, Sarah Patton Boyle, Lillian Smith, C. Vann Woodward, and others—crossed over the bridge that their various traditions afforded to become the New Liberals, they were playing with fire and wind. The transition was never sudden, and it was never easy. In order for an individual white person to let black people go, to free black people from the tyranny of a white imagination that would make of them either angels or devils, the white person, in a sense, had to die, had to cease to be in an important way what he or she had been. Just as Eve White and Eve Black had to die so that Jane could come to the fore, so too with the Conservative and Radical mentalities in the Southern white mind. Southern white identity at any given time was intimately bound up with the Southern white image of the Negro, however unreal that image might have been. To let that image go, to see black people as people, was a precarious and exceedingly dangerous venture that exposed the individual to alienation from his natal culture and to the loss of his sense of self. It was a matter of declaring, essentially, "I am not going to be me anymore." That seemingly wonderously complete and whole Southern person, in his own conscious mind so happily superior, had to be roughly brought down from his cloud and footed securely on earth. He had psychologically, quite literally, to be "born again." In their minds, Southern white people have used black people to make themselves whole, to supply their missing parts, good or bad, and to smooth over the crudely sewn seams of their lives. To surrender the use of blacks was to give up a rather handy, attractive, seemingly necessary suit of mental clothing. Having blacks vulnerable led to needing blacks vulnerable, and to surrender the manipulation of black people in this fashion has proved to be a highly hazardous undertaking for Southerners. To yield the crutch gracefully requires an extraordinary effort, a capacity to risk the destruction of one's sense of self, to risk appearing and possibly being less of a man or less of a woman, and, equally frightening, less than purely good. A very large part of the race problem in the South resolves itself into the question of how one takes the racism, the unreality of seeing black either as child or beast, out of the Southern mind without killing the Southerner. How does one excise an integral and functioning part of the body and yet preserve the life of the patient? Ultimately, it would profit the Southern white Liberal little to save the whole world, if his own soul went floating in the doing.

The South at large has never been receptive to racial Liberalism, and it was not receptive to the New Liberalism in race in the mid-twentieth century. The most the New Liberal could hope for was permission to breathe, and often enough even that seemed precarious. The attitude of Southern society is easily comprehensible. In part, the South depended for its sense of identity upon

images of blackness that Liberalism tended to dissolve, and it worshipped at
the shrine of stability. Liberals made the paranoia of Conservatism seem not
paranoid. There were indeed enemies of good order in their very midst, previously hidden, now shedding their disguises. Native white Liberals were the
weak link in the solid chain of racism in the South. They looked like the other
links, and seemed decidedly strong ones, by class, by education, dress, manners, family name, and in every other way. But their very Southerness made
their defection all the more pernicious. The white Liberal who was deeply and
persistently Southern was, indeed, a powerful foe against racial orthodoxy. He
or she would not simply go North and do other things as did Cable, nor die
as did Haygood, nor fall silent as did Sledd and other critics of the racial establishment. With undeniably legitimate Southerners persisting in asserting that
things were not good, that, in fact, things were bad, then with black people
reinforcing that assertion with legal actions, boycotts, and demonstrations,
and, finally, with various persons and elements in the national government
joining in, racial orthodoxy in the South was soon sorely embattled.

Clearly, the New Liberals began their conversion as Conservatives in pain
and seeking relief. Like Eve White, they were inwardly unhappy with themselves and their society. Things were not right racially, yet rebellion in the
South, seemingly like everything else, is very difficult. Ultimately they resorted
to radical measures—shock treatments—in efforts to alter both themselves
and their society. They suffered the results, and they struggled to hold their
balance. Sarah Patton Boyle, as we have seen, fought back from the effort to
let black people go to find herself a new Christian, a happy person somewhat
lost to the life of this world by association with the life of the next. She gloried
in the fact that the Ku Klux Klan burned a cross, the symbol of Jesus' sacrifice,
in front of her Charlottesville home. Finally, she retreated into a deepened
sense of herself as a Christian, and there, again, she felt herself whole. Lillian
Smith launched in *Strange Fruit* both the boldest and most pointed indictment
of the goodness of the "good white men" of the elite class yet made. Effectively, she chose inter-racial sex as her weapon. The South counterattacked
with charges that Lillian Smith had sold out to the North, that she was bad,
and, finally, with whispers that she was not a woman to men. When Lillian
Smith died in 1966, she was still struggling to find her way back to some seat
of soul, some method that would allow her to let black people go and preserve
her sense of self. Lillian Smith, like Sarah Boyle, felt literally the fires of Southern censure as they burned, not merely a cross in front of her home, but the
home itself.

William Faulkner could not be labeled a racial Liberal, yet he too shared
the plight of the Liberal who remained in the South and criticized the people
who determined its racial establishment. Faulkner remained, not just in the
South, but even on that little postage stamp of geography in north-central Mis-

sissippi he knew best. There he made his criticism to Southerners who never seemed to understand—at least not in his lifetime—the significance of what he said. Faulkner was critical of the South for its failure to rise to its potential, for its rape of the land, this Southern Garden of Eden, and the license it gave to the practice of inhumanity by man to man. The South, he declared, had not met its history. It had not coped with its past.

Faulkner was critical of the South for what it had become; C. Vann Woodward defended the South for what it might yet be. *The Strange Career of Jim Crow* was a prescription for the racial salvation of the South, but it was an invitation that the South did not accept. In 1952 he had written an essay entitled "The Irony of Southern History." In 1960 he re-published that essay in a book he called *The Burden of Southern History.* Woodward pointed out that Southerners had shared the common lot of mankind in ways that other Americans had not. Southerners, unlike other Americans, had known military defeat, occupation by an alien army, and reconstruction, and they had known poverty and guilt. These experiences had set them upon common ground with the great mass of humanity in the world, and conditioned them to serve all by turning American power to the service of humanity.[41] Woodward and Faulkner shared a faith that somewhere in the history of the South lay the source of its problem. Faulkner declared that the South had not met its history, not coped with its past. Woodward was trying to find that history, not just in slavery or civil war, but in Reconstruction and after, in defeat, occupation, and poverty. Finally, both men shared a driving necessity to restore that Southern Eve to the garden, to say to the white South: "Yes, you are worthy too." Faulkner said it simply by not letting the much-abused body die; Woodward said it by active search and exhortation. Southerners deeply needed affirmation from Faulkner and Woodward, and whoever else might offer it with eloquence, art, and conviction, because, after 1955, Sambo was not saying it anymore. Indeed, in the next decade Sambo virtually evaporated.

BLACK BREAKOUT

Sambo did go, and that, more than Northern re-entry into the race problem and Southern liberal defection, bent the back of Southern Conservatism for a time. Before Montgomery in 1955, white people, at the sight of black bumptiousness, had been able to come down from the cloud for quick, firm, and violent sorties against assertive blacks. They could beat or lynch a black man, either with or without the help of the police, for what they considered to be the black man's insanity or even his simple stupidity in trifling with their property, lives, or women. But they did these things with the certainty that when the job was done, they could climb back up on the cloud and sail smiling and smoothly on. It was a sort of calculated insanity, a controlled fury that was compartmentalized and sharply focused. Perhaps whites were capable of the most awfully extravagant violence precisely because its object was limited. It was almost as if Southerners sometimes said to themselves, "Today I'm going to go deliberately crazy, but tomorrow I will be sane again."

The game of black balk and white bust, so familiar to the white South in the process of keeping black people under control, suddenly stopped on a city bus in Montgomery, Alabama, in December 1955, when a black woman named Rosa Parks refused to yield her seat to a white person. She would not move and the driver would not move the bus until she yielded. Myth has sometimes painted Rosa Parks as simply a black woman of middle years, making her way home from work as a seamstress in a downtown department store. She was tired, she had suffered a lifetime of discrimination, and when the demand came from the driver, she simply refused. She was all of that and she did refuse, but she was also an active member of the local NAACP, she had been trained in leadership in an Association school near Monteagle, Tennessee, and the local chapter had been planning to stage just such a demonstration using a younger black woman before that woman became pregnant. Rosa Parks did do it on her own, but it was not exactly unplanned. What flowed out of her action was a boycott of the city's buses that had been long and carefully considered. Within hours of the incident local black leaders had asked the twenty-six-year-old minister of the Dexter Avenue Baptist Church, Martin Luther King, Jr., to lead them. After a night of soul-searching, he agreed, and shortly an organization was launched to boycott the buses and provide transportation for black people about the town using privately owned vehicles. The movement began with the objective of asking for equal accommodations with whites, not integration. Shortly, it moved on to realize that separate would always be unequal in a white-controlled city in a white-controlled state. For a year, the blacks fought, and in the end they won. The buses were desegregated. Out of the struggle came the method that would tear at the structure of institutional discrimination in the South with great effect— the non-violent demonstration. Also out of the struggle came the prime organization in using the method, the Southern Christian Leadership Conference, and its charismatic leader, Martin Luther King.[42]

With the emergence of Martin Luther King, Jr., and the Southern Christian Leadership Conference, the lodestone of black leadership moved from North to South. During the turn-of-the-century years it had centered on Tuskegee with Booker T. Washington. After Washington's death in 1915, leadership moved North and found its center in the NAACP with headquarters in New York. In 1955 it came to the deep South again, and it drew its primary strength from roots that had not been specially tapped by either Washington or the NAACP. Whereas they had been carefully secular, black leadership in the first phase of the civil-rights movement drew its power from the church.

After Montgomery there was a pause in the civil-rights movement. The Supreme Court had made its decision, but neither Congress nor President leapt to enforce it. Those schools that wanted to desegregate did so. Those that did not had trouble. Most conspicuous among the latter was Central High School in Little Rock, Arkansas. Those were the Eisenhower years, and the President was neither outstanding as a friend of black people nor vigorous in the exercise of central power. Finally, Eisenhower did order federal intervention in Little Rock, but only after it appeared that the authority of the national government was being challenged. The conflict ended in the closing of the schools. In February 1960, the movement of the waters quickened rather suddenly again when, in Greensboro, North Carolina, several students from the state's black A & T College sat in at the lunch counter of the local Woolworth department store. Among those students was Jesse Jackson, soon to become a minister and one of Martin Luther King's immediate lieutenants. Black students were getting restless, and, almost certainly, if they had not sat-in in Greensboro first, they shortly would have done so in any one of a score of other towns. After the Greensboro demonstration, the sit-in movement spread all over the South. Presently, black students were joined by white students. Out of this came another key organization, the Student Non-Violent Co-ordinating Committee, commonly called "Snick" for its initials, SNCC. Sit-ins were followed by "ride-ins," which became the specialty of an inter-racial group formed in the war, the Congress of Racial Equality. Soon the movement spread to include the registration of black voters, a move fraught with difficulty for white people in the black belt areas. There, majority rule meant black rule.

Such organized and persistent demonstrations from black people were revolutionary in race relations in the South, and, ultimately, in the nation. Brief and violent sorties by whites did not suffice to destroy rebellions as they had in the past. Rosa Parks did not leave the bus quietly; the students did not shuffle away from the lunch counter; and they sat-in again and again. Moreover, the persistent Christian nature of the demonstrations shamed the opposition. Doubtlessly racial extremists would have preferred violent protests from blacks that they could have met with furious and unrestrained violence. But the facts that the demonstrators often came directly out of the black churches; that they were led by ministers, and that they did such things as stand, hold hands, and sing "We Shall Overcome" as if it were a hymn and they were Christians in the lions' den reached the whites where they lived. Southern whites saw themselves as specially Christian people, and they could not turn a deaf ear and an endlessly violent hand to these people who behaved so much, it seemed, as Christ would have behaved in their situation. The movement built and maintained a communication with the whites and with the white elite, whether the whites willed it or not. Whites had long heard what they wanted to hear from black people, and they had heard it from whomever they chose to hear it. The message that they had heard was that black people liked it down there. Now the message from blacks jangled back along white nerves to an unhappy, resistant, but hearing white mind. "We don't like it down here," it insisted. "We don't like it at all." White poeple did not respond positively and say, "Of course you don't, who would?" What the movement accomplished in the white mind was, rather, confusion, doubt, anger, and resentment. But most of all it accomplished the nearly total destruction of neo-Sambo. The traditional idea—applied in this case to say that "our" blacks would be happy blacks if Martin Luther King, the agent of the Communists, had not stirred them up—became absurdly weak when white people saw that many trusted local black leaders (heretofore trusted by them as their fathers had trusted Booker T. Washington and his clones) were not only in the opposition, but helping to lead it. They would have preferred to believe that the demonstrators were all imported from the North, but there were among them too many familiar faces to allow that self-deception to persist for long. Furthermore, there were too many native whites among the demonstrators. All the old devices of control, thoroughly tried, availed naught in the decade after 1955, and die-hard racial Conservatives knew not what to do. Their arsenal of violence was, after all, relatively thin, and when no weapon seemed successful in quelling the rebellion, the firing grew hesitant and half-hearted. With the March on Washington in 1963, with the opening of public accommodations equally to all persons by the Civil Rights Act of 1964 and the polls and politics by the Voting Rights Act of 1965, the fight went out of the Conservatives. They fell silent, and seemed to yield, at least to the law of the land.

There can be no doubt that the Southern white psyche in 1965 had reached a new low. The Southern sense of self had been brought from the heights to nearly nothing with defeat in the Civil War a century before. During the next forty years, Southerners slowly regained the sense that they were specially spiritual relative to Northerners. In 1912 they helped elect what was at least a Southern-born President to the White House, filled his cabinet in 1913, and rose to prominent chairmanships in the Congress. There was a complacency about the white South in the 1920s and 1930s that passed into anxiety in the 1940s, and became hysteria in the 1950s and early 1960s. The Southern psyche was long driven to seek respect from the North and love from the Negro. Southerners might survive a lack of respect from the North, but they could not survive continuing manifestations of hate from black people. Blacks were too numerous, too close, and, traditionally, too necessary to the Southern sense of self. Whites might go on and become what they would become and blackness need not ever be a vital part of their lives again. Or blacks might jerk the invisible string and whites respond, not in any certain style, but variously and with biases unpredictable and especially their own. Blacks do have a rather miraculous power over Southern whites, not to control them, but to upset them and drive them to frenzy.

The agony in the Southern white mind at the prospect of a black invasion of white culture was still building in 1964 and 1965 when a shadow of relief appeared. Black people were finding that there was a difference between sitting in and being in. A legal and a physical revolution, putting black bodies among white bodies in either token or massive numbers, had not produced a revolution in white attitudes. Indeed, many blacks found that being close to whites was much more painful than being away from them. The closer they got, the greater the pain. The white South, grudgingly, under pressure from court orders, television cameras, and the ultimate police power, accommodated black people in places where they had never been before. In particular, local business interests concerned themselves with projecting to the rest of the nation that the accommodation had, indeed, been completely made. The message of each was that their community had adjusted to the new reality, that peace and good order did prevail, and that outside commerce and industry could now safely invest in that locality.[43] But all of the physical evidences of a change in race relations did not mean that the white mind was revolutionized. Bodies were more easily mixed than minds. The white mind was, as I have said, shaken, but it was not converted. Probably the sum total of white prejudice remained largely unchanged by physical integration alone, and white words, looks, and deeds—often subtle, sometimes thoughtless, and even unintentional—cut like razors. Many black people, especially children, were not prepared for such emotional mayhem. Psychologically wounded and bleeding, some black children among the first integrated came reeling back out of the schoolhouse doorway to a black world that seemed somehow blessedly sweet.

> Holy Mother Blackness,
> Take me
> Make me . . . whole,
> Save my soul.

There is a paradox in race relations in the South and in America. It is that black people have to get out of white society in order to get into it, and they have to get into it in order to get out. They have to get into the society to get a minimum of those palpable things that people need in order simply to survive—material goods, education, government, a minimum of justice, law, and order. But yet because white people are prejudiced and have the power to manifest their prejudices in a multitude of ways, they have to get out, to withdraw to themselves in some degree, to maintain a sense of worth and self-esteem. In 1965, having gotten in as far as they had and having the promise of further entry by the law of the land, having suffered the slings and arrows of white prejudice as they had, and having the surety of further hurts by the laws of inertia and momentum, some black leaders began a move to pull black people away from white people. This separatist effort had a vast impact on the civil-rights movement. In the next five years conspicuous leadership in the black world changed hands from those who had led the fight to get in to those who led the fight to get out. Black leaders in the civil-rights movement had not been very old, but the new leadership was very young. Stokeley Carmichael, H. "Rap" Brown, and Huey Newton were now the names at the forefront. It was a quality of leadership vastly different from what had gone before, and they advocated very different programs under slogans of Black Power, Black Separatism, Black Nationalism and Black Is Beautiful. Black Separatism, the withdrawal, had the effect of ending the intimacy between black and white activists that had obtained during the civil-rights movement. In 1966, SNCC, by then under the direction of Stokeley Carmichael, dramatically expelled its white membership.[44] The assassination of Martin Luther King, Jr., in 1968 symbolized, horribly, the fact that the civil-rights phase of the Black Revolution was over. No single person was widely recognized as King's successor, and there was no one organization that headed up black leadership. Furthermore, goals, like leadership, became diffused, diverse, and sometimes unclear. "Burn, baby, burn" was understandable as a reaction against the past, but it was not a very clear prescription for a livable future. It was almost as if the resources for a drive to get in had been exhausted, and the only way to go now was out. More positively, in the process of withdrawal DuBois's concept of black soul was revived. The Harlem Renaissance, black culture, the African past, and slavery were re-discovered, raised up, and drew vast interest among black artists, intellectuals, and youth. In the late 1960s integration in the older sense of the term had lost meaning and power as the cutting edge of the Black Revolution.

Even as Black Separatism was getting under way, another highly important phenomenon occurred. In the summer of 1965 a riot broke out in Watts, a large and sprawling section of Los Angeles occupied by blacks. In twenty days of burning, smashing, looting, and sniping, some two hundred city blocks were laid waste. In a sense black people took charge of their homes and neighborhoods—mostly white owned—and they burned them down. The usual, and probably accurate, interpretation was that black people not just in the South, but all over America had been promised a better life by the civil-rights movement, and those things had not been forthcoming. Somehow, the nation had lost sight of the fact that the promise of equality and a better life for black people applied not only to black people in the South, but to black people in the North and West as well, and that these were rapidly becoming the majority of the Negro population in America.

There had been race riots before, of course, but the new riot was basically the doing of black people, and they attacked not so much white persons as white property inside the black ghetto. Harlem, apparently, had established the model in the 1930s, and, indeed, there was such a riot in Harlem in 1964. But Watts compelled attention because it was the first dramatic exportation of the model. The camera eye of the nation switched rather rapidly away from the South to the North and West as city after city, even Washington, burned and smoked in imitation of Watts. The meaning was as obvious as the fire and smoke: the racism and its physical results that white America had, heretofore, preferred to see and attack in the South was not merely Southern. Indeed, perhaps in its most awful modern manifestations it was Northern and Western as evidenced in the inner cities where black ghettoes were deteriorating materially, socially, and morally, with devastating effects upon the lives of millions of individuals. White racism clearly was national, and black protest must be made national also. In the South, protest could take form in non-violent assaults upon legal segregation and disfranchisement. In the North and West, other targets would have to be chosen, and other means of assault devised. For some ten years, from Watts in 1965 to Chelsea, Massachusetts, in 1975, urban racial violence in the North and West gave demonstration after demonstration that white racism and the white South were by no means co-terminal, and that the Black Revolution begun in the South had become national.

THE CONSERVATIVE RESURGENCE

Southern leaders in the mid-twentieth century had great difficulty understanding that black people had been treated unfairly. They were convinced that blacks were innately inferior to whites, and segregation was not only necessary and fair, it was a triumph of statesmanship as well. They understood that not every American agreed with them, but the Brown decision in May 1954 left them shocked and disbelieving. Surely the North could not be so mean. Southern leadership had, indeed, honored the implicit bargain struck two generations before with the decline of Populism. The South had surrendered claim to substantial economic and political power in the nation in return for social and racial autonomy at home. Probably no state had honored that bargain more faithfully than Mississippi. In 1954 it was both the blackest and poorest state in the nation. With the organization of a White Citizens' Council in Indianola in July 1954, it was also the first to offer organized and conspicuous defiance to the High Court's ruling.

In May 1955 the Supreme Court handed down orders for the implementation of its decision. Primary responsibility was lodged with local school boards, while federal district courts were charged with overseeing the process.

Some Southern leaders saw great relief in the arrangement. There was no pre-scribed timetable, and district judges were virtually always fully established members of the local ruling elite. "Thank God," declared Georgia's lieutenant governor, "we've got good Federal judges."[45] Hope rapidly faded as district judges, almost to a man, interpreted the High Court's prescription for "delib-erate speed" to mean "begin now." Lower courts repeatedly smashed state laws mandating segregation and quickly brushed aside delaying tactics by local school boards.

Segregation was ultimately broken not by white people in general, nor even by federal judges in particular. It was broken by the first black child to walk through the doors of the traditionally white schoolhouse. It was further broken by the tens, thousands, and millions who followed that first one. Behind those children stood black families, black communities, and a black leadership. That action, and the actions after 1960 of other blacks who "sat-in" at lunch counters, on buses, and elsewhere evoked the violence that brought traditional segregation to an end. Probably, the crucial turn came when a black student, James Meredith, insisted upon entering the Law School of the University of Mississippi in September 1962. In the struggle that fol-lowed, 320 federal marshals supported by soldiers fought a minor war to keep Meredith in school. When the dust settled, the campus resembled a war zone.[46] Leaders in other Southern states, many of which were vying with each other for new investments in business and factories from the North and abroad, carefully avoided repeating the Mississippi experience. Desegregation came, but it did not end either discrimination or racism. Indeed, segregation was but an outwork in the front-line defenses of the Southern racial establishment. Hardly had that outwork succumbed before relief appeared on the horizon in the form of the self-segregation of black people and the rise of blatant racism outside the South.

Die-hard racial Conservatives in the South were delighted to see a vigorous racism in the North and West, and they often worked diligently to show that it more than matched their own. George Wallace came out of the deep South in 1968 and 1972 to win amazingly high percentages of votes in several North-ern states in the Democratic presidential primaries. In 1968, for instance, he shocked the liberal nation by garnering 40 percent of the Democratic primary vote in sometimes famously progressive Wisconsin, home state of Senators Robert La Follette and William Proxmire. Southern Conservatives at large were greatly relieved to see racism everywhere but at home. They suddenly recognized racism with surprise and delight not only in the North, but in South Africa, Russia, and, finally, even in mother England. By comparison, Southern racism appeared to be of the mildest sort, and even to approach the benign. Again, the myth began to rise that Southern white people understood black people better than anyone else. Hence race relations in the South were better, so ran the thought, and more susceptible to easy improvement.

Racism in foreign parts was a great comfort to Southern white Conservatives, but more important to them, as always, was what black people at home seemed to be doing. Black separatism was, of course, sweet music to their ears. The very best people, the ruling elite, the most exquisite and untouched among Conservatives, and their sons and daughters carefully nurtured in racial hothouses developed a strangely Mona Lisa cast to their smiles as they looked at Afro hairdos, dress, and dance. There grew up in the South a sort of two-part harmony in the dialogue between the Conservative elite and the more extreme black separatists. "I'm black," declares the Negro. "Yes," replies the Conservative, "indeed you are." "And I am beautiful," concludes the black. "Yes," responds the white, "Yes, you are." The Conservative then turns to his Liberal white friends with a look that says: (sigh) "See, I told you so. Negroes are different; they have a very special and a rather appealing thing, don't you think?" Beneath this is written in a hand quivering with relief: "THEY DON'T WANT IN, NOT REALLY THEY DON'T."

For roughly a decade after 1965 black separatism had great strength. Because of that fact, black culture today is stronger than ever before, more sophisticated, and self-conscious. Black people as a whole people are not, and now show little promise of ever again being willing to totally surrender their destiny to predominantly white culture. By the late 1970s, however, separatism had lost power. In the early eighties young black people as individuals evinced an obvious desire to get a fair share of the good things of American life, not to settle for being out and beautiful, but rather to insist upon being in and affluent.

Things have changed in this last generation, and they are better. Black people in the South and in America are better able to live the life they were previously led to idealize but denied the means to achieve. There is more freedom. There are black legislators, black mayors, black Congressmen, and even judges, sheriffs, and generals. There are black lawyers, professors, physicians, teachers, and ministers who have graduated from superb and heretofore all white schools and serve white clients. Clearly, many more are coming. But, it is also clear that the "in" phase of the Black Revolution has reached a high tide and is receding. Counterforces against the further integration of black people are rising in an often hostile and always power-packed white world. Prejudice in white minds is still rampant and discrimination, visible and invisible, witting and unwitting, exists on every hand. Nevertheless, among whites awareness of prejudice and feelings of guilt about discrimination are diminishing. The very success of some blacks in taking advantage of opportunities afforded by an America officially committed to racial equality in its fundamental legal and social constitutions is serving to diminish the reservoir of white guilt upon which so much of the progress of the civil-rights movement was built.

Conservatives in the early 1980s seemed bound for the promised land of racial unawareness. One can almost hear the click as black people in the white mind slip snugly back into that comfortable slot defined by things that white people need from blackness. Conflict gives way to complementarity, fear slides to love; a happy face rotates to the fore, locks in place, and, behold, again there is no race problem. One might well begin to look in the white mind for the recurrent Sambo, some neo-neo-Sambo to replace the image of the black militant in the style of either Martin Luther King, Jr., or Stokeley Carmichael. A decade or so after Nat Turner came Sambo. A decade or so after Reconstruction saw his pale revival. A decade after the Atlanta riot neo-Sambo appeared. Perhaps, a decade or so after the Chelsea riot we shall get the new stereotype. Perhaps, in that brave new world, the Conservative mind of the white South will generate for itself yet another racial soma pill in the form of a new model Negro. Last time they drove the model into place with rope and faggot. This time, it might be that they will pull him there bound in fur-lined manacles and with chains of gold. They need him, and they will pay a certain price to get him. Indeed, they might well come to see all the physical and emotional pain preceding the achievement of the new plateau of inter-racial peace as worth while. If one shares in the pleasantly complete logic of the very best Conservatives in the late 1890s, if one were, say, a providentially long-lived Edgar Gardner Murphy and could see the seeming conflict as in reality a divinely organized and inscrutable machine working to wear the hard rocks of life into the finely smoothed stones of God's current wish for man, the new separatism and the awful violence that have been our national lot of late could be as warmly welcomed as a second coming. Indeed, it has within itself the promise of still another redemption for the South and of paradise regained. Southern blacks are finding their proper places, it declares, and Southern whites are becoming once more—a beautiful people.

Conclusion

THE GREAT CHANGEOVER:
An Interpretation of White Culture and
Race Relations in the American South

Between 1850 and 1915 white culture and race relations in the South under-went a drastic and fundamental change. During this time the South switched from a racial pattern in which black people were firmly included in the society by way of slavery to one in which they were effectively excluded. The change-over was a complex movement in itself, but it was integrally tied to a larger and even more complex transition in the whole of American society and, indeed, in the Western world. At the heart of the change stood the industrial revolution, pioneered in the first half of the nineteenth century by the textile industry in England, Belgium, and New England. Earlier, in the seventeenth and eighteenth centuries, the American South had developed plantation slav-ery to contribute significant quantities of tobacco, rice, and sugar to world commerce. In the first decades of the nineteenth century it expanded the vast productive power of plantation slavery to supply most of the cotton that fed the mills of Manchester, Ghent, and Lowell.

Because of the climatic requirements of the cotton plant, the lower South in particular became the great cotton-producing area of the United States. Slaves from the upper South poured southward in and after the 1820s, and the lower South soon outstripped the world in cultivating the fleecy staple. The planter elite in the lower South came to presume that their place at the very fountainhead of the industrial revolution gave them great power. James Henry Hammond of South Carolina spoke well the sentiments of his class when he declared on the floor of the United States Senate in 1858 that "Cotton *is* king," and asserted that "no power on earth" dared make war against it. In 1850

Southern blacks were bound intimately to the industrial revolution through the institution of slavery. By 1915 they were no longer centrally involved in that process, and, as technology progressed, increasingly marginal in their participation in it. Both in slavery and afterward, blacks in America generally have been steadily and firmly excluded from enjoying an appreciable share of the benefits of industrialization. In the economic sphere, the story of race relations in the South and in America at large in the twentieth century is the story of black people struggling to re-enter the industrial revolution and win a larger portion of its abundant material rewards.

Culturally, the story of race relations during the changeover transcends economics and is vastly more complicated. However, the process might be roughly schematized in the form of a triangle (See Figure 1). At each corner stands one of three important groups of people in the South: the white elite, the black mass, and the white mass. In 1850 the white elite, comprised of some 10,000 large slaveholders and their professional allies, had built a strong connection with the black mass through slavery. It was through the device of plantation slavery that they gained and held the power to control society. Especially in the lower south, the white elite strengthened its hold over the black mass by a cautious alliance with free people of color of the greatest affluence, sophistication, and status. The power line in the triangle, thus, ran from the white elite to the black mass. On the other side, the white elite maintained a rather tenuous, uncertain connection with the white mass. The prime objective of the elite on that side was to neutralize the mass of white people, to keep them in place in the system and to minimize their capacity to damage the sources of power of the white elite. Most critically, the white mass must not be allowed to tamper with the institution of slavery.

By 1915 the white elite had largely abandoned the black connection. In that process, beginning in the 1850s in the lower South, it turned away from its alliance with the free mulatto elite and moved to the relegation of all people of any color to the black mass. Simultaneously, the free mulatto elite was, of its own volition, moving away from its semi-alliance with the white elite toward a firm and lasting alliance with the black mass. That engagement was greatly advanced in Reconstruction and reached a consummation in the 1920s in the era of the Harlem Renaissance.

On the other side of the race line, in 1915 the white elite was busy bonding itself to the white mass. Over three generations the crucial line of power in the triad shifted from that which joined the white elite to the black mass through the institution of slavery to that which joined the white elite to the white mass through institutions that were, in the broad sweep of Southern history, essentially new. The end result was a culture in the South in which black people were practically excluded from influence upon the ruling power, and ruling power was devoted almost exclusively to the benefit of white people. The third possible power line in the schematic, an effective and durable alliance between the black mass and the white mass, has never occurred in the South.

In race relations in the South there have been "hot" times, as we might label them, and "cool" times. The evolution of race relations is continuous, of course, but it is in the "hot" times that the evolution is more rapid, its parts more evident, and a better subject for study. Two hot times did most, first to establish the triadic relationship that prevailed in 1850, then to effect the changeover to the array described in 1915 and, hence, to give shape and substance to race relations and white culture in the South in the twentieth century.

The first hot time occurred in the last generation of slavery, in that hard-soft period that evolved after 1831 in which the South engaged itself in an alteration and re-ordering of its parts to constitute a new regime that would, in its own judgment, bring it powerfully into the modern commercial and industrial world and preserve stability at home. In that process it commenced to evolve the idea and the reality of an organic society with black Sambo tightly fixed on the one side, the mass of white people loosely held and deferential on the other, and a paternalistic chivalry at the top. In the rising order of the late Old South black people and slavery received a vast amount of attention from the white elite, while the white mass received only that minimum necessary to render it relatively quiescent and powerless to interfere with the "peculiar institution."

The second hot time occurred between 1889 and 1915 when the white elite acted vigorously to diminish substantially its previous heavy reliance upon black people as the mudsills of a higher cultural order and moved into the process of constructing instead a cultural system that put black people firmly to one side and tied the mass of white people tightly to the white elite. The final crusade for whiteness produced, among many other things, all-white factories, all-white one-party politics, compulsory public education for every white child, public health campaigns that favored whites, segregation, a rage against miscegenation, and the relatively total divorce of white religion, language, and music from black. By 1915, the changeover begun in the 1850s, had been effectively completed. Blacks had been set aside, and the institutions that would bind the white mass to the white elite in the twentieth century were in place and rapidly doing their work. Race relations and Southern culture in the twentieth century, race relations and Southern culture today, can be described substantially in terms of the end result of the changeover in the line of power in the triad. It was as if the threads in the cloth of Southern life were taken apart strand by strand and rewoven, with new threads added, in a different pattern. The power line of the organic society in late slavery was one between the white elite and the black mass; the power line in the organic society in the twentieth century was one between the white elite and the white mass. In the first order, the white mass was necessarily there but marginal; in the second order the black mass was necessarily there but marginal.

Racial Radicalism as we have described it fits integrally into this schematic as one of the key mechanisms by which the substantial detachment of the black mass from the white elite was achieved. It was as if the white elite had assigned some of their people, theretofore Conservatives, to the task of working out a rhetoric that produced a tremendous violence against black people and, in the black belts, the near destruction of that bond. The rhetoric featured black retrogression, and the end of retrogression was, of course, the dissolution of black people in America. As the Radicals painted the picture, there would be finally no black mass at all, and America would be totally white. Inevitably, the white elite and the white mass would be joined. The Radical vision of the future was clear, and the rhetoric produced action that worked toward the end envisioned. Among other things, it produced atrocities against black people unmatched in quantity or kind and an aura of threat unsurpassed in intensity in America before or since. Never before in the South had black people in such numbers been sometimes skinned alive and often burned to death before audiences that took hours and even days to assemble and rose not merely to the hundreds but to the thousands. Never before in the South had white people raked through the still smoldering ashes of murdered blacks to find teeth and bits of bones to save as if they were somehow religious relics. Radicalism gave black people a vicious push away from white people, and it did so precisely in those regions where blacks were most numerous.

Overt violence of the Radical sort diminished as the decades passed, but racial extremists of the Radical order had roles in the creation of institutional structures—such as those of public schools, public health, segregation, disfranchisement, police, courts, and prisons—that would rule much of thought and behavior in the South in the twentieth century. Their participation worked to shape those institutions in a highly significant degree upon the assumption that black people were savage and bound for dissolution. Thus, even after Radicalism as a mode of thinking about race relations was gone and practically forgotten and Conservatism again reigned virtually undisputed, there was much in Southern life that assumed the demise of black people. The society functioned, in a great measure, to make the assumption real. Blacks disappeared, for instance, behind the walls of segregation, behind the walls of prisons, and, most of all, in mid-century by emigration in great numbers to the North and West. Posthumously, the extremists very nearly achieved precisely the all-white world they had envisioned, if not in the body, then surely in the mind. When an individual black in contact with whites stepped out of his place and waxed assertive, when he ceased to be the neo-Sambo whites insisted upon seeing, he became, as Ralph Ellison so perfectly said for that age, "invisible man." In a major way, the civil-rights movement was a struggle by black people, first, simply to regain visibility in the eyes of white people.

In the changeover, the work of Radicalism was essentially negative; it was to destroy the lingering connection between the white elite and the black mass. In contrast, the work of Volksgeistian Conservatism was relatively constructive. Volksgeistian Conservatives made legitimate the separation of black from white that Radicalism had effected. They made "another place" for black people away from whites. Further, they tended to tame, refine, and harness the tremendous social energy generated by Radical racism among Southern whites and to turn that energy into strengthening the bond between the white elite and the white mass. In their minds and in their rhetoric, white racism was progressivism.

Both Radicalism and Volksgeistian Conservatism were born of the Conservative mainline, but each was in fact, revolutionary, patricidal to the traditional triadic Conservative order. Radicals would erase the black connection entirely, leaving only a white elite and the white mass. Volksgeistian Conservatives would fan the flames of whiteness to fuse the white mass up into the white elite. In the Volksgeistian utopia, all whites would rise to become equal citizens in the cultural state, leaving only blacks on one side and whites on the other. Persisting Conservatives, who did in the end prevail, worked steadily to build a system that pulled back from both extremes. They sought to preserve the basic triad, but to alter the valence of relationships between its parts. The great changeover represented a tremendous shift in the foundation of Southern culture from a black to a white base. The truly amazing success of Conservative leadership in effecting that change was possible, in large measure, precisely because Radicals and Volksgeistian Conservatives had done their work so thoroughly, each swinging wide like a pendulum, first to one side in an attempt to destroy the old connection and then to the other in an effort to construct one that was fundamentally new. After 1915, Conservativism, resurgent and virtually unchallenged, perfected a New Orthodoxy in race relations in which black people were held down and out as never before, but they were not erased, and white people were pulled upward and in but only within a hierarchy that was, essentially, traditional. In the New Orthodoxy the white elite ceased to splinter, rebels dissolved almost as fast as they appeared, and in the mind of the South, as I have said, all blacks looked alike while every white person was regarded as an individual in an ordered universe of individuals.

In constructing the New Orthodoxy, Conservatives before and after 1915 worked astutely with the materials at hand. In relation to blacks, they tended to reject the DuBoisian system as removing the black mass too far from white control, and they gladly welcomed the advent of Booker T. Washington. It was true wisdom that led his biographer, Louis Harlan, to paint Washington as the Moses of his people. Like Moses his mission was to lead his race out of Egypt. Washington was to relieve the white elite of the burden of leading the black mass after slavery. He was the definitive Conservative answer to leaders such as Atticus Haygood who would, of course, have the white elite do precisely that task. Washington would be the surrogate for the white elite in the up-from-slavery phase of black social evolution. In a racially separated world, he would become the wise and patient paternalist, gently but firmly guiding his people to the promised land across a providentially parted sea. Conservatives relished his image of the hand with fingers spread. But they also liked the fingers closing at will to make a fist. They wanted the blacks solidly separated and out there, but they also wanted them held tightly in check and ready to close harmoniously with the white world when the summons came. It turned out that the white elite itself had the power to part the sea whenever it was necessary, as in World Wars I and II, to bring the children of Israel back again into Egypt land and to enlist them for labor in Pharaoh's service.

In politics, the Populist leaders—like the Radical, Liberal, and Volksgeistian leaders in race—were splinters of the basically Conservative white elite. Their ultimate mission in the changeover was to work up a new political bond between the white elite and the white mass. In brief, they were to work toward a finally all-white Democracy that was to dominate Southern politics for most of the twentieth century. This was no easy task. Slaveholders had sometimes been highly vocal in their dedication to white democracy, but there seemed to be some slip between the lip of promise and the cup of positive benefits, such as in public education and bases of taxation. Often the most aristocratic of the slaveholders were not very vocal in favoring democracy, and some of them clearly tended in the other direction. No one ever accused John C. Calhoun or Jefferson Davis of being a common man, each would have resented the allegation, and the president of the Confederacy never made an address extolling government of the people, by the people, and for the people. Even in the Redemption movement in the deep South, the rhetoric did not always run to a high commitment to an all-white democracy, and there was little in the background of the Redeemers that would lead one to expect such. Wade Hampton, for instance, in redeeming South Carolina declared himself for free men, free schools, and free ballots, but that slogan itself was an appeal for a resurrection of the old black connection, and not the clear clarion call to pure whiteness that some of his followers more in tune with the wave of the future would have liked. In Reconstruction, Redemption, and in the Bourbon era there was simply too much of that old order still operative for an explicitly exclusively white political line to gain sway and lock into place. Even so, Liberals such as Haygood and Cable, who in the 1880s would have forced the pendulum back toward the old connection between the white elite and the black mass, soon learned to their bitter disappointment that the power line in

Southern society was swinging irresistibly in the opposite direction. In the 1890s, the Populists indirectly gave the *coup de grâce* to the Bourbons and then, having done their work, dissolved much as did the racial Radicals. They left a virtually all-white but largely ineffectual Republican party and a Democratic party that suffered not the slightest confusion about how it stood on the matter of black people in politics.

On the way to achieving that end, the Populists carried out another, collateral, and seemingly contradictory mission. The Populists probed, at least rhetorically, the bottom line in the triad. Whatever their real feelings were about joining the white mass with the black mass in politics to effect economic reforms that would get both out of the ditch, the probe showed that it would not work. There was life in that line—a truly democratic promise, but also death, and the life proved so fragile politically as to be not worth a hard and persistent test.[1] Much the same experiment in much the same mood had been made by Carpetbaggers and Scalawags in Reconstruction. It was almost as if the attempt had to be made and the failure witnessed yet again so that the new order of whiteness could get on to realizing itself without inhibiting doubts.

The Confederate myth, as we have seen, worked to bond the white elite and the white mass together. It also worked to shift the basis of Southern white identity from the black mass to the white mass. In the myth, the common Southern soldier was bravely fighting for liberty not slavery—he was in fact doing nothing more than fighting a second War of American Independence. In reality, apparently, immediately after the war the private Confederate soldier was not so much honored. "Praise for the soldier can be found, of course," thought a very close student of the subject, "but not so often as criticism, especially when compared with later periods." The shift in attitude suggested in the rhetoric was also carved in marble. The same scholar, surveying postwar statuary dedicated to the Confederate military, found that only 22 percent of the statues erected before 1885 featured the Confederate private. Between 1885 and 1899 that proportion rose sharply to 62 percent, and in the twelve years after 1900 rose still again to 81 percent.[2] Tom Dixon, U. B. Phillips, Edgar Gardner Murphy, and people of that generation came of age, then, amidst a laudatory statuary of slaveholding colonels and generals. William Faulkner, Wilbur Cash, Margaret Mitchell, C. Vann Woodward, and millions of other Southern youths grew up in the twentieth century in towns and counties where the central square pedestalized the common Confederate soldier and through him raised all whites into the sacred circle. Giants in gray remained on their pedestals, but men in butternut now rose to join them. As the beauty of the Southern folk was evoked, as the Confederate myth grew, as the common soldier was brought in stone from the graveyard to the courthouse square and deified, the necessity of looking to black people as a source of Southern white identity diminished. Blacks were still in the identity triangle as symbols vaguely complementary to whites, but the real source of identification was the soul of whiteness.

Literature, too, added its weight to dissolve the black bond and thicken the white. Ellen Glasgow pioneered in that labor in 1900 when she raised Nicholas Burr from his dirt-farmer origins to the governorship of Virginia in her novel *Voice of the People*.[3]

In the next generation, Margaret Mitchell in telling the story of *Gone with the Wind* moved Southern white culture after the Civil War quickly away from antebellum life and a dependence upon either slaves or blacks. In 1865 Tara itself is nearly denuded of blacks, and Will Benteen, the plain Cracker, perfectly true Confederate private from the wiregrass country of southern Georgia soon marries Suellen, Scarlett's sister, and sits as the man at a Tara that has, he declares, made the transition from plantation to farm. Will *is* Miss Minerva's bright schoolboy, the folklorist's soul of white wisdon, a potential Nick Burr, and the simon-pure Confederate soldier from the courthouse square all rolled snugly into a single character by Mitchell and cast backward to save what was good in the old order for use in the new.[4]

Faulkner, beginning in the late 1920s and still pressing the quest for Southern soul through the 1950s, got very close to what whites were in his own time, and how they should relate to blacks. He was far more concerned with blackness than most Southern writers in the century. But he was also a genius in the search for whiteness. He wanted homogeneity. Only in homogeneity, he declared, do a people achieve anything at all worthwhile. The Sartorises, Compsons, Sutpens, and even the Snopses and Gowries must in the end combine simply because they are white. Blacks are already homogeneous, more so than the whites, and that is why they have survived. Blacks are related to whites as moon to earth, two worlds in distant conjunction, a dance without touching.

Race relations in the South over the last century and a half have not been purely a Southern matter; they have also steadily involved the North and the nation at large. At the same time that it undertook to adjust race relations at home, the white elite has been forced to adjust relations between North and South. In that process it moved the South from a position of increasing antagonism toward the North during the last generation of slavery to one of accommodation in the twentieth century (See p. 519).

In pressing that early antagonism to the extreme of war, they overplayed their hand and lost. Southern leadership lost power in the nation, and they lived for a time in an economic and political colony, a South nearly totally at the mercy of the imperial nation. They were forced to negotiate successive settlements from weakness rather than strength. By the early years of the new century, however, they had brokered out an arrangement in which they settled

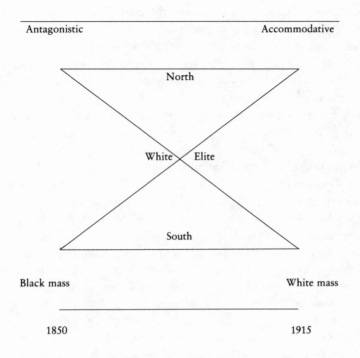

for markedly less wealth in the South and less power in the nation in return for a high level of power for themselves at home. Because politics both at home and away no longer carried great power, politics and politicians became less important. Southern politics rapidly degenerated into something very close to entertainment, and politicians often became more showmen than statesmen. They were, figuratively, the new minstrels, white men in white face displacing white men in black face, each attesting in very different ways to the same fact that black men were powerless. By the second quarter of the century, remnants of the slaveholding elite had passed away, and the white elite, no longer based on a single institution, would be found somewhere among the array of lawyers, businessmen, bankers, industrialists, ministers, newspaper editors, professors, educators, writers, intellectuals, dentists, and physicians, as well as large farmers and locally powered politicians, and the wives, mothers, and daughters of all these. The white elite varied widely in its constituency from one community to the next. In one it might center in the Men's Bible class in the First Baptist Church, in another the country club. In the Old South, the ruling element in the white elite had been powered by slavery; in the twentieth century they were powered by a capacity to organize and stabilize the white community, and either to exclude alien influences or tame them.

In the last quarter of the twentieth century it appears that the Southern white elite has managed superbly its campaign to retain local power. The all-white alliance in the South—in spite of the civil-rights movement, in spite of the drive by blacks for a fully equal participation in education, politics, and economics and the successes that they have achieved—remains in place and secure. Moreover, with well over fifty million people, the white South is gaining power in the nation, slowly and subtly in economics and politics, but rapidly and markedly in religion and race.

The Southern share of religious power in America is on the rise and already no less than astounding in its magnitude. On Sunday mornings from Castine, Maine, to Coos Bay, Oregon, it is easily possible to tune one's television set to a Southern evangelist. Indeed, in those still most segregated hours in America, if the set is on and the dials are turned, it is almost impossible not to hear Jerry Falwell from Lynchburg, Virginia, the Louisianian Jimmy Swaggart, Jim Bakker from Charlotte, or Oral Roberts from Oklahoma. Billy Graham, first and most famous, has achieved invasions of the North that Robert E. Lee might well envy, having stormed Washington several times and occupied the White House once or twice. The power of Southern evangelists in national religion is vast, not always recognized, and when it is recognized not usually welcomed. It smacks too much, for instance in the "Moral Majority," of St. Augustine presuming after all to bring the City of God down to Rome.

On the other hand, the rise of the South again to leadership in matters of race is recognized and, nearly universally, approved. In the twentieth century, it seems clear that the white South and the white North, in spite of their real cultural differences, have reached a practical congruence in their behavior in regard to black people. In all regions, when black people in large numbers have become relatively assertive in their pursuit of a fair share of the good things in life, white people have proved themselves ready for violence. Racially speaking, Chelsea in 1975 was not many miles from Birmingham in 1963. In a dozen years, the North had clearly lost legitimate claim to moral superiority in passing judgment on race relations in the South. Thereafter, an embarrassed North virtually ceased to shout "racist" at the South. By the time Alex Haley's *Roots* as book and film had run its course in 1976 and 1977, the North seemed to lose any inclination to pass judgment at all. There had been a horrible racism down there in the South back then, ran the response to that work, but there was none in the nation now and hence no reason why white people should feel guilty. The racist South had been cursed, whipped, and cured, and white America thereby cleansed and forgiven. In the new dispensation, Southern white leaders were seen to have some special affinity for dealing with black people, and it seemed best to leave local racial matters again in their hands. Most recently, one hears much about how the South has better relations between the races and hence should point the way to national progress in the future. Thus, within the twentieth century, the needle of leadership in matters racial in the nation has swung full compass and found no solution. The *style* of race relations in the South is certainly different from that of the North, but it is not at all clear that it is better.

Economic power, also, is moving southward—to centers such as Atlanta, Miami, Houston, and Dallas, not only in the form of sophisticated new factories, but even in the more vital spheres of communications, image-making, money, banking, and credit. That power is national, but it is also distinctly international and promises, vaguely, therein to bypass the North and West. The "Sunbelt" phenomenon as economics is new and real, and the end effect seems to be an evolving Southernization of national business as it operates in the South rather than a nationalization of Southern culture by way of business.

In politics, the South has recently produced a President who took office from the South and returned to the South when he had served his term. Even with that President's defeat in his bid for re-election, the South switched parties and maintained a measure of power in Washington. The most conspicuous new ambassadors of the region in the nation's capital are Republicans, and, at least presently, they are generally in tune with the rest of the country. These Republicans pose no threat to the traditional balance in the South; there is virtually no reason to expect that they will attempt to bring black power into play again. On the contrary, there is no history among the best known and most powerful of Southern Republicans in Congress that would lead one to suspect that they might favor black people in any substantial way. The long-sought two-party South has arrived, but it promises no revolution in either race relations or Southern culture, and it offers no invitation to the North to attempt again to reconstruct the South in its own image.

As the Southern white elite works to accommodate itself to Northern desires at the national and international level, local power is more assuredly in their hands. They can yield or not yield, as they choose, a great deal to black people without significantly threatening their power at home. After their momentary fright in the 1950s and 1960s, the Conservative elite in the South has come to realize that the civil-rights movement has resulted in no great revolution in race relations. In spite of strenuous efforts to do so, it has not pushed the power line back again toward an alliance between the white elite and the black mass, and there is no compelling evidence that the white mass and the black mass might soon combine against the white elite. The revolutionary but tentative experiments of Reconstruction and the Populist era on that bottom line were repeated with much the same result. Things are better, and blacks are more free in this last quarter of the twentieth century; but while the white elite might not have everything just the way they want it all the time in relations with black people, they generally have them so. On the other hand, over time they virtually always get exactly what they want from the mass of white people. The self-conscious all-white communion is still in place in the South, and, sadly, it is spreading to cover the nation. The Black Revolution appears to have been literally that, a revolution of awareness on the black side of the line not the white. Indeed, the Black Revolution seems, in a very large way, a reflection of the realization by black people that the all-white system still lives and grows and that the heartland of white exclusiveness remains intact.

There are, essentially, no such things as "black" people or "white" people. The overlapping of physical traits between the so-called races is so great that it is impossible to define a certain line to divide one group from another. Undeniably, there is a black culture and a white culture, but there is nothing in the physical structure of a person who seems to be white that precludes his or her being culturally black, any more than there is anything in one's physical structure that precludes one's being Moslem, Buddhist, or Chinese. Yet, it has happened that the power in the South has perceived a necessity for designating some people as black and keeping those people firmly separated from others called white. Physical separation has promoted cultural separation, and yet the separation has never been so great as to prevent a steady stream of interaction in which each culture took rather liberally from the other. The struggle to maintain distance in the face of inevitable and ongoing kinship has created a profound tension in Southern society. It is a tension that ramifies into areas of Southern life that seem to have nothing to do with race, and it is a tension that all America has come to share. The simple fact is that white America is married to black America by the space of national geography and by centuries of time. More importantly, they are married because each has given to each so much, and taken so much. Culturally, black America is so much white; and white America, in its stubborn and residual racial egotism, resists the realization of how very deeply and irreversibly black it is, and has been. The struggle against that awareness, the rage against the realization of their blackness and its legitimacy is the struggle of white people in race relations. To recognize and respect the blackness that is already within themselves would be to recognize and respect the blackness that is within the nation, and, functually, to surrender the uses, physical and psychological, that they have learned to make of blacks as a separate people. It is an unhappy world that white America has made, and it is unnecessary. Ultimately, there is no race problem in the South, or in America, that we, both black and white, do not make in our own minds.

NOTES

PREFACE

1. C. Vann Woodward, *The Strange Career of Jim Crow*, 1st ed. (New York: Oxford Univ. Press, 1955), xvii.
2. Vernon Lane Wharton, *The Negro in Mississippi, 1865–1890*, James Sprunt Studies in History and Political Science, Vol. XXVIII (Chapel Hill: Univ. of North Carolina Press, 1947); George Brown Tindall, *South Carolina Negroes, 1877–1900* (Columbia: Univ. of South Carolina Press, 1952); Charles E. Wynes, *Race Relations in Virginia, 1870–1902* (Charlottesville: Univ. of Virginia Press, 1961); Richard C. Wade, *Slavery in the Cities: The South, 1820–1860* (New York: Oxford Univ. Press, 1964).

INTRODUCTION

1. Wilbur J. Cash, *The Mind of the South* (New York: Knopf, 1941), 38–39, 83–85, 108-10.
2. Ralph Ellison, *Invisible Man* (New York: Random House, 1952).
3. Joseph L. Morrison, *W. J. Cash, Southern Prophet: A Biography and Reader* (New York: Knopf, 1967).
4. Marvin Meyers, *The Jacksonian Persuasion: Politics and Belief* (Stanford: Stanford Univ. Press, 1957), 9–10.
5. Arthur F. Wright, *The Confucian Persuasion* (Stanford: Stanford Univ. Press, 1960), 3.

I. THE GENESIS OF THE ORGANIC SOCIETY

1. Evarts Boutell Greene and Virginia D. Harrington, *American Population before the Federal Census of 1790* (New York: Columbia Univ. Press, 1932), 136–40, 125–26, 173; Abbott Emerson Smith, *Colonists in Bondage: White Servitude and Convict Labor in America, 1607–1776* (Chapel Hill, Univ. of North Carolina Press, 1947), 335; Peter H. Wood, *Black Majority: Negroes in Colonial South Carolina from 1670 through the Stono Rebellion* (New York: Knopf, 1974), 36.
2. Dumas Malone, *Jefferson and His Time*, 4 vols. (Boston: Little, Brown 1948), 1:20–21.
3. Malone, *Jefferson*, 1:222; Carl L. Becker, *The Declaration of Independence: A Study in the History of Political Ideas* (New York: Knopf, 1956), 212–14.

4. Malone, *Jefferson*, 1:413–14.

5. Eugene A. Berwanger, *The Frontier against Slavery: Western Anti-Negro Prejudice and the Slavery Extension Controversy* (Urbana: Univ. of Illinois Press, 1967), 7.

6. Arthur Zilversmit, *The First Emancipation: The Abolition of Slavery in the North* (Chicago: Univ. of Chicago Press, 1967).

7. Winthrop D. Jordan, *The White Man's Burden* (New York: Oxford Univ. Press, 1974), 201, 205–14.

8. Paul J. Staudenraus, *The African Colonization Movement, 1816–1865* (New York: Columbia Univ. Press, 1961), 23–35, 251.

9. Herbert Aptheker, *American Negro Slave Revolts* (New York: International Publishers, 1943), 298–300.

10. Joseph B. Robert, *The Road from Monticello: A Study of the Virginian Slavery Debate of 1832* (Durham: Duke Univ. Press, 1941), 31–32; Alison Goodyear Freehling, *Drift Toward Dissolution: The Virginia Debate of 1831–1832* (Baton Rouge: Louisiana State Univ. Press, 1982).

11. Bureau of the Census, *Negro Population in the United States, 1790–1915* (Washington, D. C.: Government Printing Office, 1918), 57.

12. Clement Eaton, *The Freedom of Thought Struggle in the Old South* (Durham: Duke Univ. Press, 1940), 113–14; John Hope Franklin, *The Free Negro in North Carolina* (New York: Russell & Russell, 1943), 223; Francis Butler Simkins and Robert Hilliard Woody, *South Carolina During Reconstruction* (Chapel Hill: Univ. of North Carolina Press, 1932), 383.

13. Ulrich B. Phillips, *American Negro Slavery: A Survey of the Supply, Employment and Control of Negro Labor as Determined by the Plantation Regime* (New York: Appleton, 1918), 497–98.

14. Howell Meadoes Henry, *The Police Control of the Slave in South Carolina* (Emory, Va.: n.p., 1914); Benjamin F. Callahan "The North Carolina Slave Patrol" (Master's thesis, University of North Carolina at Chapel Hill, 1973). There does not exist any comprehensive history of the patrol. The discussion in the text is drawn heavily from these two very detailed studies for South Carolina and North Carolina. I am especially indebted to Benjamin Callahan for the many references he made to the patrol in other Southern states.

15. James M. Merrill, *William Tecumseh Sherman* (New York: Rand McNally, 1971), 133–35.

16. Francis Butler Simkins and Robert Hilliard Woody, *South Carolina during Reconstruction* (Chapel Hill: Univ. of North Carolina Press, 1932), 381–83, 55; Joel Williamson, *After Slavery: The Negro in South Carolina during Reconstruction 1861–1877* (Chapel Hill: Univ. of North Carolina Press, 1965), 197, 198, 47.

17. Donald G. Mathews, *Religion in the Old South* (Chicago: Univ. of Chicago Press, 1977), 137–250.

18. William Sumner Jenkins, *Pro-Slavery Thought in the Old South* (Chapel Hill: Univ. of North Carolina Press, 1935).

19. Stanley M. Elkins argued otherwise in *Slavery: A Problem in American Institutional and Intellectual Life* (Chicago: Univ. of Chicago Press, 1959), esp. pp. 82–139.

20. Lawrence W. Levine, *Black Culture and Black Consciousness: Afro-American Folk Thought From Slavery to Freedom* (New York: Oxford Univ. Press 1977), 90–101.

21. The phrases are derived from David Riesman with Nathan Glaser and Reuel Denney, *The Lonely Crowd* (Garden City, N.Y.: Doubleday, 1953), 22.

22. Kenneth M. Stampp, *The Peculiar Institution: Slavery in the Ante-Bellum South* (New York: Knopf, 1956), 30–31.

23. Barbara Welter, "The Cult of True Womanhood," *American Quarterly* 18 *(Summer 1966): 151–74.*

24. David Donald, *Charles Sumner and the Coming of the Civil War* (New York: Knopf, 1960), 288–97.

25. Clement Eaton, *Jefferson Davis* (New York: Free Press, 1977), 3.

26. John Lide Wilson, *The Code of Honor: or Rules for the Government of Principals and Seconds in Duelling* (Charleston: Thomas J. Eccles, 1838 (rev. ed. 1858), 13, 16.

27. James Marion Sims, *The Story of My Life* (New York: Appleton, 1884), 88. For a thoroughly researched and highly thoughtful inquiry into the place of honor in the evolution of antebellum Southern culture, see: Bertram Wyatt-Brown *Southern Honor: Ethics and Behavior in the Old South* (New York: Oxford Univ. Press, 1982).

28. John Lide Wilson, *Cupid and Psyche: A mythological tale, from the "Golden Ass" of Apuleius. . . .* (Charleston: n.p., 1842).

29. John Lide Wilson, *Abstract of a System of Exercise and Instruction of Field Artillery, and the Exercise of Heavy Artillery in Battery and Some Directions for the Laboratory, Together with the Sword Exercise . . . , for the use of the South Carolina Militia* (Charleston: n.p., 1834), 57. I am indebted to William Henry Longton for first bringing John Lide Wilson's work to my attention. See: William Henry Longton, "Some Aspects of Intellectual Activity in Ante-bellum South Carolina, 1830–1860: An Introductory Study" (Ph.D. dissertation, Univ. of North Carolina at Chapel Hill, 1969), 379–81.

30. Economic historian Gavin Wright caught admirably the material basis for the sense of power and euphoria that came to Southern leadership in the 1850s. In that decade, for instance, he found that the value of slaves doubled while their numbers increased only 10 percent. In 1860 the average slaveholder was five times as rich as the average Northerner. In the South as a whole, almost a quarter of the whites belonged to slaveholding families, and in the lower South, the Cotton Kingdom, almost half did. It was but symptomatic of the Southern sense of self that James Henry Hammond of South Carolina could declare on the floor of the United States Senate in 1857, "Cotton is King." Gavin Wright, *The Political Economy of the Cotton South: Households, Mobility, and Wealth in the Nineteenth Century* (New York: Norton, 1978), 35–42, 88, 154.

31. Ira Berlin, *Slaves without Masters: The Free Negro in the Antebellum South* (New York: Pantheon, 1974), 316–18, 341–44; Joel Williamson, *New People: Miscegenation and Mulattoes in the United States* (New York: Free Press, 1980), 65–67, 75–76.

32. Williamson, *New People*, 63, 71, 73–75.

33. Richard C. Wade, *Slavery in the Cities: The South, 1820–1860* (New York: Oxford, Univ. Press 1964).

34. Edward A. Pollard, *Black Diamonds Gathered in the Darkey Homes of the South* (New York: Pudney & Russell, 1859). 54–58, 22; Jack Pendleton Maddex, Jr., *The Reconstruction of Edward A. Pollard: A Rebel's Conversion to Postbellum Unionism*, James Sprunt Studies in History and Political Science, vol. 54 (Chapel Hill: Univ. of North Carolina Press, 1975), 24–27, 34–35.

35. Pollard, *Black Diamonds*, 54.

36. Dorothy Ann Gay, "The Tangled Skein of Romanticism and Violence in the Old South: The Southern Response to Abolitionism and Feminism, 1830–1861" (Ph.D. dissertation, University of North Carolina at Chapel Hill, 1975), 133–65, esp. 147–48, 150–51.

37. Stampp, *The Peculiar Institution*, 322–82.

38. Ella Gertrude (Clanton) Thomas diary, May 2, June 24, 1855, Ella Gertrude (Clanton) Thomas Papers, Duke University, Durham, North Carolina.

39. "Recollections of a Life Time and More," Henry B. Ansell Recollections, Southern Historical Collection, University of North Carolina at Chapel Hill.

40. Williamson, *New People*, 64–65, 118.

41. Ibid., 42–59, esp. 55–59, 67–68.

42. Mary Boykin Chesnut, *Mary Chesnut's Civil War*, C. Vann Woodward (New Haven: Yale University Press, 1981), 168–69.

43. The story of the Townsends, black and white, is contained in the Townsend and Cabaniss Collection, University of Alabama, Tuscaloosa.

44. For a deeply researched and highly provocative view of how the slaveholders made their world and how that world was flawed, see: James Oakes, *The Ruling Race: A History of American Slaveholders* (New York, Knopf, 1982), esp. the Epilogue, "The Slaveholders' Revolution," 225–42.

II. BLACK LIFE IN THE SOUTH, 1865–1915

1. For an excellent and exhaustive description of black people in transition from slavery to freedom, see: Leon F. Litwack, *Been in the Storm So Long: The Emergence of Black Freedom in the South* (New York: Knopf, 1979).

2. R. B. Anderson to his wife, Sep. 11, 1865, R. B. Anderson Papers, Southern Historical Collection, University of North Carolina at Chapel Hill.

3. Ralph Ellison, *Invisible Man* (New York: Random House, 1952).

4. Charles N. Hunter to H. Schuyler (Rector of Trinity Church, Trenton, N.J.), Feb. 20, 1902, Charles Norton Hunter Papers, Duke University, Durham, N. C..

5. C. H. Hopkins, "Founder's Day Address," pp. 165–66, cited in Robert Glenn Sherer, Jr., "Let Us Make Man: Negro Education in Nineteenth Century Alabama" (Ph.D. dissertation, University of North Carolina at Chapel Hill, 1969), 169–71.

6. Lawrence D. Rice, *The Negro in Texas, 1874–1900* (Baton Rouge: Louisiana State Univ. Press, 1971), 246–50.

7. Franz Fanon, *The Wretched of the Earth* (New York: Grove Press, 1963). There is no modern study of violence among black people in the South in the post-Reconstruction decades. Highly suggestive is an article by Sheldon Hackney examining aspects of Southern violence between 1920 and 1964. Blacks in the South, Professor Hackney concluded, were much more likely (by a ratio of about two or three to one) to be involved in homicides than whites in Western civilization, in the North, or even in the South. Sheldon Hackney, "Southern Violence," *American Historical Review* 74 (Feb. 1969): 906–25.

8. James A. Whitted to Charles N. Hunter, Nov. 24, 1890, Hunter Papers.

9. Osborne Hunter, Jr., to George T. Wassom, Oct. 20, 1886, Hunter Papers.

10. Maggie Whiteman to George T. Wassom, Oct. 21, 1886, Hunter Papers.

11. G. W. Murray to Whitefield McKinlay, Nov. 14, 1898, Whitefield McKinlay Papers, Carter G. Woodson Collection, Library of Congress, Washington, D.C.

12. Booker T. Washington to T. Thomas Fortune, Nov. 7, 10, 1899, Booker T. Washington Papers, Manuscripts Division, Library of Congress, Washington, D.C.

13. Charles Waddell Chesnutt diary, July 22, 1875, Charles Waddell Chesnutt Collection, Fisk University Library, Nashville, Tenn.

14. Chesnutt diary, April 23, 1879; Helen M. Chesnutt, *Charles Waddell Chesnutt, Pioneer of the Color Line* (Chapel Hill: Univ. of North Carolina Press, 1952), 25. Charles Chesnutt's biography has been well done in Frances Richardson Keller, *An American Crusade: The Life of Charles Waddell Chesnutt* (Provo, Utah: Brigham Young Univ. Press, 1978). For a well-balanced and insightful treatment of his writings see: William L. Andrews, *The Literary Career of Charles W. Chesnutt* (Baton Rouge: Louisiana State Univ. Press, 1980).

15. Chesnutt diary, June 7, 1875.

16. Ibid., July 31, 1875.

17. Interestingly and probably revealingly, Chesnutt wrote "nigger wenches" in his journal and then, apparently upon second thought, lined out "nigger." Possibly he resented the romantic interest of some of the darker young women in him. Ibid., Aug. 23, 20, 1875.

18. Ibid., April 23, 1879.

19. Charles Waddell Chesnutt journal, II, n.d. [early summer, 1879], Chesnutt Collection.

20. Chesnutt diary, April 23, 1879.

21. Ibid., March 30, 1880.

22. Ibid., May 8, 1880.

23. Ibid., May 29, 1880.

24. Ibid., June 25, 1880

25. Ibid., March 16, 1880.

26. Ibid., May 29, 1880.

27. Chesnutt journal, July 7, 1880.

28. Ibid., Jan. 3, 1881.

29. Ibid., Feb. 2, March 4, May 4, 1881; Feb. 18, 1882.

30. Ibid., March 7, 1882.

31. Ibid., March 7, 1882.

32. Letter of recommendation from T. D. Haigh, June 27, 1883, Chesnutt Collection.

33. C. N. Hunter to J. A. Dodson, May 27, 1907, Hunter Papers.

34. C. N. Hunter to H. Schuyler, Feb. 20, 1902, Hunter Papers.

35. Emancipation Day Address in Raleigh, 1910, Hunter Papers.

36. Letters to C. N. Hunter from Kemp Battle, Jr., Oct. 28; Ernest Haywood, Oct. 28; and Thomas M. Gorman (secretary to Julian S. Carr) Oct. 24, 1913, Hunter Papers.

37. H. A. Parris to C. N. Hunter, Aug. 23, 1913, Hunter Papers.

38. George W. Henderson to Charles W. Chesnutt, Feb. 28, 1899, Chesnutt Collection.

39. For a comprehensive and exhaustive treatment of black thought in this era, see: August Meier, *Negro Thought in America, 1880–1915: Racial Ideologies in the Age of Booker T. Washington* (Ann Arbor: Univ. of Michigan Press, 1963).

40. Louis R. Harlan, *Booker T. Washington: The Making of a Black Leader, 1856–1901* (New York: Oxford Univ. Press, 1972), 204–21.

41. Ibid., 308–9.

42. W. E. B. DuBois, "Strivings of the Negro People," *The Atlantic Monthly* 80 (Aug. 1897): 194–98: *The Conservation of Races,* American Negro Academy, Occasional Papers, Paper No. 2, 1897.

43. Meier, *Negro Thought in America,* 178.

44. Ibid., 178–79.

45. Ibid., 181–83.

46. For a close description of the connection between the abolitionists and the NAACP see: James M. McPherson, *The Abolitionist Legacy: From Reconstruction to the NAACP* (Princeton Univ. Press, 1975), esp. 385–93.

47. Charles W. Chesnutt to Hugh M. Browne, June 20, 1908, Chesnutt Collection.

48. The distance, and the lack of distance, between Washington and DuBois, has been carefully measured by Louis R. Harlan in the second and final volume of his deeply researched biography of the Tuskegean. Louis R. Harlan, *Booker T. Washington: The Wizard of Tuskegee,* 1901–1915 (New York: Oxford Univ. Press, 1983), esp. 84–85, 174–75.

III. THE CONSERVATIVE RESTORATION AND THE LIBERAL REVOLT

1. S. W. Ferguson to Theodore G. Barker, January 7, 1876, Martin Witherspoon Gary Papers, South Caroliniana Library, University of South Carolina, Columbia.

2. Joel Williamson, *After Slavery: The Negro in South Carolina During Reconstruction, 1861–1877* (Chapel Hill: Univ. of North Carolina Press, 1965), 408–12.

3. Charles Waddell Chesnutt diary, March 25, 1880, Charles Waddell Chesnutt Collection, Fisk University, Nashville, Tenn..

4. Chesnutt diary, Jan. 15, 1881.

5. Harold W. Mann, *Atticus Greene Haygood: Methodist Bishop, Editor, and Educator* (Athens: Univ. of Georgia Press, 1965), *Passim*.

6. Atticus Greene Haygood, *Our Brother in Black, His Freedom and His Future* (New York: Phillips, 1881), *passim.*

7. Mann, *Haygood,* 190–91.

8. C. W. Miller to the *Advocate,* Sep. 8, 1883., Atticus Greene Haygood Collection, Emory University, Atlanta.

9. G. G. Smith to the *Advocate,* March 4, 1882, Haygood Collection.

10. *The Wesleyan Christian Advocate,* Dec. 17, 1881, Haygood Collection.

11. "Changing for the Wrong Thing," A. G. Haygood to *The Wesleyan Christian Advocate,* Aug. 17, 1887, in "Some Lineage of Atticus G. Haygood," a notebook compiled by Mrs. Hugh T. Trotti, Haygood Collection.

12. Clipping from the Atlanta *Constitution,* March 27, 1962, Atticus Haygood Papers, Georgia State Department of Archives and History, Atlanta.

13. Warren A. Candler to R. J. Bigham, Sep. 21, 1899, Warren A. Candler Collection, Emory University, Atlanta.

14. R. M. Johnson to A. G. Haygood, Feb. 12, 1885, Haygood Papers.

15. *Advocate,* June 20, 1883, cited in Mann, *Haygood,* 190.

16. A. G. Haygood to W. A. Candler, Aug. 30, 1881, Candler Collection.

17. *Georgia Enterprise* (Covington), Feb. 9, 1882, cited in Mann, *Haygood,* 189.

18. Atticus G. Haygood, "The Negro Problem: God Takes Time—Man Must," a typescript for *The Methodist Review,* Sep.–Oct. 1895, Haygood Papers.

19. Arlin Turner, *George W. Cable: A Biography* (Durham, N.C.: Duke Univ. Press, 1956), 3–34.

20. Ibid., 46, 74–75.

21. Ibid., 13–78. Much of this material is from Cable's unpublished "My Politics," George Washington Cable Collection, Tulane University, New Orleans. See also: Louis R. Harlan, "Desegregation in New Orleans Public Schools during Reconstruction," *American Historical Review* 67 (April 1962): 663–75, esp. 671–72; John W. Blassingame, *Black New Orleans, 1860–1880* (Chicago: Univ. of Chicago Press, 1973), 112–22; and Roger A. Fischer, *The Segregation Struggle in Louisiana, 1862–77* (Urbana: Univ. of Illinois Press, 1974), 119–32.

22. Ibid., 131–49, 171–93, esp. 187.

23. Arlin Turner, "George W. Cable's Revolt against Literary Sectionalism," *Tulane Studies in English* 5 (1955): 5–27. Cable's speech is reprinted in Turner's article, note esp. pp. 20–21.

24. Turner, *Cable,* 158–59, citing "My Politics."

25. "The Freedman's Case in Equity." *Century Magazine* 29 (Jan. 1885): 409–18.

26. Ibid., 415-16.

27. Turner, *Cable,* 207.

28. New Orleans *Times-Democrat,* Jan. 11, 22, 26, 1885, cited in Mary Scott Duchien, "Research on Charles Etienne Arthur Gayarré" (Master's Thesis, Louisiana State University, 1934), 85–86.

29. Duchien, "Gayarré," 87–89, 103, 105–110.

30. C. E. A. Gayarré to Mrs. King (probably the mother of Grace King), March 16, 1885, Charles E. A. Gayarré Papers, Grace King Collection, Department of Archives, Louisiana State University, Baton Rouge.

31. Marion A. Baker to George W. Cable, Feb. 5, 1885, Cable Collection.

32. Marion A. Baker to G. W. Cable, June 19, 1885, Cable Collection.

33. Paul M. Gaston, *The New South Creed; A Study in Southern Mythmaking* (New York: Knopf, 1970), 17–18, 48–49; Henry W. Grady, "In Plain Black and White," *Century Magazine* 29 (April 1885): 909–17.

34. George Washington Cable, "The Silent South," *Century Magazine* 30 (Sep. 1885): 674–91.

35. P. H. Hayne to "My Dear Friend," Aug. 23, 1883, Paul Hamilton Hayne Papers, Duke University, Durham.

36. P. H. Hayne to "My Dear Friend," Dec. 16, 1884, Hayne Papers.

37. P. H. Hayne to C. E. A. Gayarré, Jan. 18; February 4, 1885, Hayne Papers.

38. P. H. Hayne to "My Dear Friend," Jan. 22, 1885, Hayne Papers.

39. P. H. Hayne to "My Dear Friend," May 19, 1885, Hayne Papers.

40. E. A. Gayarré to "My Dear and most valued Friend," [P. H. Hayne], May 1885, Hayne Papers.

41. C. E. A. Gayarré to P. H. Hayne, Jan. 23, 1885; P. H. Hayne to C. E. A. Gayarré, Jan. 29, Sep. 17, 1885, Hayne Papers.

42. C. E. A. Gayarré to "My Dear Mrs. Hayne," July 1, 1885, Hayne Papers.

43. P. H. Hayne to C. E. A. Gayarré, Feb. 4, 1885, Hayne Papers.

44. P. H. Hayne to "My Dear Judge Gayarré," April 14, 1885, Hayne Papers.

45. C. E. A. Gayarré to "My Dear Mr. Hayne," April 17, 1885, Hayne Papers.

46. Turner, *Cable*, 223.

47. P. H. Hayne to "Mr. Dear and Honored Friend," Sep. 17, 1885, Hayne Papers.

48. *Nashville American*, Jan. 12, 1890, cited in Turner, *Cable*, 268–69.

49. Turner, *Cable*, 242–72.

50. William H. Harris to W. M. Baskerville, May 20, 1889, Cable Collection.

51. William R. Moore to Atticus G. Haygood, Jan. 23, 1889, Cable Collection.

52. R. Bingham to G. W. Cable, Feb. 13, 1889, Cable Collection.

53. Randall M. Ewing to W. M. Baskervill, June 2, 1889, Cable Collection.

54. J. S. Brown to W. M. Baskervill, May 23, 1889, Cable Collection.

IV. THE RISE OF THE RADICALS

1. Newspaper clipping, folder labeled "Racial Problems," Rebecca Latimer Felton Papers, University of Georgia, Athens.

2. William M. Baskervill to George Washington Cable, December 5, 1888, G. W. Cable Collection, Tulane University Library, New Orleans.

3. Clarkson's story can be traced in the voluminous James S. Clarkson Papers, Manuscripts Division, Library of Congress, Washington, D.C.

4. Allen J. Going, "The South and the Blair Education Bill," *Mississippi Valley Historical Review* 44 (Sep. 1957): 267–90.

5. Richard E. Welch, Jr., "The Federal Elections Bill of 1890: Postscripts and Prelude," *Journal of American History* 52 (Dec. 1965): 511–26, esp. 524. See also: James M. McPherson, *The Abolitionist Legacy: From Reconstruction to the NAACP* (Princeton: Princeton Univ. Press, 1975), 128–37.

6. William F. Holmes, "Whitecapping: Agrarian Violence in Mississippi, 1902–1906," *Journal of Southern History* 35 (May 1969): 166–67.

7. William F. Holmes, *The White Chief: James Kimble Vardaman* (Baton Rouge: Louisiana State Univ. Press, 1970), 134–45.

8. Bureau of the Census, *Negro Population in the United States, 1790–1915* (Washington, D.C.: Government Printing Office, 1918), 558.

9. Tillman gave this speech many times. This particular version is from the *Congressional Record*, 59th Cong., 2d sess. (Jan. 21, 1907) 41: 1441.

10. One close student of lynching thought in 1905 that interest in the subject had increased markedly only after about 1891. James Elbert Cutler, *Lynch-Law, an Investigation into the History of Lynching in the United States* (New York: Longmans, Green, 1905), 155.

11. A study published in 1905 indicated that of the 2,060 blacks lynched in the twenty-two years, 1881–1903, only 34.3 percent were accused of assaults or attempted assaults upon females. Ibid., 171, 174, 175.

12. The *Chicago Tribune*, beginning in 1882, was the pioneer in collecting statistics concerning lynching. In the 1890s Tuskegee Institute followed suit, significantly backdating its count to begin with the year 1889. Finally the NAACP picked up the count

in its publication, *Thirty Years of Lynching in the United States, 1889–1918* (New York: NAACP, 1919), 30, and supplements published through 1931.

13. Atticus Greene Haygood, "The Black Shadow in the South," *Forum* 16 (Oct. 1893): 167–75.

14. George Harvey, "The New Negro Crime," *Harper's Weekly* 48 (Jan. 23, 1904): 120–21.

15. Charles Carroll, *The Negro a Beast: or In the Image of God* (St. Louis: Adanier, 1900).

16. It is striking that from neither the Conservative nor the Radical camp was there a multi-authored widely accepted *Summa Theologica* of racism as there had been at least two such grandly synthetic statements defending slavery published in the last decade before the war: William Harper *et al., The Pro-Slavery Argument* as maintained by the most distinguished writers of the Southern states. . . . (Charleston, Walker, Richard & Co., 1852); and E[benezer] N[ewton] Elliott *et al., Cotton Is King, and Pro-Slavery Arguments.* . . . (Augusta, Ga.: Pritchard, Abbott & Loomis, 1860).

17. Nathaniel Southgate Shaler, "The Negro Problem," *Atlantic Monthly* 54 (Nov. 1884): 703.

18. Nathaniel Southgate Shaler, "Science and the African Problem," *Atlantic Monthly* 66 (July 1890): 42.

19. Nathaniel Southgate Shaler, *The Neighbor: The Natural History of Human Contacts* (Boston and New York: Houghton Mifflin, 1904), 34, 134, 136, 148–49.

20. Ibid., 151–54, 186–89.

21. Phillip Alexander Bruce, *The Plantation Negro as a Freeman* (New York: Putnam, 1889), 129, 256, 83, 84.

22. Frederick L. Hoffman, *Race Traits and Tendencies of the American Negro,* Publications of the American Economic Association (New York: Macmillan, 1896), 52, 55, 60, 95.

23. Ibid., pp. 220, 229, 230, 217, 230–31.

24. Ibid., pp. 329, 312.

25. Frederick L. Hoffman, *History of the Prudential Insurance Company of America [Industrial Insurance] 1875–1900,* prepared for the Paris Exposition of Nineteen Hundred (n.p.: Prudential Press, 1900), 137, 138, 201, 153, 211.

26. Walter Burdette Weare, *Black Business in the New South: A Social History of the North Carolina Mutual Life Insurance Company* (Urbana: Univ. of Illinois Press, 1973), 3–4, 16, 16 fn.44, 24 fn.64.

27. Harry Herbert Pace, "The Attitudes of Life Insurance Companies Toward Negroes," *Southern Workman* 57 (Jan. 1928): 4–5.

28. *The National Cyclopaedia of American Biography* (New York: James T. White, 1930), Vol. A, 345–46: Hugh C. Bailey, *Edgar Gardner Murphy: Gentle Progressive* (Coral Gables, Fla.: Univ. of Miami Press, 1968), 46; Walter F. Willcox in Joseph Alexander Tillinghast, *The Negro in Africa and America,* Publications of the American Economic Association, 3rd Series, Vol. III, No. 2 (May 1902): 1–231, printed by Macmillan, New York, p. i.

29. *National Cyclopaedia,* Vol. 7, 474; *America's Race Problems: Addresses at the Annual Meeting of the American Academy of Political and Social Science,* Philadelphia, April Twelfth and Thirteenth, MCMI (published for the Academy by McClure, Phillips & Co., New York, 1901), 198–99.

30. Hilary A. Herbert, "The Race Problem at the South," Publication of the American Academy of Political and Social Sciences No. 309. Undated. Hilary A. Herbert Papers, Southern Historical Collection, University of North Carolina at Chapel Hill.

31. Rebecca Latimer Felton, *Country Life in Georgia in the Days of My Youth* (Atlanta: Index Publishing Co., 1919), 58, 60, 62, 72, and *passim.*

32. John E. Talmadge, *Rebecca Latimer Felton: Nine Stormy Decades* (Athens: Univ. of Georgia Press, 1960), 20, citing *Atlanta Journal,* Nov. 11, 1928. See also: Scrapbook 24, p. 33; Scrapbook 32, p. 7, Felton Papers.

33. *Country Life,* 85–86, 88–89.

34. Talmadge, *Felton,* 22–136, *passim.*

35. Rebecca L. Felton to W. H. Felton, March 15, 1893, Felton Papers.

36. Leonidas F. Scott to R. L. Felton, May 30, 1894, Felton Papers.

37. Rebecca L. Felton to the Atlanta *Constitution,* December 19, 1898, clipping in Scrapbook 24, pp. 76–77, Felton Papers.

38. Clipping, Felton Papers.

39. Rebecca L. Felton to the Atlanta *Constitution,* Dec. 19, 1898, Scrapbook 24, pp. 76–77, Felton Papers.

40. Charles E. Felton (no relation) to R. L. Felton, Nov. 17, 1898, Felton Papers.

41. Fannie H. Williams to R. L. Felton, Nov. 18, 1898, Felton Papers. See also: Thomas L. Collins to R. L. Felton, Nov. 24, 1898; Ulla G. Hardeman to R. L. Felton, Dec. 22, 1898; D. P. Hale to R. L. Felton, Dec. 27, 1898; J. A. Cunningham to R. L. Felton, Jan. 1, 1899; "One of Southern warp Northern woof" to R. L. Felton, Aug. 16, 1900, Felton Papers.

42. John Temple Graves to Rebecca L. Felton, Oct. 16, 1899; T. W. Watson to Rebecca L. Felton, July 9, July 18, 1902, Felton Papers.

43. Ms., "Race Antipathy in the United States," and Ms. of a revision entitled, "The Race Problem in the United States," Felton Papers.

44. The account that follows draws heavily upon a close reading of the Benjamin Ryan Tillman Papers in the Robert Muldrow Library, Clemson University, Clemson, S. C.. General biographical information is drawn from Francis Butler Simkins, *Pitchfork Ben Tillman: South Carolinian* (Baton Rouge: Louisiana State Univ. Press, 1944).

45. G. W. Shell to B. R. Tillman, October 14, 1889, Tillman Papers.

46. W. T. Martin to B. R. Tillman, Oct. 16, 1890; Tillman Papers.

47. W. H. C. to B. R. Tillman, Oct. 21, 1890; W. T. Martin to B. R. Tillman, Oct. 22, 1890;

48. Printed "Inaugural Address," Dec. 4, 1890, John [?] H. Woodrow, State Printer, Columbia, S. C., Tillman Papers.

49. Ibid.

50. B. R. Tillman to John M. Nicholls, Sep. 29, 1891, Letterbooks, Tillman Papers.

51. Quoted in the Charleston *News and Courier,* July 7, 1892. For similar expressions, see Tillman's own letters to _____. _____. Hall, June 1, 1892, and to William J. McPherson, July 1, 1892, Tillman Papers.

52. D. H. Thompkins to S. G. Mayfield, April 18, 1893, Tillman Papers.

53. Simkins, *Tillman,* 224–25, citing the Columbia *State,* April 26, 1893.

54. Typescript, Tillman Papers. Apparently an autobiography, probably dictated by Tillman, the typescript bears corrections in ink written in Tillman's hand. See also: The act as passed in *Statutes of South Carolina,* vol. 20, p. 1084; then repealed in vol. 21, p. 429.

55. Cutler, *Lynch-Law,* 183.

56. Simkins, *Tillman,* 296; George Brown Tindall, "The South Carolina Constitutional Convention of 1895" (Unpublished master's thesis, University of North Carolina at Chapel Hill, 1948), 66, 152–53.

57. *Congressional Record,* 57th Cong, 2d sess. (Feb. 19, 1903) 36: 2564, 2556–66. See also: B. R. Tillman to B. R. Tillman, Jr., Nov. 17, 1913, Tillman Papers.

58. *Congressional Record,* 57th Cong. 2d sess. (Feb. 23, 1903) 36: 2511–15.

59. Ibid., 56th Cong., 1st sess. (Feb. 26, 1900) 33: 2245.

60. Baltimore *American,* Jan. 5, 1907, cited in *Congressional Record,* 59th Cong., 2d sess. (Jan. 21, 1903) 36: 1044.

61. *Congressional Record,* 57th Cong., 2d sess. (Feb. 24, 1903) 36: 2564–65. See also: B. R. Tillman to _____. _____. Chandler, Nov. 25, 1911; B. R. Tillman to Sophia Tillman Hughes (his daughter), May 4, 1912, Tillman Papers.

62. B. R. Tillman to Captain Moorer, March 4, 1912; B. R. Tillman to A. E. Leland, Dec. 8, 1911, Tillman Papers.

63. See Simkins, *Tillman,* 23–37, for a highly perceptive discussion of Tillman's youth.

64. *Congressional Record,* 57th Cong., 2d sess. (Feb. 23, 1903) 36: 2512, (Feb. 24, 1903) 36: 2564–65.

65. Manuscript, "My Childhood Days," Tillman Papers.

V. TOM DIXON AND *THE LEOPARD'S SPOTS*

1. Thomas Dixon, Jr., *The Leopard's Spots: A Romance of the White Man's Burden—1875–1900* (New York: Doubleday, Page 1902).

2. Raymond Allen Cook, *Fire from the Flint: The Amazing Careers of Thomas Dixon* (Winston-Salem, N. C.: John F. Blair, 1968), 3–6. Much of the following account of Dixon's personal life is taken from Professor Cook's study. He, in turn, was privileged to use "Southern Horizons," an autobiography Dixon wrote in his last years and never published.

3. Thomas Dixon, Jr., to Helen Dixon, February 26, 1927, Amzi Clarence Dixon Papers, Archives of the Baptist Historical Society, Nashville, Tennessee.

4. Cook, *Fire from the Flint,* 8–12, 20–21.

5. Ibid., 35–49.

6. Ibid., 50–52.

7. Mollie to "My dear Parents," [May?] 23, 1884, Dixon Papers.

8. Cook, *Fire from the Flint,* 55–56.

9. Ibid., 56–61.

10. Ibid., 61, 64–65.

11. Ibid., 63–64, 65–66.

12. Ibid., 67–73.

13. Ibid., 73–81.

14. Ibid., 90, citing the N.Y. *Times,* March 11, 1895, p. 8.

15. Ibid., 91.

16. Ibid., 91–95.

17. Thomas Dixon, Jr., to Marion Butler, December 16, 1896, Marion Butler Papers, Southern Historical Collection, University of North Carolina at Chapel Hill.

18. Thomas Dixon, Jr., to Marion Butler, April 19, 1898, Butler Papers.

19. Thomas Dixon, Jr., to Marion Butler, June 27, 1898, Butler Papers.

20. Cook, *Fire from the Flint,* 95–97.

21. Ibid., 95–97, 101–2.

22. Ibid., 105–12.

23. Thomas Dixon to Helen Dixon, February 26, 1927, Dixon Papers.

24. Thomas Dixon to Helen Dixon, March 2, [1927], Dixon Papers.

25. Thomas Dixon to Helen Dixon, January 10, 1929, Dixon Papers.

26. Helen C. A. Dixon, *A. C. Dixon: A Romance of Preaching* (New York: Putnam, 1931), 9–12.

27. Cook, *Fire from the Flint,* 28–29, 66.

28. Ibid., 38–40.

29. Thomas Dixon to Helen Dixon, February 26, 1927, Dixon Papers.

30. Dixon, *The Leopard's Spots,* 326.

31. "White nigger" was a term that came to be used especially in the white supremacy campaign in North Carolina in 1898. For instance, in that year a Populist leader overheard Robert Glenn, a future governor of the state, declare that the Democrats

needed to make their race on issues of "the white man's rule" and "down with the white-niggers." Morrison Caldwell to Marion Butler, May 30, 1898, Butler Papers.

32. Dixon, *The Leopard's Spots, 101–02.*
33. Thomas Dixon to Helen Dixon, February 26, 1917, Dixon Papers.
34. Dixon, *The Leopard's Spots,* 30–32.
35. Ibid., 32, 140.
36. Ibid., 449.
37. Ibid., 81.
38. Ibid., 82.
39. Ibid., 256–64, 321–27.
40. Cook, *Fire from the Flint,* 21–23.
41. Thomas Dixon, Jr., *The One Woman* (New York: Doubleday, Page, 1903).
42. Cook, *Fire from the Flint,* 17–18.
43. Dixon, *The Leopard's Spots,* 245.
44. Ibid., 443, 445-46.
45. Ibid., 125–26.
46. Thomas Dixon to Helen Dixon, February 26, 1927, Dixon Papers.
47. Dixon, *The Leopard's Spots,* 371–75.
48. Cook, *Fire from the Flint,* 126, 131.
49. Dixon, *The Clansman,* (New York: Doubleday, Page, 1905) 303–8.
50. Ibid., 302–14, 317.
51. Cook, *Fire from the Flint,* 137–38.
52. Ibid., 122.
53. Dixon, *The One Woman.*
54. Cook, *Fire from the Flint,* p. 149.
55. Ibid., 116, citing letter dated May 10, 1902, private papers of Clara Dixon Richardson.
56. Ibid., 153–56.
57. Ibid., 150–53.
58. Ibid., 161–68.
59. Ibid., 169–73.
60. Ibid., 184–202, 208–12, 223–26.
61. "Governor Vardaman on the Negro," *Current Literature* 36 (March 1904): 270–71.
62. Thomas Nelson Page, "The Lynching of Negroes—Its Cause and Its Prevention," *North American Review* 178 (January 1904): 36–46.
63. Allen W. Trelease, *White Terror, The Ku Klux Klan Conspiracy and Southern Reconstruction* (New York: Harper and Row, 1971), 172.

VI. IN VIOLENCE VERITAS

1. For an excellent and exhaustive account of the kind of interracial violence that occurred in Reconstruction, see: Allen W. Trelease, *White Terror, The Ku Klux Klan Conspiracy and Southern Reconstruction* (New York: Harper and Row, 1971).
2. *The Caucasian,* Sep. 26, 1889.
3. Ibid , Oct. 31, 1889.
4. Ibid., Sep. 10, 1891.
5. The National Association for the Advancement of Colored People, *Thirty Years of Lynching in the United States, 1889–1918* (New York: NAACP, 1919); James Elbert Cutler, *Lynch-Law, an Investigation into the History of Lynching in the United States* (New York: Longmans, Green, 1905); Frederick L. Hoffman, *Race Traits and Tendencies of the American Negro,* Publications of the American Economic Association (New York: Macmillan, 1896).
6. Atticus Greene Haygood, "The Black Shadow in the South," *Forum* 16 (Oct. 1893): 167–75.

7. B. O. Flower, "The Burning of Negroes in the South: A Protest and a Warning," *Arena* 7 (April 1893): 630–40. Flower took his description from a local resident who also sent him a clipping from the St. Louis *Daily Republic*. See also: Robert Wilson Shufeldt, *The Negro a Menace to American Civilization* (Boston: R. G. Badger, 1907) 138–39.

8. Shufeldt, *The Negro a Menace*, 117–38, 224.

9. Thomas Dixon, Jr., *The Leopard's Spots* (New York: Doubleday, Page, 1902), 378.

10. Albert Bushnell Hart, "The Outcome of the Southern Race Question," *North American Review* 188 (June 1908): 56.

11. George Brown Tindall, *South Carolina Negroes, 1877–1900* (Columbia: Univ. of South Carolina Press, 1952), 255–56, citing the Charleston *News and Courier*, Feb. 23, 1898.

12. Edward T. Clark to Marion Butler, April 4, 1898; A. A. White to Marion Butler, March 21, 1898; James A. White to Marion Butler, March 18, 1898; Fabious H. Busbee to Marion Butler, March 17, 1898, Marion Butler Papers, Southern Historical Collection, University of North Carolina at Chapel Hill.

13. K. Leggett to Marion Butler, March 18, 1898, Butler Papers.

14. W. A. Dunn to Marion Butler, March 16; March 28, 1898, Butler Papers.

15. W. A. Dunn to Marion Butler, April 19, 1898, Butler Papers.

16. Ms. Affadavit of B. D. Webb, Scotland Neck, North Carolina, April 23, 1898, Butler Papers.

17. W. A. Dunn to Marion Butler, July 22, 1898, Butler Papers.

18. *Congressional Record*, 57th Cong., 2d sess. (Feb. 23, 1903) 36: 514–15.

19. Helen G. Edmonds, *Fusion Politics in North Carolina* (Chapel Hill: Univ. of North Carolina Press, 1951), 99. The cartoon was described to Helen Edmonds by Young's daughter in an interview. The charge was made in the *Democratic Handbook, 1898*, 146, 147–48.

20. Joseph Marion King to Marion Butler, Oct. 25, 1898, Butler Papers.

21. Benjamin F. Keith to Marion Butler, Oct. 26, November 2, 1898, and a rough draft of his withdrawal statement, n.d., Butler Papers.

22. Ms. letter of recommendation, John K. Ruffin, March 21, 1898; Ms. Commission; Ms. petition by several dozen citizens of Wilson, May 26, 1898 (a typed copy); "Mamma" (probably Mrs. H. G. Connor) to Kate, Nov. 13, Henry Groves Connor Papers, Southern Historical Collection, University of North Carolina at Chapel Hill.

23. Rountree's account is contained in a typescript, "Memorandum of My Personal Recollection of the Election of 1898," in the Connor Papers. While the authorship of the memorandum is not absolutely certain, Dr. Hugh T. Lefler, a senior North Carolina historian, attributed it to Rountree.

24. Wilmington *Record*, Aug. 18, 1898, North Carolina Collection, Wilson Library, University of North Carolina at Chapel Hill.

25. Clipping from the Atlanta *Journal*, n.d., Scrapbook, Felton Papers, University of Georgia.

26. The account that follows relies heavily upon the superb and close study of Robert Charles and the riot by William Ivy Hair, *Carnival of Fury: Robert Charles and the New Orleans Race Riot of 1900* (Baton Rouge: Louisiana State Univ. Press, 1976). For a survey of the city before the riot, see: Dale A. Somers, "Black and White in New Orleans: A Study in Urban Race Relations, 1865–1900," *Journal of Southern History* 40 (Feb. 1974), 1942. For Turner and the back-to-Africa movement, see: Edwin S. Redkey, *Black Exodus: Black Nationalist and Back-to-Africa Movements, 1890-1910* (New Haven: Yale Univ. Press, 1969). Edwin Redkey was the first scholar to give Robert Charles extended recognition. Before his book appeared, students could only read the sketch in John Smith Kendell, *History of New Orleans*, 3 vols. (Chicago: Lewis Publishing Company, 1922) 2: 538–40.

27. New Orleans *L'Abeille (The Bee)*, July 25–28, 1900.

28. Hair, *Carnival of Fury,* 184–85.

29. The account of the riot that follows relies heavily upon the intensive research accomplished by Professor Charles Crowe and published in *The Journal of Negro History* in two articles: "Racial Violence and Social Reform—Origins of the Atlanta Riot of 1906," *Journal of Negro History* 53 (July 1968): 234–56; and "Racial Massacre in Atlanta, Sep. 22, 1906," *Journal of Negro History* 54 (April 1969): 150–75.

30. B. R. Tillman to Dr. W. A. Ross, October 6, 1913, Benjamin Ryan Tillman Papers, Clemson University, Clemson, S. C.

31. Dewey W. Grantham, Jr., *Hoke Smith and the Politics of the New South* (Baton Rouge: Louisiana State Univ. Press, 1959), 3–21, 25, 40–55.

32. Ibid., 131-42.

33. For a close view of how Hoke Smith worked to take advantage of both the corporate rule and race issues in the around Clarke County (Athens), see the correspondence of his chief manager in the area, E. K. Lumpkin, for the period June 15-Aug. 18, 1906. Judge E. K. Lumpkin Papers, University of Georgia, Athens.

34. Grantham, *Hoke Smith* 142–54.

35. C. Vann Woodward, *Tom Watson: Agrarian Rebel* (New York: Macmillan, 1938), 379, citing the Atlanta *Journal,* Aug. 1, 1906.

36. Raymond Allen Cook, *Fire from the Flint: The Amazing Careers of Thomas Dixon* (Winston-Salem, N. C.: John F. Blair, 1968), 143, citing the Atlanta *Constitution,* Oct. 31, 1905, p. 2.

37. Ray Stannard Baker, "Following the Color Line," *American Magazine* 63 (April 1907):564–66.

38. Ibid., 566.

39. Ibid., 568.

40. Ibid., 570; *Southwestern Christian Advocate,* Sep. 27, 1906 (Vol. 40, No. 39).

41. Baker, "Following the Color Line," 570.

42. Ibid., 571–72.

43. Ernest Sevier Cox to Emma and Edward Pines, Sep. 29, 1906, Ernest Sevier Cox Papers, Duke University, Durham, N. C.

44. Two pages of this letter are in the "1905–1906" file of the Henry P. Farrow Papers, University of Georgia, Athens. Unfortunately, the remainder of the letter is missing. It is signed "Your devoted Mother" and was probably written by Mrs. Henry P. Farrow. The Farrows sometimes lived in Gainesville, and he was originally from the vicinity of Greensville, South Carolina; hence the reference to those towns. Interestingly, he was a leader in the Republican party in Georgia.

45. Baker, "Following the Color Line," 575–79.

VII. DEPOLITICALIZATION AND THE SEPARATION OF THE RACES

1. George Brown Tindall, *South Carolina Negroes, 1877–1900* (Columbia: Univ. of South Carolina Press, 1952), 56–58, 310, 286–88; B. R. Tillman to F. P. Colcock, May 30; June 3, 1913 (copies); B. R. Tillman to Mrs. Tillman, June 3, 1913 (copy), Benjamin Ryan Tillman Papers, Clemson University, Clemson, S. C..

2. The study of race relations in Tennessee after Reconstruction had been blessed by a rich flow of recent scholarship. For an excellent overview, see: Joseph H. Cartwright, *The Triumph of Jim Crow, Tennessee in the 1880's* (Knoxville: Univ. of Tennessee Press, 1977). For the story in Nashville, see: Howard N. Rabinowitz, *Race Relations in the Urban South, 1865–1890* (New York: Oxford Univ. Press, 1978), 283–98, 324–27. For a close description of how the black vote was reduced, see J. Morgan Kousser's superb study, *The Shaping of Southern Politics: Suffrage Restriction and the Establishment of the One-Party South, 1888–1910* (New Haven: Yale Univ. Press, 1974), 104–30.

3. Carl N. Degler, *The Other South: Southern Dissenters in the Nineteenth Century* (New York: Harper and Row, 1974), 270–315.

4. Quoted in C. Vann Woodward, *The Origins of the New South, 1877–1913* (Baton Rouge: Louisiana State Univ. Press, 1951), 340, citing *Proceedings of the Constitutional Convention of Alabama, 1901* 3: 2837, 2841; 4: 4302–03.

5. A close view of Braxton and the convention can be obtained from the Braxton Family Papers, a very large collection of letters, notes, and documents, held in the Alderman Library of the University of Virginia, Charlottesville. Much of what follows was taken from those papers.

6. A. C. Braxton to William A. Anderson, April 13, 1901, Braxton Family Papers.

7. A. C. Braxton to Fergus Reid, Nov 14, 1901, Braxton Family Papers.

8. A. C. Braxton to John T. Morgan, June 1; to Martin P. Burks, July 11, 1901, Braxton Family Papers.

9. E. W. Kruttschnitt to A. C. Braxton, Oct. 31, 1901; A. C. Braxton to "Secretary Constitutional Convention, Montgomery, Alabama," Sep. 6, 1901, Braxton Family Papers.

10. A. C. Braxton, duplicate texts to the governor and attorney general of Florida, Nov. 4, 1901; A. C. Braxton to the governor of Arkansas, Oct. 28, 1901, Braxton Family Papers.

11. Charles Curry to A. C. Braxton, July 19, 1901, Braxton Family Papers.

12. Braxton's notes for "Suffrage Conference," Braxton Family Papers.

13. W. Nevin Fishburne to A. C. Braxton, Dec. 6, 1901, Braxton Family Papers.

14. Braxton's notes for "Suffage Conference," Braxton Family Papers.

15. A. C. Braxton to R. D. Haislip, March 22, 1902, Braxton Family Papers.

16. A. C. Braxton to Robert Turnbull and many other members of the Convention, June 18, 1902, Braxton Family Papers.

17. Arthur Lincoln Tolson, "The Negro in Oklahoma Territory, 1889-1907: A Study in Racial Discrimination" (Ph.D. dissertation, University of Oklahoma, 1966), 117, 2.

18. Printed copy, "Republican Platform, adopted at the Tulsa Convention, August 1, 1907," 2-3, Coleman Collection, Oklahoma University Western Collection, University of Oklahoma, Norman.

19. Laura Clay to Benjamin R. Tillman, Dec. 31, 1906, Laura Clay Papers, University of Kentucky, Lexington.

20. Keith L. Bryant, Jr., *Alfalfa Bill Murray* (Norman: Univ. of Oklahoma Press, 1968), pp. 93–95

21. T. P. Gore, to R. L. Williams, Nov. 4, 1915, Governors' Papers, Oklahoma Archives, Oklahoma City.

22. Tom G. Taylor to R. L. Williams, Dec. 8, 1915, Governors' Papers. W. L. Garner, the representative from Choctaw County, made the same statement about the southeast. W. L. Garner to R. L. Williams, Nov. 6, 1915, Governors' Papers.

23. C. C. Hills (Washita) to R. L. Williams, Nov. 8, 1915; Lee Howe (Delaware) to R. L. Williams, November 11, 1915, Governors' Papers. See also: H. S. Sitton (Lawton) to R. L. Williams, Nov. 9, 1915, Governors' Papers.

24. Tolson, "The Negro in Oklahoma Territory," 150.

25. B. R. Tillman to J. R. Chandler, April 20, 1914, Tillman Papers.

26. B. R. Tillman to J. K. Vardaman, Oct. 8, 1913, Tillman Papers.

27. Ms., "The Race Problem in America" (probably written in 1916), "Speeches," Rebecca Latimer Felton Papers, University of Georgia, Athens.

28. In 1964, Richard C. Wade published the pioneer study of segregation in the immediately prewar South. He found that it was an urban phenomenon and came on strongly in the larger cities in the 1850s as the white elite moved to control blacks, slave and free, who were getting out of hand. See Richard C. Wade, *Slavery in the Cities: The South, 1820–1860* (New York: Oxford Univ. Press, 1964), 266–77. Ten years later Ira Berlin published an exhaustive and excellent history of free Negroes in the prewar South. He found that in the eighteenth century there were few places where

free blacks and whites might come together in ways that threatened the whites. By 1860, however, there had been a proliferation of these places as public institutions for the infirm and the criminal were established by states, various private organizations were founded, and public carriers came into being. "As these institutions and facilities appeared and grew," he concluded, "whites applied their racial assumptions by systematically excluding Negroes from or segregating Negroes within them." See Ira Berlin, *Slaves without Masters: The Free Negro in the Ante-bellum South* (New York: Pantheon, 1974), 321.-22, 383. Leon Litwack, publishing in 1961, found that segregation was by no means absent in the antebellum North. On the contrary, he concluded that segregation was the general rule in the North, in spite of steady opposition from the black community and some significant success for those efforts in Massachusetts. See Leon F. Litwack, *North of Slavery: The Negro in the Free States, 1790–1860* (Chicago: Univ. of Chicago Press, 1961), 97–100, 103–12.

29. The separation of the races on the urban frontier in the South in the generation after emancipation has been thoroughly studied in Howard N. Rabinowitz, *Race Relations in the Urban South,* 182–97.

30. Louis R. Harlan, "Disintegration in New Orleans Public Schools during Reconstruction," *American Historical Review* 67 (April 1961): 633–75.

31. *Proceedings of the Constitutional Convention of South Carolina Held in Charleston, South Carolina, beginning January 14th and ending March 17th, 1868* (Charleston, Denny & Perry, 1868), 691–94, 702–6.

32. Barnas Sears to R. C. Winthrop, Sep. 18, 1870, J. L. M. Curry Papers, Alabama Department of Archives and History, Montgomery.

33. Barnas Sears to Robert C. Winthrop, January 8, 1874, Curry Papers.

34. *Acts of the General Assembly of the State of Virginia, 1899–1900,* pp. 236–37; *Code of Virginia* (1904), 681.

35. George N. Henderson to C. N. Hunter, Nov. 3, 1892, Charles Norton Hunter Papers, Duke University, Durham, N. C.

36. For one view of the separation of cultures, see: Joel Williamson, *New People: Miscegenation and Mulattoes in America* (New York: Free Press, 1980).

37. For some comprehensive displays of names borne by black people, see Herbert G. Gutman, *The Black Family in Slavery and Freedom, 1750–1925* (New York: Pantheon, 1976), esp. Chart 1 facing p. 86, and Charts 14 and 15 facing p. 180.

38. William Ivy Hair, *Carnival of Fury: Robert Charles and the New Orleans Riot of 1900* (Baton Rouge: Louisiana State Univ. Press, 1976), 11–12.

39. Ray Stannard Baker, *Following the Color Line; An Account of Negro Citizenship in the American Democracy* (New York: Doubleday, Page, 1908).

VIII. THE CONSERVATIVE RESPONSE TO RADICALISM

1. Andrew H. Sledd, "The Negro: Another View," *Atlantic Monthly* 90 (July 1902): 65–73.

2. Atlanta *Constitution,* Aug. 3, 1902.

3. Madison Bell to Rebecca Felton, July 29, 1903 (misdated by the author, actually 1902); George T. Smith to Rebecca Felton, Aug. 4, 1902, Rebecca Latimer Felton Papers, University of Georgia, Athens.

4. Andrew H. Sledd to Warren A. Candler, Aug. 27, 1902, Warren A. Candler Collection, Emory University, Atlanta.

5. J. E. Dickey to W. A. Candler, Nov. 26, 1902, Candler Collection.

6. R. D. Bingham to W. A. Candler, Nov. 26, 1902, Candler Collection.

7. James E. Dickey to W. C. Lovett, Aug. 30, 1902; W. C. Lovett to W. A. Candler, Sept. 1, 1902; James E. Dickey to W. A. Candler, Nov. 26, 1902; W. A. Candler to James E. Dickey, Nov. 28, 1902; J. E. Dickey to W. A. Candler, Dec. 1, 1902; W. A. Candler to J. E. Dickey, Dec. 13, 1902, Candler Collection.

8. J. W. Madison to W. A. Candler, Sept. 9, 1903, Candler Collection.

9. W. A. Candler to J. T. Graves, Sept. 11, 1903, Candler Collection.

10. Peyton McCrary, "John Spencer Bassett: The Scholar as Social Critic" (Master's thesis, University of Virginia, 1966), 1-41, *passim.*

11. John Spencer Bassett, "Stirring up the Fires of Race Antipathy," *South Atlantic Quarterly* 2 (Oct. 1903): 297–305.

12. J. S. Bassett to Walter Hines Page, Feb. 8, 1904; Dec. 14, 1904, Walter Hines Page Papers, Houghton Library, Harvard University.

13. Raleigh *News and Observer,* Nov. 1, 1903.

14. Ibid., Nov. 27, 1903.

15. Resolutions of the Methodist Episcopal Church, Smithfield, Nov. 11, 1903, Trinity College Papers, Duke University, Durham, N. C.

16. John F. Bruton to James H. Southgate, Nov. 14, 1903, Trinity College Papers.

17. W. H. Page to Benjamin Duke, Thanksgiving Day, 1903, Trinity College Papers.

18. Jacob A. Long to James H. Southgate, Nov. 20, 1903, Trinity College Papers.

19. Warren A. Candler to James H. Southgate, November 30, 1903, Trinity College Papers.

20. Report of an interview with John Spencer Bassett, dated Nov. 7, 1903, by an archivist, Trinity College Papers. William K. Boyd added a note on June 1, 1910 to the effect that Professor Flowers, the manuscript collector, informed him that Kilgo was the reporter in this case.

21. Transcript of the diary of E. C. Perrow, Trinity College Papers.

22. A very rough manuscript, written in pencil, and apparently a first draft of the minutes of the meeting itself, Trinity College Papers.

23. James P. Albright to James H. Southgate, Dec. 3, 1903, Trinity College Papers.

24. Fred Peacock to B. N. Duke, Dec. 4, 1903, Trinity College Papers.

25. G. S. Bradshaw to J. G. Southgate, Dec. 4, 1903, Trinity College Papers.

26. H. K. Boyer to J. H. Southgate, Nov. 23, 1903; Jan. 12, 1904, Trinity College Papers.

27. The announcement of their decision by the Board of Trustees, Trinity College Papers.

28. "A Statement by the Faculty of Trinity College," Trinity College Papers.

29. J. S. Bassett to Charles Francis Adams, Jr., Nov. 3, 1911, Bassett Papers, Milton, Mass., cited in McCrary, "John Spencer Bassett," 106.

30. John Spencer Bassett, review of *The Leopard's Spots* in *South Atlantic Quarterly* 1 (April 1902): 188–89.

31. J. S. Bassett to H. B. Adams, Oct. 23, 1899 (photocopy), Herbert Baxter Adams Letters, Duke University, Durham, N. C.

32. J. S. Bassett to H. B. Adams, July 31, 1895, Adams Letters.

33. J. S. Bassett to H. B. Adams, Dec. 7, 1900, Adams Letters.

34. "Johns Hopkins Negro Lectures," "The Period of American Freedom," cited in McCrary, "John Spencer Bassett," 87–88.

35. J. S. Bassett to H. B. Adams, Oct. 23, 1899, Adams Letters.

36. J. S. Bassett to H. B. Adams, Sep. 26, 1897, Adams Letters.

37. J. S. Bassett to H. B. Adams, Dec. 16, 1898, Adams Letters.

38. J. S. Bassett to H. B. Adams, May 22, 1898, Adams Letters.

39. J. S. Bassett to W. H. Page, February 8, 1904, Dec. 14, 19__, Walter Hines Page Papers.

40. See, for example, Bassett's review of Moncure D. Conway's memoirs in *South Atlantic Quarterly* 4 (Jan. 1905): 82-9.

41. Printed handbill, with the results indicated in ink, "Craven Memorial Hall, Saturday Evening, December 17, 1904. . . ." Trinity College Papers.

42. J. S. Bassett to W. H. Page, May 29, 1906, Page Papers.

43. E. Robert Bennett to Joshua Kimber, June 6, 1910; Bishop Edwin G. Weed to Hugh L. Burleson, July 16, 1910, Papers of the Domestic and Foreign Missionary Society of the Protestant Episcopal Church, Church History Society, Austin, Texas.

44. Robert A. Gibson to David H. Greer and Edwin S. Lines, April 7, 1909: Edwin G. Weed to John W. Wood, March 12, 1909, Missions Papers.

45. Edwin G. Weed to John W. Wood, Feb. 7, 1907, Missions Papers.

46. Robert A. Gibson to David H. Greer and Edwin S. Lines, April 7, 1909, Missions Papers.

47. *National Cyclopaedia of American Biography* 33: 501–2.

48. Brooke G. White to S. Lloyd, May 28, 1900, Missions Papers.

49. W. A. Candler to "My Dear Doctor" (W. P. Thirkield) April 10, 1899, W. P. Thirkield Papers, Interdenominational Theological Center Library, Atlanta.

50. W. A. Candler Papers, Emory University, *passim.* The Candler Papers offer a very clear record of evangelical imperialism among Southern Methodists.

51. Davis C. Hill, "Southern Baptist Thought and Action in Race Relations, 1940–1950" (Ph.D. dissertation, Southern Baptist Theological Seminary, 1952), 16-19.

52. Terry Lawrence Jones, "Attitudes of Alabama Baptists toward Negroes, 1890–1914" (Master's thesis, Stamford University, Birmingham, Ala., 1968), *passim.*

53. Ibid., 48, 100–106.

54. Hugh A. Brimm, "The Social Consciousness of Southern Baptists in Relation to Some Regional Problems, 1910–1935" (Ph.D. dissertation, Southern Baptist Theological Seminary, 1944), 9–47, *passim.*

55. Jones, "Attitudes of Alabama Baptists," 38, 64, 76.

IX. INTERFACE: CONSERVATIVES AND RADICALS

1. C. Vann Woodward, *Tom Watson: Agrarian Rebel* (New York: Macmillan, 1938), 351–52, 381–82, 401–2.

2. Lewis Harvie Blair, *The Prosperity of the South Dependent upon the Elevation of the Negro (1889)*, ed. C. Vann Woodward (Boston: Little, Brown, 1964); Isaac DuBose Seabrook, *Before and After,* ed. John Hammond Moore (Baton Rouge: Louisiana State Univ. Press, 1967); Quincy Ewing, "The Heart of the Race Problem," *Atlantic Monthly* 103 (March 1909): 389–97. See also Charles E. Wynes, "Lewis Harvie Blair, Virginia Reformer: The Uplift of the Negro and Southern Prosperity," *Virginia Magazine of History and Biography* 72 (Jan. 1964): 3–18.
Classifying Lewis Harvie Blair as a Conservative poses a problem. If one takes the language in his 1889 book as the basis for judgment, then surely he did exhibit those qualities of open-endedness, adventurousness, and willingness to experiment that marked a Liberal. Furthermore, in publishing in *Arena* and speaking at the Chicago World's Fair he was persistently active in the cause. On the other hand, unlike Cable and Haygood, Blair finally defected. At some point before his death in 1916, he rejected his 1889 position. In an undated manuscript, he asserted that Negroes were permanently and inherently inferior to whites, and that "the only logical position for the Negro is absolute subordination to the whites." He called for the repeal of the Fourteenth and Fifteenth Amendments, complete disfranchisement, and total segregation. Thus, apparently, Blair ultimately approached, but did not achieve, a Radical position. His travel was unusual. Typically, when the Conservative became either a Radical or a Liberal, he or she remained so for life. Yet, at another level, Blair's shift is not shocking; it merely illustrates that extremes do meet. In this case, the straight line spectrum from Radical at the bottom through Conservative to Liberal at the top actually bends to the left at both extremes and touches ends to form a circle. The most extreme Liberal and the most extreme Radical join in their sense of the need to do something drastic, almost revolutionary, about the gap between where the Negro is and where he ought to be. Blair simply lost faith in the capacities of black people. It was not the first time that an

angel had fallen, nor the last. For Blair's transition, see: C. Vann Woodward's introduction to Blair, *The Prosperity of the South,* xliv–xlv.

3. Address to the Evengelical Ministerial Association of Atlanta, September 4, 1911, "Christianity and the Negro Problem in Georgia," William J. Northen Papers, Georgia Department of Archives and History, Atlanta.

4. W. J. Northen to B. M. Turner, Oct. 20, 1892, scrapbook, Northen Papers.

5. W. J. Northen to M. C. Hazzard, June 8, 1899, Northen Papers.

6. W. J. Northen to W. F. Willcox, Aug. 4, 1899, Northen Papers.

7. W. F. Willcox to W. J. Northen, Aug. 2, 1899, Northen Papers.

8. W. J. Northen to the editor of the Boston *Transcript,* June 23, 1899, Northen Papers.

9. Editorial in *The Fitzgerald Enterprise,* Feb. 26, 1907, Northen scrapbook, Northen Papers.

10. Typescript with emendations by Northen, probably written in the summer of 1907, Northen Papers.

11. Clipping from the Dublin (Georgia) *Courier Dispatch,* Nov. 23, 1909, Northen Papers.

12. "Christianity and the Negro Problem in Georgia," Northen Papers.

13. John I. Hall to W. J. Northen, March 27, 1899; W. J. Northen to the editor of *The Georgian,* March 18, 1906, Northen Papers.

14. W. J. Northen to Shailer Mathews, June 22, 1907, Northen Papers.

15. "Christianity and the Negro Problem in Georgia," Northen Papers.

16. W. J. Northen to Victor I. Masters, Dec. 18, 1911, Northen Papers.

17. John Spencer Bassett, "An Exile from the South," *South Atlantic Quarterly* 1 (Jan. 1905): 32–90.

18. William Watts Ball, *The State That Forgot: South Carolina's Surrender to Democracy* (Indianapolis: Bobbs-Merrill, 1932), 295.

19. Clement Eaton, *Freedom of Thought in the Old South* (Durham, N. C.: Duke Univ. Press, 1940), ix.

20. Thomas E. Watson to R. L. Felton, Nov. 6, 1908; March 1, 1909, Rebecca Latimer Felton Papers, University of Georgia, Athens.

21. Thomas Dixon to A. C. Dixon, Jan. 27, 1901, Amzi Clarence Dixon Papers, Archives of the Baptist Historical Society, Nashville, Tenn.; Raymond Allen Cook, *Fire from the Flint: The Amazing Careers of Thomas Dixon* (Winston-Salem, N. C.: John F. Blair, 1968), 39.

22. Andrew Sledd to W. A. Candler, Nov. 8, 1902, Warren A. Candler Collection, Emory University, Atlanta.

23. Edgar Gardner Murphy, "The Task of the Leader," *Sewanee Review* 15 (Jan. 1907): 5.

24. This ploy has been identified by Eric Berne in his book *Games People Play* as the game: "Now I've Got You, You Son-of-a-Bitch." In the game, the gamesman tracks the person who projects himself as perfect until he finds a flaw or discovers some peccadillo. The gamesman exposes the heretofore paragon of perfection to the public for condemnation or ridicule. The "payoff" is that the exposed person is rudely made conscious of the fact that he is not what he pretended to be, everyone knows it, and especially he knows that it is the gamesman personally who cut him down. According to Berne, it is a game that people play who are suffering from acute feelings of "jealous rage." Eric Berne, *Games People Play: The Psychology of Human Relationships* (New York: Grove Press, 1964), 85–87.

25. Rebecca Latimer Felton, *Country Life in Georgia in the Days of My Youth* (Atlanta: Index Publishing, 1919), 118.

26. For a very provocative discussion of this subject, see Carl Degler, *At Odds; Women and the Family in America from the Revolution to the Present* (New York: Oxford Univ. Press, 1980), especially his chapter entitled "Women's Sexuality in 19th-

Century America," 249-78. Professor Degler argues that it was women, not men, who were the prime movers in the reduction of sexual activity in the late nineteenth century.

27. William Faulkner, *Light in August* (New York: Harrison Smith and Robert Haas, 1932), 439-40.

28. Thomas Dixon, Jr., *The Leopard's Spots* (New York: Doubleday, Page, 1902), 39-40.

29. Ibid.

30. Raymond Allen Cook, *Fire from the Flint;* 73-79, 81-83.

31. Ulrich Bonnell Phillips, "The Central Theme of Southern History," *American Historical Review* 34 (Oct. 1928): 30-43.

32. Roger L. Ransom and Richard Sutch, *One Kind of Freedom: The Economic Consequences of Emancipation* (Cambridge Univ. Press, 1977), 195-96.

X. THE NORTH AND THE NEGRO IN THE SOUTH

1. Whipple N. Potter to Margaret Neel, Nov. 27, 1893; Margaret Neel to Whipple N. Potter, Nov. 29, 1893, Horace M. Bumstead Papers, Atlanta University, Atlanta, Ga..

2. M. D. Chase to "Mr. Hinck," July 9, 1894, Bumstead Papers.

3. Jenkins Lloyd Jones to Katherine M. Marvin, March 18, 1896; Thomas Van Ness to Katherine M. Marvin, Feb. 22, 1896, Bumstead Papers.

4. Edward T. Ware to "Miss Dodd," May 24, 1900, Bumstead Papers.

5. Warren W. Greene to Margaret Neel, Nov. 9, 1893; April 12, 1894; Warren W. Greene to Katherine M. Marvin, June 10, 1897, Bumstead Papers.

6. Mary E. Putney to Edward T. Ware, Feb. 12, 1913, Bumstead Papers.

7. Paul M. Gaston, *The New South Creed; A Study in Southern Myth-making* (New York: Knopf, 1970), 86-91.

8. Lyman Abbott to E. G. Murphy, Dec. 31, 1906, Edgar Gardner Murphy Papers, Southern Historical Collection, University of North Carolina at Chapel Hill.

9. Joseph H. Choate to E. G. Murphy, Jan. 26, 1906, Murphy Papers.

10. J. Thomas Heflin to J. K. Vardaman, Nov. 21, 1906, James K. Vardaman Papers, Mississippi Department of Archives and History, Jackson.

11. William F. Holmes, *The White Chief: James Kimble Vardaman* (Baton Rouge: Louisiana State Univ. Press, 1970), 198-99.

12. B. R. Tillman to S. B. Hershey, Sep. 14, 1901, Benjamin Ryan Tillman Papers, Clemson University, Clemson, S. C..

13. B. R. Tillman to John M. Maxwell, Dec. 5, 1906, Tillman Papers.

14. Brown McCrary to B. R. Tillman, March 13, 1913 (Iowa): C. N. Thompson to B. R. Tillman, March 12, 1913 (Minnesota); James T. Ronald to B. R. Tillman, March 17, 1913 (Washington), Tillman Papers.

15. Clipping from the Richmond *Times-Dispatch,* Feb. 7, 1905, Edwin A. Alderman Papers, University of Virginia, Charlottesville.

16. Charles W. Eliot to W. G. Brown, Jan. 18, 1909, William Garrott Brown Papers, Duke University, Durham, N. C.

17. Willard B. Gatewood, Jr., *Black Americans and the White Man's Burden, 1898-1903* (Urbana: Univ. of Illinois Press, 1975), 47-53.

18. C. P. Purvis to Whitefield McKinlay, July 29, 1909, Whitefield McKinlay Papers, Carter G. Woodson Collection, Manuscripts Division, Library of Congress, Washington, D. C.

19. George H. Lorimer to J. C. Harris, Nov. 23, 1899, Joel Chandler Harris Papers, Emory University, Atlanta, Ga.

20. C. M. Thompson to William Garrott Brown, Aug. 15, 1913, W. G. Brown Papers.

21. Hamilton Holt to W. G. Brown, June 18, 1909, Brown Papers.

22. Clipping from the Springfield *Republican,* July 1, 1909, Jacob McGavock Dickinson Papers, Tennessee State Library and Archives, Nashville.

23. Asa H. Gordon to "My Dear Friends," n.d. (probably 1913), Bumstead Papers.

XI. NORTHERN REPUBLICANS AND SOUTHERN RACE RELATIONS, 1895–1912

1. Vincent R. DeSantis, *Republicans Face the Southern Question: The New Departure Years, 1877–1897* (Baltimore: John Hopkins Univ. Press, 1959); Stanley P. Hirshon, *Farewell to the Bloody Shirt: Northern Republicans & the Southern Negro, 1877–93* (Bloomington: Indiana Univ. Press, 1962.)

2. Olive Hall Shadgett, *The Republican Party in Georgia, from Reconstruction through 1900* (Athens: Univ. of Georgia Press, 1964), 122–36.

3. Louis R. Harlan, *Booker T. Washington: The Making of a Black Leader 1865–1901* (New York: Oxford Univ. Press, 1972), 205–21.

4. Samuel R. Spencer, Jr., *Booker T. Washington and the Negro's Place in American Life* (Boston and Toronto: Little, Brown, 1955), 105.

5. For data concerning that reduction see: J. Morgan Kousser, *The Shaping of Southern Politics: Suffrage Restriction and the Establishment One-Party South, 1880–1910* (New Haven and London: Yale Univ. Press, 1974), 130.

6. Powell Clayton to H. L. Remmel, May 18, 1897, H. L. Remmell Papers, University of Arkansas, Fayetteville.

7. Clayton Powell to H. L. Remmel, June 7, 1897, Remmel Papers.

8. H. L. Remmel to Clayton Powell, Oct. 18, 1899, Remmel Papers.

9. Powell Clayton to R. L. Remmel, Oct. 23, Nov. 4, 1899, Remmel Papers.

10. Marcus A. Hanna to Richard A. McCurdy, June 21, 1900 (copy), Remmel Papers.

11. Powell Clayton to H. L. Remmel, Aug. 20, 1901, Remmel Papers.

12. Powell Clayton to Jacob Trieber, Nov. 6, 1901, Remmel Papers.

13. William Garrott Brown to C. W. Eliot, Jan. 26, 1908 (Brown misdated this letter; the year was actually 1909), William Garrott Brown Papers, Duke University Library.

14. Whitefield McKinlay to B. T. Washington, Oct. 28, 1901; B. T. Washington to Whitefield McKinlay, Oct. 31, 1901, Whitefield McKinlay Papers, Carter G. Woodson Collection, Manuscripts Division, Library of Congress, Washington, D.C.

15. Henry F. Pringle, *Theodore Roosevelt: A Biography* (London: Jonathan Cape, 1931), 249; Whitefield McKinlay to B. T. Washington, Oct. 28, 1901, McKinlay Papers.

16. Warrington Dawson to Major Daniel L. Sinkler, Nov. 14, 1934, Francis Warrington Dawson, II, Papers, Duke University, Durham, N. C. See also: Francis W. Dawson, II, *Le Negre aux Etats-Unis* (Paris, Libraire Orientale & Americaine, 1912), 201–2; and Isaac Fisher to B. T. Washington, March 26, 1912, Booker T. Washington Papers, Manuscripts Division, Library of Congress, Washington, D. C.

17. B. T. Washington to Whitefield McKinlay, Jan. 22, 1902, McKinlay Papers.

18. James S. Clarkson to Whitefield McKinlay, Oct. 13, 1902, McKinlay Papers.

19. Extract from a Roosevelt letter of Nov. 26, 1902, Francis Warrington Dawson, II, Papers. This extract was among materials sent by Roosevelt's direction from the offices of *The Outlook* to Warrington Dawson on Nov. 18, 1911, doubtlessly in answer to Dawson's request for material for a book. Warrington Dawson to "My dear Colonel," Versailles, Oct. 8, 1911, Francis Warrington Dawson, II, Papers.

20. Kermit Roosevelt to Warrington Dawson, Dec. 17, 1911, Francis Warrington Dawson, II, Papers.

21. G. W. Murray to Whitefield McKinlay, May 5, 1904, McKinlay Papers.

22. Whitefield McKinlay to P. B. S. Pinchback, July 13, 1903, McKinlay Papers.

23. Whitefield McKinlay to C. B. Purvis, May 1, 1913, McKinlay Papers.

24. G. W. Murray to Whitefield McKinlay, May 13, 1902; E. G. Deas to Whitefield McKinlay, March 27, 1903; S. W. Bennett to Whitefield McKinlay, Dec. 17, 1902; L. W. C. Blalock to Whitefield McKinlay, March 14, 1903, McKinlay Papers.

25. Theodore Roosevelt to Senator Galliger [probably Ballinger], May 9, 1906, McKinlay Papers.

26. E. M. Barrow to J. McG. Dickinson, Jan. 1, 1904, Jacob McGavock Dickinson Papers, Tennessee State Library and Archives, Nashville.

27. Clipping, *The Nashville American,* Feb. 24, 1909, and *passim,* Dickinson Papers.

28. J. McG. Dickinson to Theodore Roosevelt, Jan. 13, 1905, Dickinson Papers.

29. Theodore Roosevelt to J. McG. Dickinson, May 2, 1905, Dickinson Papers.

30. John D. Weaver, *The Brownsville Raid* (New York: Norton, 1973), 28–33. See also: Ann J. Lane, *The Brownsville Affair, National Crisis and Black Reaction* (Port Washington, N.Y.: Kennikat, 1971).

31. Theodore Roosevelt to Booker T. Washington, Nov. 5, 1906 (copy), McKinlay Papers. For reference to extreme secrecy, see: B. T. Washington to Whitefield McKinlay, Oct. 25, 1906, McKinlay Papers.

32. Weaver, *The Brownsville Raid,* 96–98.

33. Daniel Charles Needham, "William Howard Taft, the Negro, and the White South, 1908–1912" (Ph.D. dissertation, University of Georgia, 1970), 24–25.

34. W. G. Brown to Charles Byer, Oct. 13, 1910, William Garrott Brown Papers, Duke University, Durham, N. C.

35. Thomas Nelson Page to J. McG. Dickinson, March 19, 1909; W. H. Taft to J. McG. Dickinson, Sep. 11, 1909, Dickinson Papers.

36. J. McG. Dickson to W. H. Taft, Feb. 25, 1909, Dickinson Papers.

37. Frank S. White to J. McG. Dickinson, Feb. 23, 1909, Dickinson Papers.

38. J. McG. Dickinson to W. H. Taft, Sep. 8, 1909, Dickinson Papers.

39. J. McG. Dickinson to *The Forum,* Sep. 20, 1917, Dickinson Papers.

40. Needham, "Taft," 89, 136.

41. Thomas L. Grant to Whitefield McKinlay, Oct. 21, 1909, McKinlay Papers.

42. Needham, "Taft," 90–93, 129, 137, 161–66, 171–72.

43. Richard T. Greener to Whitefield McKinlay, Aug. 1, 1910, McKinlay Papers.

44. Charles Banks to Emmett Scott, Nov. 1, 1909, Washington Papers; Needham, "Taft," 152–54.

45. Needham, "Taft," 145–51.

46. William Garrott Brown, *The Lower South in American History* (New York: Macmillan, 1902).

47. Thomas Settle to John Spencer Bassett, May 9, 1917, Brown Papers.

48. W. G. Brown to S. P. Andrew, Sep. 11, 1910, Brown Papers. See also: W. G. Brown to E. S. Martin, Nov. 27, 1911; Thomas Settle to W. G. Brown, July 27; Aug. 3, 1910, Brown Papers.

49. W. G. Brown to Charles Dyer Norton, Oct. 13, 1910, Brown Papers.

50. A. Piatt Andrew to W. G. Brown, Nov. 3, 1910, Brown Papers.

51. William H. Taft to W. G. Brown, Nov. 3, 1910, Brown Papers.

52. W. G. Brown to W. H. Taft, May 30, 1911; A. Piatt Andrew to W. G. Brown, June 1, 1911, Brown Papers.

53. Charles D. Hilles to W. G. Brown, June 17, 1911, Brown Papers. See also: A. Piatt Andrew to W. G. Brown, June 18, 1911, Brown Papers.

54. W. G. Brown to Woodrow Wilson, Oct. 30, 1911, Brown Papers.

55. W. G. Brown to A. Piatt Andrew, Nov. 1, 1911, Brown Papers.

56. W. G. Brown to E. S. Martin, Nov. 10, 1911, Brown Papers.

57. W. G. Brown to A. Piatt Andrew, Nov. 10, 1911, Brown Papers.

58. W. G. Brown to E. S. Martin, Nov. 17, 1911, Brown Papers.

59. William F. McCombs to W. G. Brown, Dec. 10, 1911, Brown Papers.

60. W. G. Brown to J. Stewart Bassett, Dec. 31, 1911, Brown Papers.

61. J. S. Bassett to W. G. Brown, Jan. 8, 1912, Brown Papers.

62. *Harper's Weekly,* Nov. 16, 1912, from W. G. Brown scrapbook, Brown Papers.

63. Needham, "Taft," 177–89.

64. P. B. S. Pinchback to Whitefield McKinlay, July 12, 1912, McKinlay Papers.

65. Needham, "Taft," 305–17.

66. T. P. Gore to R. L. Williams, Nov. 29, 1915, Governors' Papers, Oklahoma Archives, Oklahoma City.

67. Whitefield McKinlay to P. B. S. Pinchback, Aug. 16, 1912, McKinlay Papers.

XII. RADICAL SWAN SONG: RADICALISM AND CONSERVATISM IN WASHINGTON UNDER WOODROW WILSON

1. August Meier and Elliott Rudwick, "Rise of Segregation," *Phylon* 18 (1967): 178–84.

2. Woodrow Wilson to John Sharp Williams, April 2, 1914, John Sharp Williams Papers, Manuscripts Division, Library of Congress, Washington, D.C.

3. O. G. Villard to George Foster Peabody, Aug. 14, 1912, George Foster Peabody Papers, Manuscripts Division, Library of Congress, Washington, D.C.

4. Lemuel C. Moore to John Sharp Williams, May 2, 1913, John Sharp Williams Papers, Mississippi Department of Archives and Library, Jackson.

5. P. S. Golden to J. S. Williams, May 7, 1913, Williams Papers, Library of Congress.

6. Charles W. Anderson to Booker T. Washington, April 2, 1913, Booker T. Washington Papers, Manuscripts Division, Library of Congress, Washington, D.C.

7. Whitefield McKinlay to Emmett J. Scott, March 18, 1913; William G. McAdoo to Whitefield McKinlay, June 16, 1913 (copy), Washington Papers.

8. T. P. Gore to W. G. McAdoo, Oct. 1, 1913; W. G. McAdoo to T. P. Gore, October 10, 1913 (copy), William Gibbs McAdoo Papers, Manuscripts Division, Library of Congress, Washington, D.C.

9. R. W. Thompson to Emmett Scott, April 18, 1913, Washington Papers.

10. William Gibbs McAdoo to O. G. Villard, Oct. 17, 1913, in Arthur S. Link, ed., *The Papers of Woodrow Wilson,* vol. 18 (Princeton: Princeton University Press, 1978), 453–55.

11. John M. Mecklin to J. S. Williams, Nov. 22, 1913, Williams Papers, Mississippi Department of Archives and Library.

12. J. S. Williams to J. M. Mecklin, Nov. 24, 1913, Williams Papers, Mississippi Department of Archives and Library.

13. May Childs Nerney to W. L. Stoddard, Nov. 12, 14, 1913; W. L. Stoddard to M. C. Nerney, Nov. 13, 1913, Administrative Files, NAACP Papers, Manuscript Division, Library of Congress, Washington, D.C. Hereafter cited at NAACP Papers.

14. W. Ernest Douglas, "Retreat from Conservatism: The Old Lady of Broad Street Embraces Jim Crow," *The Proceedings of the South Carolina Historical Association* (1958), 3–11, esp. pp. 5–6.

15. Manuscript entitled "Washington," Nov. 19, ____, Hemphill Family Papers, Duke University, Durham, N. C.

16. Henry E. Baker to O. G. Villard, Sep. 9, 1913, NAACP Papers.

17. O. G. Villard to "Dear Friend," Aug. 18, 1913: May Childs Nerney to Jessie Fauset, Sep. 11, 1913, NAACP Papers.

18. J. S. Williams to James L. Wilmeth, July 12, 1913 (copy), NAACP Papers.

19. Scrapbook entitled *"Treasury News* (Williams)," in files labelled *"Treasury News* (General)," dated May 3 - Aug. 23, 1913, in Treasury Department files, National Archives, Washington, D.C.

20. Typed ms., untitled, dated Washington, Sep. 22, Washington Papers. The manuscript was probably sent to Tuskegee by Charles W. Anderson. For Williams's general views on segregation see: Untitled ms. by Godfrey Nurse, New York, Dec. 17, 1914, "Speeches," Felton Family Papers, University of Georgia, Athens.

21. Typed manuscript from Washington, D.C., Sep. 22, ____, Washington Papers.

22. Memorandum by Nerney, "Segregation in Washington Departments," *ca.* Sep. 9, 1913, NAACP Papers.

23. Memorandum by Nerney, "Segregation in Washington Departments," *ca.* Sep. 9, 1913; Thomas H. R. Clark to M. C. Nerney, Sep. 11, 1913; Thomas H. R. Clarke, to Jessie Fauset, Sep. 10, 1913, NAACP Papers.

24. *Passim,* Albert Sydney Burleson Papers, University of Texas Archives, Austin.

25. Untitled ms. describing the pattern of segregation in the Post Office, NAACP Papers.

26. L. M. Hepborn to M. C. Nerney, Sep. 11, 1913, NAACP Papers.

27. Untitled ms., Oct. 20, 1913; L. M. Hepborn to M. C. Nerney, Sep. 11, 1913, NAACP Papers.

28. Untitled ms., Oct. 20, 1913, NAACP Papers.

29. Thomas H. R. Clarke to M. C. Nerney, Sep. 6, 1913, NAACP Papers.

30. L. M. Hepborn to M. C. Nerney, Sep. 11, 1913, NAACP Papers.

31. William W. McCary to M. C. Nerney, Oct. 27, 1913, NAACP Papers.

32. Thomas H. R. Clarke to Jessie Fauset, Sep. 10, 1913, NAACP Papers.

33. Osward Garrison Villard to A. S. Burleson, May 6, 1913, Burleson Papers, University of Texas Archives.

34. M. C. Nerney to George Packard, July 18, 1913; O. G. Villard to "Dear Friend," Aug. 18, 1913, NAACP Papers.

35. "A letter to President Woodrow Wilson on Federal Race Discrimination from the NAACP," Aug. 14, 1913 (copy), Burleson Papers.

36. M. C. Nerney to W. L. Stoddard, Nov. 12, 14, 1913, NAACP Papers.

37. M. C. Nerney to Jessie Fauset, Sep. 11, 1913, NAACP Papers.

38. M. C. Nerney to Dr. Lucy E. Moten, Oct. 14, 1913; M. C. Nerney to A. H. Grimké, Nov. 25, 1913, NAACP Papers. Villard sent an early copy of the Nerney Report to Wilson. See: O. G. Villard to Woodrow Wilson, Oct. 14, 1913 (with enclosure) in Link, *Papers of Woodrow Wilson,* 28: 401–10.

39. Thomas H. R. Clarke to Jessie Fauset, Sep. 10, 1913, NAACP Papers.

40. George Foster Peabody to W. G. McAdoo, Sep. 6, 1913, McAdoo Papers.

41. B. R. Tillman to William Kent, 1913, Benjamin Ryan Tillman Papers, Clemson University, Clemson, S. C.; William Kent to Florence Kelley, Sep. 17, 1913; Florence Kelley to William Kent, Sep. , 1913, NAACP Papers.

42. Rolfe Cobleigh to M. C. Nerney, Oct. 23, 1913, NAACP Papers.

43. Scrapbook entitled *"Treasury Notes* (Williams)," Treasury Department files, National Archives, Washington, D.C.

44. L. M. Hershaw to James Weldon Johnson, May 9, 1923, NAACP Papers.

45. O. G. Villard to Garrett A. Morgan, Sep. 19, 1913, NAACP Papers.

46. M. C. Nerney to J. E. Spingarn, Dec. 1, 1913, NAACP Papers.

47. Link, *Papers of Woodrow Wilson,* 29: 105.

48. Thomas H. R. Clarke to M. C. Nerney, Sep. 11, 1913, NAACP Papers.

49. Clipping, James Kimble Vardaman Scrapbook, James K. Vardaman Papers, Mississippi Department of Archives and Library, Jackson.

50. Joseph Blotner, *Faulkner, a Biography,* 2 vols. (New York: Random House, 1974), 1: 340–41; William F. Holmes, *The White Chief, James Kimble Vardaman* (Baton Rouge: Louisiana State Univ. Press, 1970), p. 380.

51. Henry E. Baker to O. G. Villard, Sep. 9, 1913, NAACP Papers.

52. Clipping from the *Washington Post,* Jan. 7, 1914, Vardaman Scrapbook.

53. C. W. Anderson to B. T. Washington, April 4, 1913, Washington Papers.

54. C. W. Anderson to Emmett J. Scott, Oct. 24, 1913, Washington Papers.

55. R. R. Moton to George Foster Peabody, Sep. 3, 1913 (copy), Washington Papers.

56. R. R. Moton to B. T. Washington, Sep. 3, 1913, Washington Papers.

57. B. R. Tillman to B. F. Mauldin, March 18, 1913, Tillman Papers.

58. Clipping from the Washington *Herald,* Feb. 6, 1914, Vardaman Scrapbook.

59. John Sharp Williams to Woodrow Wilson, April 13, 1914, Williams Papers, Library of Congress.

60. Newspaper clipping, datelined Crookston, Minn., July 12, ____ (probably 1914 or 1915), Vardaman Scrapbook, p. 299.

61. Clipping from the *Magnolia Gazette,* Oct. __, 1913, Vardaman Scrapbook.

62. Newspaper clipping, datelined Washington, Sep. 30 (1913), Vardaman Scrapbook.

63. Clipping from the Norfolk (Virginia) *Pilot,* datelined Washington, Feb. 6 (1914), Vardaman Scrapbook.

64. Newspaper clipping, datelined Washington, July 17 (1913), Vardaman Scrapbook.

65. Clipping from the *Times-Democrat,* datelined Washington, Aug. 7 (1913); clipping from *The Issue,* datelined Jackson, Mississippi, Aug. 21, 1913, Vardaman Scrapbook.

66. B. R. Tillman to John Skelton Williams, April 16, 1913 (copy), Tillman Papers.

67. B. R. Tillman to J. S. Williams, July 12, 1913 (copy), Tillman Papers.

68. B. R. Tillman to an unknown person, archivist's date "October, 1913," (copy), Tillman Papers.

69. Thomas Dixon to B. R. Tillman, July 17, 1913, Tillman Papers.

70. B. R. Tillman to H. C. Tillman, July 19, 1913, Tillman Papers.

71. Clipping from *The Issue,* July 13, 1913, Vardaman Scrapbook.

72. B. R. Tillman to J. E. Osborne, Aug. 1, 1913 (copy); B. R. Tillman to W. G. Hughes, Aug. 1, 1913 (copy), Tillman Papers.

73. B. R. Tillman to an unknown person, archivist's date "October, 1913," (copy), Tillman Papers.

74. B. R. Tillman to H. C. Tillman, July 29, 1913, (copy), Tillman Papers.

75. B. R. Tillman to W. C. Rogers, Feb. 5, 1914 (copy), Tillman Papers.

76. B. R. Tillman to J. S. Williams, May 10, 1913, Williams Papers, Mississippi Department of Archives and Library; B. R. Tillman to J. Tumulty, July 25, 1913 (copy), Tillman Papers.

77. Herbert D. Brown to A. S. Burleson, March 20, 1915, Burleson Papers.

78. B. R. Tillman to J. E. Ransdell, May 3, 1913 (copy), Tillman Papers.

79. B. R. Tillman to F. P. Colcock, May 30; June 3, 1913 (copies); B. R. Tillman to Mrs. Tillman, June 3, 1913 (copy), Tillman Papers.

80. B. R. Tillman to J. F. Byrnes, June 16, 1913 (copy); B. R. Tillman to W. G. McAdoo, June 23, 1913 (copy), Tillman Papers.

81. Typed "Memorandum for the President To Go For What They Are Worth," March 8, 1913 (copy), Tillman Papers.

82. B. R. Tillman to John W. Dorrill, May 5, 1913 (copy), Tillman Papers.

83. B. R. Tillman to A. S. Burleson, March 13, 1913 (copy), Tillman Papers.

84. B. R. Tillman to A. S. Burleson, May 12, 1913 (copy), Tillman Papers.

85. B. R. Tillman to A. S. Burleson, May 29, 1913 (copy), Tillman Papers.

86. B. R. Tillman to Z. T. Thomas, March 21, 1914 (copy), Tillman Papers.

87. Broadside, from the Thomas P. Gore Papers, Western History Collection, University of Oklahoma, Norman.

88. For example, see: *Amory* (Mississippi) *Times-Press,* Sep. __, 1913, Vardaman Scrapbook.

89. Clipping from the Columbia (S.C.) *State,* July 29, 1913, Vardaman Scrapbook.

90. Wise and interested observers understood well the primary reason for Wilson's and McAdoo's behavior in the segregation matter. See: John Palmer Gavit to O. G. Villard, Sep. 26, 1913, Link, *Papers of Woodrow Wilson,* 28: 332.

91. Clipping from the *Vicksburg Herald,* Aug. 31, 1913, Vardaman Scrapbook.

92. Clipping from the *Washington* (D.C.) *Post,* n.d., Vardaman Scrapbook.

93. Clipping from the *Washington* (D.C.) *Star,* Oct. 5, 1913, Vardaman Scrapbook.

94. Memorandum entitled "Segregation in Washington Departments," Sep. 9, 1913, NAACP Papers.

95. W. G. McAdoo to Woodrow Wilson, Sep. 20, 1913, McAdoo Papers.

96. Pamphlet entitled "Opinion" (probably from the *Crisis*, about Nov. 1914), in the Peabody Papers.

97. New York *Evening Post,* Dec. 12, 1913, citing the Boston *Advertiser*, "*Treasury News* (General)," May 3 - Aug 23, 1913, in Treasury Department files, National Archives.

98. C. P. Woolley to O. G. Villard, Dec. 2, 1913, NAACP Papers.

99. B. R. Tillman to John G. Richards, Dec 2, 1913, Tillman Papers.

100. Clipping from the *Biloxi* (Mississippi) *Herald,* Jan. 27, 1914, Vardaman Scrapbook.

101. Clipping from the *Hattiesburg News,* Feb. 26, 1914, Vardaman Scrapbook.

102. Woodrow Wilson to John Sharp Williams, April 2, 1914, Williams Papers, Library of Congress.

103. J. S. Williams to Woodrow Wilson, March 31, April 13, 1914; Woodrow Wilson to J. S. Williams, April 2, 1914, Williams Papers, Library of Congress.

104. Ms., "A Question of Color," Felton Family Papers.

105. Unidentified clipping, Vardaman Scrapbook.

106. A. J. McKelway to A. S. Burleson, July 30, 1914, Albert Sydney Burleson Papers, Manuscripts Division, Library of Congress.

107. B. T. Washington to Woodrow Wilson, June 8, 1914; Woodrow Wilson to A. S. Burleson, June 9, 1914; G. F. Peabody to A. S. Burleson, June 11, 1914; Seth Low to Woodrow Wilson, June 11, 1914, Burleson Papers, Library of Congress.

108. M. C. Nerney to Charles Edward Russel, March 6, 1914 (telegram), NAACP Papers.

109. A. H. Grimké to M. C. Nerney, March 8, 1914, NAACP Papers.

110. Copy of H. R. 20329, 63rd Cong., 3d sess., December 23, 1914, NAACP Papers.

111. Josephus Daniels to Frank Porter Graham, Nov. 5, 1936, President's Papers, University of North Carolina Archives, Chapel Hill.

112. Woodrow Wilson to George Creel, June 18, 1918, George Creel Papers.

113. Claude G. Stotts to W. G. McAdoo, Nov. 13, 1914; Claude G. Stotts to John Skelton Williams, Nov. 13, 1914, McAdoo Papers.

114. Lou Cretia Owen diary, Nov. 18, 30, 1918, and *passim,* Tennessee State Library and Archives, Nashville.

115. Untitled ms., n.d. (ca. 1918), Charles Norton Hunter Papers, Duke University, Durham, N. C.

116. Files of the Navy Department, National Archives, Washington, D.C.

117. L. M. Hershaw to James Weldon Johnson, May 9, 1923; J. W. Johnson to L. M. Hershaw, May 14, 1923, NAACP Papers.

118. Shelby J. Davidson to Walter F. White, Oct. 18, 1923, NAACP Papers.

119. Mimeographed report, Aug. 10–17, 1928, Administrative Files, NAACP Papers.

120. L. M. Hershaw to J. W. Johnson, Aug. 2, 1927, NAACP Papers. For a brief discussion of segregation in the federal service under Harding, Coolidge, and Hoover, see: Meier and Rudwick, "Rise of Segregation," 181–84.

121. For a close and insightful description of Penn School throughout this general process see: Elizabeth Jacoway, *Yankee Missionaries in the South: The Penn School Experiment* (Baton Rouge: Louisiana State Univ. Press, 1980).

XIII. THE SOULS OF BLACK FOLK

1. DuBois first published his "Strivings" essay in *The Atlantic Monthly* in 1897. With only minor revisions, he republished it in 1903 as the first chapter of *The Souls of Black Folk*. W. E. B. DuBois, "Strivings of the Negro People," *Atlantic Monthly* 53 (Aug. 1897): 194–98; W. E. B. DuBois, *The Souls of Black Folk, Essays and Sketches,* 3rd ed. (Chicago: A. C. McClurg, 1903), 1–12. The materials that follow are taken from

the latter source in order to use the most matured version of his thought in this vein. *The Conservation of the Races* appeared in the second *Occasional Paper* of the American Negro Academy (Washington, D. C., 1897).

2. Georg Wilhelm Friedrich Hegel, *The Philosophy of History* (New York: Dover Publications, 1956), 98.

3. Ibid., 80.

4. Francis L. Broderick, *W. E. B. DuBois, Negro Leader in a Time of Crisis* (Stanford: Stanford Univ. Press, 1959), 21.

5. Hegel, *Philosophy of History,* 1-79, *passim,* esp. p. 19.

6. Ibid., 341ff.

7. Ibid., 103.-10, 112-15.

8. DuBois, *Souls,* 3.

9. Hegel, *Philosophy of History,* 86-87.

10. DuBois, *Souls,* 2.

11. W. E. B. DuBois, *The Autobiography of W. E. B. DuBois, A Soliloquy on Viewing My Life from the Last Decade of Its First Century* (New York: International Publishers, 1968), 105-8, 113-20, 132.

12. Ibid., 133.

13. Samuel E. Morison, ed., *The Development of Harvard University, Since the Inauguration of President Eliot, 1869-1929* (Cambridge: Harvard Univ. Press, 1930), 30; Ralph Barton Perry, *The Thought and Character of William James* (New York: Braziller, 1954), 161.

14. DuBois, *Autobiography,* 113.

15. Perry, *William James,* 161-62.

16. George Santayana, *Persons and Places: The Background of My Life* (New York: Scribner's, 1944), 1: 241.

17. DuBois, *Autobiography,* 143.

18. Morrison, *Development of Harvard,* 319.

19. For instances of Shaler's thought see: Nathaniel Southgate Shaler, "The Negro Problem," *Atlanta Monthly* 54 (Nov. 1884): 696-709; "Science and the African Problem," *Atlantic Monthly* 66 (July 1890): 35-45; *The Neighbor: The Natural History of Human Contacts* (Boston and New York: Houghton Mifflin, 1904).

20. DuBois, *Autobiography,* 143.

21. Broderick, *DuBois,* 15-17.

22. DuBois, *Autobiography,* 146.

23. Ibid., 148.

24. Broderick, *DuBois,* 26-27

25. DuBois, *Autobiography,* 164.

26. Broderick, *DuBois,* 18-19, quoting DuBois's diary for Feb. 23, 1893, DuBois Papers. See also: DuBois, *Autobiography,* 170-71.

27. DuBois, *Autobiography,* 126.

28. Hegel, *Philosophy of History,* 29-31.

29. Broderick, *DuBois,* 18-20.

30. Ibid., 227.

31. Ibid., 128, quoting *Crisis* 27 (April 1924): 274.

XIV. WHITE SOUL

1. Typescript, "Resolutions on 'Paris Lynching,' 1893," Edgar Gardner Murphy Papers, Southern Historical Collection, University of North Carolina at Chapel Hill; Hugh C. Bailey, *Edgar Gardner Murphy, Gentle Progressive* (Miami: Univ. of Miami Press, 1968), pp. 1-10.

2. "Race Problems in the South—Report of the Proceedings of the First Annual Conference Held under the Auspices of the Southern Society for the Promotion of the

Study of Race Conditions and Problems in the South . . . at . . . Montgomery, Alabama, May 8, 9, 10, A.D. 1900" (Richmond: B. F. Johnson, 1900).

3. "The Montgomery Conference," *The Churchman* 81 (May 26, 1900): 634.

4. Bailey, *Edgar Gardner Murphy,* 48–52.

5. Edgar Gardner Murphy, *Problems of the Present South: A Discussion of Certain Educational, Industrial and Political Issues in the Southern States* (New York: Macmillan, 1904); *The Basis of Ascendancy: A Discussion of Certain Principles of Public Policy Involved in the Development of the Southern States* (New York: Longmans, Green, 1910).

6. Afflicted with rheumatic fever since childhood, Murphy's health failed rapidly. He died in 1913 at the age of forty-four. Bailey, *Edgar Gardner Murphy,* 65–108, 138–85, 213–14.

7. Murphy, *Basis of Ascendancy,* 79.

8. W. E. B. DuBois, *The Souls of Black Folk* (New York: A. C. McClurg, 1903), 52. Murphy expressed his philosophy of race most lucidly in his book *The Basis of Ascendancy,* published in 1910. As the title itself suggests, Murphy argued that the basis of progress was racial self-consciousness. See especially pages 79– 81, 201–4, 209–17, 242–48.

9. *Problems of the Present South,* 34–35, 273–74.

10. Ibid., 273, 279, 277.

11. Printed report of a speech given in New York, April 15, 1903, Murphy Papers.

12. Murphy, *Problems of the Present South,* 17.

13. Ibid., 156.

14. Ibid., 272.

15. Ibid., 281.

16. Ibid., 18–19.

17. Walter Hines Page, "The Rebuilding of Old Commonwealths," *Atlantic Monthly* 89 (May 1902): 651–61. "The Forgotten Man" was published in Walter Hines Page, *The Rebuilding of Old Commonwealths* (New York: Doubleday, Page, 1902), 2–35.

18. Murphy, *Problems of the Present South,* 14–19.

19. Ibid., 255, 263, 264.

20. Ibid., 21.

21. Ibid., 15–16, 31–32.

22. Ibid., 46–50.

23. Page, "Rebuilding Old Commonwealths," 460.

24. Murphy, *Problems of the Present South,* 47.

25. Manuscript (apparently an address to the students at the University of South Carolina by Mitchell), n.d., Samuel Chiles Mitchell Papers, South Caroliniana Library, University of South Carolina, Columbia.

26. For a history of Mitchell and his presidency of the University of South Carolina, see: Daniel Walker Hollis, *University of South Carolina,* vol. 2: *College to University* (Columbia: Univ. of South Carolina Press, 1956), 241–60.

27. *The National Cyclopaedia of American Biography* (New York: James T. White, 1916) 15: 276.

28. Monroe Lee Billington, *The American South: A Brief History* (New York: Scribner, 1971), 256; Laurence Shore, "Daniel Augustus Tompkins and Blacks: The New South Faces the Race Question," Honors Essay, Department of History, University of North Carolina, Chapel Hill, 1977, pp. 63–64, citing the Daniel Augustus Tompkins Papers, Folders 107, 115, 188, 191, and 274, in the Southern Historical Collection, University of North Carolina, Chapel Hill; Ben F. Lemert, *The Cotton Textile Industry of the Southern Appalachian Piedmont* (Chapel Hill: University of North Carolina Press, 1933), p. 121.

29. Murphy, *Problems of the Present South,* 102, 103.-05, 125.

30. Broadus Mitchell, *The Rise of the Cotton Mills in the South* (Baltimore: Johns Hopkins Univ. Press, 1921), vii–viii.

31. Thomas F. Parker to S. C. Mitchell, Jan. 30, 1911, Mitchell Papers.

32. S. C. Mitchell to T. F. Parker, Feb. 10, 1911, Mitchell Papers.

33. Mitchell, *Rise of Cotton Mills,* 69–86, 89, 94.

34. Ibid., pp. 102–4. For the same interpretation, see: Murphy, *Problems of the Present South,* 10–11; and Daniel Augustus Tompkins, "The South's Vast Reserves," *World's Work* 14 (June 1907): 8951–52.

35. Mitchell, *Rise of Cotton Mills,* 132.

36. Broadus Mitchell, *The Industrial Revolution in the South* (Baltimore: Johns Hopkins Univ. Press, 1930), 70–73, 78–80; Shore, "Daniel Augustus Tompkins," 8, 22;-23. 32–33. 37–38, 40, 61–63.

37. Broadus Mitchell, *Rise of Cotton Mills,* 162ff., 168–69; Broadus Mitchell, *William Gregg: Factory Master of the Old South* (Chapel Hill: Univ. of North Carolina Press, 1928).

38. Mitchell, *Rise of Cotton Mills,* 265–66.

39. Ibid., 136–37, citing hearing before the committee of Judiciary, House of Representatives, April 29, 1902, p. 11 ff.

40. James L. Orr, "The Negro in the Mills," *The Independent* 53 (April 11, 1901): 845–46.

41. Mitchell, *Rise of Cotton Mills,* 214, 217–18.

42. Marcus Wayland Beck Diary, May 29, June 5, 19, 21, 1899, University of Georgia, Athens.

43. Murphy, *Problems of the Present South,* 103–4; Lemert, *Cotton Textile Industry of the Southern Appalachian Piedmont,* 65.

44. Mitchell, *Rise of Cotton Mills,* 90, 161.

45. Ibid., pp. 161, 162, 169.

46. William Garrott Brown, *The New Politics and Other Papers* (Boston and New York: Houghton Mifflin, 1914), 114–15.

47. Interview with a *News and Courier* reporter, Blackburn, cited in Mitchell, *Rise of Cotton Mills,* 217.

48. Orr, "The Negro in the Mills," 846; Tompkins, "The South's Vast Resources," 8952.

49. Mitchell, *Rise of Cotton Mills,* 95.

50. Ibid., 160–61.

51. Joseph L. Morrison, *W. J. Cash, Southern Prophet: A Biography and Reader* (New York: Knopf, 1965).

52. Wilbur J. Cash, *The Mind of the South* (New York: Knopf, 1941), 205.

53. Murphy, *Problems of the Present South,* 143.

54. Orr, "The Negro in the Mills," 846.

55. Clippings from several newspapers, Murphy Papers.

56. S. C. Mitchell to H. B. Frissell, May 13, 1910, Mitchell Papers.

57. Mitchell, *Rise of Cotton Mills,* vii, 153–54.

58. U. S. Dept. of Agriculture, *Agricultural Statistics, 1941* (Washington: Government Printing Office, 1941), 116–17.

59. Lemert, *Cotton Textile Industry,* 116–19, 140; Mitchell, *Industrial Revolution in the South,* 72–73; Melvin Thomas Copeland, *The Cotton Manufacturing Industry of the United States* (Cambridge: Harvard Univ. Press, 1912), 221, 224.

60. Mitchell, *Industrial Revolution in the South,* 70–73, 78–80; Shore, "Daniel Augustus Tompkins," 61–63; Page, "Rebuilding Old Commonwealths," 658.

61. Murphy, "The Task of the Leader," *Sewanee Review* 15 (Jan. 1907): 5.

62. The changeover in philosophic systems has been closely studied in South Carolina by William Henry Longton in "Some Aspects of Intellectual Activity in Ante-

Bellum South Carolina, 1830–1860: An Introductory Study" (Ph.D. dissertation, University of North Carolina at Chapel Hill), 1969, esp. pp. 272, 273.

63. For a very perceptive discussion of Jeffersonian thought in the Old South and the New, see: Merrill D. Peterson, *The Jeffersonian Image in the American Mind* (New York: Oxford, Univ. Press, 1960), 38–82, 211–16.

64. Margaret Mitchell, *Gone with the Wind* (New York: Macmillan, 1936), 422–28; Sidney Howard, *GWTW, The Screenplay,* ed. Richard B. Harwell (New York: Collier Books, Macmillan, 1980), 242–44.

65. Ibid., 3–5.

66. Daniel Robinson Hundley, *Social Relations in Our Southern States* (New York: Henry B. Price, 1860).

67. Mitchell, *Gone with The Wind,* 429, 428, 1037.

68. William Heyward to James Gregorie, Jan. 12, 1868, Gregorie-Ellison Papers, Southern Historical Collection, University of North Carolina at Chapel Hill.

69. The best short account of the anti-hookworm campaign is by Page himself: Walter Hines Page, "The Hookworm and Civilization," *World's Work* 24 (Sep. 1912): 504–18.

70. Ibid., 509–11, 513.

71. Liesa Stamm Auerbach, an anthropologist, spent several months in Mississippi in 1967 studying the state's midwife program in Holmes County. In that program white public health nurses trained black women to serve as midwives, presumably to black women only. The program was established in 1921 for the officially stated purpose of upgrading the practice of midwives to meet modern standards. In addition, however, it was begun because the older doctors, who were called "country doctors" and who had previously served rural black women in this way, were dying out. They were being replaced by younger physicians who settled in the towns and were no longer readily available to black people in the country. Black professionals were thus left to minister to black patients. Interestingly, Dr. Auerbach observed that these white nurses oversaw their trainees only loosely, and that the latter derived a part of their medicine from black culture rather than white. Interview by the author with Liesa Stamm Auerbach (Lecturer in Anthropology, University of Wisconsin, Milwaukee) at the Center for Advanced Study in the Behavioral Sciences, Stanford, California, Aug. 5, 1980.

72. Ellen Glasgow, *The Voice of the People* (New York: Houghton Mifflin, 1900). For reference to the death of Nicholas Burr, see pages 423, 440–42.

73. Ibid., 443–44.

74. William Faulkner, *Intruder in the Dust* (New York: Random House, 1948), 153–56.

75. Murphy, *Problems of the Present South,* 19.

76. W. E. B. DuBois, *The Souls of Black Folk* (New York: A. C. McClurg, 1903), 52.

XV. LEGACY: RACE RELATIONS IN THE TWENTIETH-CENTURY SOUTH

1. Pamphlet, "The Struggle of 1876," delivered in Anderson, S. C. Aug. 25, 1909, n.p., n.d., Benjamin Ryan Tillman Papers, Clemson University, Clemson, S. C.

2. J. S. Basnight to Marion Butler, Jan. 13, Feb. 9, 1898; G. L. Hardison to Marion Butler, Jan. 25, Feb. 18, 1898; Ralph Howland to Marion Butler, Jan. 29, 1898; H. H. Perry to Marion Butler, Jan. 31, 1898, Marion Butler Papers, Southern Historical Collection, University of North Carolina at Chapel Hill.

3. Thomas Dixon, *The Leopard's Spots* (New York: Page, Doubleday, 1902), 81–81, 173–75, 256–64, 320–27.

4. Helen G. Edmonds, *The Negro and Fusion Politics in North Carolina, 1894–1901* (Chapel Hill: Univ. of North Carolina Press, 1951), 97–99.

5. For a description of the changeover from relative tolerance of mulattoes in the lower South to intolerance, see: Joel Williamson, *New People: Miscegenation and Mulattoes in the United States* (New York: Free Press, 1980), 61–109.

6. Thomas Dixon, Jr., *The Sins of the Father: A Romance of the South* (New York: Grosset and Dunlap, 1912).

7. Harry Lewis Golden, *A Little Girl Is Dead* (Cleveland: World Publishing Company, 1965), 6–25, 36, 50, 54. Harry Golden, the Charlotte, N. C., journalist, did excellent historical detective work on the Frank case. This account relies heavily upon his book, and that of Leonard Dinnerstein, *The Leo Frank Case* (New York: Columbia Univ. Press, 1968).

8. Ibid., 90, 98–99.

9. Ibid., 62–65, 75–84, 115–26.

10. Ibid., 127–37.

11. For a rendition of this phenomenon in fiction, see: William Faulkner, *Light in August* (New York: Smith and Haas, 1932), 275–77.

12. Golden, *A Little Girl is Dead*, 284–93.

13. Ibid., 231–33.

In 1982, Alonzo Mann, who had been a 14-year-old office boy in the factory at the time of the murder, declared that he had seen Conley carrying the body toward a trapdoor that led to the basement. Conley wheeled on him and threatened, "If you ever mention this I'll kill you." Mann, on the advice of his mother and father, decided not to testify to what he saw. Conley, himself, died in 1962. Washington *Post*, March 8, 1982.

14. Harry Golden described most of these connections in *A Little Girl Is Dead*, 209–10.

15. David M. Chalmers, *Hooded Americanism: The First Century of the Ku Klux Klan, 1865–1965* (New York: Doubleday, 1965), 3–5, 29–31.

16. *Watson's Jeffersonian Weekly*, Jan. 25, 1912.

17. Sarah Patton Boyle, *The Desegregated Heart: A Virginian's Stand in Time of Transition* (New York: Morrow, 1962), 14, 16.

18. Dan Carter, *Scottsboro: A Tragedy of the American South* (Baton Rouge: Louisiana State Univ. Press, 1969).

19. Howard Odum, *Race and Rumors of Race* (Chapel Hill: Univ. of North Carolina Press, 1944), 86–88, 97–104, 135.

20. Pamphlet, "The Value of Southern Idealism," Edwin A. Alderman Papers, Alderman Library, University of Virginia, Charlottesville.

21. Gary Thomas Scott, "The Kappa Alpha Order, 1865–1897; How It Came To Be and How It Came To Be Southern" (Master's thesis, University of North Carolina, 1968).

22. Susan Spear Durant, "The Gently Furled Banner; the Development of the Myth of the Lost Cause, 1865–1900" (Ph.D. dissertation, University of North Carolina, 1972); Gaines M. Foster, "Ghosts of the Confederacy: Defeat, History and the Culture of the New South, 1865–1912" (Ph.D. dissertation, University of North Carolina, 1982).

23. Douglas Southall Freeman, *Robert E. Lee, A Biography*, 4 vols. (New York: Scribner's 1942–45); *Lee's Lieutenants, A Study in Command*, 3 vols. (New York: Scribner's 1942–44).

24. Jervis Anderson, *A. Philip Randolph: A Biographical Portrait* (New York: Harcourt, Brace, Jovanovich, 1972), 252–61.

25. Richard M. Dalfiume, *Fighting on Two Fronts: Desegregation of the Armed Forces, 1939–1953* (Columbia: Univ. of Missouri Press, 1969), 92–103.

26. Ibid., 201–19.

27. George Brown Tindall, *The Emergence of the New South, 1913–1945*, vol. 10: *The History of the South* (Baton Rouge: Louisiana State Univ. Press, 1967), 175–77; Jacqueline Dowd Hall, *Revolt Against Chivalry: Jessie Daniel Ames and the Women's*

Campaign Against Lynching (New York: Columbia Univ. Press, 1979), *passim;* Morton Sosna, *In Search of the Silent South: Southern Liberals and the Race Issue* (New York: Columbia Univ. Press, 1977), 20–41.

28. Tindall, *Emergence of the New South,* 719–20; Sosna, *In Search of the Silent South,* 152–63.

29. Harry Ashmore, *An Epitaph for Dixie* (New York: Norton, 1957), 11–12, 160–61.

30. James F. Byrnes, *All in One Lifetime* (New York: Harper, 1958), 407–9.

31. Ashmore, *Epitaph for Dixie,* 161–62.

32. Sarah Patton Boyle, *A Desegregated Heart.*

33. Lilliam Smith, *Killers of the Dream* (New York: Norton, 1949); *Strange Fruit: A Novel.* (New York: Reynal and Hitchcock, 1944); Sonsa, *In Search of the Silent South,* 174–94.

34. Sonsa, *In Search of the Silent South,* 42–59.

35. C. Vann Woodward, *Tom Watson: Agrarian Rebel* (1938) (New York: Oxford Univ. Press, 1963).

36. C. Vann Woodward, *The Strange Career of Jim Crow,* (New York: Oxford, 1955), vii–ix, 3–95.

37. C. Vann Woodward, *Origins of the New South, 1877–1913,* vol. 9: *The History of the South* (Baton Rouge: Louisiana State Univ. Press, 1951).

38. Boyle, *A Desegregated Heart,* 201–2.

39. Corbett H. Thigpen and Hervey M. Clerkley, *The Three Faces of Eve* (London: Secker and Warburg, 1957), esp. 1–11, 23, 26–34, 97, 107–8, 143, 158, 221, 222–34.

40. Ibid., 15.

41. C. Vann Woodward, *The Burden of Southern History,* 2nd ed. rev. (Baton Rouge: Louisiana State Univ. Press, 1969), 187–211, esp. 190.

42. Eugene P. Walker, "Montgomery Revisited," a paper presented at the First Anniversary Meeting of the State Committee on the Life and History of Black Georgians, Feb. 9–11, 1978. See also: David Levering Lewis, *King A Critical Biography* (New York: Praeger, 1979), 446–84; and Coretta Scott King, *My Life with Martin Luther King, Jr.* (New York: Holt, Rinehart and Winston, 1969), 108–15.

43. For a close study of this process, see: D'Etta Barnhardt Leach, "Desegregation in Charlotte, North Carolina: A Study in Business Leadership," (M.A. thesis, University of North Carolina, 1976). For the Greensboro story, see: William Henry Chafe, *Civilities and Civil Rights: Greensboro, North Carolina, and the Black Struggle for Equality* (New York: Oxford Univ. Press, 1980).

44. Clayborne Carson, *In Struggle: SNCC and the Black Awakening of the 1960s* (Cambridge: Harvard, Univ. Press, 1981), 235–42.

45. C. Vann Woodward, *The Strange Career of Jim Crow,* 3d ed. (New York: Oxford Univ. Press, 1974), 153.

46. Ibid., 174–75.

CONCLUSION

1. For an incisive account of the Populist effort, see: Lawrence Goodwyn, *Democratic Promise: The Populist Movement in America* (New York: Oxford Univ. Press, 1971), 273–306.

2. Gaines M. Foster, "Ghosts of the Confederacy: Defeat, History, and the Culture of the New South, 1865–1912" (Ph.D. dissertation, University of North Carolina, 1982), ch. 4, fn. 44.

3. Ellen Glasgow, *The Voice of the People* (New York: Doubleday, Page, 1900).

4. Margaret Mitchell, *Gone with the Wind* (New York: Macmillan, 1936), 501–5, 707–8, 962.

INDEX

abolitionism, 14
accommodationism, 70, 71–73
African survivals, 37–38, 401
Alabama: miscegenation, 41–42;
    disfranchisement, 234; Baptists and
    blacks, 282
Alderman, Edwin A., 274
Alexander, William W., 485
American Colonization Society, 14–15
Ames, Jessie Daniel, 485
Anderson, Charles, 376–78
anti-Communism, 473–74, 474–75
anti-Semitism, *see* religious prejudice; (Leo)
    Frank case
aristocracy in the South: black, 54; white, 25,
    28, 29, 33–34, 102–3, 237–38, 287–88,
    293, 301; *see also* chivalry; class lines;
    code of behavior; feudalism in the South
Arkansas: Brooks-Baxter War, 179; post-
    Reconstruction Republican politics, 346–49
Army of Northern Virginia, 480, 481–82
Army of Tennessee, 481
Ashmore, Harry, 486–87
assimilationism, 70, 76–77
Association of Southern Women for the
    Prevention of Lynching, 485
Atlanta: Cotton States Exposition, 71;
    Compromise, 71; riot, 209–23; University,
    328; Leo Frank case, 468–72
Australian ballot, 228

Baker, Ray Stannard, 215, 221, 222
Bakker, Jim, 520
Ball, William Watts, 293
Baptists, Southern Home Missionary Board,
    128

Barringer, Paul B., 177, 275
Baskervill, William M., 105, 106
Bassett, John Spencer, 261–71, 293
"beat," as related to the slave patrol, 19
Bible Belt, 81, 312–17
(The) Birth of a Nation, 140, 175–76, 304,
    336, 472
black belts, 114, 181–82; *see also* population,
    black
black matriarchy, 59, 213; *see also* gender
    roles: black women
black militants, 202, 390–93, 506, 510
Black Nationalism, 49, 506
Black Reconstruction, 44–50, 491
Black Revolution, 501–7, 509, 522
"Black Second" Congressional District in
    N.C., 191, 226
"black and tans," 344, 349, 357, 362
blacks, *see* culture; disfranchisement: of
    blacks; education: of blacks; emigration
    of blacks from South; names of blacks;
    patronage, political: for blacks;
    population, black; property, black
    attitudes toward; religious influence of
    blacks on whites; resettlement of blacks;
    separatism; soul: black; subordination of
    blacks; suffrage for black men; voting: by
    blacks
blacks in government, 191–94, 225–29, 245,
    344–45, 351–53, 355, 357–58, 360, 362–
    63, 365–67, 374–92, 466–67; *see also*
    desegregation: of the military; patronage,
    political: for blacks; segregation: in
    federal service, in the military
blacks in the military, 338–39, 354–55, 393,
    483–84; *see also* desegregation: of the
    military; segregation: in the military

555